CW00486474

Poverty, Charity and Social Welfare in Central Europe in the 19th and 20th Centuries

Poverty, Charity and Social Welfare in Central Europe in the 19th and 20th Centuries

Edited by

Olga Fejtová,
Milan Hlavačka,
Václava Horčáková
and Veronika Knotková

Cambridge
Scholars
Publishing

Poverty, Charity and Social Welfare in Central Europe in the 19th
and 20th Centuries

Edited by Olga Fejtová, Milan Hlavačka, Václava Horčáková,
Veronika Knotková

This book first published 2017

Cambridge Scholars Publishing

Lady Stephenson Library, Newcastle upon Tyne, NE6 2PA, UK

British Library Cataloguing in Publication Data
A catalogue record for this book is available from the British Library

The preparation for the English edition of this book was supported
by the Prague City Archives and the Institute of History,
Czech Academy of Sciences.

ISBN (10): 1-4438-9871-6
ISBN (13): 978-1-4438-9871-3

TABLE OF CONTENTS

Part II: Case Studies

Part III: Institutions, Instruments, Discourses

LIST OF ILLUSTRATIONS

LIST OF TABLES

ACKNOWLEDGEMENTS

The idea to put this book together came about during the annual international conference dedicated to urban history called "For you always have the poor with you" – From Charity to the Social Politics Within Cities in the 18th–20th Century, jointly organised by the Prague City Archives, the Institute of History of the Academy of Sciences of the Czech Republic and by the Faculty of Humanities at Charles University, which was held in Prague in 2013. Stimulating and inspiring discussions as well as the high quality of submitted studies related to modern social policy of the 19th and 20th centuries led editors to the idea of making the most interesting papers from this conference available to a wider international audience.

The editors of the book would like to express heartfelt thanks not only to all authors, but at this point also to their collaborators, without whose unselfish efforts this book would never have been published – especially to Dr Klára Polasek for translations into English and to Steven Conway and Sharon King for revision of English texts; we are equally grateful to Dr Nina Lohmann for revision of the German texts.

Last but not least, without the extraordinary understanding and generous support of both the Institute of History of the Academy of Sciences of the Czech Republic and the City of Prague (Prague City Archives), this book would never have been published.

Veronika Knotková

INTRODUCTION

OLGA FEJTOVÁ, MILAN HLAVAČKA, VÁCLAVA HORČÁKOVÁ AND VERONIKA KNOTKOVÁ

The issue of poverty is currently an important one. The renewed interest in this topic led the organisers of traditional scientific meetings dealing with the comparative history of cities (meetings which have been taking place in the Prague City Archives since the 1980s) to the idea to organise a conference which would focus on poverty and social care in Prague and in other cities throughout Central Europe from the Enlightenment reforms to the destruction of the system of municipal social care in the Czech Lands by the Nazis in the 1940s. The conference took place on October 8–9, 2013 under the title "'For you always have the poor with you' ...from charity to municipal social policy" in Clam-Gallas Palace in Prague. The organisers were the Prague City Archives, the Institute of History of the Academy of Sciences of the Czech Republic and the Faculty of Humanities at Charles University in Prague.

The conference also marginally dealt with development in earlier periods, i.e. during the Early Modern era, where the roots of modern development of social welfare are to be found. Yet the basic question remained the same: what was symptomatic of the social problems of cities in the 19th and early 20th centuries in the Czech Lands? At the beginning, the Austrian state took over a considerable portion of the care for the poor from churches, private charitable organisations and cities. However, the state gradually began to return the provision of social care back to the competence of municipal administrations. Expanding and internally differentiated social care in Austria (unlike Prussia) had reached a level at which carrying out social care became unmanageable on the state level, financially as well as organisationally. Thus, municipalities, as evidenced by the excellent example of Prague, began to intensively cultivate this sphere of their duties. During the inter-war period, municipalities managed to polish the social care system to relative perfection despite the severe effects of the economic crisis. Yet it was the state again (specifically the

Nazi Reich and afterwards socialist Czechoslovakia) that took this agenda away from municipalities only to return it to them in the form of delegated powers.

Conference discussions mainly focused on contemporary reflection and argumentation against the background of key reforms as well as on internal and public debate associated with them. Furthermore, institutional forms, which came into existence to ensure steps towards dealing with repeatedly escalating social problems in cities, were also examined at the conference.

Topics concerning the transformation of the poor and social policy in the urban environment occurred as well, since municipalities in general began to change dramatically due to mass migration and rapid urbanisation from the 1860s. The organisational, financial and institutional base required for coping with social (and subsequently socio-medical) problems of the metropolitan population constituted another set of conference topics.

The related issues of the coexistence of state and municipal institutions as well as the constant renewing of the network of religious and/or various types of associational social institutions, i.e. ties between public and private care for the poor, completed the set of conference topics.

The topic of the evolution of the perception of poverty and its professional reflection was also included. The conference participants dealt with both the literary (journalistic) and fine art reflection on poverty as well as with the gradual reshaping of its image in the eyes of the urban public. Poverty (including its most drastic public manifestations, as well as the impact of the specific mental world of the "modern" precariat on the "cultivated, middle class" parts of the city) was an integral (functional) part of everyday city life. Thus the conference also included debate on the organisational and financial "management" of poverty including a debate on the diverse political instrumentalisation of social issues in its urban instantiation as poverty issues became a part of the permanent repertoire on the political scene (not just local).

To understand the development of the care for the poor and social policy in Prague, or in the Czech Lands generally – which aimed to remove, the practice of alms-giving in favour of general social insurance – it was necessary to compare the practice carried out by the city of Prague with other examples, both domestic and foreign (Cisleithanian and Transleithanian municipalities, as well as with a wider European horizon).

The abovementioned conference topics subsequently became the decisive criterion for the selection of papers included in this volume. From a total of 34 participants at the conference – the dealings are described in detail in a report by Martina Maříková and Martina Power, which was published on the website of the Institute of Historical Sciences of the Humboldt University Berlin, H-Soz-Kult – twenty of them were asked to produce studies based on their conference papers, chronologically defined by period from the beginning of the 19th century to the 1940s. At the centre of their attention was Prague with the Austro-Hungarian, or rather the European, context of its development in the social sphere. The entirety of all papers presented at the conference in 2013 is being published in parallel in the journal Documenta Pragensia (no. 34/2015) in the form of separate studies in the original languages.

PART I:

TENDENCIES OF DEVELOPMENT

CHAPTER ONE

"FOR YOU ALWAYS HAVE THE POOR WITH YOU…": FROM CHARITY TO MUNICIPAL SOCIAL POLICY

OLGA FEJTOVÁ AND MILAN HLAVAČKA

Abstract: Any urban organism has faced the problem of poverty throughout its existence. In the Middle Ages and early modern times, poverty policy in the European context oscillated between care, control and repression. In the early modern period we can trace the roots of modern European poverty policy, based on the belief that care for the poor is not just a matter of private and religious facilities, but one of the main tasks of the state. Old age, illness and unemployment were the three basic causes of poverty during the examined time period: the Austrian, and in particular Czech approach to poverty eradication at the end of the 18th and beginning of the 19th centuries was determined by connection of the state with the church and municipal bodies of the care for the poor through the so-called "Poor Institutes", active in the area of open care for the poor. The system of institutional care then connected the areas of health care and poverty care. The original system, installed during the Enlightenment era, which centralised care for the poor mainly in the hands of the state, was transformed in the 19th century due to financial problems. Thus, the obligation to care for the poor was transferred onto the shoulders of municipalities where the given individual in need had his permanent residence. A new approach to solving both the traditional poor and newer workers' issues was tried at the end of the 19th and beginning of the 20th century, resulting in a merger of all these issues into a single "humanitarian" area. This new concept of social policy subsequently served as a basis for the reorganisation of social policy in Czechoslovakia, whereas the central problem of the system continued to be the issue of unemployment.

Poverty is a concept that has to be always regarded with a respect for the contemporary political, economic, social and psychological context.

The definition of poverty has always been dependent on the perception of contemporary subsistence minimum within a certain social group, which has always been a relative value, related specifically and exclusively to the socio-economic circumstances of that given social group.[1] Yet poverty cannot be reduced only to material poverty, it is also a social exclusion, accompanied by discrimination at the level of social opportunities.[2] The poor, the elderly, as well as sick or orphaned individuals have become recipients of systematic care.[3] Poverty and beggary have primarily been related to the urban environment.[4]

The problem of poverty has accompanied cities and their inner functioning throughout their development. The urban organism has always had to react to problems associated with the daily life of the lowest classes, to individuals on the outskirts of the city or to individuals entirely excluded. The church has played a dominant role in this area since the Middle Ages. In addition, there have also been various private initiatives, coupled with activities of individuals and local communities (e.g. guilds) – or their administrative institutions respectively – and the royal initiative cannot be forgotten either. In the long term – and in the context of the European situation – fighting poverty has evolved from non-systematic care provided by individual donations to collectively organised and managed care for the poor, resulting in systematic social care in the 19th century, adopting a form of targeted social policy, provided by the state or municipal institutions.[5]

In the Middle Ages and Early Modern era, the poverty policy ranged between care, control and repression. A widely shared view that poverty actually constituted "God likes it like that" status in the medieval European Christian society, and therefore there was no distinction between

---

[1] Poverty was a caused as well as accidental, both absolute and relative phenomenon of a group or individual character, subjective or objective, caused by natural and social conditions, individual destinies and their own actions, or a combination of those all phenomena. Cf. Bohumil Geist, *Sociologický slovník* [Dictionary of Sociology], 1st edition, s.v. "chudoba" [poverty], (Praha: Victoria Publishing, [1993]), p. 116.

[2] Bedřich Loevenstein, "'Každý svého štěstí strůjcem?' Chudoba: evropské percepce a praktiky" ['Every man is the architect of his own fortune.' Poverty: European perception and practice], *Dějiny a současnost* 34 (2012), no. 1: p. 24.

[3] Wolfgang von Hippel, *Armut, Unterschichten, Randgruppen in der Frühen Neuzeit* (München: Oldenbourg, 1995), p. 45.

[4] Andrea Iseli, *Gute Policey. Öffentliche Ordnung in der Frühen Neuzeit* (Stuttgart: Ulmer, 2009), p. 45.

[5] Geist, *Sociologický slovník*, p. 409.

the worthy and unworthy poor, and care for the needy was actually a basic task of contemporary society, had its limitations.[6] On one hand, protecting the poor and weak represented both an important element of legitimising medieval reign and also a contemporary ideal way of life. Additionally, Christian alms was a ritual, a question of social prestige as well as a "heavenly" reward.[7] At the theological level, there has been a differentiation between "the poor with Peter", i.e. ecclesiastical persons who had voluntarily chosen poverty, and "the poor with Lazarus", i.e. secular people who found themselves in need.[8] On the other hand, the medieval Christian concept has also reflected the principle of "culpable" or "honour" poverty.[9] In relation to this phenomenon, there can be identified both a generally declared sympathy and an extreme aversion to healthy individuals who made their living by begging. There was a persistent theoretical debate in the medieval Christian intellectual environment, which attempted to address the question of who to support – all the "needy" or just those who were in their regrettable situation involuntarily.[10]

The Christian teaching perceived the poor primarily as an object of mercy and therefore primarily cared about the people who actually provided the support.[11] Almsgiving (support) was supposed to create a "mutuality between the donor and the recipient."[12] In the late Middle Ages and in early modern times, however, a tightened regimentation and control occurred. Christian mercy, based on the principles of Christian ethics, remained merely one of the motives for supporting the poor. A structural change in perception of the relationship between poverty and work, associated with the implementation of the ideas of humanism and the Reformation, began to play an important role at that time – contemporary society consistently began to distinguish poverty as a result of the inability

[6] Loevenstein, "Každý svého štěstí strůjcem?," pp. 24–25.
[7] Ibid., p. 25.
[8] Bronisław Geremek, *Slitování a šibenice* [Mercy and gallows] (Praha: Argo, 1999), p. 33.
[9] Ibid., pp. 26–27.
[10] Wolfram Fischer, *Armut in der Geschichte. Erscheinungsformen und Lösungsversuche der "Sozialen Frage" in Europa seit dem Mittelalter* (Göttingen: Vandenhoeck und Ruprecht, 1982), p. 41; Geremek, *Slitování a šibenice*, p. 24; Lukas Clemens, "Armenfürsorge in den mittelalterlichen Städten Westeuropas," in *Armut. Perspektiven in Kunst und Gesellschaft*, eds. Herbert Uerlings et al., (Darmstadt: Primus Verlag, 2011), p. 116; *Milosrdenství ve středověkých městech*, [Mercy in Medieval towns] (= Documenta Pragensia Supplementa 4), ed. Kateřina Jíšová (Praha: Scriptorium, 2013).
[11] Geremek, *Slitování a šibenice*, pp. 33–34.
[12] Loewenstein, "Každý svého štěstí strůjcem?," p. 25.

to work, lack of income from work, lack of job opportunities or the poverty caused by a lack of willingness to work.[13] This approach resulted in the gradual establishment of new types of facilities for the poor in cities. These facilities actually expanded the functionality of originally generously and fairly universally conceived spitals/hospitals (these medieval hospitals combined health care and care for the poor). In the 16th century, European cities also started to operate facilities whose purpose was to identify the poor who were able to work and who claimed various forms of support in order to compel them to work. The very first facility of this type was established in England in 1555 and spread to the continent about four decades later (Amsterdam).[14] These institutions spread through Western Europe from the second half of the 17th century. Their statutes declared that education of the poor but physically able to work was their priority, in full accordance with the principles of Christian morality. Such re-educated individuals could be re-integrated into municipal communities. These hybrid spital-prison institutions – although they could acquire the form of "houses of work", "correctional facilities" or "houses of forced labour" (house of correction) – often had a less clear-cut form, focused on the effort to isolate the poor.[15] In practice, these "hospitals" (in contemporary terminology) accepted the sick, the elderly and the physically and mentally disabled. Sooner or later, they outnumbered the employable inmates, who had been accepted for re-education. Thus the original educational purpose of these institutions was never fully met, mainly due to economic problems, hand in hand with a lack of cooperation with the surrounding municipal communities.[16]

The requirement for the internment and segregation of the poor who were able to work appeared in the European context before the Enlightenment era, and such requirement actually did not compromise the continuity of traditional Christian mercy.[17] Therefore, establishing these large spitals – or types of criminal detention facilities – cannot be considered exclusively

---

[13] Hippel, *Armut*, p. 4.
[14] Franz Dorn et al., "Zucht- und Arbeitshaus," in *Armut. Perspektiven in Kunst und Gesellschaft*, eds. Herbert Uerlings et al., (Darmstadt: Primus Verlag, 2011), p. 68.
[15] Geremek, *Slitování a šibenice*, pp. 220–228.
[16] Iseli, *Gute Policey*, pp. 48–49. The year of 1656 represents the beginning of such policy in Europe – a decree confirming the establishing of a "General Spital" in Paris was issued. It was an administrative unit with a half-court character and a clear-cut repressive purpose – cf. Michel Foucault, *Dějiny šílenství v době osvícenství* [Madness and Civilization: A History of Insanity in the Age of Reason], (Praha: Nakladatelství Lidové noviny, 1994), pp. 7, 37–38.
[17] Geremek, *Slitování a šibenice*, pp. 150–180, 227.

as a product of the Enlightenment era.[18] The Enlightenment reality merely provided them with a universal character and made their massive expansion possible in connection with the development of charitable activities promoted and organised by the state. Besides, in the pre-Enlightenment era, there were partial attempts (conducted by the state administrative) to record the number of the poor, to fund their support and to distribute these financial means through an organised network of secular and religious institutions.[19] Similarly, we cannot fully agree with Michel Foucault, who argues that it was the Enlightenment era which created a "dividing line between work and idleness." [20]

Requirements for dividing the poor into two groups: employable beggars and vagrants living on alms, and the poor who were unable to provide sustenance for reasons of age or other serious conditions, had existed within the secular government throughout the entire early modern period. The Enlightenment époque only triggered the institutionalisation of tackling this problem in an urban environment.[21] A trend of centralisation and rationalisation is therefore associated with the advent of the early modern period of European history.[22] Behind the new, largely rational approach to poverty in the early modern times stood new ideas of mercantilism, which perceived poverty in people able to work as a failure of the sovereign or the state.[23]

Poverty was definitely not a marginal problem for urban settlements in the early modern period. Numbers of people reliant on alms undoubtedly differed, not only locally, depending on the size and nature of cities, but also depended on various critical moments that periodically affected early modern cities (wars, epidemics, fires, etc.). The latest research suggests that up to one third of all households may have been reliant on alms in the early modern cities and up to a half of all burgesses were not able to generate savings, i.e. they were constantly teetering on the brink of poverty.[24] Until the early modern period, care for the poor had been private and church business. In the 16th century, municipal or aristocratic

---

[18] Foucault, *Dějiny šílenství*, p. 40.
[19] Geremek, *Slitování a šibenice*, pp. 150–180.
[20] Foucault, *Dějiny šílenství*, p. 49.
[21] Ibid., p. 174. Forced labour was a "coercive measure" in such correctional institutions.
[22] Loewenstein, "Každý svého štěstí strůjcem?," p. 25.
[23] Sebastian Schmidt, "Armut und Arme in Stadt und Territorium der Frühen Neuzeit," in *Armut. Perspektiven in Kunst und Gesellschaft*, eds. Herbert Uerlings et al., (Darmstadt: Primus Verlag, 2011) pp. 127–128.
[24] Ibid., p. 121.

institutions became increasingly involved in this sphere as well.[25] In early modern times, the poor policy gradually became a part of disciplinary measures enforced by the temporal power, which standardised public and moral life in Prague via police orders and regulations. The "poor police" featured, together with interventions in the field of religion, health, economy and construction, a basic means of regulating everyday life.[26] In this respect, the poor policy represented a part of measures called "gute Policey" – an instrument for achieving a "public good" – a desired order of early modern urban society.[27] The poor police measures mainly concerned traditional forms of dealing with poverty, i.e. institutional, closed hospital care, the practice of alms, etc. They were still based on the principles of Christian ethics along with regulating the occurrence of beggars.[28]

A decisive period that changed the perception of poverty and sought new ways to solve it was the 18th century. On one hand, this was the era when the development of early modern society was crowned, and on the other hand it was a period of anticipating the development of poverty based on new principles brought by the industrial period. In the 18th century, the urban poor policy was affected by the principles of communisation, rationalisation, bureaucratisation and last but not least by education.[29] Generally, cities tried to improve the organisation of care for the poor by concentrating its financial funding in the hands of the municipal administration, as well as by keeping lists of the poor, by provisions of job opportunities for the poor and especially by ensuring their education for work, or ultimately for a bourgeois morality.[30] During that period, however, new requirements started to be implemented in the ongoing system of care for the poor. These new elements actually hinted at – at least in some aspects – the concept of future modern poor care of the

---

[25] Ibid., p. 120.

[26] Cf. Olga Fejtová, *"Já pevně věřím a vyznávám…" Rekatolizace na Novém Městě pražském v době pobělohorské* ['I firmly believe and confess…' Counter-Reformation in Prague New Town during the post-White Mountain period] (Praha: Scriptorium, 2012), p. 82 – the anti-luxurious agenda occurred only in a limited way in Prague, when compared to foreign countries.

[27] For more on the "gute Policey" and on the poor police see Iseli, *Gute Policey*, pp. 8–31, 45–49.

[28] Cf. Robert Jütte, *Obrigkeitliche Armenfürsorge in deutschen Reichsstädten der frühen Neuzeit. Städtisches Armenwesen in Frankfurt am Main und Köln*, (Köln et al.: Böhlau, 1984), pp. 331–340.

[29] Hippel, *Armut*, p. 47.

[30] Ibid.; Fischer, *Armut in der Geschichte*, p. 41 – a need to force the poor to work was already being emphasised by the mercantilism at the end of the 17th century.

19th century, including principles of subsidiarity, individualisation, right of domicile and also discipline.[31] The official state policy interfered in the sphere of urban poverty, seeking to enforce the abovementioned principles.[32] Specifically, it was mainly an effort to concentrate funds dedicated to the care for the poor in the hands of the municipal administration. And it was also the municipality that was supposed to synchronise all activities of other entities engaged in the area of poor care (churches, charitable societies, guilds, etc.).

The roots of modern European poor policy clearly lie in the early modern period. It was then concluded that poor care is not merely a matter of private and church facilities, but also one of the basic tasks of the state. Nevertheless, solving the problem of poverty in early modern states – setting up a facility that could provide work for the poor as well as their education – proved to be of limited efficacy. The "coercive workhouse" was a place intended to offer integration into the civic society instead of punishment and banishment from the city to those capable of work but living on begging. Besides, the integration of their inmates into urban society was equally important. Yet the achievements of such types of corrective facilities had been poor and stigmatised people who found themselves in them. As early as in the 18th century, it was obvious that the coercive workhouses did not solve the problem of urban poverty.[33]

The fundamental triad of causes of poverty at the threshold of the 19th century were: old age, various illnesses and unemployment.[34] Estimates valid for the urban population of European capitals in this period indicate that about 20–30% of the entire urban population was constantly balancing at subsistence level. Individuals belonging to this set were constantly threatened by relegation to the social bottom and a possible subsequent sentence to live on various forms of support for the poor. On average, 10–20% of the urban population was dependent on various forms of support.[35] The abovementioned facts were the main reasons for starting to think about various ways to minimise the consequences of two basic life

---

[31] Ibid.

[32] In some parts of the Reich, the urban poor care was already under state (or monarchal) supervision at the beginning of the 17th century, e.g. in Berlin. Compare Wolfgang Radtke, *Armut in Berlin. Die sozialpolitischen Ansätze Christian von Rothers und der Königlichen Seehandlung im vormärzlichen Preußen* (Berlin: Akad.-Verl., 1993), p. 55.

[33] Schmidt, "Armut und Arme in Stadt und Territorium der Frühen Neuzeit," p. 128.

[34] Fischer, *Armut in der Geschichte*, pp. 82–83.

[35] Ibid.

handicaps – illness and old age. The output of such efforts was the birth of social insurance, which, however, in the first phase was earmarked merely a form of health or accident insurance.[36]

In the 19th century, the socio-economic reality changed rapidly as the industrialisation process expanded the traditional issues of poverty also regarding workers. Solving the issues of the poor and other social issues in the 19th century influenced the shaping of liberal constitutional states. The state theory (and the law system as well) subsequently changed the view of the relationship between the state and an individual. This development opened a substantial debate on to what extent the state should act as a central provider of poor care. Debates on who is really poor, and who is therefore entitled to receive support from public institutions were endless. Another widely debated topic was the responsibility of the society/state for the lowest strata of society and its responsibility for improving the situation of the poorest. Especially in the second half of the 19th century, the answers to this question ranged from liberal stances, through Christian ones, to new socialist views. In liberal theory, (which massively influenced political systems of European states in the first half of the 19th century), the "absolute definition of poverty" was heavily promoted. Poverty meant merely a lack of the necessary material means for physical survival (food, clothing, housing).[37] This strict approach resulted in deriving a definition of the poor which represented only persons who could not solely for reasons of old age, disease and/or juvenile age (in the case of orphans) provide for themselves. However, practical implementation of this definition was rather rare, e.g. in England. In the 1830s, the British Poor Law allowed financial support only to those who were willing to enter the coercive workhouses and work there under very difficult circumstances. In other countries, the category of persons who should be supported by the state or municipalities was not that radically and extremely determined. Nevertheless, the general tendency was to differentiate support given to the needy according to their current situation.[38]

The social question became one of the major themes of social discourse in the Czech Lands in the 19th century as well, since it represented a fundamental aspect of the transformation of the estates-feudal agrarian society to a modern industrial society.[39] In the first half of

---

[36] Ibid., p. 85.
[37] Andreas Gestrich, "Armut im Liberalen Staat," in *Armut. Perspektiven in Kunst und Gesellschaft*, eds. Herbert Uerlings et al., (Darmstadt: Primus Verlag, 2011), pp. 130–131.
[38] Ibid., p. 132.
[39] Werner Drobesch, "Die 'soziale Frage' in der Habsburgermonarchie im

the 19th century, initial responses to problems of arising industrial society
– along with rather limited discussions on poor care issues and newly,
social issues too – were mostly non-systematic solutions focused on
particular issues. Contemporary debates and subsequent proposals oscillated
between bureaucratic interventions – which were still ideologically
anchored in guild-feudal estates establishment and took the form of
"reform from above" – and considerations which led to social utopianism
on the opposite side of the sphere.[40]

In the Habsburg monarchy, a model of "social state" by Lorenz von
Stein became the defining idea of theoretical discussions dedicated to
solving social issues. Basically, it was a concept of "conservative
modernisation", which distanced itself from the positions of both
liberalism and the emerging socialist concepts. Stein's proposals aimed at
achieving social harmony between capital and labour, through social
reforms under the auspices of the state.[41] This model sought the third way
between capitalism and socialism and from the era of Taaffe's government
it became part of the official state-bureaucratic discourse and influenced
political reform steps of the state. The idea of social reforms also
penetrated political concepts, forming political blocs and programmes of
various national groupings.[42] When confronted with the need to solve
poverty and other social issues – which greatly increased during the 19th
century – the state power had to accept a series of compromising procedures
that required state intervention, and thus ultimately strengthened the
position of the state in this area.

At the very beginning of state reforms, the issues concerning both the
poor and working class (social issues) were to be separated (first
administratively and later also fiscally).[43] Traditional poverty was supposed

---

zeitgenössichen gesellschaftwissenschaftlichen Diskurs, *Moderní dějiny. Časopis pro dějiny 19. a 20. století* 20 (2012), no.1: p. 2.

[40] Ibid., pp. 2–4. On one hand, it was a concept by Matthias Koch, Albert Hummelauer, Johann Perthaler, and on the other hand it was a theory by Bernard Bolzano.

[41] Ibid., pp. 4–5.

[42] Ibid., pp. 5–6.

[43] Milan Hlavačka, "Chudinství a sociální politika: terminologické vyjasnění, historický přehled a koncepce řešení" [Care of the poor and social policy: terminology, histrorical survey, concepts of solution] in *Chudinství a chudoba jako sociálně historický fenomén: ambivalence dobových perspektiv, individuální a kolektivní strategie chudých a instrumentária řešení* [Care for the poor and poverty as a social and historic phenomenon], eds. Milan Hlavačka and Pavel Cibulka (Praha: Historický ústav, 2013), pp. 40–58; *Ottův slovník naučný* [Otto's encyclopaedia] (further referred to as OSN) vol. 12, 1st edition, s.v. "chudinství"

to be managed by municipal and private initiatives and the new "workers' poverty" was subject to state social regimentation.[44] Fundamentals of social legislation in the monarchy were formed in the 1880s, when the state significantly interfered into the relationship of employee and employer, both by setting up factory inspections and by the amendment to the Trade Act governing overall working conditions (working hours, child labour, etc.).[45] Protective (social) legislation was not left behind either and both health and accident insurance were embodied into the legal system. The overall level of social reforms in the last third of the 19th century put the entire Cisleithanian region in many ways ahead of Germany, its contemporary role model.[46] The level of state involvement in the field of social reforms entrenched in the Habsburg monarchy a general feeling (persisting till the outbreak of the First World War) that such state interventionism was a legitimate means of addressing social issues. A socially active state complemented the existing liberal law state, while discussions were held only on the form and intensity of interventions.[47] This situation largely copied general trends of European development, as the policy of social liberalism became commonly applied at the turn of 19th century.

   The strategy of solving issues concerning the poor in European countries in the 19th century was not directed merely by government policies – private activities still played an important role (stemming from the middle class environment based on Christian traditions). In many countries, such private activities aimed at assisting the poor were more or less integrated into the system of public services. Such integration was typical for regions where the poor care remained rooted in its conservative-paternalistic traditions.[48] It primarily concerned the reality of the monarchy during the first half of the 19th century, when patriarchalism (*Herr-im-Haus-Prinzip*) was a prevailing organisational style, even though it more matched the

---

[care of the poor], (Praha: J. Otto, 1897), p. 431.
[44] Nevertheless, this premise did not exclude private activities in the field of the establishing of workers' societies, mainly for educational purposes. Cf. Gunilla Budde, *Blütezeit des Bürgertums. Bürgerlichkeit im 19. Jahrhundert* (Darmstadt: Wiss. Buchges. 2009), pp. 100–101.
[45] Michael Borovička et al., *Velké dějiny zemí Koruny české* vol. 12a [History of the Lands of the Bohemian Crown], (Praha: Paseka, 2012), pp. 450–453.
[46] Cf. a review by Josef Harna, "Jan Janák, Příčiny vzniku předlitavské sociální správy, Brno 1970" [Jan Janák, Origins of Cislethanian social administration], Časopis Matice moravské 90 (1971): pp. 369–370.
[47] Drobesch, "Die 'soziale Frage' in der Habsburgermonarchie," pp. 8–9.
[48] Gestrich, *Armut im Liberalen Staat*, p. 132.

tradition of estates-feudal agrarian society than the modern, industrial one.[49]

The Austrian, or more specifically Czech, approach towards poverty eradication was characterised by both formal and informal interconnections of state activities with the church and municipal ones through so-called "poverty institutes." These "institutes" were built on a voluntary basis, but state bureaucracy as well as the monarch and his court administration considered the creation of a dense network of such institutions as an expression of loyalty of both the wealthier population and religious circles to the state policy. The influence of the Catholic Church on the practical implementation of poor policy lasted until the liberal era, when it was replaced by local administrations, i.e. the institute of "home village." The poverty institutes channelled their activities into so-called "open care for the poor" and worked under the supervision of the state apparatus, or under the supervision of state and ecclesiastical officials. The second sphere of the newly-organised poor care in the monarchy became institutional care, which interconnected health and poor care. In keeping with the Josephine reforms, the guarantor of the entire system of poor care was the state. In the case of poverty institutes, the state provided the capital and then controlled their activities. Centralised, institutional medical-poor care (poorhouses, spitals, etc.) was directly responsible to government administration. Only the Jewish population was excluded from this newly created system.[50]

Financial problems of poor care in the post-Josephine era actually freed up a space for new reform proposals around the late 1820s. Yet the majority of them only concerned bureaucratic measures and efforts to obtain additional funds from municipalities, although they were supposed to be – if they operated the "poverty institutes" in accordance with royal directives from the Josephine period – free of any additional financial contributions.[51] However, bigger problems beset the provincial institutional poor care institutes, as they provided care for poor people for free. The share of municipal finances was rising during the first half of the 19th

---

[49] Budde, *Blütezeit des Bürgertums*, p. 99. Entrepreneurs often played the role of "pater familias" in their businesses.
[50] Hlavačka, "Chudinství a sociální politika," pp. 54–57.
[51] Petr Svobodný and Ludmila Hlaváčková, *Pražské špitály a nemocnice* [Prague spitals and hospitals] (Praha: Nakladatelství Lidové noviny, 1999), pp. 38–39, Olga Fejtová, "Organizace chudinské péče v letech 1781–1922" [Care of the poor within 1781–1922] , in *Osm století pražské samosprávy* [Eight centuries of Prague's self-government], eds. Václav Ledvinka et al. (Praha: Scriptorium, 2000), pp. 135–136.

century and gradually became a fundamental source of financial security in the field of poor care. A logical consequence of this development was re-transferring of the obligation to care for the poor back onto the community – or onto the home village – which culminated in the release of a new imperial municipal law. Subsequently, a Domicile Act (1862, 1863) was released.[52] Even though this step theoretically presented a unifying solution for the entire Empire, it was actually never quite achieved, since individual units of the Habsburg Empire implemented the domicile law to differing extents. While in some provincial units of the monarchy the care provided by parishes was formally abolished (concurrently with the issuance of the Domicile Act), the network of open care systems provided by single parishes in the Czech Lands was merely reorganised. Yet from the early 1860s, the actual administration of care for the poor did not have a direct connection with the church. This statutory norm, i.e. the Domicile Act, brought a significant financial burden, especially for smaller communities. This was caused by the fact that individuals in social need – who had spent their productive age in industrialised urban centres – were transported back to their home village after having become "unproductive" due to age, illness or disability.

The system of home villages remained the basis of the organisation of poor care in Cisleithania. In the context of solving issues concerning the poor abroad, mainly in neighbouring German states, it was one of the basic models of poor care. The second model was the Prussian one, based on the current residence of the person in need, so ultimately the state was responsible for the care of the poor. Thus local communities were not functioning as a starting point for ensuring the care for the poor, but they actually functioned as its providers.[53]

The organising principle based on the home jurisdiction was confirmed by the Czech edition of the Act of Relief of the Poor in 1868. Its wording already reflected the extraordinary financial demands that burdened the municipal budgets, and returned at least a part of this agenda – especially

---

[52] Imperial Act no. 18/1862, article V (March 5, 1862); Act on Right of Domicile no. 105/1863, part IV, obligation of municipalities to provide for the poor – articles 22–31 (December 12, 1863).

[53] *OSN* vol. 12, 1st edition, s.v. "chudinství" [care of the poor], pp. 434–435; Martin Krauß, *Armenwesen und Gesundheitsfürsorge in Mannheim vor der Industrialisierung 1750–1850/60* (Sigmaringen: Thorbecke, 1993), pp. 146–150; Christoph Sachße and Florian Tennstedt, *Geschichte der Armenfürsorge in Deutschland* vol. 1, (Stuttgart: Kohlhammer, 1998), second edition, pp. 195–205; Susanne F. Eser, *Verwaltet und verwahrt – Armenpolitik und Arme in Augsburg: Vom Ende der reichsstädtischen Zeit bis zum Ersten Weltkrieg* (Sigmaringen: Thorbecke, 1996).

when coupled with medical care – back to the state or provincial administration respectively.[54] Yet the debates about financial demands of the care of the poor agenda in the municipal budgets concerned especially smaller towns and villages. A closer look at the situation, for example in Prague, reveals a gradual increase in municipal spending on individuals in need, though it was a matter of only a few percent.[55]

After the transfer of the agenda onto the municipalities, the increasing financial demands on managing the issues of the poor in the Czech Lands became an important impetus for further modernisation measures in this area. Efforts to achieve a greater efficiency led the municipal administration in a number of towns to implementing the so-called "Elberfeld system." This mechanism reorganised the sector of open care for the poor and its main advantage was that the active care for the poor was carried out without the participation and/or support of the church. The Elberfeld system also counted on volunteer activity and was based on principles of directness, individualisation and decentralisation of care. It was applied especially in border areas of the Czech Lands (Trutnov, Liberec, Karlovy Vary, Varnsdorf, Bílina, etc.).[56] Soon it became apparent that this system, though based on rigorous control activities, did not bring the expected substantial savings.[57]

The second trend which influenced modernisation of the care for the poor at the turn of the century was a change in the perception of care for the poor, which was also reflected at a terminological-semantic level. The terms "poverty" or "the state of being poor" were then replaced by "care for human well-being," or humanistic care (*Wohlfahrtspflege*). Obviously, this was not only a matter of terminology. It was a general change in the overall approach to the poor and to social issues globally. In other words, it meant an attempt to unify all the procedures in this area. Poverty should

---

[54] *OSN* vol. 12, 1st edition, s.v. "chudinství" [care of the poor], p. 436.
[55] The budget of the city of Prague included expenses for the poor (both open care and institutional as well). In the 1870s it was 5%–6%, in the 1890s it was ca. 8% and in 1900–1910 it reached 10%. Cf. *Finanční předchozí rozvrh obecních důchodův a zvláštních fondův královského hlavního města Prahy na rok 1879* [Financial previous budget of municipal incomes and particular funds of the royal capital of Prague for the year 1879] (Praha: V. Nagl, 1878), pp. 62–63; *Předchozí rozpočet král. hlavního města Prahy na rok 1896* [Previous budget of the royal capital of Prague for the year 1896] (Praha: E. Beaufort, 1895), pp. 178–180; *Obecní rozpočty král. hlav. města Prahy 1905* [Municipal budgets of the royal capital of Prague 1905] (Praha: E. Beaufort, 1904), pp. 278–279 (section XI., Předchozí rozpočet [Previous Budget]).
[56] *OSN* vol. 12, 1st edition, s.v. "chudinství" [care of the poor], p. 436.
[57] Hlaváčka, "Chudinství a sociální politika," p. 57.

be further mitigated by comprehensive measures, which would be based on improving the economic situation of the lower classes, whose standard of living should be increased by a set of procedures (legal standards, compulsory insurance, recruitment and job creation).[58] On the other hand, traditional practices of a preventive, control and corrective character, were also incorporated into the new system. All types of activities in this area were supposed to be coordinated (i.e. private and municipal/state activities) at the same time. The expected result of these changes should be a new type of institution called "humanitarian," which was supposed to "morally and materially uplift humanity."[59] In practice, this meant mainly the interconnection of management of services such as poorhouses, orphanages, spitals with hospitals and prisons (prisons actually newly functioned as shelters for the poor to prevent them from loitering), with the entire spectrum of care facilities for children and youth, including corrective ones. Besides, the agenda of wageworkers was also included in the new "humanitarian system." In addition, problems of unemployment and housing issues became an integral part of the urban social policy.[60]

However, these mechanisms could not fully develop before the First World War so that their effectiveness in municipal administrative practice could not be assessed. The abovementioned new approach to solving traditional issues of the care for the poor, along with newer workers' issues, resulted in their revolutionary uniting into a single "humanitarian" area. This newly devised system actually became the basis of the reorganisation of the entire social sphere within both the state and municipal administration in Czechoslovakia. Unemployment issues were the focus of social policy both at the state and municipal level in Czechoslovakia and they escalated during the world economic crisis. Besides, housing issues quickly became urgent at the level of municipal administration. Yet the original idea that all expenses on unemployment benefits would be fully guaranteed and assumed by the state was abandoned due to the financial cost in the early 1920s. Thus the First Republic system of social care adopted the Ghent system in 1921. It was an arrangement whereby the main responsibility for unemployment benefits was held by labour unions, with some financial assistance from the state.[61] Yet this support was in many respects limited, with the result

---

[58] Ibid.
[59] *OSN* vol. 11, 1st edition, s.v. "humanitní ústavy" [humanitarian institutions], p. 870.
[60] *Almanach král. hlav. města Prahy na rok 1908* (Praha: E. Stivín, 1908), p. 121.
[61] Jakub Rákosník, "Gentský systém v období I. Československé republiky" [The Ghent system in the era of the 1st Czechoslovak Republic], *Časopis Národního*

that more than 40% of the unemployed found themselves outside the
system. Since the outbreak of the Great Depression, the benefit system
became supplemented by extraordinary aid from state resources, flat-
allocated according to the degree of social necessity. This emergency
assistance took the form of both financial benefits which were paid
regionally according to the degree of unemployment, and besides that
help, there were other forms of relief (free distribution of bread, etc.).
Nevertheless, a significant part of the solution to the problem of
unemployment still burdened municipalities all across Czechoslovakia.[62]

The newly organised social security system was intended to function
primarily on full professionalisation, for the first time in its history.
Working and housing issues, alongside social care for adults and youth
affairs, remained the core problem to tackle. The aim was to carry out the
active social policy based on prevention and effective control. Yet the
basic social measures remained the financial support (whether regular or
extraordinary) which was paid out by municipalities outside of the Ghent
system.[63]

On the example of Prague, we can demonstrate that the basic assumptions
of municipal social care relied on minimal state interference in the period
between the wars. Furthermore, the entire system was based on
decentralisation and individualisation of subsidies, and on the other side
stood the centralisation and specialisation of institutional care. Prevention
and mobilisation of unemployed (but capable of work) individuals was
also emphasised during the whole inter-war period. Activation was also
associated with an active approach to the various forms of social
insurance. However, the city of Prague also purposefully and deliberately
channelled public investments into the health system, sanitation, housing
and education. Interestingly, despite a relatively generous social policy,
the amount of money spent on welfare was not higher than in pre-war
times, even during the Great Depression.[64] The above characteristics

---

muzea – řada historická 170 (2001), no. 3–4: pp. 84–105, p. 85 specifically.

[62] Ibid., pp. 88–92.

[63] Olga Fejtová, "Od chudinské k sociální péči v Praze 19. a první poloviny 20.
století" [From the care for the poor to the social welfare in Prague of the 19th and
first half of the 20th centuries] in *Sociální myšlení a sociální praxe v českých
zemích 1781–1939. Ideje – legislativa – instituce* [Social thought and social praxis
in the Czech Lands 1781–1939. Ideas—legislation—institutions], eds. Milan
Hlaváčka et al. (Praha: Historický ústav, 2014), pp. 223–314, here pp. 288, 291–
314.

[64] In the budget of 1923, these expenses accounted (after extending the social
agenda, which had been excluded from education) for ca. 9% of the total budget
(i.e. less than in the pre-war period). In 1929, the social expenses accounted for

suggest that social care in Prague oscillated between liberal and socialist elements. What is more, in many aspects it still implemented more conservative and old paternalistic models. While a liberal approach was promoted in the branch of open social care and its principles in this area were significantly violated only in times of crisis, institutional care tended towards a rather socialist model. The traditional paternalistic model was still typical for the organisational structure of social bodies of Prague, as it leaned towards – and often actually duplicated – the older pre-war tradition of poor care.[65] On the municipal level, inter-war Prague exercised in its social policy a number of procedures and solutions, applying a model of a democratic welfare state that later became leading trends in social policy in European countries after the Second World War.[66]

11% of Prague's budget and they stayed at this level in the 1930s. Cf. *Rozpočty obce hlav. města Prahy na rok 1923* [The budgets of municipality, capital of Prague for the year 1923] (Praha: Českomoravské podniky tiskařské a nakladatelské, 1922), pp. iii–iv; *Rozpočty obce hlav. města Prahy na rok 1929* [The budgets of municipality, capital of Prague for the year 1929] (Praha: Tiskárna "politika," 1928), p. 116; *Rozpočty obce hlav. města Prahy na rok 1934* [The budgets of municipality, capital of Prague for the year 1934] (Praha: Tiskárna "politika," 1933), p. 84.

[65] Fejtová, "Od chudinské k sociální péči v Praze," p. 312.

[66] Winfried Thaa and Markus Linden, "Armut im demokratischen Wohlfahrtsstaat," in *Armut. Perspektiven in Kunst und Gesellschaft*, eds. Herbert Uerlings et al., (Darmstadt: Primus Verlag, 2011), pp. 141–142.

CHAPTER TWO

FROM HEGEMONY TO MARGINALISATION: TRENDS IN THE CARE FOR THE POOR IN THE CZECH LANDS IN THE YEARS 1863–1956

JAKUB RÁKOSNÍK

Abstract: This article deals with the development of the care for the poor and social care in the Czech Lands and in Czechoslovakia since 1863, when the Act on the Right of Domicile of December 3 came into effect (this act formed a basic framework of the care for the poor) to the release of the Social Security Act in 1956, which ultimately replaced all previous legislation regarding care for the poor stemming from the 19th century. The overall development of the care for poor is divided into three thematic areas: legal regulation of this area, institutions involved in the care for the poor. Finally, the study evaluates and compares statistical data on poverty.

The years cited in the title of the article may seem completely arbitrary only at first sight,[1] as these are literally breakthrough dates in the history of care for people in need. The Act on Right of Domicile was passed in 1863 and it provided exact general rules for municipalities in the field of support for the poor. In 1956, the Social Security Act created a new legal basis for social policy, which completely replaced all previous legislation regarding care for the poor stemming from the 19th century. This act remained effective without any major changes until the beginning of the transformation of social policy in 1990. The title "From hegemony to marginalisation" expresses the process of the declining significance of the care for the poor in the complex of public-law social protection. Aside from private philanthropy and self-help associations according to the

---

[1] This article was written within the project Prvouk P12, whose bearer is the Faculty of Arts of Charles University (History in interdisciplinary perspective).

Mining Act (Coll. no. 146/1854) and the trade order, respectively (Coll. no. 227/1859), care for the poor actually constituted an almost hegemonic tool of public-law social protection during the 1860s. Thanks to the subsequent development of other instruments during the century that followed, the importance of the poor law was gradually weakening, and we can talk about its utter marginalisation after 1948. Care for the poor, or social welfare, in general, was considered something unsystematic, inappropriate, even unworthy of a society embracing socialism.[2]

This article focuses on the following topics: legal regulations of the area of the care of the poor, the institutions involved in the care for the poor and an evaluation and comparison of statistical data on poverty.

Legal regulations

The terms "poverty"/"pauperism" [*chudinství*] and "care for the poor"/"poverty care" [*chudinská péče*] carry a hint of archaism in contemporary Czech language. Despite the fact that we stopped using these terms in the legal sphere a long time ago, a continuity between the past and present still exists – perhaps it is actually stronger than we would ever be willing to admit (testing social necessity, without which current social care cannot do, stigmatisation and social marginalisation of beneficiaries of support, etc.). In the inter-war period, the term "poverty"/"pauperism" was rapidly being eliminated as politically incorrect and replaced by other, less stigmatising terms – especially by terms such as "social welfare," or less frequently by the expression "social assistance." In this aspect, the Czech Lands did not prove to be any exception, as they pursued rather broader contemporary European trends (similarly, Great Britain switched from the traditional "poor law" to "social assistance" at the same time).

The roots of modern legislation on the care for the poor can be seen in the Revolution of 1848. The Provisional Municipal Law was issued under Coll. no.170/1849 and it anchored the legal right of members of a given community to "provision by proven needs" (Article 22 of the cited Law). Being a member of that given community meant by law having a right of domicile in that particular community. In practice, however, this was not a fundamental change, as it actually presented a legislative response to the abolition of landlords-subjects relations and the associated disintegration of the previous patrimonial administration. Basically, nothing changed in the institutional structure of the care for the poor,[3] as it had been

---

[2] Cf. *Od národního pojištění k dnešku* [From national insurance to the present], *Sociální zabezpečení* 17, no. 4 (1968): p. 1.

[3] For more see Jiří Pražák, *Rakouské právo správní* [The Austrian administration

continuously evolving since the time of Joseph II and the Municipal Law
Coll. no. 18/1862 which had set the duty of the community "care for its
poor and for communal charitable institutions" (Article V.). This act was
followed by the implementing act Coll. no. 105/1863, called the Act on
Right of Domicile.[4] The Act on Right of Domicile actually did not
introduce anything groundbreaking into the existing practice, since it only
specified general provisions of municipal governing rules, which also
included the obligation of communities to care for their poor.[5] In addition,
some countries of the Habsburg monarchy adopted special regulations on
the care for the poor. The (Provincial) Poor Law for the Czech Kingdom
(Coll. no. 59/1868) was of that character. It specified the following
conditions for a legal claim for receiving assistance in poverty: right of
domicile, poverty, incompetence and lack of ability to provide for oneself
as well as a lack of persons capable of providing for the particular
individual in need. Yet these abovementioned points only constituted a
factual expansion of previously applicable principles included in existing
regulations, and therefore we can fully agree with the contemporary
assessment made by Friedrich Kleinwächter in 1870, when he aptly stated
that this law "does not enforce any new pathways, nor does it contain any
special, remarkable provisions."[6]

The general legal parameters of the care for the poor remained
basically unchanged until the dissolution of the Habsburg monarchy. But
this cannot be said about their practical application. The most serious
problem was the excessive generality of these rules. The former legislation
lacked any precise determination of an existence minimum. On the other
hand, this is fully understandable, when taking the huge regional divergence
of the entire monarchy into account. Clearly, it was impossible to determine
a uniform rate that could be applied to all corners of the monarchy – in rich

---

law] (Praha: Jednota právnická, 1906), pp. 322–323.

[4] In this sense, the Czech (Provincial) Poor Law Coll. no. 59/1868 as well as the
Act on Right of Domicile Coll. no. 105/1863 acted as implementing acts. Moravia
lacked a specific modification to care for the poor at the provincial level. Although
this issue was repeatedly discussed at the Moravian Provincial Assembly, for
reasons of political disputes an approval of some law analogous to that which was
in force in Bohemia never occurred. Thus in practice, only the general provisions
of the Municipal Law remained as the single directive.

[5] Zdeňka Stoklásková, "Zákonné rozlišení „domácích" a „cizích" – Vývoj
domovského práva v Rakousku 1750–1863" [The legal distinction of "locals" and
"foreigners" – the development of the right of domicile in Austria], *Český časopis
historický* 102 (2004): pp. 297–341.

[6] Arwed Emminghaus, *Das Armenwesen und die Armengesetzgebung in
europäischen Staaten* (Berlin: F. A. Herbig, 1870), p. 455.

and poor areas, in rural as well as in industrial regions. Thus a framework of legal provisions fell into the competence of courts. A quite rich judicature of the courts actually developed over the following decades and eventually it became relatively stable and contained constant features. What was typical for this practice was a very narrow, even restrictive interpretation of the eligibility for entitlement to benefits as well as to poor provisions. An employable poor individual could not receive any benefit under any circumstances. In actual practice, however, the situation was not so strict, as is evidenced in archival material of 1931: "Until the post-war period [...] municipalities had been ignoring [...] this integral character to define poverty. A detailed knowledge of the local and personal circumstances of those individuals in need was decisive enough for the municipal authorities to approve or reject benefit claims and to implement care for the poor effectively. Therefore, the moment of eligibility to work was being completely disregarded and decisions were made based only upon personal experience, sound reasoning, and especially on the state of community finances."[7]

In 1918, the newly formed Czechoslovak state entered the field of social legislation very ambitiously and it seemed that care for the poor would undergo fundamental reform. In the beginning, an assumption stood, matching the wording of the amendment to Article 20 of Amendment to the Municipal Law (Coll. no. 76/1919): this regulation assumed that the care for the poor as well as charitable institutions would be transferred from municipalities to either the state or to some higher degree of local governments in the context of comprehensive welfare reform. Further developments, however, proceeded to go in a different direction. A fatal problem of the care for the poor was its connection to the community via the right of domicile. This arrangement favoured industrial cities where young people came to work. When these individuals aged, they would become dependent on care for the poor, and would be sent back to their home community (mostly in rural areas). Thus the reform plan of 1919 would surely have helped relieve municipal budgets throughout the country. However, the legislature eventually chose another path. New support tools were introduced instead of overall reform of the care for the poor.

---

[7] Péče o chudé a péče o mládež ochrany potřebnou v Republice československé v roce 1931. díl 1, veřejná péče o chudé v obcích, okresech a zemích republiky československé [Care for the poor and care for the youth in need of protection within the Czechoslovak Republic in 1931, vol. 1: public care for the poor within municipalities, districts and lands of the Czechoslovak Republic], (Praha: Státní úřad statistický, 1935), p. 22.

These additional regulations can be divided into two main branches. First was social insurance. Insurance is a form of protection, which is untested – after all, whoever pays premiums and is affected by a negative social occurrence (e.g. illness, disability, injury, old age, unemployment, etc.) is not required to prove their being in need to receive benefits. The peak of reform efforts in the field of insurance legislation was undoubtedly Act Coll. no. 221/1924, which introduced pensions for all employees, not just for privileged groups such as higher officials or "white collar workers" from higher private sector services. Yet small business owners, entrepreneurs and other independent workers were still not included and Act Coll. no. 148/1925, which gave the right to pensions to these individuals, never actually took effect. Because senior citizens unable to work made up a large group of persons requiring social assistance, improving and expanding the social insurance system meant indirect relief for funding the care for the poor.[8]

Secondly, tools similar to care for the poor also existed, but they were explicitly taken out from the legal and institutional framework of social assistance. The similarity resided in the fact that this form of care was tested, i.e. subject to the criteria of social necessity. In inter-war Czechoslovakia, such measures presented a subsidiary state non-contributory old-age pension plan and catering for the unemployed, a support action run by the state, introduced by Act Coll. no. 74/1930. Those who did not qualify for aid under the Ghent System, were supposed to obtain food vouchers – in contemporary parlance, widely known as "begging vouchers." A subsequent negative evaluation of this state action stemmed from multiple causes. Firstly, the law regulated this action only generally and its specific implementation was governed by internal regulations of the Ministry, which were not publicly known. Therefore, the entire action inevitably created the impression that the limited resources were being distributed among districts unfairly and on a partisan basis. Yet the government had good reason for such a strategy. A proper statutory regulation would have made municipalities eligible for financial allocations and the government definitely wanted to avoid imposing such obligations on itself, with respect to the uncertain outlook of the state budget in times of the Great Depression.[9] The second major shortcoming

---

[8] Cf. Zdeněk Deyl, "Z historie přípravy a vzniku zákona o pojištění zaměstnanců pro případ nemoci, invalidity a stáří" [Few moments from the history of preparation and origin of the on the Employees' Insurance Act in case of illness, disablement and old age], *Československý časopis historický* 21 (1973): pp. 527–552.
[9] Therefore, there consistently appeared criticism (especially in the party press)

presented low allocations to individuals. The minimum voucher was worth 10 Czechoslovak Crowns per week, which could be further supplemented by municipalities at any amount (from their own resources), but obviously, this was definitely not a common practice due to deep financial difficulties municipalities faced at that time.[10]

The subsidiary state non-contributory old-age pension was introduced by the Act Coll. no. 43/1929 for elderly persons not entitled to a pension from insurance. As its name suggests, it was a form of financial support provided by the state, even though the law commanded that their payout would be contributed by a 10–20% premium from the budget of the community where that given person resided (Article 4). People older than 65 years of age, being "poor and incapable of earning" (Article 1) were entitled to receive this benefit. The state old-age pensions were abolished in 1948 when the introduction of the National Insurance (Coll. no. 99/1948) came into effect. This act introduced a new subsidiary called a "social pension", fully replacing the prior system of old-age pensions. However, in terms of conducting the care for the poor in the inter-war Czechoslovakia, both the above analysed measures had a positive effect – relieving municipal finance (from which the care for the poor was covered) as well as increasing the share of the state budget for care for people in need.

After the Second World War, the care for the poor was transferred into the competence of a newly organised system of national committees. At that time, however, care for the poor represented a completely marginal segment of social protection of the Czechoslovak population. The only fundamental conceptual change meant a repeal of the right of domicile, embedded in the Act Coll. no. 174/1948. If there occurred an entitlement to the poor provision after December 31, 1948, providing such social protection to the person in need was on the shoulders of the municipality where the concerned person in need had his permanent residency – and if that given person had no permanent residency, then the municipality where he was currently living (Article 2). The position of social welfare in

---

that some districts received unjustly more than others and that the German borderland was hungry at the expense of the Czech interior, or, conversely, that the German Minister of Social Welfare (Ludwig Czech) favoured his fellows and forgot the poor areas in Slovakia. There also occurred fraudulent machinations with the "begging vouchers."

[10] For more detail, see Jakub Rákosník, *Odvrácená tvář meziválečné prosperity: Nezaměstnanost v Československu v letech 1918–1938* [The reverse side of inter-war prosperity: Unemployment in Czechoslovakia within 1918–1938] (Praha: Karolinum 2008), pp. 233–246.

Czechoslovakia after 1948 can be eloquently summarised by one comment from 1968: "Willy-nilly, the national insurance plunged social care to a certain pathway, somewhat on the margins of society, and so it happened that it was merely passively surviving, instead of being adjusted to the new conditions. Irresponsibly running permanent reorganisations caused individual agendas to become scattered in various departments/ministries where they actually almost never belonged. A necessary understanding has never occurred, [the reorganisations] existed only on paper and where they existed in a tangible form (e.g. in institutional care), they became slashed to eternal fame of other areas."[11] The new legal basis for social care was laid out by the Act on Social Security Coll. no 55/1956. Despite the fact that this act did not explicitly mention the abolition of the old Poor Law of 1868, we may conclude that its effectiveness really ceased only in 1956 and not in 1948, when the right of domicile was abolished.

Institutional care

Even though we can track some sort of care for the poor in every country across the European continent in the 19th century, there were not many common denominators. Differences related to the degree of involvement of individual providers, among which local public-law institutions (from the state to municipalities), churches and philanthropic organisations played a major role. Transferring the care for the poor to the scope of communities in the 1860s meant that various extant institutions involved in the care for the poor lost their status of public-law corporations and became ordinary private charitable institutions – assuming they had not been transferred under the community administration before.

A large plurality of institutional providers was typical for both the Austrian and later Czechoslovak system of the care for the poor – assuming that the care was not provided directly by the inhabitants of a given municipality. This method, when the inhabitants of a given municipality took care of their poor directly and together (could be described as a "circulation of the needy persons around the village"), was following a path of a permanent, noticeable decline in the course of the time, in parallel with a progressive development of other methods of social security. Statistics from 1931 categorically claim: "The circulation was mostly typical only for the poor people of mature age and for old people, unable to work. We can see that practice in Czechoslovakia actually tends to legal conclusions that providing for the poor by applying a circulation is

---

[11] "Od národního pojištění k dnešku," p. 1.

inappropriate. Moreover, it is completely contemptible for children and juveniles from the standpoint of educational, moral, ethical and hygienic, it is inappropriate even for adults because of the same reasons, to which adds a security aspect. Harmful consequences of such a method of procurement cannot be compensated even by economic and administrative reasons. Circulation is of its nature close to begging, and it is a good school and preparation for vagrancy and crime craftsmanship."[12] In addition, Otakar Klapka concluded in the 1920s that the system of "circulation" was controversial from a legal perspective as well, "because the burden of social care should be borne by the municipality as a public corporation and not individual citizens."[13]

From the institutional point of view, a community stood for a primary liable subject. Communities were entitled to establish appropriate administrative commissions and to operate institutions of care for the poor (ranging from so-called "municipal herdsman's huts" to large social institutes in bigger cities). Since the operation of such institutions was often expensive, municipalities could organise "poverty care unions" and the financial burden could be shared among more administrative units this way. Occasionally, also even higher levels of public administration interfered: e.g. in Bohemia in 1902, a provincial orphan fund (Coll. no. 78/1902) was established on the initiative of the Land Committee. Its administration fell within the authority of the Land Committee in close cooperation with district committees and consequently, district committees of youth care were being created at that time as well. According to data from 1911, there were around 90 such committees in Bohemia, supervised by the Land Committee of Youth Care. In 1911, the fund cared for nearly 6,000 orphans. Yet given the fact that at the beginning of the century the number of such needy children in the Czech Lands was estimated at 50,000, the fund covered only a fraction of them.[14]

In the then legal jargon, district committees of youth care had the status of "semi-official institutions."[15] In 1921, the Ministry of Social

---

[12] *Péče o chudé a péče o mládež ochrany potřebnou,* p. 53.

[13] Otakar Klapka, *Chudí v obci – stručný výklad předpisů o chudinství* [The poor in a community – a concise explanation of the regulations on care for the poor] (Praha: Čsl. obec samosprávná, 1924), p. 12.

[14] Miloslav Martínek, "Přehled vývoje rakouského zákonodárství v oblasti chudinství, zdravotnictví a sociální správy" [An overview of the development of the Austrian legislation in the spheres of poor care, health care and social administration], *Sborník k dějinám 19. a 20. století* 4 (1977): pp. 70–71.

[15] In the then language a "semi-official" organization/institution meant that although such bodies had public funds available to them for the purpose of caring for youth and children in need, these bodies did not lose their federal character, i.e.

Welfare issued new model regulations, which finally became normative guidelines for their further activities. As their name suggests, the objects of their care were mainly children and adolescents in need of special care either because of orphanhood or a dismal family background. Nevertheless, a comprehensive reform was carried out as late as during the Third Republic (in April 1947). The Act On the Organisation of Youth Care Coll. no. 48/1947 confined this agenda exclusively to the state administration. District national committees and land national committees (district national committees and the Nominee of Social Care in Slovakia) were obliged to establish special commissions called "District Youth Care" and "Land Youth Care" respectively. The existing voluntary charities were all cancelled.

The "Czechoslovak protection of mothers and children", a central authority for all organisations that focused their activities on these categories of the population, could also trace its roots back to the pre-war times. In addition, the Masaryk League against tuberculosis continued the pre-war activities of the "Czech assistant land association for ill with pulmonary diseases in Bohemia," which was founded in 1899 by the Act on the Right of Association. Another major organisation was the Czechoslovak Red Cross, founded in 1919, which dealt with general social and health care on the battlefield and beyond.[16]

Private charities provided a wide range of services – from counselling on vocational training, counselling for "deviant children", counselling for mental health, counselling for mothers with children, to venereal and tuberculosis clinics. Sometimes such bodies managed to gain a "semi-official" status, which allowed them to raise some means from public financial resources. In exceptional cases, the public administration actually took over such private institutions or, on the contrary, it suppressed their existence. This was the case with private employment agencies, which – after years of pressure stemming from expert groups and trade unions – were intended to gradually disappear after implementation of new legislation in 1936.[17] On the other hand, these private employment agencies were not typical tools of the care for the poor, because their task was to find work for the unemployed and not to provide them with food and/or other necessary care. All in all, the usual practice was that even in every smaller

---

they did not become state or self-governmental bodies.

[16] For more details, see Milan Pátra, "Chudinská péče v Čechách v letech 1918–1938 a její historické kořeny" [The care for the poor in Bohemia in 1918–1938] (M. A. thesis, Charles University in Prague, 2009).

[17] For more details, see Rákosník, *Odvrácená tvář meziválečné prosperity*, pp. 358–369.

or medium-sized town, there operated a network of various associations and foundations having the common purpose of solving social problems in that particular municipality and their heyday belonged mainly to the second half of the 19th century.[18]

The only fundamental change in performing care for the poor during the Second World War – from the institutional point of view – meant creating the so-called "Czech Social Assistance" [*Česká sociální pomoc*] – a body whose goal was conducting charity care as well as coordinating private and semi-official philanthropic associations. After the year of 1945, its position became highly uncertain. This body was originally founded as the "National Assistance" [*Národní pomoc*] in 1938, and after the war it was renamed as the "Social Assistance for Bohemia and Moravia" [*Sociální pomoc pro Čechy a Moravu*], and eventually it became the "Czech Social Assistance" [*Česká sociální pomoc*] and it operated under this name well after the war.[19] This organisation actually came into being as a rather spontaneous citizens' initiative for assistance to people fleeing from the borderlands to the interior of former Czechoslovakia in 1938 and it united representatives of different philanthropic institutions in a common effort to coordinate the performance of care for the needy, including distribution of funds to individual sectors of social care. The "Czech Social Assistance" continuously carried out its activities after the war as well, although it often endured criticism that it had been a purely collaborationist organisation. Its clientele consisted mainly of self-employed workers who were not covered by social insurance and found themselves in existential problems for various reasons, then families with numerous offspring as well as unmarried individuals or older couples or anybody who lacked the means of subsistence from social insurance.

The importance of this organisation is definitely supported by the fact that around 200,000 citizens applied for a one-time or permanent assistance every year.[20] Yet the "Czech Social Assistance" was quickly losing its justification within the system of social care as the historical development was proceeding more and more rapidly towards nationalisation.

---

[18] Cf. e.g. Eva Šmilauerová, *Poděbrady v proměnách staletí*, [The town of Poděbrady in the metamorphosis of centuries], vol. 1 (until 1850), (Praha: Scriptorium 2009), pp. 213–214.

[19] Denisa Hriňová, "Problémová mládež v českých zemích v první polovině 20. století aneb Mládež „mravně vadná"" [Problematic youth in Czech Lands in the 1st half the 20th century, or "Morally defective" youth] (M. A. thesis, Charles University in Prague, 2008), p. 42.

[20] See Jan Auředníček, "Jde o sedm procent českého národa" [It is about seven percent of the Czech nation], *Sociální revue* 21 (1946): pp. 202–204.

Eventually, the "Czech Social Assistance" organisationally merged with the Czechoslovak Red Cross in 1948.[21]

Statistics on the care for the poor

Legal and institutional aspects of the care for the poor are not able to reveal much about how many persons were actually poor, and what the composition of this population group was like. For this purpose, it is necessary to use sources of a statistical nature.[22] Due to the limited range of this study, we will deal only with a few parameters of the care for the poor, which we consider to be representative: (a) the total number of supported; (b) regional differences; (c) the age structure of supported persons; (d) the structure of supported persons by gender; (e) the structure of supported persons by their marital status.

To point (a) In the national dimension, the care for the poor did not cover more than 1–2.5% of the population in the late 19th century – roughly the same proportion as after 1950, but there constantly occurred significant local and regional imbalances over the examined period. According to the statistics from 1890, only 1.62% of the population was being supported in Bohemia. Yet this figure showed only the number of breadwinners in the household – after including the other family members,

---

[21] A more detailed analysis on legal and institutional aspects of social care in the Czech Lands see Jakub Rákosník, *Sovětizace sociálního státu: Lidově-demokratický režim a sociální práva občanů v Československu 1945–1960* [Sovietization of a welfare state. People's democratic regime and social rights of citizens in Czechoslovakia 1945–1960] (Praha: Filozofická fakulta Univerzity Karlovy, 2010); Jakub Rákosník and Igor Tomeš, *Sociální stát v Československu: právně-institucionální vývoj v letech 1918–1992* [A welfare state in Czechoslovakia: legal and institutional development in 1918–1992] (Praha: Auditorium, 2012).

[22] Today's researcher is fortunate that comprehensive statistical overviews on the care for the poor were regularly conducted. The first summary statistics within the followed period were organised on the initiative of the Land Committee in Bohemia in 1886 (completed by another survey in 1890, published in 1894). The second one was conducted in 1902 (publ. 1906) already for all Czech Lands. The third was taken in 1906, and Karel Engliš proceeded its outputs into statistical publications and articles in the journal of Economic Horizon [*Obzor národohospodářský*] (1909). The fourth time, in 1912, the statistics were valid only for Bohemia, but the survey results have never been published. The fifth survey was carried out in 1921 (Antonín Tvrdoň worked the outputs for the journal of Czechoslovak Statistics [*Čs. statistika*], vol. 19) and the sixth one was conducted in 1932 (publ. 1935).

it was 2.25% of the entire population.[23] In 1902, the figure was similar – 2.4% of the entire population. Yet in 1921 it was only 1.4% of the Czechoslovak population. This decline is relatively easy to explain – there occurred a boom of accompanying social legislation, particularly the enactment of means-tested unemployment benefits in December 1918, followed by care for war invalids as well as state maintenance allowances responding to wartime and post-war inflation. These abovementioned tools functioned beyond the care for the poor and they supported persons who would otherwise have fallen on the shoulders of the system of the care for the poor. In 1931, during the Great Depression, around 2.19% of the population was being financially supported.[24] It seems that the difference is only small – from a statistical point of view – but considering the population growth it meant an increase to double in absolute numbers. However, if we counted the people who were supported merely due to being unemployed, the figure would be 1.47% in the year 1931, i.e. almost the same as the relative number reached at the census in 1921.

We should remain very cautious when processing information from statistical sources on the number of supported poor. A telling example can be the experience of neighbouring Germany from the era of the Great Depression in the 1930s.[25] In the period of presidential cabinets of Heinrich Brüning, the number of persons applying for poverty subsidies was rapidly increasing. At first sight, we would have simply concluded that, given the worsened living conditions of the population as a result of the crisis, such an increase seems quite logical. However, this is only part of the truth. The main reason lies in the fact that the Chancellor sought to relieve the increasing financial deficit of the Imperial Authority for Supporting the Unemployed (*Reichsanstalt für Arbeitsvermittlung und Arbeitslosenversicherung*). Therefore, the Chancellor decided to begin reducing unemployment insurance benefits and to move the financial burden of caring for people in need onto the shoulders of municipalities, i.e. to the sphere of social assistance. At the same time, the Czechoslovak government, with respect to the dire state of public finances, could not afford[26] to pursue such a strategy. Many municipalities balanced on the

---

[23] Karel Adámek, *Příspěvky k upravení chudinství* [Contributions for adjustment of the care for the poor] (Chrudim: Ad. Eckert, 1896), pp. 4–5.

[24] *Péče o chudé a péče o mládež ochrany*, p. 40.

[25] David Crew, *Germans on Welfare: From Weimar to Hitler* (Oxford: Oxford University Press, 1998).

[26] Cf. Jiří Šouša jr., *Obecní majetek v Čechách 1848–1938: Základy právní úpravy komunálního majetku v Čechách v letech 1848–1938* [Municipal assets in Bohemia in 1848–1918: Grounds of legal adjustment of municipal assets in Bohemia in

verge of bankruptcy, and therefore the government opted for implementing the aforementioned catering for the unemployed (a state run action), which was basically a type of care for the poor, but it was completely separated from its legislative and institutional structure. Thus this form does not occur in cited statistics and therefore the costs of the care for the poor, at least at first sight surprisingly, did not rise significantly during the Great Depression.

To point (b) As we have already noted above, significant differences are to be found between the number of supported in different municipalities and districts respectively across all studied statistics. This phenomenon cannot be explained by putting a single cause on the table. What is certain is that neither ethnic factors nor the economic structure of a given region play any role. In 1906, the highest rate of supported persons occurred in those districts: Polná (6%), Kašperské Hory (5.2%) and Stříbro (4.9%). In 1931, the largest number (almost 10%) showed districts of Jablonec (9.41%), Aš (8.07%), Přísečnice (9.7%). Obviously, there occurred a change in most affected districts – despite the fact that in 1931, the most struck districts were those lying in the German borderland, there cannot be inferred any ethnic correlation, because this rate was rather unusual number even among German districts in Czechoslovakia. Moreover, other cities in northern Bohemia inhabited in majority by Germans such as Nejdek or Kraslice, which traditionally showed the highest unemployment rate in Czechoslovakia in the 1930s, had relatively low numbers of persons supported in the framework of the care for the poor. The overall provincial average for Bohemia was 2.34% of people dependent on care for the poor in 1931. Even statisticians themselves could not adequately explain these discrepancies. They referred to unemployment, but that was no reason that could be generalised. What seems to have played a crucial role in different numbers of people dependent on care for the poor were probably local traditions as well as actions of local elites and, finally, a number of institutions in a given municipality which focused on philanthropy and care for the poor.[27]

Despite that, however, we can trace some regularity, e.g. falling average amounts paid on social benefits going geographically from west to east across Czechoslovakia – according to the statistics from 1921, the city of Prague spent six times more on one poor individual than municipalities in the eastern parts of the republic such as Martin in Slovakia or cities in

---

1848–1918] (Praha: Karolinum, 2009); Karel Maier, *Hospodaření a rozvoj českých měst 1850–1938* [Management and development of Czech cities in 1850–1938] (Praha: Academia, 2005), pp. 344–350.

[27] *Péče o chudé a péče o mládež ochrany potřebnou*, p. 42.

Ruthenia. The similar trend could be also observed in the statistics 10 years later. Furthermore, it seems that industrial areas spent more money on the poor than agricultural areas, although there existed significant local variations. In general, it is true that larger municipalities spent on average more money on their poor than smaller municipalities. Karel Engliš, a Czech economist, formulated another interesting correlation in 1909 – he compared the standard of living in a municipality (according to the average amount paid on direct taxes per capita – the higher, the better life in a given place) and the number of people dependent on the care for the poor. It must be said that this is a very imprecise indicator – and the author himself was well aware of that – but there was no other, more precise source available in existing statistical materials. His conclusion, based on this comparison, was that with the increasing number of the poor, there occurred an increased number of people dependent of the care for the poor. The regions with the lowest paid taxes per capita showed 3% supported individuals, while in regions with higher averagely paid taxes, the number of supported person went down to ca. 1.5%.[28] However, it definitely does not mean that poor municipalities supported their poor at the highest possible level – it was exactly the opposite, as evidenced by statistics from the First Republic. The poorest communities in Slovakia and Ruthenia also showed the lowest percentage of supported persons: "Those poor persons are reliant on support by any other means than from empty municipal coffers," statisticians noted in 1931.[29] According to the statistics from the year 1921, merely 1.77% of the total population was supported in Bohemia, 1.59% in Moravia, 1.54% in Silesia, 0.43% in Slovakia and in Carpathian Ruthenia it was only 0.13% of the entire population.[30]

To point (c) Another relevant factor is the age structure of the supported persons. According to the statistics from 1890, a full 53% of supported persons were over 60 years. Nearly 24% came from the age cohort of 40–60 years of age. The remaining less than a quarter of supported persons was made up by younger people, whereas children under 14 years old accounted for nearly one tenth of the total.[31] Karel

---

[28] Karel Engliš, "Počet a osobní poměry chudých v království českém" [The number and personal circumstances of the poor in the Czech Kingdom], *Obzor národohospodářský* 14 (1909): p. 214.

[29] *Péče o chudé a péče o mládež ochrany potřebnou*, p. 42.

[30] *Veřejné chudinství v Republice československé v roce 1921* [Public care for the poor in the Czechoslovak Republic in 1921] (Praha: Státní úřad statistický, 1924), p. 9.

[31] *Statistika veřejného chudinství v království Českém* [Statistics on the public care

Engliš stated in 1909 that every 140th child under 14 years of age was supported, added by every 200th person of working age and by every 10th person in the post-productive age (over 60 years of age).[32] According to the statistics from 1931, every 70th child was supported, then every 125th person of working age and every 12th person in the post-productive age.[33] What do these development trends show? One obvious thing is a quantitative increase in child care. Yet we must not put the falling birth rate aside and therefore, the result is not that brilliant, when we think in absolute numbers. In 1930, the number of children under 14 years of age in the former Czechoslovakia was 15% smaller, compared to the year of 1900.[34] Yet despite that, there is no reason to doubt the numerical growth of institutional facilities caring for youth in inter-war Czechoslovakia. The increase in the number of supported persons of working age was undoubtedly caused by mass unemployment due to the Great Depression. The decrease observed in the number of older persons can be misleading, but in absolute numbers, the total number of supported persons remained still more or less the same. However, we must consider the phenomenon of an aging population, which was already apparent in the 1930s. In Czechoslovakia in 1930, there was about one third more people older than 60 years of age, compared to the year of 1900. This statistic data therefore demonstrates the importance of social insurance law from the year of 1924, and particularly the state old-age pension system launched in 1929, which significantly relieved the system of the social assistance, especially in its subfield of care for the elderly.[35]

To point (d) There was one single feature of poverty that can be easily generalised for the entire European continent – women were increasingly

---

for the poor in the Czech Kingdom] (Praha: [Statistická kancelář zemědělské rady pro Království české], 1894), p. xviii.
[32] Engliš, "Počet a osobní poměry chudých v království českém," p. 268.
[33] *Péče o chudé a péče o mládež ochrany potřebnou*, p. 48.
[34] Cf. *Demografická příručka 1959* [The handbook of demography 1959], eds. Milan Kučera and Dagmar Vysušilová (Praha: Státní úřad statistický, 1959), p. 18.
[35] We use data from 1890 and 1906, which both indicate the causes why individuals fell onto the shoulders of the care for the poor care despite the fact that the criteria in these two statistics are not fully compatible. In 1890, the leading causes were: age (40.9%), injury, physical or mental disability (25%), widowhood or breakup with the breadwinner (12.9%), the high number of offspring (2%) and unemployment (also 2%) of all supported persons. In 1906, the statistical survey revealed the causes of poverty: 46.8% due to an advanced age; 21.6% due to injury, physical or mental disability; 10.5% due to widowhood or breakup with the breadwinner; 9.6% was caused by a high number of offspring and 3.4% of the total number of supported persons became poor due to their unemployment.

becoming dependent on the care for the poor. At the beginning of the 20th century, men accounted for 30%, women for 50% of all clients of the system and the remaining 20% were made up by children.[36] What is interesting is the changing proportion of men and women in different age cohorts which differed quite significantly. The statistics from the year of 1890 showed a clear rule that, in the age cohort of children, boys greatly prevailed over girls, while in cohorts of productive and post-productive age, the proportion of women significantly strengthened. This phenomenon is quite understandable in older age groups and the reasons are obvious: first, women live longer on average. Second, there is also the dangerous impact of widowhood, as well as motherhood, which puts women at greater risk of poverty in productive years. If we look at the data about 30 years earlier (from the early 1930s), the statistics are significantly different from each other, but this is easily explainable as well. Generally, there are no significant changes in a cohort of post-working age during the Great Depression. But a closer look at the productive category now reveals that there are a fifth more supported men than women. This phenomenon occurred due to mass unemployment.[37] Yet explaining why there is such a significant predominance of boys over girls in the cohort of children is not so clear. Czech statisticians offered the following explanation, applicable to the situation at the end of the 19th century: "Girls in general, and especially in the lower classes of society, begin making a living by themselves earlier than boys. Girls already during school and [it is typical] especially in recent years, babysit small children and do all types of house chores and enter the working process as maids, nannies, etc. right after finishing school. Boys, on the other hand, continue from [elementary] school in schooling by entering apprenticeships, which, however, means a need of auxiliary [financial] means."[38]

To point (e) According to the statistics from the year 1890, a significant percentage of supported persons were those who had lost a partner. Widows and widowers together accounted for nearly half – a total of 48%.[39] Persons living in marriage accounted for 18.2% of all supported persons and the remaining 32.1% supported persons were single.[40] In

---

[36] Engliš, "Počet a osobní poměry chudých v království českém," p. 267.

[37] *Péče o chudé a péče o mládež ochrany potřebnou*, p. 47.

[38] *Statistika veřejného chudinství v království Českém*, p. xix.

[39] Inconsistency with the figures presented in footnote no. 35 is caused by the fact that those figures are widows and widowers included in other categories – especially in the category of "old age," but they can be expected to be included to some extent in other categories as well.

[40] The remaining percentage included persons who were divorced, separated,

1931, the figures differed significantly: 36.6% of all supported persons were widowed, 37.2% of them were living in a marriage and the remaining 21.2% were single (whereas the rest were either separated or divorced).[41] Statisticians did not pay any attention to this discrepancy and did not offer any rational explanation for the abovementioned change in those numbers. It must have been rising unemployment – with regard to the middle-aged cohort, of which this group consisted – that caused a higher proportion of those who lived in a marriage and were receiving support.

Conclusion

We miss such thorough and representative official records that would have covered the period after the Second World War. The national committees implemented two forms of social care: individual care and a specialised one. The Individual Social care [*Individuální sociální péče*] functioned as a tool to help needy persons using the funds of national committees, unless other system utilities were unable to provide a minimal (but undefined) standard to a given individual in need. This tool represented additional support in cases where the citizen, for whatever reason, did not have sufficient means of subsistence and the national committee recognised him as worthy of support. In practice, this form of care was quite marginal, because if that given person was capable of work, he was immediately sent to work in an enterprise or factory in his community or nearby. An average of 1–2% of the regional population was being supported in this way in the 1950s. There were, however, not uncommon cases where such persons made up less than 1% of the regional population. With some generalisation, we can say that the level of economic backwardness of individual Czechoslovak regions was reflected in the number of clients of individual social care.[42]

Given the vagueness of the definition of "being poor", the changes in absolute numbers are unable to denounce anything either about the growth or decline of poverty, or the quality of care for the poor. The only way to learn more about its quality is creating microprobes from the opposite side – to examine the lives of individuals and study what benefits were granted to the poor in a given area. A statistical analysis of funding of care for the

---

abandoned or persons of unidentified marital status. See *Statistika veřejného chudinství v království Českém*, p. xvii.

[41] *Péče o chudé a péče o mládež ochrany potřebnou*, p. 50.

[42] For more details on the beginnings of the social care during the early period of building socialism in Czechoslovakia, see Rákosník: *Sovětizace sociálního státu*, pp. 385–408.

poor and of its forms would require a separate study, and sources cited therein actually to contain enough representative quantitative data. The real living standards of persons living on the means of care for the poor eloquently testifies a laconic sigh by Czechoslovak statisticians from 1931: "Only a fifth of the poor in Bohemia and a quarter of the poor in Moravia is sufficiently humanly provided for."[43] In effect, only the largest municipalities were capable of providing such benefits and services that would reach more or less the breadline.[44]

---

[43] *Péče o chudé a péče o mládež ochrany potřebnou*, p. 50.
[44] *Veřejné chudinství v Republice československé v roce 1921*, p. 17.

CHAPTER THREE

THE STORY OF POVERTY: AN INTERPRETATION OF THE CONCEPT OF POVERTY IN CZECH ECONOMIC THOUGHT IN THE 19TH AND 20TH CENTURIES

ANTONIE DOLEŽALOVÁ

Abstract: This paper focuses on the concept of poverty in Czech economic thought in the late 19th and early 20th centuries. It was a time of radical changes in the concept of poverty: the changes not only touched upon the perception of this phenomenon in society, but also the ways in which it could be dealt with. Poverty had separated itself from the concept of mercy embodied in thousands of years of Jewish and Christian tradition, and become a subject of interest of the state in the social sector. This paper is based on the thesis that the concept of poverty in Czech economic thought was shaped and influenced by three factors: the Christian and Jewish approach to poverty as a necessity calling for mercy and helping one's neighbour, the development of economics as a scientific discipline and, finally, the transfer of experience in the social sphere among European states, which led to the intervention of the state into the social sphere in the Habsburg monarchy. The paper seeks to answer the question of what the concept of poverty in Czech economic thought was like, and what causes of poverty were identified by the economists of the time.

Poverty, Czech economic thought, social issue, social policy, social legislation, the causes of poverty, charity

This study builds on previously published studies on poverty in which I outlined how the concept of poverty developed from the Old Testament connection with the term "justice" to the Christian concept of mercy and to social engineering which treated poverty – and still treats it – as statistical data.[1] The definition of "what poverty is" had been changing over the

---

[1] Antonie Doležalová, "Příběh chudoby. Mezi spravedlností, milosrdenstvím a

course of centuries and what continues to persist is only one of its characteristics – that it is ambiguous. The myriad conceptual changes influenced not only the perception of this phenomenon in society, but also the ways to approach it and deal with it.

At the turn of the 19th and 20th century, we can talk about a definite paradigm shift in the understanding of the concept of poverty: in the course of one or two centuries, poverty became disconnected from the principles of mercy based upon thousands of years of Jewish and Christian tradition, and became the subject of interest of the state in the social sector. While throughout the entire 19th century, poverty meant dependence on charity and the support of neighbours and community, in the first twenty years of the 20th century poverty was seen as insufficient income, and states focused on determining the level of such income, and set out to find ways to increase it through social transfers.

For the concept of poverty, the turn of the century was to be a turbulent time as poverty became a subject of interest for Czech economic thought. This study focuses on how the concept of poverty was seen by representatives of Czech economic thought in the late 19th and early 20th centuries. In my opinion, the concept of poverty was shaped and influenced by three main factors at that time: the Christian and Jewish approach to poverty as an impulse calling for mercy and helping our neighbour, the development of economics as a scientific discipline and its relation with ethics (or conversely, its release from ethics) and lastly, the interaction between the domestic economic situation and international competition, which resulted in the transfer of experience among individual countries, and ultimately led to interventions in the social sphere within the Habsburg monarchy as well. This study is focused on the third factor – the origin and development of the social policies of the state and is based on the following issues: (1) the concept of poverty in Czech economic thought and (2) causes of poverty identified by the economists of the era.

Social policy of the state as a source of the concept of poverty in Czech economic thought

The Reformation not only led to a distinction in the approach to poverty between Catholicism and Protestantism, but also to the seizure of

---

statistikou" [The story of poverty. Among justice, mercy and statistics] in *Chudinství a chudoba jako sociálně historický fenomén* [Care for the poor and poverty as a social and historic phenomenon], eds. Milan Hlavačka and Pavel Cibulka (Praha: Historický ústav Akademie věd ČR, 2013), pp. 61–65.

church property, which had previously served for charitable functions of the church. This paved the way for the intervention of secular power into the existing church domain. Those social functions, formerly church responsibilities, had to be secured by institutions which obtained the seized church property, i.e. municipalities or state administrations. The accession of secular power brought regulations defining who, where and under what conditions someone may beg; so-called "begging passports" served as evidence of having the right to beg. These seemingly insignificant and perhaps even practical regulations fundamentally changed the paradigm of poverty: it was no longer about who gives alms, but who may beg for it. Yet the nature of institutions caring for the poor remained ecclesiastic, based on the Christian concept of mercy. And the resources for the care for the poor continued to be of the same origin – possessions which had been confiscated from churches, religious orders and church foundations. However, two major changes occurred under the state administration of the care for the poor. Expenses on care for the poor dramatically increased within a few years,[2] and a new idea on a certain standard of living, which was to be reached by all individuals, penetrated society. From this moment on, the state took on the task of ensuring not only the care for the poor, dependent children, widows and orphans, but it was also supposed to secure employment for everybody capable of work. Industrialisation significantly contributed to these dynamic processes, as it acted as an accelerator of social change. Its most visible aspect was the increase in the number of the poor, occurring at irregular intervals dependent on the cyclical fluctuations of the level of production. Nevertheless, all European governments somehow moved into the social sphere at the end of the 19th century.[3]

Both the foundation and the ultimate goals of social policy were in agreement among European countries and the policy's means were often identical across Europe at the end of the 19th century. England is generally considered to be a cradle of social legislation – despite the fact that before the creation of the very first of the relevant English laws, social laws had originated in Austria and Switzerland. Social laws focused on two areas – laws to protect workers and insurance.

---

[2] Albín Bráf, *Almužna a mzda* [Pittance and Wages] (Praha: J. Otto, 1893), p. 8.
[3] See Antonie Doležalová, "Welfare State or Social Reconciliation? A Social Question from the Perspective of an Economist (Albín Bráf)," in *Theory and practice of the Welfare State in Europe in the 20th century. Ways towards the Welfare State*, eds. Zlatica Zudová-Lešková and Emil Voráček, (= Práce Historického ústavu AV ČR/Opera Instituti Historici Pragae, A, Monografia, vol. 49), (Praha: Historický ústav Akademie věd ČR, 2013): pp. 177–198.

Chronologically, the first chapter in the evolution of social legislation are the laws to protect workers. In Austria-Hungary, two basic laws existed that regulated employment of workers and women as well as working hours and a day of rest on Sunday in the mining industry.[4] The second area of social legislation was insurance – accident, health or old age pensions and unemployment benefits. Insurance as a whole had different forms in European states and did not always cover all listed areas. In Austria-Hungary, the only mandatory types of insurance were health insurance along with accident insurance. Both workers and employers contributed to these two types of insurance. In addition, several fraternal societies operated in the mining industry, and were primarily intended to support labourers, widows and orphans, but were also helpful in cases such as serious illness, accidents or funeral costs.[5]

Caring for the poor was firmly in private hands for centuries – the church, later private associations and corporations, either in the form of alms or foundations (since the end of the Middle Ages). Yet beginning in the 15th century, municipalities and the state itself began to get involved in dealing with the issues of the poor – Emperor Joseph II established the parish and the poor institutes.[6] At the turn of the 19th and 20th centuries, fighting poverty in Austria-Hungary constituted a branch of social care, represented by a set of institutions and measures in the interests of the poor. Compared to the previous concept of "free poverty", we are here talking about "closed poverty" at that time.[7] Care for the poor was organised according to Sections 22–31 of the Domicile Act of December 3, 1863 no. 105, the Land Poor Act for the Czech Lands of December 3, 1868 no. 59 with the amendment of May 13, 1896 no. 46 article XXII of 1886, and the articles VIII and XXI from the year 1901. Under the enumerated acts, care for the poor was to be covered by municipalities (usually under the right of domicile) and in case of emergency (e.g. illness) by the municipality of current residence. Municipal councils catered to the care for the poor, sometimes supported either by a "commission of the poor" or by "fathers of the poor" (persons who acted

---

[4] The Act of March 8, 1885 which extended and amended the trade act.

[5] See Doležalová, "Welfare State or Social Reconciliation?"

[6] Antonie Doležalová, *Hlávkovi předchůdci a pokračovatelé: právní postavení a sociální funkce nadací v českých zemích a v Československu od jejich vzniku do současnosti* [Hlávka's predecessors and successors. Legal status and social functions of foundations in Czechoslovakia from their establishment up to the present] (Praha: Národohospodářský ústav Josefa Hlávky, 2014).

[7] *Masarykův slovník naučný* [Masaryk's encyclopaedia], vol. 3, 1st edition, s.v. "chudoba" [poverty].

as social secretaries). This was typical for smaller communities. Sometimes, local councils were assisted by a social office, a social department or by social counselling (which maintained a list of people in need). In cities, the care for the poor was organised in accordance with poverty regulations. According to the Poor Act 59/1868, the birthplace community was obliged to take care of its poor members, individuals unable to work due to physical inadequacy – i.e. being too young, too old or ill. This assistance usually consisted of a food provision, health care and child rearing help – but only if such individuals could not help themselves, or if they did not receive any charity and/or private foundation support. The initial attempt to somewhat systemise the support for the poor resulted in the creation of a voucher system (for meals, finding a job, youth care), which aimed both at increasing the individual independence of a given recipient and also at eliminating begging and alms in general.

Expenses on the care for the poor belonged (along with payments of the city debt and salaries of city officials) to the mandatory expenses of urban budgets; while debt payments in Prague totalled more than a quarter of all regular expenses. Revenues flowed from the profits of municipal enterprises and tolls on bridges, as well as from municipal levies. These municipal levies were formed by separate sorts of taxes in accordance with provincial laws (e.g. property tax, taxes on alcohol and beer) as well as by surcharges on state taxes (if such surcharge exceeded 25%, the approval of the Land Committee and Governor's Office to collect such special tax was required. If it exceeded 50 %, the approval of a special provincial law was needed).[8]

The concept of poverty in Czech economic thought in the 19th and 20th centuries

The development of independent Czech economic thought is widely considered to have begun around the middle of the 19th century, when Czech economic thought separated from the German spiritual and educational

---

[8] In the budget of the City of Prague in 1905, mandatory expenses amounted to 11.816 million crowns. The poor policy comprised CZK 1.1 million, all city authorities amounted to CZK 1.4 million, and the city's debt amortisation totaled CZK 2.9 million. The revenues from municipal levies amounted to CZK 5.7 million, revenues from municipal enterprises were CZK 0.837 million and from bridges CZK 0.989 million. Cyril Horáček, "Několik dat o hospodářských a sociálních poměrech pražských" [A few data of Prague's economic and social conditions], *Obzor národohospodářský* 10 (1905): p. 262. Available at www.bibliothecaeconomica.cz/library/.

climate.[9] A strong emphasis on social issues had been typical for this thought from its inception in various forms and with various theoretical focuses. This emphasis was driven by three key factors: the urgency of social issues in Czech public space, the presence of two main currents of thought which were then playing crucial roles in the foundations of Czech economic thought (both accentuated the social question: cooperatives and the German historical school),[10] and lastly, the focus on the ethical dimension of economics (shaped by notable figures and the time in which Czech economic thought was being constituted).

Albín Bráf (1851–1912), who is broadly regarded as the founder of Czech economic thought, strongly defended the position that economic development must progress with respect to the ethical aspects of social development. According to Bráf, social issues arose when a violation of the fundamental rules for the functioning of society occurred. Among the fundamentals he included a monogamous marriage, legal equality, and the individual ownership of the means of production. He introduced this topic to the Czech economic community and consequently set the course for dealing with issues concerning social concepts. This way he defined a space within the Czech intellectual environment in which the solving of the issues of poverty was to be dealt with in the coming decades. With regard to the ethical dimension of the emerging economic thinking, morality remained a key category for understanding the nature of poverty as well as for related considerations of a moral uplift of contemporary society. The question of poverty continued to be primarily a question of ethics (I emphasise that on the part of donors as well as recipients of aid), followed by all the organisational issues and the financial issues.

The approach to social issues was divided by two aspects. First, by a social group whose specific problems were supposed to be solved: not only the question of poverty itself, but also workers' questions, small business issues, issues concerning the middle class, women's issues, children's issues and lastly, the issue of education. The second aspect meant those parts of social life in which the approach intervened. The social question was therefore defined – and solved – as a moral issue (and ethical, legal and political or economic, respectively). A deep sense of the connection between economics and social issues resonated in thoughts about social justice.[11] In a broader context of social issues in the Czech

---

[9] Milan Sojka, *Dějiny ekonomických teorií* [History of economic theories] (Praha: Vysoká škola ekonomická, 1998), p. 391.

[10] Antonie Doležalová, *Rašín, Engliš a ti druzí* [Rašín, Engliš and others] (Praha: Oeconomica, 2007), pp. 34–37.

[11] Albín Bráf recognised two branches of national economic science – theoretical

environment, the workers' question was the most frequently analysed. The interest of economists of the time actually followed common contemporary trends, ranging from passing laws to protect the workers to social security. On the issue of poverty, economists sought to answer three things: what poverty is, explaining the causes of poverty and proposing a possible solution.

The content of the term "poverty"

The actual content of the word "poverty" remained unclear both in Czech economic thought as well as in public discourse. Throughout the 19th century, poverty meant dependence on charity and support of the neighbourhood and community, while at the turn of the 19th and 20th centuries the definition of poverty was based on the minimum wage, influenced by Malthusian population theory[12] and exposed to the first attempts of statistical quantification.

When we search for the real content of the term "poverty", we cannot avoid the concept of "well-being", because poverty has been explained as its opposite. Yet well-being has been understood as individual and social, as well as material and spiritual – these four dimensions have determined the quality of a human life; poverty has also had all these dimensions. The meaning and content of the term well-being varied in the eyes of individual economists – even in the question to what extent well-being is a measurable indicator, to what extent it is related to the satisfaction of an individual, how much it is connected with one's ethical values, and how deeply the feeling of well-being is connected with the idea of the moral right to promote one's own interests.[13] The phenomenon of well-being closely

---

and practical. The ethical was possible to be required only after the practical science, whereas he considered the theoretical branch as ethically neutral, "[...] all theories are ethically neutral, including even the ethics itself, unless the name is often understood – in more recent times – as a theory about the origin and evolution of moral stances and negotiations, rather than a normative doctrine." Albín Bráf, "Věda národohospodářská počátkem XX. věku" [The economic science at the beginning of 20th age] in *Albín Bráf, Život a dílo*: Díl 2., *Výbor statí z nauky národohospodářské* [Albín Bráf, Life and Works, vol. 2: Anthology of essays on economic and social politics], eds. Cyril Horáček and Josef Gruber (Praha: Vesmír 1923), pp. 27–56, here pp. 38–39.

[12] Malthusian population theory belonged to the economic canon in the Czech Lands: all the books of the national economy – well into the early 1920s – include a "population question" as one of the first and key chapters.

[13] Antonie Doležalová, "Blahobyt, luxus …a štěstí v ekonomickém myšlení 2. poloviny 19. století" [Prosperity, luxury… and luck in economic thought of the

met poverty when it came to determining the minimum level of well-being – below which any given individual would fall into poverty. It is truly remarkable that material and individual well-being was the pole opposite of poverty, but the argument for the elimination of poverty was a requirement for general social well-being as it actually refers to the social dimension of human existence, because it belonged to the emerging concept of social justice. No matter how poverty was defined and even when a subjective evaluation was excluded from its indicators, poverty was closely associated with the inability of individuals to participate in society. The term "poverty" included both purely normative aspects (poverty as evil), and positive ones (quantification of poverty as a part derived from the distribution of income in the economy).

Ultimately, poverty was seen as an insufficient income regardless of the source of the income. Karel Engliš considered "poor" the segment of the population that "due to the circumstances of the individual and under the prevailing socio-economic system cannot make a living even to the scantiest degree, and not having even any private titles of subsistence that would be given to them by the third parties, they are forced to look for some sort of support either by benefactors or by the general population."[14] Thus we can see attempts to define poverty by setting a minimum family budget which should include contemporarily and locally accepted basic needs and their financial demands. In addition, the economists not only collected and evaluated statistical data, but they also conducted research on lifestyles of families in different social classes and in different cultural conditions (in cities, in the countryside, teaching professions). Yet all the effort to define the content of the term "poverty" ultimately ended in defining the category of persons who can be considered poor, and such quantification apparently had its limits. And this was for two reasons:

First, when defining who is poor, the criteria of either a zero-tax minimum or breadline was applied. Both, however, differed according to location, time and segment of the economy. In addition, individual municipalities paid various allowances to the poor according to the degree

second half of the 19th century], *Hospodářské dějiny* 25, no. 1 (2010): pp. 77–92.
[14] For the calculation of these quotas, he differentiated the population according to the level of income, where individuals show the lowest level in a variety of incomes (or zero income). According to Karel Engliš, the poverty itself reflects the inequality in the distribution of income. Karel Engliš, "Počet a osobní poměry chudých v království Českém" [The number and personal circumstances of the poor in the Czech kingdom], *Obzor národohospodářský* 14, (1909): pp. 209–217, 265–271, 314–320, here p. 209. Available at www.bibliothecaeconomica.cz/library/.

of their "humanity" – meaning that a person in need would be supported from public funds in some municipalities, whereas they would not be supported if living in another place. A specific situation occurred in agriculture – quite different mechanisms of private charity activities and social solidarity existed than in urban or industrial areas.[15]

Second, statistical research was still in its infancy and the data was highly imprecise, often distorted and misinterpreted. Data was collected via questionnaires in which supporting institutions were mentioned; yet it often turned out that multiple forms of support were reported as support to more persons. Outside of any statistical surveys there were obviously a group of individuals who concealed their poverty and did not claim any support. Some social groups could not be found among the poor at all – for example, vagrants and Gypsies.[16] However, the poor were supported by a number of other, private, institutions that did not know about each other, and did not provide information for statistical surveys – with the exception of municipalities and associations.[17] Unfortunately, municipalities did not proceed consistently when conducting the statistical surveys and on top of that, the surveys were conducted using different methodologies in different years. Given that no clearly defined poverty line existed, the statistics did not provide any real number of the poor, but only the number of supported individuals. Therefore, such outputs had almost zero informative value and it is not possible to trace any trend here.[18]

---

[15] Antonie Doležalová, "Prolegomena ke studiu spolkové činnosti zemědělců" [Prolegomena to resesearch of farmers'associations] in *Agrární strana a její zájmové, družstevní a peněžní organizace* [Agrarian party and its interest, credit and financial organizations], ed. Blanka Rašticová (Uherské Hradiště: Slovácké muzeum, 2010), pp. 93–105.

[16] A decree issued by Leopold I ruled that Gypsies are outside the law and anyone who caught them is entitled to hang or shoot them. This law was valid until 1697. Dr. K., "Tuláci a nynější trestní praxe k jejich potlačení" [Tramps and the current penal practice to suppress them], *Obzor národohospodářský* VII, (1902): pp. 165–170, here p. 167. Available at www.bibliothecaeconomica.cz/library/.

[17] In 1901, municipalities in the Czech Kingdom supported 152,705 individuals and a year later 156,938 individuals. Engliš, "Počet a osobní poměry chudých v království Českém."

[18] We can extract the number of supported persons in the population from the statistics – it reached 2.5% in 1900. Of this number, 50% were women, 30% were children under 14 years of age and 20% were men; in other words, municipalities supported every 140th child under the age of 14, every 200th person of working age and one in ten people over the age of 60 years. Engliš, "Počet a osobní poměry chudých v království Českém," p. 268.

Thus, when Czech economists spoke about the poor in this period, they were speaking of those who were entitled to receive any form of support. When they spoke about the poverty line, it was a locally valid indicator that did not take into account all possibilities to fulfil the principle of social solidarity. And when they spoke about poverty, they said almost nothing about the real situation of the poor, did not understand the roots of poverty, the process of the formation of different groups of the poor, nor the factors that affected it. Yet these were questions they desired to answer.

The causes of poverty

As the question of the nature of poverty faded in academic debate, Czech economists became focused on identifying the factors that led to the emergence of groups that meet the conditions for the disbursement of aid to the poor; therefore, such factors were considered the causes of poverty. According to Albín Bráf, poverty had both subjective and objective causes. Among the objective causes he included such diverse factors as the legal system, geographical and climatic conditions, advances in science and technology and resulting changes in the division of labour as well as economic cycles or economic policies, i.e. factors out of the control of an individual. Among subjective causes he included physical and psychological disposition of a given human being as well as their moral and volitional qualities – adding that even these factors are not always entirely in the hands of the individual concerned.[19]

A few years later, Karel Engliš argued that the causes of poverty are actually the same factors that determine the distribution of income.[20] He also distinguished individual and social causes of poverty. By setting this characteristic, Karel Engliš tried to make a distinction between the causes of impoverishment and the circumstances for granting aid; thus he actually answered the question why at some point an individual needs some support, and why he cannot provide for himself. Both situations resulted from either a worsening financial situation or from the inability to obtain earnings. In addition, he identified the contemporaneous economic and legal situation acting as social causes of poverty.

However, there was a sharp contrast with what poor individuals (supported persons) reported in statistical surveys. They themselves reported physical decrepitude (468), physical ailments (183), a large number of

---

[19] *Albín Bráf – Život a dílo*, Díl 3., *Výbor statí z hospodářské a sociální politiky* [Albín Bráf – Life and works. Vol. 3, Anthology of essays on economic and social politics], eds. Josef Gruber and Cyril Horáček (Praha: Vesmír 1923), p. 140.
[20] Engliš, "Počet a osobní poměry chudých v království Českém."

children (96), death of the breadwinner (86) and drunkenness (14) as reasons why they were actually poor.[21] Important progress was being made in the perception of poverty. It stopped being explained only as a consequence of alcoholism, laziness, incompetence or moral decay, but came to be seen as a result of certain social realities (meaning the institutional and economic framework that significantly influenced individual causes of poverty). A poor individual would not necessarily be uneducated, unable to care for themselves and their loved ones. The state of poverty could befall an entrepreneur or a businessman and affect their children, if they had not created sufficient financial reserves. Or poverty could hit hard the family of a terminally ill person.

At the end of the 19th century, unemployment became the most urgent issue among social (objective) causes of poverty. It had become a pressing problem after the onset of industrialisation in the Czech Lands. The economists of the time distinguished three categories of unemployed individuals, two being of the "classic" variety: persons unable to work and those who were work-shy. Yet the third category was new, brought about by modern times: persons who were able to work and wanted to work, but sadly, no employment was available for them. The emergence and consequent rapid growth of this third category usually strengthened arguments for deeper involvement by the state, because the financial power (disposable financial means) of municipalities could not sufficiently meet this challenge.

This brings us to a paradox. The most frequently cited cause of poverty, from the perspective of the economists of the time, was the act of specific laws that had been created to tackle the problem of poverty. Economists criticised the unclear definition of poverty and all applicable regulations concerning it as well as the ways in which the fight against poverty was being waged. In their opinion, the reason lay not so much in the absence of relevant laws, but rather in their non-fulfilment in practice: to put it briefly, the authorities were reluctant to apply the related laws and regulations in practice. In this respect, the Domicile Act of 1863 serves as an ideal example of such neglect. The Domicile Act assigned the care for the poor to be carried out by hometowns. This duty was precisely formulated as follows: if the provision of any given poor individual went beyond the responsibilities and resources of their hometown's institutes and foundations, the responsibility to support such a poor individual was transferred to the municipal authority. The most common target of criticism was the fact that the right of domicile was formulated in favour of industrial cities and the period required for acquisition of the right of

---

[21] Ibid., p. 317.

domicile for people over 24 years old was set at 10 years. Statistics on poverty in the Czech Kingdom from 1894 show that only 31% of supported people lived outside their hometown and only 41% of them for more than 10 years[22]. In terms of the total number, it was a very small group, which was becoming even further diminished by the process of merging municipalities into larger urban areas. Other persons remained completely outside any municipal support and thus fell out of any sort of social insurance.

This paradox – claiming that a legislative step towards tackling poverty is actually a cause of poverty – brings us to a discussion on specific ways to solve the problem of poverty. Indeed, the economists of the time agreed that the Domicile Act of 1863 was inadequate for changing the social position of the poor and discussed how to reset the parameters of social policy so there would be no reason for any aid to the poor. This miraculous tool would be workers' insurance – the introduction of which should have led to both a change in social habits of the lowest social classes in the sense of starting to "save for the future" as well as raising the minimum wage to a level that would increase the living standard of the poorest working classes.[23]

Conclusion

Czech economic thought finally broke free from the German environment in the middle of the 19th century and from almost the beginning it has given a strong emphasis to social issues, poverty included. Due to the time of its inception, Czech economic thought has both Christian and pre-Christian conceptions of the relation to the poor in its genetic code. Furthermore, it was influenced by the Reformation, industrialisation, the emergence of civil rights and the encroachment of secular power into the care for the poor. This complex of factors was reflected within the transformation of the paradigm of poverty in economic thought. At the end of the 19th century, the social dimension of being became both a new facet of the idea of poverty as well as an argument for caring for the less fortunate members of society, taking as its cue the Christian maxim "love thy neighbour". In the 20th century, poverty was no longer merely seen as a consequence of subjective reasons on the part of individuals, but as a result of a certain social reality – created by an

---

[22] Vladimír Fáček, "Studie o našem chudinství veřejném" [The study on our public care for the poor], *Obzor národohospodářský* II (1897): pp. 17–19, 33–38, 69–72, 85–89, here p. 18. Available at www.bibliothecaeconomica.cz/library/.

[23] Bráf, *Almužna a mzda*.

institutional and economic framework. Poverty was seized by rational science; Christian mercy was replaced by fiscal calculating. From that moment on, the state took on the duties of providing care for the poor. The range of tasks was informed by the emerging concept of social policy as a tool for solving social issues as well as the development of the concept of fiscal policy as a tool for the redistribution of wealth.

The Czech economists of the time did not go deeply after the real causes of poverty, they merely stuck to statistical surveys, and based on them, tried to conclude what poverty was. The condition of "being poor" varied according to the location and time of the assessment and was practically exhausted by a mere statement of the number of supported individuals. This quantity did not say anything about a subjective perception of the state of "being poor", let alone the factors that affect poverty.

Czech economists, however, managed to broadly reflect on the causes of poverty and identified subjective and objective causes, subjecting them to a thorough analysis. Poverty was now explained not only as a consequence of alcoholism, laziness, incompetence or of moral decay, but also as a result of certain social realities. We would now say that poverty is a result of the current economic order and even of moral and social crises. Unemployment is therefore considered a fundamental cause of poverty (not caused by an individual worker, but by economic fluctuations) and, paradoxically, so is the inability of the state to set up and enforce fundamental principles of caring for the poor.

It is significant that when one speaks of "the state of poverty", this does not only mean individual experience of poverty and ways of determining its borders, but also how to tackle poverty, and this – the how – is denounced. The cause and effect are often confused – when a specific law is referred to as the cause of poverty and this particular law was supposed to be a tool to tackle it. Yet the Austrian legislation was undoubtedly very advanced and offered many good and effective tools for fighting poverty; unfortunately, those tools were not widely applied, solutions were bureaucratic, discouraging, individuals in need were often ignored and a further pauperisation of society occurred.

CHAPTER FOUR

SOCIOLOGICAL RESEARCH CONDUCTED ON THE POOR IN INTER-WAR PRAGUE

ZDENĚK R. NEŠPOR

Abstract: The paper describes and analyses the first two sociological surveys dealing with the poor conducted in Prague in the 1920s and 1930s. The first was initiated by Alice Masaryková and based upon the tradition of American "social surveys" and the second was carried out by Otakar Machotka, a leading figure of the Prague sociological school. The latter used more modern tools. The author describes the background, the context, as well as the practical implementation and results of both surveys. He stresses that the surveys were very rare not only within the Czech environment, but also within the entire contemporary European context. It can be said that the execution of both surveys had a greater influence on the development of Czech sociology than on finding practical solutions to issues related to poverty as a whole. However, the development of sociology as an academic discipline did not last long, as this science was banned after the communist coup and both surveys became quite forgotten. Today, they can serve as a source of historical data as well as an inspiration for public engagement of academic staff to become involved in solving burning social issues.

We tend to consider sociology to be a much more traditional and "longer-living" field of science than it actually is. Leaving aside social reformers of the Enlightenment period or even before, we consider Auguste Comte to be the founder of sociology, as he directly declared sociology as an independent science and also Karl Marx, whose opinion was, however, a bit restrained.[1] Yet we keep forgetting that sociology was in the mid-19th century at most a theoretical concept constructed by a few intellectuals of differing disciplines, whose academic background was either marginal or close to zero, and whose social influence was at best

---

[1] For more details, see Jan Keller, *Dějiny klasické sociologie* [History of classical sociology], (Praha: Sociologické nakladatelství, 2004).

problematic, if at all. Leaving aside the specific situation of this young
discipline in the United States, sociology as a science partially established
itself at the beginning of the 20th century and became fully rooted only in
the inter-war period, and even then only in certain European countries.[2]
Moreover, sociology at that time was far from the present form of
sociology, or from that form which was being formed after the Second
World War. Sociology at that time was mostly about theoretical
speculations and was not clearly separated from the social reformism of
various characters and last but not least, the then sociology was quite
boundless, occasionally involving virtually any stream of thinking and all
sorts of discussions about contemporary society, its structure, functioning
and development. Empirical material and/or a coherent theoretical system
only started to be applied at the end of the inter-war period, propping up
prior reflections and ideas. Consequently, sociology itself started to
present a specialised scientific mainstream only after the Second World
War.

The problematic, unanchored character of sociology corresponded to
its long-lasting precarious position among academic disciplines. After its
initial boom of the late 19th and early 20th centuries, a period of decay
followed everywhere (apart from the United States) – even in those
countries where sociology established itself at universities or technical
universities in the early 20th century, only solitary individuals or small and
fairly closed groups of scientists kept the fire burning (in France, Italy,
Germany, Poland, Romania, temporarily in Russia). Moreover, sociology
could not develop naturally during the period of the onset of authoritarian
or totalitarian regimes between the two world wars. In virtually all
countries where something like this occurred, sociology was either
completely banned or severely restricted (Germany, Russia, Spain), if it
was ever given the opportunity to develop in even its most basic stages
(Hungary or Austria).[3] By contrast, Czech (Czechoslovak) sociological
efforts thrived as an exception to the rule. In Howard Becker's words,

---

[2] Chales-Henry Cuin and François Gresle, *Dějiny sociologie* [History of
sociology], (Praha 2004); for Czech environment Zdeněk R. Nešpor, *Republika
sociologů. Zlatá éra české sociologie v meziválečném období a krátce po druhé
světové válce* [Republic of sociologists. Golden age of Czech sociology in the
inter-war period and shortly after the Second World War], (Praha: Scriptorium,
2011).

[3] For a very good, yet partially biased overview, see *Social Thought from Lore to
Science Sociological Trends Throughout the World to the Start of the Twentieth
Century's Seventh Decade*, vol. 3, eds. Howard Becker et al. (New York: Dover
Publications, 1961), pp. 793–1174.

"there is no other land of the same size, which could boast such a significant number of contemporary sociologists or such scope and intensity of sociological work. Here [i.e. Czechoslovakia] is again one brilliant point on the sociological map."[4]

The reasons, the form as well as the practical results of the Czech (Czechoslovak) exceptionality have been analysed in detail elsewhere.[5] Czech sociology in the inter-war period indeed experienced unprecedented growth and produced many valuable results. The most important of these, substantively and methodologically "time-resistant" – or they could have been if given the opportunity – were two surveys of Prague's poor from the 1920s and 1930s, which we will examine below. However, we must add that this boom of sociological efforts in the inter-war period and shortly also in post-war Czechoslovakia certainly did have some shortcomings. As in other countries, sociology largely represented only a theoretical, rather speculative and inward-looking discipline. Additionally, its development was hindered by a constant shortage of scientists and funds as well as by mutual sharp disagreements among its main protagonists. Lastly, there was in general a very small number of empirical studies that would have led to a more respectable anchoring of the scientific work. These shortcomings were interconnected and mutually reinforced each other. Otakar Machotka, one of the leading representatives of Czech inter-war sociology could enthuse that "the need for objective scientific study of social reality will be increasingly recognised and that will happen in the foreseeable future within the rational control of social developments. We believe that institutions for social research will become as common and widely recognised as chemical or biological laboratories. We have no doubt that it will become universally recognised that social research must be expensive if it is to bring genuine recognition. One cannot build a social science without financial backing, just as you cannot discover anything in the natural sciences without funding either. Mere common sense, along with the personal experience that had sufficed for many sociologists to conduct scientific work up to now, has proved to be

---

[4] Ibid, p. 1067 (the new edition of the book reprinted unchanged characteristics originally written in 1938, although the situation in the early 1960s was already completely different). The Czech translation is quoted by the *Sociological Review* 9 (1938), pp. 89–92, here p. 91.

[5] Nešpor, *Republika sociologů*, especially pp. 37–70. To a relationship of Czech (and for a long time practically non-existing) Slovak sociology, see Zdeněk R. Nešpor, "Čeští sociologové v počátcích slovenské sociologie" [Czech sociologists in the beginnings of Slovak sociology], *Sociológia* 45 (2013): pp. 27–47.

an insufficient source of knowledge."[6] Yet this was just wishful thinking and this much coveted background was not created even during the inter-war "Republic of sociologists."

Worldwide, when the national sociological traditions – with the exception of the USA – stagnated or even disappeared as a whole, Czech sociology developed vigorously and a substantial portion of this exemption was represented by the empirical research of Prague. The reasons were obvious: the capital of the new state was undergoing major social transformations, having formed an excellent "laboratory" for studying all possible positive and negative impacts. In addition, it was the closest and most accessible research terrain, because the vast majority of researchers resided and worked in Prague. Thus, Czech sociologists (or researchers working in Czechoslovakia) were capable of organising five major empirical investigations before the rise of Marxism. And it should not be surprising that three of them were dedicated to Prague: first, it was research on the organisation of social care conducted under the leadership of Ruth Crawford in 1919. Second, it was research on socially needy families, led by Otakar Machotka in 1931. Third, it was research on urbanising the areas around Prague, carried out by Zdeněk Ullrich in 1936 (not examined in this study).[7] In addition, the population of Prague became the subject of a number of other, smaller studies or sociologically inspired analyses of statistical data.[8] Although we can complain about the

---

[6] Otakar Machotka, *Sociálně potřebné rodiny v hlavním městě Praze* [Socially needy families in the Capital of Prague], (Praha: Orbis, 1936), p. 202.

[7] The outcomes of this research were published in: *Soziologische Studien zur Verstädterung der Prager Umgebung*, ed. Zdeněk Ullrich (Prag: Im Verlage der Revue "Soziologie und soziale Probleme," 1938); a shortened version: Zdeněk Ullrich, *Nástin sociologické analysy pražského okolí* [An outline of sociological analysis of the Prague's environs], (Praha: Sociologický seminář VŠPS, [1948]). Cf. Nešpor, *Republika sociologů*, pp. 152–153.

[8] One of the most influential was a study on zoning in Prague by A. Boháč (Antonín, Boháč, "Hlavní město Praha. Studie o obyvatelstvu" [Capital of Prague. Study on the Inhabitants], *Československý statistický věstník* 3 [1922]: pp. 353–480; 4 [1923]: pp. 325–425); research on high school graduates by J. Doležal and Z. Ullrich (Jan Doležal and Zdeněk Ullrich, "Výzkum abiturientů českých středních škol v zemi České a Moravskoslezské ve škol. roce 1933/34" [Research on graduates of Czech secondary schools in Bohemia and Moravia in the school year 1933/34], *Statistický obzor* 16 (1935): pp. 191–203, 314–344, 455–486); practically oriented statistics by the *Krematorium* Association (analyzed by Zdeněk R. Nešpor, "Socioekonomie spalování mrtvol, aneb neznámá kapitola z dějin české sociologie a pojišťovnictví" [Socioeconomy of cremation, or unknown chapter of the history of Czech sociology and insurance], Pantheon 6, no. 2 (2011): pp. 22–47); or a survey on upbringing and religiosity in Prague by J. Šíma (Jaroslav

lack of empirical investigation in Czech pre-Marxist sociology, Prague was definitely the most common field of research and all the results should draw attention even today – if, it must be said, someone were aware of their existence. The following pages introduce as well as analyse two of the abovementioned studies.

Research on organisation of social care in Greater Prague (1919)

Although the first small attempts at conducting sociological research are older and of domestic origin,[9] the Czech environment had the opportunity to first meet with extensive and thoroughly prepared social research thanks to American researchers after the First World War. There were several reasons for their engagement in Czechoslovakia – and it had no parallel throughout Europe in its time period, and it did not occur again. First, there was an effort to help war-affected Europe, second, there was the strong interest of the newly established Ministry of Social Welfare and of other institutions or individuals interested in this field, and finally, the personal impact of the daughter of the first Czechoslovak president, Alice Masaryková, who played a significant role. During her studies in the United States, she gained contacts among (proto-) sociologists working in Chicago,[10] and in the inter-war period, she invited those American researchers to Prague to perform exemplary social research. In her own words: "A practical sociologist needs diagnosis, if he wants to start working. Whether he regards the reduction of infant mortality – or any other certain field of social work [...] he needs to have a survey of the social relations in general, and this summary is "Survey." Whosoever

Šíma, *Sociologie výchovy* [Sociology of upbringing], Praha: Československá grafická unie, (1938), pp. 77–96).

[9] For example, E. Chalupný and J. Pavlík's survey on workers in Tábor: Emanuel Chalupný and Josef Pavlík, *Poměry dělnictva táborského* [Conditions of Tábor's workers], (Tábor: Dělnický spolek, 1903); a research on the small town "spirit" by I. A. Bláha in his unpreserved dissertation thesis, which were partially published – see Inocenc Arnošt Bláha, "*Maloměstská morálka*" [Provincial morals], *Česká mysl* 13 (1912): pp. 96–102; Inocenc Arnošt Bláha, "K psychologii malého města" [A contribution to the psychology of a small town], *Lidové noviny* 21 (1913), no. 199: pp. 1–2; no. 213: pp. 1–2; no. 223: pp. 1–2; no. 254: pp. 1–2; no. 268: pp. 1–2; no. 274: pp. 1–2; *Lidové noviny*. 22 (1914), no. 30: pp. 1–2; no. 35: pp. 1–2; no. 41: pp. 1–2; no. 65: p. 1; no. 72: pp. 1–2.

[10] Radovan Lovčí, *Alice Garrigue Masaryková. Život ve stínu slavného otce* [Alice Garrigue Masaryková. Life in the shadow of the famous father], (Praha: Univerzita Karlova v Praze, Filozofická fakulta v nakladatelství Toga, 2007), pp. 57–67.

wants to do a good job needs to search for good work that has been already done."[11] Therefore, it seemed obvious to invite relatively experienced American experts and give them the task of analysing one of the most burning social problems – the rapidly growing capital city of Prague, affected by the war and by other negative impacts. Masaryková accomplished this through her former American protector Mary McDowell, who reacted by sending eight researchers of the YWCA Chicago led by Ruth Crawford. The Minister of Social Welfare, Lev Winter, provided her team with 35 Czech collaborators and technical workers.

The research, carried out in 1919, sought to perform a description of local organisations and institutions of social assistance/care and to evaluate their effectiveness[12] (such sociological procedure had already become common in the United States). Apart from a purely descriptive directory – whose creation was entrusted to a Czech worker – the research was supposed to include the area of public health, individual social care, education, recreation and employment of women.[13] In the case of the first, second and fourth areas, the research actually succeeded[14] via a form of

---

[11] Alice Masaryková, "Proslov" [the Speech], in Mary Emerson-Hurlbutt, *Sociální péče o jednotlivce v Praze. Přehled sociálních zařízení Velké Prahy* [Social welfare of individuals in Prague], (Praha: Ministerstvo sociální péče republiky Československé, 1920), pp. 7–8, here p. 7. The "relative experience" of American researchers was a result of the fact that they had graduated in degree programs, otherwise – with the exception of the head of research – those researchers were only fresh/recent graduates without their own research experience. Interestingly, the research was conducted (similarly to the first Czechoslovak census of February 1921) throughout Greater Prague, although the Act on Greater Prague was adopted only in February 1920 and came into force at the beginning of 1922 (Act Coll. No. 114–117/1920.).

[12] Although the American scholars came from Chicago, they did not represent the famous Chicago school. They were socially conscious "practical sociologists" whose activities preceded the Chicago school. On the Chicago School in Czech see Jan Balon, *Sociologie v USA. Historické kontextualizace* [Sociology in the United States. Historical contextualizations], (Praha: Sociologické nakladatelství SLON, 2011), pp. 52–62; Jiří Musil, "Chicagská škola a česká sociologie" [Chicago school and Czech sociology], *Lidé a města* 14 (2012): pp. 395–419.

[13] Masaryková, "Proslov," p. 8; cf. also Ruth Crawford, "Předmluva" [Preface], in *Adresář sociálních zařízení Velké Prahy* [A directory of social facilities of Greater Prague], ed. Jaroslav Janko (Praha: Ministerstvo sociální péče republiky Československé, 1919), pp. v-vii.

[14] Apart from the already cited publication by Emerson-Hurlbutt, there were other publications, e.g. Philip Skinner Platt, *Přehled veřejného zdravotnictví Velké Prahy* [Survey of public health care of Greater Prague], trans. Pavla Molnárová (Praha: Ministerstvo sociální péče, 1920); Anne Rylance Smith, *Rekreační přehled*

knowledgeable interpretations combining social statistics with the study of documents and direct observation. The aim was not only to describe the status quo, but to also subject it to critique and suggest corrective measures. In general, research of this type had a "preaching dimension", which resulted from the religious basis of their authors. While in the United States this stood as a common and generally approved practice,[15] the situation was different in Czechoslovakia as the field of social care became, in effect, monopolised by the Social Democrats.[16] Even though some representatives of the religious version of sociological research became members of various social institutions, such as in the case of Bedřich Vašek and the Social Institute of the Czechoslovak Republic, they clearly remained on the margins and their real influence on the formation of inter-war social policy was minimal.

Mary Emerson-Hurlbutt dealt with the research on the organisation of social care for the poor and she focused on institutions providing assistance to mothers and infants, addicted children, delinquents, war invalids and on medical facilities supplying institutions of social care.[17] Although the research was directed primarily at creating an inventory, description and analysis of the aforementioned organisations, the author also paid attention to sources of poverty, among which she particularly emphasised the importance of family and its proper functioning: heredity, social influences and living conditions as a source of social deviance.[18] Moreover, she considered the family to be a much more effective institution in correcting social deviances than any available support and social facilities. Thus her recommendations for city, state, but also civic as well as religious institutions included in particular care for a functioning family, rather than any further development of institutional care – especially not its extensive branching (being divided into a number of small organisations whose resources and expertise did not reach the

---

Prahy [Recreation survey of Prague], trans. Jarmila Mašková (Praha: Ministerstvo sociální péče, 1920).

[15] Cf. Otakar Machotka, *Americká sociologie. Sociální podmínky vzniku a rozvoje* [American sociology. Social conditions of its origin and development], (Praha: Melantrich 1938).

[16] Cf. Jakub Rákosník, "Sociální ústav 1920–1941. Mozkové centrum československé sociální politiky" [The Social Institute 1920–1941. Brain center of Czechoslovak social politics], in *Svět historie – historikův svět. Sborník profesoru Robertu Kvačkovi* [A world of history – a historian's world. A Festschrift in honor of professor Robert Kvaček], (Liberec: Technická univerzita v Liberci, 2007), pp. 296–316.

[17] Emerson-Hurlbutt, *Sociální péče o jednotlivce v Praze*.

[18] Ibid., pp. 186–190.

required level). According to Emerson-Hurlbutt, social work as a whole should be profoundly professionalised and restructured, but anyway, her vision was that social work remain only secondary, an exceptional safety net in case of the dysfunction of standard social institutions that should be supported in their individuality and variability. While in the first section, the author certainly agreed with domestic representatives of social care institutions, her second set of recommendations was not in accordance with their vision, or at least not in its entirety – different, ideologically conditioned "input assumptions", jointly caused her research and recommendations for all intents and purposes to not find any response.

Although the Ministry of Social Welfare sponsored and co-organised the work of the American researchers, it did not make any use of the results and nor did anybody else. The only output was a publication with small number of copies, containing translated monographs. After the American researchers returned to the United States, all discussions ended. Sadly enough, the research did not have any practical application. Moreover, no use of the research was made on the pages of Social Revue[19] either (a periodical issued by the Ministry of Social Welfare, dedicated to social issues). The "American" research remained unknown and unused in academic sociological work as well.[20] In the second case, it was due to the "very practical" and "preaching" orientation from which inter-war Czech sociology shied away, leaving it in the hands of lawyers and other experts on social policy. As for the first case, the reasons for omitting the outputs of the "American" research were probably different value backgrounds as well as a different mindset and the professional status of Czech workers collaborating with the Americans. Nobody fancied adopting views of "inexperienced foreigners." Moreover, they were a generation younger than the Czechs involved in the project. And nobody actually asked to continue dealing with their findings. Mary Emerson-Hurlbutt did not make any use of her significant experience gained in Prague either. She probably devoted herself to family life and left research work after returning to the United States.[21] In summary, the extensively and for its time (in the Czech

---

[19] For more on this periodical, see chapter "Sociální revue" [Social Revue], in *Edice českých sociologických časopisů* [Editions of the Czech sociological journals], eds. Zdeněk R. Nešpor and Anna Kopecká, Praha 2011

[20] Nešpor, *Republika sociologů*, pp. 82–83; Jiří Musil, "Alice Masaryková jako sociolog" [Alice Masaryková as a sociologist], *Sociologické aktuality* 3 no. 2, (1992): pp. 23–24.

[21] The fate of Emerson-Hurlbutt after her return to the USA is not known. Her only other publication is a much more recent study on migrants near Pittsburgh: Mary E. Hurlbutt, *New Americans in Allegheny County: A Cultural Study* (New York, N.

environment) exceptionally well-conceived research did not have any real impact.

Research on needy families in Prague (1931)

The second survey, this time based on socially needy families, was ordered by the city of Prague through its Central Social Board. Its implementation was entrusted to a team led by Otakar Machotka, a sociologist representing the Prague sociological school.[22] Machotka had already emphasised the need for empirical sociological research in his earlier works. He understood them to serve as a basis for responsible social policy, though at the same time he clearly circumscribed the possibilities of scientific work – its results could be a basis for practical or political activity, but not its "justification."[23] In these terms he also prepared research on family (never conducted in practice),[24] basing current approaches of French and later American sociologists (younger Durkheim followers and a tradition of French social policy, the Chicago school respectively). As one of the key representatives of the Prague sociological school, Machotka pushed for implementing the latest international approaches – mainly quantitative empirical methodology to capture the actual state of social problems, where the subsequent solutions should be the responsibility of public social policy (state, municipal, etc.). Conducting this research also meant an extra income to his bureaucratic

---

Y.: The New York, school of social work, 1937); the estate archived at Indiana University contains only letters from Prague and trips to London 1919–20.

[22] For the Prague sociological school in detail, see Nešpor, *Republika sociologů*, pp. 137–162.

[23] Cf. Otakar Machotka, *Mravní problém ve světle sociologie. Názory, methody, kritika* [A moral problem in the light of sociology. Opinions, methods, criticism], (Praha: Orbis, 1927); Otakar Machotka and Zdeněk Ullrich, *Sociologie v moderním životě. Směry, organisace, úkoly* [Sociology in the modern life. Specialization, organization, tasks], (Praha: Orbis, 1928). The Prague sociological school was later wrongfully accused of not being involved in current social issues – e.g. Jiřina Šiklová, "K dějinám pražské sociologické školy mezi světovými válkami" [A contribution to the history of Prague's sociological school in the inter-war period], *Acta Universitatis Carolinae – Phil. et His.*, no. 4 (1968), pp. 13–25 – but in fact it was just about the consistent separation of scientific research and its practical application.

[24] Otakar Machotka, *K sociologii rodiny. Příspěvek k metodám empirické sociologie – metoda statistická a individuální* [A contribution to the methods of empirical sociology—statistical and individual method], (Praha: Nákladem Státního úřadu statistického, 1932), pp. 98–212 in particular.

post at the State Statistical Office, because his university engagement began several years later.[25]

The research assignment was to determine the structural, demographic, social, educational and religious characteristics of needy families, their housing conditions, economic conditions and forms of participation in money-making activities, as well as their spatial dislocation in the capital city. Machotka did not apply a mere "legalistic" definition of poverty – measured through social benefits and so on, but he set his own indicators and statistical analysis and his results led to (for the time) an unprecedented depth – the publication, containing his research outputs, includes a series of 68 detailed tables, topically ranging from basic questions to analysis of the condition and functional separation of flats, their natural and artificial light, or even locating where the laundry was being done.[26] His research, implemented in 1931, was based on observation and on a questionnaire survey. Machotka engaged almost 50 social workers of the Central Social Board, and included nearly 14,000 families actually living in the capital city of Prague. He eventually processed data from 12,000 families, as these met Machotka's definition of poverty. Thus his research sample actually included the entire poor population of Prague – Machotka did not work with a method of random selection, which in the world of sociology was naturalised during the 1930s but the Czech academic environment only became familiar with in the following decade.[27] However, this was virtually the only difference from modern empirical research, which became mainstream in sociological work after the Second World War; in

---

[25] We naturally cannot determine from the extant sources how strong the stated motivation was, but it paid off nevertheless. First, he applied the experience of the research on Prague's poor later in an even larger investigation on urbanisation processes around the capital: the study *Soziologische Studien zur Verstädterung der Prager Umgebung*, ed. Ulrich; for more cf. Zdeněk Ullrich, "Sociologické výzkumy skupiny Sociálních problémů" [Sociological researches of the group Social problems], *Sociologie a sociální problémy* 5 (1937): pp. 53–60, 306–320 and in some theoretical studies, e.g. Otakar Machotka, "Rodinná pouta ve městě a na venkově" [Family ties in cities and countryside], *Statistický obzor* 20 (1939): pp. 261–272); but above all in practical terms, because Machotka could "return" to the Central Social Office of the capital city of Prague after the closure of Czech universities, where he, among other things, first organised marriage counseling.

[26] Machotka, *Sociálně potřebné rodiny*, pp. 205–290.

[27] František Egermayer, "Náhodný výběr v representativní metodě" [A random choice within the representative method], *Statistický obzor* 22 (1941): pp. 424–435; Čeněk Adamec, "Výzkum veřejného mínění a sociální vědy" [A public opinion poll and social sciences], *Sociologie a sociální problémy* 7 (1947): pp. 34–40.

most other aspects, Machotka's research, with its sophisticated preparation, methodology, statistical analyses of empirical material followed by sober interpretation, is fully equivalent to modern research.

Its main outputs include not only a description of the objective characteristics of the Prague poor, which could have been used by municipal social policy makers, but it also determines the negative factors contributing in individual cases to falling into poverty. In addition to the societal conditions such as the impact of the economic crisis, the high cost of housing and the like, Machotka identified the other most important indicators: the character of education, social background, education, the strength of family ties and working conditions.[28] He also thought a lot about the "moral and intellectual inferiority of the poor" compared to the middle class, meaning that he – yet in a very rudimentary form – anticipated a much younger conceptualisation of the "culture of poverty" by American sociologist Oscar Lewis. Unfortunately, the analysis of the results had to be postponed – in contemporary circumstances, when all the calculations had to be done by hand, it was a laborious and especially costly procedure. The city did not release funds for carrying out such calculations until 1934, and even then only because this money could be used to involve the unemployed intelligence within the so-called "working colonies."[29]

Professional sociological processing and subsequent publications then took another two years. In other words, although the city of Prague through its Central Social Board (after reorganisation: the Central Social Office) released considerable resources to implement such demanding sociological research – and occasionally also boasted about it[30] – the municipality actually did not make much real use of its outcomes. Reports published by the Journal of the City of Prague show no signs of the implementation of the research outcomes, even in a period when its initiator Petr Zenkl became mayor.[31] The reason for this could be that the

---

[28] Machotka, *Sociálně potřebné rodiny*, pp. 193–195.

[29] Ibid, p. 16.

[30] For example, Otakar Urbánek, "Můj program sociálně hygienický pro nejbližší dobu" [My social and hygienical program for the nearest future], *Věstník hlavního města Prahy* 42, no. 27–31 (1935): pp. 549–551; Petr Zenkl, "Péče o bydlení nejchudších vrstev obyvatelstva" [The care of the housing of the poorest inhabitants], *Věstník hlavního města Prahy* 43, no. 13 (1936): pp. 257–259. It is significant that P. Zenkl in his lecture did not consider it necessary to name the author of the research. He also incorrectly localized it in time and interpreted its results quite arbitrarily.

[31] Cf. also Zenkl's programme essays Petr Zenkl, "Slovo mají nezaměstnaní..." [It's the jobless' turn to speak...], *Věstník hlavního města Prahy* 42, no. 46 (1935):

reform of municipal social welfare had only recently been carried out[32] and the municipality officials feared that further changes in this area would bring only more complications.

The other modern-conceived sociological research of the Prague poor therefore did not bring any practical implications for the (municipal) social policy, which was in direct conflict with the interests of its author. The organisation of social care kept following its own patterns, entirely practical, as if it actually did not need any professional background. Not surprisingly, carrying out such extensive research turned out to be much more fundamental for sociology itself, at least in the intentions of the Prague sociological school: "For the first time, this research brought important yields for the accurate differentiation of certain social strata, especially with regard to the differences in their characters, intellectual and moral and material,"[33] which was later used in the implementation of the aforementioned research on the urbanisation of greater Prague, i.e. the widest Czech sociological survey before the Second World War.

Further fates of both studies on poverty

Seeing as two major sociological surveys of the poor population of the capital city of Prague took place in the inter-war period, and globally, the quantitative empirisation of sociological research in progress occurred at the same time, we could assume that the development of sociology after the Second World War would lead to a further multiplication or even to a deepening of these above mentioned methods. In reality, nothing of the sort occurred. Czech wartime and briefly also post-war sociology had other concerns,[34] then the communist coup came in 1948 and sociology – being considered a "bourgeois pseudoscience" – was completely eliminated. Otakar Machotka, who was among the leaders of the National Socialist Party, left for exile soon after 1948, where he became a member of the

---

pp. 803–804; Petr Zenkl, "Úkoly sociální péče v obraně národa" [Tasks of the social welfare within the national defense], *Věstník hlavního města Prahy* 44, no. 23, (1937): pp. 445–447.

[32] It is surely possible that some of Zenkl's reforms might be inspired by the research carried out by Machotka, or by other informal contacts with Machotka, who devoted to handling these issues in the long term; Zenkl was indeed in contact with Machotka also because both were members of the National Socialist Party. However, it must be noted that the mutual contacts were never too warm and a direct inspiration of Zenkl's reforms by Machotka's research cannot be proved.

[33] Ullrich, "Sociologické výzkumy skupiny Sociálních problémů," p. 60.

[34] Nešpor, *Republika sociologů*, pp. 189–238.

Council of Free Czechoslovakia (later a member of the committee). He was often cited as an exemplary case. His research became misinterpreted, as it allegedly harmed the interests of the lower social strata.[35]

The opportunity to conduct social research was not completely thwarted, although it was only done under the cover of other disciplines. However, what became problematic was the topic of poverty itself – while historians and propagandists used historical material to demonstrate high levels of inter-war poverty and its alleged removal after the communist coup,[36] it was automatically assumed that poverty had been eradicated.[37] The Ministry of Labour and Social Welfare was temporarily cancelled without establishing any substitutional institution. Any investigation that would identify the real social problems in Czechoslovakia, including poverty in the communist-controlled society, almost amounted to treason. Some architects and other specialists began (very carefully) to raise such questions in the late 1950s.

Yet the need for an overview on the real social situation, associated with the reformist economic and political programs, eventually led to the preparation and implementation of the largest Czechoslovak sociological research in the 1960s. Its objective was the investigation of social stratification and mobility, carried out under the leadership of Pavel Machonin.[38] In many aspects, this research featured themes and/or methods used by the inter-war Prague sociological school, yet it was a "magic of unwanted." Machonin and his colleagues definitely did not pick up the threads of Machotka's pre-war work (they did not quote him either, unlike for example the inter-war research dedicated to the prestige of various occupations in Czechoslovakia, carried out by Antonín Obrdlík). They drew inspiration mainly from a combination of theoretical and methodological approaches of contemporary American sociology with Marxist rhetoric. The results of this research, in addition to showing

---

[35] For example, *Obraz "zlatých" časů* [A picture of a "golden" age], *Rudé právo,* February 17, 1952, p. 6.

[36] For example, Antonín Chyba, *Postavení dělnické třídy v kapitalistickém Československu* [A status of the working class in the capitalist Czechoslovakia], (Praha: Svoboda, 1972).

[37] For more on the communist social policy in its widest context, see Jakub Rákosník, *Sovětizace sociálního státu. Lidově-demokratický režim a sociální práva občanů v Československu 1945–1960* [Sovietization of a welfare state. People's democratic regime and social rights of citizens in Czechoslovakia 1945–1960], (Praha: Filozofická fakulta Univerzity Karlovy, 2010).

[38] The input of the research is Pavel Machonin et. al., *Československá společnost. Sociologická analýza sociální stratifikace* [Czechoslovak society. Sociological analyzis of social stratification], (Bratislava: Epocha, 1969).

income equality within society (and the authors of the research criticised that fact) also pointed to the threats of falling into poverty to certain social groups (especially pensioners). Surely enough, those outcomes did not match with the emerging "Normalisation" political strategy, and were therefore silenced again. Empirical research on the poor and poverty could only be renewed after 1989.[39]

The implementation of new sociological research on social inequalities, exclusion, poverty and other topics was related to their newly gained importance in the process of social transformation, as well as with massive development of social and public policies. Thus within this scenario, Machotka's requirement (cited in the introduction) for methodologically challenging, well-researched and extensively funded sociological research became a reality. Yet there was almost too much research to be adequately processed.[40] However, it does not appear that the results would have had a more practical application than in the case of the earlier forms of research. The realms of sociology and social policy do not have much in common even today, they mostly remain unrelated and actual social policy is entirely determined by non-scientific considerations and arguments.

Conclusion

In terms of its era, high quality sociological research work developed during inter-war Czechoslovakia and in many aspects it greatly exceeded the then foreign (European) field standards. Poverty and related social problems of the capital city of Prague was one of the most important topics which were handled in the framework of sociological surveys. Whether it was research on organising social care, conducted by American researchers at the end of the second decade of the 20th century, or modern-conceived research on needy families under the leadership of Otakar Machotka from the early 1930s, both turned out to be high quality investigations. In many ways, their findings compare very favourably with any ahistorical criticism. Both studies were completely unique projects in the framework of contemporary Europe. Despite that (or maybe because of that) the results of both studies actually had very little – if any – impact on

---

[39] Jiří Večerník, "Empirický výzkum chudoby v českých zemích ve třech historických obdobích" [Empirical research of poverty in Czech lands within three historical periods], *Data a výzkum – SDA Info* 5, no.2, (2011): pp. 133–146.

[40] Cf. *Cesty k datům. Zdroje a management sociálněvědních dat v České republice* [Ways to the data. Resources and management of social and scientific data in Czech Republic], eds. Jindřich Krejčí and Yana Leontiyeva (Praha: Sociologické nakladatelství SLON, 2012).

actual contemporary social policy. In the latter case, the research at least influenced the development of the Czech sociological community, or part of it, but it did not last long and the awareness of such a great project became lost even among the academic community. When we recall these studies today, it is partly because they can serve as a valuable source of data for social historians, and partly because they can stand as a memento for the Czech community of the social sciences, rich in terms of scope and funding, but not very strong in results.[41]

---

[41] Cf Zdeněk R. Nešpor, "Před ¾ stoletím… Kvantifikovaný esej o časopisecké produkci české sociologie před nástupem marxismu a dnes" [A three-quater century ago… A quantificational essay on journals' production of the Czech sociology before the onset of Marxism, and today], *Sociologický časopis/Czech Sociological Review* 43 (2007): pp. 397–422; Josef Baslet al., *Publikační výsledky české sociologie v odborných časopisech v posledních deseti letech* [Publication outcomes of the Czech sociology in scientific journals within the last decade], Praha 2009.

PART II:

CASE STUDIES

CHAPTER FIVE

VON DER ARMENPFLEGE ZUR SOZIALHILFE. KOMMUNALE „DASEINSVORSORGE" IN WIEN VOM 19. JAHRHUNDERT BIS IN DIE GEGENWART

ANDREAS WEIGL

From the care for the poor to social assistance: Municipal "services for the public" in Vienna from the 19th century to the present

Abstract: The genesis of municipal care for the poor in Vienna goes back to the pre-March period, but in Lueger's era, Viennese authorities began to play a more active role. After the outbreak of the First World War, the activities of the municipality in the social sphere focused on large population groups. In the inter-war period, a strictly organised network of social care was formed and its focus areas presented targeted care for families as well as for youth. Yet under the pressure of a worsening situation during the world economic crisis, a number of activities in the field of social care had to be significantly limited. Nevertheless, this successful model of social care survived periods of austrofascism and the National Socialist regime. After the Second World War – with a regard to changing societal conditions – classic social care transformed into social work. The issues of an aging population as well as the increase in the number of migrants stand as its two main challenges these days.

Kommunale „Armenpflege" bis zum Ersten Weltkrieg

Vor den 1780er Jahren lag die Armenfürsorge in Wien in erster Linie im Aufgabenbereich der Pfarren. Mit dem Bürgerspital und dem Großarmenhaus bestanden darüber hinaus große Institutionen, die sich auf Basis städtischer und landesfürstlicher Stiftungen und der Zahlungen der Bruderschaften der Kranken- und Armenpflege widmeten.[1] Schon am Beginn des 18. Jahrhunderts wurde mit der Schaffung der „cassa pauperum" der Versuch unternommen, alle gespendeten Mittel in einer vom Statthalter, Landmarschall und Erzbischof kontrollierten Kasse zu bündeln und damit auch deren Verteilung, einschließlich der Mitfinanzierung einschlägiger Anstalten, effizienter zu gestalten.[2] Die unter Kaiser Joseph II. durchgeführten aufgeklärt-absolutistischen Reformen hatten eine Zentralisierung des Armenwesens in staatlichen Händen und seine Trennung vom Gesundheitswesen zum Ziel. Dazu diente die Auflösung des Großarmenhauses, auf dessen Areal das Allgemeine Krankenhaus errichtet wurde, welches in seiner Funktion einem modernen Spital entsprach. Die im Großarmenhaus versorgten Armen wurden in verschiedene Versorgungshäuser verlegt.[3] Auch innerhalb der nunmehr reinen Armenpflege kam es zu einer institutionellen Trennung. Schon unter Maria Theresia war es primär unter Verfolgung merkantilistischer Konzepte zu einer Reorganisation des Waisenhauses am Rennweg mit dem Ziel der Einbindung der Insassen in den Produktionsprozess der Textilmanufakturen gekommen. Dieser Form der „Jugendfürsorge" war freilich kein kommerzieller Erfolg beschieden.[4] Erst unter der Alleinregentschaft Josephs II. wurde mit dem Gebär- und Findelhaus eine eigene, auf die Säuglings- und Kinderfürsorge spezialisierte Institution ins Leben gerufen, die sich allerdings für Säuglinge und Mütter auf Grund der dort verbreiteten Infektionskrankheiten, vor allem des Kindbettfiebers, für viele Jahrzehnte als wahre Todesfalle erwies.[5] Im Rahmen der Armenfürsorge erwachsener Personen wurde durchaus mit gewissem

---

[1] Vgl. dazu Josef Holzinger und Michael Altmann, Das Wiener Bürgerspital. Zur Erinnerung an die Eröffnung des neuen Bürger-Versorgungshauses in der Alservorstadt (Wien: Selbstverlag des Bürgerspitalamtes, 1860); Die Blumen des Bösen. Eine Geschichte der Armut in Wien, Prag, Budapest und Triest in den Jahren 1693 bis 1873 Bd. 2, Hrsg. Nora Fischer-Martin und Gerhard Fischer (Wien: Daedalus, 1994).
[2] Hannes Stekl, Österreichs Zucht- und Arbeitshäuser 1671–1920. Institutionen zwischen Fürsorge und Strafvollzug (Wien: Verlag für Geschichte und Politik, 1978), S. 27.
[3] "Altes Allgemeines Krankenhaus," in Felix Czeike, Historisches Lexikon Wien Bd. 3 (Wien: Kremayr und Scheriau, 2004), S. 591–593.
[4] Peter Feldbauer, Kinderelend in Wien. Von der Armenkinderpflege zur Jugenfürsorge (17.–19. Jahrhundert) (Wien: Verlag für Gesellschaftskritik, 1980), S. 48–53.
[5] Verena Pawlowsky, Mutter ledig – Vater Staat. Das Gebär- und Findelhaus in Wien 1784–1910 (Innsbruck et al.: Studien-Verlag, 2001), S. 209–215.

Erfolg der Versuch unternommen, möglichst viele „Arbeitsfähige" aus der Anstaltsbetreuung zu entlassen und die Versorgungshäuser zu reinen Pflegeheimen für Hochbetagte und chronisch Kranke umzufunktionieren.[6] Im Zuge der Reform wurden im Jahr 1783 die bestehenden Bruderschaften aufgelöst und deren Vermögen zur Hälfte dem neu gegründeten „Wiener Armeninstitut" überschrieben. Dieses diente als Sammel- und Verteilungsstelle der Armengelder. Über ehrenamtlich tätige „Armenväter" wurden die gespendeten Almosen unter Kontrolle der Pfarrer an die Bedürftigen verteilt. Diese Reorganisation der offenen Armenpflege blieb jedoch hinter den Erwartungen zurück, weil die Pfarrer mit der organisatorischen Aufgabe heillos überfordert waren und die spendenwillige Bevölkerung an den traditionellen Formen des Almosengebens festhielt.[7]

Als sich in der ersten Hälfte des 19. Jahrhunderts der Pauperismus zu einem Signum der frühindustriellen Epoche entwickelte, erwiesen sich die Aufnahmekapazitäten der bestehenden Einrichtungen der Armenpflege zunehmend als völlig unzureichend. Ausdruck des restaurativen Klimas jener Zeit war jedoch die Indifferenz von Herrscher, Regierung und Behörden gegenüber der wachsenden Armut. Impulse in der Armenfürsorge kamen lediglich von privater Seite. Im Zeitraum von 1810 bis 1848 entstanden insgesamt 22 private, teilweise sehr gut dotierte Wohltätigkeitsvereine, die unter loser staatlicher Kontrolle standen. Da sich die Vereine statutengemäß unterschiedlichen Gruppen von Armen – Kleinkindern, Schulkindern, Studierenden, Invaliden, geistig Kranken, Erwerbslosen, ehemaligen Häftlingen und vielen mehr – widmeten, trat dadurch eine weitere Spezialisierung der Armenpflege ein. Angesichts des Massenelends – im Jahr 1807 dürften 18 Prozent der Bevölkerung Almosenempfänger gewesen sein – blieb die Wirkung dieser privaten Gründungen aber sehr beschränkt.[8]

Die Genesis der kommunalen Armenfürsorge reicht in den späten Vormärz zurück. Im Jahr 1842 wurden alle bestehenden Fonds der Armenhilfe im „Allgemeinen Versorgungsfonds" vereinigt und vom Magistrat in dessen Verwaltung übernommen – zunächst noch im Auftrag der Regierung, nach dem 1849 erlassenen provisorischen Gemeindegesetz

---

[6] Hannes Stekl, "Vorformen geschlossener Altenhilfe in Österreich. Ihre Entwicklung von Joseph II. bis zur ersten Republik," in *Der alte Mensch in der Geschichte*, Hrsg. Helmut Konrad (Wien: Verlag für Gesellschaftskritik ,1982), S. 122–147, hier S. 124–126.
[7] Peter Feldbauer und Hannes Stekl, "Wiens Armenwesen im Vormärz," in Renate Banik-Schweitzer et al., *Wien im Vormärz* (Wien: Jugend und Volk, 1980), S. 175–201, hier S. 178.
[8] Ebenda, S. 176, 190 f.

dann in eigener Regie.[9] Im Grundsatz verstand sich die kommunale Armenfürsorge als Verwaltung bestehender Stiftungen und strebte eine ausgeglichene Bilanz durch sparsamen Umgang mit den vorhandenen Mitteln an. Die „allerhöchste Entschließung" vom 26. Februar 1842 bürdete dem Magistrat der Stadt Wien die Pflicht auf, Ausgaben der Armenhilfe, die aus dem Versorgungsfonds nicht gedeckt waren, aus eigenen Mitteln abzudecken.[10] Die starke Zuwanderung und die damit verbundene Wohnungsnot ließ die Zahl der zu versorgenden Armen weiter ansteigen. Die daraus resultierenden finanziellen Belastungen wurden zwar durch das Heimatrecht, insbesondere die Heimatrechtsnovelle von 1863,[11] limitiert, Handlungsbedarf war aber dennoch gegeben. Der Bau des Bürgerversorgungshauses in den Jahren 1858 bis 1860 stellte eine erste größere Investition in die geschlossene Armenpflege dar. Zudem zog die Gemeinde im Jahr 1862 die Waisenpflege an sich, was den Bau kommunaler Waisenhäuser und die Rekrutierung von Waisenvätern und -müttern bedingte.[12] Bezogen auf die Einwohnerzahl nahm der Anteil der Unterstützungsfälle in den folgenden Jahrzehnten erheblich zu, doch waren es nicht die öffentlichen, sondern die privaten Fonds, die den steigenden Bedarf zum größeren Teil finanziell abfederten.[13] Allein bis zum Jahr 1888 stieg die Zahl privater Humanitätsvereine auf beinahe 250 rasant an. Zu den prominentesten zählten der im Jahr 1849 gegründete „Wiener Centralverein für Krippen", die „unentgeltliche Knabenbeschäftigungs-Anstalt" (1854), der „Centralverein zur Beköstigung armer Schulkinder in Wien", der „Wiener Kreuzer-Verein zur Unterstützung der Gewerbsleute" (1847) und der „Allgemeine Wiener Hilfs- und Sparverein" (1847). In den 1870er Jahren kamen dazu auch neu gegründete Volksküchen sowie Suppen- und Teeanstalten.[14] Trotz dieser umfangreichen Vereinsaktivitäten wurden die Stimmen nach einer Reform der Armenfürsorge immer lauter.

[9] Karl Weiß, Geschichte der öffentlichen Anstalten, Fonde und Stiftungen für die Armenversorgung in Wien (Wien: Kraumüller, 1867), S. 344.
[10] Elisabeth Rachholz, "Zur Armenfürsorge der Stadt Wien von 1740 bis 1904. Von der privaten zur städtischen Fürsorge" (Diss. Wien, 1970), S. 94.
[11] Sylvia Hahn, Migration – Arbeit – Geschlecht. Arbeitsmigration in Mitteleuropa vom 17. bis zum Beginn des 20. Jahrhunderts (Göttingen: V&R unipress, 2008), S. 137 f.
[12] Weiß, Geschichte, S. 350, 355, CLXXXII.
[13] Rudolf Kobatsch, Die Armenpflege in Wien und ihre Reform (Wien: s. t., 1893), S. 83–85.
[14] Friedrich von Radler, "Gesellschaftliche Wohlthätigkeitspflege," in Wien 1848–1888. Denkschrift zum 2. December 1888 Bd. 1., Hrsg. Gemeinderath der Stadt Wien (Wien: Carl Konegen, 1888), S. 321–396, hier S. 335–362.

Bewegung in die Armenpolitik kam jedoch erst durch die überfällige Lockerung des Heimatrechts. Eine im Jahr 1901 in Kraft getretene Novelle sah einen Rechtsanspruch auf Heimatzuständigkeit nach zehnjährigem, freiwilligem ununterbrochenen Aufenthalt vor,[15] allerdings unter der Bedingung der Großjährigkeit der Antragsteller und -stellerinnen. Zudem durften im Zeitraum der „Ersitzung" keine Mittel aus der öffentlichen Armenfürsorge beansprucht worden sein.[16] Trotz dieser Einschränkungen nahm infolge der geänderten Rechtslage die Zahl der in Wien Heimatberechtigten sprunghaft zu, wobei es sich bei den Antragstellern im erheblichen Maß gerade um ältere Personen handelte, die als „Risikogruppe" im Sinn der Armenfürsorge zu betrachten waren.[17] Das Heimatrecht blieb allerdings auch in der Folge bis in die austrofaschistische Ära ein Mittel, um einen Teil der städtischen Bevölkerung von Leistungen der Armenfürsorge auszuschließen oder zumindest deren Erlangung zu erschweren.[18]

Die seit 1897 an der Macht befindlichen Christlichsozialen hatten keineswegs eine grundlegende Neuorientierung der Armenpflege im Sinn, orientierten sie sich doch auf diesem Gebiet am patriarchalisch-repressiven Vorbild der Vergangenheit. Die in der Regierungszeit Bürgermeister Karl Luegers (1896–1910) verfolgte, groß angelegte Kommunalisierung berührte daher die Armenpflege nur am Rande. Unter dem Druck des demographischen Wachstums und einer steigenden Lebenserwartung wurde eine Ausweitung der Altenpflege wie auch der Säuglings- und Kinderfürsorge dennoch unumgänglich.

Die wichtigsten sozialpolitischen Leistungen der Lueger'schen Ära auf dem Gebiet der Armenpflege bestanden im Ausbau der geschlossenen Fürsorge. Zu den bestehenden sechs Versorgungshäusern[19] gesellte sich mit dem Versorgungsheim (1904) und dem 1908 fertig gestellten Jubiläumspital in Lainz ein Zentrum der Altenfürsorge von beachtlicher Dimension. Die Kapazität des Versorgungsheimes wurde innerhalb weniger Jahre auf nahezu 5.000 Insassen erhöht,[20] die Betriebskosten

---

[15] Reichsgesetzblatt 222/1896.

[16] Ludwig Spiegel, "Heimatrecht," in *Österreichisches Staatswörterbuch. Handbuch des gesamten österreichischen öffentlichen Rechtes* Bd. 2, Hrsg. Ernst Mischler und Josef Ulbrich (Wien: Hölder, 1906), S. 809–843, hier S. 823 f.

[17] Hahn, *Migration*, S. 152 f.

[18] Gerhard Melinz und Gerhard Unger, *Wohlfahrt und Krise. Wiener Kommunalpolitik 1929–1938* (Wien: Deuticke, 1996), S. 7–17.

[19] Kathrine E. Kogler, "Die geschlossene Armenpflege in Wien vor Bau des Lainzer Versorgungsheimes," in *„In der Versorgung". Vom Versorgungsheim Lainz zum Geriatriezentrum „Am Wienerwald"*, Hrsg. Ingrid Arias et al. (Wien: Verlag-Haus der Ärzte, 2005), S. 11–26, hier S. 15.

[20] Christiane Feuerstein, *Vom Armenhaus zur sozialen Infrastruktur.*

kletterten infolgedessen auf über 3 Millionen Kronen.[21] Für Bürgermeister Lueger bot das Prestigeprojekt nicht nur eine willkommene Möglichkeit, bürgerliche Armenfürsorgevorstellungen zu verwirklichen, sondern gegen Ende seiner Amtszeit auch der Selbstverherrlichung in der auf dem Gelände des Heimes errichteten Kirche zu huldigen: „Ventures like Lainz were definitely charity and not social welfare."[22]

Auch in den Bereich der Kinder- und Jugendfürsorge kam in der Lueger-Ära etwas Bewegung. Schon im Jahr 1902 wurden im Zuge einer Reform der kommunalen Armenkinderpflege die bis dahin fungierenden Waisenmütter durch Armenrätinnen und Armenräte ersetzt, die nun mit der Überwachung der Pflege- und Kostkinder betraut waren. Für eine Ausweitung der kommunalen Armenkinderpflege im Rahmen des Vormundschafts-, Familien- und Fürsorgerechts sorgte die Einführung der Berufsvormundschaft für unehelich geborene Kinder ein Jahrzehnt später. Diese bedingte den Aufbau eines administrativen Apparats: So wurde ein Amt für städtische Berufsvormünder gegründet und städtische Bezirkswaisenräte, vorerst allerdings nur in zwei Bezirken, eingerichtet.[23]

Einen wichtigen Professionalisierungsschritt in der Fürsorge brachte der Beschluss des Gemeinderates vom 6. September 1912, der die Schaffung kommunaler Säuglingsfürsorgestellen vorsah. Zu diesem Zweck wurden Säuglingspflegerinnen eingestellt, die ein- bis zweimal monatlich unehelich geborene Säuglinge besuchen, deren Pflegebedingungen kontrollieren und den Müttern Kenntnisse der Säuglingspflege vermitteln sollten. Diese Säuglingspflegerinnen können als die ersten „Sozialarbeiterinnen" im kommunalen Dienst bezeichnet werden.[24]

Insgesamt lässt sich in den Jahren vor Ausbruch des Ersten Weltkriegs eine gewisse Sozialpolitisierung feststellen, die durch die politische Auseinandersetzung zwischen den beiden Massenparteien, den regierenden

---

Altersversorgung in Wien (Weitra: Verlag Bibliothek der Provinz, Ed. Seidengasse, 2009), S. 76.
[21] Kathrine E. Kogler, "‚Daß auch der wahrhaft Arme als ein Mensch behandelt werde …'," in *„In der Versorgung". Vom Versorgungsheim Lainz zum Geriatriezentrum „Am Wienerwald"*, Hrsg. Ingrid Arias et al. (Wien: Verlag-Haus der Ärzte, 2005), S. 41–62, hier S. 50.
[22] John W. Boyer, *Culture and Political Crisis in Vienna. Christian Socialism in Power, 1897–1918* (Chicago und London: Univ. of Chicago Press, 1995), S. 18 f.
[23] Gudrun Wolfgruber, *Von der Fürsorge zur Sozialarbeit. Wiener Jugendwohlfahrt im 20. Jahrhundert* (Wien: Löcker, 2013), S. 22.
[24] Susanne Birgit Mittermeier, "Die Jugendfürsorgerin. Zur Professionalisierung der sozialen Kinder- und Jugendarbeit in der Wiener städtischen Fürsorge von den Anfängen bis zur Konstituierung des Berufsbildes Ende der 1920er Jahre," *L'Homme* 5 (1994): S. 102–120, hier S. 108–110.

Christlichsozialen und den oppositionellen Sozialdemokraten, wichtige
Impulse erhielt.[25] Aber auch auf staatlicher Ebene wurde Kinderschutz ein
Thema. Im Jahr 1907 fand der Erste Österreichische Kinderschutzkongress
in Wien statt, der sich dem Problem der „Verwahrlosung" von Kindern
widmete. Dabei wurden die Unzulänglichkeiten der Jugendfürsorge und
eine „falsche Kriminalpolitik" gegenüber straffällig gewordenen Jugendlichen
kritisiert sowie zugleich ein stärkeres finanzielles Engagement der
Öffentlichkeit gefordert.[26] Tatsächlich verschoben sich die Gewichte
zwischen öffentlichen und privaten Mitteln erheblich. Am Ende der
liberalen Ära wurden die Ausgaben für die „Armenpflege" noch zu mehr
als 60 Prozent durch Einnahmen gedeckt, in den Jahren vor Ausbruch des
Ersten Weltkriegs kam der überwiegende Teil der Mittel aus dem
Gemeindebudget. Im Jahr 1913 entfielen von den Ausgaben in der Höhe
von etwa 23 Millionen Kronen rund 13 Millionen auf die offene
Armenpflege. Für gemeindeeigene Armen- und Versorgungshäuser fielen
bereits 6,5 Millionen an.[27]

„Kriegsfürsorge"

Der Ausbruch des Ersten Weltkriegs stellte für die Kommunalpolitik
und die kommunale Verwaltung eine enorme Herausforderung dar, da
schon in den ersten Tagen des Krieges Versorgungsschwierigkeiten
auftraten, die sich in der Folge immer mehr verschärften, und die Not
immer größere Teile der städtischen Bevölkerung erfasste. Die prekäre
Versorgungslage nötigte die Stadtregierung zur Schaffung von
Dienststellen, die sich mit der Lebensmittel- und Heizmittelversorgung
befassten und ab April 1917 in einem Bezirkswirtschaftsamt zusammengefasst
wurden. Im Februar 1918 trat dazu noch ein Städtisches Landwirtschaftsamt.[28]

[25] Gerhard Melinz und Susan Zimmermann, Über die Grenzen der Armenhilfe.
Kommunale und staatliche Sozialpolitik in Wien und Budapest in der
Doppelmonarchie (Wien und Zürich: Europaverlag, 1991), S. 175.
[26] Edmund Gayer, "Welches sind die Ursachen und die Erscheinungsformen der
Verwahrlosung von Kindern und Jugendlichen?," in Die Ursachen,
Erscheinungsformen und die Ausbreitung der Verwahrlosung von Kindern und
Jugendlichen in Österreich. Einzeldarstellungen aus allen Teilen Österreichs, Hrsg.
Joseph M. Baernreither (Wien: Manz, 1906), S. 111–171.
[27] Eigene Berechnungen nach Statistisches Jahrbuch der Stadt Wien XIII. (1895)
(Wien: Magistrat, 1897), S. 123, 133, 136; XXXI. (1913) (Wien: Magistrat, 1916),
S. 155, 169, 175.
[28] Christian Mertens, "Die Wiener Stadtverwaltung im Ersten Weltkrieg," in Im
Epizentrum des Zusammenbruchs. Wien im Ersten Weltkrieg, Hrsg. Alfred Pfoser
und Andreas Weigl (Wien: Metroverlag, 2013), S. 284–291, hier S. 286 f.

Bereits Ende Juli 1914 wurde die kommunale „Zentralstelle der Fürsorge für Soldaten und ihre Familienangehörigen und für die im Krieg in Not Geratenen" ins Leben gerufen. Sie entfaltete eine umfangreiche Tätigkeit, die von Geldunterstützungen über Vermittlung von Arbeit, öffentliche Ausspeisungen, Lebensmittelabgaben an Mindestbemittelte bis zur „Bekleidungsfürsorge" reichte.[29] Angesichts schwindender Ressourcen geriet die Kriegsfürsorge immer mehr zu einer „Verwaltung der Not".

Durch die eintretende Massenarmut wurde die traditionelle Armenfürsorge immer mehr in den Hintergrund gedrängt. Da die Armen- und Versorgungshäuser teilweise zu (Ersatz-)Lazaretten umfunktioniert wurden und die Insassen der verbliebenen Einrichtungen lediglich die rationierten Mengen an Lebensmitteln erhielten, war die Sterblichkeit unter den in Armenhäusern versorgten Menschen besonders hoch.[30]

Besonders schlimm traf der Krieg auch Kinder und Jugendliche, von denen viele mehr oder minder auf sich alleine gestellt waren und ums Überleben kämpfen mussten. „Verwahrlosung" und Kleinkriminalität waren die Folge.[31] Die verbreitete schwere Unterernährung der Kinder und Jugendlichen sorgte in der Folge auch für einen massiven Anstieg der Sterbefälle im schulpflichtigen Alter, Kriegsjahr für Kriegsjahr um etwa 20 Prozent. Im Jahr der Grippeepidemie 1918 kam es zu einer weiteren Verdoppelung.[32] Die Not vieler Kinder zwang die Gemeinde zu einer Erweiterung der Kinder- und Jugendfürsorge. Das Amt der städtischen Berufsvormundschaft entsandte Pflegerinnen in die Gebärkliniken, um möglichst früh unterstützungsbedürftige Kinder und deren Mütter zu erfassen.[33] Vor allem mit Bezug auf die heranwachsenden Kinder und Jugendlichen blieb vorerst eine Fürsorgelücke bestehen, die eine organisatorische Veränderung veranlasste. Die Berufsvormundschaft wurde nun auf alle unehelich geborenen Kinder ausgedehnt. Im Jahr 1917

[29] *Die Gemeindeverwaltung der Stadt Wien in der Zeit von 1. Jänner 1914 bis 30. Juni 1919*, (Hrsg.) Wiener Magistrat (Wien: s. t., 1923), S. 153–167.
[30] Martina Gamper, "Nudelexpress, Hungerration und Zwetschkenknödel," in *„In der Versorgung". Vom Versorgungsheim Lainz zum Geriatriezentrum „Am Wienerwald"*, Hrsg. Ingrid Arias et al. (Wien: Verlag-Haus der Ärzte, 2005), S. 129–153, hier S. 139 f.
[31] Maureen Healy, *Vienna and the Fall of the Habsburg Empire. Total War and Everyday Life in World War I.* (Cambridge: Cambridge Univ. Press, 2004), S. 247–255.
[32] Clemens Pirquet, "Ernährungszustand der Kinder in Österreich während des Krieges und der Nachkriegszeit," in *Die Volksgesundheit im Krieg* Bd. 1, Hrsg. idem (Wien und New Haven: Hölder-Pichler-Tempsky et al., 1926), S. 172 f.
[33] *Ein Jahr Kriegsfürsorge der Gemeinde Wien*, Hrsg. Gemeinde Wien (Wien: Gerlach & Wiedling, 1915), S. 24–31.

nahm das Wiener Jugendamt in der Nachfolge des Amtes städtischer Berufsvormünder seinen Betrieb auf.[34] Eine weitere Ausweitung des Fürsorgeapparats wurde bereits während des Krieges von leitenden Verwaltungsbeamten als zukünftig erforderlich erachtet.[35]

Lediglich im Bereich der Säuglingsfürsorge gelang es einigermaßen, die schädigenden Wirkungen des Krieges zu begrenzen. Die im Jänner 1915 als privater Verein ins Leben gerufene „Kriegspatenschaft" baute auf Spenden wohlhabender Familien, die bedürftige Jungmütter finanziell bis zum 10. Lebensmonat des neugeborenen Kindes unterstützten. Stillende Mütter erhielten eine doppelt so hohe Förderung.[36] Über ein Netz von Mutterberatungs- und Säuglingsfürsorgestellen gelang es dem Verein, etwa jedem zweiten neugeborenen Kind und dessen Mutter während der Kriegsjahre Hilfen zukommen zu lassen. Wie eine Subventionszusage des k. u. k. Ministeriums für Volksgesundheit an den Verein „Kriegspatenschaft" vom 20. August 1918 zeigt, wurde die Bedeutung der Aktion auch staatlicherseits erkannt und gefördert.[37] Der „Kriegspatenschaft" war es maßgeblich zu verdanken, dass die Säuglingssterblichkeit während des Krieges kaum stieg. Allerdings fiel sie auch nicht, wie es in den Jahren vor dem Krieg zu beobachten gewesen war. Ihr kam somit eine wichtige Vorreiterrolle für die Kinder- und Jugendfürsorge im „Roten Wien" zu.

Soziale Wohlfahrt und Armenfürsorge im „Roten Wien"

Bereits während des Ersten Weltkriegs war es zu einem anlassbezogenen Ineinandergreifen staatlicher und kommunaler Sozialpolitik gekommen. Mit der Gründung der Republik setzte nun auf staatlicher Ebene ein sozialpolitischer Reformschub ein, der Österreich bis zum Auseinanderbrechen der Koalition zwischen Sozialdemokraten und Christlichsozialen im Sommer 1920 eine der fortschrittlichsten Sozialgesetzgebungen Europas bescherte. Seit dieser Reformperiode ist es sinnvoll, von einem „ersten", staatlichen, und einem „zweiten",

---

[34] *70 Jahre Wiener Jugendamt*, Hrsg. Jugendamt der Stadt Wien (Wien: Jugendamt, 1987), S. 11.
[35] Andreas Weigl, "Kommunale Daseinsvorsorge. Zur Genesis des ‚Fürsorgekomplexes'," in *Im Epizentrum des Zusammenbruchs. Wien im Ersten Weltkrieg*, Hrsg. Alfred Pfoser und Andreas Weigl (Wien: Metroverlag, 2013), S. 336–347, hier S. 346 f.
[36] Leopold Moll, "Vier Jahre ärztliche Fürsorgearbeit in der Kriegspatenschaft nebst kurzen Bemerkungen zu meinem Vorschlage der Mutterräte," *Wiener klinische Wochenschrift* 27 (1919): S. 9–18.
[37] Wiener Stadt- und Landesarchiv, M.Abt. 119, A 32: 4949/1927.

vorrangig kommunalen, sozialen Netz in Österreich zu sprechen. Für die kommunale Fürsorge war es dabei bedeutsam, dass im Zuge dieser Reform die allgemeine Krankenversicherung auf alle Lohnarbeiter und auf die öffentlich Bediensteten ausgedehnt wurde. Mit dem Angestelltenversicherungsgesetz von 1926 und dem Arbeiterversicherungsgesetz von 1927 wurde zudem die Kranken-, Unfall- und Altersversicherung der überwiegenden Mehrheit der unselbstständig Erwerbstätigen und deren Angehöriger eingeführt, die Altersversicherung der Arbeiter vorerst allerdings nur provisorisch und finanziell ungenügend.[38] Dennoch sicherte das staatliche Sozialnetz nur Erwerbstätige, „Erwerbsfähige" und einen Teil der Angehörigen. Andere von Armut bedrohte Bevölkerungsgruppen blieben auf Basis der Landesgesetzgebung der neugeschaffenen Bundesländer auf die Länder und Gemeinden verwiesen. Dieses „zweite soziale Netz" erfuhr nun ebenso wie das staatliche eine deutliche Erweiterung.[39]

Als im Mai 1919 die Sozialdemokraten in Niederösterreich die Wahlen gewannen und wenig später aus dem ehemaligen Kronland Niederösterreich die Bundesländer Wien und Niederösterreich entstanden, bot sich für die sozialdemokratische Stadtregierung die Chance, jenes spätaufklärerische Modell einer umfassenden Wohlfahrtspolitik zu implementieren, welches unter dem Signum „Rotes Wien" auch international große Beachtung fand.[40] Die Eckpfeiler dieser Politik erklären sich einerseits aus der katastrophalen Ausgangslage, andererseits aus einem ideologisch begründeten Bruch mit der reaktiven Armenpolitik der Vergangenheit. Nach Kriegsende waren erhebliche Teile der Wiener Bevölkerung schwer unterernährt und vom Hungertod bedroht. Der Ernährungszustand vieler heranwachsender Kinder war verheerend. Nach Untersuchungen aus dem Jahr 1920 unter 145.000 Wiener Kindern lag der Anteil unterernährter Kinder bei 75 bis 80 Prozent.[41] Wenig besser war es um die erwachsene Bevölkerung, vor allem um die Kriegshinterbliebenen und ihre Angehörigen, bestellt. Nach einer Erhebung unter Angehörigen von Gefallenen oder Vermissten knapp vor Kriegsende waren ein Drittel der Ehefrauen und 22 Prozent der Lebensgefährtinnen zum Zeitpunkt der

---

[38] Emmerich Tálos, *Staatliche Sozialpolitik in Österreich. Rekonstruktion und Analyse* (Wien: Verlag für Gesellschaftskritik, 1981), S. 193–204.
[39] Gerhard Melinz, "Das ‚zweite soziale Netz' – Kehrseite staatlicher Sozialpolitik," in Emmerich Tálos et al., *Handbuch des politischen Systems Österreichs. Erste Republik 1918–1933* (Wien: Manz, 1995), S. 587–601.
[40] Helmut Gruber, *Red Vienna. Experiment in Working-Class Culture 1919–1934* (New York und Oxford: Oxford Univ. Press, 1991), S. 65–73.
[41] Pirquet, "Ernährungszustand," S. 161–165.

Erhebung krank.[42] Nach Schätzungen von Verena Pawlowsky und Harald
Wendelin lebten im Jahr 1922 etwa 40.000 Kriegsbeschädigte in Wien. Sie
und ihre Familien mussten sich mit einer kümmerlichen staatlichen
Unterstützung durchs Leben bringen.[43]

Angesichts der Massenarmut richteten sich die Anstrengungen der
Stadtregierung zunächst auf die Minderung der ärgsten Not. Auf Basis der
gesetzlich vorgesehenen Armenfürsorge erhielten beispielsweise Mitte der
1920er Jahre in der offenen Armenfürsorge etwa 38.000 in Wien
heimatberechtigte   Personen   und   ihre   Angehörigen   laufend
Erhaltungsbeiträge.[44] Dazu kamen die weiterhin bestehenden Leistungen in
der geschlossenen Fürsorge, die sich auf den Ausbau dieser Einrichtungen
in der Lueger-Ära stützen konnten.[45] In diesem Bereich der Armenpflege
kam es nun zu einer Ausdifferenzierung und Spezialisierung, die an das
Konzept der josephinischen Reform anknüpfte. Während „pflegebedürftige
Sieche" je nach Krankheitstyp in verschiedenen Pavillons des
Versorgungsheimes Lainz von spezialisiertem Pflegepersonal betreut
wurden, dienten andere Heime den „bloß Erwerbsunfähigen".[46]

Die sozialdemokratische Stadtregierung strebte jedoch mehr an. Mit
ihrem Protagonisten Universitätsprofessor Julius Tandler an der Spitze
wurde eine umfassende Reform der kommunalen Fürsorge auf Basis eines
wohlfahrtsstaatlichen Konzepts implementiert. Nun ging es nicht mehr um
eine Reaktion auf soziale Problemlagen, sondern um Armutsprävention,[47]
nicht um die Fürsorge nur für soziale Randgruppen, sondern für die
gesamte Stadtbevölkerung. Im Mittelpunkt des Fürsorgekonzeptes standen
dabei die Kinder. „Den Höhepunkt des gesamten Strebens", wie Tandler
nicht ohne Pathos in einer offiziösen Leistungsschau feststellte, „stellt die
Sorge um unsere Kinder dar, des höchsten vielfach einzigen Gutes, das uns
geblieben […]. Denn Sinn und Zweck des Daseins einer Generation kann
nur die Sorge um die nächste sein."[48] Im öffentlichen Diskurs über die

---

[42] "Ergebnisse der Zählung der Kriegshinterbliebenen in Wien," *Blätter für das Wohlfahrts- und Armenwesen der Stadt Wien* 17 (1918): Nr. 204.
[43] Verena Pawlowsky und Harald Wendelin, "Der Krieg und seine Opfer. Kriegsbeschädigte in Wien," in *Im Epizentrum des Zusammenbruchs. Wien im Ersten Weltkrieg*, Hrsg. Alfred Pfoser und Andreas Weigl (Wien: Metroverlag, 2013) S. 310–317, hier S. 312.
[44] *Das Neue Wien. Städtewerk II.* (Wien: Elbemühl, 1927), S. 352–356.
[45] Stekl, "Vorformen," S. 140.
[46] Feuerstein, "Vom Armenhaus," S. 79–81.
[47] Gudrun Wolfgruber, "Messbares Glück? Sozialdemokratische Konzeptionen zu Fürsorge und Familie im Wien der 1920er Jahre," *L'Homme* 10 (1999), S. 277–294, hier S. 280.
[48] *Das Neue Wien II.*, S. 340 f.

Kinder- und Jugendwohlfahrt konstruierten die Sozialdemokraten das „Rote Wien" als „Über-Mutter" aller Wiener Kinder.[49] „Jedes Kind ist von Natur aus arm und hilfsbedürftig und bleibt dies so lange, bis es die Erziehung zu einem brauchbaren Menschen gemacht hat."[50] Die besondere Hinwendung zum Kind bedingte eine Schwerpunktsetzung im Bereich der Kinder-, Jugend- und Familienfürsorge, die eugenisch und bevölkerungspolitisch legitimiert wurde.

Organisatorisch wurden im Zuge der neuen Geschäftseinteilung des Wiener Magistrates von 1920 alle Sparten der Fürsorge im Wohlfahrtsamt gebündelt. Diesem unterstanden als Abteilungen das Jugendamt, die Armenpflege, die Pflegeanstalten, die Notstandsfürsorge, das Gesundheitsamt und die Abteilung für Friedhofsangelegenheiten.[51] Damit wurde dem Anspruch einer Betreuung „von der Wiege bis zur Bahre" theoretisch voll Rechnung getragen. Es bedurfte jedoch eines entsprechend ausgebildeten Personals, um ihn auch in der Praxis umzusetzen. Eine wichtige Rolle kam dabei der Berufsgruppe der „Fürsorgerinnen" zu, die nun in größerer Zahl von der Gemeinde Wien aufgenommen wurden. Fürsorgerinnen waren in den Mutterberatungsstellen tätig, machten Hausbesuche, übergaben Säuglingswäschepakete und kontrollierten und überwachten die Betreuung und Pflege der Kinder, insbesondere im Fall unehelicher Geburten und schwieriger sozialer Verhältnisse. Da ihre Angaben bis zur behördlichen Kindeswegnahme führen konnten, waren sie unter den sozial Schwachen unbeliebt, gefürchtet, zum Teil auch gehasst. Das schwierige Verhältnis zu ihrer Klientel wurde verschärft durch ihre soziale Herkunft aus dem zumeist bürgerlichen Milieu. So fehlte es oft am nötigen Verständnis für soziale Problemlagen, obwohl auch der Wiener Mittelstand unter den Wirkungen des Weltkrieges schwer gelitten hatte.[52] Mit dem Ausbruch der Weltwirtschaftskrise und dem drastischen Absinken der Geburtenzahlen verlagerte sich zu Beginn der 1930er Jahre der Schwerpunkt der Tätigkeit der Fürsorgerinnen zur Erwachsenenfürsorge, was das Konfliktpotential noch erhöhte, da nun die

---

[49] Dieses Bild fand auch in der zeitgenössischen, von der Gemeinde Wien beauftragten Plastik, in der die Stadt Wien als „Fürsorgende Mutter" dargestellt wurde, ihren offiziösen Ausdruck. Vgl. dazu Wiener Stadt- und Landesarchiv, Fotosammlung Gerlach: C 18604M, ca. 1930.
[50] Wolfgruber, *Von der Fürsorge*, S. 30.
[51] Felix Czeike und Peter Csendes, *Die Geschichte der Magistratsabteilungen der Stadt Wien 1902–1970* (Wien und München: Jugend und Volk, 1971), S. 38.
[52] Zusammenfassend dazu Andreas Weigl, ",Fürsorgliche Belagerer'. Bürgerliche Fürsorgerinnen im ‚Roten Wien'," *Jahrbuch des Vereins für Geschichte der Stadt Wien* 66 (2010), S. 319–335.

Zuerkennung oder Aberkennung von Kranken- und Armenunterstützungen
die soziale Distanz vieler Fürsorgerinnen zu ihrer Klientel noch deutlicher
zu Tage treten ließ.[53]

Die „Fürsorge" bildete aber bei weitem nicht das einzige Feld
kommunaler Wohlfahrtspolitik im „Roten Wien". Im Sinne des Konzeptes
einer ganzheitlichen Daseinsvorsorge gingen die Aktivitäten der
Gemeinde Wien zur Bekämpfung der Armut und Not über den Bereich der
Fürsorge deutlich hinaus und erzielten auf dem Gebiet der
Wohnungsversorgung besonders große Wirkung. Ein im Jahr 1923
beschlossenes großes Wohnbauprogramm setzte nach damaligen Begriffen
neue, moderne Wohnstandards, die über die Ausstattung mit Innen-WCs,
kollektiv genutzten Waschküchen und begrünten Innenhöfen und nicht
zuletzt niedrigen Mieten auch gesundheits- und sozialpolitisch von großer
Relevanz waren. Die Ausgaben für den kommunalen Wohnbau bewegten
sich in der zweiten Hälfte der 1920er Jahre in etwa in der Höhe der
Ausgaben für das Wohlfahrtsamt, sanken aber dann in der Folge deutlich
darunter. Dies ist ein Hinweis darauf, dass der Fürsorge in der
Weltwirtschaftskrise höchste Priorität beigemessen wurde.[54]

Die Schwerpunktverlagerung der Fürsorge von der Armen- zur Kinder-,
Jugend- und Familienfürsorge wäre ohne die sozialpolitischen Reformen auf
staatlicher Ebene aus den Jahren 1918 bis 1920 nicht möglich gewesen. Mit
der sich verschlechternden ökonomischen Situation erweiterte sich jedoch
zu Beginn der 1930er Jahre der Kreis jener Personen, die durch das erste
soziale Netz fielen, „ausgesteuert" wurden und anlassbezogenen oder
dauernd finanzielle Unterstützungen seitens der Gemeinde Wien erhielten.
Vor allem aber stieg der Aufwand für „Erhaltungsbeiträge" für Alte, Kranke
und Berufsunfähige nicht nur als Folge der Wirtschaftskrise, sondern nicht
zuletzt aufgrund der gestiegenen Lebenserwartung Jahr für Jahr an, ein
Trend, der durch Einsparungsmaßnahmen weder unter der
sozialdemokratischen noch unter der ihr folgenden autoritären
austrofaschistischen Stadtregierung gestoppt werden konnte.[55] Erhebliche
Mittel erforderte auch der Betrieb bestehender Einrichtungen der
geschlossenen Fürsorge wie des Versorgungsheims Lainz und der acht
Bezirksarmenhäuser.[56]

---

[53] Gruber, *Red Vienna*, S. 71.
[54] Felix Czeike, *Wirtschafts- und Sozialpolitik der Gemeinde Wien in der Ersten Republik (1919–1934)* Bd. 2 (Wien: Verlag für Jugend und Volk 1959), S. 35 f.; Melinz und Unger, *Wohlfahrt und Krise*, S. 46 f.
[55] Melinz und Unger, *Wohlfahrt und Krise*, S. 58–60, 66–69.
[56] Feuerstein, "Vom Armenhaus," S. 80.

Das austrofaschistische Intermezzo

Gemäß der Ideologie des im Februar 1934 endgültig an die Macht gelangten austrofaschistischen Regimes, dessen Protagonisten aus den Reihen der Christlichsozialen Partei stammten, versuchte die neue Stadtregierung, eine rückwärtsgewandte katholische Armen- und Fürsorgepolitik zu forcieren, die sich auf die Enzyklika *Quadragesimo Anno* zu stützen vorgab. Das „Recht auf Fürsorge" wurde nun durch die „Pflicht zur Nächstenliebe" der Fürsorgenden und die Dankbarkeit der Befürsorgten ersetzt.[57] In diesem Sinn sollte privaten, karitativen Organisationen eine größere Rolle zukommen. Sozialpolitische Zielsetzung war eine Verbesserung der Zusammenarbeit zwischen öffentlichen und privaten Fürsorgeorganisationen, wie dem „Josefswerk" – einer auf eherechtliche Fragen und Familienseelsorge spezialisierten Institution – und dem „Mutterschutzwerk der Vaterländischen Front".[58]

Angesichts der Weltwirtschaftskrise und des eingeschränkten finanzpolitischen Spielraums betrieb die Regierung ein scharfes Kürzungsprogramm, welches für immer größere Löcher im staatlichen Sozialnetz sorgte.[59] Auf kommunaler Ebene fiel der Versuch, öffentliche Mittel nur noch „Bedürftigen" zukommen zu lassen, äußerst widersprüchlich aus. Die Heimatgesetznovelle von 1935 suchte die Regresspflicht der Heimatgemeinde für nicht heimatzuständige „vorübergehend Anwesende" einzuschränken, was in der Praxis permanente Konflikte mit der Aufenthaltsgemeinde provozierte, die intendierte Beseitigung der „Bettlerplage" jedoch nicht beförderte.[60] Auch in der Familien- und Jugendfürsorge gab es widersprüchliche Tendenzen. So sank die Zahl der ausgegebenen Säuglingswäschepakete zwar auf etwa die Hälfte, wozu auch der Geburtenrückgang beitrug, gleichzeitig sah sich die politische Führung aber genötigt, eine Jahr für Jahr wachsende Zahl an Lebensmittelpaketen an Familien auszugeben, was mit einer Kostensteigerung von rund 40 Prozent verbunden war.[61] Insgesamt sanken die Ausgaben für

---

[57] Gerhard Melinz, "Fürsorgepolitik(en)," in *Austrofaschismus. Politik – Ökonomie – Kultur 1933–1938*, Hrsg. Emmerich Tálos und Wolfgang Neugebauer (Wien: Lit, 2005), S. 238–252, hier S. 240 f.
[58] *70 Jahre Wiener Jugendamt*, Hrsg. Jugendamt der Stadt Wien, S. 31 f.
[59] Emmerich Tálos, "Sozialpolitik im Austrofaschismus," in *Austrofaschismus. Politik – Ökonomie – Kultur 1933–1938*, Hrsg. Emmerich Tálos und Wolfgang Neugebauer (Wien: Lit, 2005), S. 221–235, hier S. 228–230.
[60] Melinz, "Fürsorgepolitik(en)," S. 242 f.
[61] *Statistisches Jahrbuch der Stadt Wien NF III. (1930–1935)* (Wien: Magistrat, 1936), S. 64; *NF 4 (1937)*, S. 57.

das Wohlfahrtswesen im Vergleich zum Gesamtbudget daher weit unterdurchschnittlich. Vielfach wurden die im „Roten Wien" entwickelten Aktivitäten wenig verändert übernommen. Das bildete sich auch in der Verwaltungsorganisation ab. Unter dem breiten Dach des Wohlfahrtsamtes wurde sogar eine weitere Abteilung, ein Amt für Sozialpolitik, eingerichtet.[62] Nur der kommunale Wohnbau wurde nahezu eingestellt.[63]

An der praktischen Arbeit im Bereich der Fürsorge änderte sich wenig.[64] Der Versuch, mit der Schaffung von Familienasylen neue Akzente zu setzen, blieb ohne größere Wirkung. An den praktischen Gegebenheiten der Weltwirtschaftskrise kam die weitgehend reaktive Sozialpolitik ohnehin nicht vorbei.

„Armenpolitik" im NS-Staat

In der NS-Zeit erfuhr die kommunale Sozialpolitik einen radikalen Wandel. Traditionelle Armenfürsorge gab es nun nach den Intentionen der neuen Machthaber zumindest nicht mehr. Mit dem Inkrafttreten des Deutschen Sozialversicherungsgesetzes per 1. Jänner 1939 und der Reichsversicherungsordnung über die Kraft-, Unfall- und Rentenversicherung der Arbeiter weitete sich das lückenhafte staatliche „soziale Netz" mit Bezug auf die Alters- und Invaliditätsversicherung der Arbeiter und deren Angehöriger erheblich aus. Die Bestimmungen wurden nach Ende der NS-Herrschaft im Wesentlichen übernommen.[65] Die Kehrseite der „NS-Sozialpolitik" war die gleichzeitige Ausgrenzung, Verfolgung und Ermordung des nicht zur „Volksgemeinschaft" zählenden Teils der Bevölkerung. Neben Unterstützungen für kinderreiche „arische" Familien, „Ehestandsdarlehen" und Kinderbeihilfen traten massive Repression und Zwangsmaßnahmen gegen rassisch und ethnisch Verfolgte, politisch Oppositionelle und „Nicht-Unterstützungswürdige".

Auf kommunaler Ebene verschmolzen „erstes" und „zweites" soziales Netz zu einem Fürsorgeapparat im Dienst des nationalsozialistischen Rassenwahns. Der engen Verschränkung von sozialen und rassenbiologischen Kriterien wurde auch organisatorisch durch die Zusammenlegung der kommunalen Jugend- und Gesundheitsfürsorge Rechnung getragen.[66] Das

[62] Czeike und Csendes, *Die Geschichte der Magistratsabteilungen*, S. 41.
[63] Melinz und Unger, *Wohlfahrt und Krise*, S. 132–135.
[64] Wolfgruber, *Von der Fürsorge*, S. 43 f.
[65] Walter Peissl, *Das „bessere" Proletariat. Angestellte im 20. Jahrhundert* (Wien: Verlag für Gesellschaftskritik, 1994), S. 136.
[66] Herwig Czech, Erfassung, Selektion und „Ausmerze". Das Wiener Gesundheitsamt und die Umsetzung der nationalsozialistischen

Berufskonzept der Fürsorgerin wurde durch jenes der „Volkspflegerin" ersetzt. Letztere besaß im Rahmen der nationalsozialistischen „Erb- und Rassenpflege" eine für Einzelne oder Gruppen gefährliche Denunziationsmacht, die zumindest manche von ihnen zu Handlangerinnen und Unterstützerinnen der NS-Vernichtungsmedizin machte.[67]

Die praktische Wirkung ideologischer, ausbildungsbezogener und personeller Veränderungen im Bereich der Fürsorge wurde allerdings durch die Tatsache beschränkt, dass die „Soziale Frauenschule der Stadt Wien" als Ausbildungsstätte für „Volkspflegerinnen" erst im Jahr 1940 ihren Dienst aufnahm,[68] der Bedarf an weiblichen Arbeitskräften in der Kriegsindustrie groß war und die „Kriegsfürsorge" mit Fortdauer des Krieges einen immer größeren Platz einnahm. Gegen Ende des Krieges kamen nach offizieller Darstellung die Angestellten der Bezirksfürsorgeämter fast zur Gänze, jene des „Hauptwohlfahrtsamtes" immerhin zum größten Teil in den Obdachlosensammelstellen und Betreuungsstellen für „Ausgebombte" zum Einsatz.[69]

Ins Visier der nationalsozialistischen Biopolitik der „Ausmerzung" gerieten neben rassisch Verfolgten auch Geisteskranke, Trinker, Prostituierte, Geschlechtskranke, „schwer erziehbare" Kinder, die in Heimen untergebracht waren, und Kinder, die Hilfs- oder Sonderschulen besucht hatten. In weiterer Folge dehnte sich die kumulative Stigmatisierung durch das Regime auf immer größere Bevölkerungsteile aus.[70] Besonders fatal erwies sich das für Personen, die sich bereits in „geschlossener Fürsorge" befanden, nicht zuletzt Kinder. Die Nationalsozialisten nützten dabei die bereits in der Zwischenkriegszeit geschaffenen Einrichtungen, die ja bereits einem bevölkerungspolitischen und eugenischen Konzept folgten. Die zeitgenössische Heilpädagogik hatte die „Verwahrlosung" von Kindern und Jugendlichen mit dem

---

„Erbgesundheitspolitik" 1938–1945 (Wien: Deuticke, 2003).

[67] Katja Geiger, ",Im Dienst der Volksgesundheit'. Fürsorgerinnen bzw. Volkspflegerinnen im nationalsozialistischen Wien," in Im Dienste der Volksgesundheit. Frauen – Gesundheitswesen – Nationalsozialismus, Hrsg. Ingrid Arias (Wien: Verlag-Haus der Ärzte, 2006), S. 177–209, hier S. 187–194.

[68] Werner Steinhauser, Geschichte der Sozialarbeiterausbildung (Wien: Österr. Komitee für Soziale Arbeit, 1994), S. 60–62.

[69] Die Gemeindeverwaltung des Reichsgaues Wien vom 1. April 1940 bis 31. März 1945. Verwaltungsbericht, Hrsg. Magistrat der Stadt Wien (Wien: Magistrat, o. J.), S. 155.

[70] Herwig Czech, "Die Inventur des Volkskörpers. Die erbbiologische Bestandsaufnahme im Dispositiv der NS-Rassenhygiene in Wien," in Eugenik in Österreich. Biopolitische Strukturen von 1900 bis 1945, Hrsg. Gerhard Baader et al. (Wien: Czernin, 2007), S. 284–311, hier S. 291 f., 310 f.

defizitären elterlichen Milieu begründet. Daraus wurde das Recht der Kommune auf möglichst frühe „Kindesübernahme" abgeleitet. Dieses massive Interventionsrecht griffen die Nationalsozialisten auf, um nun nicht auf Basis einer sozialen, sondern rassenbiologisch behaupteten Asozialität „volksschädliche Elemente" „umzuerziehen" und in manchen Fällen auch zu ermorden.[71] Die schlimmsten Folgen hatte der nationalsozialistische Repressionsapparat für Kinder und Jugendliche mit geistiger Behinderung, die in der Jugendfürsorgeanstalt „Am Steinhof", 1941 euphemistisch zur „Heilpädagogischen Klinik" „Am Spiegelgrund" umbenannt, verbracht wurden. In der Anstalt wurden mindestens 800 Kinder und Jugendliche ermordet.[72]

Die Zweite Republik

Nach Ende des Zweiten Weltkrieges und der Wiederherstellung demokratischer Verhältnisse stand zunächst die Nachkriegsnot im Mittelpunkt kommunaler Maßnahmen der Armenfürsorge. Der Kampf gegen den Hunger und die Wiederherstellung zerstörter oder schwer beschädigter Wohnungen sowie der städtischen Infrastruktur waren die dringendsten Erfordernisse. Dank eines beeindruckenden Wohnbauprogramms gelang es bis zu Beginn der 1960er Jahre, die Zahl der Gemeindewohnungen zu verdoppeln. In der Folge erlaubte die Einführung des Montagebaus Neubauleistungen pro Jahr von teilweise weit über der Zehntausendergrenze.[73] Ende der 1960er Jahre wurde jedoch von der reinen Objektförderung abgegangen und mit der Subjektförderung auf die Erfordernisse der werdenden Wohlstandsgesellschaft reagiert.[74]

Im Bereich der klassischen Armenhilfe sorgte die in den frühen 1950er Jahren einsetzende und bis zum „Ölschock" im Jahr 1973 anhaltende Hochkonjunktur für einen kontinuierlichen Rückgang der Unterstützungsempfänger. Unterstützungen erhielten nun primär in Not Geratene. Während im Jahr 1947 noch fast 40.000 Personen dauerhaft „Sozialhilfe" erhielten, waren es 1955 nur noch 16.000, 1960 etwa 9.500

---

[71] Reinhard Sieder und Andrea Smioski, Der Kindheit beraubt. Gewalt in den Erziehungsheimen der Stadt Wien (1950er bis 1980er Jahre) (Innsbruck et al.: StudienVerlag, 2012), S. 36–39.

[72] Czech, Erfassung, S. 105.

[73] Andreas Weigl, "Zeitreihen zu Ökologie, Soziales, Verkehr, Verwaltung und Freizeit 1945–2002," *Statistische Mitteilungen der Stadt Wien* 2 (2003): S. 3–96, hier S. 22.

[74] *60 Jahre kommunaler Wohnbau* (Wien: Compress, 1983), S. 52 f.

und zu Beginn des 21. Jahrhunderts lediglich 3.500.[75] Von noch größerer längerfristiger Bedeutung war die Ausweitung des staatlichen Sozialnetzes. Mit dem Allgemeinen Sozialversicherungsgesetz vom 9. September 1955 erhielten die sozialrechtlichen Bestimmungen für alle Dienstnehmer in fast sämtlichen Zweigen der Sozialversicherung eine einheitliche Norm.[76] Zudem enthob das „Gewerbliche Selbständigen-Pensionsversicherungsgesetz"[77] seit dem Jahr 1958 die Stadt der Aufgabe der Existenzsicherung alter Kleingewerbetreibender.[78] Klein- und Kleinstpensionen schützten jedoch vor Armut nicht. Eine Untersuchung aus dem Jahr 1974 erbrachte einen Gesamtstand von 3,3 Prozent oder fast 25.000 Haushalten, die sehr arm waren, davon mehr als die Hälfte Pensionisten, vor allem ältere Frauen.[79]

Programmatisch griff die sozialdemokratische Stadtregierung auf Konzepte und Leistungen des „Roten Wien" zurück. In einer im Jahr 1958 erschienenen offiziösen Leistungsschau erhielt das einschlägige Kapitel den vielsagenden Titel: „Die Stadt Wien als große Mutter". Wie sich dem Bericht unschwer entnehmen lässt, stand erneut die Kinder- und Jugendfürsorge im Mittelpunkt des sozialpolitischen Interesses. Mutterberatungsstellen, Säuglingswäschepakete, Kindergärten, Horte und Jugendhilfswerke bestimmten das Fürsorgeprogramm.[80]

Nach Kriegsende übernahmen temporär zunächst bezirksweise eingerichtete Fürsorgekommissionen die Aufgaben der Fürsorgeämter, die im Jahr 1946 wieder in Funktion traten. Die unbefriedigende Personalsituation – das Personal der Fürsorgeämter bestand hauptsächlich aus Kanzleikräften – ließ das Image der Fürsorge innerhalb und außerhalb des Magistrates sinken.[81] Dazu trug auch bei, dass die Klientel sich immer mehr auf soziale Problemfälle beschränkte. Das Aufgabenspektrum der

---

[75] Weigl, "Zeitreihen," S. 36.

[76] Peissl, Das „bessere" Proletariat, S. 137 f.

[77] Bundesgesetzblatt 292/1957 vom 31.12.1957.

[78] Feuerstein, "Vom Armenhaus," S. 82.

[79] Armut in Wien. Eine Untersuchung der Wirtschaftswissenschaftlichen und der Statistischen Abteilung der Wiener Kammer für Arbeiter und Angestellte (1974), Hrsg. Kammer für Arbeiter und Angestellte für Wien (Wien: Verlag des Österreichischen Gewerkschaftsbundes, 1974), S. 108.

[80] Anton Tesarek, "Die Stadt Wien als große Mutter," in Wien um die Mitte des XX. Jahrhunderts. Ein Querschnitt durch Landschaft, Geschichte, soziale und technische Einrichtungen, wirtschaftliche und politische Stellung und durch das kulturelle Leben, Hrsg. Ferdinand Lettmayer (Wien: Verlag für Jugend und Volk, 1958), S. 491–509.

[81] Herbert Drapalik, Geschichte der Wiener Sozialverwaltung von 1945–1985 (Wien: s. t., 1990), S. 24 f.

Fürsorgerinnen und der wenigen Fürsorger engte sich während der
Wirtschaftswunderjahre auf die Überwachung und Betreuung städtischer
Mündel ein. Sie stand nun bis in die 1980er Jahre im Mittelpunkt ihrer
Tätigkeit.[82] Die im Rahmen dieser Tätigkeit von den Fürsorgerinnen und
Fürsorgern vollzogene „Erziehungsberatung" erwies sich als besonders
problematisch. Sie diente der Einweisung in Kinder- und Jugendheime und
machte   manche   Fürsorgerinnen   in   mehrfacher   Hinsicht   zu
„Schreibmaschinentäterinnen":[83] im engeren Sinn durch die in den
Heimen vorherrschende Repression, die erst in den letzten Jahren durch
die Arbeit mehrerer Historikerkommissionen ans Licht trat,[84] im
Allgemeinen dann durch eine spezifisch gegen Mädchen und Frauen
gerichtete Durchsetzung einer konservativ-reaktionären Geschlechterordnung.
Erst mit der „Heimreform 1998", die mit der Schließung von Großheimen
einherging und die Betreuung auf Kleingruppen verlagerte, kam es zu
einer grundlegenden Änderung der bestehenden Strukturen in der
„geschlossenen" Kinder- und Jugendfürsorge.[85]
    Inhaltlich wandelte sich die Fürsorge erst langsam zu moderner
Sozialarbeit, von der Bekämpfung sozialer Not zur Unterstützung bei
psychosozialen Problemen von Familien in schwierigen Lebenslagen.
Diese Schwerpunktverlagerung erfolgte unter dem Schlagwort „Wiener
Weg in der Jugendwohlfahrt".[86] Deren Berufskonzeption orientierte sich
nun am „social casework" mit methodischer Kompetenz, was nicht
bedeutet, dass damit alle Defizite in der Sozialarbeit mit einem Schlag
behoben gewesen wären.
    Eine quantitative und inhaltliche Erweiterung des Aufgabengebiets von
Sozialarbeitern und Sozialarbeiterinnen bedingte die seit der zweiten
Hälfte der 1960er Jahre anlaufende „Gastarbeiterwanderung" und die sich
in   weiterer   Folge   intensivierende   Arbeitsmigration,   aber   auch
Flüchtlingsbewegung von bildungsfernen Schichten. Die Arbeit mit
Kindern und Jugendlichen mit Migrationshintergrund nimmt mittlerweile
einen wichtigen Platz in der Sozialarbeit in Wien ein, was nicht weiter
verwundert, besitzen doch gegenwärtig von 1,73 Millionen Wienerinnen

---

[82] Wolfgruber, Von der Fürsorge, S. 97.
[83] Gertrude Czipke, ",Die Schreibmaschinentäterinnen'. Die Wiener
Jugendfürsorge in den Jahren 1945 bis 1970 und ihr Beitrag zur Durchsetzung
einer gegen Mädchen, Frauen, ,uneheliche' Mütter und deren Kinder gerichteten
Geschlechterordnung" (Diplomarbeit, Universität Wien, 2013).
[84] Sieder und Smioski, Kindheit.
[85] Wolfgruber, Von der Fürsorge, S. 12.
[86] *70 Jahre Wiener Jugendamt*, Hrsg. Jugendamt der Stadt Wien, S. 55.

und Wienern fast 400.000 einen Nicht-EU-Migrationshintergrund.[87] Innerhalb der zweiten und dritten „Gastarbeiter"-Generation hat sich zwar eine Vielfalt an soziokulturellen Milieus herausgebildet, aber eine soziale Schieflage, meist in Verbindung mit defizitärer Ausbildung, bleibt bis heute bestehen. Vor allem Konflikte zwischen dieser Generation und der Schicht sozial schwacher Autochthoner gehören zum Alltag der gegenwärtigen Sozialarbeit in Wien.

Schon in den 1950er Jahren zeigte ein Blick auf die Bevölkerungsstatistik, dass Wien nicht nur ein ausgeprägtes Geburtendefizit aufwies, sondern auch die „Überalterung" der Bevölkerung rasch voranschritt. Die großen Geburtenjahrgänge der Jahrzehnte um 1900 rückten nunmehr in das Rentenalter auf und sorgten für erheblichen sozialpolitischen Bedarf. Bereits Ende der 1950er Jahre wurde festgestellt, dass rund 24.000 alte Menschen in ihren Haushaltungen völlig auf sich allein gestellt lebten.[88] Wohl erreichte die Wiener Bevölkerung den höchsten Anteil älterer Menschen bereits zu Beginn der 1970er Jahre und ist seitdem nicht unerheblich jünger geworden. Dennoch ist nicht zu verkennen, dass der kontinuierliche, in Zeiten des „Roten Wien" nicht vorstellbare weitere Anstieg der Lebenserwartung in Verbindung mit immer neuen Innovationen im Bereich der modernen Medizin die kommunale Daseinsvorsorge vor (budgetäre) Herausforderungen stellte. Auf diese Veränderungen der Altersstruktur wurde schon früh reagiert. Während sich in den unmittelbaren Nachkriegsjahren die Stadtverwaltung noch mit dem Problem herumschlagen musste, die rund 10.000 Pfleglinge in den Wiener Altenheimen in den durch Bombentreffer beschädigten und teilweise von den Alliierten belegten Gebäuden unterzubringen,[89] konnte bereits wenige Jahre später das Angebot in der geschlossenen Altenfürsorge erweitert werden. Seit 1952 wurden „Heimstätten für ältere Menschen" als erste Sozialwohnform errichtet,[90] 1960 das „Kuratorium Wiener Pensionistenheime" gegründet[91] und in weiterer Folge die Infrastruktur für ältere Menschen Schritt für Schritt ausgebaut. Ab den

---

[87] *Statistisches Jahrbuch der Stadt Wien 2012* (Wien: Magistrat, 2012), S. 66.

[88] *Altersprobleme in Wien. Ergebnisse einer Forumsdiskussion*, in *Die Großstadt Wien als Lebensstätte der Wiener. Ein Arbeitsbericht der Forschungsgemeinschaft für Großstadtprobleme* (Wien: Institut für Wissenschaft und Kunst, 1957), S. 105–124, hier S. 110.

[89] Drapalik, *Geschichte*, S. 31.

[90] Feuerstein, "Vom Armenhaus," S. 83–89.

[91] Anton Tesarek, "Im Mittelpunkt der Mensch," in *Wiedergeburt einer Weltstadt. Wien 1945–1965*, Hrsg. Karl Ziak (Wien: Jugend und Volk, 1965), S. 35–46, hier S. 37.

1970er Jahren kam es zu einem Paradigmenwechsel in der stationären Versorgung, der einerseits durch eine weitere Spezialisierung, andererseits durch den Trend zu Mischformen von ambulanter und teil-stationärer Betreuung gekennzeichnet war.[92]

Im besonderen Maß von Altersarmut bedroht war und ist die Bevölkerungsgruppe der „Gastarbeiter". Nach einer im Jahr 2006 publizierten Befragung konnten sich in der Gruppe der über 50-Jährigen 18 Prozent der aus der Türkei und 15 Prozent der aus Ex-Jugoslawien Stammenden keine neue Kleidung leisten, 14 Prozent beziehungsweise 11 Prozent vermochten die Rezeptgebühr nicht zu bezahlen.[93] Aus der ökonomischen Notlage resultierten weitere Unsicherheiten. So fühlten sich 46 Prozent der über 50-jährigen Arbeitsmigrantinnen und Arbeitsmigranten psychosozial belastet, im Unterschied zu 26 Prozent der autochthonen Vergleichsgruppe.[94] Die Akzeptanz von sozialen Diensten und Versorgungsangeboten war und ist bei diesen Migrantinnen und Migranten schwieriger als bei der einheimischen Bevölkerung herzustellen. So stellen stationäre Einrichtungen für Zuwanderer aus der Türkei hierfür in weit geringerem Maße eine Option dar als diejenigen für andere Migrantengruppen. Das weitgehende Fehlen kultursensibler Angebote spielt dabei eine große Rolle.[95]

Die strukturellen Veränderungen der letzten Jahrzehnte im Bereich kommunaler Sozialpolitik schlugen sich auch in der Budgetgestaltung nieder. Innerhalb der Ausgabengruppe „Soziale Wohlfahrt und Wohnbauförderung", die weiterhin rund ein Fünftel des Wiener Gesamtbudgets umfasst, entfällt gegenwärtig der größere Teil der Ausgaben auf soziale Belange (1,2 Mrd. €), und zwar fast eine halbe Milliarde Euro in Form allgemeiner Sozialhilfe und eine Dreiviertelmillion als Budget des „Fonds Soziales Wien". Dieser im Jahr 2001 in Betrieb gegangene Fonds dient der Förderung von sozialen Einrichtungen und Projekten, aber auch der direkten Personenförderung auf Basis des Wiener Sozialhilfegesetzes.[96] In etwa in der Dimension der Sozialausgaben

---

[92] Feuerstein, "Vom Armenhaus," S. 102–131.
[93] Christoph Reinprecht und Anne Unterwurzacher, *Lebenslagen und Lebensqualität, Sonderauswertung des Datensatzes „Leben und Lebensqualität in Wien"* Bd 2. *Forschungsbericht. Institut für Soziologie* (Wien: s. t., 2006).
[94] Christoph Reinprecht, *Nach der Gastarbeit. Prekäres Altern in der Einwanderungsgesellschaft* (Wien: Braumüller, 2006), S. 58.
[95] Nevin Altintop, "Wie sich türkischsprachige Migranten in Wien ihre Zukunft im Alter vorstellen" (Diplomarbeit, Universität Wien, 2010).
[96] Wiener Sozialhilfegesetz vom 11.3.1973, in Landesgesetzblatt 11/1973 und Novellen.

bewegt sich auch das Budget des Gesundheitswesens (1,4 Mrd. €). Diese beiden Budgetposten übertreffen damit die Ausgaben für den Wohnbau (677 Mio. €) recht deutlich.[97] Innerhalb der Sozialhilfe ist im langfristigen Vergleich die Zahl der Dauerunterstützungen kontinuierlich gefallen, diejenige der einmaligen Geldaushilfen hingegen tendenziell gestiegen. Der größte Teil der finanziellen Zuzahlungen entfiel zuletzt auf Geldleistungen für Personen in Alten- und Pflegeheimen.[98] Damit ist auch für das „zweite soziale Netz" ein vorhersehbarer Trend für die Zukunft benannt.

---

[97] *Rechnungsabschluss der Bundeshauptstadt Wien für das Jahr 2012* (Wien: s. t., 2013).
[98] Ulrike Pailer, "Sozialhilfe in Wien von 1946 bis 2000," *Statistische Mitteilungen der Stadt Wien* 31 (2001): S. 4–21.

CHAPTER SIX

FROM MERCY AND CHARITY TO THE SYSTEM OF STATE AND MUNICIPAL CARE FOR THE POOR IN PRAGUE IN THE LONG 19TH CENTURY

OLGA FEJTOVÁ

Abstract: The study deals with the fundamental problems of the development of the care for the poor in Prague during the long 19th century. The study highlights the conflict between state and municipal concepts for providing social care. The development of open care for the poor is thus introduced at the beginning of the study. It was organised in the framework of the "Poor Institute", based on voluntary work and in cooperation with the church. Institutional care was transferred to the supervision of the state after the Enlightenment reforms. Both areas of care for the poor were being shaped during the 19th century by the influence of the municipality of Prague, resulting in the strengthened position of the city in the entire system of the care for the poor. At the beginning of the second half of the 19th century, care for the poor came to be carried out fully under the city administration. During the long 19th century, Prague experienced repeated poverty care reform interventions that definitely led to improvements within its management, administration and bureaucratisation. Additionally, a partial professionalisation of care for the poor occurred as well and the entire system became fully independent of the church.

When the cities of Prague merged into one large metropolis in 1784, the city had actually already undergone a major overhaul of its care for the poor before the merger. The royal capital city of Prague adopted the standard defined by the Josephine prescriptive rules from 1781, which attempted to solve the problem of poverty in the monarchy at the level of individual state authorities and their metropolitan areas based on centralisation of both care for the poor and health care, including the establishment of specialised institutes and the separation of state care systems from charities, other private initiatives and church institutions.[1] The reform measures of Joseph II relied upon the separation of care for the poor into two branches: institutional care under state competence (the care for the poor-health care-repressive institutions) and private charity activities channelled into the area of open care for the poor (to those who were both unable to work and poor). This system was designed to be based on cooperation among single charities and churches.[2]

"The roots of modern European social policy [...] lie in the early modern period."[3] This thesis, by German historian Sebastian Schmidt, fully applied describing to development in the Czech Lands. Christianity, in the European context, perceived the poor primarily as objects of mercy and alms as its main expression. Christian mercy, rooted in the principles of Christian ethics, remained throughout the early modern period one of the main incentives for supporting the poor. However, the advent of humanism and the Reformation brought a significant change in the perception of poverty as a whole.

Merciful activities carried out by private charities in the cities of Prague differed significantly in the period before and after the Battle of White Mountain in 1618. This situation is illustrated by preserved testaments in which charitable donations appear.[4] The Utraquist environment prior to the White Mountain times distributed aid to the poor rationally and equally among institutionalised facilities of the care for the poor – especially hospitals. The contemporary society also cared for the poor inhabitants of the city dwelling outside of hospitals and the system did not omit poor students of local Latin and parish schools. The latter case undoubtedly reflected a situation specific to the Czech pre-White Mountain educational system that actually attained a level of exceptional quality in the European context – inter alia, with the support of townspeople. We can observe links between charitable activities with

---

[1] Cf. Olga Fejtová, "Organizace chudinské péče v letech 1781–1922" [Organization of the care for the poor within 1781–1922], in *Osm století pražské samosprávy* [Eight centuries of Prague's self-government], eds. Václav Ledvinka et al. (Praha: Scriptorium, 2000), pp. 133–134.

[2] Antonín Pokorný, *1000 let chudinství v Praze* [A thousand years of the care for the poor in Prague], (Praha: Nákladem vlastním, 1940), pp. 33–34.

[3] Sebastian Schmidt, "Armut und Arme in Stadt und Territorium der Frühen Neuzeit," in *Armut. Perspektiven in Kunst und Gesellschaft*, eds. Herbert Uerlings et al. (Darmstadt: Primus, 2011), p. 129.

[4] Olga Fejtová, "„Já pevně věřím a vyznávám…" Rekatolizace na Novém Městě pražském v době pobělohorské" ['I firmly believe and confess…' Counter-Reformation in Prague New Town during the post-White Mountain period], (Praha: Archiv hlavního města Prahy and Scriptorium, 2012), pp. 200–233.

some sort of demonstrations of professional and social identities of the townspeople who used the charity as a tool to help the community and to the city administration or how to support the guilds. The form of the testaments clearly reflected changes that had occurred in the perception of charitable activities in the Protestant environment in general – i.e. the ethical, rational and practical aspects of helping others.[5] Charity represented a significant part of Catholic piety as well, because at the time charitable activities represented a way to ensure the salvation of one's soul, and contributed to the salvation of the souls of loved ones as well. Therefore, during the post-White Mountain period, this intention became clearly manifest by a much higher number of testimonies in favour of charitable institutions. Support for institutional care for the poor became less important to Catholic townspeople, because they started to donate their material and financial means to poor individuals living from poor care institutions. When doing so, they actually did not follow a punitive aristocratic policy and its efforts to divide the poor according to the criterion of being able to work.[6]

Humanism and the Reformation substantially contributed in modifying the view of the relationship between poverty and work – society began to consistently distinguish poverty as a result of the following: the inability to work, lack of income from work, insufficient income from work, lack of job opportunities or lack of willingness to work.[7] Therefore, a new type of institution, whose purpose was to concentrate on poor individuals capable of work and who at the same time claimed various forms of aid, was being established during the 16th century. Establishment of these institutions represented a portion of the disciplinary measures the then-current power used to regulate basic spheres of life of urban society in public and private, as well as in the work environment.[8] Standardisation of the urban population came about by covering both traditional forms of poverty, i.e. the institutional, closed, hospital care and the practice of giving alms along with regulating the movement of beggars.[9] In the Prague of the early modern period, the policy regulating the poor was closely bound to the

---

[5] Schmidt, "Armut und Arme," p. 123.

[6] Fejtová, „Já pevně věřím a vyznávám... ", pp. 209–232

[7] Wolfgang von Hippel, *Armut, Unterschichten, Randgruppen in der Frühen Neuzeit* (München: Oldenbourg Wissenschaftsverlag, 1995), p. 4.

[8] Gerhard Oestereich, "Strukturprobleme des europäischen Absolutismus," in *Geist und Gestalt des frühmodernen Staates* (Berlin: Dunckel & Humblot, 1969), p. 193.

[9] Cf. Robert Jütte, *Obrigkeitliche Armenfürsorge in deutschen Reichsstädten der frühen Neuzeit. Städtisches Armenwesen in Frankfurt am Main und Köln* (Köln – Wien: Taschenbuch, 1984), pp. 331–340.

post-White Mountain disciplinary religious measures, following the official royal policy, the so-called "gute Policey." Therefore, these new forms began to regularly appear in the 1620s, concentrating on the regulation of the free movement of beggars and vagrants.[10] The municipal authorities in Prague were determined to register and separate those people. Persons in real need (because of age or infirmity) were required to wear a visible sign (a coat of arms of the city) which had been provided to them by the city council, and based on that they were entitled to ask for alms in a specific area of the city.[11] The poor care policy for dealing with the rest of the poor was either to physically coerce capable beggars and vagrants to work or to confine the remaining poor, physically incapable individuals to hospitals.[12]

As in other parts of Europe, hospitals had functioned as facilities providing constitutional provision since the Middle Ages.[13] A large number of these facilities were set up in the Prague towns in the 16th century, and this trend fully corresponded to trends in Western Europe.[14] During the 18th century the state gradually gained oversight of individual hospitals in Prague, at least economically. The state controlled hospitals and other foundations through the so-called "foundation committee", which began operation in the 1820s.[15] Yet Prague hospitals in the 17th and 18th centuries cannot be seen simply as devices whose primary objective was disciplining inmates, even though certain rules of behaviour were enforced. Most of Prague's hospitals in the Early Modern period maintained their original character as universally organised facilities which combined elements of health care and care for the poor.[16]

The requirement for the separation those able to work – and their compulsion to work – from the poor in need had become manifest in royal decrees addressed to all Prague towns[17] since the mid-17th century. But the existing hospital facilities definitely did not provide sufficient space. Thus, a penitentiary was opened in the Old Town in 1674, where prisoners

---

[10] Fejtová, „Já pevně věřím a vyznávám... ", p. 151.
[11] The Prague City Archives (further referred to as AHMP), The Collection of Manuscripts, no. 753, The Book of Decrees issued by the New Town of Prague, collection 109r–110v, 10. 10. 1675 (here are the links to previous city standards).
[12] Fejtová, „Já pevně věřím a vyznávám... ", p. 151.
[13] Cf. Petr Svobodný and Ludmila Hlaváčková, Pražské špitály a nemocnice [Prague's spitals and hospitals], (Praha: NLN, 1999).
[14] Bronisław Geremek, Slitování a šibenice [Mercy and gallows], (Praha: Argo, 1999), pp. 17–19.
[15] Ibid., pp. 17–19.
[16] Svobodný and Hlaváčková, Pražské špitály, pp. 8–46.
[17] Fejtová, „Já pevně věřím a vyznávám... ", pp. 151–152, 174.

had to work to provide for themselves as they were no longer provided for by the municipal administration.[18] Some of the penitentiary inmates were vagrants and the work undoubtedly represented "coercive" means. Yet it was not a classic early modern, prison-like-hospital facility, quite common in other European metropolises.[19]

The municipal councils of the Prague towns responded to the contemporary demands for modernisation of the care for the poor by attempting to establish a general poorhouse in 1733. Its ambition was to create the basis for the separation of the poor unable to work and their consequent placement in this facility, which was designed to serve all towns of Prague.[20] Moreover, in the 1730s construction of an accommodation facility for military invalids began outside the walls of Prague (what is now Karlín). Military veterans had been supported by single towns of Prague in their institutions at their own cost until then. Yet the establishment of a specialised institute for military invalids did not free the city from paying a special tax which was levied at the city gates and whose purpose was to cover general expenses on the military invalids throughout the monarchy. This tax was abolished by the Josephine reforms.[21]

The creation of a joint facility for the poor of three towns of Prague (Hradčany joined the project later) reflected the fact that poor persons often wandered throughout the entire metropolis uncontrolled and it was difficult or even impossible to determine in which part of the city they were entitled to claim support.[22] The management of this institute was entrusted in the hands of municipal inspectors, but gradually the impact of the governor's (provincial) office grew stronger and control over this institution passed to the "foundation committee."[23]

The regulations for the operation of the general Prague poorhouse accentuated both the provision of elementary education and apprenticeships for children and youth as well as the provision of work for adult inmates who were capable of work.[24] Since the poorhouse was not

---

[18] Lucie Pokorná, "Spolek na podporu bydlící chudiny. Reflexe chudých na počátku 19. století" [Association for supporting the resident poor. Reflection of the poor at the beginning of the 19th century], (M.A. thesis, University of South Bohemia in České Budějovice, 2012), p. 32.

[19] Cf. Geremek, *Slitování a šibenice*, pp. 220–228.

[20] Pokorný, *1000 let chudinství*, p. 23.

[21] Ibid., pp. 29–31.

[22] Cf. Fejtová, „*Já pevně věřím a vyznávám...* ", pp. 151–152.

[23] Pokorný, *1000 let chudinství*, p. 29.

[24] Ibid.

associated with a specific workshop or manufactory, the rules related to work duties of adult inmates were rarely encountered in its operation. The poorhouse was complemented by the establishment of a foundling home in 1765 and later by a maternity hospital in the New Town of Prague. Yet the foundling home faced financial problems throughout its entire existence and therefore it was organisationally merged with the Italian hospital in 1775.[25]

Negotiations on the establishment of a classical penitentiary and workhouse in the cities of Prague were launched in 1739. The so-called "*špinhaus*", which was located in the Old Town, was named after the workshops where the inmates processed wool, cotton and silk. At the beginning there were only convicts working there and only gradually did the involvement of those for whom the penitentiary and workhouse was originally intended occur, i.e. vagrants, beggars and the temporarily unemployed – "loafers" in the parlance of the times.[26]

Another initiative in setting up this type of coercive institution was associated primarily with the activities of the state, or provincial government. Markvart Koc of Kobrš, a provincial administrator, founded several "temporary workhouses" on a trial basis throughout the cities of Prague. The most important of these were located on the left bank of the Vltava River in the Lesser Town, and in the New Town. Their operation, however, depended on financial support from the residents of the Prague conurbation from their inception. The contributions came from public collections, which no longer appealed to Christian mercy, but to new "civic" virtues, including patriotism. The ultimate failure of penitentiary and workhouses was not caused solely by their economic problems, mostly related to problematic labour productivity. A fundamental reform of care for the poor, which was carried out by Joseph II in the 1780s and which no longer relied on institutions of this type, also played a significant role.[27]

The first steps of the Josephine reforms included a gradual phasing-out of traditional urban hospitals, whose properties and assets were used to create the financial background of the newly established institutions for the care for the poor in the form of secular foundations. The area of

---

[25] Ibid., p. 32.

[26] Alena Petráňová, "K využití práce žebráků a tuláků v textilní výrobě v Praze kolem r. 1781" [A contribution to the research on the use of beggars' and tramps' work within the textile production in Prague around 1781], *Československý časopis historický* 60 (1962): p. 98.

[27] Pokorná, "Spolek na podporu bydlící chudiny," pp. 33–34; Pokorný, *1000 let chudinství*, p. 33.

"open" care for the poor (alms) was supposed to be regulated by a newly
formed institution called the "Poor Institute", which was subject to
supervision by provincial, i.e. state administration.[28] The new system was
based on a newly created network of 20 districts, which copied the current
shape of parochial districts, headed by the local clergy. Alongside them,
two "Fathers of the poor" worked in each district. These "Fathers" were
city residents who held these posts unpaid as volunteers. They were
actually responsible for the registration of poor individuals within their
districts and for collecting donations. The entire system of raising funds
for the poor and their subsequent distribution ran on this voluntary basis,
including the head of the whole system – a chief directorate of the "Poor
Institute", which was being gradually formed during the first half of the
19th century. This new system of open care for the poor in Prague faced
two primary challenges: a critical problem with the insufficient number of
volunteers and a significant lack of funding.[29] The new "Poor Institute"
functioned by the means which it had obtained from the transfer of
property of abolished religious brotherhoods and foundations that were
dedicated to the care for the poor of all categories in the historical towns of
Prague. However, the whole system was still designed to operate mainly
on voluntary contributions from collections and inheritances. In addition to
these voluntary dispositions, its budget was increased by obligatory
contributions of voluntary auctions, court and police fines and fees from
public performances, i.e. from funds earmarked for the state budget. The
"Poor Institute" was also supposed to create its own foundations'
resources.[30]

The entire system of the open care for the poor in Prague was propped
up by activities of civic associations from the beginning of the 19th
century. "The private association for supporting poor households"
[Soukromý spolek ku podporování domácích chudých] held an almost

[28] Josef Vlk, Chudinství královského hlavního města Prahy [Care for the poor in
the royal capital of Prague], (Praha: Nákl. král. hlavního města Prahy, 1901), pp.
20–21.
[29] Pokorný, 1000 let chudinství, pp. 23–24; AHMP, Magistrát hlavního města
Prahy I. [Municipal Office of the City of Prague I.] (further referred to as MHMP
I.), Rankeum, Praha – Úřady – Instrukce – "Ch" – Chudinský ústav.
[30] Pokorný, 1000 let chudinství, s. 36–37; AHMP, MHMP I., Rankeum, Praha –
Úřady – Instrukce – "Ch" – Chudinský ústav. There was a ball being organised to
raise money for the Poor Institute – cf. AHMP, MHMP I., Presidium rady a
magistrátu hlavního města Prahy (further referred to as Presidium), man. 1831–
1835, no. F 10/4, box 48, a fundraising ball for the poorhouse of St. Bartholomeus,
ticket sale; man. 1836–1840, no F 10/1, box 66, a ball with musical shows and
raffles; man. 1841–1845, no. F 10/2, box 78, etc.

monopolistic position in providing physical care for the needy in Prague during the first half of the 19th century (heating, food, clothing and bedding). Its activities expanded during the 19th century when the association began to be supplemented by other charitable societies, already focusing on particular or specific problems/needs of the care for the poor. Yet it was only "The private association for supporting poor households" which managed to retain its status of an official partner to the state and later to the municipality in the field of open care for the poor. This tie between the state and private activities became even stronger in the course of the second half of the 19th century, as the activities of the association became adapted to the structural layout of the poor districts. Members of the association were especially wealthy Prague businessmen, officials and clergy. No less important supporters, however, were noble persons and the monarch himself. They provided assistance during the establishment of foundations or via participation in financial collections.[31]

Despite a relatively wide and differentiated allocation of financial sources, the "Poor Institute" was forever on the edge of its financial capabilities during the entire first half of the 19th century. However, the difficulties of finding new volunteers presented an even more serious problem. Their honorary positions were time-consuming and required some clerical skills. An average of more than 1,200 people were supported throughout the poor districts during the first two decades of the 19th century. This number far exceeded the real capabilities of the "Poor Institute" and its staff. Critical comments made by volunteers involved in this system emphasised the fact that there had been a failure to effectively distinguish the truly needy persons from those who just abused the system. Another aspect which was also loudly criticised was that the basic components of incomes for the "Poor institute" were still voluntary collections that definitely did not represent a guarantee of stable income, even though the "Fathers of the poor", the representatives of Prague guilds and even school children worked hard to raise cash for the Institute.[32]

Based on this experience, the first major reorganisation of Prague open care for the poor occurred in the years 1825–1828. At the directorate of the "Poor Institute" as well as of the poor districts persons of noble origin came to replace the clergymen. These new leaders were employed in

---

[31] Cf. *Statuten des Privatvereines zur Unterstützung des Hausarmen Prag* (Praha, 1876; *Zpráva účetní soukromého spolku pro podporování domácích chudých v Praze* [Final accounts of the Home poor's private supporting association], (Praha, 1899; Pokorná, "Spolek na podporu bydlící chudiny," pp. 38–46.

[32] Ferdinand Kindermann z Schulsteinu, *Péče o chudé* [Care for the poor], ed. Josef Vlk (Praha: Důchody hlavního města Prahy, 1904), pp. 4–7.

various positions in the state administration – in the words of contemporary
sources, they were the "first men of the public."[33] Yet the actual
performance of open poor care in Prague continued to be organised
through the "Fathers of the poor", but their number was being gradually
increased depending on the size of the poor district (the number of
"Fathers" ranged from 4 to 15).[34] The poor districts became reorganised as
well – they were divided into smaller areas, each managed by one Father
of the poor. Each of them was given only a few houses, in which he
carried out his inspection activities, counted the poor in his district and
verified their claims for help.[35] The alms were also paid at the respective
parishes once a week in all districts on one day – every Friday. Everyone
who was entitled to receive the alms had to prove his claim by presenting
the "alms book." This document accompanied the lives of the poor in
Prague throughout the entire 19th century.[36] A person who was granted the
alms had to respect a strict ban on begging on the streets, in homes, in
churches or cemeteries. The ban also applied to the sending of "begging
letters." In case of violation of this regulation they were punished by the
loss of the alms ration.[37]

Changes that occurred in the system of open care for the poor in the
late 1820s implemented several basic organisational principles, which
were a couple of decades later applied in the so-called "Elberfeld model",
i.e. a system of rationally organised open care for the poor. The oldest
Elberfeld poverty care order dates back to 1852 and its basis lay in the
consistent application of decentralisation of the management of care for
the poor and in promoting individualisation of the care for the poor under
the motto "*Hilfe von Mensch zu Mensch.*"[38] The main principle of the
Elberfeld system was primarily transferring the organisation of open care
for the poor from religious institutions/societies to civic society, and at the
same time streamlining its implementation, which was supported by
rigorous and continuous control. The entire distribution sector was
continuously controlled, as were those who claimed the support. The
system distinguished only two basic categories of people in need, i.e. those
capable of work and those incapable of work. The first category should
have a job guaranteed and the second one should be provided with

---

[33] Vlk, *Chudinství*, p. 27.
[34] Ibid., pp. 27–31.
[35] Ibid., p. 27.
[36] Ibid., p. 31.
[37] Ibid.
[38] Christoph Sachße and Florian Tennstedt, *Geschichte der Armenfürsorge in
Deutschland I.* (Stuttgart: Kohlhammer, 1980), pp. 214–222.

adequate financial support.[39] Job opportunities were to be provided by the municipality. The distribution of financial support, as well as controlling individual beneficiaries, was supposed to be carried out by citizens who would do the job for free as an "honorary function." The basic aim of the Elberfeld system was to convert public care for the poor into a system based on volunteering. All these steps aimed at making the entire care system more effective, along with its individualisation, decentralisation and limiting the long-term and ineffective provision of financial support.[40] The success of the model was based not only in its undeniable material savings in the first decade of its application, but also by the "material" involvement of wealthy residents of the city as they basically had to accept those honorary positions under the new system of the care for the poor, because rejecting such an "honorary function" would have resulted in an increase in tax payments and the loss of certain privileges.[41] However, the Prague system of open care for the poor in the first half of the century was not connected with the municipal administration, which could have otherwise provided employment to able-bodied poor individuals. Moreover, accepting a post of a "Father" was not obligatory for Prague residents either. Consequently, the Prague system of the care for the poor engaged substantially fewer people than was demanded by the Elberfeld model. Obviously, it also significantly limited the outputs of the reorganisation of the Prague "Poor Institute" in the late 1820s. Another major issue which the abovementioned reorganisation in Prague could not solve was the inefficient collection of financial contributions. Archival documents show that even after the reform, up to a tenth of homeowners did not contribute to the care for the poor at all, and if they did, it was only a minimal amount. The budget for the care for the poor clearly needed to find new resources. Fortunately, it became significantly stabilised thanks to contributions coming from the Prague guilds and municipal officials in later years.[42]

The second area of the care for the poor, which was largely influenced by the Josephine reforms, was institutional care. The centrally planned

---

[39] Ibid., p. 215.

[40] Ibid., pp. 215–216.

[41] Ibid., pp. 215–216.

[42] AHMP, MHMP I., Presidium, man. 1831–1835, F 10/1a, box 48, 1832 contributions made by municipal officials to the newly reorganised Poor Institute; man. 1836–1840, F 10/3, box 66, 1840 contributions made by municipal officials to the newly reorganised Poor Institute – 162 Fl. 10 Kreutzer; man. 1841–1845, F 10/7, box 78, 1841–1842 contributions made by municipal officials to the newly reorganised Poor Institute; 135 Fl. 24 Kreutzer and 141 Fl. 20 Kreutzer.

establishment of many specialised facilities in the poverty and health care spheres appeared on the basis of directive rules. A novelty was the inclusion of care for the mentally ill into the care for the poor.[43] A new complex of a combined medical-poor care facilities was supposed to be concentrated in the southern part of the New Town[44] and financially secured from a newly established fund, which accumulated assets from closed hospitals and endowments. Yet not all the planned facilities were built. The maternity hospital *U Apolináře* and a hospital for incurables in Karlov were put into operation in 1789 and a year later, a general hospital with a hospital for the mentally ill at Charles Square was opened. A poorhouse, located in the former hospital of St. Bartholomew joined the complex of new facilities after a significant delay in 1809 and an orphanage was established in 1875, and this was purely a municipal institution from its inception. All institutions were planned to serve nationally. Their management was therefore not delegated to the city of Prague, but to the Governor's Office. This fact had been criticised from the beginning by the Governor's Office, by provincial estates, and also by the Prague municipal authorities. Anyway, the drawbacks of this unilateral concept soon became apparent.[45]

The city of Prague could influence the activities of the aforementioned institutions only through its own foundations. Despite this minimal impact, the Municipal Office was obliged to compensate for financial deficits that emerged in the management of the abovementioned institutions. This became a bone of contention between the municipality and the Governor's Office, since money in the treasury of secular foundations was already totally insufficient for covering all financial demands in the first half of the 19th century.[46]

In the first half of the 19th century, the two basic poverty care tools under the administration of the chief directorate were a poorhouse and a hospital for incurables. The establishment of a poorhouse in 1809 was accompanied by the issuing of a royal decree, which dedicated 10,000 Florins to its initial operation and simultaneously ordered the city of Prague to partially cover the activities of this newly established facility

---

[43] Cf. the review: Olga Fejtová, "Dějiny Chudinství v Praze, Vídni, Budapešti a Terstu 1693–1873" [History of care for the poor in Prague, Vienna, Budapest and Trieste 1693–1873], review of *Die Blumen des Bösen II*, by eds. Nora Fischer et al., *Pražský sborník historický* 28 (1995): p. 201.

[44] Svobodný and Hlaváčková, *Pražské špitály*, pp. 48–50.

[45] Fejtová, "Organizace chudinské péče," p. 136.

[46] Svobodný and Hlaváčková, *Pražské špitály*, pp. 38–39; Fejtová, "Organizace chudinské péče," pp. 135–136.

from its budget. The rationale for this step referred to the obligation of the municipality to take care of the poor people who were to be admitted to this institution. The amount for it was not fixed. Given the fact that during the first half of the 19th century the number of inmates almost doubled, it was not a negligible amount.[47] The very first statutes of the poorhouse characterised the institute – despite being originally declared as national – as a local institution, i.e. the facility of the city of Prague. Therefore, only poor persons from Prague, who were too old to work or disabled, could actually be admitted. They could not, however, be afflicted by contagious or "ugly" diseases. For these kinds of handicaps another special facility was established – a hospital for incurables. In practice, the poorhouse inmates were only persons older than 50 (the elderly, from the contemporary perspective).[48] The supervision over both institutions was gradually entrusted to two commissioners during the first half of the 19th century, one representing the political district of police administration, the other municipal administration.[49] Thus the poorhouse of St. Bartholomew was from the beginning under the administration of the Governor's Office, but with respect to its financial support by the city of Prague, the municipal administration gradually gained some influence over its management.[50]

All poorhouse inmates were entitled to receive a regular daily food provision. The statutes even specified its composition, which should consist of nutritionally rich food – soup, a portion of meat and either a vegetable meal or a flour-based meal. Everybody was eligible to a pound of bread per day. During feast days they were given roasted meat of various kinds. Everybody was also provided with a bed with a mattress, pillow, blanket and bed linens as well as uniform clothing. At the expense of the poorhouse, heating and lighting were provided, as well as laundry service. There was also a physician (usually from the staff of the general hospital) available as well as a healer, who also worked in a hospital for

---

[47] When the poorhouse was opened, there were 213 poor individuals accommodated and in 1843 there were 470 people living there. *Dějiny obecní správy Král. hlav. města Prahy za léta 1860–1880 I. Léta 1860–1870* [History of the municipal administration of the Royal capital of Prague for the years 1860–1880, vol. 1, 1860–1870], ed. Vojtěch Kraus (Praha: Obec král. hlav. města Prahy, 1903), p. 182. Wilhelm Rud. Weitenweber, *Die medicinischen Anstalten Prag's nach ihrem gegenwärtigen Zustande geschildert* (Prag: Borrosch & André, 1845), pp. 156–157. Females clearly dominated – in 1843 there were 152 males and 318 females.
[48] Weitenweber, *Die medicinischen Anstalten Prag's*, p. 156.
[49] Ibid., p. 157.
[50] *Dějiny obecní správy I.*, p. 182; Fejtová, "Organizace chudinské péče," pp. 134–135.

incurables in Karlov. Auxiliary works around the poorhouse were actually carried out by the inmates themselves and they were also sent to help in other medical or poor care facilities throughout the entire city of Prague.[51]

The hospital for incurables – the second fundamental facility of the care for the poor in Prague – had been originally designed for sickly persons who did not have any other support, and for persons suffering from some "untreatable infirmity", without distinction of age.[52] For this reason, even small children were placed there. The provincial administration originally sought to find a location outside the city walls or in the country, but no suitable space was found. Eventually, the facility was moved to the building of a former Augustinian Monastery in Karlov (now administrative district Prague 2).[53] Although the hospital for incurables, unlike the poorhouse, was from its inception designed to care for Prague residents, the applicants for admission from the countryside were not entirely excluded (but in fact only in exceptional cases). The hospital for incurables could accept a poor person with a military background (only women and children), if they received some sort of financial support. This way the hospital for incurables actually extended the capacities of the provision of this category of the poor, hitherto fully reliant on services provided by *Invalidovna* (a shelter for military disabled persons).[54] As with the poorhouse, the Prague hospital for incurables was subordinated to the Governor's office, i.e. provincial administration. The hospital for incurables was also often used as a back-up place when the hospitals faced repeated problems of insufficient capacity. Thus mentally ill persons were temporarily housed there, as well as venereal patients or short-term sick persons during extensive epidemics.[55]

The hospital provided its inmates with a particular diet that consisted of one basic meal at lunchtime and two portions of soup every morning and evening. The lunch menu was nutritionally a much richer food than in the poorhouse because it consisted of soup, a main dish in the form of meat-based food with a side dish. Material support included a provision of

---

[51] *Dějiny obecní správy I.*, p. 182.

[52] Ibid., p. 208.

[53] Ibid., p. 202.

[54] Ibid., p. 208; *Dobročinné ústavy Královského hlavního města Prahy* [Charitable institutions of the royal capital of Prague], (Praha: Nákladem Obce pražské, 1891), p. 19.

[55] *Chrorobinec na Karlově (1759) 1789–1862* [Hospital for incurables at Karlov (1759) 1789–1862. Inventory of the record series], (Praha: Archiv hlavního města Prahy, 1998), p. iii; Weitenweber, *Die medicinischen Anstalten Prag's*, p. 100; *Dobročinné ústavy*, p. 20.

clothing as well. It was a uniform, similar to that used in the Prague poorhouse in the first half of the 19th century.[56]

Unlike the poorhouse, the hospital for incurables relied more on labour carried out by its residents, which was supposed to activate them. This was a fairly significant difference that was even noticed by an impartial observer. Thanks to a travelogue by Wilhelm Horn from the early 1830s, which was specifically focused on European cities and their care for the poor as well as medical facilities, we have both a precise description of the Prague hospital for incurables and a description of the poorhouse, including an evaluation of their quality. Horn appreciated the better material security provided to the residents of the hospital. He considered the other facility, the poorhouse of St. Bartholomew, to be a hospital for incurables as well, because of the care for the sick and elderly which it provided (regular "clients" in European hospitals for incurables). In assessing the quality of Prague's poorhouse we can note some trauma which the author suffered due to seeing the inmates, who were mostly bedridden due to their age, with no prospect of any improvement in their condition. He also observed the fact that even people in relatively better condition had no real life in this institution and that their daily routine was not filled with any activity, he merely notes that "Alle thun nichts."[57] In the end, however, when describing the situation in the sphere of the institutional care for the poor in Prague, he sounds quite positive. In his book, a pragmatic evaluation prevails, reflecting a complicated and often only limited solution to the situation of the poor in many European cities: "[...] I am pleased that the people, when they are no longer usable, are kept better than horses that you leave to die."[58]

The residents of the Prague hospital for incurables also participated in daily laundry service for their facility, and they even did the job for other poverty care and medical facilities in Prague. They also worked as watchmen and gatekeepers, caretakers or teachers for child inmates in hospital. Sadly enough, all attempts to organise education for the residents of the hospital of school age in school facilities outside the premises of the hospital did not work out well. Educating children from the hospital for incurables in local schools failed due to complaints made by the public because the children from the hospital became the targets of jokes due to

---

[56] *Dějiny obecní správy I.*, p. 208–209; *Dobročinné ústavy*, pp. 18–19.
[57] Wilhelm Horn, *Reise durch Deutschland, Ungarn, Holland, Italien, Frankreich, Grossbritanien und Irland in Rücksicht auf medicinische und naturwissenschaftliche Institute, Armenpflege u.s.w. I.* (Berlin: Verlag von Th. Fr. Chr. Enslin, 1831), p. 55.
[58] Ibid.

their disabilities and the entire situation "aroused indignation among the public."[59] The employment of the hospital inmates reached its peak during the reforms of poverty care facilities in the city of Prague during the second half of the 1820s, when most of the professional staff were laid off due to financial problems and thus their role had to be taken over by those hospital residents who were physically and mentally capable of caregiving.[60] Generally, the residents of the hospital for incurables had to follow much stricter rules than the inmates of the poorhouse.[61]

The numbers of the hospital for incurables inmates settled at the amount of about 300 people at the beginning of its operation and gradually increased.[62] The nature of the hospital is well illustrated by the fact that apart from a negligible number of inmates who annually left the institute voluntarily or fled, nearly half of them died in the first years of its operation.[63] The number of deaths dropped in the following years and eventually stabilised at around one fifth of hospital capacity.[64] Most of them were decrepit old people, blind, mentally and physically disabled, epileptics, patients afflicted by gout or cancer patients. During the first half of the 19th century, the hospital for incurables cared almost exclusively for terminal patients.[65]

Fortunately, the hospital for incurables did not struggle with enormous financial problems as did the poorhouse. Yet its daily operation also depended on subsidies provided by the city of Prague. The yearly sum was fixed at 1000 Fl.[66]

The deficits in budgets of all Prague poor care facilities were caused by the fact that the vast majority of their inmates did not pay for their stays as they were poor. The duty to pay for their stays was legally supposed to be covered by municipalities, yet this duty was widely circumvented, with the exception of Prague. In the late 1820s, the growing deficits in the financing of some Prague poor care facilities resulted in a search for new ways to fund these institutions. Such deficit growth had its roots in two

[59] *Dobročinné ústavy*, pp. 20–21; *Dějiny obecní správy I.*, pp. 221–222.
[60] *Dějiny obecní správy I.*, pp. 217–218; *Dobročinné ústavy*, p. 19.
[61] *Dějiny obecní správy I.*, pp. 211–212.
[62] In 1844, there were 385 sick persons (295 females and 90 males); cf. Weitenweber, *Die medicinischen Anstalten Prag's*, p. 102. In 1863, after the takeover of the hospital under the city administration, there were 286 people; cf. *Dějiny obecní správy I.*, p. 230.
[63] *Dobročinné ústavy*, p. 19. During the year of 1791, 154 persons came to stay in the hospital and 148 of them died over the same period of time.
[64] Weitenweber, *Die medicinischen Anstalten Prag's*, p. 103.
[65] Ibid., p. 104.
[66] *Dobročinné ústavy*, p. 17.

aspects: as a result of the facilities' maintenance and in particular, due to the city of Prague's generous support, which was given even to those persons without permanent residency.[67] The Governor's Office first suggested covering the deficits by a lump sum from the state finance, but the emperor's reaction was clearly negative. For the first time – as early as in 1818 – Prague municipal finance was used to cover the debts of the poor care institutions and this practice persisted throughout the entire first half of the 19th century.[68]

In the early 1850s, the overall problems of the Prague poverty care escalated again, and not only due to lack of funds. It turned out that the reorganisation from the 1820s did not produce the desired effect either in the open or in the institutional. The impetus for the new reform was the appointment of Count Franz Thun-Hohenstein in the post of the director of the "Poor Institute." Thun-Hohenstein was also the chairman of "The private association for supporting poor households." His basic concept for the maintenance and further development of the system of the care for the poor in Prague was the consistent centralisation of both charitable and institutional care, hand in hand with systemic changes. He drew inspiration for his reforms mainly from England. His first and fundamental reform step was therefore a merger of all private activities in the open care for the poor. It was necessary to merge the directorate of "Poor Institute" (newly a collective body), which managed the open care for the poor within Prague, with the leadership of the "The private association for supporting poor households." Within each poor district, he subsequently significantly increased the number of the "Fathers of the poor."[69] These reform steps promoted by Count Thun-Hohenstein focused primarily on the open care for the poor, brought about a temporary improvement in the financial situation, which, however, did not last long. The reform itself did not affect the entire system of financial security of the care for the poor, but only its organisation and staffing.[70]

---

[67] Antonín Pokorný, "Několik poznámek o vzniku a právním poměru všeobecné nemocnice v Praze" [A couple of comments on the origin and legal conditions of the General Hospital in Prague], *Věstník hlavního města Prahy* 35, no. 7 (1928): p. 170. On the other hand, in 1843 the Prague hospital for incurables as well as the poorhouse obtained an increased amount of finance and their yearly incomes exceeded expenses, albeit not significantly. Cf. Weitenweber, *Die medicinischen Anstalten Prag's*, pp. 104, 158.

[68] Ibid.

[69] Cf. Vlk, *Chudinství*, pp. 33–36; Josef Vlk, *Chudinství královského hlavního města Prahy* (Praha, 1900), pp. 17–18.

[70] There even existed a plan to set up a regular lottery to fund care for the poor. Cf. AHMP, MHMP I., Presidium, man. 1848–1851, F 10/9, box 101, 1851 a proposal

It is no accident that an intense effort to seek a solution to the difficult social situation of the inhabitants of Prague occurred in the second half of the 1840s. Rapid economic development, new construction and the overall industrial development of the capital led to a growth of unemployment problems the likes of which neither state nor municipal administration had any experience of dealing with.[71] And because of this rather uncontrolled economic boom, coupled with complications with food supplies, such as those experienced in 1846 (in connection with crop failures), some sort of social unrest seemed quite likely. It increased the pressure on the quest for effective organisation of the Prague care for the poor. This situation was more manifest in particular steps made by the Municipal Office than by the state administration. Since the late 1840s, the Municipal Office began to understand the issues of the poor in a broader context, including newly emerged workers' issues. By doing so, the Municipal Office was actually reacting to these new issues earlier than the provincial government.[72] The issue of the care for the poor was embodied in the agenda of Municipal Office of the City of Prague throughout the entire first half of the 19th century. The city of Prague partly intervened into the direct subsidies, and even through its own foundations, i.e. by controlling of appointments of the foundations' boards,[73] it provided direct financing of these institutions, and revised the jurisdiction of Prague's poor and dealt with "foreign" poor persons (i.e. people without permanent residency in Prague). [74] After the first reorganisation of the Prague system of care for the poor in the 1820s, the city initiated intensive negotiations with the state administration about the situation in this area. The provincial government required a consistent implementation of the "poor policy" – meaning crackdowns on begging, etc. The city of Prague reciprocally achieved participation in the control of the budgets for poor care in the early 1830s and it achieved supervision of collecting financial contributions for the open care for the poor.[75] The alpha and omega of mutual communication between the state and the

of the „Lotterie-Eröffnung-Anträge" for charity purposes.
[71] Václav Ledvinka and Jiří Pešek, *Praha* [Prague] (Praha: NLN, 2000), pp. 448–449.
[72] AHMP, MHMP I., Presidium, man. 1848–1851, F 10, 10a, 10b, 10/6, box 100–101, 1848–1849, documents on care for the poor, special funds for unemployed persons, work in the quarry in Prague-Strahov, soups and bread for the poor, etc.
[73] Ibid., man. 1819–1825, F 28/1, box 18, 1806–1820 subsidies for the poor.
[74] Ibid., man. 1826–1830, F 7/2, box 30, 1829–1830 control of permanent residency of poor persons and the deportation of "foreign" ones.
[75] Ibid., man. 1831–1835, F 10/8, box 48, 1831 controls of the financial reserves for the care for the poor.

municipal administration remained the issue of financing care for the poor in Prague.[76] The city proposed solving the financial deficit at the "Poor Institute" by establishing a new fund to cover the needs of open care for the poor, with the participation of the city. However, the city of Prague conditioned its financial involvement by the implementation of consistent and accurate records of all recipients of financial support, including the degree of their dependence on benefits.[77] In the framework of Prague institutional care for the poor, the Municipal Office secured its biggest influence on the poorhouse, whose activities were subsidised by regular contributions. The city could involve some significant investments in the development of the poorhouse[78].

The period of gradual transfer of competencies from state to municipal administration, however, started at the administrative level as late as 1850. This transition of the Prague institutional and open care for the poor under the municipal administration happened primarily because of the abovementioned financial problems that were associated with budget deficits of the institutional care administered by the state, but also due to increasing costs of open care for the poor based primarily on the private sector. Moreover, there was an effort to synchronise the entire system of the care for the poor in accordance with the wording of the Prague Provisional Municipal Law from 1850. Its Article 85 decreed that "providing care for the poor belongs to the affairs of the municipality. If the funds of private charitable institutions and private charitable foundations are insufficient, the municipality is obliged to make a necessary provision of equipment as well as make sure that local charitable institutes have good manners and are well managed."[79]

The reorganisation of the Prague system of the care for the poor lasted from 1850 to 1864.[80] The overall delay in conducting the reform was

---

[76] Ibid., man. 1841–1845, F 10/7, box 78, 1844 the contributions made by the city officials for the "Poor institute".

[77] Ibid., man. 1831–1835, F 10/10, box 48, 1832 expertise on centralising the open care for the poor in Prague; F 10/12, box 48, 1832 alms books.

[78] Ibid., man. 1831–1835, F 10/27, box 48, 1835 the erection of the new pavilion of the St. Bartholomew poorhouse; Ibid., man. 1841–1845, F 10/4, box 78, 1842 documents on the economic situation of this facility.

[79] Municipal Law of 1850, Article 85. There was an amendment of February 7, Coll. no. 76/1919, which further confirmed the obligation of municipalities to care for their poor (Article 20).

[80] Administrative changes happened between 1851–1864 and resulted in "Ordinance to the district directorates of the poor in royal capital of Prague" [*Naučení okresním řiditelstvům chudých v král. Hlav. městě Praze*], which only confirmed the newly established processes – see *Naučení okresním ředitelstvům*

partly caused by implementing additional legal norms. In 1862, the Imperial Municipal Law declared the obligations of municipalities in their direct competency in the sphere of the care for the poor as follows: it is their duty to "care for the poor and general charitable institutes."[81] A year later, the Law on the Right of Domicile[82] confirmed the commitment of municipalities to provide for their poor residents – an obligation to provide assistance to impoverished community residents.

The two most important Prague poor care facilities – the indebted poorhouse of St. Bartholomew and the hospital for incurables in Karlov – were both transferred under the administration of the Prague municipality in the early 1860s. In the same period, the municipality normatively defined open care for the poor, which, however, remained in the same form which it had acquired during the reforms in the first half of the 19th century, i.e. based on poor districts, "Fathers of the poor" and on private philanthropy. Fundamental changes concerned only staffing of the chief directorate of the "Poor Institute", whose employees were newly elected by the city council and director was elected by the by the Board of Aldermen. This body gradually gained the form of an office and it coordinated the whole area of the care for the poor (open and institutional care together).

The final form of the system of the care for the poor was anchored in the act on "the custody of the poor" in 1868.[83] The so-called "poor law" specified the organisation of the care for the poor in keeping its current form as a prime duty of the municipality (which was already defined as a "political community") according to the law on the right of domicile (from 1863) and if necessary, the state was then supposed to secure the care.[84] The "poor law" also strictly forbade any form of begging and specified various forms of aid, which could be required by a member of the poorest strata of the society – and this was first and foremost, employment. The old practice of coercion and punishments should have served as a tool to enforce employment of physically fit individuals. Caring for the poor who

---

chudých v král. Hlav. městě Praze (Praha, 1864).

[81] The Imperial Law Coll. no. 18/1862, part V (March 5, 1862).

[82] The Imperial Law Coll. no. 105/1863, part IV – About the duty of a community to care for its poor residents – Articles 22–31 (December 3, 1863).

[83] The Imperial Law Coll. no. 59/1868 (December 3, 1868).

[84] Ibid., Articles 2, 3, 25, and 26. If the community was unable to provide necessary care, it was supposed to ask for help at the district board of representatives, and at the provincial board of representatives. These bodies were directly responsible for charitable institutions on the district and provincial level. Ibid., Articles 27 and 28.

were unable to work was channelled into the hospitals for incurables, where persons stricken by incurable, contagious, as well as "detestable" diseases and also patients with psychiatric diagnoses were concentrated.[85] That practice reflected not only contemporary efforts to include persons with apparent physical and mental disabilities into institutional care, but by concentration of the care it also enabled smaller municipalities and communities to provide care for their physically and mentally disabled residents. Unlike Prague, smaller towns and communities could not provide care in specialised facilities, i.e. hospitals separated from hospitals for incurables as well as from psychiatric hospitals. Furthermore, particular attention was devoted to poor, orphaned and abandoned children, who should be provided education, training and/or apprenticeships by municipalities.

The "poor law" from 1868 exhaustively defined ways of raising funds to provide care for the poor. In addition to specially defined basic capital enriched by testamentary dispositions and donations; other sources were to be used by the law: finances and voluntary contributions. If these resources were not enough, a given community had the obligation to help from its budget.[86] Basic poverty care assets were legally reproduced in a certain portion by inheritances from clerics, by a percentage of the sale of goods at various auctions, as well as by finance and properties that had been confiscated in criminal cases. The community could also supplement these revenues through specially introduced taxes and charges.[87] The law also appealed to municipalities to be more active in attracting voluntary contributions for the care for the poor through collections and other legal means. In addition, the duty of municipalities to oversee the establishing and functioning of treasuries of fraternal and self-help groups in factories, steel mills and mines was newly embodied in this law. The official state policy actually wanted employees to set up the treasuries of these self-help associations.[88] Municipalities throughout the Czech Lands were also encouraged to be actively involved in the establishment and operation of institutions that facilitated either job opportunities for the poor or assisted them in procuring cheap food. Furthermore, these institutions looked after persons who could not take care of themselves due to their old age or physical or mental disabilities. In addition, this law also confirmed the role of the clergy in terms of the care for the poor organised by a municipality. Clerics started to have, from now on, a mere advisory vote when the

---

[85] Ibid., Article 12.
[86] Ibid., Article 16.
[87] Ibid., Articles 20–22.
[88] Ibid., Article 29.

municipal bodies were deciding on matters of the poor. The fundamental place in the performance of municipal care for the poor was again confirmed to the "Fathers of the poor." They were elected by the municipal boards and they were supposed to "directly and personally care for the poor."[89] Finally, the law confirmed to municipalities the execution of the poor police, whose main tasks were both preventing begging and controlling the proper management of the assets dedicated to the care for the poor.[90] The entire system of the care for the poor was definitively and completely taken over by municipalities in the course of the 1860s.

The basic principles of the care for the poor in Prague became stabilised after the release of the "poor law" in 1868 and maintained their form – with some formal and rather minor changes – until 1918. The care for the poor in Prague was completely entrusted to the municipal authorities. Yet that does not mean that there would be no further attempts to reform the system. The inspiration provided the already mentioned "Elberfeld system," whereas some other suggestions reflected solutions to poverty care issues chiefly in a number of Austrian and German cities. Their systems usually oscillated between the Prussian model, which was based on support in the current place of residence, thus ultimately accentuated the responsibility of the state, and the Bavarian system, relying on the old principle of the right of domicile.[91] Several reform attempts took place under the Prague municipal administration in the 1880s and 1890s, when the municipal authority tried to streamline its most problematic part – the open care for the poor. The objective was to strengthen the role of the chief directorate as well as the transfer of the actual administration of the care for the poor from various departments of the Municipal Office to the chief directorate.[92] The proposals also aimed both at increasing the social prestige of the Fathers of the poor and at ensuring their more frequent contact with the poor. Also, the proposals promoted more active work with children and youth at risk of poverty. Yet all in all, the proposed reform was again a mere compromise between the open care for the poor organised by the city and private charity.[93]

---

[89] Ibid., Article 32.

[90] Ibid., Article 33.

[91] *Ottův slovník naučný* (further referred to as OSN) [Otto's encyclopaedia] 12, 1st edition, s.v. "chudinství" [care for the poor], pp. 434–435; Sachße and Tennstedt, *Geschichte der Armenfürsorge in Deutschland I.*, pp. 195–214.

[92] AHMP, MHMP I., Rankeum – Praha – Chudinství – vol. 1897–1898 – Karel Vendulák, a report for the city council of March 5, 1897, pp. 14–18.

[93] *Almanach královského hlavního města Prahy na rok 1901* [Annual of the royal capital of Prague for the year of 1901], ed. Vojtěch Kraus (Praha: tiskem Dra E.

However, the only particular outcome was a consolidation of the control mechanisms.[94]

An element which defined further development of the care for the poor from the 1860s was a change in the approach to the whole set of issues related to poverty. The issues of the care for the poor had their roots in the 1840s when the very first attempts appeared to connect poverty-related problems and working class issues (i.e. social). The whole topic came to be seen within the broader concept of "humanistic care." Poverty should be further mitigated by a set of measures primarily relying on improving the economic situation of the lower classes. Their standard of living was supposed to be increased by a whole complex of measures, ranging from new legal standards, compulsory insurance, and facilitating employment by creating new jobs.[95] The new system also integrated the old, traditional practices of a preventive, control, and corrective character. Moreover, the newly set processes were to coordinate all private and municipal (state, respectively) activities in poverty care. [96]

The above analysed change definitely brought a more proactive approach by the municipality at the conceptual level. The aim was to achieve an effective implementation of public care for the poor, to regulate and support private philanthropy, but also to prepare measures to prevent the spread of poverty and to provide general support to lower social classes. Social work was concentrated in a new municipal department called "humanitarian", which started to function in 1901. Its scope of activities reflected the penetration of new social problems into the traditional concept of poverty policy.[97] This department primarily focused on preventive measures, but it also dealt with the issues of children and youth in need, and pursued an active policy of support of overall employment and social housing. A wide spectrum of "humanitarian" facilities existed under the municipal administration at that time – alongside traditional institutions, a new municipal orphanage operated (founded in 1875), several re-education institutions, shelters for youth, but

---

Grégra, 1901), p. 213.

[94] *Řád ústavu chudinského královského hlavního města Prahy* [Rules of the Institute of the poor of the royal capital of Prague], (Praha: Obec pražská, second edition 1901), p. 7.

[95] Ibid.

[96] *OSN* 11, 1st edition, s.v. "humanitní ústavy" [humanitarian institutions].

[97] "Zprávy. Referát popisní a humanitní" [News. Department of Registration and Humanitarian Department], *Věstník obecní královského hlavního města Prahy* 8, no. 19 (1901): p. 173. The "humanitarian department" was already established in 1899.

also a prison. Prisons – in terms of humanitarian care – served as shelters for the poor as well as protection against vagrancy. Additionally, the agenda of the "humanitarian department" included providing assistance in searching for work and dealing with alcoholism or prostitution.[98]

After the re-organisational measures in the 19th and 20th centuries, the overall system of social care in Prague was still largely funded from special municipal funds, of which the beneficiary fund was the most significant.[99] A significant part was still provided by various private foundations. Yet even in this period, the city struggled with financial problems and welcomed any additional voluntary support in favour of the "Poor Institute." Thus even at the turn of the century, the municipal administration had to rely on contributions coming from fees levied by the police directorate for permitting theatrical or musical productions and donations from various associations, brotherhoods and of course from individuals.[100]

The measures which were implemented by the "Chief directorate of the Poor Institute" in the early 20th century (functioning under the name the Chief Directorate of the Poor Office since 1914),[101] partially mitigated the most pressing problems of poverty, but in general, they did not go beyond the conservative paternalistic model of poverty policy that characterised the care for the poor in Prague throughout the entire 19th century. In 1909, the chief directorate of the "Poor Institute" adopted the last pre-war

---

[98] *Administrativní zpráva královského hlavního města Prahy a spojených s městskou statistickou kommisí obcí Karlína, Smíchova, Král. Vinohradů a Žižkova za léta 1900 a 1901* [Administrative report of the royal capital of Prague along with communities of Karlín, Smíchov and Královské Vinohrady and Žižkov], eds. Josef Erben and Jan Srb (Praha: Statistická komisse král. hlavního města Prahy, 1904), pp. 711, 734–735; Václav Hlavsa et al., *Archiv hlavního města Prahy. Průvodce po fondech a sbírkách* [Prague City Archives. A guidebook] (Praha: Archivní správa ministerstva vnitra ČSR, 1955), p. 51.

[99] Cf. AHMP, Record Office, ref. MHMP 70076/2007, research done by Hana Svatošová, *Obročnický fond hl. m. Prahy* [Beneficiary fund of the capital of Prague], Prague, July 25, 2007.

[100] "Zprávy. Dobrovolné příspěvky fondu pražského ústavu chudinského" [News. Voluntary contributions to the fund of the Prague's Institute of the Poor], *Věstník obecní královského hlavního města Prahy* 8, no. 26 (1901): pp. 239–240.

[101] *Administrační zpráva král. Hlav. města Prahy za léta 1908, 1909, 1910 II.* [Administrative report of the royal capital of Prague of the years 1908, 1909, and 1910, vol. 2.], ed. Josef Šiška (Praha: Statistická komisse královského hlavního města Prahy, 1915), p. 888; *Almanach král. hlav. města Prahy na rok 1914* [Annual of the royal capital of Prague for the year of 1914], ed. Vojtěch Kraus (Praha: Obec královského hlavního města Prahy, 1914), p. 127.

proposals to reform the Instruction of the care for the poor, which were gradually implemented until 1914. Social care for children and young people became epicentres of its activity and in addition, the "Poor Institute" had to deal with social care in the new parts of the growing city.[102] The standard provision in its facilities as well as financial support in the form of alms were in the pre-war period complemented by a range of activities, especially at the initiative of Social and Humanitarian Commission at Prague Municipal Office. This body became not only the bearer of conceptual changes in the social sphere, but it also practically implemented proposals for specific measures, such as providing subsidised heating fuel, tax credits for homes with small apartments intended for socially disadvantaged residents, interventions to the selling food at regulated prices, further expansion of mandatory minimum old-age insurance for municipal employees and construction of affordable workers' apartments.[103]

At the same time, the city fought unemployment primarily by organising community services or other types of subsidised work.[104] Such subsidised work became part of the so-called "ancillary actions", through which the municipal authorities sought to alleviate the effects of unemployment, with the aim not only to provide work for the unemployed, but also to provide food to unemployed individuals at the same time. These actions were regularly organised by the city of Prague in winter months, when the situation of unemployed persons was most difficult. Their economic revenue was indeed minimal, yet in the opinion of the municipal administration, much larger problems (such as assurance of financial support for the unemployed and the difficulties in securing public order) were thus avoided. Therefore, the municipal administration decided to create a permanent system of these works to overcome the prevalent practice of one-time support activities. These organised actions of providing work for the unemployed did not distinguish whether any given person got into his/her bad financial situation by careless behaviour or whether this was his/her fault.

---

[102] AHMP, MHMP I., Presidium, man. 1914–1937, no. 56/7, 1918–1920 a proposal of the Chief Directorate of the Poor Office on re-organisation of the care for the poor in Prague.

[103] *Administrační zpráva královského hlavního města Prahy za léta 1905, 1906, 1907 II.* [Administrative report of the royal capital of Prague of the years 1905, 1906, and 1907, vol. 2], ed. Josef Husák (Praha: Statistická komisse královského hlavního města, 1911), p. 889.

[104] "Zprávy. Proti nezaměstnanosti" [News. Against unemployment], *Věstník obecní královského hlavního města Prahy* 8, no. 24, (1901): p. 218.

The populations of surrounding villages sought unemployment assistance in Prague in rather large numbers and securing these individuals was beyond the capabilities and capacities of the Prague municipal social care system. Subsidised works were mostly carried out on the demolition of the city walls, road construction and their regular maintenance, regulation of watercourses, as well as other construction projects throughout the capital city.[105] These one-time actions typically employed 500 to 700 workers.[106]

Despite all possible problems, and the overall condition of municipal care for the poor (and lately the newly formed system of the social care in the period before the First World War), the municipal administration perceived its state, chiefly rightly, as fairly satisfactory. Not surprisingly, the city administration tried to present the results of its social measures nationwide and consequently at the international level as well. On the other hand, no really large and successful project occurred that would transcend contemporary quality standards in the care for the poor. The Viennese Caring Home [*Versorgungsheim*] in Lainz (Vienna) can serve as an example of such a large and generous project.[107] The Prague municipal administration started to establish similar facilities with a delay in the post-war period. The delegation of poor care competencies to the city administration brought new elements into the traditional poverty care system: firstly, the streamlining of both management and centralisation of the administration of the institutional care for the poor. Secondly, it was the bureaucratisation and professionalisation of a significant part of the care for the poor, with the exception of direct disbursement of financial aid within the traditional system of the poor districts. Dependence of the care for the poor on the church was completely removed as well. Furthermore, a plethora of private charitable activities intensively developed on an associations basis in this period. In addition, the issues of children and youth unemployment represented another major theme of municipal social policy. Yet the financial demands associated with the implementation of municipal poor and social policy after the mid-19th century represented a not negligible part of the city budget; despite this, the financial needs of

[105] *Administrační zpráva... za léta 1905, 1906, 1907 II.*, p. 926.
[106] Josef Vlk, *Zpráva o nezaměstnanosti a akci pomocné z doby minulé na přítomnost se vztahující a směry do budoucnosti naznačující* [Report on unemployment and on a relieve campaign in the past, with a relation to the present and with implying prospect for the future], (n.p.: Vrchní ředitelství ústavu chudinského král. hlav. města Prahy, 1902).
[107] "Zusammenfassung der historischen Fakten und der Bürgerversammlung vom 8. April 2010," Ober St. Veit an der Wien, accessed October 14, 2015, http://www.1133.at/document/view/id/389.

the care for the poor did not represent a chief impulse for the reformist efforts in this aspect. After delegating social care issues to city authorities, the expenses in this area represented 5–6% of the municipal budget (in the 1870s). This share doubled after embodying all adjustments and reform interventions before the First World War – undoubtedly in connection with the centralisation of various social agendas under the so-called "humanitarian department."[108] However, the newly applicable principles of the humanitarian agenda could not fully develop at the municipal level during the pre-war period, because the municipal social policy impinged on limits of official state social policy. These limits were loosened as late as after 1918, with the reorganisation of the state administration, hand in hand with new social legislation, when democratic Czechoslovakia came into being.[109]

---

[108] Cf. *Finanční předchozí rozvrh obecních důchoduv a zvláštních fonduv královského hlavního města Prahy na rok 1879* [Financial previous budget of municipal incomes and particular funds of the royal capital of Prague for the year 1879], (Praha: V. Nagl, 1878), pp. 62–63; *Předchozí rozpočet král. hlavního města Prahy na rok 1896* [Previous budget of the royal capital of Prague for the year 1896], (Praha: E. Beaufort, 1895), pp. 178–180; *Obecní rozpočty král. hlav. města Prahy 1905* [Municipal budgets of the royal capital of Prague 1905], (Praha: E. Beaufort, 1904), pp. 278–279 (XI. Previous budget).

[109] Cf. Jakub Rákosník, "Gentský systém v období I. Československé republiky" [The Ghent system in the era of the 1st Czechoslovak Republic], *Časopis národního muzea – řada historická*, 170, no. 3–4 (2001): pp. 84–105; a summary of legislative tools to fight unemployment, compare: Jan Cerman, *Podporování nezaměstnaných podle předpisů o státním příplatku k podpoře nezaměstnaných* [Supporting the unemployed according to the regulations on the state supplementary allowance for supporting the unemployed], (Praha: Sociální ústav ČSR, 1938).

Fig. 6-1 Masaryk Homes in Prague-Krč ca. 1930 (AHMP, Photographs, sign. I 1601)

Fig. 6-2 Municipal Poorhouse of St. Bartholomew No. 427 Vyšehradská Str., Prague II, New Town ca 1925 (AHMP, Photographs, sign. II 547)

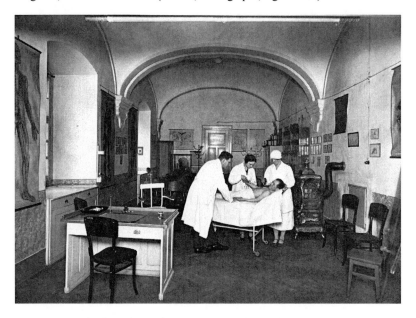

Fig. 6-3 Examination of a patient, 1921. Hospital for incurables "Na Karlově", former Augustinian monastery, No. 453, Prague II, New Town, 1921 (AHMP, Photographs , sign. II 529)

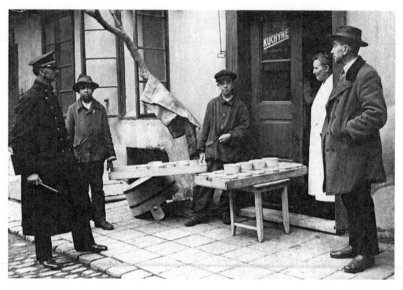

Fig. 6-4 Meal distribution at the Municipal prison and Station for expellees "Fišpanka", 1921, under Emauzy No. 374, Prague II, New Town (AHMP, Photographs, sign. II 1007)

Kostelík sv. Bartoloměje a chudobinec
Vyšehradská třída č. pop. 435-II.
Zbořeno r. 1884.

Fig. 6-5 Municipal poorhouse with the church of St. Bartholomew, ca 1880, Vyšehradská str. No. 427, Prague II, New Town (AHMP, Photographs, sign. VI 30/27b)

CHAPTER SEVEN

„SOZIALE FRAGE" UND ARMENFÜRSORGE IM GEFOLGE DER „GROßEN DEPRESSION" (1873) IN EINER SEMIINDUSTRIELLEN GESELLSCHAFT: DIE PROVINZHAUPTSTADT KLAGENFURT

WERNER DROBESCH

"The social question" and care for the poor as a consequence of the "Great Depression" (1873) in semi-industrial society: the regional capital of Klagenfurt as a case study

Abstract: Like other cities in Cisleithania, Klagenfurt was touched by the "social question", although the city was not developing so rapidly. The transition to a modern industrial society was happening slowly. One of the groups of problems that the city had to cope with was the "social question." In this context, issues of housing and social care were especially important. Construction of residential houses was supposed to gradually improve the housing situation of workers. The initiative also started to develop in care for the poor. Based on the "Statute for the Poor" (*Armenstatut*), the city administration started to interfere into this field, albeit initially in a restrained way. As for the forms of social care, the local practice was rather diverse. The number of persons who were served by municipal facilities was continuously growing until 1914. In addition to the city's social activities, private institutions, civic associations and churches also took care of those people in need. Such persons received rations of fuel wood, modest financial assistance, food and/or, if necessary, they were assigned accommodation. Furthermore, a "people's kitchen" (*Volksküche*) was set up so that everyone could afford food. In comparison to the 1870s, the individual parts of the social safety net became more closely interconnected on the eve of the First World War.

„Der Bürgermeister berichtet hinsichtlich der Delogierung mehrerer obdachloser Armen, die im Stadtrathaus untergebracht sind. Die eingeleiteten Schritte zur Aufbringung geeigneter Wohnungen seien erfolglos geblieben, daher müsse man auf die eigenen Gebäude [...] zurückgreifen, in welchen der Gemüsekeller für die Unterbringung dieser Leute [...] adaptiert werden könnte. Die Lokalität wurde durch den Stadtphysikus bereits untersucht und [...] als Wohnung vollkommen geeignet befunden. [...] Bei diesem Anlass wünscht Gemeinderat Canaval, dass die Wohnungsfrage mit Nachdruck behandelt und zu ihrer Lösung [...] ein Komitee eingesetzt werde."[1]

Das hält das Protokoll des Klagenfurter Gemeinderates über die aktuelle Situation im städtischen Wohnungswesen ein Jahr nach der „Großen Depression" des Jahres 1873 fest. Die Wohnungsfrage war auch in Klagenfurt ein Aspekt der „sozialen Frage", die das Gesellschaftsgefüge der Stadt zwar nicht erschütterte, aber doch nicht spurlos an der Politik und ihren Entscheidungsträgern vorüberging. In der politischen Diskussion und im öffentlichen politischen Diskurs der Stadt, die als eine „Mittelstadt" sowie „Dienstleistungsstadt im Industrialisierungsprozess" zu klassifizieren ist,[2] begann sie seit den frühen 1870er Jahren eine immer gewichtigere Rolle zu spielen. Das Fehlen einer nachhaltigen Industrialisierung war wohl auch ein Grund dafür, dass in ihr die Lebensverhältnisse „generell etwas günstiger als in den neuen Industriestädten" waren.[3] Das bedeutete aber nicht, dass es im Rahmen der industriekapitalistischen Modernisierung und des sozioökonomischen Wandels zu keiner Freisetzung breiter Bevölkerungsgruppen aus ihren Sozial- und Arbeitsbindungen kam. Damit verbunden waren moderne Formen der Subsistenz- und Obdachlosigkeit. Ebenso gewannen Lebensrisiken wie Alter, Krankheit und Unfall einen neuen Charakter, weil Teile der Bevölkerung nicht in die neuen industriellen Erwerbsverhältnisse integriert werden konnten. Mit der sich daraus ergebenden Ungesichertheit des Broterwerbs und der Lebenssituation sahen sich die industriellen, aber

---

[1] Kärntner Landesarchiv Klagenfurt (weiter KLA Klagenfurt), Stadtarchiv Klagenfurt II, Schachtel 127, Protokoll über die ordentliche Sitzung des Gemeinderates Klagenfurt, 13.1.1874.
[2] Vgl. Renate Banik-Schweitzer, "Der Prozess der Urbanisierung," in *Die Habsburgermonarchie 1848–1918 IX. Soziale Strukturen, 1. Tl.bd. Von der feudal-agrarischen zur bürgerlich-industriellen Gesellschaft, Tl.bd. 1/1. Lebens- und Arbeitswelten in der industriellen Revolution*, Hrsg. Helmut Rumpler und Peter Urbanitsch (Wien: Verlag der Österreichischen Akademie der Wissenschaften, 2010), S. 183–232, hier S. 211 ff.
[3] Ebenda, S. 211.

auch semiindustriellen Zentren konfrontiert. Per se entwickelte sich die „soziale Frage" zu einem gesellschaftspolitischen Thema der Kommunalpolitik – auch in Klagenfurt. Die Stadt verzeichnete im ausgehenden 19. Jahrhundert eine wenig dynamische Bevölkerungsentwicklung, das demographische Wachstum fiel im Vergleich zu anderen „Mittelstädten" eher unspektakulär aus. Wohl verzeichnete Klagenfurt von 1851 bis 1880 mit einem Plus von 54,9 Prozent noch einen erheblichen Zuwachs an Bevölkerung (1851: 12.101; 1880: 18.747 Einwohner). Danach jedoch verflachte die Wachstumskurve. Zwischen 1880 und 1890 betrug die Zunahme der Bevölkerung nur mehr 5,4 Prozent, zwischen 1901 und 1910 trotz der Eingemeindung von Vororten 19,1 Prozent. Das war im Vergleich zu anderen Städten im Alpenraum eine unterdurchschnittliche Steigerungsrate. Am Vorabend des Ersten Weltkrieges zählte die Stadt 28.911 Einwohner.[4] Die Zunahme resultierte nur zu einem geringen Teil aus einer sinkenden Sterbe- und steigenden Geburtenrate, sondern war das Ergebnis einer Binnenmigration. Der Anteil der aus den Bezirken Kärntens, aber auch aus anderen Kronländern zugewanderten Bevölkerung nahm zu. Das spiegelt sich in der Heimatberechtigung der anwesenden Bevölkerung wider (Tabelle 1).

Tabelle 7-1: Anwesende Bevölkerung nach Heimatberechtigung in Klagenfurt 1880–1910, in Prozent

Heimatberechtigung	1880	1890	1900	1910
Klagenfurt	31,7	28,5	24,5	32,3
anderer Bezirk Kärntens	41,6	49,2	45,6	37,7
anderes Kronland	21,8	18,1	25,6	25,1
Ausland	4,9	4,3	4,3	4,0

Quelle: *Österreichische Statistik* Bd. 1, 1. Heft, S. 47; *Österreichische Statistik* Bd. 32, 2. Heft, S. 6 f.; *Österreichische Statistik* Bd. 63, 2. Heft, S. 20 f.; *Österreichische Statistik* N. F. Bd. 2, 1. Heft, S. 214

Im Rahmen der Armenfürsorge war dieser Umstand nicht unwichtig. Das Heimatrechtsgesetz des Jahres 1863 verpflichtete die Gemeinden zur Armenversorgung, und zwar für den Fall, dass „sich der Arme den notwendigen Unterhalt nicht mit eigenen Kräften zu verschaffen" vermochte, wie auch „auswärtigen Armen im Falle augenblicklicher

---

[4] Wilhelm Hecke, "Die Städte Österreichs nach der Volkszählung vom 31. Dezember 1910," *Statistische Monatsschrift* N. F. 18 [29] (1913): S. 179–221, hier S. 212.

Bedürfnisse die nötige Unterstützung" nicht versagt werden durfte.[5] Bis 1900 wurde dieses seitens der Stadtverwaltung wohl aus ökonomischen Überlegungen rigoros gehandhabt. Oft wurden Zuwanderer, die im Wohnort keine Heimatberechtigung und daher auch keinen Anspruch auf Armenfürsorge hatten, wieder in ihre Heimatgemeinde zurückgeschickt.[6] Die deutliche Zunahme der in Klagenfurt Heimatberechtigten von 1900 bis 1910 war auf das neue Heimatgesetz des Jahres 1901 zurückzuführen. Dieses ermöglichte nach zehnjährigem Aufenthalt („Ersitzung") in der Gemeinde die Antragstellung auf Heimatberechtigung am Wohnort, wenn „das Ersitzungssubjekt während der Ersitzungsfrist der öffentlichen Armenversorgung nicht anheimgefallen" war.[7]

Die wenig spektakulären Zuwachsraten in der Bevölkerungszahl hingen mit der nur langsam in Gang kommenden Industrialisierung zusammen. „Die Stadt reckt und streckt sich nach allen Seiten, legt einen großstädtischen Anzug an, der überall schlottert",[8] stellte der Bürgermeister Franz Glöckner 1890 fest. Aber eine Großindustrie entstand nicht. Auch konnte die schmale Basis klein- und mittelindustrieller Unternehmen, die das Stadtbild noch im Vormärz geprägt hatte, nicht erweitert werden, ihre Zahl hielt sich in Grenzen.[9] Die Tabakfabrik mit über 1.000 Beschäftigten um 1900 war das größte Unternehmen in der Stadt, die erst 1863 an das Eisenbahnnetz angeschlossen und damit in den interregionalen Verkehr integriert worden war.

Gemächlich gestaltete sich der Wandel von der altständischen Welt zu einer modernen Industriegesellschaft. Das hing damit zusammen, dass die Bewohner nach „einer Form kontrollierter Urbanität [...], die Problemzonen einhegte und überschaubar hielt", strebten.[10] Aus diesem

---

[5] Reichsgesetzblatt 105/1863 v. 3.12.1863.

[6] Hermann Blodig jun., "Heimatrecht," in *Österreichisches Staatswörterbuch. Handbuch des gesamten österreichischen öffentlichen Rechtes* Bd. 2, Hrsg. Ernst Mischler und Josef Ulbrich (Wien: Hölder, 1896), S. 71–78, sowie Ludwig Spiegel, "Heimatrecht," in *ebenda*, S. 809–843.

[7] Spiegel, "Heimatrecht," S. 824.

[8] Eduard Skudnigg, "Die freigewählten Bürgermeister von Klagenfurt," in *Die Landeshauptstadt Klagenfurt. Aus ihrer Vergangenheit und Gegenwart* Bd. 2 (Klagenfurt: Selbstverlag der Landeshauptstadt, 1970), S. 305–318, hier S. 310.

[9] Werner Drobesch, "Die Provinzhauptstadt Klagenfurt – gesellschaftlicher Wandel und Vereinskultur im ‚peripheren Zentrum' (1965–1914)," in *800 Jahre Klagenfurt. Festschrift zum Jubiläum der ersten urkundlichen Nennung,* (Klagenfurt: Geschichtsverein für Kärten 1996), S. 311–326, hier S. 312.

[10] Hannes Steckel und Hans Heiss, "Klein- und mittelstädtische Lebenswelten," in *Die Habsburgermonarchie 1848–1918 IX. Soziale Strukturen, 1. Tl.bd. Von der feudal-agrarischen zur bürgerlich-industriellen Gesellschaft, Tl.bd. 1/1. Von der*

Ansinnen heraus wurde „eine ungebremste Zunahme der Unterschichten
[...] erfolgreich vermieden, Aufsteiger und Leistungsträger verstärkt in die
kommunale Partizipation integriert. [...] Aus dem vergleichenden Blick
auf die Großstädte" schätzten die Klagenfurterinnen und Klagenfurter die
„maßvolle Urbanität" ihres Lebensraumes, „wo sich die Vorzüge von
Stadtleben und Naturnähe verbinden ließen, während die negativen Seiten
des ‚Molochs Großstadt' nur in Ansätzen spürbar wurden".[11]

Die Klagenfurter Bevölkerung entsprach mehr dem Typus einer
agrarisch-bürgerlichen Übergangsgesellschaft. Der zahlenmäßige Anstieg
der Arbeiterschaft ging nicht auf die Gründung privater Industrieunternehmen
zurück, sondern basierte auf einer Ausweitung des öffentlichen Sektors.
Innerhalb der „Hauptberufsklassen" nahm das Segment „Industrie" von
1890 bis 1910 sogar ab (Tabelle 2). Hatte dieses 1890 noch einen Anteil
von 27,9 Prozent gehabt, so reduzierte sich Letzterer bis 1910 auf 22,5
Prozent. Innerhalb der Industriebeschäftigten dominierten die Bekleidungs-
und Textilindustrie (1890: 1.311 Beschäftigte; 1910: 1.462 Beschäftigte)
sowie die Genußmittelindustrie (1890: 1.112 Beschäftigte; 1910: 932
Beschäftigte).[12] Die anderen Industriesparten spielten eine untergeordnete
Rolle.

Tabelle 7-2: Bevölkerung nach Hauptberufsklassen 1890–1910, in Prozent

Hauptberufsklassen	1890	1900	1910
Land- und Forstwirtschaft	1,9	1,9	1,3
Industrie	27,9	27,8	22,5
Handel und Verkehr	13,2	12,8	17,9
Öffentlicher Dienst, Militär	46,0	46,9	49,4

Quelle: *Österreichische Statistik* Bd. 33, 5. Heft, Tabelle 1; *Österreichische
Statistik* Bd. 66, 5. Heft, S. 2 ff.; *Österreichische Statistik N. F.* Bd. 3, 5. Heft, S. 3
ff.

Nahezu die Hälfte des prozentuellen Anteils der Berufstätigen entfiel
auf die Kategorie „Öffentlicher Dienst und Militärdienst", welche
aufgrund der erhöhten militärischen Präsenz sogar einen Anstieg von 46,0

Stände- zur Klassengesellschaft, Hrsg. Helmut Rumpler und Peter Urbanitsch
(Wien: Verlag der Österreichischen Akademie der Wissenschaften, 2010), S. 561–
619, hier S. 617.
[11] Ebenda.
[12] *Österreichische Statistik* Bd. 33, 5. Heft, Tabelle 1; *Österreichische Statistik N.
F.* Bd. 3, 5. Heft, S. 3 ff.

Prozent (1890) auf 49,4 Prozent (1910) verzeichnete.[13] Der Anteil der Taglöhner verringerte sich von 2,4 Prozent im Jahre 1880 auf 0,8 Prozent im Jahre 1910.[14] Ein städtisches Industrieproletariat war kaum vorhanden. Ungeachtet dessen kam es in Klagenfurt zu einem Wandel im Lebensalltag, in dem der „sozialen Frage" seit den frühen 1880er Jahren in Weiterführung der sozialpolitischen Ambitionen der Regierung Eduard Graf Taaffes und in Anlehnung an den nun intensiver geführten sozialpolitischen Diskurs eine größere Aufmerksamkeit als zuvor geschenkt wurde. Sozialproteste, Streiks und militante Ausschreitungen hielten sich in Grenzen. Neben den gesamtstaatlichen Aktionsfeldern wie der Auseinandersetzung um die Arbeitszeit und höhere Löhne, um die Schaffung besserer Arbeitsbedingungen und den Ausbau der Arbeiterschutzgesetzgebung sowie um eine Verbesserung der Altersversorgung und der Versorgung im Krankheitsfall, deren sich die diversen Fach- und Gewerkschaftsvereine annahmen, konkretisierte sich die „soziale Frage" im städtischen Lebensalltag primär in der Wohnungsfrage, in der Armenfürsorge, aber auch im Gesundheitswesen. Mit diesen Bereichen war die Kommunalpolitik unmittelbar konfrontiert.

Außer Frage steht, dass Klagenfurt angesichts der Bevölkerungszunahme – auch wenn diese moderat ausfiel – von einer Wohnungsnot tangiert war, wenngleich der Zuzug der Landbevölkerung in die Stadt deutlich geringer ausfiel als in anderen innerösterreichischen Städten, wie etwa in Triest.[15] Im Rahmen der kommunalen Politik hatten die Wohnungsfrage und die damit in Zusammenhang stehenden Wohnverhältnisse eine sozialpolitische Brisanz. Denn in der Stadt gab es zu wenige Wohnungen, vor allem solche, die finanziell leistbar waren und über Mindeststandards verfügten. Ab den 1890er Jahren begann man seitens der Stadtregierung, in der die „Deutsche Volkspartei" den Ton angab, unter dem Einfluss der Wohnreformbewegung gegen die Wohnungsmisere mit Bauprogrammen entgegenzusteuern,[16] um das Wohnraumdefizit zu beseitigen. In dieses Konzept fügte sich der Beitritt der Stadt zur „Zentralstelle für

[13] Ebenda.
[14] *Österreichische Statistik* Bd. 33, 5. Heft, S. 35; *Österreichische Statistik N. F.* Bd. 3, 5. Heft, S. 3.
[15] Vgl. Sabine Rutar, "Wohnen in Triest um die Jahrhundertwende," in *Wohnen in der Großstadt 1900–1939. Wohnsituation und Modernisierung im europäischen Vergleich*, Hrsg. Alena Janatková (Stuttgart: Franz Steiner Verlag 2006), S. 55–75.
[16] Vgl. Eberhard Kraigher, "Städtebauliche Planungen und ihre Verwirklichung in Klagenfurt von der Mitte des 19. Jahrhunderts bis 1914," in *Klagenfurt. Festschrift zum Jubiläum der ersten urkundlichen Nennung* (Klagenfurt: Geschichtsverein für Kärten 1996), S. 345–369.

Wohnungsreform" ein.[17] Es war das Ziel, für die breiter werdende
Arbeiterschicht adäquate Wohn- und Lebensverhältnisse zu schaffen, die
über das Zimmer-Küche-Wohnschema hinausgingen. Um 1890 begann
man mit dem Bau von Arbeiterwohnhäusern.[18] Im privaten Wohnbau tat
sich gleichfalls einiges. Im letzten Dezennium vor dem Ersten Weltkrieg
erlebte die Stadt einen Bauboom (Tabelle 3).

Tabelle 7-3: Häuserzahl und Wohnparteien 1857–1910

Jahr	Häuserzahl	Wohnparteien	Wohnparteien/ Bevölkerungszahl
1857	760	2.288	5,89
1880	803	3.194	5,86
1890	870	3.547	5,56
1900	1.096	4.602	5,27
1910	1.326	5.558	5,20

Quelle: Österreichische Statistik Bd. 1, 1. Heft, S. 46 ff.; Österreichische Statistik
Bd. 32, 1. Heft, S. 11 f.; Österreichische Statistik Bd. 63, 2. Heft, S. 11 f.;
Österreichische Statistik N. F. Bd. 1, 1. Heft, S. 8; Österreichische Statistik N. F.
Bd. 3, 2. Heft, Tafel 24a.

Innerhalb eines halben Jahrhunderts hatte sich die Zahl der Häuser
nahezu verdoppelt (1857: 760; 1910: 1.326), von denen mehr als die
Hälfte (434) zwischen 1890 und 1910 erbaut wurde. Ebenso erhöhte sich
die Zahl der Wohnparteien (1857: 2.288; 1910: 5.558). Nahezu
unverändert blieb der Verteilung der Wohnparteien pro Haus (Tabelle 4).
Hatten 1890 35,7 Prozent der Häuser drei bis fünf Wohnparteien und 5,1
Prozent mehr als zehn Wohnparteien aufzuweisen, waren es 1910 35,3
Prozent bzw. 5,2 Prozent.

[17] KLA Klagenfurt, Stadtarchiv Klagenfurt II, Schachtel 155, Protokoll über die
ordentliche Sitzung des Gemeinderates Klagenfurt, 13.8.1912.
[18] Skudnigg, "Freigewählte Bürgermeister," S. 309.

Tabelle 7-4: Häuserzahl und Wohnparteien 1890 und 1910

Zahl der Wohnparteien	1890		1910	
	Häuser	%	Häuser	%
1	170	20,2	266	20,8
2	149	17,7	202	15,8
3–5	301	35,7	451	35,3
6–10	179	21,3	291	22,8
11–20	41	4,9	59	4,6
21–30	2	0,2	5	0,4
31–50	0	0	2	0,2

Quelle: *Österreichische Statistik* Bd. 32, 4. Heft, S. 12 f.; *Österreichische Statistik N. F.* Bd. 4, 1. Heft, S. 29.

Angesichts der nicht in Massen vorhandenen Industriearbeiterschaft gab es für den Bau von „Mietskasernen" wie in den Industriestädten keine Notwendigkeit, wenngleich nun doch auch Häuser, die mehr Wohnparteien Platz boten, errichtet wurden. Ihre Zahl blieb aber gering. 1910 gab es in der Stadt nur zwei Häuser mit mehr als 30 Wohnparteien und fünf Häuser mit 21 bis 30 Wohnparteien. Die Wohnungsgröße – d. h. die Wohnfläche und die Zahl der Wohnräume – blieb nahezu unverändert. 1910 dominierten noch immer, wie schon zwei Jahrzehnte zuvor (1890: 42,0 Prozent), Klein(st)wohnungen mit entweder zwei Wohnungsbestandteilen (Zimmer oder Kabinett und Küche) oder nur einem Wohnraum (Tabelle 5). 41,7 Prozent der Wohnungen waren dieser Kategorie zuzuordnen. Diese „Arbeitermietshäuser" entsprachen dem Trend der Zeit, das heißt, sie hatten keine sanitären Einrichtungen im Wohnungsverband. Diese befanden sich im Bereich der geschlossenen Gänge und wurden von den Mietern gemeinsam genutzt.[19] 1910 verfügten nur mehr 18,9 Prozent der Wohnungen über einen Raum und bereits 22,7 Prozent über zwei Räume.

---

[19] Vgl. Banik-Schweitzer, "Prozess der Urbanisierung," S. 224.

Tabelle 7-5: Wohnungen nach Räumen 1890, 1900 und 1910

Jahr	1 Raum		2 Räume		3–5 Räume		6–10 Räume		mehr als 10 Räume	
1890	811	22,9	677	19,1	1.382	39.0	585	15,9	112	3,2
1900	1.099	24,1	956	20,9	1.728	37,8	681	14,9	105	2,3
					3–4 Räume		mehr als 5 Räume			
1910	1.041	18,9	1.251	22,8	1.541	27,7	1.683	30,1		

Quelle: *Österreichische Statistik* Bd. 32, 4. Heft, S. 44 f.; *Österreichische Statistik* Bd. 45, 2. Heft, S. 25 ff.; *Österreichische Statistik N. F.* Bd. 4, 1. Heft, S. 16.

Im Vergleich zu 1890, als noch 22,9 Prozent der Wohnungen nur einen Raum und 19,1 Prozent zwei Räume gehabt hatten, war das ein Fortschritt. Es ermöglichte ein Leben in bescheidenen Verhältnissen. Das Gros der Industriearbeiterschaft lebte in wenig komfortablen, beengten Kleinstwohnungen. Viele wurden als die „unsanitärsten und bedenklichsten Lokale" klassifiziert. Zugleich verringerte sich der Anteil der Aftermieter und Bettgeher von 12,8 Prozent (1890) auf 8,0 Prozent (1910).[20] Diese waren in Arbeiterhaushalten anzutreffen. Denn nur auf diese Weise war es ledigen Zuwanderern in die Stadt möglich, sich eine kostengünstige Unterkunft zu leisten.

Ein weiteres zentrales, wenn nicht das zentrale Problemfeld, mit dem die Kommunalpolitik beschäftigt war, bildete die Armenfürsorge. Zu den Hauptfeldern der klassischen Fürsorge und Armenpolitik zählten die Armenfürsorge für Erwachsene, die Kinder- und Jugendfürsorge sowie die Obdachlosen- bzw. Wohnungsfürsorge. Beginnend mit der Gemeindeverordnung des Jahres 1862 und dem Heimatgesetz des Jahres 1863 war die Armenpflege zu einer kommunalen Angelegenheit geworden. Im Falle der Alpenländer führte das dazu, dass in den Städten „die Armengesetzgebung und das Interesse der Landesverwaltung für dieses Gebiet der sozialen Verwaltung auf einer höheren Stufe" stand.[21] Dem Gesetz nach galt eine Person, die nicht imstande war, „durch eigene

---

[20] Reinhard Eichwalder, "Wohnverhältnisse in den größeren Städten Österreichs in der zweiten Hälfte des 19. und zu Beginn des 20. Jahrhunderts," in *Geschichte und Ergebnisse der zentralen amtlichen Statistik in Österreich 1829–1979. Festschrift aus Anlass des 150jähr. Bestehens der zentralen amtlichen Statistik in Österreich,* Hrsg. Österreichisches Statistisches Zentralamt (Wien: Österreichische Staatsdruckerei, 1979), S. 559–574, hier S. 573 f.
[21] Ernst Mischler, "Die Armenpflege in den österreichischen Städten und ihre Reform," *Statistische Monatsschrift* 15 (1889): S. 493–522, hier S. 514.

Kraft oder Mittel sich und der Familie den unentbehrlichen Lebensunterhalt zu verschaffen", als „arm".[22] Die Versorgung sah eine Unterbringung im Armenhaus, die Beteiligung mit Geld oder Naturalien sowie die Verpflegung und ärztliche Versorgung im Krankheitsfall vor. Im Falle des Todes hatte die Stadt auch für die Beerdigung zu sorgen. „Von den größeren Städten der Alpenländer" besaß Klagenfurt nach der Aufhebung der „Pfarrarmeninstitute" „im Verhältnis zu seiner Volkszahl" ein „gutes Armenstatut".[23] Auf dessen Grundlage entfaltete die Stadtregierung zunächst eine vom Umfang her noch zurückhaltende, von den Formen her aber vielfältige Praxis der Armenversorgung. Armenfürsorge und -versorgung waren ein Teil der Stadtpolitik. Fernab klassisch-liberalen gesellschaftspolitischen Denkens war die Versorgung mittel- und obdachloser Menschen zu gewährleisten. 1886 wies die offizielle Statistik für Klagenfurt 1.000 Personen als „Arme" aus, für die die öffentliche Armenpflege zuständig war.[24] Das waren 5,3 Prozent der städtischen Bevölkerung, für die seitens der Gemeindekasse 33.000 fl. aufgewendet wurden. Aufgrund der Übergabe des Vermögens der Pfarrarmeninstitute an die Gemeinden – im Falle Klagenfurts belief sich die Summe auf 48.948 fl.[25] – war die Stadt imstande, die vordringlichen sozialen Aufgaben zu bewältigen, zumal seit 1871 die „formale Leitung der Armenpflege der Gemeindebehörde, die Beschlussfassung den Armencommissionen und die Hilfsaction den Armenpflegern und ihren Collegien" per legem übertragen war.[26] Diese beackerten das Feld der kommunalen Sozialaktivitäten, die durch private und kirchliche Initiativen ergänzt wurden.

---

[22] Hugo Wachner, *Österreichische Sanitätsgesetze und Verordnungen. Mit besonderer Berücksichtigung der einschlägigen Erlässe der k.k. Landesregierung von Kärnten zum Gebrauche für Amtsärzte, Districtsärzte, Staats- und Gemeindeämter, Physicatscandidaten, Apotheker etc.* (Klagenfurt: Kleinmayr, 1896), S. 358.

[23] Mischler, "Armenpflege," S. 515.

[24] Rudolf von Mandorff, "Die öffentliche Armenpflege in Kärnten," in *Österreichs Wohlfahrtseinrichtungen 1848–1898. Festschrift zu Ehren des 50jährigen Regierungsjubiläums Seiner k. u. k. Apostolischen Majestät des Kaisers Franz Joseph I.* Bd. 1, Hrsg. Commission der Österreichischen Wohlfahrts-Ausstellung Wien 1898 (Wien: Verlag von Moritz Perles, 1899), S. 80–103, hier S. 85.

[25] Ebenda, S. 82.

[26] Heinrich von Cardona, "Das städtische Armenwesen in Österreich," in *Österreichs Wohlfahrtseinrichtungen 1848–1898. Festschrift zu Ehren des 50jährigen Regierungsjubiläums Seiner k. u. k. Apostolischen Majestät des Kaisers Franz Joseph I.* Bd. 1, Hrsg. Commission der Österreichischen Wohlfahrts-Ausstellung Wien 1898 (Wien: Verlag von Moritz Perles, 1899), S. 366–389, hier S. 376 f.

Den Kern der Armenfürsorgeklientel bildeten Witwen, Waisen, erwerbsunfähige alte, kranke sowie physisch bzw. geistig beeinträchtigte Menschen. Und die Zahl derer, die über die „Armen-Versorgungsanstalten" sowie „Armen-Institute" versorgt wurden, wuchs seit den 1870er Jahren kontinuierlich an. Damit korrespondierte ein Anstieg der beteilten Armen (Tabelle 6).

Tabelle 7-6: Zahl der in „Versorgungshäusern" untergebrachten Personen pro 10.000 Einwohner 1880–1905

Jahr	Untergebrachte Personen	Jahr	Untergebrachte Personen
1880	182,4	1893	174,1
1881	185,4	1894	173,5
1882	183,0	1895	193,3
1883	180,6	1896	187,7
1884	171,6	1897	205,2
1885	184,9	1898	237,4
1886	176,4	1899	254,9
1887	177,6	1900	217,8
1888	174,6	1901	217,3
1889	172,8	1902	246,0
1890	170,7	1903	260,8
1891	167,9	1904	268,6
1892	165,1	1905	282,5

Quelle: Sandra Salbrechter, "Gesundheit, Krankheit und Tod im Herzogtum Kärnten während des ‚langen' 19. Jahrhunderts – Zwischen staatlichem Wohlfahrtsdenken und ökonomischer Nützlichkeit" (Masterarbeit, Universität Klagenfurt, 2012), S. 102.

Waren es 1880 pro 10.000 Einwohner noch 182,4 gewesen, stieg ihre Zahl bis 1905 auf 282,5 Personen an, wobei sich die Zahl der Frauen innerhalb dieses Zeitraumes fast verdoppelte: von 94 bei insgesamt 201 unterstützten Personen im Jahr 1880 auf 184 von 313 unterstützten Personen im Jahre 1900.[27] Verbunden mit dem Anstieg der von der Gemeinde versorgten Bedürftigen war eine Erhöhung der Finanzmittel: von 21.968 fl. (1880) auf 76.247 Kronen (1900).[28] Bezogen auf den Einzelnen blieben die Geldmittel für die Armenunterstützung im Falle der

---

[27] *Österreichische Statistik* Bd. 37, 2. Heft, S. 271; *Österreichische Statistik N. F.* Bd. 3, 7. Heft, Tafel 24a.
[28] Ebenda.

„Versorgungsanstalten" nur im Wesentlichen konstant. Ähnlich gestaltete sich die Entwicklung im Falle der „Armen-Institute". Die Zahl der „beteilten Armen und Pfleglinge" nahm zu. Mehrheitlich handelte es sich bei den Versorgten um Frauen. 1890 betrug der Frauenanteil mit 310 beteilten Armen fast 70 Prozent,[29] was teils altersbedingte Ursachen hatte. Denn Frauen wurden älter als Männer und konnten im Alter oft keinem Erwerb mehr nachgehen. Viele waren zeit ihres Lebens ledig geblieben, oder sie waren kinderlos verwitwet. Daraus ergab sich ihre Armut. Mit der Zahl der beteilten Personen lag Klagenfurt, wo 1880 247,7 Menschen pro 10.000 Einwohner in den „Armen-Instituten" versorgt wurden (Tabelle 7), weit über dem Landesdurchschnitt.

Tabelle 7-7: Beteilte Personen in den „Armen-Instituten" pro 10.000 Einwohner 1880–1893

Jahr	Beteilte Personen	Jahr	Beteilte Personen
1880	247,7	1887	276,1
1881	231,4	1888	283,9
1882	211,4	1889	261,0
1883	202,4	1890	247,6
1884	216,9	1891	230,6
1885	197,5	1892	234,6
1886	247,7	1893	215,4

Quelle: Salbrechter, "Gesundheit, Krankheit und Tod", S. 102.

Die ökonomische Krise um die Jahrhundertwende verstärkte die Armut in der Stadt. Im Rahmen der Kommunalpolitik bedingte das einen erhöhten Stellenwert der Armenversorgung. Bis Ende der 1870er Jahre waren – dem Trend der Zeit entsprechend – die Normen und Praktiken der Stadtpolitik darauf ausgerichtet gewesen, „Hilfeleistungen für erwerbsfähige Erwachsene weitestgehend hintan zu halten und [...] Geldaushilfen nur an völlig verarmte Alte und chronisch Kranke sowie verwaiste und verlassene Kinder zu vergeben."[30] Mit den sozialpolitischen Bestrebungen der Regierung Taaffe änderte sich das. Die kommunale Armenfürsorge und Sozialpolitik bildeten auf der untersten staatlichen Ebene in dem seitens der Regierung forcierten modernen System sozialer Absicherung einen

---

[29] *Österreichische Statistik N. F.* Bd. 3, 7. Heft, Tafel 24a.
[30] Gerhard Melinz, "Armutspolitik und Sozialversicherungsstaat. Entwicklungsmuster in Österreich (1860 bis zur Gegenwart," *Österreich in Geschichte und Literatur* 47 (2003), S. 135–161, hier S. 140.

wichtigen Mosaikstein. Es ging nicht bloß um die Bereitstellung von
Finanzmitteln zur Linderung der Armut, sondern auch um Fragen der
Nahrungsmittelversorgung   oder   um   die   Bereitstellung   von
Schlafunterkünften. Nicht immer konnte der Hunger gestillt werden. „Die
armen   Leute   waren   angewiesen,   in   Boutiquen   und   sonstigen
Ankauflokalen ihre Nahrung zu suchen, die ihnen in der Regel ziemlich
theuer und noch dazu schlecht gebothen […] waren. Eine andere
Nahrungsweise war den Armen, insbesondere den von Taglohn lebenden
Arbeitern gar nicht möglich, weil ihnen eben die Mittel mangeln, eine
ordentliche Nahrung sich zu verschaffen", hielt ein Bericht an das k.k.
Landespräsidium fest.[31] Und am Vorabend des Ersten Weltkrieges gab es
noch immer solche Fälle, wie auch den Fall, dass eine Schlafstätte gesucht
wurde. So genehmigte der Gemeinderat für „Fräulein Charlotte Heifler
eine Schlafstelle im Bürgerspital".[32] Die Linderung der Armut erforderte
entsprechende Finanzmittel. Die Ausgaben für die „soziale Infrastruktur"
wurden so innerhalb des Stadtbudgets zu einem Faktor, auch wenn dieser
staatlicherseits mehr oder weniger aufgezwungen war. Tendenziell nahm
der Anteil der Sozialausgaben, insbesondere für die Armenversorgung,
kontinuierlich zu. Der prozentuelle Anteil am städtischen Gesamtbudget
blieb aber gering. Die durchschnittlichen Fürsorgeausgaben pro
Einwohner bewegten sich auf einem bescheidenen Niveau. 1910 waren u.
a. für „klassifizierte Institutsarme" 465 K, für die „Ortsarmenbeteiligung"
31.482 K, für die „Kinderbeteilung" 9.000 K, für Naturalien 1.677 K, für
Medikamente 700 K, für auswärtige Arme 9.959 K, das Siechenhaus
24.354 K und das Asylhaus 1.030 K an Aufwendungen vorgesehen.[33]
    Die kommunale Armenfürsorge bildete nur eine Säule in der
Versorgung von in Not geratenen, bedürftigen Personen – vom Kind und
Jugendlichen bis zum alten Menschen. Wer durch das Netz der
öffentlichen Unterstützung fiel, war auf die private Wohltätigkeit und die
Fürsorgeaktivitäten der Kirchen angewiesen. Vor dem Hintergrund des
Wandels von einer feudalen Bischofskirche zu einer Volkskirche
intensivierte sich seitens des Katholizismus die Beschäftigung mit sozialen

---

[31]   KLA Klagenfurt, Stadtarchiv Klagenfurt II, Schachtel 156, Bericht
[Bürgermeister] an k.k. Landespräsidium, 31.8.1876, Zl. 9323.
[32]   Ebenda, Schachtel 219, Protokoll über die ordentliche Sitzung des
Gemeinderates Klagenfurt, 23.9.1913.
[33]   Ebenda, Schachtel 155, Protokoll über die ordentliche Sitzung des
Gemeinderates Klagenfurt, 10.12.1910, Beilage: Bericht und Antrag des
Verwaltungsausschusses über den Rechnungsabschluss des Stadtgemeindefonds
und der übrigen städtischen und unter städtischer Verwaltung stehenden Fonde für
das Rechnungsjahr 1910.

Belangen. Das Ergebnis war als Ausdruck des Prinzips der christlichen Nächstenliebe die Gründung sozial-caritativer Institutionen und kirchlicher Organisationen. Sie boten mit einer starken Ausrichtung auf moralische Ziele die Möglichkeit, spezialisierter auf die Bedürfnisse der Notleidenden einzugehen. Zudem stand das Wohl von besonders unterstützungswerten Gruppen wie Kindern, Jugendlichen und Frauen im Zentrum der Aktivitäten, deren Finanzierung durch Sammlungen, Spenden, Kostgelder, private Stiftungen, aber auch durch Subventionen seitens der Stadt erfolgte. So wurden durch die „Bürgerspitalssektion" veranlasst, „dass die Vertheilung des Joh[ann] Messnerschen Legates pr. 100 fl. unter die Armen im Bürgerspitale vorgenommen worden ist und dass von den 63 Armen jeder 1 fl. 57 kr. – 1 fl." erhielt.[34] 1909 gewährt die Stadt dem „Wohltätigen Frauenverein für die Kleinkinder-Bewahranstalt" eine Subvention in der Höhe von 1.800 K. Das war ein beachtlicher Betrag und ein Viertel der Gesamteinnahmen, zu denen noch u. a. eine Subvention der „Kärntner Sparkasse" (1.200 K), zwei Legate sowie Mitgliedsbeiträge kamen.[35]

Die dynamische Entwicklung im Vereinswesen erfasste im ausgehenden 19. Jahrhundert auch den Typus des sozial-caritativen Vereins. Den Wohltätigkeits- bzw. Sozialfürsorgevereinen fiel eine wichtige Aufgabe zu. Der Vorstand bestand aus Bürgerlichen, Adeligen und im Falle der kirchlichen Vereine aus Geistlichen, so auch im Falle des „Asylvereins für weibliche Dienstboten". Diesen leitete 1906 Marie von Jovanovič, ihre Stellvertreterin war Therese Edle von Metnitz, die Funktion der Schriftführerin und Kassierin bekleidete Josefine Puck.[36] Im Gegensatz zu den Gewerkschafts- und Fachvereinen, deren primäres Ziel die Interessenvertretung und die soziale Versorgung der berufstätigen Bevölkerung war, sowie den humanitären Hilfsvereinen (Gesellenvereine; Krankenunterstützungs- und Leichenbestattungsvereine; Unterstützungsvereine) waren die Wohltätigkeits- und Sozialfürsorgevereine (Tabelle 8) in ihren Aktivitäten ganz auf die Fürsorge für die Armen fokussiert.

---

[34] Ebenda, Schachtel 127, Protokoll über die ordentliche Sitzung des Gemeinderathes Klagenfurt, 9.12.1874.
[35] Ebenda, Schachtel 226, Bericht und Jahresrechnung des „Wohltätigen Frauenvereines für die Kleinkinder-Bewahranstalt" für das Jahr 1909.
[36] F[riedrich] Engel, *Die charitativen und humanitären Vereine und Anstalten im Herzogtume Kärnten* (Wien: Verlag des Reichsverbandes d. Kathol. Wohltätigkeitsorganis., 1908), S. 73 f.

Tabelle 7-8: Wohltätigkeits- bzw. Sozialfürsorgevereine 1867–1914

Verein	gegründet
Elisabethen-Verein der werktätigen Liebe	Oktober 1871
Verein vom hlg. Vinzenz von Paul für freiwillige Armenpflege	Dezember 1872
Verein der Volksküche	Mai 1875
Asylverein für weibliche Dienstboten	13.6.1891
Knabenhort	14.10.1891
Verein zur Bekämpfung der Trunksucht	1899
Wärmestubenverein	1903
Jüdischer Frauen- und Wohltätigkeitsverein	3.7.1908
Verein Jugendfürsorgestelle	29.7.1908
Verein Deutsches Mädchenheim	30.6.1911
Wohlfahrtsverein „Deutsche Hilfe"	24.12.1911
Mädchenwohlfahrt	13.6.1912

Quelle: Vereinskataster – KLA Klagenfurt

Die Befürsorgten erhielten Brennholzzuteilungen, bescheidene Geldhilfen oder Nahrungsmittel, dem einen oder anderen wurde, wenn sich die Notwendigkeit ergab, eine Unterkunft zugewiesen. Den Waisenhäusern, in der Regel unter kirchlicher Leitung, fiel eine besondere Aufgabe in der sozialen Integration der Kinder und Jugendlichen zu. Das Knaben-Waisenhaus des „Vereines vom hlg. Vinzenz von Paul für freiwillige Armenpflege", „der es sich zur Aufgabe gemacht hat[te], das Elend der Mitmenschen aufzusuchen und dasselbe nach Möglichkeit […] mit Wort und That zu lindern", widmete sich den in Not geratenen Jugendlichen.[37] Damit deckte der „Vinzenz-Verein" ein Feld ab, das der Stadtpolitik zu einem Anliegen geworden war: „Eine besondere Obsorge des Gemeinderates wird die Entwicklung der Kinder- und Waisenfürsorge bilden, die […] bereits in günstigen Bahnen ist",[38] stellte Bürgermeister Gustav von Metnitz anlässlich seiner Angelobung fest. Aber die soziale Fürsorge um die Jugendlichen war nur ein Teil der Vereinsaktivitäten, ein anderer Teil konzentrierte sich auf die Versorgung verarmter Familien. Zu diesem Zweck besuchten die Vereinsmitglieder einmal in der Woche für die Unterstützung in Frage kommende Arme, „um ihre Noth genauer

---

[37] KLA Klagenfurt, Stadtarchiv Klagenfurt II, Schachtel 219, Jahresbericht des Vereines vom hlg. Vincenz von Paul für freiwillige Armenpflege, erstattet in der Generalversammlung am 8.12.1873.
[38] Ebenda, Schachtel 155, Protokoll über die ordentliche Sitzung des Gemeinderates Klagenfurt, 6.8.1912.

kennen zu lernen und für entsprechende Unterstützung an Lebensmitteln, Brennmaterialien, Haus- und Arbeitsgeräthen [...] Sorge zu tragen."[39] 1875 wurden „35 Partheien, und zwar 19 Familien und 16 einzelne Arme unterstützt".[40] Im Detail wurden „889 Laib Brot im Wert von 151 fl. 13 kr., 565 Pfund Fleisch (134 fl. 52 kr.), 70 Pfund Milch (5 fl. 4 kr.), 176 Pfund Reis (23 fl. 33 kr.), 23 Pfund Stockfisch (2 fl. 53 kr.), 5 Paar Schuhe (12 fl. 35 kr.), Kleidungsstücke (32 fl. 84 kr.), 2 Klafter Holz (7 fl. 45 kr.), Quartiergeld-Beitrag (30 fl. 50 kr.) sowie Verpflegungskosten (156 fl.)" an die Armen der Stadt verteilt.[41] Die budgetären Mittel für seine Aktivitäten waren begrenzt. 1892 betrugen die Aufwendungen 2.443 fl. 65 kr., ein Jahr später 2.381 fl. 87 kr.[42] Neben dem Knaben-Waisenhaus des „Vinzenz-Vereins" widmete sich das Mädchen-Waisenhaus der Ursulinen, das 1896 120 Pflegekinder zählte, der Ausbildung weiblicher Waisen zu Dienstboten.[43] Letzteren diente das 1892 gegründete „Dienstmädchen-Asyl", das sich um „ältere Dienstboten, die [...] schwer irgendwo Unterkunft" fanden, kümmerte und in dem „gegen ein kleines Entgelt für Wohnung, Beheizung und Beleuchtung [...] Dienstmädchen aus allen Gegenden Kärntens während der [...] Dienstlosigkeit aufgenommen" wurden.[44] Der „Elisabethen-Vereine" fokussierte sich auf die „religiöse und moralische Hebung der Armen und besonders der Kinder und weiblichen Jugend", wobei ihm „die christliche Erziehung verwahrloster Mädchen aus der Klasse der Armen" besonders am Herzen lag.[45] Zu diesem Zweck errichtete er außerhalb der Stadt in Maria Saal eine eigene Anstalt.

Neben den kirchlich-konfessionellen Sozialinstitutionen, deren Gründung das Ergebnis des verstärkten kirchlichen Engagements in der „soziale Frage" war, nahm sich seit den 1890er Jahren ein dichter werdendes Netz

---

[39] Alois Cigoi, *Das sociale Wirken der katholischen Kirche in der Diöcese Gurk (Herzogthum Kärnten)* (Wien: Selbstverlag, 1896), S. 178.

[40] KLA Klagenfurt, Stadtarchiv Klagenfurt II, Schachtel 219, Dritter Jahresbericht des Vereines vom heiligen Vinzenz von Paul für freiwillige Armenpflege in Klagenfurt, erstattet in der Generalversammlung am 8. Dezember 1875.

[41] Cigoi, *Das sociale Wirken der katholischen Kirche*, S. 178.

[42] Ebenda.

[43] Johann Max Hinterwaldner, "Waisenhäuser, Kinderasyle, Internate," in *Österreichs Wohlfahrtseinrichtungen 1848–1898. Festschrift zu Ehren des 50jährigen Regierungsjubiläums Seiner k. u. k. Apostolischen Majestät des Kaisers Franz Joseph I.* Bd. 1, Hrsg. Commission der Österreichischen Wohlfahrts-Ausstellung Wien 1898 (Wien: Verlag von Moritz Perles, 1899), S. 93–178, hier S. 176 f.

[44] Cigoi, *Das sociale Wirken der katholischen Kirche*, S. 158.

[45] Engel, *Die charitativen und humanitären Vereine*, S. 85.

privater sozial-caritativer Vereine der Stadtarmen an. Dazu zählte unter
anderem der „Wohltätige Frauenverein", der sich in seiner „Kleinkinder-
Bewahranstalt" um Kinder im Alter von zwei bis sechs Jahren kümmerte,
um diesen eine „ihrer körperlichen und geistigen Kräften entsprechende
Erziehung zu gewähren".[46] Hinzu kamen der Verein „Knabenhort", der
„Verein zur Bekämpfung der Trunksucht", der „Fürsorgeverein für
Kärntner Krüppelkinder", der „Unterstützungsverein für entlassene
Häftlinge sowie hilf- und schuldlose Familienmitglieder", der „Verein für
Kinderschutz- und Jugendfürsorge", der Verein „Mädchenwohlfahrt" oder
die „Jugendfürsorgestelle", welche „die planmäßige [...] Fürsorge für die
Jugend in Klagenfurt, insbesondere die Fürsorgearbeit an Kindern und
Jugendlichen beiderlei Geschlechts bis zum 18. Lebensjahr, die
Beschaffung der Mittel zur Durchführung der Fürsorgearbeit und die
Sammlung arbeitswilliger Hilfskräfte" für die Vereinsarbeit bezweckte.[47]
Als Mittel zur Erreichung des Vereinszieles dienten u. a. die „Erforschung
der Unterstützungsbedürftigkeit von Kindern und Jugendlichen, denen es
an leiblicher und an sittlicher Pflege" mangelte, weiters die Erteilung von
Auskünften und Ratschlägen, die Kontaktierung der Behörden in Fällen
körperlicher oder sittlicher Schädigung von Kindern und Jugendlichen, die
„Gewährung einmaliger oder wiederkehrender Unterstützungen in Geld
(als Lehrgelder u. a.) oder Naturalien (als Medikamente, Nahrungsmittel,
Kleider, Lernbehelfe u. a.)", die „Unterbringung der Schützlinge in
geeigneten Familien, Dienstorten und Erziehungsanstalten" sowie die
„Aufklärung der Bevölkerung über Notwendigkeit des Kinderschutzes und der
Jugendfürsorge".[48]

Von weitreichender Bedeutung für den Lebensalltag wurde der Verein
„Volksküche",[49] der 1875 das gleichnamige Ausspeisungslokal gründete.
Seitens der Stadtpolitik wurde die Gründung unterstützt. Bis zu diesem
Zeitpunkt waren die armen Leute darauf angewiesen gewesen, sich in
Lokalen ihre Nahrung zu besorgen, welche teuer und zudem von
schlechter Qualität waren. Viele Stadtbewohner konnten sich immer
weniger ein sättigendes Mittagessen leisten. Mit der Schaffung einer
„Volksküche" war es nun möglich, zu leistbaren Preisen zu essen. Die
Notwendigkeit einer günstigen Verköstigungsmöglichkeit für die ärmeren
Bevölkerungsgruppen stand außer Frage: „Daß die Volksküche eine
wirtschaftliche Notwendigkeit für Klagenfurt ist, daß sie vielen

---

[46] KLA Klagenfurt, Stadtarchiv Klagenfurt II, Schachtel 207, Statuten des
"Wohltätigen Frauenvereines in Klagenfurt," 21.2.1902.
[47] Ebenda, Schachtel 212, Satzungen des Vereins „Jugendfürsorge", 1906.
[48] Ebenda.
[49] KLA Klagenfurt, Vereinskataster.

Minderbemittelten und Armen die einzige Möglichkeit bietet, in diesen teuren Zeiten ihre Existenz zu fristen, beweist der steigende Besuch derselben, der oft so groß ist, daß man von einem Massenandrang sprechen kann."[50] Und die Zahl der Konsumenten stieg kontinuierlich an. 1897 wurden fast 700 Personen verköstigt, 1898 waren es schon etwa 1.000 Personen.[51] Vor dem Hintergrund von Lebensmittelpreissteigerungen und der ökonomischen Krise wurde die „Volksküche" zu einer wichtigen Institution für die Ausspeisung der Klagenfurter Bevölkerung. 1905 wurden schon 16.989 Portionen à 24 Heller Fleisch mit Gemüse, 59.180 Portionen à 18 Heller Fleisch mit Gemüse, 80.489 Portionen Suppe à 8 Heller, 37.730 Portionen Suppe à 10 Heller, 14.761 Stück Mehlspeisen à 20 Heller und 34.734 Stück Brot à 4 Heller in einem Gesamtwert von 29.283 Kronen habgegeben.[52] In Zeiten schwieriger ökonomischer Verhältnisse konnte sich aber nicht jeder eine „große Portion" mit Fleisch und Gemüse leisten. Als 1907 der Preis für die „große Portion" von 18 auf 20 Heller angehoben wurde, ging die Zahl der „großen Portionen" von 16.582 auf 12.854 zurück, während die Zahl der preislich günstigeren „kleinen Portionen" von 62.012 auf 68.675 anstieg.[53] Mancher konnte sich gar nur eine Suppe um 8 Heller leisten. 1913 heißt es im Jahresbericht: „Von Jahr zu Jahr begnügt sich […] der größte Teil unserer Besucher, von der Not gezwungen, mit Suppen- und Gemüseportionen zu 10 und 8 Hellern."[54] Der Armenverpflegung verschrieb sich auch der „Wärmestubenverein", in dessen Räumlichkeiten die Bedürftigen „Suppe, Tee und Milch mit Brot zu […] billigen Preisen" erhielten.[55]

Mit der sozialen Frage in Zusammenhang stand indirekt auch das Gesundheitswesen, dessen Ausbau seit der Ära Taaffe forciert wurde. Damit einher ging eine Verdichtung und Modernisierung der gesundheitlichen Versorgung im urbanen Bereich. Auch Klagenfurt schloss sich dieser Entwicklung an, das Netz der ärztlichen Versorgung wurde ausgebaut: Entfielen 1880 auf 10.000 Einwohner 12,89 Ärzte,

[50] *36. Jahresbericht der Klagenfurter Volksküche für das Jahr 1910* (Klagenfurt: Kleinmayr, s. a.).
[51] *23. Jahresbericht der Klagenfurter Volksküche für das Jahr 1897* (Klagenfurt: Kleinmayr, s. a.); *24. Jahresbericht der Klagenfurter Volksküche für das Jahr 1898* (Klagenfurt: Kleinmayr, s. a.).
[52] Engel, *Die charitativen und humanitären Vereine*, S. 75.
[53] *33. Jahresbericht der Klagenfurter Volksküche für das Jahr 1907* (Klagenfurt: Kleinmayr, s. a.).
[54] *39. Jahresbericht der Klagenfurter Volksküche für das Jahr 1913* (Klagenfurt: Kleinmayr, s. a.).
[55] Engel, *Die charitativen und humanitären Vereine,* S. 89.

waren es 1906 bereits 17,57 Ärzte.[56] Ferner wurde 1896 ein neues Krankenhaus eröffnet, 1907 kam noch ein Sanatorium hinzu. Somit verfügte die Stadt 1910 über vier Krankenhäuser mit 550 Betten. Im Vergleich zu 1880 war das eine Zunahme von 200 Betten. Hand in Hand damit ging eine Zunahme der in den Krankenanstalten aufgenommenen und behandelten Personen. Waren 1880 pro 10.000 Einwohner 2.027 Patienten behandelt worden, stieg die Zahl der Behandelten bis 1910 auf 2.981 Patienten an.[57] Im Zusammenhang mit dem Sanitätswesen und der Armenfürsorge standen die „Humanitätsanstalten", zu denen u. a. Kinderkrippen, „Kinderbewahranstalten" sowie Taubstummen- und Blindenerziehungsinstitute gezählt wurden. Die Zahl der in ihnen betreuten Personen nahm zu, obwohl die Zahl der Blinden und Taubstummen seit den 1890er Jahren kontinuierlich abnahm. Die „Kinderbewahranstalten" wiederum waren ein Auslaufmodell, da nun an ihre Stelle der öffentlich-städtische Kindergarten trat, in dem die Drei- bis Sechsjährigen während der elterlichen Berufstätigkeit betreut wurden.

Die Prinzipien der staatlichen Sozialpolitik, wie sie von der Regierung des „Eisernen Ringes" und den Nachfolgeregierung entsprechend den Konzepten zur Lösung der „sozialen Frage" umgesetzt wurden,[58] fanden im Falle von Klagenfurt im ausgehenden 19. und beginnenden 20. Jahrhundert seitens der Stadtregierungen eine adäquate Berücksichtigung. Wie in anderen Städten Cisleithaniens erlebte die kommunale Fürsorgepolitik auch in Klagenfurt eine Reformperiode. Das soziale Netz und die Armenversorgung wurden in kleinen Schritten ausgebaut, wobei das Prinzip der „offenen" Fürsorge Priorität hatte. Ungeachtet der Relevanz der „sozialen Frage" und – damit im Zusammenhang stehend – der Armenfürsorge verfügte die Stadt Klagenfurt am Vorabend des Ersten Weltkrieges im Vergleich zu den 1870er Jahren über eine dichter gewordene Infrastruktur sozialer Institutionen zur Linderung der Not der Stadtarmen. Die Weichen in Richtung einer aktiven städtischen Wohlfahrtspolitik waren gestellt.

---

[56] Sandra Salbrechter, "Gesundheit, Krankheit und Tod im Herzogtum Kärnten während des ‚langen' 19. Jahrhunderts – Zwischen staatlichem Wohlfahrtsdenken und ökonomischer Nützlichkeit" (Masterarbeit, Universität Klagenfurt, 2012), S. 52.
[57] Ebenda, S. 72.
[58] Vgl. Werner Drobesch, "Ideologische Konzepte zur Lösung der ‚sozialen Fragen'," in *Die Habsburgermonarchie 1848–1918 IX. Soziale Strukturen, 1. Tl.bd. Von der feudal-agrarischen zur bürgerlich-industriellen Gesellschaft, Tl.bd. 1/ 2. Von der Stände- zur Klassengesellschaft*, Hrsg. Helmut Rumpler und Peter Urbanitsch (Wien: Verlag der Österreichischen Akademie der Wissenschaften, 2010), S. 1419–1563.

Fig. 7-1 10. Oktober-Straße 1909 (Fotonachweis: Privatsammlung Joachim Eichert; für die Gewährung des Copyrights sei Herrn Eichert herzlich gedankt)

Fig. 7-2 Heuplatz, um 1890 (Fotonachweis: Privatsammlung Joachim Eichert)

Fig. 7-3 Siechenhauskaserne o. J. (Fotonachweis: Privatsammlung Joachim Eichert)

Chapter Eight

Municipal Social Welfare in Bratislava during the 19th and Early 20th Centuries: Examples and Modernisation Trends

Gabriela Dudeková

Abstract: A study on the modernisation of the municipal social care in Bratislava/Pressburg in the 19th and early 20th centuries. The study characterises the main principles, forms of organisation and stages of modernisation of the care for the poor in Hungary at both the municipal and the state level. It follows the processes of secularisation, specialisation, rationalisation, bureaucratisation, professionalisation and humanisation, as well as the degree of participation of the state in organising the care for the poor and the social policy in Hungary. Hungary specifically – compared to Cisleithania – only to a small extent shared of the state in the organisation and financing of overall social care. A strongly decentralised system of care for the poor existed in Hungary, based on the duty of the home municipalities. This practice continued until the dissolution of the Habsburg Monarchy. The vast majority of charitable, social and socio-health facilities remained under the control of single municipalities, churches and various civic associations. This insufficient system of social policy in Hungary resulted in omitting large groups of socially dependent people from state and municipal social assistance.

The study[1] aims to define the main principles and forms of the organisation of public social care in Bratislava during the long 19th century. Subsequently, the study describes their transformation into a form which already contained elements of the municipal social policy. We focus on both the development stages and modernisation of the welfare system, particularly on the poverty policy. The development stages and trends are

---

[1] The research for this article was done within the Project APVV-00119-11 at the Institute of History, Slovak Academy of Sciences, Bratislava.

demonstrated in the example of selected institutions and organisers which provided care for the poor and operated in the city over a longer period of time and are thus marked by long continuity – a city hospital, infirmary, workhouse and Women's charitable society.

As for the name of the city, we use its then-contemporary Slovak name – Pressburg[2] – to cover the period before the collapse of the Habsburg Monarchy. The city was renamed Bratislava in March 1919.

The gradual evolution from decentralised care to a systematic municipal social policy was characterised by a number of fundamental trends. While in the 18th century numerous charitable institutions related to the church dominated social care, during the 19th century specialised local civic associations gained superiority and dominance and worked alongside institutes within particular religious communities. At the turn of the 19th and 20th centuries, the state significantly entered into municipal social care and the socio-health sphere as a whole. Nationalisation of the care for certain categories of socially dependent persons (e.g. orphans) and (partial or complete) state take-over of institutions became common in the then Hungary. The main features of the modernisation process in the field of social care were gradual secularisation, specialisation, rationalisation, bureaucratisation, professionalisation and humanisation, accompanied by efforts to nationalise originally religious and/or municipal facilities.

These processes were obviously determined by developments in the political status of the city and its economic and social character during the period. Since the late 18th century, the city had been transformed from a temporary capital of Hungary into one of the most important, yet still only provincial centres, a so-called "municipality." Due to urbanisation and industrial development, the city changed from a craft-trade town into an industrial centre, with a corresponding influx of population, resulting in the emergence of new specific social problems. Thanks to such a boom, the city proudly carried the attribute "the second city of Hungary." In 1910, Pressburg had nearly 80,000 inhabitants and a multicultural population – Germans traditionally accounted for the majority, the second

---

[2] German equivalent of the historical name of the city was Pressburg and Pozsony in Hungarian. See Elena Mannová and Gabriela Dudeková, "Komu patrí Bratislava? Multietnické mesto ako miesto lokálnej, národnej a nadnárodnej reprezentácie" [To whom belongs Bratislava? A multiethnic city as a place of local, national and transnational representation] in *Medzi provinciou a metropolou. Obraz Bratislavy v 19. a 20. storočí* [Between a province and a metropolis. Reflection of Bratislava in the 19th and 20th centuries], ed. Gabriela Dudeková et al. (Bratislava: Historický ústav SAV, 2012), p. 12 and following for more details on using the historical names for the city.

largest group were Hungarians, followed by Slovaks. Religious affiliation played an extremely important role in the organisation of social welfare in the city. In terms of religion, Pressburg was at that time comprised of two-thirds Roman Catholic, about a third Protestant, and approx. 8–10% Jewish.

The status of the city had a significant impact on the level and organisation of social policy. Current research confirms findings of contemporary authors – given its status of "a substitute capital," public social care in Pressburg was much more advanced and its institutions much more efficient and more differentiated than in other Hungarian cities, and in some respects even better than Budapest (resp. Buda and Pest),[3] as some social care institutions located in Pressburg at the time were of all-Hungarian importance.[4] Even after the decline of the prestigious political importance of Pressburg in the middle of the 19th century, its developed network of charitable and social institutions continued to function without any significant changes.

The provision of social welfare in urban areas was carried out on the fundamental principles of poverty policy within the state. Contemporary attitudes toward socially needy people also played a role. The organisation of care for the poor had retained two fundamental principles in Hungary – and throughout the entire Habsburg Monarchy – since the 16th century. The first was the obligation of municipalities to deliver basic social assistance to its population under the right of domicile and legal

---

[3] See Anna Falisová and Gabriela Dudeková, "Úroveň zdravotníctva ako znak veľkomesta. Plusy a mínusy zdravotníckej starostlivosti v Prešporku/Bratislave" [The level of health care as a feature of a metropolis], *Medzi provinciou a metropolou. Obraz Bratislavy v 19. a 20. storočí* [Between a province and a metropolis. Reflection of Bratislava in the 19th and 20th centuries], ed. Gabriela Dudeková et al. (Bratislava: Historický ústav SAV, 2012), pp. 143–160.

[4] Ingrid Kušniráková, "Vplyv konfesionálneho rozdelenia spoločnosti na systém sociálnej starostlivosti v Bratislave v období 17. – 18. storočia" [The impact of confessional division of a society on the system of social care in Bratislava in the 17th and 18th centuries], *Történeti Tanulmányok* 15, Acta Universitatis Debreceniensis Series Historica, no. 59 (2007): pp. 141–151; Ingrid Kušniráková, "Mecenáši, dobrodinci a patróni. Komemoratívna kultúra uhorských spoločenských elít v Prešporku raného novoveku" [Benefactors, philantropists and patrons. Comemmorative culture of Hungarian social elites in Presburg in Early Modern era] in *Medzi provinciou a metropolou. Obraz Bratislavy v 19. a 20. storočí* [Between a province and a metropolis. Reflection of Bratislava in the 19th and 20th centuries], ed. Gabriela Dudeková et al. (Bratislava: Historický ústav SAV, 2012), pp. 78–82.

residence.[5] And the second was the principle of subsidiarity – the principle that the abovementioned obligation of municipalities to support persons in need began only when all other options within existing social safety nets had been exhausted (meaning close and extended family, neighbourhood community, charitable activity of the church and the civic charity). An important criterion for deciding to grant or deny social assistance was the assessment of "eligibility"/"necessity." Yet this was primarily based on moral criteria and contemporary understanding of the causes of poverty and not on the real social situation of a particular needy person. These principles of an organised welfare system also became its greatest weakness. As a result of the application of such criteria during the rapid growth of mass poverty in the period of industrialisation, entire population groups remained completely outside of the public social safety net.[6]

The reform of social care by Joseph II was to all intents and purposes not carried out in Hungary.[7] A strongly decentralised way of organising

---

[5] The oldest regulation which obliged municipalities to look after their poor is the police order by Ferdinand I from 1552. It cracked down on beggars and vagrants as it considered them to be socially undesirable. Harald Wendelin, "Schub und Heimatrecht," in *Grenze und Staat. Paßwesen, Staatsbürgerschaft, Heimatrecht und Fremdengesetzgebung in der österreichischen Monarchie (1750–1867)*, eds. Waltraud Heindl and Edith Sauer (Wien – Köln – Weimar: Böhlau Verlag, 2000), p. 181; Ernst Bruckmüller, *Sozialgeschichte Österreichs* (Wien – München: Oldenbourg Wissenschaftsverlag, 1985), p. 183; Ilse Reiter, *Ausgewiesen, abgeschoben. Eine Geschichte des Ausweisungsrechts in Österreich vom ausgehenden 18. bis ins 20. Jahrhundert* (Frankfurt am Main: Peter Lang, 2000), p. 148; Andor Csizmadia, *A szociális gondoskodás változásai Magyarországon* (Budapest: MTA Állam. es Jogtud. Int., 1977), p. 139ff. Later, this principle was embedded in Hungarian acts on municipalities from 1871 and 1886.
[6] For more details, see: Gabriela Dudeková, "Právo alebo milosrdenstvo? Domovská príslušnosť ako základný princíp sociálnej starostlivosti v Uhorsku" [Law or mercy? Domicile as a basic principle of social welfare in Hungary], in Dušan Kováč et al., *Sondy do slovenských dejín v dlhom 19. storočí* [Sondes into Slovak history in the long 19th century], (Bratislava: Historický ústav SAV, 2013), pp. 196–213.
[7] Joseph II attempted to establish a poverty policy system under state control in Hungary. Yet in the end it was only state supervision over financial expenses of individual facilities that was implemented. Additionally, some particular facilities were somewhat reformed. Yet neither a network of institutes for the care of the poor (Armeninstituten) nor specialized institutes under state supervision came into being. See Ingrid Kušniráková, *Piae fundationes. Zbožné fundácie a ich význam pre rozvoj uhorskej spoločnosti v ranom novoveku* [Piae fundationes. Pious foundations and their significance for the development of Hungarian society in the Early Modern era], Bratislava 2009, p. 156.

social care existed there, based on the responsibilities of municipalities with only minimal state interference. This system functioned until the end of the Habsburg Monarchy. The vast majority of charitable, social and socio-health facilities worked within the framework of churches and charitable associations. The specifics of Hungary compared to Cisleithania was the small measure of the share of the state in the organisation and financing of social care. The main part of the care for the poor rested on the shoulders of municipalities. The overall level and efficiency of social care in Hungary remained insufficient for these reasons and its organisers/organisations struggled with a constant lack of financial resources.[8]

While in rural areas a simple traditional and easily controllable form of social assistance prevailed, in major cities quite mature and systematised communal social work developed during the 19th century. It was conducted by institutions managed by urban municipal authorities, religious communities and burgher's associations (charitable or self-help). The motive for the reorganisation of social welfare in municipalities as well as at a state level was to increase its efficiency and to achieve the greatest possible centralisation of financial resources. Both better coordination and centralisation were supposed to guarantee more efficient controls against the misuse of social assistance as well.

Hospital versus Lazaret

In the examples of the earliest social care facilities in Pressburg – Hospital and Lazaret – we can observe progress in the gradual transformation of the original church and municipal institutions in the longer term. In the case of the so-called "Hospital", this transformation meant a gradual shift from centuries-old tradition of self-management to subsidisation by the city of Pressburg and on to its complete takeover in the management by a civic association running the Hospital in 1830. This institute, which was the oldest in the city[9] (originally under church administration), had a universal character as a home for elderly people as well as being a poorhouse. Obviously, it also served as a medical centre and a social institution with accumulated functions. Later, this Hospital was passed to city administration and to municipal property.[10] In 1769, the

---

[8] Dudeková, *Právo alebo milosrdenstvo*, pp. 201–202.
[9] The Pressburg Hospital dates back to the 12th century and the first reliable document on its existence comes from 1309. Anton Špiesz, *Bratislava v 18. storočí* [Bratislava in the 18th century], Bratislava 1987, p. 220.
[10] This institute carried the name "Hospital" until the 1830s, regardless of the

Hospital came under strong pressure from the Hungarian Royal Chamber in order to reach the transformation of its relatively large real estate into capital assets.[11] However, the early 19th century brought an economic crisis into this institution and for this reason it was transformed into a civilian associational facility under the supervision of the municipal administration in the 1830s. From 1830 it began to operate under the name Catholic burghers' nursing home (Katholische Bürgerversorgungsanstalt) as a facility for the care of old impoverished citizens of Catholic faith with permanent residency in Pressburg.[12]

Unlike the Hospital, the so-called "Lazaret" was established in the 17th century from the beginning as a municipal facility. It served as a general poorhouse. In the 18th century, a shift in the organisation of communal care for the poor occurred, moving it from the Hospital to Lazaret. During the reorganisation of social care at this time, Lazaret was reconstructed and its capacity expanded to accommodate socially dependent old persons, foundlings and the mentally ill. This intention was successfully carried out thanks mainly to the generous financial support of Maria Theresa.[13] The development of Lazaret in the next century reflects the process of specialisation and professionalisation of institutional care, when specialised institutions of social and socially-medical care for different categories of persons were created under the aegis of the city of Pressburg. During the 19th century, the Lazaret building served not only as a general poorhouse, but it also housed other social institutions and facilities operated by the city, as these facilities were not being provided by any specific building. The municipal administration temporarily placed orphans there, another part of the premises served for a brief time as a

---

change of its original purposes. First, it was originally under the management of the Catholic Church (order Antonito). Since 1309 it functioned as a municipal institute for the care of the poor and in 1397 it became city property. Stefan V. Vámossy, *Die katholische Bürgerversorgungs-Anstalt in Preßburg. Festschrift aus Anlaß des fünfhundertjährigen Bestehens der Anstalt* (Preßburg: Im Verlage der Anstalt, 1898), p. 19.

[11] Špiesz, *Bratislava*, pp. 221–222.

[12] The name of the association managing this facility was "Catholic civil caregiving association" (Katholischer Bürgerversorgungs-Verein). Vámossy, *Die katholische Bürgerversorgungs-Anstalt*, p. 3.

[13] The reconstructions and extensions were finished in 1735 and in 1778. Károly Kanka, "Adatok Pozsony városának orvosi helyrajzásához," in *Pozsony és környéke. A magyar orvosok és természetvizsgálók 1856 évben Pozsonyban tartott XI. nagy-gyülésén emlékéül* (Pozsony: Wigand, 1865), p. 223; Tivadar Ortvay, *Pozsony város utcái és terei. A város története utca- és térnevekben*, Pozsony 1905 [Reprint Budapest 1991], p. 40.

general municipal hospital, while another part served temporarily as a children's hospital until the city completed the construction of its own building (in 1894).[14]

Lazaret and Hospital differed significantly from each other in their capacity and in the level of care. While Lazaret provided only basic accommodation to its inmates, who had to cover all other expenses by themselves (typically from alms), until the end of the 17th and beginning of the 18th centuries, Hospital was able to ensure a full provision to its inmates thanks to its property and in-house management. While the Lazaret capacity was still expanding, the hospital constantly ensured a provision of about 30 to 40 persons.[15] Since the 1860s, the Hospital clearly fulfilled the function of a selective retirement home, which provided a significantly higher standard. In the 1830s, the management of this Catholic citizens' nursing home of St. Ladislaus (commonly called by its colloquial name "Burgher hospital") decided to erect a new building modelled on the Vienna Bürgerspital.[16] Thus its capacity rose to about 40 inmates (who received full support, including clothing). In addition, it also provided open social care through the allocation of cash and in-kind benefits.[17] In 1898, on the occasion of the 500th anniversary of the passing of the property to the city, a new building with 26 rooms for 62 inmates was erected for the "Burgher hospital." There was surprisingly a high quality of diet – the inmates received meat up to five times a week, except for fast days.[18] The social origin of its residents also matched the standard

---

[14] A part of the building served as a municipal hospital until 1857, between 1856–1864 there was a regional eye hospital. Ortvay, *Pozsony város*, p. 40.

[15] Špiesz, *Bratislava*, pp. 220–222; Karl Uhl, *Ueber die frühern Schicksale und den jetzigen Bestand des Bürger-Spitals und der dazu gehörigen Kirche zum h. Ladislaus in Preßburg. Nebst einer Aufforderung an die Bewohner dieser k. Freistadt, zur thätigen Mitwirkung bei der beabsichtigen neuen Gestaltung derselben* (Preßburg: Karl K. Snischek, 1830), pp. 21–22.

[16] In 1830, the then administrator and a religious leader called on the public for financial support for the reconstruction of the old building and the erection of a new building. The old one was significantly damaged by the flooding of the Danube. At this time, the institution cared for 26 persons. Uhl, *Ueber die frühern Schicksale*, pp. 3–10, 40–42.

[17] István Vámossy, *A pozsonyi katholikus polgári ápoló intézet. Fennállásának ötszáz évfordulója alkalmából* (Pozsony: Az intézet kiadványa, 1898), p. 96.

[18] Since 1875, a newly established city cookery, so-called "Municipal people's kitchen" provided the inmates with food. The diet composition showed a high standard: 0.3 litre of coffee with a bun for breakfast; lunch consisted of 0.3 litre of soup + 100 g of cooked meat with a side dish and a dessert, once a week instead of soup there was a goulash with potatoes; on Fridays it was soup, lentils or vegetable

selection and focus of this retirement home: its residents were impoverished local artisans and wine growers (in particular widows coming from the same social groups). Of the 20 women residing there, 15 were widows and 2 were unmarried. The age of male residents ranged from 69 to 82, female residents were 69 to 89 years old (3 of them were of age 89). Interestingly, there are also records confirming a division of married couples into two different nursing homes: Maria Babosch (75 years old) had been living in the Hospital of St. Ladislaus, whereas her husband was in the care of the Lutheran almshouses.[19] In the early 20th century, this institution accommodated 20 men and 20 women, and each room was shared by two inmates. Their social and medical care was provided by St. Vincent de Paul nuns. Medical supervision was conducted by a municipal doctor.[20] The selective character of this facility was anchored in its statutes. According to the Statutes, the Hospital was dedicated to look after "local impoverished citizens of Catholic faith, who have always led a proper way of life, and – apart from truly exceptional unfortunate cases – have fulfilled their citizens' obligations and who have duly paid legal tax and diligently run their businesses for at least 20 years."[21]

In contrast, the city poorhouse was called Lazaret, and it was primarily designed for poor people unable to work who had permanent residency in Pressburg. Its occupants were generally people from the lowest social classes. The key conditions for being admitted to Lazaret were both permanent residency in Pressburg and the inability to secure a livelihood on their own due to old age or illness. A special municipal committee decided on admission to this institution. The capacity of this facility was always being expanded: during the 18th century, it reached a capacity of nearly 200 inmates (from an original 30 beds),[22] In the 1860s, Lazaret could accommodate approximately 150 persons. In addition, the inmates

---

side dish with pasta; on Sundays it was a thick soup + 100 g of cooked meat + 150 g rice or boiled potatoes and a dessert. Roasted meat and wine were on the menu on public holidays.

[19] Namensverzeichniß der Pfründner zu Anfang 1898, in Vámossy, *Die katholische Bürgerversorgungs-Anstalt*, pp. 129–130.

[20] Gábor Pávai-Vajna, "Pozsony sz. kir. város egészségügyének fejlődése az utóbbi ötven év alatt. 1856–1906," in *1856–1906 Emlékmű. Kiadja a Pozsonyi Orvos-Természettudományi egyesület fennállásának ötvenedik évfordulója alkalmából*, eds. Jakab Fischer et al. (Pozsony: Bratislava Orvos-természettudományi egyesület, 1907), p. 123.

[21] Statuten des Preßburger kath. Bürgerversorgungs-Vereines zum heil. Ladislaus, Article 1, in Vámossy, *Die katholische Bürgerversorgungs-Anstalt*, p. 133.

[22] Spiesz, *Bratislava*, p. 222.

were provided with food and clothing.[23] In the early 20th century, in connection with the acceleration of Pressburg's industrialisation, the number of those in poverty increased and in the words of municipal doctor Gabor Vajna "due to the menacing rise of pauperism", it was necessary to enlarge its capacity by purchasing the adjacent building in 1906. The average number of residents was thereby increased up to 90–100 females plus 50 to 60 male inmates.[24] The care for inmates in Lazaret was, compared to St. Ladislaus Hospital, at only a basic level. The Municipal People's Kitchen provided both Lazaret and a city workhouse with food. It was merely a monotonous diet and meat was only served twice a week.[25]

Since both the Hospital and Lazaret retained an exclusively Catholic character, Protestant and Jewish religious communities founded special nursing homes serving the members of these two communities under their own administration in the 1880s and 1890s.[26]

From a sweathouse to asylum for the homeless

The organisation of the poverty policy took the form of a combination of social assistance to selected categories of those in poverty accompanied by repressive measures. The development of the institution of forced labour in the form of so-called "workhouses" illustrates not only a degree of repression against people on the margins of society, but also changing attitudes toward poverty and unemployment as a result of progressive urbanisation and industrialisation. The procedures of an enlightened state – seeking to ensure state control and discipline of all social groups – resulted in a change of existing attitudes to poverty. The idea of sacred poverty was replaced by the negative stereotypical image of a work-shy beggar with criminal tendencies, who had to be put back on track and punished by forced labour. The Emperor Joseph II intended to establish a network of so-called "parish poor institutions" (Pfararmen-Instituten) as central authorities for local care for the poor. These assumed a strict distinction of beggars under the category of employability. Traditional recipients of the

---

[23] Kanka, *Adatok*, p. 223.

[24] Pávai-Vajna, *Pozsony*, p. 124.

[25] A typical lunch during the working week consisted of 700 ml soup, sauce, 500 g rye bread; on Sundays and Thursdays there was an extra portion of 90 g beef meat. Ortvay, *Pozsony város*, p. 409.

[26] The evangelical community founded its nursing home in 1885 and it provided indigent care for 23 elderly and sick inmates of evangelical religion around 1900, the Jewish nursing home was founded in 1895 to look after 31 indigent members of the Jewish religious community. Ibid, pp. 126–127.

care for the poor, such as widows, orphans, physically and mentally handicapped and elderly persons, were considered "worthy" of aid. They were strictly distinguished from the "undeserving" able-bodied beggars. Moreover, police actions against beggars became codified in the Criminal Code of Joseph II from 1787, presenting a conditional mercy with a constant threat of repression.

In Pressburg, the "poor institute" was founded in November 1787 by detailed regulations drawn up by Joseph II (the order of the Hungarian Royal Regency Council from September 1787). At the same time, the city established a prohibition on begging. A newly established workhouse also functioned as a tool for tackling problems of poverty and begging in the city. From the first month of its activity it supported over 300 poor persons in three categories.[27] According to regulations made by the Royal Regency Council, the individuals on welfare were obliged to carry a special badge, which showed a city coat of arms, mark of the category and the relevant urban district.[28] In subsequent periods, the poor institute became further adapted to the local conditions and later incorporated into the already existing network of municipal social welfare.

The example of the Pressburg institution of forced labour illustrates the gradual removal of repressive measures against people without work. Partly, it was the result of a new understanding of poverty and unemployment, and partly this phenomenon was dismissed due to the humanisation of social care. The development of the institution of forced labour in Hungary also shows that this trend could be disrupted and reversed.

The city workhouse (*Domus laboratoria, Arbeitshaus, Dologház*) was established by a municipal council in Pressburg in 1809 as a tool for forced labour of formerly prosecuted persons. Practically from its inception,

---

[27] *Preßburg*, Preßburger Zeitung, November 24, 1787, no. 94, p. 1; *Rechnungsauszug. Über Empfang und Ausgaben des Armeninstituts in der Königl. Frey-Stadt Preßburg für das Monat Novemb. Und Decemb. 1787*, Preßburger Zeitung, January 2, 1788, no. 1, p. 8.

[28] In this regulation, the special badge for poor individuals was described as follows: "Unter dem Zeichen verstehet man ein blechenes Schild, worin die Stadtwappe und unterhalb, die Klasse, in welche der Arme eingesetzet sich befindet, nämlich in der erster Klasse I. C. in der zweyten II. C. und in der Dritten III. C. einzuprägen ist, mit derley Zeichen müssen demnach die institutsmässigen Armen versehet werden, theils weil sie bey der Betheilung diese Zeichen dem Armenvater vorweisen müssen, theils weil hinkünftig nach den Direktivregeln keine andere Armen in einer institutsmässig regulirten Stadt gedultet werden dürften." Concl. Cons. No. 29259, die 4. Sept. 1787 Instituta pauperum. Franciscus Xav. Linzbauer, *Codex sanitario-medicinalis Hungarie*, vol. 3/1, Budae 1853, p. 383.

the workhouse also contained a so-called "voluntary part", where the able-bodied inmates were transferred from Lazaret. Attempts to turn it into a prison-type institution with a broader regional scope (for the entire territory of the district of Pressburg) – promoted by provincial authorities during the Bach neo-absolutism – were unsuccessful.[29] The city strongly fought against nationalisation of this facility and insisted on maintaining its municipal character as well as on the existence of the voluntary part of the workhouse (under threats that they would close the workhouse as a whole). After restoring legislative conditions in Hungary (from 1860) a return to the original legal status occurred at the Pressburg workhouse. In 1862, the municipality renamed this facility as the "Asylum for the Homeless", and the forced and voluntary parts were strictly separated. A further weakening of the punitive function of the Asylum occurred in the late 1860s – in 1869, the inmates in the forced part rebelled against adhering to existential and substandard working conditions.[30] The original workhouse was thus transformed into a facility for the homeless, which was dominated by voluntary work.[31] The reasons why the Town Police Office (the so-called "town capitanate") placed detained persons into the Asylum during the 1870s were as follows: the inability to prove employment or property sufficient to ensure the livelihood, begging, vagrancy and exceptionally also drunkenness. People placed in the Asylum were largely craftsmen's helpers, day labourers or persons without employment; the gender composition was as follows: a third were female and two thirds male[32] (in other types of social institutions the ratio was generally reversed).

In the early 20th century this institution was named "Urban Asylum or so-called workhouse", and it stated "employment of wicked homeless and placement of the homeless" to be its two main tasks.[33] Its inmates were busy doing tailoring work, shoemaking, carpentry and other craft work, while some of them worked on maintenance of roads and streets. Expenses

---

[29] In February 1855, the central authorities placed in sweatshops prisoners without the consent of the municipality and installed their own personnel, while the municipality lost the right of decision on placing inmates. Norbert Duka, *K histórii robotárne a jej budovy v Bratislave* [A contribution to the history of the workhouse and its building in Bratislava], *Spisy Mestského múzea v Bratislave*, a yearbook, vol. 4 (1969): pp. 167–206, here pp. 196–198.

[30] For more details on this rebellion: *Unser Arbeitshaus I. – IV.*, Preßburger Zeitung, September 22 – 25, 1869, p. 2.

[31] For more details on humanitarian transformation of this facility: "Unser 'freiwilliges Arbeitshaus,'" Preßburger Zeitung, November 20, 1869, pp. 2–3.

[32] Duka, *K histórii robotárne*, p. 200.

[33] Pávai-Vajna, *Pozsony*, p. 125.

for their provision were deducted from their earnings and what remained
was paid in cash on release from the Asylum. Increasing unemployment
was reflected in the upward trend of the number of inmates placed in both
parts of the Asylum (while in the 1890s there were around 180 people
accommodated, in 1905 it had increased to more than 400 persons per
year).[34] The level of provided care was very basic and monotonous when
compared to the quality of the Lazaret provisions.[35]

In general, the sweathouses became transformed into voluntary
asylums for the homeless in other Hungarian cities during the second half
of the 19th century. Escalating poverty, unemployment and population
migration to larger cities for work evoked repeated criticism of the
inefficient organisation of the Hungarian system of social care. Various
solutions were proposed by politicians and social reformers at that time, in
particular the ones based on positive experience from abroad – a greater
involvement of the state in the organisation – in particular in financing of
care for the poor and other sectors of social policy. Other proposals were
intended to coordinate and centralise the existing parts of the social safety
net. Yet the increase in the number of beggars and vagrants encouraged
efforts to reinforce control and enforcement. Despite the criticism of such
practices and despite arguing that the institute of forced labour in the past
did not bring the expected results, a new law aimed against "publicly
dangerous loafers" became effective in Hungary in 1913 and it re-enacted
the existence of forced labour duty as well as re-introducing workhouses.[36]

The Pressburg Charitable Women's Association and the reorganisation of the municipal system of the care for the poor

While the organisation of poverty policy, built on a network of
poorhouses, orphanages and other institutions under the supervision of the
state, failed to be implemented in practice in Hungary, the idea of
establishing a central municipal office – respecting religious and civic
charitable institutions – became widely accepted. Increasing charitable
activities of civic societies during the first third of the 19th century led to

---

[34] Ortvay, *Pozsony város*, pp. 408–410; Duka, *K histórii robotárne*, pp. 202–203.
[35] The Asylum residents were given a thick soup for breakfast, the lunch was
brought from Lazaret (see note 24), and the lunch leftovers were consumed for
dinner. Ortvay, *Pozsony város*, pp. 408–409.
[36] For more details, see the study and the sources cited in Dudeková, *Právo alebo
milosrdenstvo*, pp. 210–212.

the stabilisation of both the care for the poor and the general social care in Hungarian cities. Its fundamental principle was the cooperation of charitable religious societies and civic charities with municipal self-governments. This model was followed in Pressburg as well. A significant reorganisation of social care in Pressburg was carried out in 1834–35 by establishing a central body called the "Association for the care of the poor" (Armenversorgunsverein) whose headquarters directed activity of various social institutions and associations throughout the city. The basis of this reorganising lay in the cooperation of voluntary civic associations with the municipality in order to optimise spending, achieve centralisation and to increase targeting of social assistance. This central body directed the actions of committees for different social institutions under the supervision of the city. The city workhouse was controlled by a special commission. In addition, a commission for the management of the municipal poorhouse existed – Lazaret (at that time, orphans were also housed in its building) and a special commission operated for the open form of care for the poor, i.e. granting cash benefits to the poor (in fact, previous Armeninstitut).[37] The question of financing municipal care for the poor in Pressburg was centrally solved by collecting contributions in the city surcharges on the property tax.[38] The Pressburg Charitable Women's Association (Preßburger Wohltätige Frauenverein) also worked under the auspices of the central association. At its inception in 1830–31 two main objectives of their prospective activities were set: to establish and manage an orphanage and children's care centres.

Hungarian women's associations, whose scope was primarily charity, in the second half of the 19th century formed more than half of all charitable associations in Hungary.[39] Women could act there as patrons, representatives, honorary members, as well as eager volunteers and pragmatic organisers. The status of women in society and their limited

---

[37] *Achter Jahresbericht über die in Pressburg erzielte Abstellung der Gassenbettelei. Zeitraum vom 1. November 1842 bis 31. Oktober 1843. Nebst einem kurzgefassten Berichte über die hiesigen Wohltaetigkeitsanstalten*, Pressburg, n. d., pp. iii–vi.
[38] *Vierter Jahresbericht die in der königlichen Frei- und Krönungsstadt Preßburg zu stande gebrachte Abschaffung der Gassen- und Strassenbettelei, den Zustand des damit in Verbindungen gebrachten Arbeitshauses, des Armeninstituts, der Verwaltung des städtischen Lazareths und die aus dessen Fond verpflegten Findel- und Waisenkinder. Für den Zeitabschnitt vom 1. Nov. 1838 bis 31. Okt. 1839.* n. p., n. d.; Kanka, *Adatok*, p. 224.
[39] Gyula Vargha, *Magyarország egyletei és társulatai 1878-ban. Hivatalos Statisztikai Közlemények* (Budapest: Az Athenaeum r. társ. könyvnyomdája, 1880), pp. v–xxxxi.

access to education was also reflected in the organisational structure of women's associations, as until nearly the end of the 19th century the professional functions (Treasurer, Executive Chairman, Secretary) were mostly carried out by men. This was true even for the Pressburg Women's Association,[40] which was in existence for quite some time (this association functioned in the years 1830 to 1945).[41] A contemporary model of gender order as well as gender stereotypes elbowed women out of the public sphere and predetermined their activities mainly within the private sphere eventually only into the realm of so-called "public maternity." Nevertheless, the charity meant a space for public activities for women in the conservative Hungarian environment.[42]

Charitable women's associations had particular importance in providing social care in Hungary. They mainly specialised in the care and education of the poor, especially children. In many ways, they actually conducted those activities that were under the state administration in the Cisleithanian part of the Austro-Hungarian empire. In Buda and Pest, local women's charities actually took over the duties of municipal government related to care for the poor – Pest's women's association originally founded and administered the poorhouse, workhouse and the eye hospital for the poor.[43]

The Pressburg Women's Association serves as a typical example of cooperation with municipal authorities. The immediate impetus for its

[40] See Archív města Bratislavy [The City Archives of Bratislava], sign. XI, Mestské zariadenia, year 1880, box 2828, no. 25, the statutes of Pressburger women's association: *Neunundvierzigster Jahresbericht über die in den kön. Freistadt Preßburg bestehenden christlichen Klein-Kinderbewahranstalten bezüglich dreiundzwanzigsten Jahresbericht des Franz-Josef-Kleinkinder-Spitales und neunten Jahresbericht der hießigen Krippe (Creche) Vom 1. Januar bis Ende Dezember 1879*, Preßburg 1880.
[41] For more details, Gabriela Dudeková, "Frauenbewegung in der Slowakei bis 1918," in *Wie Frauenbewegung geschrieben wird. Historiographie, Dokumentation, Stellungnahmen, Bibliographien*, eds. Johanna Gehmacher and Natascha Vittorelli (Wien: Erhart Locker, 2009), pp. 329–349.
[42] For more details on women's charities and their role in the process of emancipation, see: Elena Manová, "Mužské a ženské svety v spolkoch" [Men's and women's worlds within associations] in Gabriela Dudeková et al., *Na ceste k modernej žene. Kapitoly z dejín rodových vzťahov na Slovensku* [On the road towards a modern woman. Chapters from the history of family relations in Slovakia], (Bratislava: Veda, 2011), pp. 175–195.
[43] "Pesther Wohltätige Frauenverein" was founded in 1817. Árpád Tóth, *Önszervező polgárok. A pesti egyesületek társadalomtörténete a refromkorban* (Budapest: L'Harmattan, 2006), pp. 59–94 and specifically pp. 60–91.

establishment were the consequences of cholera epidemics, where many children were orphaned, as well as the general objectives of the eradication of poverty and begging in the city. Theresa Brunswick, a strong advocate for the Pestalozzi movement to establish day-care centres for children in Hungary, founded an "Association to promote the good and useful" (Verein zur Beförderung des Guten und Nützlichen) in Pressburg at the end of 1830. At the same time, another association came into being, aimed at the establishment and management of children's care centres. This association was soon renamed to the "Pressburg voluntary association."[44] During the 1830s, the "Pressburg charitable society" founded and managed an orphanage, three children's care homes, a day nursery and later even a Children's Hospital (the opening ceremony was held in 1857). All these institutions were supervised by the city authorities. Moreover, the city regularly subsidised the activities of the association, provided the orphanage building and managed its finances. The city of Pressburg also assisted the institutions under the management of the Association by providing and financing medical personnel, etc. Gradually, the city and/or the provincial authorities began to be more and more involved in the management of the Association's facilities – e.g. the orphanage was fully transferred to the city administration. The new building of the Children's hospital, equipped with the latest medical equipment (completed in 1894) acquired the right to public and therefore state subsidies, yet the Pressburg Women's Association stayed involved in its management until 1918 (the hospital was nationalised in January 1918).[45] The day nursery and the children's care homes remained under the management of the Association during the entire inter-war period. The Association was abolished after the Second World War.

Stages of modernisation and measures of the effectiveness of municipal social welfare

While rural communities with small populations coped with their obligation to care for the poor by applying simple and easily controllable methods, the organisation of social care in large cities developed into a

---

[44] Paul Ballus, *Geschichte der Entstehung und Gründung des Waisenhauses in der. k. freien Krönungstadt Preßburg* (Preßburg: Ludwig Weber, 1833), pp. 34–42, Beilage I.; *Kurze Geschichte der Entstehung und Wirksamkeit des Preßburger Frauenvereines. Vom Jahre 1830 bis März 1873* (Preßburg, 1873), pp. 3–5.
[45] Ludwig Kemény, *Hundert Jahre der Wohltätigkeit gewidmet 1830–1930. Rückblick auf die Vergangenheit des Preßburger Wohltätigen Frauenvereines* (Bratislava – Preßburg: Wigand, 1930).

rather complicated system. During the 19th century, every municipal social institution in Pressburg had its own administrator as well as its own administrative committee, which was subject to the municipality. Gradually, all departments responsible for monitoring social care institutes, care for orphans and other forms of social welfare were subsumed under the framework of various municipal authorities. In terms of so-called "municipal laws", the management of social care facilities became divided into specialised sections and commissions during formal reorganisation which took place from the 1880s to the 1890s. Yet the basic principles of the organisation of social welfare remained unchanged – it was a collaboration among different forms of associations with city authorities and with various religious communities. By the end of the 19th century, virtually all basic social care institutions were present within each religious community in Pressburg (Catholic, Protestant, Jewish Orthodox and Neolog separately) – manging old people's homes, a poorhouse, an orphanage, cash subsidies to the poor and the like. An extremely specialised form of welfare existed within Jewish communities.

Based on processes and examples covering the entire century, we can now summarise the development of social care into three basic stages: (1) The very first attempts of Joseph II to centralise care for the poor and its partial implementation; (2) The centralisation of social care in the 1830s, when begging was banned as well. This reform, based on cooperation between municipal authorities and civic societies/associations was a response to the economic and social crises in order to achieve increased efficiency and control of welfare expenditures; (3) The efforts to incorporate care for the poor into the emerging system of municipal social policy at the beginning of the 20th century. At this stage, the existing network of religious, civic and municipal institutions began to be significantly supplemented by self-help societies as well as trade union societies. Another significant change in this period is the entrance of state funding and the state organisation of social care for selected categories of persons.[46]

At the beginning of the 20th century, municipal social welfare in Pressburg acquired a new quality by focusing on population groups that had been previously excluded from social assistance, ssuch as the unemployed, single mothers, morally vulnerable children, individuals suffering from tuberculosis. Another sign of the formation of systematic

---

[46] For more details on the stages and typology of the reorganization of the social care system in Pressburg, see Gabriela Dudeková, "The System of Social Care in the 19th Century Bratislava and its Modernization around 1900," *Historický časopis* 63, no. 5 (2015): pp. 847–876.

municipal social policy was the creation of a new commission called the "social welfare commission" in 1906. Its task was "studying fundamental social questions" and based on their findings, the commission members were supposed to prepare proposals for the city council to address on all social issues.[47] Given the Hungarian reality, municipal support for a model project of social housing for workers called the "Schulpe colony" was exceptional. The same applies to the construction of 120 flats in the so-called "Ten houses," as well as other flats serving as alternative accommodation after the fire of Pressburg-Podhradie in 1913.[48]

The much desired entry by the state into the area of poverty policy brought about improvements in financing, but it also meant jurisdictional disputes with the incumbent managers of social care institutions. A certain curtailing of municipal power was the intention of the "municipal laws" introduced in Hungary in the 1880s. State intervention into the organisation of social welfare did not always have positive consequences. For example, the nationalisation of the care for orphans and abandoned children under 7 years should have contributed to the overall improvement of their situation as well as ensuring sufficient financing. However, the excessive state efforts to centralise and enforce "patriotic" (in practice, Magyarisation) education in childcare resulted in the resistance of Pressburg city administration to such state interference. This was reflected in the jurisdictional dispute about the local orphanage. The state sought to take over the existing orphanage Izabella and to transform it into a state orphanage called the "Children's Asylum." Later, state authorities gave up on their plan due to the "German character of the city", but anyway, the orphanage was closed in 1904.[49] The city of Pressburg fought to keep the orphanage under local government administration and the dispute finally ended with the construction of a new municipal orphanage with the

---

[47] *Pozsony szab. kir. város törvényhatóságának szervezési szabályrendelete*, Pozsony 1913, p. 40.

[48] For more details, see Viera Obuchová and Marta Janovíčková, *Každodenný život a bývanie v Bratislave v 19. a 20. storočí* [Everyday life and housing in Pressburg in the 19th and 20th centuries], (Bratislava: Marenčin PT, 2011); Gabriela Dudeková, "Das soziale Wohnmodell für Arbeiter in Pressburg am Ende des 19. Jahrhunderts," in *Städtisches Alltagsleben in Mitteleuropa vom Mittelalter bis zum Ende des 19. Jahrhunderts: Die Referate des Internationalen Symposions in Častá-Píla vom 11.–14. September 1995*, eds. Viliam Čičaj and Othmar Pickl (Bratislava: Academic Electronic Press, 1998), pp. 339–346; Gábor Gyáni, "Lakáshelyzet és otthonkultúra a munkásság körében," *Századok* no. 3–4 (1990): p. 375; Gábor Gyáni, *Bérkaszárnya és nyomortelep. A budapesti munkáslakás múltja* (Budapest: Magvető, 1992), pp. 96–99.

[49] Pávai-Vajna, *Pozsony*, p. 132.

capacity of 120 children. A magnificent newly built orphanage called "Protected by Our Lady" was completed in 1900. Its scope was expanded and it took up educational functions as well. Its administration was carried out by the city council.[50]

The very advanced – and in the context of the contemporary situation – systematised communal welfare in Pressburg in the early 20th century contrasted sharply with the situation in rural areas. Traditional forms of welfare still largely dominated in Hungary, also due to very low village budgets. The system of municipal social policy in Pressburg was in many ways comparable to the principles and types of institutions in Budapest (which had 800,000 inhabitants at that time). The available statistical data can be used to determine a number of social institutions in Hungarian cities at that time. In 1908, sixty institutions of closed social care were operating in the territory of Slovakia. The largest part of them (26) functioned as "general poorhouses", followed by nursing homes for the elderly, orphanages and "other types of institutions." In the city of Pressburg, nine social care institutions were operating, followed by the cities of Trnava and Rožňava (four institutions). Pressburg excelled in comparison to other cities in Hungary. Together with Oradea it had the largest number of social care institutions after Budapest (25 social care institutions). Yet the capacities of such facilities varied significantly. While in small towns social institutions cared for an average of 10 to 20 people, two Budapest-based "general poorhouses" provided care for almost 3,500 individuals – representing up to one-third of all persons living in residential social care in Hungary. In the then Pressburg, there were about 500 individuals in institutional care.[51]

Despite emphasising the high level of municipal social care, the city of Pressburg spent on average only 2.5% of the annual municipal budget on municipal social care (excluding expenditures on education and school as a whole). Thanks to this, the city of Pressburg, like Timisoara, ranked second in the proportion of social policy expenditure in Hungary, right

---

[50] In 1913, there were 113 children accommodated – only a third of them were orphans, more than a third were made up by paying inmates, whereas the state covered the cost for only eight children. István Vámossy, *Jelentés a Mária Oltalma árvaház és nevelőintézet Pozsonyban, 1913 működésséről*, Pozsony 1914, pp. 14–15. Cf.: *A pozsonyi szent Erzsébet gyermekotthon-egyesület jelentése az 1909. Évi egyesületi működésről és ezt megelőző szt. Erzsébet jubileumi mozgalomról*, Pozsony 1910, pp. 10–15.

[51] Gusztáv Thirring, *A magyar városok statisztikai évkönyve. A magyar városok országos kongresszusának iratai II.*, Budapest 1913, pp. 548–549, 554.

after the capital of Budapest.[52] Compared to the nearby metropolis of Vienna, however, Pressburg lagged far behind – during the same period, the expenses of the Vienna city administration on the care for the poor amounted to nearly 11% of the total annual budget.[53]

As for the qualitative comparison with Budapest (the capital of Hungary), there were virtually identical types of social care institutions in Pressburg, with the difference that in the former there were nationwide social care institutes with an incomparably higher capacity (nationwide children's asylum, mental hospital, etc.). Budapest was the only Hungarian city to have its own "poverty policy regulations" – the highest share of state contributions for municipal poor relief flowed to Budapest. The origins of civic activities had deeper roots in Budapest than in Pressburg – two women's associations (in Pest and Buda), which operated a poorhouse, orphanage, children's nursing homes, as well as workhouses, date their founding back to 1817.

The modernisation of the social welfare system in Pest essentially went through the same stages of development as in Pressburg. Its centralisation under the supervision of the municipal authorities was carried out in 1833. After the unification of Buda and Pest in 1872 (resulting in the establishment of the so-called "Greater Budapest"), a further centralisation and bureaucratisation occurred (special municipal departments responsible for single segments of poverty policy came into being). Until 1918, no further significant reorganisation took place, the "poverty policy regulations" from 1875 continued to be effective, supplemented by a decree from the years of 1903–1904.[54] Due to the size of population and the importance of Budapest as a major industrial centre in Hungary, the

[52] *Magyarország városaink háztartása az 1910 évben. Magyar statisztikai közlemények. Új sorozat, 58. kötet.* Budapest 1916, pp. 266–267; Péter Ágoston, *A szegényügy, Városi szemle,* 1910, no. 11, pp. 806–807.
[53] Friedrich Gottas, "Zur Armenpflege in Budapest und Wien in der zweiten Hälfte des 19. Jahrhunderts," in *Zentrale Städte und ihr Umland. Wechselwirkungen während der Industrialisierungsperiode in Mitteleuropa,* eds. Monika Gletter et al. (St. Katharinen: Scripta Mercaturae, 1985), pp. 172–201, here p. 190; Gerhard Melinz and Susan Zimmermann, Die aktive Stadt. Kommunale Politik zur Gestaltung städtischer Lebensbedingungen in Budapest, Prag und Wien (1867–1914)," in *Wien – Prag – Budapest. Blütezeit der Habsburgermetropolen. Urbanisierung, Kommunalpolitik, gesellschaftliche Konflikte (1867–1918),* eds. Gerhard Melinz and Susan Zimmermann (Wien: Promedia, 1996), pp. 158–159.
[54] For more details: József Kőrösy, *Budapest székesfőváros szegényügye az 1900–1902 években,* Budapest 1905; Susan Zimmermann, *Prächtige Armut. Fürsorge, Kinderschutz und Sozialreform in Budapest. Das "Soziallaboratorium" der Monarchie im Vergleich zu Wien 1873–1914* (Sigmaringen: J. Thorbecke, 1997).

enormous problem of the increasing number of socially deprived persons without permanent residence in the capital became critical at the end of the century. It led to reinventing ideas about the introduction of more stringent punitive measures. Attitudes towards this ostracised segment of the population (and towards poverty as a whole) can be characterised by two important factors: (1) persistence in the practice of refusing to grant a permanent residence to needy persons; (2) repeated proposals for the restoration of the institute of forced labour.

The effectiveness of the existing system of state and municipal poverty policy in Hungary remained insufficient. Unfortunately, the basic principles of social policy in Hungary remained unchanged, therefore entire segments of the population remained permanently outside of the social safety net. Although Pressburg had a wide and specialised network of social institutions and self-help associations, charities and other charity-like organisations as well as the municipality trying to entrench a targeted and effective system of municipal social policy, its overall effectiveness remained limited. Despite its modernisation, the entire system struggled with improving public social care availability as well as with expanding access to it for new categories of the needy. Large groups of socially dependent persons remained without support. Its biggest limit remained an insufficient and inadequate system of the care for the poor in Hungary as a whole and the weak rate of development of state social policy in general. In democratic Czechoslovakia, state social policy was based on new concepts, which created a more favourable place for the implementation of more adequate and better quality municipal social policy.

Chapter Nine

Armut, Armenfürsorge und Disziplinierung von Armen in Landshut in der zweiten Hälfte des 19. Jahrhunderts

Peter Heumos

Poverty, care for the poor and their disciplining in Landshut in the second half of the 19th century

Abstract: In the last quarter of the 19th century, two percent of the population in Landshut lived below the politically defined poverty line and these individuals were recipients of poverty aid. The real poverty rate can be found when taking into account the relative poverty derived from income. The care for the poor became embodied in the city administration in 1816. Yet private charity organised in civic associations continued to play an important role. The practice of public care for the poor was tied into traditional pre-industrial forms and developed only a limited understanding of different conditions, causing poverty in the industrial age in the second half of the 19th century. The providers of care for the poor in Landshut did not agree with the state's approach to the problem of the growing number of poor, which meant the criminalisation of begging (in the context of politically organised Catholicism); on the other hand, the problem of care for the poor in Landshut could not be solved by developing alternative solutions.

Im November 1810 schrieb der königliche Polizeikommissar in Landshut, Gruber, in seinem Jahresbericht: „...Wohlhabenheit ist in Landshut fremd. Mangel an Ackerbau, das Element des Nationalreichtums, ist hier die Quelle eines höchst mittelmäßigen Zustandes, und die Industrie in den Gewerben ist hier sowie in anderen Städten Bayerns noch zu weit zurück, um den Bürger einem wohlhabenden Bauersmann gleichzustellen... Industrie herrscht in dieser Klasse [der Handwerker – P. H.], wenn man da irgend einen eigenen Zweig ausgeigen sollte, keine außerordentliche. Der Bürger arbeitet für seinesgleichen, für den Tag und den Ort, und einer nährt so ziemlich konventionell den anderen, um wieder genährt zu werden, wie dieses in kleinen Städten der Fall ist...“[1] Gruber illustrierte das selbstgenügsame, handwerklich geprägte Erwerbsmilieu Landshuts an den sechs Mühlen der Stadt, die zwar in der lokalen Rangordnung des „Gewerbeflors“ an der Spitze lagen, deren Inhaber aber seiner Meinung nach nicht „industriös“ genug waren, um sich gegen auswärtige Konkurrenz behaupten zu können. Auch der kulturelle Gesichtskreis der Landshuter Gesellschaft erschien Gruber lokal begrenzt; er vermutete, dass daran die Personalpolitik der katholischen Kirche, der mehr als 90 Prozent der Einwohner der Stadt angehörten, ihren Anteil hatte. Da es zur Gewohnheit geworden sei, den Prediger bis zu seinem Tod an demselben Ort zu lassen, werde der „Volksunterricht auf der Kanzel“ immer einfallsloser. Der Prediger wisse schließlich nicht mehr, „was er sagen muß, und das Volk nimmt Ekel an dem Oftwiederholten...“[2]

Der Polizeikommissar schätzte die soziale und wirtschaftliche Perspektive Landshuts offenbar richtig ein. Mehr als 50 Jahre später, in den Jahren 1866–1867, ergab eine Erhebung der bayerischen Staatsregierung, dass Landshut mit fast 50 Armen (d. h. Empfängern von Armenunterstützung) auf 1.000 Einwohner zu den Städten Bayerns mit den höchsten Armenquoten zählte.[3]

I.

Die Entstehungsbedingungen gesellschaftlicher Armut im 19. Jahrhundert sind oft beschrieben worden[4] und müssen nicht noch einmal dargestellt werden. Der Übergang von vorindustrieller Armut, die durch die Krisen

---

[1] Stadtarchiv Landshut (StAL), B 1, Bd. 5, Jahres-Bericht für 1809–10 des Königlichen Polizeikomissariates Landshut, S. 45. Für freundliche Unterstützung danke ich den Mitarbeitern des Stadtarchivs Landshut, besonders Mario Tamme und Gerhard Tausche.

[2] Ebenda, S. 44. Zum breiteren Zusammenhang der Kritik Grubers an der katholischen Kirche in Landshut s. Thomas Götz, "Ordnungen des Glaubens im Umbruch. Religiöse Lebenswelten zwischen Barockfrömmigkeit, katholischer Aufklärung und bürokratischem Staatsabsolutismus 1750–1830," *Verhandlungen des Historischen Vereins für Niederbayern* 129–130 (2003–2004): S. 215–242.

[3] *Zeitschrift des Koeniglich Bayerischen Statistischen Bureau* 1 (1869): S. 107. Exakt entfielen in Landshut 48,6 Arme auf 1.000 Einwohner, im Landesdurchschnitt waren es 18,2 Arme. Ebenda.

[4] Vgl. Christoph Sachße und Florian Tennstedt, *Geschichte der Armenfürsorge in Deutschland* Bd. 1. *Vom Spätmittelalter bis zum 1. Weltkrieg* (Stuttgart: Kohlhammer, 1998²).

des „alten Typs", vor allem durch Missernten, Teuerungen und Seuchen, verursacht wurde,[5] zu den Krisen des „neuen Typs", den Wechsellagen der industriellen Produktion,[6] zog sich bis in die 1840er Jahre hin.

Aufgrund seiner sozialen und gewerblichen Struktur gehörte Landshut zum Typus der Ackerbürgerstadt; noch in den 1880er Jahren arbeiteten knapp zehn Prozent der Einwohner in der Landwirtschaft.[7] Das Bevölkerungswachstum Landshuts beruhte im Untersuchungszeitraum im Wesentlichen auf den Wanderungsverlusten des bäuerlichen Umlandes.[8]

Das Handwerk als der dominierende gewerbliche Sektor Landshuts setzte der industriellen Entwicklung, die in Bayern später begann als in anderen deutschen Staaten,[9] ein konservatives Programm entgegen.[10] Nachdem das Zunftwesen 1804 durch die Aufhebung der realen Gewerbe und das Prinzip der staatlichen Gewerbekonzession zum Teil beseitigt worden war, die Gemeinden sich jedoch 1834 das unbedingte Vetorecht gegen Konzessionisten gesichert hatten, wurde die partiell schon eingeführte Gewerbefreiheit wieder eingeschränkt.[11] Vor allem die niederbayerischen Städte (Landshut, Passau, Straubing) nutzten nun ihren Einfluss auf das Konzessionswesen,[12] um die traditionelle Gewerbeverfassung

---

[5] Wilhelm Abel, *Massenarmut und Hungerkrisen im vorindustriellen Deutschland* (Göttingen: Vandenhoeck und Ruprecht, 1972); speziell zu Bayern siehe Angelika Baumann, *„Armut ist hier wahrhaft zu Haus…" Vorindustrieller Pauperismus und Einrichtungen der Armenpflege in Bayern vor 1800* (München: UNI-Druck in Komm., 1984); Michael Doege, *Armut in Preußen und Bayern 1770–1840* (München: Uni-Druck, 1991).
[6] Für eine bayerische Stadt dazu Karl G. Kick, *Von der Armenpflege zur Sozialpolitik. Die Entwicklung des Fürsorgewesens im 19. Jahrhundert am Beispiel Regensburgs* (Regensburg: Univ.-Verl. Regensburg, 1995).
[7] *Beiträge zur Statistik des Königreichs Bayern* 48 (1885): S. 200 ff.
[8] Peter Reinhold Preißler, "Wirtschaft und Gesellschaft in Landshut 1834–1914," (Diss. phil., Universität Erlangen-Nürnberg, 1973), S. 90.
[9] Im Überblick dazu Wolfgang Zorn, "Gesellschaft und Staat im Bayern des Vormärz," in *Gesellschaft im deutschen Vormärz 1815–1848*, Hrsg. Werner Conze und Theodor Schieder (Stuttgart: Klett, 1962), S. 113–142.
[10] Dies gilt für große Teile Bayerns. Berichte der Bezirksärzte aus den frühen 1860er Jahren zeigen, dass das konservative gewerbliche Programm in manchen Regionen zugleich explizit industriefeindlich war. In anderen Landesteilen (Augsburg, Textilgewerbe im Allgäu) wurde die industrielle Entwicklung positiv rezipiert, u. a. auch deshalb, weil sie zum Rückgang der Armut führte. Vgl. Wolfgang Zorn, "Medizinische Volkskunde als sozialgeschichtliche Quelle. Die bayerische Bezirksärzte-Landesbeschreibung von 1860/62," *Vierteljahrschrift für Sozial- und Wirtschaftsgeschichte* 69 (1982): S. 219–231.
[11] Vgl. dazu Zorn, "Gesellschaft und Staat," S. 118.
[12] Die Entscheidung über die Erteilung der Gewerbekonzession lag bei

zu konservieren.[13] Die Verhältnisse in Landshut kamen dem besonders entgegen: Nach der Gewerbezählung von 1823 waren von den 553 Gewerbebetrieben der Stadt (mit durchschnittlich einem Gesellen) noch 407 oder 74 Prozent zünftig organisiert.[14]

Die langfristigen Auswirkungen der Konzessionspolitik werden in der Literatur überwiegend negativ gesehen. Danach befand sich das bayerische Handwerk um 1860 infolge dieser Politik – noch bevor es die Auswirkungen der Industrialisierung in stärkerem Maße zu spüren bekam – in einer „fast trostlosen Situation."[15] Hier interessiert nur der mit unserem Thema verknüpfte Aspekt dieser Situation: der Zerfall der korporativen Bindungen im Handwerk, die in der Regel den Versorgungszwang gegenüber den Gesellen einschlossen, also potentiell Armut linderten.[16]

Die restaurative Gewerbepolitik mit ihrer Stoßrichtung gegen „fremde Concurrenten"[17] produzierte im Handwerk 1847–1861 in mehr als der Hälfte aller bayerischen Städte einen Gesellenstau. Während Landshut in diesem Zeitraum einen Zuwachs der Gesellen und Lehrlinge um mehr als sieben Prozent verzeichnete, ging die Zahl der Meister um über 20 Prozent zurück,[18] d. h. der Gesellenstau machte über 27 Prozent aus. Stark

---

„Kommissären", die die lokalen Gewerbsvereine leiteten und den Einfluss der bayerischen Staatsregierung auf das Konzessionsverfahren sicherstellen sollten. Da sie aus den Mitgliedern des städtischen Magistrats bzw. des jeweils zuständigen Landgerichts bestellt wurden, waren sie in der Regel Anwälte lokaler Interessen.

[13] Vgl. dazu bes. Kapitel 3 und 4 der Untersuchung von Gerard Schwarz, *„Nahrungsstand" und „erzwungener Gesellenstand". Mentalité und Strukturwandel des bayerischen Handwerks im Industrialisierungsprozeß um 1860* (Berlin: Duncker & Humblot, 1974).

[14] StAL, B 2, Nr. 12071, Gewerbe der Stadt Landshut 1823, Conspect ueber die Anzahl der Gewerbe im Polizei-Bezirke Landshut im Isarkreis (II).

[15] So die überwiegende Einschätzung der zeitgenössischen Sachkenner. Schwarz, *„Nahrungsstand"*, S. 70.

[16] Die Formen dieses Sozialprotektionismus im zünftig gebundenen Handwerk waren vielfältig. Es sollte darauf hingewiesen werden, dass sich dieser auch während noch intakter Zunftverhältnisse auflösen konnte. Das galt nicht zufällig vor allem für saisonale Gewerbe mit langer Winterarbeitslosigkeit und einem entsprechend hohen Unterstützungsaufwand. Vgl. Wolfgang Renzsch, "Bauhandwerker in der Industrialisierung," in *Handwerker in der Industrialisierung. Lage, Kultur und Politik vom späten 18. bis ins frühe 20. Jahrhundert*, Hrsg. Ulrich Engelhardt (Stuttgart: Klett-Cotta, 1984), S. 589–602.

[17] Worunter von den Gegnern der Gewerbefreiheit in aller Regel die ganze Bandbreite ausländischer u n d inländischer Gewerbe verstanden wurde. Schwarz, *„Nahrungsstand"*, S. 66.

[18] Ebenda, S. 84.

eingeschränkt wurden die sozialen Aufstiegsmöglichkeiten der Landshuter Gesellen außerdem durch die restriktive Gesetzgebung über Verehelichung und Niederlassung.[19]

Daraus resultierten erhebliche Spannungen zwischen Gesellen und Meistern. Um 1860 war die Auflösung der von der moralischen Ökonomie des Handwerks getragenen patriarchalischen Hausgemeinschaft schon weit fortgeschritten.[20] Zwar zog sich die Emanzipation der Gesellen vom Meisterhaushalt bis in die 1880er Jahren hin,[21] der korporative Nexus bestand jedoch längst nicht mehr. Konflikte zwischen Gesellen und Meistern wurden in Landshut nicht mehr in überlieferten Handlungsmustern ausgetragen, sondern – wie z. B. 1868 im Maurerhandwerk – vor Gericht entschieden.[22] Die „Anbahnung eines freundschaftlichen Verhältnisses zwischen Meister und Gesellen", das Ziel des 1865 gegründeten Landshuter Handwerkervereins,[23] beschwor nur noch eine ins Unverbindliche entglittene Tradition.

Erste Anzeichen der Erosion der absolutistischen öffentlichen Wohlfahrt im Hinblick auf Marktüberwachung und Konsumentenschutz findet man in Landshut im frühen 19. Jahrhundert. So erwähnt Gruber in seinem Bericht, der Magistrat, der den Verkauf von preisgünstigem Getreide in der örtlichen Getreideschranne[24] kontrollierte, habe gegen die Preistreiberei der „Kornkäuflerzunft" in der Schranne „streng" einschreiten müssen.[25]

---

[19] Aufgehoben wurden die Beschränkungen der Verehelichung und Niederlassung mit dem Gesetz vom 16. April 1868 über Heimat, Verehelichung und Aufenthalt. Text in: *Gesetzblatt für das Königreich Bayern 1866–1869* München: s. t., s. a.), S. 357–402.

[20] Schwarz, *„Nahrungsstand"*, S. 169.

[21] In einer vom Landshuter Armenpflegschaftsrat 1882 zusammengestellten Liste unterstützungsbedürftiger Personen wird deren monatliche Miete („Hauszins") ausgewiesen. Handwerksgesellen, die in dieser Liste auftauchen, wohnten nur noch ausnahmsweise beim Meister. StAL, B 2, Nr. 14668, Statistik des Armenwesens und der Wohltätigkeitsvereine 1870–1894.

[22] Theo Herzog, *Zur Geschichte des Bauhandwerks in Landshut vom 14.–19. Jh.* (Landshut: Bauinnung,1963), S. 96.

[23] Franz Paul Weber und Otto Marschall, *Aus dem Leben der Kreishauptstadt Landshut. Sechs Jahrzehnte, die Jahre 1834 mit 1893 umfassend. Mit Fortsetzung, für die Jahre 1893–1908* (Landshut: Stadtmagistrat, 1916), S. 58.

[24] Bezeichnung für die seit dem Mittelalter bestehende Verkaufsstelle der Bäcker, in der die Qualität des Brotes überprüft und dieses ebenso wie Getreide zu obrigkeitlich festgesetzten Preisen verkauft wurde.

[25] StAL, B 1, Bd. 5, Jahres-Bericht für 1809–10 des Königlichen Polizeikommissariates Landshut, S. 60. Zum breiteren gesellschaftlichen Zusammenhang, in dem diese Auseinandersetzung um den Brotmarkt im Europa des 18. und frühen 19. Jahrhunderts stand, siehe Edward P. Thompson, "Die ‚sittliche Ökonomie' der

Später wandten sich vor allem die Bäcker gegen die sozialprotektionistische Politik der Stadt; sie setzten 1876 die endgültige Schließung des seit dem Mittelalter bestehenden Brothauses durch, das Brot zu Preisen unter dem ortsüblichen Niveau anbot.[26] Schrittweise übernahm allerdings auch die Stadtverwaltung die neue Wirtschaftsgesinnung. Noch vor 1848 begann der Magistrat darüber nachzudenken, wie Armenfürsorge „rentabel" gemacht werden könne,[27] und nachdem er in den 1860er Jahren die Entwicklung der Gewerbe bilanziert hatte, die der Stadt im Zuge der Säkularisation zugefallen waren, wurden die Mühle und die Brauerei des Landshuter Heilig-Geist-Spitals wegen „geringer Rentabilität" verkauft.[28]

Reste alter Gemeinwohlvorstellungen sind in Landshut noch um 1880 zu erkennen, wie noch gezeigt wird. Im Handwerk erhielten sich unter den Gesellen hier und da Formen korporativer Solidarität. Der 1854 gegründete Katholische Gesellenverein und der seit 1863 bestehende Verein der Metzgergesellen[29] boten wandernden Gesellen, wie von alters her, unentgeltlich Unterkunft und Verpflegung in der Herberge.[30] Insgesamt aber entwickelte das Handwerk aus sich heraus kein Rezept gegen die Krisen des neuen Typs. Die Abschaffung der alten Gewerbeverfassung, so hieß es in Landshut, würde dem „gottlosen Liberalismus" Tür und Tor öffnen.[31] Anderswo in Niederbayern vermutete man, hinter der Gewerbefreiheit müsse „Garibaldi" stecken.[32] Auch als die Zeichen längst auf Wandel standen, hielt das niederbayerische Handwerk zäh an den althergebrachten Verhältnissen fest. Drei Jahre vor Einführung der Gewerbefreiheit (Gesetz vom 30. Januar 1868[33]) lehnte der Landshuter

---

englischen Unterschichten im 18. Jahrhundert," in *Wahrnehmungsformen und Protestverhalten. Studien zur Lage der Unterschichten im 18. und 19. Jahrhundert*, Hrsg. Detlev Puls (Frankfurt am Main: Suhrkamp, 1979), S. 13–80.

[26] *Kurier für Niederbayern* 188 (12.7.1876).

[27] Theo Herzog, "Krankenhäuser und medizinische Unterrrichtsanstalten in Landshut," *Verhandlungen des Historischen Vereins für Niederbayern* 91 (1965): S. 5–82.

[28] Heinrich Karl, *Das heilig Geistspital zu Landshut. Seine Geschichte und seine Wirtschaft II./B* (Landshut, s. t., 1942), S. 510 ff. und S. 557 ff.

[29] Vgl. *Chronik. 100 Jahre Metzger-Innung Landshut* (Landshut: s. t., s. s.), S. 18.

[30] Weber und Marschall, *Aus dem Leben*, S. 59.

[31] Im Landshuter Vormärz ein häufiger Topos. Vgl. Heinrich Egner,"Das Aufkommen politischer Parteien in Landshut vor 1848," *Verhandlungen des Historischen Vereins für Niederbayern* 129–130 (2003–2004): S. 267–348.

[32] Vgl. die Stellungnahme einer niederbayerischen Gemeinde bei Schwarz, „*Nahrungsstand*", S. 43.

[33] Text in: *Gesetzblatt für das Königreich Bayern 1866–1869*, S. 309–328.

Gewerbeverein in einer Adresse an das zuständige Staatsministerium die Aufhebung des Konzessionswesens noch einmal nachdrücklich ab.[34]

Zwischen 1861 und 1895 wuchs, wie Tabelle 1 zeigt, der Gewerbesektor Landshuts rascher als die Bevölkerung, der städtische Markt verengte sich also. Das gewerbliche Wachstum war zugleich ein Verdrängungsprozess. Allein zwischen 1870 und 1881, im Wesentlichen also im ersten Jahrzehnt der Gewerbefreiheit, mussten nach Ausweis des Gewerbekatasters 482 Gewerbetreibende ihren Gewerbeschein zurückgeben.[35]

Tabelle 9-1: Bevölkerungs- und gewerbliches Wachstum in Landshut 1861–1895[36]

Jahr	reales und prozentuales Bevölkerungswachstum		reales und prozentuales Wachstum der Gewerbebetriebe*		Einwohner auf 1 Gewerbebetrieb
1861	12.135	100	381	100	32
1895	20.553	169	906	238	23

*Berücksichtigt werden nur produzierende Gewerbe.

Erwerbslosigkeit und damit Armut als Folge dieses Verdrängungsprozesses pendelte sich in Landshut zwischen 1877 und 1895 bei knapp zwei Prozent ein. Damit lag die Stadt unter dem Landesdurchschnitt. In Landshut entfielen im Zeitraum 1877–1895 auf 1.000 Einwohner durchschnittlich 19 Arme, in Bayern zwischen 1881 und 1900 auf 1.000 Einwohner 32 Arme.[37] Den größten Anteil an den Armen / Erwerbslosen stellten in Landshut mit einem Drittel Tagelöhner, die sozial Schwächsten der arbeitenden Bevölkerung, gefolgt von Maurern, Zimmerleuten, Schuhmachern, Pflasterern und landwirtschaftlichen Arbeitern.[38]

---

[34] Weber und Marschall, *Aus dem Leben*, S. 58.

[35] StAL, B 2, Nr. 14671, Gewerbestatistik 1870–1929.

[36] Quellen: *Die Bevölkerung und die Gewerbe des Königreichs Bayern nach der Aufnahme vom Jahre 1861, die Gewerbe in Vergleichung mit deren Stande im Jahre 1847*, Hrsg. k. statistisches Bureau (München: Cotta, 1862), Tab. XIV.; Preißler, "Wirtschaft und Gesellschaft," S. 106.

[37] Vgl. *Das Heimat- und Armenwesen in Bayern: statistische Unterlagen zur Reform der bayerischen Heimat- und Armengesetzgebung*, Hrsg. Statistisches Landesamt, (München: Lindauer, 1911), S. 51.

[38] StAL, B 2, Nr. 14668, Statistik des Armenwesens und der Wohltätigkeitsvereine

Wie wurden die Hilfsbedürftigen unterstützt? Richtsätze der Unterstützung kannte die öffentliche Armenfürsorge nicht.[39] Ihre vordringliche Aufgabe sah sie darin, Armenunterstützung vom niedrigsten Arbeitslohn abzugrenzen. Das hieß in Landshut Abgrenzung vom Arbeitslohn eines Tagelöhners, der zwischen 1877 und 1895 im Durchschnitt täglich zwei Mark verdiente.[40] Aus den Gesamtausgaben der öffentlichen und der privaten Armenfürsorge sowie aus den Zahlen der Armen in Tabelle 2 errechnet sich für 1877–1895 eine Armenunterstützung pro Kopf und Tag zwischen 40 und 50 Pfennig,[41] d. h. rund ein Viertel des Tagesverdienstes eines Tagelöhners. Die Gesetzgebung definierte Armenunterstützung als „Gewährung des zur Erhaltung des Lebens und der Gesundheit Unentbehrlichen"[42] – für Landshut ein frommer Wunsch, denn mit 40 bis 50 Pfennig pro Tag war der Arme zusätzlich auf Betteln angewiesen. Damit folgte die Stadt einer im Deutschen Reich weit verbreiteten Praxis der Armenunterstützung.[43]

1870–1894. Eine Liste von Armen vom September 1882 in diesem Faszikel führt unter 143 Erwerbslosen, bei denen der Beruf angegeben wurde, 48 Tagelöhner an.
[39] Richtsätze in der Armenunterstützung wurden erst in der Weimarer Republik eingeführt. Vgl. Stephan Leibfried, "Existenzminimum und Fürsorge – Richtsätze in der Weimarer Republik," *Jahrbuch für Sozialarbeit. Geschichte und Geschichten* 4 (1981), S. 469–523.
[40] Vgl. Johann Sommer und Nikolaus Sommer, *F. J. Sommer, Maschinenfabrik Landshut. Denkschrift zum 25jährigen Geschäftsjubiläum* (Landshut: s. t., 1895), S. 23.
[41] Bei der Festsetzung der Höhe der Armenunterstützung unterschied der Armenpflegschaftsrat zwischen monatlicher und jährlicher Unterstützung. In beiden Kategorien war der Unterstützungssatz nicht einheitlich, sondern wurde entsprechend der jeweiligen materiellen Situation des Armen festgelegt. Für den Zeitraum 1877–1895 unterscheiden die Armenverzeichnisse nicht durchgehend zwischen Personen mit monatlicher und mit jährlicher Unterstützung. Deshalb wird hier ein durchschnittlicher Unterstützungssatz verwendet.
[42] Text des Gesetzes die öffentliche Armen- und Krankenpflege betr. vom 29. April 1869, in: *Gesetzblatt für das Königreich Bayern 1866–1869*, S. 1094–1126.
[43] Vgl. Sachße und Tennstedt, *Geschichte der Armenfürsorge* Bd. 1, S. 210.

Tabelle 9-2: Arme und Armenunterstützung in Landshut 1877–1895[44]

Jahr	Bevölkerung*	Arme	Arme in % der Bevölkerung	Ausgaben der öffentlichen Armenfür- sorge (in Mark)**	Ausgaben der privaten Armenfür- sorge (in Mark)	Gesamtaus- gaben der Armenfür- sorge (in Mark)	tägliche Armen- unterstützung pro Kopf (in Mark)
1877	14.780	316	2,1	40.326	8.004	48.330	0,42
1881	17.225	267	1,6	35.235	6.266	41.501	0,52
1890	18.862	365	2,0	34.767	22.322	57.089	0,43
1895	20.553	378	1,8	28.000	39.575	69.575	0,51

* Für 1877 wurde der Stand des Jahres 1875, für 1881 der des Jahres 1880 zu Grunde gelegt, da Angaben zur Einwohnerzahl für diese beiden Jahre fehlen. Das Bevölkerungswachstum Landshuts betrug zwischen 1861 und 1895 im jährlichen Durchschnitt ziemlich regelmäßig zwei Prozent (siehe Tabelle 1), sodass beide Veränderungen nicht zu ins Gewicht fallenden Verzerrungen bei der Berechnung des Anteils der Armen an der Bevölkerung und der Höhe der Armenunterstützung führen.

** Nicht einbezogen in die Ausgaben der öffentlichen Armenfürsorge wurden die Verwaltungskosten für die Armenbeschäftigungsanstalt (Armenhaus) in Landshut, die rund zehn Prozent des Etats der Armenfürsorge ausmachten. Im Landshuter Armenhaus wurden regelmäßig auch Personen untergebracht, die nicht in die Kategorie der Armen fielen, die in diesem Beitrag verwendet wird, d. h. keine Armenunterstützung erhielten.

II.

Zuständig für die Armenfürsorge war in Bayern seit 1816 die Gemeinde.[45] Uneingeschränkt wahrnehmen konnte sie diese Aufgabe allerdings erst nach der Einführung der kommunalen Selbstverwaltung im April 1869,[46]

---

[44] Quellen: StAL, B 2, Nr. 14650, Lokalarmenpflege / Rechnungsstellung 1874–1907; Nr. 14668, Statistik des Armenwesens und der Wohltätigkeitsvereine 1870–1894; Preißler, "Wirtschaft und Gesellschaft," S. 198 und 267.

[45] Zur Vorgeschichte der gesetzlichen Regelung von 1816, die eng mit der Frage verknüpft war, wie weit die bayerische Staatsregierung ihre traditionelle Zuständigkeit für die Armenfürsorge an die Gemeinde zu delegieren gedachte, siehe *Handbuch der bayerischen Geschichte* Bd. 4. *Das neue Bayern. Von 1800 bis zur Gegenwart. Erster Teilband: Staat und Politik*, Hrsg. Alois Schmid (München: Beck, 2003), S. 92.

[46] Gesetz, die Gemeindeordnung für die Landestheile diesseits des Rheins betr. vom 29. April 1869, in: *Gesetzblatt für das Königreich Bayern 1866–1869*, S.

die denn auch eine gleichzeitige Neuregelung der Armenfürsorge erforderte.[47]
Seit der Regierungsverordnung vom 22. Februar 1808 zeichnete sich ab,
dass die bayerische Staatsregierung mit der Säkularisation, die durch die
Aufhebung der Klöster und Orden die jahrhundertelange Dominanz der
kirchlichen Armenpflege beendet hatte,[48] eine andere Armenpolitik einleiten
wollte. Die Regierungsverordnung führte dazu aus, der Armenpflege sei
zwar stets „besondere Aufmerksamkeit" gewidmet worden, ein „der
Wichtigkeit des Gegenstandes [...] entsprechender Erfolg" könne aber
bislang nicht verzeichnet werden.[49] Hier klingt die in der Zeit verbreitete
Kritik an der kirchlichen Armenpflege an. Ihr wurde ein „mißverstandener
Begriff der religiösen Pflicht des Wohlthuns" und vor allem vorgeworfen,
durch zu große Freigiebigkeit das Bettlerwesen gefördert zu haben.[50]

Auf die Mitwirkung der Kirche in der Armenfürsorge wollte allerdings
niemand im Ernst verzichten. Die katholische Kirche stellte in Bayern
auch in der zweiten Hälfte des 19. Jahrhunderts vor allem für die
geschlossene Armenfürsorge in reichem Maße Pflegepersonal zur
Verfügung,[51] richtete schon in den 1850er Jahren neue Anstalten der

---

866–1006.

[47] Quelle wie Anm. 42. Die in den Jahren 1868–1869 erlassenen Gesetze über
Gewerbefreiheit, Heimat und Verehelichung, Selbstverwaltung und Armenfürsorge
fungierten in der zeitgenössischen Literatur als „Social-Gesetze" Bayerns. Eine
Analyse dieser Gesetze im Zusammenhang mit der sozialen, wirtschaftlichen und
politischen Entwicklung Bayerns bei Horst Hesse, *Die sogenannte
Sozialgesetzgebung Bayerns Ende der sechziger Jahre des 19. Jahrhunderts*
(München: Stadtarchiv; Kommissionsbuchhandl. Wölfle, 1971).

[48] Zu den wirtschaftlichen und sozialen Folgewirkungen der Säkularisation in
Niederbayern am Beispiel einer Abtei und ihrer Propsteien siehe Andreas
Schlittmeier, *Die wirtschaftlichen Auswirkungen der Säkularisation in
Niederbayern, untersucht am Beispiel der Abtei Niederaltaich und seiner
Probsteien Rinchnach und Sankt Oswald* (Landshut: Histor. Verein f.
Niederbayern, 1961).

[49] Zit. nach: *Koeniglich-Baierisches Regierungsblatt* Bd. 12 (Muenchen: s. t.,
1808), S. 594.

[50] Das Zitat nach Karl Biedermann, *Deutschland im achtzehnten Jahrhundert* Bd. 2
(Leipzig: J. J. Weber, 1880), S. 405. Grundsätzliche Einwände gegen diese Kritik
bei Franz Xaver Bärlehner, "Die Entwicklung der karitativen Wohlfahrtpflege in
Bayern unter besonderer Berücksichtigung des Kreises Niederbayern und der
Städte München, Augsburg, Bamberg, Würzburg, Nürnberg, Regensburg, Passau,
Landshut und Straubing," (Diss., Universität Erlangen, 1927), S. 109 f.

[51] Für Schwaben dazu im Einzelnen Gert Paul Tröger, *Geschichte der Anstalten
der geschlossenen Fürsorge im bayerischen Regierungsbezirk Schwaben
insbesondere während des 19. Jahrhunderts* (München: Stadtarchiv; Wölfle,
1979).

Armenpflege ein, und einige der nach der Säkularisation wiedergegründeten Klöster orientierten ihren Schulunterricht auch an den Bedürfnissen der ärmeren Klassen. So boten die Zisterzienserinnen im 1836 wiedererrichteten Kloster Seligenthal in Landshut neben dem allgemeinen Unterricht eine Industrieschule für „arme Mädchen" an.[52] Nach dem Gesetz über die Armenfürsorge vom 29. April 1869 sollten dem Armenpflegschaftsrat – als dem für die Gestaltung und praktische Durchführung der Armenfürsorge verantwortlichen Gemeindeorgan – sämtliche Pfarrvorstände der Gemeinde angehören.[53] Insofern blieb ein erhebliches Maß an Kontinuität der kommunalen Armenfürsorge mit der staatlichen Armenpflege des Spätabsolutismus gewahrt. Die erwähnte Regierungsverordnung aus dem Jahr 1808 hatte den Pfarrern ebenfalls eine Reihe von Aufgaben in der Armenpflege zugewiesen.[54]

Das Gesetz vom April 1869 sah für die kommunale Armenfürsorge diese Einnahmequellen vor: 1) den dem Lokalarmenfonds zugewiesenen Anteil am Gemeindevermögen, 2) Wohltätigkeitsstiftungen, die bis 1818 vom Staat, dann von der Gemeinde verwaltet wurden,[55] 3) die gesetzlich für die Armenfürsorge vorgesehenen Mittel, 4) örtliche Abgaben für öffentliche Veranstaltungen (Hochzeiten in öffentlichen Wirtschaften, Pferderennen, Theatervorstellungen, Tanzveranstaltungen etc.), 5) Zuschüsse der Gemeindekasse, 6) Schenkungen, Vermächtnisse und die Erträge von Sammlungen.[56]

---

[52] *Seligenthal. Zisterzienserinnenabtei 1232–1982. Beiträge zur Geschichte des Klosters*, Hrsg. Zisterzienserinnenabtei Seligenthal Landshut (Landshut: Zisterzienserinnenabtei Seligenthal, 1982), S. 199.

[53] Vgl. Art. 22 des in Anm. 42 zit. Gesetzes.

[54] Vgl. Art. 29 und 30 der in Anm. 49 zit. Verordnung.

[55] Tröger, *Geschichte der Anstalten*, S. 39. Die Quellenlage zu den wohltätigen Stiftungen in Landshut ist so fragmentarisch, dass dieser Aspekt der Armenfürsorge hier nicht systematisch berücksichtigt werden kann. Die vereinzelten Quellen zur Tätigkeit der Stiftungen haben außerdem den Nachteil, dass sie entweder nur Angaben zum Vermögensstand der jeweiligen Stiftung enthalten oder bloß summarische Beträge ihrer Spenden für kulturelle, schulische oder wohltätige Zwecke ausweisen. Nur in ganz wenigen Fällen finden sich exakte Angaben zur Verteilung von Spenden aus dem Stiftungsvermögen an Arme, wobei dieser Vorgang so abgewickelt wurde, dass der Armenpflegschaftsrat einen Antrag an die jeweilige Stiftung stellte und die gespendeten Beträge (meist in der Form von „Renten") dann über den Armenfonds verteilt wurden. Vgl. dazu das Verzeichnis von 12 Armen mit den ihnen im Haushaltsjahr 1852–1853 aus der Bernegger-Stiftung gewährten Stiftungsrenten. StAL, B 2, Nr. 14537, Die fundationsmäßige Verteilung der Berneggerischen Stiftungsrenten an den Armenfonds und die Kirche St. Martin 1844.

[56] Vgl. Art. 18 des in Anm. 42 zit. Gesetzes.

Auf den ersten Blick flossen die Quellen offenbar reichlich. So verfügte beispielsweise die Heilig Geist-Spital-Stiftung, die in Landshut – wie in vielen anderen bayerischen Städten – ein Spital unterhielt, im Jahr 1889 über ein rentierendes Vermögen von 1,6 Millionen Mark.[57] Wenn die kommunale Armenfürsorge das Existenzminimum der Armen dennoch nicht sicherte, dann wohl auch deshalb, weil die Armenunterstützung – in der Reaktion auf die als zu generös betrachtete kirchliche Armenpflege – von politisch erwünschten sozialen Verhaltensmustern abhängig gemacht und in diesem Sinne eingeschränkt werden sollte. Die verschärften Kontrollen der Empfänger von Armenunterstützung durch das Gesetz vom April 1869 deuteten das schon an: Die Mitglieder des Armenpflegschaftsrates waren berechtigt, sich jederzeit Zutritt zu den Wohnungen der Armen zu verschaffen.[58]

Ein anderer wesentlicher Grund für die „zurückhaltende" Ausgabenpolitik des Magistrats in der Armenfürsorge[59] lag darin, dass sich die Stadtverwaltung stets eines erheblichen Beitrags privater Wohltätigkeit sicher sein konnte. Darin folgte sie dem Geist der Regierungsverordnung vom Februar 1808.[60] Wie extensiv diese ausgelegt werden konnte, zeigte sich im September 1846, als private Wohltätigkeit in Landshut nicht das gewohnte Ausmaß erreichte. Der Armenpflegschaftsrat gab daraufhin bekannt: „…Sollte sich für den Monat Oktober eine hinreichende Sammlungsquote nicht ergeben, so würde sich der Armenpflegschaftsrath veranlaßt sehen, an den Magistrat und die Gemeinde-Bevollmächtigten

---

[57] StAL, Titel VIII, Erhebungen über den Stand der Stiftungen, Abteilung A, 499/12.
[58] Vgl. Art. 36 des in Anm. 42 zit. Gesetzes.
[59] Preißler, "Wirtschaft und Gesellschaft," S. 266, reduziert dieses Defizit einseitig auf mangelnde staatliche Fürsorge „bis zur Sozialgesetzgebung in den 80er Jahren". Bis zu diesem Zeitpunkt sei die unzureichende Fürsorge des bayerischen Staates durch die „caritative Einstellung einiger wohlhabender Bürger, der Kirchen und Klöster" etwas kompensiert worden. Da er keine Zahlen zum Beitrag der privaten Wohltätigkeit anführt, bleiben die konkreten Anteile der öffentlichen und der privaten Karitas am materiellen Gesamtaufwand der Armenfürsorge im Dunkeln.
[60] Nach Art. 20 dieser Regierungsverordnung waren die Erträge von Sammlungen zugunsten der Armen Teil des so genannten Ergänzungsvermögens der Armenpflege, das dann in Anspruch genommen werden sollte, wenn das Fundierungsvermögen nicht ausreichte, um den Bedarf der Armenpflege zu decken. Art. 20 lässt jedoch offen, welche Bestandteile des Ergänzungsvermögens (Armensteuer, Sammlungen, Vermächtnisse, Strafgelder etc.) zwangsweise zum Ausgleich des Etats verwendet werden sollten und welche aus freiem Ermessen der Kommune zur Verfügung gestellt werden konnten.

den Antrag zu stellen, daß nach sorgfältiger Etatsermittlung eine allgemeine Konkurrenz von Pflichtbeiträgen ermittelt werde...“[61] Die von den privaten Wohltätigkeitsvereinen aufgebrachten Mittel wurden nicht von diesen selbst an die Armen verteilt, sondern an den vom Armenpflegschaftsrat verwalteten Lokalarmenfonds abgeführt.

Das Gesetz über die Armenpflege vom April 1869 plante private Wohltätigkeit ein und bot in gewissem Sinne eine Gegenleistung an. Die Mitglieder des Armenpflegschaftsrates sollten nicht – wie bei kommunalen Organen sonst üblich – ausschließlich vom Magistrat ernannt, sondern zum Teil direkt aus der Bürgerschaft gewählt werden. Dem Magistrat wurde nahe gelegt, sich bei diesen Wahlen durch die Vorsitzenden der privaten Wohltätigkeitsvereine zu verstärken.[62] Ausdrücklich erwähnt wird private Wohltätigkeit in dem Gesetz im Übrigen nur insofern, als die Vereine dem Armenpflegschaftsrat Auskünfte zu erteilen hatten, die dieser zur Durchführung seiner Aufgaben benötigte.[63]

Den Nährboden privater Wohltätigkeit in Landshut bildete eine breite Strömung christlich motivierter Nächstenliebe quer durch alle sozialen Klassen, von der Kellnerin bis zum Fabrikanten.[64] Damit ging ein Verständnis von Armut einher, das – wie noch gezeigt wird – mit bestimmten Zielsetzungen der staatlichen Armenpolitik kollidierte.

Privates Engagement entlastete die kommunale Armenfürsorge offenbar in einem Maße, dass diese sich über ihre Politik kaum je den Kopf zerbrechen musste. In der Tat machte sie 1869 dort weiter, wo die spätabsolutistische Armenpolitik aufgehört hatte. Dies gilt z. B. für die bei Teuerungskrisen übliche Zuteilung von Getreide aus dem städtischen Getreidemagazin an „ärmere und unbemittelte Familien“, die nach 1848

---

[61] *Landshuter Wochenblatt* 40 (4.10.1846): S. 334.

[62] Vgl. Art. 22 des in Anm. 42 zit. Gesetzes. Im Jahr 1873 zählte der Armenpflegschaftsrat 20 Mitglieder, von denen acht direkt aus der Bürgerschaft gewählt wurden. StAL, B 2, Nr. 2678, Armenpflegschaftsrat, Einladung des Armenpflegschaftsrates zu seiner Sitzung am 9.1.1873, Protokoll der Sitzung des Armenpflegschaftsrates vom 9. 1. 1873.

[63] Vgl. Art. 28 des in Anm. 42 zit. Gesetzes.

[64] Dokumentiert wird dieses volkstümliche karitative Verhalten in Landshut durch zahlreiche Spenden, Schenkungen und Vermächtnisse aus allen Schichten der Bevölkerung. So vermachte beispielsweise die Kellnerin Barbara Straßburger vor ihrem Tod den „hiesigen Armen“ fünf Gulden. Vgl. *Landshuter Wochenblatt* 45 (8.11.1807). Zur karitativen Tätigkeit der wohlhabenden Schichten: StAL, B 2, Nr. 1445, Die Vermächtnisse des ehem. Papierfabrikanten u. Magistratsrates Joh. Georg Schmid zu den städt. Kultus-, Unterrichts- und Wohltätigkeitsstiftungen 1824–1894.

eine selbstverständliche Maßnahme der Armenfürsorge blieb.[65] Auch
solche Maßnahmen erfüllten selbstverständlich ihren Zweck, konservierten
aber zugleich eine bestimmte Sicht der sozialen Realität. Krisen des alten
Typs, die weit ins 19. Jahrhundert hineinreichten, wurden vom Magistrat
schärfer wahrgenommen und energischer bekämpft als Krisen des neuen
Typs. Als die Cholera 1873 in Landshut über 70 Tote forderte, stellte der
Magistrat umgehend beträchtliche Mittel für den Bau eines
Epidemienhauses zur Verfügung und ließ im gesamten Stadtgebiet
umfangreiche sanitäre Maßnahmen (Erneuerung von Brunnen, Beseitigung
von Stallungen, Verbesserung der Kanalisation, Abdichtung von
Abortgruben) durchführen.[66] Dagegen wusste er sich mit den Krisen des
neuen Typs keinen Rat. Als sich 1867 die „konskribierten" Armen, deren
prozentualer Anteil an der Bevölkerung Landshuts sich seit 1852
verfünffacht hatte,[67] mehrheitlich aus Erwerbslosen rekrutierten,[68]
gründete der Magistrat – getreu seiner Maxime, Armenfürsorge müsse
rentabel sein – „im Interesse der ärmeren Klassen der Bevölkerung" eine
städtische Pfandleihe.[69]

Auch langfristig änderte sich an dieser Perspektive des Magistrats
wenig. Die ersten gesetzlichen Regelungen zum Arbeiterschutz auf
Reichsebene in den 1880er Jahren lösten in Landshut nicht mehr als eine
Debatte darüber aus, wie am besten kontrolliert werden könne, dass die
Beiträge zur Krankenversicherung ordnungsgemäß abgeführt wurden.[70]
Gegen Ende des 19. Jahrhunderts klagte der Magistrat zwar häufig über
die beträchtliche Erhöhung der Lasten der Armenfürsorge,[71] nahm aber
bedrückende soziale Missstände in der Stadt oft erst dann wahr, wenn aus
München interveniert wurde. So brachte nur das Eingreifen der
bayerischen Staatsregierung den Magistrat 1899 dazu, die desolaten
Wohnverhältnisse der „Arbeiter und Minderbemittelten" in Landshut
überhaupt erst einmal zur Kenntnis zu nehmen.[72] Schließlich geht aus
Tabelle 2 hervor, dass die Ausgaben der öffentlichen Armenfürsorge in
den Krisenjahren der Großen Depression sanken und die Bewältigung der

[65] Vgl. Weber und Marschall, *Aus dem Leben*, S. 25 und 35.
[66] Vgl. Otto Schreyer, *Landshut, seine sanitären Mißstände und deren Verbesserung* (Landshut: Thomann,1878), S. 114–121.
[67] Im Jahr 1852 betrug der Anteil der Armen an der Bevölkerung Landshuts 0,9 Prozent. Joseph Georg Egger, *Medizinische Topographie und Ethnographie von Niederbayern* (Passau: s. t., 1861), S. 19–166, hier S. 69.
[68] Vgl. Anm. 3.
[69] Weber und Marschall, *Aus dem Leben*, S. 63.
[70] StAL, B 2, Nr. 2642, Krankenversicherung in einzelnen Betrieben s. d.
[71] Weber und Marschall, *Aus dem Leben*, S. 194.
[72] *Kurier für Niederbayern* 25 (22.11.1899), S. 2.

sozialen Folgen der Depression nur durch eine enorme Ausweitung des Beitrags der privaten Fürsorge ermöglicht wurde. Dieser überstieg 1895 erstmals die Ausgaben der kommunalen Armenfürsorge.

Die privaten Wohltätigkeitsvereine haben früher gesehen, wie Armut unter den Bedingungen der Industrialisierung zweckmäßig bekämpft werden musste. Bereits 1861 war in Landshut ein mehr als 600 Mitglieder zählender Verein gegründet worden, der sich der sozialen Misere der weiblichen Dienstboten annahm. Diese war kein spezifisch lokales Problem, sondern hing – wie der hohe Anteil von weiblichem ländlichen Gesinde und Tagelöhnerinnen vom Lande an den aus Landshut wegen Bettel ausgewiesenen Personen belegt[73] – eng mit der Landflucht und insofern mit der industriellen Entwicklung zusammen. Der Verein, der seit 1870 über ein eigenes Haus verfügte,[74] bot in Not geratenen und Arbeit suchenden Dienstmägden Unterkunft und richtete für sie eine Arbeitsvermittlungsstelle ein.[75] Auf die Idee einer solchen Maßnahme zugunsten der „Wanderarmen" kam die niederbayerische Regierung erst nach 1900.[76]

Wie die Lasten der Armenfürsorge in Landshut zwischen öffentlicher, privater und kirchlicher Wohltätigkeit bis in die 1870er Jahren verteilt waren, sei kurz dargestellt.

---

[73] StAL, B 2, Nr. 2166, Stadtverweise. Die in dieser Akte zusammengestellten Fälle von Stadtverweisen wegen Straßenbettel fallen überwiegend in die frühen 1870er Jahre.

[74] Weber und Marschall, *Aus dem Leben*, S. 83.

[75] StAL, B 2, Nr. 2689, Der St. Johannisverein für freiwillige Armenpflege in Bayern 1893–1915. Im Jahr 1893 beherbergte der Landshuter „Verein für weibliche Dienstboten" 345 Dienstmägde und vermittelte offenbar den meisten einen Arbeitsplatz. Die Kosten dafür betrugen 3.428 Mark. Ebenda. Zu den sozialen Problemen in der bayerischen Landwirtschaft vgl. Axel Schnorbus, "Die ländlichen Unterschichten in der bayerischen Gesellschaft am Ausgang des 19. Jahrhunderts," *Zeitschrift für bayerische Landesgeschichte* 30 (1967): S. 824–852. Vgl. ferner Günther Kapfhammer, "Wanderarbeiter und Gesindemärkte in Niederbayern. Ein Beitrag zur regionalen Volkskunde und Agrargeschichte," *Verhandlungen des Historischen Vereins für Niederbayern* 112–113 (1986–1987): S. 230–236.

[76] In Niederbayern wurde 1905 die erste Arbeitsvermittlungsstation für „Wanderarme" eingerichtet. Vgl. *Das Heimat- und Armenwesen in Bayern*, S. 74. Die ersten Versuche, dem Wanderbettel nicht mit sozialer Diszplinierung und der Strategie der Kriminalisierung, sondern mit sozialpolitischen Maßnahmen entgegenzutreten, gingen auch in anderen deutschen Staaten von der privaten Wohltätigkeit aus. Vgl. Sachße und Tennstedt, *Geschichte der Armenfürsorge* Bd. 1, S. 236.

Nach Ausweis des kommunalen Etats für 1864–1865 trug die öffentliche
Armenfürsorge die Kosten folgender Einrichtungen: des städtischen
Armenhauses, des städtischen Waisenhauses und der städtischen
Kleinkinderbewahranstalt. Die Höhe dieser Kosten ist nicht festzustellen,
da der Etat nur Gesamtkosten für sämtliche Gemeindeanstalten anführt.[77]
Neben den Mitteln für die karitativen Einrichtungen wurden 1864–1865
von der Gemeinde für wohltätige Zwecke einschließlich der
Verwaltungskosten des Armenfonds 274 Gulden zur Verfügung gestellt.[78]
Im nächsten Jahrzehnt kam zu den Gemeindeanstalten das erwähnte
Epidemienhaus hinzu.

In die Zuständigkeit der öffentlichen Armenfürsorge fielen nach dem
Gesetz über die Armenpflege vom April 1869 wohltätige Stiftungen, also
auch das Landshuter Heilig-Geist-Spital, dessen Kosten die gleichnamige
Stiftung trug. Der Magistrat nahm auf die karitative Tätigkeit des Spitals
einen gewissen Einfluss, als er 1870 in dem Spital eine Suppenküche für
Arme und schlecht bezahlte Arbeiter einrichten ließ.[79]

Das Heilig-Geist-Spital gilt als die bedeutendste Wohltätigkeitseinrichtung
Landshuts bis zur Jahrhundertwende.[80] Im Untersuchungszeitraum
entwickelte es sich im Wesentlichen zu einem Altersheim, in dem seit
1868 rund 100 alte und gebrechliche Personen versorgt wurden. Bei diesen
„Pfründnern" wurden drei Klassen unterschieden, die reichen, die
mittleren und die armen Pfründner, wobei Letztere im Spital nur Wohnung
und ein bescheidenes Wochengeld erhielten, im Krankheitsfall jedoch auf
Spitalkosten behandelt wurden.[81] Die Kostordnung des Landshuter Heilig-
Geist-Spitals zeigt diese Unterscheidung, da neben der unentgeltlichen
Verpflegung auch Gerichte angeboten wurden, die der Pfründner selbst zu
bezahlen hatte.[82]

Einen wirksamen Beitrag zur Bekämpfung der Armut leistete das
Spital vermutlich nicht: Stiftungsgemäß wurden nur Personen
aufgenommen, die die Bürgerrechte besaßen und unbescholten waren.[83]

---

[77] StAL, B 2, Nr. 14602, Gemeinde-Haushalt 1864/65.
[78] Ebenda.
[79] Zit. nach Anton Mößmer, *Ärzte, Bürger, Herzöge. Eine Dokumentation zur
Medizinalgeschichte der Stadt Landshut* (Landshut: Attenkofer, 2004), S. 406.
[80] Preißler, "Wirtschaft und Gesellschaft," S. 265.
[81] Bärlehner, "Die Entwicklung der karitativen Wohlfahrtspflege," S. 116.
[82] StAL, B 2, Nr. 2082, Gesundheitspflege. Kostordnungen der Wohlfahrtsinstitute
1875/6, Kost-Regulativ für die Pfründpersonen im heil. Geist-Spital Landshut.
[83] Für Schwaben dazu Tröger, *Geschichte der Anstalten*, S. 52; für Landshut
Schreyer, *Landshut*, S. 20.

Noch um 1900 waren nur vier Prozent der Einwohner Landshuts im Besitz der Bürgerrechte.[84]

Das von den Barmherzigen Schwestern geleitete Armenhaus der Stadt, das auch als vorübergehender Aufenthaltsort für Geisteskranke diente,[85] stand dagegen Gemeindeangehörigen offen. Die Insassen waren zumeist ältere, arme und kranke Personen, die jedoch als erwerbsfähig galten. Sie verdienten im Armenhaus „ohne Zwang" durch „Stroharbeit" etwas Geld, mit dem sie die Kosten ihrer Kleidung bestreiten mussten. Der Verkauf der Arbeitsprodukte der Insassen deckte 12 Prozent der Unterhaltskosten der Anstalt. Der Unterschied zum Heilig-Geist-Spital lässt sich schon an der Kostordnung ablesen,[86] vor allem aber an der in jener Zeit üblichen Rede von den „verkommenen Bewohner[n]" des Armenhauses.[87]

Das städtische Waisenhaus kam im Urteil örtlicher Sachkenner trotz seiner beengten Verhältnisse für 22 Jungen und Mädchen (1878) glimpflich davon. Dagegen galt die städtische Kinderbewahranstalt mit rund 100 Kindern (1878) als der wundeste Punkt aller Wohltätigkeitsanstalten Landshuts. Nach Meinung eines Arztes glich das in einem Kellergewölbe untergebrachte Heim einer „Höhle" und war gesundheitsschädlich.[88]

Während der Magistrat die Beseitigung dieses Missstandes auf die lange Bank schob,[89] zeigte der private Vinzenzverein in einer vergleichbaren Situation größeres Engagement. Im Jahr 1851 von 260 Bürgern gegründet, um Armen „durch Verabreichung von Lebensmitteln, Holz und Kleidung"

---

[84] Manfred Krapf, "Landshut im 19. Jahrhundert. Bürgermeister und Modernisierung 1870 bis 1914," *Verhandlungen des Historischen Vereins für Niederbayern* 120–121 (1994–1995): S. 169–205. Wie die soziale Zusammensetzung der Hospitalpfründner an anderen Orten zeigt, wurde die Bestimmung über die Bürgerrechte nicht strikt eingehalten. Für Augsburg vgl. dazu Tröger, *Geschichte der Anstalten*, 172. Zur sozialen Zusammensetzung der Pfründner des Heilig-Geist-Spitals in Landshut liegen keine Angaben vor.

[85] Nach Tröger, *Geschichte der Anstalten*, S. 51 f., sammelte sich in den schwäbischen Armenhäusern zu Beginn des 19. Jahrhunderts ein „sehr gemischter Personenkreis". Insassen der Armenhäuser in Augsburg, Memmingen und Kempten waren neben Armen und Kranken auch Sträflinge, Schwachsinnige, Erwerbslose, verwahrloste Kinder und Mägde mit unehelichen Kindern.

[86] StAL, B 2, Nr. 2082, Gesundheitspflege. Kostordnungen der Wohlfahrtsinstitute 1875/6, Kost-Ordnung in der Armen-Beschäftigungs-Anstalt der königl. Kreishauptstadt Landshut. Das Essen war qualitativ schlechter und eintöniger. Morgens und abends gab es an Wochentagen nur Brotsuppe, Brot zum Abendessen musste bezahlt werden. Vgl. Schreyer, *Landshut*, S. 21.

[87] Ebenda.

[88] Ebenda, S. 23 f.

[89] Ebenda, S. 24.

zu helfen, widmete sich der Verein früh auch der Unterstützung und
Erziehung „armer und verwahrloster Knaben".[90] Die Knabenerziehungsanstalt,
zu der 1857 eine entsprechende Anstalt für Mädchen (Marienanstalt)
hinzukam, wurde zunächst im städtischen Baumagazin untergebracht. Dort
waren die Wohnverhältnisse so miserabel, dass der Vinzenzverein zwei
Grundstücke erwarb, die „sehr schön am Ostrand der Stadt frei zwischen
Gärten" lagen. Beide Erziehungsanstalten wurden dorthin umgesiedelt.[91]

Zur organisierten privaten Wohltätigkeit gehörten außerdem der seit
1829 bestehende Verein zur „Unterstützung der Armen zur rauhen
Winterszeit", der auch für die Miete einiger Armen aufkam, der 1854
gegründete St. Johannis-Verein für Armenpflege sowie seit 1862 ein
Frauenverein, der sich der Unterstützung armer Kranker widmete.[92]
Obwohl die Nähe der privaten Wohltätigkeit zur kirchlichen Armenpflege
deutlich ist,[93] verfolgten nur wenige Vereine über ihren karitativen Zweck
hinaus ausdrücklich christlich motivierte Ziele. Zu diesen gehörte der
Vinzenzverein, der erklärtermaßen für die Erhaltung einer katholischen
Lebensführung unter den kleinen Leuten eintrat.[94]

In fast allen Anstalten der öffentlichen und der privaten Armenfürsorge
lagen Pflege, Aufsicht und gegebenenfalls Unterricht bei Ordensschwestern,
in erster Linie den Barmherzigen Schwestern, Franziskanerinnen,
Dominikanerinnen, Ursulinerinnen, den Armen Schulschwestern und den
Zisterzienserinnen. Die kirchliche Armenfürsorge besaß eigene Anstalten,
ein Altersheim und das 1859 eingerichtete Dienstbotenhaus.[95] Da der
Magistrat, wie schon erwähnt, der Auffassung war, Armenpflege und
Rentabilität dürften sich nicht ausschließen, nutzte er das breite Angebot

---

[90] StAL, B 2, Nr. 2689, Der St. Johannisverein für freiwillige Armenpflege in
Bayern 1893–1915.

[91] Schreyer, *Landshut*, S. 25 f.

[92] StAL, B 2, Nr. 2689, Der St. Johannisverein für freiwillige Armenpflege in
Bayern 1893–1915.

[93] Eine genauere Untersuchung des Verhältnisses der privaten Wohltätigkeitsvereine
zur katholischen Kirche würde über den Rahmen dieses Beitrags hinausgehen. Die
Landshuter Wohltätigkeitsvereine waren zumeist Zweigvereine eines
Zentralvereins, der seinen Sitz in einer anderen Stadt hatte. Ihre Geschichte kann
insofern nur zu einem geringen Teil über lokale Quellen erschlossen werden.

[94] Werner K. Blessing, *Staat und Kirche in der Gesellschaft. Institutionelle
Autorität und mentaler Wandel in Bayern während des 19. Jahrhunderts*
(Göttingen: Vandenhoeck & Ruprecht, 1982), S. 144.

[95] Vgl. Bärlehner, "Die Entwicklung der karitativen Wohlfahrtspflege," S. 244 und
267.

an Pflegepersonal aus den Orden gelegentlich zu dem Versuch, die Löhne der Ordensschwestern zu drücken.[96]

Neben den Vereinen waren Sammlungen zugunsten der Armen ein weiteres Betätigungsfeld privater Wohltätigkeit. Sie wurden in enger Zusammenarbeit zwischen Bürgerschaft und Klerus durchgeführt, wie etwa 1883, als Bürger und Geistliche gemeinsam Abfälle sammelten, durch deren Verkauf Winterkleidung für 20 arme Schulkinder beschafft werden konnte.[97] Regelmäßiger Ort von Sammlungen waren bis 1848 die Tischgesellschaften in den Weinlokalen und Brauereigaststätten Landshuts.[98]

Auch diese wenigen Hinweise deuten an, dass private Wohltätigkeit einen Pfeiler der Armenfürsorge bildete, nicht allein aufgrund ihrer finanziellen Leistung. Früher als die öffentliche Armenfürsorge entwickelte sie jedenfalls in Ansätzen ein Verständnis für den Wandel der strukturellen Ursachen von Armut, reagierte auf kritische Situationen mit größerer Initiative und nahm die Bedürfnisse der Armen ernster als der Magistrat, wie am Beispiel des Vinzenzvereins gezeigt.

Der Magistrat ließ sich mit den Problemen der Armenfürsorge wohl auch deshalb Zeit, weil er von höherer Seite keine Kritik zu erwarten hatte. Die jährlichen Berichte über die Inspektion der karitativen Einrichtungen Landshuts durch die Distriktspolizeibehörde sind voller Wohlwollen. Die Inspektoren verloren z. B. kein Wort über den Zustand der städtischen Kinderbewahranstalt, sie rieten nur davon ab, weitere Kinder in die überfüllte Anstalt aufzunehmen.[99]

Auf lange Sicht blieb die „zurückhaltende" Ausgabenpolitik der öffentlichen Armenfürsorge nicht ohne Auswirkung auf die private Wohltätigkeit; sie bremste deren Ansätze zu einer konzeptionellen

---

[96] Vgl. Anm. 27. Die Ausbreitung der Gesetze des Marktes in der Armenfürsorge begann im 19. Jahrhundert in schwäbischen Gemeinden bei der Verköstigung in Spitälern vom Typ des Landshuter Heilig-Geist-Spitals. Die Verpflegung wurde häufig Kleinunternehmern („Akkordanten") übertragen, die auch das Küchenpersonal stellten und auf Kosten der Hospitalinsassen in die eigene Tasche zu wirtschaften pflegten. Vgl. Tröger, *Geschichte der Anstalten*, S. 50.

[97] Theo Herzog, *Landshut im XIX. Jahrhundert* (Landshut: Stadt Landshut, 1969), S. 343.

[98] Ebenda, S. 77.

[99] StAL, B 2, Nr. 2676, Die jährliche Besichtigung der Wohltätigkeitsanstalten durch die Distriktspolizeibehörde, Schreiben der Königlichen Regierung von Niederbayern an den Magistrat und Armenpflegschaftsrat der Kreishauptstadt Landshut vom 24. Januar 1859. Den unkritischen Tenor der Inspektionsberichte zeigt ein Vergleich mit der schon mehrfach zitierten Abhandlung des praktischen Arztes Schreyer, *Landshut*, der sämtliche karitativen Einrichtungen Landshuts eingehend untersucht hat.

Umorientierung. Da öffentliche und private Armenfürsorge zusammen das Existenzminimum der Armen nicht sicherten, sah sich die private Wohltätigkeit immer wieder gezwungen, erst einmal aktuelle Not lindern zu müssen. Auf diese Weise wurde die Politik des Löcherstopfens aus der ersten Hälfte des 19. Jahrhunderts fortgesetzt, wie sie noch in den 1870er Jahren Ludwig II. auf seinen Reisen durch Bayern praktizierte.[100]

Dass die Armenpflege vor 1848 – in offensichtlicher Übereinstimmung mit den Vorstellungen privater Wohltäter – keine langfristigen Überlegungen anstellte, lässt sich vielfach belegen. Die Landshuter Presse versicherte im Herbst 1807 denjenigen, die „ihre Gaben in die Hände der königlichen Armeninstitutskommission" gelegt hatten, dass diese noch am selben Tag an die Armen verteilt worden seien.[101] Ebenso waren Schenkungen und Vermächtnisse in Landshut durchweg als Ad-hoc-Maßnahmen gedacht. Ein Fabrikant vermachte 1824 den Armen der Stadt 100 Gulden; davon erhielt das Armenhaus 25 Gulden und jeder Arme einige Kreuzer auf die Hand.[102]

Jahrzehnte später zwang der knapp bemessene Etat der öffentlichen Armenfürsorge die private Wohltätigkeit, in ganz ähnlicher Weise zu verfahren: Der Vinzenzverein hatte 1881 unter seinen Mitgliedern über 5.000 Mark gesammelt, die umgehend zur Bekämpfung der Not von 280 Armen verwendet wurden. Zwei andere Wohltätigkeitsvereine teilten, ebenfalls 1881, Spenden von mehr als 900 Mark unverzüglich unter 23 Arme auf.[103] Auch Sammlungen dienten ausschließlich der Linderung aktueller Not. Dagegen deuten die wenigen Angaben zu den Stiftungen darauf hin, dass diese an die längerfristige Versorgung der arbeitsunfähigen Armen dachten. Der Beitrag der Stiftungen bestand in so genannten Stiftungsrenten.[104]

---

[100] Vgl. Hermann Rumschöttel, "König Ludwig II. und die soziale Frage," in *Götterdämmerung. König Ludwig II. und seine Zeit*, Hrsg. Peter Wolf (Augsburg: Haus der Bayerischen Geschichte, 2011), S. 122–124.

[101] *Landshuter Wochenblatt* 45 (8.11.1807).

[102] StAL, B 2, Nr. 14445, Die Vermächtnisse des ehem. Papierfabrikanten u. Magistratsrates Joh. Georg Schmid zu den städt. Kultus-, Unterrichts- und Wohltätigkeitsstiftungen 1824–94.

[103] StAL, B 2, Nr. 14668, Statistik des Armenwesens und der Wohltätigkeitsvereine 1870–1894.

[104] Vgl. Anm. 55. Wie die Bernegger-Stiftung spendete u. a. auch die Scharff von Scharffenstein'sche Wohltätigkeitsstiftung in der Regel Renten, beispielsweise 1876 fünf Witwenrenten. Vgl. Weber und Marschall, *Aus dem Leben*, S. 91.

III.

Geht man von Subsistenzsicherung im weitesten Sinne aus, gehören in unseren Zusammenhang auch freiwillige Sozialleistungen der Betriebe und Selbsthilfemaßnahmen der von Armut Betroffenen. Betriebliche Sozialleistungen freiwilliger Art waren in Landshut dünn gesät. Eine Enquete der Staatsregierung im Jahr 1874 ermittelte in Landshut vier Betriebe mit 189 Beschäftigten, die sich auf diesem Gebiet engagierten, wobei allerdings nicht nur soziale Motive eine Rolle spielten, wenn etwa der Fabrikherr den Arbeitern Wohngeld als Prämie für „Wohlverhalten" zahlte.[105]

Die Erfolge der Selbsthilfe sind ebenfalls überschaubar. In Landshut bestätigte sich, dass das Handwerk nach dem Zusammenbruch seiner Sozialverfassung und seiner kulturellen Wertorientierungen im Zuge der Anpassung an die industrielle Entwicklung häufig in einen Zustand sozialer Anomie verfiel, der mit apathischem Verhalten einerseits und den Verheißungen einer mit der Realität nicht mehr vermittelten Gegenwelt andererseits einherging.[106] Von den weit über 2.000 Arbeitern im Kleingewerbe gründeten nur die Bäcker-, Schmiede-, Wagner- und Ofensetzergesellen Krankenunterstützungsvereine und Hilfskassen.[107] Weit verbreitet unter den Gesellen war auf der anderen Seite bereits im frühen Stadium des Zerfalls der handwerklichen Arbeits- und Lebenswelt die Vision „Amerika" als Synonym für eine glückliche Welt mit weniger Plackerei und besserem Lohn.[108]

---

[105] Vgl. *Ergebnisse einer Erhebung über die in Bayerischen Fabriken und größeren Gewerbebetrieben zum Besten der Arbeiter getroffenen Einrichtungen,* königl. Staatsministerium des Innern (München: Huber, 1874), S. 14 f. Neben Wohngeld umfassten die freiwilligen Sozialleistungen insgesamt drei Kranken- und Unterstützungskassen und drei Unfallversicherungskassen. Der zitierten Quelle ist nicht zu entnehmen, ob und in welchem Maße sich die Unternehmer an den von ihnen initiierten Einrichtungen mit eigenen Beiträgen beteiligten.

[106] Am Beispiel Böhmens dazu Peter Heumos, "Bruderlade und proletarischer Tabor. Soziale Bedingungen von Aktions- und Organisationsformen tschechischer Kleingewerbe-Arbeiter 1850–1870," *Vierteljahrschrift für Sozial- und Wirtschaftsgeschichte* 69 (1982): S. 339–372.

[107] StAL, B 2, Nr. 14666, Statistik des Vereins- und Hilfskassenwesens 1877/78.

[108] StAL, B 2, Nr. 117, Das Auswanderungsgesuch des Hutmachergesellen Sebastian Niedermaier von Landshut 1850. Siehe dazu für eine Landgemeinde in der Nähe Landshuts Willibald Ernst, ",Um meine Lage zu verbessern...' Auswanderungswelle im 19. Jahrhundert im Gebiet der jetzigen Gemeinde Gangkofen," *Verhandlungen des Historischen Vereins für Niederbayern* 136 (2010): S. 5–30.

Der zögernde Verlauf einer kritischen Politisierung des Katholizismus gerade in den bayerischen Ackerbürgerstädten und der nach 1848 von der Kanzel herab gepredigte Grundsatz, „Gehorsam gegen den Landesvater als Gehorsam gegen den göttlichen Vater" zu üben,[109] werden quietistische Verhaltensmuster gefördert haben. Arbeitskämpfe etwa sind in Landshut zwischen 1850 und 1900 an einer Hand abzuzählen.[110] Sie blieben lokal beschränkt und auf Distanz zu größeren Streikbewegungen.[111] Unruhig wurde es nur, wenn der volkstümliche Konsens über legitime und illegitime Praktiken auf dem Markt verteidigt werden musste. Der Volkszorn über „ungerechte" Bierpreise konnte dann auch in Gewaltexzesse umschlagen.[112] Sie setzten die Kenntnis der örtlichen Verhältnisse voraus und zielten allein auf diese: Man wusste, wer die Schufte waren, und ließ sie in Drohbriefen wissen, was ihnen blühte.[113]

Der Lokalismus in allen seinen Spielarten, dem der eingangs zitierte Gruber so wenig abgewinnen konnte, konservierte überlieferte Volksfrömmigkeit,[114] die in ihrem Festhalten am Althergebrachten durchaus einen politischen Unterton hatte: Sie lag quer zur konservativ-autoritären Zuspitzung der Armutsproblematik im Programm des politisch organisierten Katholizismus, der Zentrumspartei,[115] die in Landshut bis

---

[109] Vgl. Blessing, *Staat und Kirche*, S. 139 und S. 144.

[110] Zwischen 1850 und 1900 streikten nur die Buchdrucker (1873 und 1891) und die Schuhmachergesellen (1875). Vgl. *Denkschrift zum 100jährigen Jubiläum der Jos. Thomannschen Buchhandlung* (Landshut: Thomann, 1893), S. 18; StAL, B 3, Nr. 559, Generalstreik der deutschen Buchdruckergehilfen; Titel VIII, Abtlg. A, Fach 499, Nr. 2, Streiks s. d.

[111] Vgl. Preißler, "Wirtschaft und Gesellschaft," S. 261.

[112] Im Januar 1880 wurde die Inneneinrichtung der Brauerei Neuhausen im Bezirksamt Landshut als Reaktion auf eine Erhöhung des Bierpreises kurz und klein geschlagen. Vgl. Barbara Kink, "Die Volksstimmung in Bayern im Spiegel der Berichte der Regierungspräsidenten 1866–1886," in *Götterdämmerung. König Ludwig II. und seine Zeit*, Hrsg. Peter Wolf (Augsburg: Haus der Bayerischen Geschichte, 2011), S. 133–142.

[113] Ebenda.

[114] Blessing, *Staat und Kirche*, S. 144. Untersuchungen zur Volksfrömmigkeit beschäftigen sich eher selten mit den sozialen Weltbildern der Volksfrömmigkeit und deren potentiellem politischen Konfliktpotential. Meistens illustrieren sie ihren Gegenstand an den manifesten Formen religiösen Lebens. Ein Beispiel ist Stephan Mokry, "Frömmigkeitsphänomene zur Zeit Ludwigs II. von Bayern," in *Götterdämmerung. König Ludwig II. und seine Zeit*, Hrsg. Peter Wolf (Augsburg: Haus der Bayerischen Geschichte, 2011), S.129–133.

[115] Zur Geschichte der Zentrumspartei, die aus der 1869 gebildeten „Patriotischen Fraktion" in der bayerischen Zweiten Kammer hervorging, siehe den Überblick in: *Handbuch der bayerischen Geschichte* Bd 4/1, Hrsg. Schmid, S. 336–350.

zum Ende des 19. Jahrhunderts dominierte und die bayerische Armenpolitik maßgeblich beeinflusste.[116] An der Frage des Bettels kann man das Sich-Einigeln der Volksfrömmigkeit gegen armenpolitische Maßnahmen der bayerischen Staatsregierung gut zeigen.

IV.

Die Bekämpfung des „Bettlerunwesens" bildete das zentrale Aktionsfeld der staatlichen Armenpolitik. Deren wichtigste Aspekte waren: Regulierung der Armut durch Trennung der einheimischen von den fremden Armen / Bettlern,[117] ihre soziale Disziplinierung[118] und Kriminalisierung durch strafrechtliche Verfolgung und geschlossene Armenpflege (Arbeitshäuser).

Nach dem Gesetz vom April 1869 erstreckte sich die Armenfürsorge der Gemeinde ausschließlich auf die „in ihr heimatberechtigten hilfsbedürftigen

---

[116] Das zeigen vor allem die Ergebnisse der Reichstagswahlen, bei denen sich das Zentrum 1874 mit 87 Prozent der Stimmen (gegen 11,3 Prozent der Nationalliberalen und 1,3 Prozent der Sozialdemokratie) in Landshut eine komfortable absolute Mehrheit sicherte, die es bis 1884 auf 98 Prozent steigerte. In den Jahren 1893 und 1898 bedrohte der Bayerische Bauernbund (36,1 bzw. 37,7 Prozent) vorübergehend die Vormachtstellung des Zentrums, das sich jedoch bis 1907 (75,6 Prozent) die Vorherrschaft zurückeroberte. Vgl. Preißler, "Wirtschaft und Gesellschaft," S. 301, Tab. 68. Bei den Wahlen zum Gremium der Gemeindebevollmächtigten entfielen im Jahr 1869 auf das Zentrum 22 Sitze, auf die Nationalliberalen 8. In den folgenden Jahren sicherten sich die Nationalliberalen die Mehrheit in diesem Gremium, ehe das Zentrum 1887 seine führende Position zurückgewann und bis 1905 behaupten konnte. Auf kommunaler Ebene bestanden zwischen dem Zentrum und den Liberalen „kaum größere Gegensätze". Vgl. Krapf, "Landshut im 19. Jahrhundert," S. 180.

[117] Die Unterscheidung zwischen einheimischen und fremden Armen bildete vom Spätmittelalter bis zum Absolutismus einen zentralen Punkt der Armenordnungen. Vgl. Sachße und Tennstedt, *Geschichte der Armenfürsorge* Bd. 1, S. 107 ff.

[118] Der Begriff der sozialen Disziplinierung ist in den 1960er Jahren von Gerhard Oestreich eingeführt worden. Sachße und Tennstedt relativieren in ihrer mehrfach zitierten Untersuchung das kritische Gesamtbild der Armenfürsorge in Deutschland am Ende dadurch, dass sie den vorher im Sinne Oestreichs benutzten Begriff aufweichen und mit der im „modernen Wohlfahrtsstaat" erforderlichen „sozialen Disziplin" in Zusammenhang bringen. Vgl. Sachße und Tennstedt, *Geschichte der Armenfürsorge* Bd. 1, S. 371. Die Kompromissformel der beiden Autoren, soziale Disziplin habe einerseits etwas mit Repression zu tun, sei andererseits eine positive, weil für die Moderne notwendige Wertorientierung, lässt so ziemlich alle Fragen offen. Es kann damit wohl nicht gemeint sein, Repression habe hinter ihrem Rücken immer auch eine „fortschrittliche" Funktion.

Personen".[119] Die Unterscheidung zwischen einheimischen und fremden Armen meinte jedoch schon lange vor 1869 nichts anderes als die öffentliche moralische und soziale Ächtung der fremden Armen bzw. Wanderbettler. Als Landshut im November 1807 abermals – um hier nur ein Beispiel anzuführen – von einer „Horde unverschämter Bettler" heimgesucht worden war, sah die lokale Presse Unheil heraufziehen und hielt die friedvollen Tage der Stadt für gezählt.[120]

Die öffentliche Debatte über „verschämte", „demütige" und „würdige" Arme einerseits und „unverschämte", „freche" und „unwürdige" Arme andererseits bildete bloß den Auftakt zu den oft geradezu hysterischen und mit weit größerem bürokratischen Aufwand betriebenen Kampagnen der Staatsregierung gegen den Wanderbettel.[121] Wie anderswo auch, produzierten diese Kampagnen massenhaft den Verdacht auf Arbeitsscheu der Bettler und Landstreicher.[122]

Maßgebend für die Sprachregelung des Problems und die Absicht der Obrigkeiten, die Bevölkerung gegen Bettler und Landstreicher zu mobilisieren, war die Bekanntmachung der niederbayerischen Regierung (mit Sitz in Landshut) vom 14. Juni 1844, die alle umherstreunenden Armen unter der Signatur „arbeitsscheues Gesindel" zusammenfasste. Polizeibehörden, Gemeindevorsteher, Ortswächter, Flurschützen[123] und

---

[119] Zit. nach Art. 10 des Gesetzes über die öffentliche Armen- und Krankenpflege vom 29. April 1869, Text in: *Gesetzblatt für das Königreich Bayern 1866–1869*, S. 1094–1126.

[120] *Landshuter Wochenblatt* 1 (8.11.1807).

[121] Die Statistiken zum „Bettlerunwesen" beschränken sich auf kleinere Zeiträume und erfassen nur gerichtlich verurteilte Bettler und Landstreicher. Daher lassen sie keine gesicherte Aussage darüber zu, ob ein Missverhältnis zwischen diesem Aufwand und der tatsächlichen Dimension des Problems bestand, wie zu vermuten ist. In Niederbayern entfielen zwischen 1862 und 1866 im Jahresdurchschnitt auf 100.000 Einwohner 691 gerichtlich verurteilte Bettler und Landstreicher. Vgl. dazu: *Ergebnisse der Strafrechtspflege im Königreiche Bayern bei den Schwurgerichten, Bezirksgerichten, Appellationsgerichten, dem Obersten Gerichtshof, den Stadt- und Landgerichten und Militärgerichten, bei letzteren bezüglich gemeiner Verbrecher, Vergehen und Uebertretungen während der Jahre 1862/63, 1863/64, 1864/65, 1865/66: nach den von dem königl. Staatsministerium der Justiz und dem königl. Kriegsministerium angeordneten Erhebungen*, (München: Gotteswinter & Mößl, 1868), S. LXXII. Im Vergleich mit anderen Landesteilen Bayerns war Niederbayern vom Problem der Bettler und Landstreicher offenbar in geringerem Maße betroffen. Von 100 aufgegriffenen Bettlern im Zeitraum 1850–1856 entfielen auf Niederbayern 10, auf die Pfalz 25. Vgl. Egger, *Medizinische Topographie*, S. 69.

[122] Vgl. Sachße und Tennstedt, *Geschichte der Armenfürsorge* Bd. 1, S. 209.

[123] Andere Bezeichnung für Feldhüter, die im Rahmen der staatlichen Feldpolizei

Schulinspektionen wurden angewiesen, Bettler und Landstreicher sofort in Arrest zu nehmen und dem zuständigen Gericht zu übergeben.[124]

Von den zahlreichen Verordnungen, Entschließungen und Instruktionen zum Problem des Bettels und der Landstreicherei[125] soll zunächst nur der Beitrag des Landshuter Magistrats näher betrachtet werden. Seine Bekanntmachung vom 10. Januar 1855[126] führt aus:

„Nachdem neuerdings eine Ueberhandnahme des Haus- und Straßenbettels den bestehenden Verordnungen entgegen sich wahrnehmen läßt, so wird hiemit zu widerholten Malen bekannt gegeben:

1. Der Bettel überhaupt, sei es unter dem Vorwande der Armuth oder sonstigen Unglückes und aus welch' immer einer Ursache, ist durchaus verboten.
2. Jede am Bettel betretene Person hat sofort körperliche Züchtigung oder Arreststrafe und wenn selbe der dießseitigen Stadtgemeinde nicht angehört, Verschubung in die Heimath zu gewärtigen.
3. Einer Arreststrafe von 1–3 Tagen oder Geldbuße von 3–10 fl. unterliegen gleichfalls jene Hauseigenthümer oder Miethbewohner, welche ohne Anzeige bei der unterfertigten Behörde Bettlern und Landstreichern Unterschlupf geben oder Almosen reichen,
4. sowie Eltern oder deren Stellvertreter, die ihre Kinder dem Bettel und Vagiren nachgehen lassen, Hausväter die solches bei ihren Dienstboten, Gesellen oder Miethleuten wissentlich dulden und Wirthe, welche derartigen Unfug in ihren Lokalitäten gestatten und überhaupt jene Vorschriften vernachläßigen, die sie rücksichtlich der Fremden zu beobachten haben.

Indem man sich der Erwartung hingibt, daß von Seiten der Einwohnerschaft die bestehenden Vorschriften eine sorgfältige Beobachtung zur Steuerung dieses lästigen Unfugs finden mögen und zwar um so mehr, da der Wohlthätigkeitssinn auf andere Weise durch mildthätige Gaben sich zu bewähren Gelegenheit hat, wird zugleich

---

Feldgrundstücke, Pflanzungen und Feldfrüchte gegen rechtswidrige Beschädigung durch Menschen oder nichtbeaufsichtigte Tiere schützten.

[124] *Königlich-Bayerisches Intelligenz-Blatt von Niederbayern* 7 (1844): S. 407 f.

[125] Eine reichhaltige Sammlung der Verordnungen, Instruktionen und Bekanntmachungen zur Problematik des Bettels findet sich im Landshuter Stadtarchiv. StAL, B 2, Nr. 2155, Generalien und Verordnungen über das Hochgericht, das Bettler- und Vagantenunwesen, Landstreicherei, Gesellenwandern, Steckbriefe, Reisepässe, Waffentragen etc. 1820–1879.

[126] Abgedruckt in: *Landshuter Wochenblatt* 49 (21.1.1855): S. 1.

bemerkt, daß die Polizei-Mannschaft zur strengsten Ueberwachung dieser
Bestimmungen beauftragt sei."

Das Dilemma des Magistrats ist in dieser Bekanntmachung nicht zu
übersehen. Der Bettel in Landshut selbst (Kinder, Dienstboten, Gesellen)
hing mit dem Wanderbettel offensichtlich aufs Engste zusammen und ließ
sich von diesem durch die administrative Teilung des Problems
(einheimische vs. fremde Bettler) nicht trennen. Dass den Vaganten in
Landshut Unterkunft gewährt wurde, macht dies besonders deutlich.

Die Skandalisierung des lokalen Resonanzbodens des Wanderbettels
setzte meistens am Kinderbettel an, der zugleich zeigt, wie lange es
dauerte, ehe die Frage des Bettels realistisch betrachtet werden konnte. Die
Bekanntmachung der niederbayerischen Regierung vom Juni 1844 führte
den Kinderbettel auf die Ansteckung durch Bettler und Landstreicher
zurück.[127] Ein halbes Jahrhundert später räumte immerhin die Landshuter
Presse ein, dass das Problem nicht von außen in die Stadt hineingetragen,
sondern durch Armut am Ort verursacht wurde.[128]

Der Landshuter Magistrat trennte sich nur schwer von der tradierten
Sicht des Wanderbettels. Wenn die „Rotten von arbeitsscheuem
Gesindel"[129] nicht mehr als das radikale Gegenbild des sesshaften,
arbeitsfrohen und gehorsamen Untertanen wahrgenommen werden
sollten,[130] dann musste die behördliche Sicht der sozialen Verhältnisse
überprüft werden. Dass die Empfänger von Armenunterstützung in
Landshut nur mit zusätzlichem Bettel überleben konnten, wollte sich der
Magistrat freilich nicht eingestehen. In seiner Bekanntmachung vom 1.
März 1880, die die niederbayerische Regierung angemahnt hatte,[131] heißt

---

[127] Vgl. dazu die in Anm. 124 zit. Bekanntmachung.

[128] *Kurier von Niederbayern* 44 (11.2.1893).

[129] Zit. nach der Bekanntmachung der niederbayerischen Regierung vom 14. Juni
1844. Vgl. Anm. 124.

[130] Die Bereitschaft, Bettler und Landstreicher zum gesellschaftlichen Sündenbock
abzustempeln, ging weit über ihren vermuteten Einfluss auf den lokalen Bettel
hinaus. Wurden „Ruhe und Ordnung" gestört, standen Bettler und Landstreicher
von vornherein als Schuldige fest. Ein Beispiel ist der Brand in einem Kuhstall in
Landshut im August 1867. Einen Tag später wurden Bettler und Landstreicher –
ohne dass irgendjemand Näheres über die Ursachen des Brandes wusste – der
Brandstiftung bezichtigt. Vgl. dazu StAL, B 2, Nr. 2159, Bettelunwesen, Haus-
und Straßenbettel und deren Bestrafung, Schreiben der niederbayerischen
Regierung an den Magistrat in Landshut vom 1. September 1867.

[131] StAL, B 2, Nr. 2159, Bettelunwesen, Haus- und Straßenbettel und deren
Bestrafung 1867–80, Schreiben der Regierung von Niederbayern an die kgl.
Bezirksämter in Niederbayern und die Magistrate der Städte Deggendorf,
Landshut, Passau und Straubing vom 15. Februar 1880.

es zu dieser Frage lediglich, dass die Armenfürsorge der Stadt „ausreichende Unterstützungen" gewähre.[132]

Völlig unzugänglich für das Elend des Bettels war der Magistrat allerdings nicht. Deutlich kann man das daran sehen, dass er die Kriminalisierung der Bettler und Landstreicher nur halbherzig mitvollzog. Die Staatsregierung und die niederbayerische Regierung mussten in Landshut immer wieder aufs Neue zum Einschreiten gegen Wanderbettler drängen und dazu auffordern, die Strenge des Gesetzes walten zu lassen. Schließlich riss der niederbayerischen Regierung die Geduld. Aufgeschreckt durch Presseberichte über Scharen von Bettlern in Landshut, deren Treiben die Stadtverwaltung, wie es hieß, untätig zusah, rügte sie in einem Schreiben an den Magistrat vom 1. September 1867 dessen „Indolenz" und wies ihn nachdrücklich an, „sofort mit aller Energie" gegen die Vaganten vorzugehen. Andernfalls werde sie die Verantwortlichen „mit empfindlicher Disziplinarstrafe unnachsichtlich" zur Rechenschaft ziehen.[133]

Eine Politik des Dreinschlagens war jedoch für Landshut angesichts der verbreiteten subversiven Reintegration der Bettler in die Gesellschaft ziemlich realitätsfern. Die Neigung zur nachsichtigen Wahrnehmung des Bettels begann bei der örtlichen Polizei und setzte sich bei Honoratioren der Stadt fort, wie man am Fall einer Landshuter Bettlerin zeigen kann.

Maria Härtl, die Witwe eines Landshuter Wagners, pflegte täglich an der Landshuter Spitalerbrücke zu betteln. In einem Polizeibericht an den Landshuter Magistrat vom 30. September 1876 heißt es, vor einigen Jahren sei man einmal gegen die „ziemlich alte, gebrechliche" Frau vorgegangen und habe sie „vom Platze geschafft". Alle späteren Versuche seien jedoch gescheitert. Die Bettlerin werde gegenüber der anrückenden Polizei „grob, schimpft und bemerkt, daß sie nicht gehe, weil der Bettel ihr Gewerbe sei". Maria Härtl bettelte nicht nur für ihren Lebensunterhalt. Einen Teil der Almosen übergab sie regelmäßig dem Kurator der Stadtpfarrei.[134]

---

[132] StAL, B 2, Nr. 2159, Bettelunwesen, Haus- und Straßenbettel und deren Bestrafung 1867–80, Handschriftliches Konzept und gedruckter Text der Bekanntmachung vom 1. März 1880.

[133] StAL, B 2, Nr. 2159, Bettelunwesen, Haus- und Straßenbettel und deren Bestrafung 1867–80, Schreiben der niederbayerischen Regierung an den Magistrat in Landshut vom 1. September 1867.

[134] StAL, B 2, Nr. 2159, Bettelunwesen, Haus- und Straßenbettel und deren Bestrafung 1867–80, Schreiben der Polizeiwache Landshut an den Landshuter Magistrat vom 30. September 1876.

Vor diesem Hintergrund war guter Rat teuer. Die Volksstimmung, die Haltung kirchlicher Vertreter und die hier und da zu erkennende Nachsicht der Polizei gegenüber den Bettlern[135] waren ausschlaggebend dafür, dass das Problem des Bettels in Landshut lange auf kleiner Flamme gekocht werden konnte. Andererseits ließ sich der Magistrat dafür nicht uneingeschränkt als Verbündeter gewinnen: Seine bloß aufschiebende und im Ganzen ambivalente Politik reichte nicht aus, um eine Barriere gegen die rigideste Form staatlicher Bettelbekämpfung zu errichten, nämlich gegen die Einweisung besonders „korrektionsbedürftiger" Bettler in die Arbeitshäuser.[136] Am Ende rangierten daher in Landshut im Kampf gegen den Bettel – nimmt man die schon erwähnte gesetzliche Verhaltensregulierung auch der würdigen Armen hinzu – das Polizei-, Straf- und Verwaltungsrecht mit weitem Abstand vor dem Fürsorgerecht, wie dies auch in anderen Teilen des Deutschen Reiches der Fall war.[137]

Auch konservative Zeitgenossen wie Hermann Wagener, Bismarcks zeitweiliger Berater in sozialpolitischen Fragen, sprachen angesichts dieser Situation von der reichsdeutschen Armenpolitik als einer Politik der Furcht und des bloß repressiven Umgangs mit einem sozialen Problem.[138] Die bayerische Bürokratie machte aus dem für sie zentralen Aspekt des Problems keinen Hehl: Die Bekämpfung des Bettels sollte dem Schutz der „Wohlhabenderen" dienen.[139] Dazu einige Erläuterungen.

Furcht verbreitete in Landshut ein Bettlertypus, der zumeist aus Böhmen oder anderen Regionen Österreich-Ungarns stammte, rebellisch gesinnt und häufig bewaffnet war, in den Gaststätten zu schreien und zu fluchen pflegte und beim Zugriff der Polizei „Widerstand gegen die Staatsgewalt" leistete.[140] Nichts deutet darauf hin, dass dieser Typus, der

---

[135] Zu diesem Tieferhängen des Problems gehörte auch, dass Bettler und Landstreicher durchweg nicht wegen des Verstoßes gegen geltende Gesetze verurteilt wurden, sondern wegen einer „Übertretung", nach damaliger juristischer Interpretation also wegen „Rechtsgefährdung". Vgl. *Ergebnisse der Strafrechtspflege im Königreich Bayern*, S. LXXII.

[136] StAL, B 2, Nr. 2473–2477, Unterbringung im Arbeitshaus s. d. In Landshut bestand kein Arbeitshaus. Bettler und Landstreicher, die das Landshuter Land- oder Stadtgericht zur Einweisung in ein Arbeitshaus verurteilte, wurden überwiegend in das Arbeitshaus Rebdorf überführt. Dort hatte der bayerische Staat 1855 in einem während der Säkularisierung aufgelösten Kloster ein Arbeitshaus eingerichtet.

[137] Vgl. Sachße und Tennstedt, *Geschichte der Armenfürsorge* Bd. 1, S. 212.

[138] Ebenda, S. 214.

[139] So die Bekanntmachung der niederbayerischen Regierung vom 14. Juni 1844. Vgl. Anm. 124.

[140] StAL, B 2, Nr. 2156, Zwangsarbeitshäuser und Strafanstalten 1816–58; Nr.

so offensichtlich anders war als der akzeptierte demütige Arme, über individuelles Sich-Durchschlagen hinaus Umstürzlerisches im Sinn hatte.[141] Obwohl die Vaganten stets in Gruppen unterwegs waren, fehlen Anzeichen dafür, dass sie als Gruppe handlungsfähig gewesen wären. Von der im 18. Jahrhundert in Bayern verbreiteten Subkultur der Wanderbettler und ihren kollektiven Verhaltensmustern, die sich z. B. in den „Armenbällen", d. h. in ausgedehnten Zechgelagen, artikulierten,[142] findet sich im 19. Jahrhundert keine Spur mehr.

Indem die Kriminalisierung des Bettels und der Landstreicherei an diesem Typus ansetzte, auf den die Masse der Stadt- und Landesverweise und der Einweisungen in die Arbeitshäuser entfiel, verband sich Arbeitsscheu als das anstößigste Merkmal des Bettels mit dem Gespenst des Umsturzes und dem Erschrecken der Behörden darüber, dass Not und Elend nicht mehr klaglos hingenommen wurden.

Mit der Realität hatte dieses öffentliche Schreckbild jedenfalls im Hinblick auf Arbeitsscheu wenig zu tun. Die Erhebung von 1885 über Verarmungsursachen im Deutschen Reich, die nur Bayern und Elsaß-Lothringen nicht erfasste, ergab, dass lediglich 1,2 Prozent aller Fälle von Verarmung auf Arbeitsscheu zurückgeführt werden konnten.[143] Da auf der anderen Seite Verarmung aufgrund von Erwerbslosigkeit mehr als fünf Prozent ausmachte,[144] Hilfsbedürftigkeit also in viel stärkerem Maße mit der Arbeitsverfassung zusammenhing, erschienen die moralische Ächtung und rechtliche Diskriminierung der Armutsbevölkerung doppelt fragwürdig.

Die um Arbeitsamkeit und Disziplin zentrierten Kampagnen gegen Bettler und Landstreicher in Bayern lassen sich vor diesem Hintergrund nicht unmittelbar mit den gesellschaftlichen Realitäten der Zeit

---

2173, Akte Joseph Fischer 1870, Akte Georg Babel 1871; Nr. 2473, Akte Franz Petrik 1893, Akte Otto Bondy 1895.

[141] Einschränkend muss dazu festgestellt werden, dass Polizeiakten (als einzige Quelle im vorliegenden Zusammenhang) für die mentale Verfassung der Bettler und Vaganten auch deshalb nicht sehr aussagekräftig sind, weil sie diesen Aspekt in aller Regel nur bei deren Ergreifung, Vernehmung und gerichtlichen Verurteilung beleuchten.

[142] Vgl. dazu den Bericht über ein Bettlerfest im Allgäu im Jahr 1797, abgedruckt bei Sachße und Tennstedt, *Geschichte der Armenfürsorge* Bd. 1, S. 134. Zum sozialen Habitus der Bettler und Landstreicher in Bayern im späten 18. Jahrhundert siehe Carsten Küther, *Menschen auf der Straße. Vagierende Unterschichten in Bayern, Franken und Schwaben in der 2. Hälfte des 18. Jahrhunderts* (Göttingen: Vandenhoeck und Ruprecht, 1983).

[143] *Statistik des Deutschen Reiches* Bd. 29 (Berlin: s. t., 1887), S. 40.

[144] Ebenda.

zusammenbringen. Zwar könnte, auf den ersten Blick, ihre Funktion
darin   bestanden   haben,   strukturelle   Voraussetzungen   des
Industrialisierungsprozesses zu schaffen, indem sie einen erzieherischen
Beitrag zur Umwandlung von Nicht-Arbeit in Lohnarbeit und zur
Kontrolle über die Anwendungsbedingungen von Arbeitskraft leisteten.[145]
Dass aber der Arbeitserziehung in der bürokratischen Praxis nur wenig
Bedeutung zugemessen wurde, zeigt die Zusammensetzung der Insassen
der Arbeitshäuser. Nachdem es bereits in den 1840er Jahren üblich
geworden war, „Krüppelhafte, Epileptische und Blödsinnige" in diese
Anstalten einzuliefern,[146] wurden auch in den folgenden Jahren wegen der
chronischen Überfüllung der bayerischen Gefängnisse immer wieder
gerichtlich abgeurteilte Verbrecher in die Arbeitshäuser verlegt.[147] Die
Arbeitsvorgänge in den Arbeitshäusern waren außerdem zu stumpfsinnig,
um die Vorstellung einer produktiven Nutzung der Arbeitskraft und des
Sinns von Arbeit vermitteln zu können.[148] In diesem Punkt unterschieden
sich die Arbeitshäuser nicht von den Armenhäusern, in denen – wie in
Landshut – freiwillig gearbeitet wurde.[149]

    Mit der sozialen Zusammensetzung ihrer Insassen knüpften die
Arbeitshäuser an die Zucht- und Arbeitshäuser des 18. Jahrhunderts an.
Deren Beitrag zur merkantilen Wirtschaftsförderung ist unbestritten.[150]
Die disziplinäre Funktion der Arbeitshäuser bei der Bekämpfung des
Bettels zielte jedoch darüber hinaus erkennbar auf die Ausgrenzung
gesellschaftlicher Randgruppen.[151] Die Zusammenführung von Verbrechern

---

[145] Zu der These, dass die Funktion sozialpolitischer Maßnahmen auf der
staatlichen Bearbeitung dieses Problems beruht, siehe Claus Offe, "Staatstheorie
und Sozialpolitik. Funktionen und Innovationsprozesse der Sozialpolitik," in ders.,
*Strukturprobleme des kapitalistischen Staates. Aufsätze zur Politischen Soziologie.
Veränderte Neuausgabe*, Hrsg. Jens Borchert und Stephan Lessenich (Frankfurt
und New York: Campus-Verl., 2006), S. 157.
[146] StAL, B 2, Nr. 2156, Zwangsarbeitshäuser und Strafanstalten 1816–58,
Schreiben der Koeniglichen Regierung von Niederbayern an den Magistrat der
Kreishauptstadt Landshut vom 29. Mai 1844.
[147] StAL, B 2, Nr. 2156, Zwangsarbeitshäuser und Strafanstalten 1816–58,
Schreiben des Präsidiums der Koeniglichen Regierung von Niederbayern an die
Landgerichts-Vorstände und Stadtmagistrate von Niederbayern vom 13. Juni 1850.
[148] Für Augsburg vgl. dazu Susanne F. Eser, *Verwaltet und verwahrt. Armenpolitik
und Arme in Augsburg. Vom Ende der reichsstädtischen Zeit bis zum Ersten
Weltkrieg* (Sigmaringen: Thorbecke, 1995).
[149] Schreyer, *Landshut*, S. 21.
[150] Sachße und Tennstedt, *Geschichte der Armenfürsorge* Bd. 1, S. 115 ff.
[151] Ebenda, S. 112. Eine Fallstudie für Bayern ist Rudolf Endres, "Das ‚Straf-
Arbeitshaus' St. Georgen bei Bayreuth," *Jahrbuch der Sozialarbeit* 4 (1981): S.

mit Bettlern, Huren, Krüppeln und Wahnsinnigen in diesen Anstalten produzierte eine illegalisierte Gegengesellschaft. Diesem Konzept blieben die bayerischen Arbeitshäuser des 19. Jahrhunderts verhaftet.

Dass die Armutsproblematik in Bayern mit vorindustriellen gesellschaftlichen Strukturen zusammengedacht wurde, lässt vor allem das „Heimatprinzip" der Armengesetzgebung vermuten, an dem Bayern im Unterschied zum Deutschen Reich bis 1916 festhielt. Die Bestimmung des Gesetzes vom April 1869, wonach Armenunterstützung nur durch die Heimatgemeinde gewährt werden konnte, war im Grunde auf eine statische wirtschaftliche Ordnung zugeschnitten; sie hemmte Mobilität, die im industriellen Zeitalter erforderliche (und durch die Gesetzgebung in Preußen schon 1842 ermöglichte) Freizügigkeit im Sinne der „Wanderung zur Arbeit". Die Novellierung des bayerischen Heimatgesetzes im Jahr 1896 erleichterte zwar in mancher Hinsicht die Gewährung des Heimatrechts, änderte aber grundsätzlich nichts an dem für die soziale und wirtschaftliche Entwicklung kontraproduktiven Auseinanderfallen von Heimat und Wohnort. Das räumten die Behörden selbst ein.[152]

Die mit dem Heimatprinzip einhergehende Verklärung der traditionalen Agrargesellschaft ist an Art. 18 des Gesetzes von 1869 abzulesen. Danach bedurfte es auf dem Lande keiner institutionellen Vorkehrungen zur Bekämpfung der Armut. Die Unterstützung der Armen in den Dörfern sollte durch das traditionelle Verfahren der „Umfuhr" gewährleistet werden, das die Bauern in einer bestimmten Reihenfolge verpflichtete, für die Verköstigung der Armen zu sorgen. In welchem Maße dabei Gemeinsinn und soziale Integrationsfähigkeit der dörflich-bäuerlichen Lebenswelt überschätzt wurden, zeigt die Situation der Armen auf dem Lande, die in Hirtenhäusern und in Kolonien auf verlassenen Höfen dahinvegetierten, auch deshalb, weil die ärmeren Bauern mit ihrem Beitrag zur Umfuhr überfordert waren.[153] Die ländliche Bevölkerung war insgesamt ärmer als die städtische Bevölkerung.[154] Wo auf dem Lande Wohltätigkeitsanstalten bestanden, erreichten sie in der Regel nur ein Drittel der finanziellen Leistungsfähigkeit entsprechender städtischer Einrichtungen.[155]

Der Rückgriff auf einen vorindustriellen *ordre naturel* orientierte sich an einer lokalen, unhinterfragt für bewahrenswert erklärten sozialen Identität. Sie war Ausdruck der Überhöhung nicht nur des ländlichen

---

89–105.
[152] Vgl. *Das Heimat- und Armenwesen in Bayern*, S. 94.
[153] Vgl. Egger, *Medizinische Topographie*, S. 104 f.
[154] *Das Heimat- und Armenwesen in Bayern*, S. 59.
[155] Ebenda, S. 61.

Milieus. Die Unterscheidung zwischen einheimischen und fremden Armen in Landshut betonte auch für den städtischen Bereich den Vorrang des Lokalen vor den in Fluss geratenen sozialen Strukturen und neigte in gleicher Weise zur Idealisierung einer überschaubaren, d. h. ortsgebundenen sozialen Realität.

Die Einbettung des Armutsproblems in eine statische wirtschaftliche Ordnung, die als sozial intakt vorgestellt wurde, deutet auf den Einfluss des Zentrums hin. Dem politisch organisierten Katholizismus ging es um die Restauration der gesamten Gesellschaft, wobei die Konservierung traditionaler agrarischer Strukturen unter Führung von Adel und Bauerntum die Hauptrolle spielte.[156] Der Volksunterricht auf der Kanzel lieferte die zu dieser Zielvorstellung passende düstere Zeitkritik: Not und Elend seien die Folge des Verfalls traditioneller Werte, der „Anmaßung" und des „liederlichen" Lebenswandels der Unterschichten.[157] Armenpflegschaftsrat und Magistrat in Landshut sekundierten dem durch Versuche, „Demut" zu fördern, und wiesen die Armen auf ihre Pflicht hin, den alljährlichen „Seelengottesdienst für die verstorbenen Wohlthäter der Armen" zu besuchen.[158]

In der Rückkehr zur althergebrachten agrarischen Lebenswelt lag für das Zentrum der Schlüssel zur Lösung des Problems der Armut; das unterstrich beispielsweise auch der Katholikentag in Landshut im September 1897. Die Generalversammlung der Katholiken Deutschlands war sich darin einig, dass die Organisation der Berufsstände auf christlicher Grundlage die entscheidende Voraussetzung für die Beseitigung von Not und Elend bildete, und diese Organisation sollte vom Bauernstand ausgehen, dem „Herz im Gesellschaftskörper".[159]

Das Roll-back zu vorindustriellen Verhältnissen konnte mit wachsendem Abstand zu diesen Verhältnissen gerade auch in der Armenpolitik immer weniger auf Momente der Repression verzichten. Vom vormodernen Konzept der öffentlichen Wohlfahrt und von vorindustriellen Gemeinwohlvorstellungen im Sinne der moralischen Ökonomie hatte sich die Gesellschaft de facto längst verabschiedet. Zwar spiegelt der oben erwähnte Landshuter Bierkrawall von 1880 noch die paternalistische Tradition moralischer Grundannahmen über eine „gerechte" Ökonomie

---

[156] Vgl. Anm. 115. In breiterem Zusammenhang zu dieser Frage Barrington Moore, *Soziale Ursprünge von Diktatur und Demokratie. Die Rolle der Grundbesitzer und Bauern bei der Entstehung der modernen Welt* (Frankfurt: Suhrkamp, 1969).

[157] Blessing, *Staat und Kirche*, S. 139 f.

[158] *Landshuter Wochenblatt* 54 (28.10.1860): S. 176.

[159] *Kurier für Niederbayern* 23 (2.9.1897).

wider, doch war die Entscheidung gegen solche traditionalistischen Standards längst gefallen. Das verdeutlichen für Landshut, wie gezeigt, die Erosion der sozialprotektionistischen Funktion der Getreideschranne, die reibungslose Liberalisierung des lokalen Brotmarktes, die Auflösung der korporativen Schutzmaßnahmen im Handwerk und schließlich auch das Rentabilitätsdenken des Magistrats in der Armenfürsorge. Was die Gesellschaft mit ihrem Tribut an die neue Ökonomie hinter sich gelassen hatte, konnte nur auf repressivem Wege wiederhergestellt werden. Der autoritäre Grundzug der öffentlichen Armenfürsorge, die Diszplinierung der verschämten und die Kriminalisierung der unverschämten Armen haben hier ihren Ursprung.

V.

Die vorangegangenen Ausführungen sind wegen der hier verwendeten Definition von Armut[160] vorläufig.

In diesem Beitrag wird ein Armutskonzept benutzt, das auf einer politisch festgelegten Armutsgrenze beruht. Der Mangel dieses Konzepts ist seine Anfälligkeit für Manipulationen, die den Umfang der Armutsbevölkerung unmittelbar beeinflussen.[161] Ein Beispiel in unserem Zusammenhang ist die zwar nie kodifizierte, in der behördlichen Praxis aber relevante Unterscheidung zwischen verschämten und unverschämten Armen, die die Gewährung von Armenunterstützung an politisch erwünschte soziale Verhaltensmuster knüpfte.

Von diesem politischen Armutskonzept unterscheiden sich andere Armutskonzepte dadurch, dass sie Selbsteinschätzung, Bedürfnisse und Lebenslagen der Armen weit mehr berücksichtigen.[162] Ihre Anwendung

---

[160] Zu den verschiedenen Armutskonzepten siehe Herbert Jacobs, "Armut," in *Soziologie des Sozialstaats. Gesellschaftliche Grundlagen, historische Zusammenhänge und aktuelle Entwicklungstendenzen*, Hrsg. Jutta Allmendinger und Wolfgang Ludwig-Mayerhofer (Weinheim und München: Juventa-Verl., 2000), S. 237–268.

[161] Ein instruktives Beispiel ist die alljährliche Debatte im Bundestag über den seit 2001 vorgelegten „Armuts- und Reichtumsbericht der Bundesregierung". Zahlreiche Hinweise auf den manipulativen Umgang der Behörden mit der Armutsproblematik am Beispiel der amerikanischen *Welfare*-Politik bei Frances F. Piven und Richard A. Cloward, *Regulating the Poor: The Functions of Public Welfare* (New York: Random House, 1971).

[162] Ansätze zu einem Konzept von Armut, das sich die Perspektive der Betroffenen zu eigen macht, finden sich für einen Teil Frankens im 19. Jahrhundert bei Gerhard Philipp Wolf, „‚Nun bin ich aber kein Bettler, sondern ein Unglücklicher!' Beobachtungen zum Armenwesen im ehemaligen Landgerichtsbezirk Pegnitz,"

setzt jedoch Quellen voraus, die einen viel genaueren Blick auf die Alltagswirklichkeit der Armen ermöglichen als die Akten der Behörden, die im vorliegenden Fall zur Verfügung standen.

Die Problematik unterschiedlicher Definitionen von Armut, die dann auch zu unterschiedlichen Aussagen über das Ausmaß der Armut kommen, kann deshalb in diesem Beitrag nur gestreift werden. Für Landshut gilt jedenfalls, dass die Zahl der Empfänger von Armenunterstützung, also der anhand der politischen Definition von Armut ermittelten Armen, wenig über das tatsächliche Ausmaß von Armut aussagt. Eine andere Dimension von Armut kommt in den Blick, wenn man über die zeitgenössischen Kategorien hinausgeht. So registriert keine Statistik im Untersuchungszeitraum Hilfsbedürftigkeit infolge relativer Einkommensarmut. Dazu ein Beispiel aus dem Landshuter Alltag: Die Wohltätigkeitsvereine, deren Tätigkeit sich auf die behördlich registrierten Armen beschränkte, versorgten diese im Winter mit Brennholz. Unterhalb der karitativen Eingreifschwelle war es jedoch eine verbreitete Erscheinung, dass die Unterschichten ihre noch nicht schulpflichtigen Kinder im Winter tagsüber in die städtische Kinderbewahranstalt schickten, weil das Geld für die Heizung der Wohnung fehlte.[163]

VI.

Gibt es einen roten Faden in der Entwicklung der Landshuter Armenfürsorge in der zweiten Hälfte des 19. Jahrhunderts? Zwei durchlaufende Linien zeichnen sich ab; sie rücken das Thema entweder näher an das 18. oder näher an das 20. Jahrhundert heran.

a) Auffällig ist das Fortwirken vorindustrieller Traditionen, vor allem die Fortführung der sozial unspezifischen Disziplinierungsstrategie der Zucht- und Arbeitshäuser des 18. Jahrhunderts. Dass in diesen Anstalten diejenigen, die Arbeit leisten konnten, nicht von Arbeitsunfähigen unterschieden wurden, verweist auf einen anderen Bedeutungsgehalt von Arbeit. Die vorindustrielle Ökonomie ignorierte den Unterschied zwischen produktiver und unproduktiver Arbeit, weil Arbeit noch nicht – wie im Handwerk besonders deutlich – aus der Einbettung in symbolische Zusammenhänge herausgelöst worden war. Maßgebend war der Gegensatz zwischen dem Faulen, der seine soziale Pflicht vernachlässigte, und dem Arbeitenden, der seiner sozialen Pflicht nachkam.[164]

---

[163] Vgl. Schreyer, *Landshut*, S. 24.
[164] Zum Übergang von Arbeit in *embedded economies* zur industriellen Lohnarbeit siehe Karl Polanyi, *The Great Transformation* (New York und Toronto: Farrar &

Die Skandalisierung des Faulenzertums in den Kampagnen der bayerischen Bürokratie gegen Arbeitsscheue bei gleichzeitigem Fehlen eines erzieherischen Konzepts zur produktiven Nutzung der Arbeitskraft zielte insofern nicht auf die Vermittlung zweckrationaler Verhaltensmuster, die die industrielle Entwicklung erforderte, sondern auf eine Universalisierung von Disziplin zur Produktion des gehorsamen Untertanen. In diesem Sinne traten die bayerischen Arbeitshäuser des 19. Jahrhunderts die Nachfolge der Zucht- und Arbeitshäuser des 18. Jahrhunderts an.

Ein zweiter Traditionsstrang ist die Terminologie der Armenfürsorge, die punktuell noch auf die Nürnberger Armenordnung von 1522[165] zurückgriff. Bis zur Jahrhundertwende ist in den Akten der Stadtverwaltung keine Rede von „Erwerbslosigkeit" bzw. „Arbeitslosigkeit", sondern allein von „Armen", von „Armenvätern", von der „Armenkasse" und von „Almosen".

Dass, drittens, Wohltätigkeit mit polizeilichen Kompetenzen verbunden wurde (Kontrolle der karitativen Einrichtungen durch die Polizei), zeigt die Nähe der Wohltätigkeit zu kameralistischen Traditionen, zur Kommerzienwirtschaft des 18. Jahrhunderts, in der die Sphären des Politischen und des Sozialen noch nicht auseinandergetreten waren. Armenpflege fiel unter vorindustriellen Verhältnissen in die Zuständigkeit der „Polizei", d. h. der Verwaltung bzw. der öffentlichen Gewalt[166] und galt von daher als Teil der – repräsentativ eingeschränkten – Öffentlichkeit (s. u.).

Die Bedeutung der Tradition tritt schließlich am paternalistischen Umgang mit der Armutsproblematik in Landshut hervor. Dessen Symbol waren die seit der Reichsgründung 1871 alljährlich veranstalteten „Armenbälle" unter dem Patronat adeliger Damen,[167] die an Theatervorstellungen „zum Besten der Armen" vor 1848 anknüpften.[168] Die Armenbälle zelebrierten Wohltätigkeit noch als „Gabe" ganz im Sinne

---

Rinehart, 1944). Wo die Anfänge dieses Übergangs liegen, ist in der Literatur umstritten. Sachße und Tennstedt, *Geschichte der Armenfürsorge* Bd. 1, S. 14 f., nehmen an, dass Arbeitsmoral und Zeitdisziplin als zwei wesentliche Bedingungen der Gewährleistung von Produktivität bereits in den spätmittelalterlichen Städten Deutschlands auf mittelständisch-handwerklicher Ebene Gegenstand systematischer Bemühungen waren.

[165] Diese ist abgedruckt bei Sachße und Tennstedt, *Geschichte der Armenfürsorge* Bd. 1, S. 67–76.

[166] Der eingangs erwähnte Landshuter Polizeikommissar Gruber war 1807 Vorsitzender der Königlichen Armen-Instituts-Kommission in Landshut.

[167] Weber und Marschall, *Aus dem Leben*, S. 211.

[168] Herzog, *Landshut*, S. 77.

von Mildtätigkeit aus herrscherlicher Gnade.[169] Sie waren von daher mit den am königlichen Hof geführten Debatten über die Lösung der sozialen Probleme verbunden. Der Kulturstaat sollte diesen Debatten zufolge die Rahmenbedingungen für die Bewältigung dieser Probleme schaffen,[170] und dies erforderte nicht geringe Anstrengungen zur Hebung der Kultur des Volkes. Die Armenbälle in Landshut zielten auf diese kulturelle „Veredelung". Mit der Anknüpfung an subkulturelle Traditionen der Armen, an die Armenbälle der Bettler des 18. Jahrhunderts, sollte die Schwelle zur Welt der Ehrbaren und Wohlhabenden gesenkt werden.

Ein Vorreiter der Rückwendung zu vorindustriellen Verhältnissen war der Landshuter Magistrat gleichwohl nicht, dazu war seine Politik zu zwiespältig und zu unentschieden. Sein geringes Verständnis für den Strukturwandel von Armut im Industriezeitalter hinderte ihn nicht daran, sich die Wirtschaftsgesinnung des neuen Zeitalters anzueignen, um Armenfürsorge rentabel zu machen. Die Disziplinierung der Armen trug er noch mit, die Kriminalisierung des Bettels aber nur auf Druck höherer Stellen. Der Grund für dieses Hin und Her lag auch darin, dass der bedeutende konzeptionelle und finanzielle Beitrag der privaten Wohltätigkeit in Landshut der Stadtverwaltung eigene Anstrengungen in der Armenfürsorge lange Zeit ersparte.

b) Nahm also der Magistrat die sich verändernden Entstehungsbedingungen von Armut deshalb kaum wahr, weil er zu tief in der Tradition vorindustrieller Armenpflege steckte? Es ist nicht auszuschließen, dass der Magistrat – und das wäre die zweite durchgehend erkennbare Linie – eine bewusste Strategie der Konfliktabwehr verfolgte.

Unter vorindustriellen Verhältnissen war es üblich, die Namen der Armen bekannt zu machen. Beispiele für Landshut sind die Jahr für Jahr in der lokalen Presse veröffentlichten Listen der Armen[171] und die alljährliche „Konstatirung des Standes der Armuth" durch den Armenpflegschaftsrat, die noch 1850 in der Öffentlichkeit, im Landshuter Rathaussaal, vorgenommen wurde.[172] Dass diese Gelegenheit genutzt wurde, um obrigkeitliche Mildtätigkeit zu demonstrieren, liegt auf der Hand. Während das Ausmaß der Armut im Behördenalltag kleingeredet wurde, lud man zu öffentlichen Verteilungen von Brot und Geld neben den konskribierten Armen auch „Hausarme"[173] ein, die keine

---

[169] Rumschöttel, "König Ludwig II.," S. 122.

[170] Ebenda, S. 124.

[171] Für 1805 und 1806 vgl. dazu: *Landshuter Anzeiger* 3 (20.1.1805); (3.2.1805); (7.2.1805); 4 (16.3.1806).

[172] Vgl. Mößmer, *Ärzte, Bürger, Herzöge*, S. 643.

[173] Diesen Begriff kannte bereits die Nürnberger Armenordnung von 1522, die

Armenunterstützung erhielten, weil sie den Behörden unbekannt waren und aus diesem Grund nur auf informellem Wege (über Angehörige und Bekannte) erreicht werden konnten.[174]

Es ging jedoch bei diesen Kundgebungen paternalistischer Fürsorge nicht in erster Linie um Selbstdarstellung. Relevant ist, dass dieser öffentliche Umgang mit Armut mit der Deutung der Krisen des alten Typs zu tun hatte. Deren ökonomische Brisanz konnte religiös weggedeutet werden, weil sie das Werk des „allmächtigen Gottes" waren, wie es ein Münchener Hofkammerrat 1774 stellvertretend für die Sicht der Zeit im Rückblick auf die Hungerkrise der Jahre 1770–1773 formulierte.[175] Wenn Hunger und Not dem Wirken Gottes zugerechnet werden konnten, dann war die Veröffentlichung der Namen der Armen nicht mit individueller Diskriminierung verbunden.

Die letzte öffentliche Darbietung des Armutsproblems in Landshut war die Versammlung der Armen im Rathaus am Allerseelentag im November 1860. An diesem Tag wurden vor dem Publikum der Wohltäter und „Menschenfreunde" der Stadt nach altem Brauch Geld und Brot an die Armen verteilt.[176] Von ungefähr kam dieser letzte öffentliche Akt nicht. Bereits 1807 war vorgeschlagen worden, die Frage der Armut künftig „im Stillen" zu regeln. Dies sei sowohl im Sinne der Wohltäter als auch der Armen; Letzteren müsse man den „harten Schritt ersparen, ihre Armuth kund zu machen".[177] Die entscheidende Wende leitete jedoch erst die staatliche Bürokratie ein, die noch vor 1848 dazu überging, mit dem verschämten Armen einen Armentypus zu favorisieren, der sein Elend nicht an die Öffentlichkeit trug.

---

allerdings vorsah, dass diese Armen, „die sich aus guten christlichen Gründen schämen zu betteln, jedoch ohne persönliche Hilfe und Handreichung nicht zu leben vermögen", von den städtischen Pflegern aufgesucht und in die Armenpflege der Stadt einbezogen werden sollten. Vgl. Sachße und Tennstedt, *Geschichte der Armenfürsorge* Bd. 1, S. 70.

[174] *Landshuter Wochenblatt* 54 (28.10.1860): S. 176. Um die Hausarmen erreichen zu können, rief der Armenpflegschaftsrat vor öffentlichen Spendenaktionen in der Presse dazu auf, dass jedermann, der einen Hausarmen kannte, dem Magistrat dessen Namen mitteilen sollte.

[175] Zit. nach Helmut Rankl, "Die bayerische Politik in der europäischen Hungerkrise 1770–1773," *Zeitschrift für bayerische Landesgeschichte* 68 (2005): S. 745–779.

[176] Vgl. dazu die Einladung des Magistrats und des Armenpflegschaftsrates zur „Allerseelenspende" im Landshuter Rathaus, abgedruckt in: *Landshuter Wochenblatt* 54 (28.10.1860): S. 176.

[177] *Landshuter Wochenblatt* 1 (8.11.1807).

Wesentlicher Bestandteil dieses Kurswechsels war die von den
Behörden geschürte Tendenz, Armut individuellen Defiziten
zuzuschreiben und in der Öffentlichkeit wie bei den Betroffenen ein
entsprechendes Bewusstsein zu erzeugen. Der Wandel der Perspektive ist
deutlich: In dem Maße, in dem die kapitalistische Produktionsweise die
vorindustrielle *embedded economy* auflöste, wurde Arbeit aus ihren
traditionalen, die Beziehung zwischen der Arbeit und dem Produkt
verbergenden soziokulturellen Bezügen herausgelöst und unter das
Produktivitätsgebot des Systems gestellt.[178] Vor diesem Hintergrund
können die Kampagnen gegen Arbeitsscheue, die kirchlichen Strafreden
über den Verfall der Sitten und das weit verbreitete Misstrauen gegenüber
Empfängern von Armenunterstützung gesehen werden, die von Amts
wegen des „Missbrauchs" öffentlicher Leistungen verdächtigt wurden.[179]

Eindämmung der öffentlichen Thematisierung von Armut und die
Delegierung der Verantwortung für Armut an das Individuum sind – bei
grundsätzlicher Akzeptanz der industriellen Entwicklung im Landshuter
Magistrat – Ausdruck der Konfliktabwehr, des Versuchs, sich der
politischen Zuständigkeit für Armut als Konsequenz der Arbeitsverfassung
der neuen Produktionsweise zu entziehen.[180] Trotz der in Bayern später
einsetzenden Industrialisierung galt dies auch für Landshut. Die Krisen des
neuen Typs hinterließen in der Stadt seit den späten 1860er Jahren ihre
Spuren, und nach 1895 verlor der handwerklich-kleingewerbliche Sektor
unter dem Druck der industriellen Entwicklung seine vorherrschende
Position. Im Endstadium der Großen Depression setzte im produzierenden
Gewerbe Landshuts ein Konzentrationsprozess ein, in dessen Verlauf sich
die Zahl der Beschäftigten in Großbetrieben (über 50 Personen) bis 1907
verdoppelte und ihr Anteil an der Gesamtzahl der Beschäftigten im
Zeitraum 1895–1907 von 24 auf 36 Prozent stieg.[181]

---

[178] Vgl. dazu Untersuchung von Polanyi, *The Great Transformation*.

[179] Aufschlussreich sind in dieser Hinsicht die Briefwechsel zwischen
Unterstützungsbedürftigen und dem Landshuter Magistrat. StAL, B 2, Nr. 14741,
Unterstützungsgesuche 1877–1911. In welchem Maße die Behörden die
Empfänger von Armenunterstützung des Missbrauchs dieser Unterstützung
verdächtigten, zeigen über 70 Stellungnahmen bayerischer Land- und
Stadtgemeinden aus den Jahren 1905–1907 zu den Ursachen von Armut, in
Auszügen abgedruckt in: *Das Heimat- und Armenwesen in Bayern*, S. 85–93.

[180] Die private Wohltätigkeit hat die Praxis der Geheimhaltung der Namen der
Armen offenbar weitgehend übernommen. Vgl. dazu den Tätigkeitsbericht des
Frauenvereins zur Unterstützung verschämter Armer in Berlin für das Jahr 1892,
abgedruckt bei Sachße und Tennstedt, *Geschichte der Armenfürsorge* Bd. 1, S.
307–30.

[181] Preißler, "Wirtschaft und Gesellschaft," S. 106.

Es gibt also Gründe für beide Interpretationen. Ob man nun die restaurativen Tendenzen oder die „kostensparende" Anpassung an die industrielle Entwicklung hervorhebt – in beiden Fällen hat die kommunale Armenfürsorge in Landshut keine konsistente Politik verfolgt. Für die Rückkehr zu vorindustriellen Verhältnissen schien ihr der Preis einer autoritären Regelung des Armutsproblems am Ende doch zu hoch. Andererseits war sie nicht bereit, die finanzielle Last „systemproduzierter" Armut in ihrem ganzen Ausmaß zu tragen.[182]

---

[182] Über das vor allem in Phasen hoher Beschäftigung von der politischen Klasse für realisierbar gehaltene Wunschbild der „Reprivatisierung des Beschäftigungsrisikos" wurde im rechten Parteienspektrum der Bundesrepublik Deutschland noch in den 1970er Jahren öffentlich diskutiert. Vgl. Claus Offe, "Klassenherrschaft und politisches System. Die Selektivität politischer Institutionen," in ders., *Strukturprobleme des kapitalistischen Staates. Aufsätze zur Politischen Soziologie. Veränderte Neuausgabe*, Hrsg. Jens Borchert und Stephan Lessenich (Frankfurt und New York: Campus-Verl., 2006), S. 95–126, hier 121.

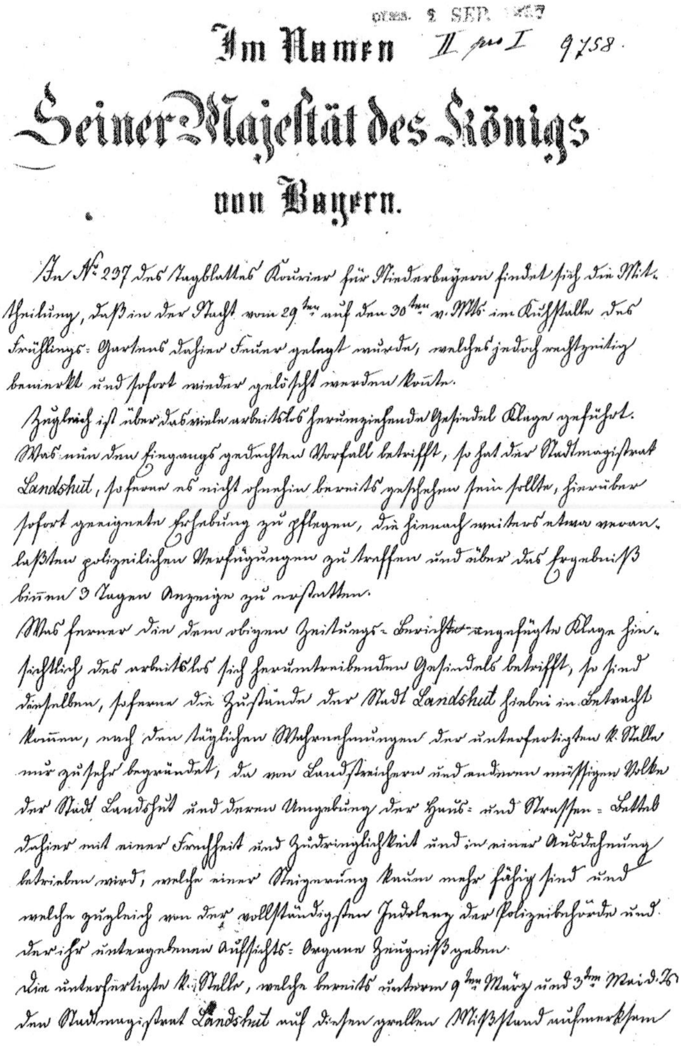

pres. 2 SEP. 1867 II pr. I 9758.

Im Namen
Seiner Majestät des Königs
von Bayern.

In No 237 des Tagblattes Kurier für Niederbayern findet sich die Mittheilung, daß in der Nacht vom 29ten auf den 30ten v. Mts im Kuhstalle des Frühlings-Gartens dahier Feuer gelegt wurde, welches jedoch rechtzeitig bemerkt und sofort wieder gelöscht werden konnte.

Zugleich ist über das viele arbeitslos herumziehende Gesindel Klage geführt.

Was nun den Eingangs gedachten Vorfall betrifft, so hat der Stadtmagistrat Landshut, soferne es nicht ohnehin bereits geschehen sein sollte, hierüber sofort geeignete Erhebung zu pflegen, die hienach weiters etwa veranlaßten polizeilichen Verfügungen zu treffen und über das Ergebniß binnen 3 Tagen Anzeige zu erstatten.

Was ferner die dem obigen Zeitungs-Berichte angefügte Klage hinsichtlich des arbeitslos sich herumtreibenden Gesindels betrifft, so sind dieselben, soferne die Zustände der Stadt Landshut hiebei in Betracht kommen, nach den täglichen Wahrnehmungen der unterfertigten K. Stelle nur zu sehr begründet, da von Landstreichern und anderem müssigen Volke der Stadt Landshut und deren Umgebung der Haus- und Strassen-Bettel dahier mit einer Frechheit und Zudringlichkeit und in einer Ausdehnung betrieben wird, welche einer Steigerung kaum mehr fähig sind und welche zugleich von der vollständigsten Indolenz der Polizeibehörde und der ihr untergebenen Aufsichts-Organe Zeugniß geben.

Die unterfertigte K. Stelle, welche bereits unterm 9ten März und 3ten Mai d. Js den Stadtmagistrat Landshut auf diesen grellen Mißstand aufmerksam

Fig. 9-1 Schreiben der niederbayerischen Regierung an den Magistrat in Landshut vom 1. September 1867. (StAL, B 2, Nr. 2159, Bettelunwesen, Haus- und Straßenbettel und deren Bestrafung.)

CHAPTER TEN

ZWISCHEN STAATLICHER FÜRSORGE UND GEWALTTÄTIGER SELBSTHILFE: DIE ARMEN IN BARCELONA WÄHREND DER ZWISCHENKRIEGSZEIT (1918–1936)

FLORIAN GRAFL

Between state care and violent self-help: the poor in Barcelona in between the World Wars (1918–1936)

Abstract: Even before the outbreak of the Spanish Civil War in July 1936, weekdays in the Catalan capital of Barcelona were strongly influenced by the endless violence that ranged from political assassinations through armed robberies to targeted sabotage in the form of arson attacks on buses and trams. In order to explain how deeply the absence of any strategy in social policy in Barcelona caused the poor to secure their livelihood by committing crimes and other violence, this paper closely monitors Spanish social policy, with a particular focus on Barcelona. In doing so, the paper deals with social reforms and associated public discussions, as well as with single institutions dedicated to eradicating poverty. This is illustrated by the example of Barcelona in the inter-war period. First, the living conditions of the poorer sections of the Barcelona population are introduced. Following this, how and to what extent attempts to improve the overall unfavourable situation were made are shown. Finally, the paper examines how much the survival of the poorer members of the city population depended on illegal means.

Einleitung

„Am späten Morgen des 7. Juni 1926 überquerte ein alter Mann in der Nähe der Bailen-Straße die Gran Via [Prachtstraße, die sich vertikal quer durch Barcelona zieht, Anm. d. Verf.] im Stadtviertel Eixample. Er war klein, mit hellblauen Augen und hatte lockige silbergraue Haare. Er trug einen abgenutzten schwarzen Anzug. Als er über die Gran Via schlurfte,

um auf die andere Straßenseite zu gelangen, schaute er weder nach rechts
noch nach links und bemerkte deshalb die herannahende Straßenbahn der
Linie 30 nicht. Er ignorierte die erklingende Alarmglocke wie auch die
warnenden Rufe der Passanten und wurde überfahren. Als die Polizei den
Kreis Schaulustiger, der sich um den Verletzten gebildet hatte,
weggescheucht hatte, stellte sich heraus, dass seine Taschen leer waren
und sich deshalb die Identität der Person nicht ermitteln ließ. Er war durch
die Räder der Straßenbahn so schlimm verletzt worden, dass vier Taxis,
die nacheinander am Unfallort vorbeifuhren, es ablehnten, ihn zu einem
Krankenhaus zu fahren. Schließlich kam ein Krankenwagen. Der Verletzte
atmete noch, roch aber nicht nach Alkohol. Seine Kleidung ließ darauf
schließen, dass er zwar arm, aber offensichtlich kein Alkoholiker war. Es
schien sich um einen der vielen heruntergekommenen Rentner zu handeln,
die einsam in den Pensionen von Barcelona lebten. So wurde er zum
Hospital Sant Creu gebracht und dort auf ein eisernes Feldbett in der
öffentlichen Abteilung gelegt. Erst am nächsten Tag, als Leute kamen, um
nach ihm zu sehen, stellte sich heraus, dass es sich bei dem Patienten um
Spaniens bekanntesten Architekten, Antoni Gaudí i Cornet, handelte.
Seine besorgten Freunde versuchten ihn in eine Privatklinik verlegen zu
lassen, aber Gaudí lehnte dieses Ansinnen ab. ‚Mein Platz', soll er gesagt
haben, ‚ist hier, unter den Armen'"[1].

Ob Antoni Gaudí, der Architekt der Sagrada Familía, der Casa Batlló
und der Casa Milà, die heute jährlich Millionen von Besuchern in die
katalanische Hafenstadt Barcelona locken, wirklich darauf bestand, im
öffentlichen Krankenhaus unter den Armen zu bleiben und ob er deswegen
wenige Tage später nach dem Unfall seinen Verletzungen erlag, bleibt
Spekulation. Was aber durch diese in Robert Hughes' weltbekanntem
Buch über Barcelona erzählte Episode deutlich wird, ist, dass Armut im
Barcelona der Zwischenkriegszeit von 1918 bis 1936 ein alltägliches
Phänomen war und Arm- oder Reichsein im Extremfall über Leben und
Tod entscheiden konnte.

Außer dem extremen Gefälle zwischen Reich und Arm war es vor
allem der Gegensatz von Glanz und Gewalt, der das Stadtleben in den
ersten Jahrzehnten des 20. Jahrhunderts entscheidend prägte. So zeugen
nicht nur die Prachtbauten Gaudís vom Aufschwung, den die Stadt um die
Jahrhundertwende erlebte, sondern auch die Tatsache, dass Barcelona
innerhalb kürzester Zeit, 1888 und 1929, zweimal die prestigeträchtige
Weltausstellung ausrichtete.[2]

---

[1] Zitiert in Robert Hughes, *Barcelona* (London: Harvill, 1992), S. 464.
[2] Martin Baumeister, "Alteuropäische Städte auf dem Weg in die Moderne.
Großausstellungen und metropolitane Identitäten in Barcelona und Turin 1884 bis

Auf der anderen Seite durchlitten die Bürger Barcelonas eine der gewaltsamsten Epochen ihrer Geschichte. Die zu Beginn der 1890er Jahre einsetzenden anarchistischen Bombenattentate machten die Stadt zum ersten Mal auch außerhalb der iberischen Halbinsel bekannt, wo sie bald als „La Ciudad de las Bombas" (Die Stadt der Bomben) in Verruf kam.[3] Neben der Radikalisierung des politischen Klimas verschärften sich zu Beginn des 20. Jahrhunderts zunehmend auch die Konflikte zwischen Arbeiterschaft und Bourgeoisie. Diese führten schließlich zu dem von 1919 bis 1923 andauernden „Pistolerismo", in dessen Verlauf mehr als 800 Personen auf offener Straße ermordet wurden.[4] Zu Beginn der 1930er Jahre machte Barcelona schließlich aufgrund der sich fast täglich ereignenden spektakulären Raubüberfälle erneut wegen seiner hohen Gewaltsamkeit von sich reden.[5]

Besonders angloamerikanische Historiker machten für die extreme Gewalt in Barcelona während der Zwischenkriegszeit vor allem die schwierigen Lebensverhältnisse der ärmeren Bevölkerung verantwortlich.[6] Um wirklich klären zu können, inwiefern die soziale Notlage den Armen

---

1929," *Historische Anthropologie* 10 (2002): S. 449–463.

[3] Angesichts der Fülle der Forschungsliteratur zum Terrorismus in Barcelona um die Jahrhundertwende sei hier nur auf das klassische Pionierwerk von Romero Maura, "Terrorism in Barcelona and its Impact on Spanish Politics, 1904–1909," *Past and Present* 41 (1968): S. 130–183 sowie auf die aktuellste Arbeit von Ángel Herrerín López, *Anarquía, dinamita y revolución social. Violencia y represión en la España de entre siglos (1868–1909)* (Madrid: Los Libros de la Catarata, 2011), hingewiesen.

[4] Auch diese Episode der Stadtgeschichte von Barcelona ist bereits gut erforscht, deshalb sei hier nur auf das neue Übersichtswerk des führenden katalanischen Historikers Albert Balcells hingewiesen: Albert Balcells, *El Pistolerisme* (Barcelona: Pórtic, 2009).

[5] Im Gegensatz zu den beiden vorher genannten Zeitabschnitten sind die kollektiven Gewaltpraktiken in Barcelona während der Zweiten Republik noch nicht so oft Gegenstand einer wissenschaftlichen Betrachtung geworden, weshalb ich mir erlaube, auf meinen eigenen Aufsatz zu diesem Thema hinzuweisen: Florian Grafl, ",¡Deú nos ens guardi, quins lladres!' Urbane Gewalt im Barcelona der Zweiten Republik (1931–1936), Gewaltpraxis, staatliche Interventionsversuche und die Reaktion städtischer Akteure," *Informationen zur modernen Stadtgeschichte* 2 (2013): S. 31–42.

[6] Exemplarisch hierfür sind besonders: Temma Kaplan, *Red city, blue period. Social movements in Picasso's Barcelona* (Berkeley: Univ. of California Press, 1992); Angel Smith, *Anarchism, Revolution and Reaction. Catalan Labour and the Crisis of the Spanish State, 1898–1923* (New York et al.: Berghahn Books, 2007) sowie Chris Ealham, *Anarchism and the city. Revolution and counter-revolution in Barcelona, 1898–1937* (Oakland et al.: AK Press, 2010).

in Barcelona keine andere Wahl ließ, als sich durch Kriminalität oder gar Gewalt ihren Lebensunterhalt zu sichern, muss die spanische Sozialpolitik, insbesondere im konkreten Bezug auf Barcelona, eingehend betrachtet werden. Das ist in der Forschung bisher lediglich bruchstückhaft erfolgt. Diesen Ansätzen folgend, sollen im vorliegenden Beitrag die sozialpolitischen Reformen und die um sie entstehenden öffentlichen Diskussionen sowie die Institutionen zur Bekämpfung der Armut am Beispiel Barcelonas während der Zwischenkriegszeit untersucht werden.

Die Lebensbedingungen der ärmeren Bevölkerungsschichten Barcelonas

Die Lebensbedingungen waren in Spanien für die ärmeren Bevölkerungsschichten zu Beginn des 20. Jahrhunderts generell sehr schwierig. Verdeutlicht wird das etwa dadurch, dass um die Jahrhundertwende die Lebenserwartung nur bei 35 Jahren lag, also im Schnitt deutlich niedriger war als in anderen Ländern Europas.[7] Die Hauptursache dafür bestand in der hohen Kindersterblichkeitsrate, die bei den ärmeren Schichten Barcelonas bei fast 20 % lag, was vor allem auf die fehlende Hygiene und die mangelhafte Ernährung zurückzuführen war.[8] Der im Vergleich zu anderen europäischen Ländern sehr hohe Kornpreis hatte nämlich überdurchschnittliche Lebenshaltungskosten zur Folge.

Der Erste Weltkrieg verschlimmerte die Situation noch einmal deutlich. So stiegen die Lebenshaltungskosten von 1914 bis 1919 um etwa 50 %.[9] Nach einer Statistik von 1919 erhielten beispielsweise weder Metallarbeiter (Tageslohn: 5–9 Peseten) noch Angestellte (Tageslohn: 3–8,5 Peseten) oder Handwerker (Tageslohn: 5–7 Peseten) die täglich für das Überleben nötigen 10 Peseten.[10] Viele Arbeiter verfielen überdies dem Alkohol, um dem grauen Arbeitsalltag zu entfliehen. So berichtet der sozialistische Arbeiterführer Manuel Vigil um 1900 über die Industriearbeiter Barcelonas sinngemäß: „Obwohl die Arbeiter keine Säufer sind, ist es durchaus üblich, dass sie gerne trinken. Sie konsumieren in der Tat auch

---

[7] Walther Bernecker, *Geschichte Spaniens im 20. Jahrhundert* (München: Beck, 2010), S. 93 f.

[8] Rafael Núñez Florencio, *Tal como éramos. España hace un siglo* (Madrid: Espasa, 1998), S. 147.

[9] Ealham, *Anarchism*, S. 25.

[10] Diese Daten finden sich in der zeitgenössischen Statistik des spanischen Arbeitsministeriums, siehe: José Luis Oyón, *La quiebra de la ciudad popular. Espacio urbano, inmigración y anarquismo en la Barcelona de entreguerras, 1914–1936* (Barcelona: Ed. del Serbal, 2008), S. 72.

relativ große Mengen und das bekommt ihnen gar nicht gut. Das tun sie vor allem, weil die Welt, in der sie leben, ihnen keine andere Zerstreuung bietet als die Flasche und das Kartenspiel."[11]

Nach der Machtergreifung von General Primo de Rivera im September 1923 verbesserte sich die Lage auf dem Arbeitsmarkt durch die großangelegten Bauprogramme des Diktators. Zwar wurde durch diese insgesamt ein wirtschaftlicher Aufschwung eingeleitet, zugleich brachten diese Maßnahmen aber massive Finanzprobleme des Staates mit sich, die neben anderen Faktoren der Grund dafür waren, dass die früheren Förderer Primo de Riveras, wie das Militär und die katalanischen Industriellen, dem Diktator schließlich das Vertrauen entzogen und dieser seine Macht verlor.[12] In der sich anschließenden Zweiten Spanischen Republik machten sich die Folgen der Weltwirtschaftskrise auch in Spanien bemerkbar und ließen die Zahl der Arbeitslosen wieder in die Höhe steigen, was wiederum einen Großteil der Arbeiterschicht Barcelonas in eine soziale Notlage brachte.

Die Armenfürsorge in Barcelona

Die Armenfürsorge war in Spanien traditionell die Aufgabe der katholischen Kirche. Allerdings gab es zu Beginn des 19. Jahrhunderts nur wenige religiöse Orden, die sich in Hospitälern und Waisenhäusern direkt um die Armen kümmerten. Die überwiegende Mehrheit der Nonnen lebte von der Welt isoliert in Klöstern, während die männlichen Geistlichen sich eher missionarisch oder in der Bildung engagierten. So bestand die Armenfürsorge der Kirche zunächst hauptsächlich darin, den Bedürftigen, die sich an den Toren der Klöster und Konvente versammelten, Almosen zukommen zu lassen.

Im Zuge der Säkularisierung wurde die Armenfürsorge dann Aufgabe des Staates, der ab 1838 versuchte, den Armen unmittelbar in ihren Behausungen Hilfe angedeihen zu lassen.[13] Als Mitte des 19. Jahrhunderts klar wurde, dass diese Initiative nicht das erhoffte Ergebnis brachte, wurde

---

[11] Sinngemäß zitiert nach Adrian Shubert, *Historia social de España (1800–1990)* (Madrid: NEREA, 1991), S. 296.

[12] Vgl. hierzu die beiden Standardwerke zur Diktatur Primo de Riveras: Eduardo González Calleja, *La España de Primo de Rivera. La modernización autoritaria 1923–1930* (Madrid: Alianza Editorial, 2005), und den neu aufgelegten Klassiker von Shlomo Ben-Ami, *El cirujano de hierro. La dictadura de Primo de Rivera (1923–1930)* (Barcelona: RBA, 2012).

[13] Vgl. William Callahan, *The Catholic Church in Spain 1875–1998* (Washington D.C.: Catholic Univ. of America Press, 2000), S. 230 f.

versucht, die Armenfürsorge zu institutionalisieren und öffentliche Krankenhäuser, Waisenhäuser und Altenheime einzurichten. Aufgrund der politischen Wirren infolge der Revolution von 1868 kam dieses Programm aber bald wieder zum Erliegen.

Mit der Stabilisierung der politischen Verhältnisse durch die Restaurationsmonarchie erhielt auch die Armenfürsorge ab 1875 wieder Auftrieb.[14] Dafür waren vor allem drei Faktoren verantwortlich. Zum einen die Tatsache, dass die religiösen Orden massiven Zulauf von Frauen erhielten, die sich in der Armenfürsorge engagieren wollten, des Weiteren das steigende Interesse der Regierung an der Lösung des Pauperismus, der als Gefährdung für die Gesellschaft angesehen wurde, und schließlich die Privatisierung der Armenfürsorge, die dazu führte, dass nun verstärkt auch private Geldgeber in die Hilfe eingebunden wurden. Das Personal für die neu entstehenden Institutionen zur Armenfürsorge stammte zunächst weiterhin aus den kirchlichen Orden.[15] Sie betrieben in Barcelona zwei Einrichtungen für Arme, von denen eine alleine um 1899 fast 1.700 Hilfsbedürftige versorgte.[16] Der Staat unterstützte die Armenfürsorge nur mit etwa 3 Millionen Peseten, sodass die Hauptlast mit 45 Millionen von den lokalen Behörden getragen werden musste. Insgesamt reichten diese Mittel aber trotzdem bei Weitem nicht aus, um die Versorgung der Armen sicherzustellen.[17] So gingen viele Institutionen dazu über, die Armen in den Arbeitsprozess zu integrieren, um so die Einrichtung finanzieren zu können. Diese Praxis führte dazu, dass die Armenhäuser von der lokalen Presse oft mit Gefängnissen verglichen wurden, in denen katastrophale Zustände herrschten und die Hilfsbedürftigen ausgebeutet wurden.[18] Ab 1899 wurden private Hilfsorganisationen offiziell zugelassen und schon kurz nach der Jahrhundertwende waren bereits über 9.000 von ihnen registriert. Sie waren von privaten Geldgebern abhängig und bezogen ihr Personal ebenfalls meist von religiösen Orden. Allerdings handelte es sich hier um einzelne Initiativen, von einem koordinierten System konnte keine Rede sein.[19]

---

[14] Vgl. Elena Maza Zorrilla, *Pobreza y asistencia social en España, siglos XVI al XX* (Valladolid: Secretariado de Publ., Univ. de Valladolid, 1987), S. 193.

[15] Vgl. Elias de Mateo Avilés, *Paternalismo burgués y beneficencia religiosa en la Málaga de la segunda mitad del siglo XIX* (Málaga: Servicio de Publicaciones, Diputación Provincial de Málaga, 1985), S. 68 ff.

[16] Vgl. Frances Lannon, *Privilege, Persecution and Prophecy. The Catholic Church in Spain* (Oxford et al.: Clarendon, 1987), S. 74.

[17] Vgl. Callahan, *The Catholic Church*, S. 232.

[18] Vgl. de Mateo Avilés, *Paternalismo burgués*, S. 72.

[19] Vgl. Callahan, *The Catholic Church*, S. 234.

Erst unter der nun folgenden Diktatur Primo de Riveras lassen sich Ansätze für eine Sozialpolitik erkennen. Die wichtigsten Projekte waren die „Casas Baratas" (dt.: Billige Häuser), Großsiedlungsprojekte, mit denen die Wohnungsnot in Ballungsgebieten wie Barcelona bekämpft werden sollte.[20] Diese Maßnahmen verbesserten die Situation der ärmeren Bevölkerungsschichten in Barcelona allerdings nur marginal, zumal Primo de Rivera wie bereits ausgeführt, bald darauf seiner Macht entbunden wurde.

Mit der 1931 neu entstandenen Republik war schließlich die Hoffnung verknüpft, dass sich nun die Lebensbedingungen für die ärmeren Bevölkerungsschichten endlich verbessern würden. Tatsächlich führte Arbeitsminister Largo Caballero eine Arbeitslosenunterstützung ein, deren Wirkung aber aufgrund der allgemein schlechten Wirtschaftslage marginal blieb.[21] Einer Studie von Albert Balcells zufolge erhielten 1933, also zwei Jahre nach Beginn der Zweiten Republik, nur 2,4 % aller Arbeitslosen Unterstützung durch den Staat.[22]

Die katalanistische Partei Esquerra Republica de Catalunya wollte das Problem der Arbeitslosigkeit dadurch bekämpfen, dass die Immigranten, die in den vorangegangenen Jahrzehnten aus ganz Spanien auf der Suche nach Arbeit nach Barcelona gekommen waren, wieder zurück in ihre Heimat geschickt werden sollten. Um dieses Vorhaben zu organisieren, wurde ein Sonderzug bereitgestellt. Das Unternehmen endete allerdings in einem Fiasko. Aufgrund eines Sabotageakts kam der Zug bereits in einem Vorort Barcelonas wieder zum Stehen. Als die Fahrt fortgesetzt werden sollte, hatten fast alle Immigranten den Zug verlassen, und zwar mit der von den lokalen Behörden bereitgestellten Verpflegung, die ihnen für ihre Bereitschaft, Barcelona zu verlassen, überlassen worden war.[23] Insgesamt blieb die Armenfürsorge während der Zweiten Republik somit weit hinter den an sie geknüpften Erwartungen zurück.

---

[20] Eine ausführliche Darstellung dieses Projektes bietet: Miquel Domingo Clota et al., *Barcelona. Les cases barates* (Barcelona: Ajuntament de Barcelona, Patronat municipal de l'Habitatge, 1999).

[21] So zumindest beschreibt es der überzeugte Anarchist Abel Paz in seiner Biographie: Abel Paz, *Feigenkakteen und Skorpione. Eine Biographie (1921–1936)* (Lich: Verl. Ed. AV, 2007), S. 55.

[22] Vgl. Albert Balcells, *Crisis económica y agitación social en Cataluña de 1930 a 1936* (Barcelona: Instituto Católico de Estudios Sociales de Barcelona y Ediciones Ariel, 1971), S. 127.

[23] Diese Episode wird beschrieben in Carles Sentís, *Viatge en Transmiserià. Crònica viscuda de la primera gran emigració a Catalunya* (Barcelona: La Campana, 1994), S. 73 ff.

Die „Selbsthilfe" der Armen

Aufgrund der harten Lebensbedingungen und der marginalen staatlichen Hilfe sahen sich die Armen meist auf sich alleine gestellt. Sie solidarisierten sich innerhalb der Nachbarschaft oder auf der Ebene ihres Stadtviertels und halfen sich in Notsituationen, etwa bei Krankheit, gegenseitig.[24] Besonders aber in der Zweiten Republik, als die wirtschaftliche Lage sich dramatisch verschlechterte, wurde darüber hinaus Kriminalität immer mehr als legitimes Mittel angesehen, um das Überleben zu sichern.

Regelmäßig wurden Lebensmittelgeschäfte oder Apotheken geplündert. Normalerweise wurde dabei so vorgegangen, dass eine einzelne Frau den Laden betrat und die Lebensmittel wie bei einem ganz normalen Einkauf einpackte. Dann aber betraten mehrere Personen den Laden, die die Entwendung der Lebensmittel sicherstellten. Meist reichte schon die Androhung von Gewalt, um den Widerstand des Ladenbesitzers zu brechen.

Eine andere Methode bestand darin, dass einzelnen Personen oder auch Gruppen in einem Restaurant oder einer Bar speisten, das Lokal dann aber verließen, ohne zu bezahlen. Gewaltsamere Praktiken bestanden in bewaffneten Überfällen. Die beliebtesten Opfer hier waren Taxifahrer, deren Dienste zunächst scheinbar von den Tätern in Anspruch genommen wurden, um zu einem abgelegenen Ort zu fahren. Dort angekommen, wurden die Taxifahrer gezwungen, ihre Tageseinnahmen herauszugeben und das Taxi zu verlassen. Die Täter fuhren dann mit der Beute im gekaperten Taxi zurück in die Innenstadt. Diese Art der „Selbsthilfe" wurde dadurch begünstigt, dass es auf dem in Hafennähe gelegenen Schwarzmarkt relativ einfach war, an Waffen zu kommen.[25]

Auch wenn die bürgerliche Presse die Vorfälle sicherlich dramatisierte, scheint es doch vielfach die gängige Praxis gewesen zu sein, dass sich die Armen Barcelonas ihren Lebensunterhalt mit kriminellen Mitteln sicherten. Zumindest ist anzunehmen, dass die Zahl derer, die zu dieser Art von „Selbsthilfe" griffen, deutlich höher war als die Zahl derjenigen, die auf die staatliche Fürsorge vertrauten.

---

[24] Die Betonung des Zusammengehörigkeitsgefühls in den einzelnen „barrios" lässt sich in vielen biographischen Darstellungen nachlesen, vgl. Ealham, *Anarchism*, S. 27.
[25] Ealham, *Anarchism*, S. 102 ff.

Resümee

Die Lebenssituation der armen Bevölkerung in Barcelona in der ersten Hälfte des 20. Jahrhunderts kann ohne Übertreibung als dramatisch bezeichnet werden. Staatliche Hilfe gab es bis auf einige wenige Initiativen nahezu überhaupt nicht. So war es vor allem die katholische Kirche, in Spanien seit jeher einen Sonderstatus genießend, die sich der Armenfürsorge annahm. Mit der Säkularisierung in Spanien, die in der Zweiten Republik ihren Abschluss fand, wurde ihr Einfluss aber zunehmend zurückgedrängt. Aufgrund seiner chronischen Finanznot konnte der Staat die Bedürftigen in keinem der drei politischen Systeme – der Restaurationsmonarchie bis 1923, der Diktatur Primo der Riveras bis 1930 und der Zweiten Republik bis zum Beginn des Bürgerkriegs im Juli 1936 – ausreichend unterstützen. Die Armen solidarisierten sich deshalb und halfen sich in Notsituationen gegenseitig. Besonders während der Wirtschaftskrise in der Zweiten Republik griffen aber immer mehr von ihnen auch zu kriminellen Mitteln, die sich von einfachen Straftaten wie Mundraub bis zu schweren Delikten wie bewaffneten Überfällen erstreckten. Zusammenfassend lässt sich bei der Betrachtung der Armenfürsorge in Barcelona während der Zwischenkriegszeit als Ergebnis festhalten, dass die Armen wegen der völlig unzureichenden offiziellen Unterstützung auf eigene, teilweise kriminelle oder gar gewaltsame Strategien angewiesen waren, um zu überleben.

CHAPTER ELEVEN

THE POOR AND ILL:
FROM CHARITY TO A DELIBERATE
ORGANISATION OF THE HEALTH CARE
FOR THE POOR IN PILSEN DURING
THE FIRST HALF OF THE 20TH CENTURY

KAREL ŘEHÁČEK

Abstract: The study summarises health care for poor citizens of Pilsen in the first half of the 20th century. Against a background of its general development, the study sums up the transition from general support for the poor to more efficient care in specialised facilities, i.e. hospitals for the poor and elderly, which were built either by municipalities or by private benefactors. The study introduces the history of Fodermayer's hospital for incurables in Pilsen and its post-war transformation within the system of centralised municipal social care in the city of Pilsen. In addition, the study cites the issues concerning poor and ill children and the financial, social and political aspects of health care for the poor.

Introduction

The poor formed a traditional strata of the urban population and their survival long depended on the mercy of others.[1] This practice continued well until the mid-19th century, when the status of the urban poor – under the influence of Enlightenment ideas and consequent social changes –

---

[1] See Marie Bláhová, "Péče o chudé a nemocné v přemyslovských Čechách" [Care for the poor and ill in the Přemyslid Bohemia], in *Curatores pauperum. Źródła i tradycje kultury charytatywnej Europy Środkowej* (Katowice: Societas Scientiis Favendis Silesiae Superioris – Intytut Górnośląski et al., 2004), pp. 114–132; Kateřina Jíšová, "Péče o nemocné a chudé na Novém Městě pražském v pozdním středověku" [Care for the ill and poor in the Prague's New Town in the Late Middle Ages], *Mediaevalia Historica Bohemica* 10 (2005): pp. 323–351.

began to gradually transform and these changes affected the Habsburg monarchy as well. Many reforms in social and health care were carried out under the rule of the Emperor Joseph II.[2] Its practical implementation, or at least the major volume of care for the poor, was transferred to communities/municipalities, which were supposed to act as guarantors of providing effective and efficient assistance to the poorest. According to Article 24 of the Imperial Law Coll. no. 105/1863, communities/municipalities were obliged to provide their poor with food and provision in case of illness. Additionally, if the subjects of the care were children, the concerned administrative unit was supposed to secure their education as well.[3] More accurate and detailed instructions on care for the poor care were brought about in the Provincial Act Coll. no. 59/1868 of December 3, 1868.

Securing care for the poor was a significant burden on communities/ municipalities, both organisationally and financially. Single administrative units were spending more and more resources on care for the poor out of municipal budgets, and in parallel, they actually could not cope without the help of various individuals and private benefactors and corporations. The expenses on the care for the poor significantly increased after the First World War, when the care for the underprivileged classes became one of the priorities for Czechoslovak municipalities and literally a showcase of many towns and cities. Modern and specialised social and health care facilities were being built during the First Republic, added to by an efficient and easily controllable system of benefits and care for the poor, ill and otherwise handicapped individuals. All these measures became a benchmark for success of Czechoslovak municipalities and for the level of humanity of their representatives, particularly those of the left-wing. The contemporary legislation in this area provided a framework which set out the rules for the provision of the care for the poor and many municipalities went about providing for their poor far beyond it.

---

[2] For more details to this transformation, see Zdeňka Stoklásková, "Osvícenství a vznik veřejného zdravotnictví" [The Enlightenment and origins of public healthcare], in *Post tenebras spero lucem. Duchovní tvář českého a moravského osvícenství* [Post tenebras spero lucem. Spiritual character of the Bohemian and Moravian Enlightenment], (Praha: Filozofická fakulta Univerzity Karlovy, 2008), pp. 88–105.

[3] The Act no. 105/1863 of December 3, 1863, Article 24: "The obligation of the community to make provision for its poor village closes in itself only a commitment to give them the nutrition needed and to administer their custody in case of illness. The obligation to make provision to the poor children also contains within itself (in addition to the abovementioned) an obligation to provide them with education."

The poor and health care

Care for the poor was not a smooth process. This particularly applied to the care for the poor and ill community members. A key platform for providing health care from the late 19th century was health insurance, yet that tool remained far from accessible to all and only a limited part of the population was covered within its framework. A positive change towards affordable health care was brought about by the Act Coll. no. 221/1924, which significantly expanded the range of compulsorily insured individuals. However, this legislation did not concern the legal regulation of health insurance for members of the poor community. Their access to health care therefore remained limited, and if they did not have funds to pay for medical care in cash, they became dependent on care for the poor.

As with health insurance companies, who paid the cost of medical care for their clients, communities/municipalities were obliged to pay the cost of health care for their poor. Bills for outpatient or inpatient care were paid directly to general practitioners, outpatient specialists and hospitals, and, to a limited extent even to spa care providers. However, considering the possibilities and the level of the then health care, such therapies were usually relatively inexpensive and time-limited: a conservative or surgical treatment resulted fairly quickly in either recovery, or conversely, in the death of the patient and compared to today, very costly subsequent therapies such as radiotherapy, chemotherapy, biological therapy, etc. mostly did not exist at all.

Thus the biggest problems local governments faced in the field of health care for the poor concerned those chronically or terminally ill poor members – their diagnosis resulted neither in recovery, nor in a rapid death. In these cases, the health condition of such poor patients usually required permanent care, yet their diagnosis was not so urgent that the patient could be transferred to a hospital. It was more like today's subsequent medical care, similar to health care clinics caring for the chronically ill, perhaps hospices.[4] And also in this case, the organisation of

---

[4] For more details on this process, see Ludmila Hlaváčková, "Od chorobinců ke geriatrickým klinikám. Vývoj specializované péče o pacienty pokročilého věku" [From hospitals for the poor and elderly to geritatric clinics. The development of specialized care for patients of advanced age], in *Vetché stáří nebo zralý věk moudrosti? Sborník příspěvků 28. ročníku sympozia k problematice 19. století. Plzeň, 28. února – 1. března 2008* [A feeble old age or a mature age of wisdom? Collection of papers of the 28th symposium to the issues of the history of the 19th century, Pilsen, February 28—March 1, 2008], (Praha: Academia, 2009), pp. 190–198.

institutional care for the chronically ill poor underwent an evolutionary development: initially, such individuals were placed in poorhouses, together with healthy occupants and something resembling systematic medical care was a mere exception in these institutions. As time went by, specialised institutes (i.e. hospitals for the poor and elderly) were gradually being founded, where those persons were kept separately from the healthy. Hospitals for the poor and elderly were supposed to be founded across the entire Habsburg monarchy by a decree of Emperor Joseph II of May 24, 1781. Some of these "model" institutions actually came into existence shortly after the release of that decree (e.g. a "large capacity" hospital for incurables in Karlov in Prague, which was opened in December 1789), yet greater efforts that would eventually lead to the establishment of such facilities occurred only gradually and reluctantly.[5]

The main limitation on the development of these institutes were the high costs required for their establishment as well as for their daily operation. Sometimes, and actually not that infrequently, private donors substituted for the role of the community/municipality/district when using their own funds for establishing private hospitals for the poor and elderly. The respective administrative units then usually took over the administration of such facilities and contributed to their upkeep. In addition, many big cities started to found their own institutions for their chronically ill and poor citizens. In the inter-war period, this sector also underwent radical changes, which were supposed to streamline the operation of fragmented and isolated municipal institutions and submit them to a central leadership.

Care for the ill poor in Pilsen in the first half of the 20th century

The abovementioned patterns of care for the ill and poor applied to the city of Pilsen as well. Their treatment as well as a provision of necessary medications and medical aids were all conducted on the basis of the resolution of the city council of October 7, 1879, which thoroughly specified rules and regulations on care for the poor.[6] The municipality paid for medical care, necessary medications, as well as for medical aids on account of the Poor Fund, designed to provide for the local poor in Pilsen. The city actually secured the same care for "foreign" (i.e. non-local) poor

---

[5] Hlaváčková, "Od chorobinců ke geriatrickým klinikám," p. 191.

[6] The City Archives of Pilsen (AMP), the municipal office (MÚ) Pilsen, magistrátní registratura (1880–1942), box 461, no. 2/I/1890, a document titled "Pravidla, podle kterých opatřovati bude obec chudé královského města Plzně," [1879], article 21.

individuals as well and then collected the expenses mostly from the communities where those individuals had a right of domicile.

The funds to cover health care for the poor in Pilsen came from several sources: first, from revenues earmarked in the municipal budget to cover the expenses on the poor, second, it was an income specified by law. The third source was voluntary donations and contributions. Finally, there were municipal incomes involved as well. The local committee for the care for the poor (later it was a council for the care for the poor) then decided on allocations of these financial means. This committee/council closely cooperated with the advisory body consisting of "Fathers of the poor", who were elected by communal/municipal councils and, on the basis of Article 32 of the Provincial Law Coll. no. 59/1868, carried out investigations about the need for care directly in families of applicants.[7] In the case of payment for health care, the municipality paid the cost directly to the providers. These rules applied until 1922, when under the Act Coll. no. 236/1922 from July 13, 1922, the personal expenses for the care of the poor were taken over by the state and municipalities were required to pay only for medication. Yet even after that, the city of Pilsen ensured specialised treatment for their poor citizens in addition to the statutory basic medical care, at least in cases that guaranteed recovery.[8]

Outpatient care for the poor in Pilsen – whether they lived in their own homes or in social institutions (poorhouses, hospitals for the poor and elderly) – was provided either by municipal or institutional doctors, and specialised care was provided by specialists. If institutional medical care was indicated, poor patients were sent to the Municipal Public General Hospital and the costs for their care (of course, at the lowest nursing class) were covered by the municipality, which subsequently received some of the money back from provincial funds. In addition, the municipality regularly paid some financial support to the hospital as a partial reimbursement of medical expenses. This money was originally intended to be paid out in cash to that given poor individual and that practice

---

[7] Act Coll. no. 59/1868 of December 3, 1868, on the care for the poor, Article 32. According to that Act, "Fathers of the poor" were supposed to "directly and personally care for the poor, to visit their households, to check on their circumstances and needs privately, to ask priests and physicians, the acquired knowledge about these things constantly maintain and to present the needs of the poor, if possible, orally to the municipal committee or to the commission of the poor."

[8] František Kříž, *Město Plzeň. Přehled složení a činnosti obecní správy za léta 1919–1924* [City of Pilsen. A survey on composition and activities of the municipal administration for the years 1919–1924], (Plzeň: Nákl. města Plzně, 1925), p. 275.

continued until early 1924. At that time, the law commission of the city of Pilsen adopted a new attitude to this practice, stemming from the period before the release of the Act Coll. no. 236/1922. On February 2, 1924, the commission decided that the municipality was no longer obliged to pay to the hospital anything which would go beyond explicitly listed items in the appropriate passage of the hospital statutes, such as paying for the clothes that the patient urgently needed, for surgical instruments, glasses, bandages, crutches, etc.; in other words, items that the discharged poor person needed to take with him when leaving the hospital.[9]

In addition, poor people who fell into financial trouble due to the cost of medical care could apply for instalment payments or could even be forgiven a part of their debt. For example: Marie Koskubová, wife of a worker in the Škoda factory in Pilsen, was hospitalised in Pilsen hospital with lung disease for a quarter of the year 1939 and after having been released, she received a bill of 1,455 Czechoslovak Crowns (CZK). Since her husband earned only 200–250 CZK per week, she was obviously unable to pay the full amount. The hospital management allowed her to pay only 200 CZK in four monthly instalments, and the remaining amount was submitted for reimbursement to the Provincial Office in Prague.[10]

The biggest problem – and definitely not only in Pilsen – was ensuring institutional care for chronically ill poor citizens. In the early 20th century, the city of Pilsen ran only two poorhouses, where ill individuals (and often the seriously ill) lived together with healthy ones. An example of such co-existence was in a poorhouse in Otakarovy Sady in 1905, when this place housed 59 persons, divided into three groups: the first consisted of persons who were supported by the Mary Magdalena Foundation. Those people were actually impoverished Pilsen burghers and their spouses. They definitely made up the group which was best off within the poorhouse, thanks to the support of the foundation. The second group consisted of other poor citizens of Pilsen without any serious health issues, and the third group was made up of poor citizens of Pilsen who suffered from an incurable disease but were not eligible for admission either to a hospital or to a mental institution. Obviously, these persons were seriously ill and needed constant supervision and care as well as medical treatment.

The medical service in this poorhouse was voluntarily conducted by city physician Rudolf Kučera, MD. Care of ill residents was ensured only

---

[9] AMP, MÚ Plzeň, magistrátní registratura (1880–1942), box. 724, no. 2/I/1924, a letter addressed to the Municipal Public General Hospital in Pilsen of April 30, 1924.
[10] AMP, MÚ Plzeň, magistrátní registratura (1880–1942), box 726, no. 2/I/1939, a letter by the Municipal Public General Hospital in Pilsen of January 9, 1940.

by a single caregiver, who, for a daily wage of 1 Krone [sic] had to oversee the mentally ill, clean all the beds, wash and iron clothes, bathe, groom and feed the poorhouse residents. Besides these duties, she had to cook for all and distribute coal to all rooms throughout the poorhouse. Regarding sanitary conditions, the city paid for cleaning once every 2 weeks, and all rooms were whitewashed twice a year. However, as the poorhouse residents brought their beds and other furniture in and they did not have enough money to have them cleaned regularly, the poorhouse became flooded with bedbugs to such an extent that "wherever you look, bedbugs can be seen in big clusters along the walls and under the pictures and in the beds too." Another problem was the hygiene of the toilets, which were open and had little drainage, resulting in a permanent situation when "the accumulated faeces smelled terribly," and the only means of hygiene was pouring chlorinated lime into them.[11]

A year later, this facility was accommodating 55 persons. Three of them were very seriously mentally ill (one in a fit of insanity had murdered his wife, another one spent a couple of years in a mental institution and the third suffered from severe epilepsy with daily seizures). Obviously, these individuals were due to "the nature of their disease very dangerous to themselves and to each other and to the whole environment." Besides these three individuals, the poorhouse was also at the time accommodating nine mentally ill women whose condition required constant supervision as well.[12]

Care for residents of this poorhouse was very demanding: they needed constant supervision and medical treatment. Moreover, in many cases, they also posed a risk (health, but also safety) to their roommates. The city officials understood the long-term need to establish a specialised institute in which the chronically or terminally ill poor could be accommodated separately from healthy poor persons. Yet financial difficulties kept preventing the city representatives from establishing any such type of city facility. Augustin Fodermayer (1829–1906),[13] one of Pilsen's philanthropists,

---

[11] AMP, MÚ Plzeň, magistrátní registratura (1880–1942), box 556, no. 2/I/1905, a report on conditions in the poorhouse in Otakarovy Sady (former Panský mlýn) by R. Kučera, M.D. of January 24, 1906.

[12] AMP, MÚ Plzeň, magistrátní registratura (1880–1942), box 556, no. 2/I/1905, a letter by city physician R. Kučera, M.D., to the Pilsen city council of January 25, 1907.

[13] A. Fodermayer was born in a poor family. Yet his innate diligence and thrift resulted in great business success and considerable wealth. His wife died in 1899 and his only son Vilém suffered from an incurable mental illness. Fodermayer therefore bequeathed all his property to charitable purposes. He died on July 5, 1906 at his villa in Pötzleinsdorf near Vienna and his remains were moved to

decided to step in and fill a gap in the provision of care for long-term or terminally ill poor citizens. In 1901, he established a foundation whose purpose was to build the first Pilsen hospital for incurables.

Fodermayer's hospital for incurables in Pilsen

Augustin Fodermayer planned to establish a hospital for incurables, in which "the unhappiest among those miserable, poor, severely and incurably ill would find a refuge after having been expelled from a hospital."[14] He also determined the main rules for the operation of the future hospital for the poor and ill. First and foremost, the proposed institution was intended to care for totally poor and incurably ill individuals and for those unable to work. They would be provided with "healthy accommodation, food, bedding, clothes, medical care, religious comfort and in case of their death also with a proper funeral."[15]

He established a foundation for a future hospital for incurables. He secured it financially by his own property (with two houses, where beer was being brewed; they were called "The Golden Keg" and located in Říšská and Školská Street no. 167 and 168). At first, Augustin Fodermayer assumed that the institution would not start operating until after his death. Yet in 1902 he changed his mind and decided to build the hospital for incurables as soon as possible. Subsequently, the municipal council donated land for the construction of a suitable building on April 18, 1902. The plans were drawn up in 1902–1903 and the construction itself began on June 27, 1904. In 1905 – in connection with the upcoming 75th birthday of Emperor Franz Joseph I – Augustin Fodermayer decided that "to permanent memory to the descendants of the famous and longstanding reign of His Majesty and fervent prayer to God to keep His Majesty to the welfare and happiness of the empire, and to his family of devoted nations in full body strength and vigour for many more years," he would donate the dedicatory charter as well as the set of the main rules to the city administration.[16]

Pilsen and displayed in the hospital for incurables on July 8. He was buried in Pilsen a day later. AMP, MÚ Plzeň, magistrátní registratura (1880–1942), box 566, no. 160/I/1906.

[14] AMP, MÚ Plzeň, magistrátní registratura (1880–1942), box 531, no. 38/I/1901, the charter of the hospital for incurables in Pilsen, November 9, 1901.

[15] AMP, MÚ Plzeň, magistrátní registratura (1880–1942), box 531, no. 38/I/1901, article 1 of the rules, November 9, 1901.

[16] AMP, MÚ Plzeň, magistrátní registratura (1880–1942), box 532, no. 38/I/1901, the dedicatory charter of June 15, 1908, p. 5.

The building of the institute (house no. 15 with a yard and a garden in Doudlevecká Street in Imperial suburb [*Říšské předměstí*], later Kuffner Pavilion) was erected by the builder Josef Houdek in 1905–1906 and finished under the supervision of architect Emanuel Klotz on September 25, 1906. Soon after, on November 25, 1906, the brand new facility was solemnly consecrated, and put into operation in early December of the same year. The total construction costs of the hospital for incurables (including equipment) amounted to 211,070 Krone (Kr).[17]

Čeněk Šimerka, MD, was appointed as the first medical director of the new hospital for incurables. The facility management as well as care for patients was entrusted to the Congregation of the Grey Sisters of the Third Order of St. Francis in Prague – in 1909, 5 nuns and 3 maids worked there.[18]

Let us now look at the changing numbers of persons accommodated in this facility. In 1906, 36 persons lived there. During the year of 1907 their number grew to 50,[19] in 1908, an increase occurred again – this time to 67 and in 1909, there were 61 persons accommodated.[20] Regarding gender and place of origin of residents of the hospital for incurables, out of the first 36 admitted persons, 17 were men and 19 women. Regarding their place of origin, 20 of them were citizens of Pilsen, another 6 persons belonged to the political district of Pilsen and the remaining 10 residents of the hospital for incurables had a right of domicile in other districts.[21] In 1909, the largest group of residents was diagnosed with weak-mindedness (congenital imbecility or idiocy affected 10 persons in that facility), followed by 7 paralysed persons, 7 other persons suffered from various kinds of chronic diseases of bones and joints. In addition, there were diagnoses such as brain softening (encephalomalacia), multiple sclerosis, polio, epilepsy, neuritis, various heart diseases, emphysema and various forms of cancer.[22] Most patients were aged between 50 and 80 years. Obviously, a large portion of the residents was made up by old and very seriously ill persons, who were bedridden and around-the-clock care for

---

[17] *Třetí zpráva o činnosti kuratoria chorobince Fodermayerova za správní rok 1909* [The third anniversary report on the activities of the Board of the Fodermayer's Hospital for the administrative year of 1909], (Plzeň: Tiskem J. Císaře v Plzni, nákladem chorobince 1909), p. 5.
[18] Ibid, p. 6.
[19] AMP, MÚ Plzeň, magistrátní registratura (1880–1942), box 532, no. 38/I/1901, a letter from the city hall in Pilsen to the Ministry of Finance in Prague, November 18, 1940.
[20] *Třetí zpráva o činnosti kuratoria chorobince Fodermayerova*, p. 8.
[21] Ibid., p. 15.
[22] Ibid, p. 16–17.

them was very demanding on the nursing staff. The capacity of the hospital for incurables reached 61 beds before the First World War. Yet the yearly turnout was much higher – mainly because of the high mortality rate, and to a small extent also due to voluntary or forced departures. In 1917, a total of 96 people spent at least some part of the calendar year in this facility.[23]

The capacity of Fodermayer's hospital for incurables could not meet the demand. For example, a former flour mill worker, Jan Ryneš (b. 1838), requested admission to this facility in February 1918. He justified his application in these words: "I am 80 years old, a widower, decrepit from work and age, I have no one to look after me until I die. I can pay neither for apartment nor for assistance, and I am an impoverished person. I am not afflicted by any repulsive disease, I am only old and weak."[24] But his application was rejected as well. The management of the hospital for incurables justified it by claiming that "Jan Ryneš does not suffer from any serious disease which would justify his admission to the hospital for incurables. He would rather qualify for the poorhouse."[25] Another example of a rejected applicant is Václav Teleš – the co-owner of a brewery house at the corner of the Sedláček and Veleslavín Street in Pilsen – this time he did not meet the criterion of complete poverty, so he was not accepted into Fodermayer's hospital for incurables either.[26] Not exceptionally, current residents were excluded from Fodermayer's hospital – mostly because of their mental instability/disorders as they posed a real threat to other occupants as well as to the staff.

The institute was managed by municipal and district councils, which managed its daily operation through a seven-member elected board of trustees (five representatives of the city plus two representatives of the district) with a three-year mandate.[27] This arrangement followed the wish of Augustin Fodermayer and the very first seven-member board of trustees

---

[23] *XI. zpráva o činnosti kuratoria chorobince Fodermayerova za rok 1917* [The 11th report on the activities of the Board of the Fodermayer's Hospital for the year of 1917], (Plzeň: Tiskem J. Císaře v Plzni, nákladem chorobince, 1918), p. 2.
[24] AMP, MÚ Plzeň, magistrátní registratura (1880–1942), box. 532, no. 38/I/1901, the application by Jan Ryneš to the Pilsen city council and to the management of Fodermayer's hospital for incurables of February 20, 1918.
[25] AMP, MÚ Plzeň, magistrátní registratura (1880–1942), box 532, no. 38/I/1901, a letter from the hospital for incurables to city hall in Pilsen of June 6, 1918.
[26] AMP, MÚ Plzeň, magistrátní registratura (1880–1942), box 532, no. 38/I/1901, a letter by Fodermayer's hospital for incurables management to the city council in Pilsen of April 2, 1908.
[27] AMP, MÚ Plzeň, magistrátní registratura (1880–1942), box 531, no. 38/I/1901, a dedicatory charter by Augustin Fodermayer, November 9, 1901.

was established in his personal presence on May 20, 1906. This body consisted of the owner of numerous pieces of real estate Emanuel Bezděka, František Částek, the retired head director of Czech secondary schools, another owner of real estate Antonín Doubek, Bernard Guldener, JD, who was a defence lawyer, the civil engineer Emanuel Klotz, chief engineer Karel Ritter of Rittershain and factory owner Bernard Říha.[28] František Částek served as a head of the board of trustees until his death on January 22, 1915. He was considered the father of the idea of founding the hospital for incurables in Pilsen, since he actually directed Augustin Fodermayer towards establishing this facility. Bernard Říha served as a deputy chairman of the board of trustees. In 1915, Josef Strnad became the new head of the board of trustees, a government counsellor as well as director of a secondary school in Pilsen.[29]

During the pre-war period, Fodermayer's hospital for incurables managed to keep a surplus in its budget – thanks to revenue from brewing houses – and this trend continued even during the First World War. In addition to the proceeds from the foundation, the hospital ran its own small farm in the courtyard and this significantly contributed to its self-sufficiency. There was a poultry farm keeping chickens and geese, a barn for pigs (sometimes up to 10 pigs per year) and part of the garden was used for growing vegetables for home use. In 1917, both income and expenses amounted to over 111,000 Czech Kr (CZK) (revenues: from its assets 89,324 CZK and from the hospital itself 22,070 CZK. Expenses: 23,802 CZK covered the expenses to the management of the foundation's assets and 87,365 CZK were spent on the operation of the hospital for incurables).[30] However, proceeds from the foundation's assets did not cover all financial needs of the hospital after the First World War, and therefore the city voluntarily started to contribute for their poor citizens by 5 CZK per person per day.

Over the years, however, it was necessary to carry out a variety of construction and adaptation works which were all relatively expensive. A significant capacity expansion of this hospital occurred in 1928–1930,

---

[28] *První zpráva o činnosti kuratoria chorobince Fodermayerova 1906–1907* [The 1st report on the activities of the Board of the Fodermayer's Hospital for the year of 1917], (Plzeň: Tiskem J. Císaře v Plzni, nákladem chorobince, 1908), p. 3.

[29] AMP, MÚ Plzeň, magistrátní registratura (1880–1942), box 531, no. 38/I/1901, a letter by Fodermayer's hospital management to the city council in Pilsen of January 26, 1915.

[30] AMP, MÚ Plzeň, magistrátní registratura (1880–1942), box 532, no. 38/I/1901, a letter by the management of Fodermayer's hospital to the city council in Pilsen of May 4, 1918.

when the Pilsen district conducted extensions and additions to the original building, thereby increasing the number of beds to 140.[31] Since the district of Pilsen contributed to the implementation of this work in the amount of 1,850,000 CZK from its budget, it logically demanded an increased influence on deciding who would be admitted to this facility. This led to a redefinition of the rules between the city of Pilsen and the district of Pilsner so that 40 places were reserved for poor Pilsen citizens, who were accommodated and treated for free (covered by the revenue from the foundation's assets), another 40 beds were reserved for poor citizens of the Pilsen district and 60 beds were filled by residents who actually paid a daily fee in the amount of 12 CZK from their own resources. Despite all abovementioned measures, the balance sheet of the hospital for incurables was still in the red and showed considerable deficits annually.[32]

The new administrative arrangement of this facility substantially increased its expenses as well as overheads costs. Thus, the board of trustees requested an increase of the contribution made by the city to 220 CZK per month (i.e. more than 7 CZK per person per day) as of September 1, 1929.[33] According to the board of trustees, this amounted to a bare minimum which did not even reach half the actual cost. The city of Pilsen did not agree with the proposed increase as of September 1929, but in 1930 the financial requirements of the hospital for incurables were finally accepted and subsequently, the hospital received a total of 105,600 CZK.[34] Yet even this financial support did not ensure a balanced budget. In 1934, the budget of the hospital was 659,400 CZK and the year ended with a deficit of more than 28,000 CZK (a year earlier, the budget deficit reached nearly 40,000 CZK).[35] In 1934, almost a third of the budget went to covering food expenses, whereas only 20,000 CZK (3%) was granted to cover medicine and medical supplies, and this amount of money was in

---

[31] AMP, MÚ Plzeň, magistrátní registratura (1880–1942), box 532, no. 38/I/1901, a letter by the city council of Pilsen to the Ministry of Finance in Prague, November 18, 1940.

[32] Ibid.

[33] AMP, MÚ Plzeň, magistrátní registratura (1880–1942), box 531, no. 38/I/1901, a letter by the management of Fodermayer's hospital to the city council in Pilsen of July 9, 1929.

[34] AMP, MÚ Plzeň, magistrátní registratura (1880–1942), box 531, no. 38/I/1901, a letter by the city department of social care in Pilsen to the city council in Pilsen of July 17, 1929.

[35] AMP, MÚ Plzeň, magistrátní registratura (1880–1942), box 532, no. 38/I/1901, the financial statement of Fodermayer's hospital for incurables—year 1934. May 21, 1935.

fact not completely used.[36] Budget deficits became standard in the coming years: in 1941, the deficit amounted to 239,000 CZK and the financial plan for the year 1942 already accounted for a deficit in the amount of 173,000 CZK.[37]

The internal situation in the hospital for incurables was quite difficult, particularly during the First World War. Complaints about the behaviour of staff towards the hospital patients were mounting and they mostly concerned theft of food, originally intended to be consumed by the hospital patients. Shortly after Czechoslovakia came into existence in October 1918, the situation in Fodermayer's hospital escalated and in late November 1918, the National Committee (NV) in Pilsen had to deal with those accumulated issues. On November 29, 1918, there was a meeting held in the presence of the Mayor of the city of Pilsen, Matouš Mandl, JD, at which it was decided to carry out an impartial investigation of all complaints by a specially appointed committee. The interrogations of patients and staff were conducted in the hospital on January 20–21, 1919 in the presence of the following officials: representative of the National Committee Josef Kozlík, city councillor Josef Petřík and district secretary František Berdych.

Most complaints were related to the management of Fodermayer's hospital and in particular to the alleged enrichment of staff at the expense of patients, as well as to small food rations, but also to ill-treatment of patients by staff. Bedřich Vobruba, one of the patients, testified: "Mother Superior scolds us as fools and oxen. The food is poor. We have had turnip without potatoes or dumplings, and without bread for four times this week. I did some masonry work, I brought coal as well chopped the wood, which is why I was entitled to get better food. When I asked about some more food, I did not get anything."[38] A mentally ill patient, Vojtěch Honzík, said: "Mother Superior laughs at us in the garden. When we did not want to go to the church, she plagued us by hunger. She often scolds us as oxen and idiots."[39]

The testimonies of patients also mentioned bullying and psychological and physical violence (e.g. beating) from the side of the personnel. Any criticism was absolutely unacceptable under threat of exclusion from the

---

[36] Ibid.
[37] AMP, MÚ Plzeň, magistrátní registratura (1880–1942), box 532, no. 38/I/1901, a letter by the management of Fodermayer's hospital to Petr Němejc, a government commissioner of the city of Pilsen, October 6, 1941.
[38] AMP, MÚ Plzeň, magistrátní registratura (1880–1942), box 532, no. 38/I/1901, a protocol of January 20–21, 1919, p. 3, testimony by B. Vobruba.
[39] Ibid, p. 4, testimony by V. Honzík.

hospital. Marie Fleisigová testified: "Once I was ill. The doctor ordered me to have bedrest. Our maid had to sweep the stairs, but she did a poor job. Then the nun came to me and wanted to slap me around. I have been here for 10 years and I have cried here more than enough. The nuns told me that I was a beggar and that I am here merely from mercy. They told me I was lazy and would prefer not to do anything. Mother Superior scolded us often. Nothing we did was trusted. We are not lazy. We like to work, but please, we should also get something to eat when we work, we should not be hungry all the time."[40] The head doctor Čeněk Šimerka, MD, and chairman of the board of trustees J. Strnad confirmed that complaints about the behaviour of the nuns were partially based on truth and that it had already been resolved. But he also added that although the nuns did not satisfy everyone in the hospital, they were basically the only option for securing care for the patients, as civil workers would have been far more expensive – the nuns received merely food plus only 25 CZK per month.[41] Nevertheless, the commission recommended terminating the contract with the congregation. Furthermore, the committee ordered improvements in the hospital diet as well as detailed record-keeping of stocks of food and the employment of an experienced official who would reside in the hospital and manage the institution on behalf of its patients[42].

Municipal hospital for incurables and the post-war centralisation of health care for the poor

The city of Pilsen decided to build its own hospital for incurables shortly before the outbreak of the First World War. The city poorhouse in Wenzig Street was completely converted into a hospital for incurables based on the resolution of the municipal council of June 10, 1913 and on February 20, 1914, the city council approved the rules of operation for this new city facility. The purpose of the new hospital for incurables was to accommodate persons from all city poorhouses who were "bedridden for any physical or mental chronic disease and thus unfit to work."[43]

The applications were supposed to be assessed by the city council upon a proposal from the city council and the municipal health and hygiene department. Medical service was entrusted to the town physician (in 1914

[40] Ibid, p. 8, testimony by M. Fleisigová.
[41] Ibid, p. 7, testimony by Č. Šimerka.
[42] Ibid, the protocol, p. 14.
[43] AMP, MÚ Plzeň, magistrátní registratura (1880–1942), box 599, no. 2/I/1912, a letter by the city council to the municipal Building Authority in Pilsen of February 20, 1914.

it was František Střízek, MD). The supervision over this new city facility was in the hands of the Poor Office along with the municipal health and hygiene department. The capacity of the new hospital reached 40 beds (29 beds in the front wing, 11 in the rear). The city council allocated 8,500 CZK to equip the new facility and its personnel came from the poorhouse in Otakarovy Sady.[44] Yet the outbreak of the war ruined all those plans, because this facility started to serve as a military hospital and its patients were treated by the Red Cross, and thus the proposed city hospital for incurables did not begin serving its purpose until January 9, 1919.

After Czechoslovakia came into existence in October 1918, social care in Pilsen underwent a huge transformation. The new city government, headed by the Social Democratic Mayor Luděk Pik, launched the era of the building of specialised social and health institutions, and sought ways to streamline their management as the cost of such care grew significantly every year. Thus the existing fragmented and incoherent social care was concentrated in a single institution – the Municipal Social Welfare Office.

Its statutes were approved by the city council on March 16, 1923 and this new proposed authority was supposed to start real work after the building of the House of Social and Health Care in Otakarovy Sady. Its construction started on December 17, 1923. The very first part of the institution was opened on July 1, 1924. Less than 9 months later, on March 14 the following year, the city hospital for incurables was moved there from Wenzig Street and the entire institution was put into full operation on March 1, 1926[45] and became the basis for quality and efficient social and health services to needy citizens of Pilsen.

Caring for the ill children of poor citizens of Pilsner

Obviously, the care for ill children of poor parents was very important. As in other branches of social care, its daily practice changed from more or less random activities to systematic and highly specialised care. The city even organised recovery trips for ill and poor children to the Adriatic Sea. Most of these children were diagnosed with scrofula.[46] The city paid

---

[44] Ibid.

[45] Kříž, *Město Plzeň.*, p. 256.

[46] A form of chronic childhood tuberculosis. Affected children used to suffer from overall weakness, developmental delay, diseases of the lymphatic system, bones, joints, and respiratory tract. In the Czech Lands, the treatment of this disease was in the scope of the Provincial Institute for Scrofula Children in Luž with a branch in Chroustovice. Cf. Archiv Kanceláře prezidenta republiky – AKPR [The Archive of the President's Office], Kancelář prezidenta republiky – KPR [The President's

for six to seven-week long stays in Grado (North Adriatic) upon recommendation of the city physician.

Children were accommodated in the so-called "First Austrian marine hospital in Grado" (*Primo Ospizio Marino Austriatico di Grado*) just across the harbour. It was a three-storey corner building and on the ground floor there was a dining room, kitchen and office. The first floor was dedicated to bedrooms for boys, whereas the girls' bedroom was located on the second floor. Each bright and airy bedroom contained 20 beds with bedside tables. Children could play in two gardens (one for boys and one for girls). The third garden was taken up by the isolation ward for infectious patients. A therapeutic sea spa was located behind the building, with a slightly sloping bank. Medical supervision of children was carried out by Rudolf Hynek, MD, for free. He was the only Czech specialist working in Grado, and the children were looked after by Italian nuns, who knew only a little German. In addition to patients with scrofula, children with eye diseases (inflammation of the corneas and conjunctiva) were also sent to Grado before the First World War. Not surprisingly, a considerable improvement occurred in virtually all diagnoses.[47]

During the first five years, a total of 59 children were sent to Grado (1907: 8, 1908: 9, 1909: 13, 1910: 14, 1911: 15).[48] The last session took place in 1914, when 19 children travelled to Grado (5 boys and 14 girls). The six-week treatment was brought to an end on August 11, 1914 as planned, but because of the complex international situation caused by the outbreak of the First World War, they could not be transported back to Pilsen. Eventually, the children stayed in Grado for 52 days and returned to Pilsen on August 24 after a four-day long train trip.

The war as well as new post-war geopolitical conditions broke the tradition of trips of children from Pilsen to Grado. After Czechoslovakia came into being, ill children were frequently sent to Yugoslav coastal resorts (e.g. Crikvenice or Baška). The city of Pilsen was no longer involved as children were being sent through specialised institutions, supported by the state (e.g. the Association of Adriatic Convalescent Homes [*Spolek jadranských ozdravoven a léčeben*] or the Czechoslovak Children's Sanatorium in Crikvenica [*Československá dětská ozdravovna v Crikvenici*]).[49]

Office] (1919) 1948–1962, box 721, no. P 14.

[47] AMP, MÚ Plzeň, magistrátní registratura (1880–1942), box 920, no. 14/II/1911.

[48] AMP, MÚ Plzeň, magistrátní registratura (1880–1942), box 920, no. 14/II/1911.

[49] For more details on these institutions and their activities, see: Národní archiv, Ministerstvo veřejného zdravotnictví a tělesné výchovy [National Archives, Ministry of public health and physical education], box 404, no. V/5/1c a V/5/5, or

In terms of providing medical care for chronically ill and otherwise handicapped children (not only for poor children), the cooperation between the city of Pilsen and the District Care for the Youth was especially important. This administrative body was established in Pilsen in 1914 as a centralised institution with various specialised departments such as the Department for the care of deaf and dumb children (since 1920, this department ran a boarding house for affected children from the areas outside of Pilsen, who attended a four-class school for the deaf and dumb in Pilsen). Furthermore, the Department for the care of mentally handicapped children also worked there (this department began to run a specialised institute in 1926) as well as the Department for the care of crippled children (this department started to run the Masaryk Institute for crippled children in November 1921).

Other organisations involved in the care for children in Pilsen area were as follows: The American Red Cross, which operated medical counselling called "*Našim dětem*" [To Our Children] in the orphanage in Otakarovy Sady and a year later, the American Red Cross organised a recovery trip for youth at risk of tuberculosis close to the pond of Šídlov. The other organisation working in social care was the Pilsen branch of the Czechoslovak Protection of Mothers and Children, which provided obstetric care to poor and needy pregnant women at a shelter in Wenzig Street almost for free.

Cost of caring for poor patients in Pilsen

We may have concluded, based on all the information above, that the situation in Pilsen was almost idyllic and that poor citizens had the same opportunities as other city dwellers. But that was not the case, because the funds were never full enough to support all needy persons, and despite the effort to adhere to the largest possible thrift, the city faced financial deficits in the sphere of the care for the poor almost constantly. This system could not provide for all needy persons before the creation of Czechoslovakia and thus a fund was created for the local poor, to which the more affluent citizens of Pilsen voluntarily contributed.[50] Yet before 1918, health care costs had not been particularly significant – due to their objective limitations as well as relatively to other expenditures of the system of the care for the poor: for example, in 1890, the municipality of

---

AKPR, KPR 1919–1947, box 55, no. D 4035.
[50] AMP, MÚ Plzeň, magistrátní registratura (1880–1942), box 504, no. 2/1/1896, a letter by the Social Care Municipal Office to the city council of June 11, 1928.

Pilsen allocated a total of 23,274 Florins to their poor members, but only 876 Fl. out of this amount was spent on "homeless and ill in the poorhouse accommodated" and another 23,725 Fl. were spent on "supporting the ill." These sums together amounted to only less than 5% of the total cost of the care for the poor (the vast majority of the money was paid out in the form of cash support for poor persons).[51]

A considerable increase in health spending came after the First World War. Apparently, this trend was primarily related to expanding possibilities of hospital treatment and therefore the financial demands became more evident. The most significant increase can be observed in the ever-growing daily rates of nursing care in hospitals: in July 1919, the daily nursing rate in the public general hospital in Pilsen in third grade equalled 4.70 CZK, in January 1924 it was 21 CZK.[52] Price increases were evident in the case of medicine and medical aids as well. Even after the year of 1922, when the state took over covering a part of the costs for treatment of the poor, the city budget was burdened by increasingly higher amounts allocated to ensuring medical care for the poor (1925: 41,579 CZK, in 1926 the amount reached 66,439 CZK, a year later it was a bit less – 45,726 CZK – and in 1928 another increase occurred to 53,318 Czechoslovak Crowns).[53] That development burdened the city budget more and more and also because of these costs, the city of Pilsen was in serious debt during the inter-war period.

The opposite trend occurred during the occupation, when the city, forced by a lack of money, had to radically reduce social spending and was forced to use self-help more than ever before. Additional support for social and health care for the poor was therefore also conducted via "voluntary" collections of the National Assistance [Národní pomoc], where the employees had to pay a certain percentage of their income (about 1% of their monthly salary).[54] This was coordinated by the district auxiliary committee of the Office of the National Assistance, whose aim was to "give the most to those who have to secure their livelihoods in dependence on the support."[55]

---

[51] AMP, MÚ Plzeň, magistrátní registratura (1880–1942), box 461, no. 2/I/1890, a balance sheet of the Poor Institute in Pilsen in 1890.
[52] Kříž, Město Plzeň., p. 386.
[53] Ibid., p. 358.
[54] AMP, MÚ Plzeň, magistrátní registratura (1880–1942), box 726, no. 2/I/1939, the appeal made by the city authority in Pilsen on October 17, 1942.
[55] AMP, MÚ Plzeň, magistrátní registratura (1880–1942), box 726, no. 2/I/1939, a letter by the Office of the National Assistance in Pilsen to the city council of October 5, 1942.

Social and political aspects of care for the ill and poor citizens of Pilsen

The provision of social aid, including medical care to the poor, especially the selection criteria of necessity, was frequently abused. There are documented cases that in the context of election campaigns, granting poor sickness benefit in exchange for voting for a particular political party (usually the "ruling" social democracy) occurred.[56] This problem was particularly apparent in the case of *Okresní nemocenská pojišťovna* [District Health Insurance Company] (ONP) in Pilsen, whose top management was dominated by Leopold Krombholz and Josef Bosák, both leaders of social democracy. There was a fight over prices, influence, as well as a political struggle in the background for supremacy in the city and surrounding areas between the ONP – which was one of the largest health insurance companies in Czechoslovakia[57] – and its smaller competitor called *Všeobecná nemocenská pojišťovna* [General Health Insurance Company], which was dominated by the national (Czechoslovak) socialists. Potential political abuse could also occur when deciding whether or not to forgive the cost of medical care for poor people who got into financial difficulties due to disease.

In addition to the abovementioned aspects, providing health care for the poor also meant an important propaganda tool. This fact became apparent in the early 1920s, when the city leaders sought to create a new, large administrative unit, Great Pilsen, i.e. to merge with several of its surrounding villages. Yet representatives of some villages did not favour the potential merger, and thus it was necessary to present the benefits that would be brought to the local rural population.

From the perspective of health care for the poor, the example of Václav Kovář from Božkov – a village that was to become (and eventually did become) one of the proposed new parts of Pilsen – was the most striking. Kovář was drafted to the 5th Border guard Battalion in Cheb in March 1922 and during training in November of that year, his lower limbs

---

[56] For more, see Karel Řeháček, "Obecní volby v roce 1919 v Plzni" [Local elections in Pilsen in 1919], *Minulostí západočeského kraje* 45 (2010): pp. 56–111.

[57] In 1938, the Okresní nemocenská pojišťovna [District Health Insurance Company] in Pilsen was the third largest health insurance company in Czechoslovakia and covered over 40,000 persons (including family members, the number exceeded 100,000 insured persons). Cf. Miloslav Bělohlávek, *Archiv města Plzně. Průvodce po fondech a sbírkách* [Archives of the City of Pilsen. A guidebook to the collections], (Plzeň: Západočeské nakladatelství, 1987), p. 255.

became paralysed and the ominous diagnosis of multiple sclerosis was determined after thorough examinations. Military authorities refused to pay for his treatment because the disease was not caused by his training. Subsequently, Kovář was released from the army and sent home.

Obviously, taking care of a patient with such a serious diagnosis was not easy. The general public hospital in Pilsen refused to admit him, because he suffered from an incurable disease. Václav Kovář was completely destitute and his mother, a widow of a fallen soldier and mother of five dependent children, said that she was unable to care for her son as she had to commute daily to Pilsen to work. Thus the community of Božkov was supposed to ensure care for him, based on his permanent residency in this village.[58] However, the Božkov community administration protested that caring for its citizen Václav Kovář was too expensive, claiming that there were no means in the community budget. Fortunately, Luděk Pik, the mayor of Pilsen, intervened upon the request of the Božkov administration and secured that "due to the upcoming merger of Božkov into Great Pilsen" Kovář would be eventually placed in Fodermayer's hospital for incurables, paying 150 CZK per month.[59] Kovář lived here until his death in 1925.

Conclusion

Health care for poor citizens underwent remarkable development during the first half of the 20th century. This process expanded the reforms which had been undertaken in the previous period, when care for the poor generally became an institutionalised form of social welfare secured mostly by communities and municipalities across the Czech Lands. A sophisticated system of health care for the poor, based on the funds of care for the poor as well as on means provided by private foundations, had been continuously formed before the First World War. That system was grounded in relatively affordable outpatient as well as inpatient care. The cost of health care for the poor was actually not that significant, since the then medical practice had limited options and treating patients (with either positive or negative results) lasted only a limited period of time.

---

[58] AMP, Archiv obce Božkov – AO Božkov (Archive of the village Božkov), box 465, a letter by the Czechoslovak Military Hospital no. 2 in Pilsen to the community council in Božkov of August 6, 1923.

[59] AMP, AO Božkov, box 465, a letter by Josef Burian, the chairman of the board of trustees of the Fodermayer's hospital for incurables to Václav Kovář of September 24, 1923; another letter by Josef Burian to the community administration of Božkov of September 24, 1923.

A much bigger issue was care for long-term and chronic illnesses, where no efficient and quick therapy was available. These patients needed long-term care, in principle different from acute hospital therapy. At first, the long-term or chronically ill were placed together with healthy persons in poorhouses and later, hospitals for the poor and elderly were founded for such patients as specialised institutes.

After the First World War, the health care system for poor Czechoslovak citizens significantly improved. Institutes specialising in providing social services were established, especially in big cities. Generally, these institutes fell under one centralised management. The costs of health care rose constantly and meaningful and wise administration was much sought to manage the chronic lack of funds. Despite all efforts, municipal budgets in many Czechoslovak cities showed large deficits caused by providing social services and thus they became heavily indebted in the inter-war period. However, modern health and social institutions could actually come into being thanks to these increased investments in social policy. In many cases, those facilities became showcases for their home municipalities and often, they continue to serve the same purpose till this day. Moreover, establishing social institutions of all types significantly contributed to the modernisation of many Czechoslovak cities.

CÍSAŘE A KRÁLE FRANTIŠKA JOSEFA I.
CHOROBINEC
ZALOŽIL AUGUSTIN FODERMAYER V PLZNI.

1912.

AUGUSTIN FODERMAYER,
čestný měšťan král. města Plzně, zakladatel chorobince
1829–1906
JEHO MANŽELKA VILEMÍNA
1839–1899.

Fig. 11-1 Mr. and Mrs. Fodermayer, Archives of the City of Pilsen (AMP)

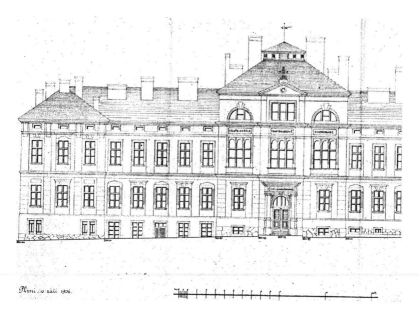

Fig. 11-2 The plan of the hospital for incurables, exterior (AMP)

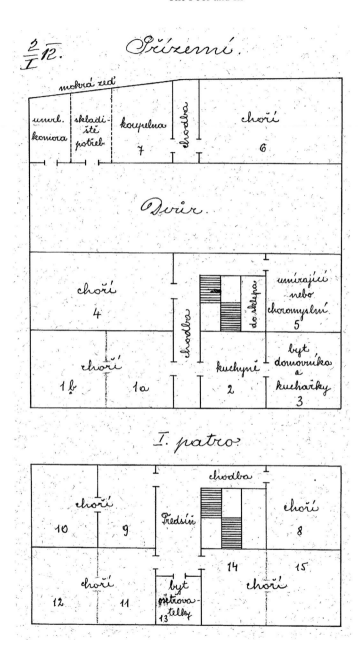

Fig. 11-3 The plan of the hospital for incurables, interior (AMP)

Fig. 11-4 The hospital for incurables, general view (Museum of West Bohemia in Pilsen – department of modern history)

Fig. 11-5 The first chairman of the board of trustees of the hospital for incurables
František Částek (AMP)

Fig. 11-6 His successor Josef Strnad (AMP)

Fig. 11-7 Luděk Pik, a social Democratic mayor of the city of Pilsen (the author's collection)

PART III:

INSTITUTIONS, INSTRUMENTS, DISCOURSES

CHAPTER TWELVE

THE PRAGUE FOUNDLING HOSPITAL AND ITS ROLE IN THE CARE FOR THE POOR

MARTINA HALÍŘOVÁ

Abstract: The paper deals with a foundling hospital in Prague and its role in child care. It briefly summarises the history of the foundling hospital, which was administered by the Provincial Maternity Hospital. The article focuses on monitoring the practice of childcare and it analyses the conditions under which children were admitted to the foundling hospital. It also focuses on foster care. The article shows how this institute recruited new foster parents and lists their responsibilities towards children. It also deals with a novelty in foster care – the so-called "two-third care", which allowed either a biological mother or other blood relatives to become a foster parent of the child. The article specifies the role of this institute within the framework of care for the poor in Prague and its achievements. The foundling hospital fulfilled its role as guardian of uncared-for children and facilitated additional education or services for its residents. In addition, this facility also provided assistance to unmarried mothers.

The provincial foundling hospital in Prague was founded on the basis of directive rules issued by Emperor Joseph II in 1781. It started operating on August 17, 1789, when children were relocated there from the closed Italian hospital.[1] This paper focuses on mapping child care provided by this foundling hospital in the years that followed and it also describes the role of this facility within the system of the care for the poor in Prague during the 19th century.

First, let us introduce the daily functioning of this institute. The foundling hospital was administratively connected with the maternity hospital in Prague. In the 1860s, when the institute came under the administration of the Czech provincial committee, its full official name was "The Provincial Maternity Hospital and Foundling Hospital in

---

[1] Thaddäus Bayer, Beschreibung der öffentlichen Armenversorgungsanstalten in der königl. böhmischen Hauptstadt Prag, Prag 1793, p. 36.

Prague."[2]. The foundling hospital, functioning as an integral part of the maternity hospital, was designed to care mainly for babies born to single mothers there. Such infants were actually rescued from a potential violently death, because killings or abandonments by mothers were nothing exceptional. The primary task of the foundling hospital was to take care of these new-born children and to protect their health. The original idea, embodied in the set of directive rules, was the establishment of an orphanage for older children (as a tool of aftercare). Yet a chronic lack of money made this impossible and the idea of founding a state orphanage was abandoned. It was later decided that the subsequent care for these children would be provided by the foundling hospital.[3] Unlike the French system, where the children received institutional care,[4] the Czech system opted for entrusting these babies into the hands of foster mothers in rural areas in order to save their lives. Only weak and sick children were supposed to stay in the foundling hospital, because their potential transport to a foster family could result in their death.

Originally a brand new building was planned to be built for the foundling hospital. In the end, it was decided that this institution would be placed in the former building belonging to the clergymen at St. Apollinaire, together with the maternity hospital. The rebuilt facility had a maximum capacity of 50 beds for mothers and 100 beds for children. Yet the demand often exceeded its capacity. Moreover, the old building was soon unable to meet contemporary hygiene and health standards. Due to a lack of space, the hospital department was extended throughout the entire building and the foundling hospital was moved to a neighbouring house. Because of the increasing number of births at the hospital, the capacity of the foundling hospital soon became insufficient and the management was forced to rent houses nearby. Another serious problem was an inadequate water supply. The overall unsatisfactory conditions resulted in the increased mortality of mothers as well as children. For this reason, it was decided to build a new, modern maternity hospital, designed by the

---

[2] To the foundling hospital Petr Svobodný and Ludmila Hlaváčková, *Pražské špitály a nemocnice* [Prague spitals and hospitals], (Praha: NLN, 1999); also Martina Halířová, *Sociální patologie a ochrana dětství v Čechách od dob osvícenství do roku 1914. Disciplinace jako součást ochrany dětství* [Social pathology and protection of childhood in Bohemia since the Enlightenment by 1914. Disciplination as a part of protection of childhood] (Pardubice: Univerzita Pardubice, Fakulta filozofická, 2012).

[3] See Bayer, Beschreibung, p. 30.

[4] The operation of foundling hospitals in France has been well documented. See e.g. *Noms et destins des sans Famille*, eds. Jean Pierre Bardet and Guy Brunet (Paris: PUPS, 2007).

architect Josef Hlávka, and this ambitious project was completed in 1875. Yet the foundling hospital itself had to wait for its new building much longer – this facility was not completed and put into full operation until 1901–1902.[5]

Let us now focus on daily childcare. The foundling hospital was headed by a special directorate (*Waisen und Pründler Oberdirektion*), which was responsible for entrusting children into foster care, supervising the foster parents and providing care for ill children.[6] A child could be taken into the foundling hospital free of charge or after paying a certain fee. Acceptance depended on the nursing class of his mother in the maternity hospital. The admission fee at the foundling hospital for children born in the maternity hospital was divided into four price categories: in the first class the admission fee was 20 Florins, in the second class the fee was 10 Fl., the placement fee for a child born in the third class was 6 Fl., whereas the fourth class was unpaid. These charges were set for the year 1789, when the facility was opened.[7]

The fee for taking a child into care gradually increased, keeping pace with the improving economic situation of the Czech Lands. Thanks to preserved admission protocols, we know that the majority of women in the

---

[5] See Svobodný and Hlaváčková, Pražské špitály a nemocnice; Ludmila Hlaváčková, "Pražské porodnictví a gynekologie před založením II. gynekologicko-porodnické kliniky " [Obstetris and gynaecology before founding of the 2nd gynaeacological and obsterical clinic] in *75 let gynekologicko-porodnické kliniky I. lékařské fakulty Univerzity Karlovy a Všeobecné fakultní nemocnice v Praze při 120. výročí otevření Zemské porodnice* [75th anniversary of gynaecological and obsterical clinic of the 1st medicinal faculty of Charles University and Universal faculty hospital in Prague, along with 120th anniversary of openning of the Land Maternity Hostpital] (Praha, 1995), pp. 12–24.

[6] The staff was comprised of a chief director, who oversaw the orphans' agenda; There was also an "orphan's visitator", whose main responsibilities were supervising the children in foster care, informing the director of his findings, making sure that the children in foster care were kept clean and properly cared for. Once the children had reached a specified age, they were supposed to attend school, and "hold for art or craft" so that after their release from the foster care they would be able to provide for themselves. The orphan's visitator also handed nursing fees to parish priests. Furthermore, there was also an "orphans' protocolist", who kept records on all the inmates, registered foster parents and transferred the children to their new foster families. According to Bayer, Beschreibung, p. 237.

[7] The National Archives (further referred to as NA) Prague, České Gubernium – Publicum (further referred to as ČG-Publ.), 1806–1815, no. 90 Záležitosti nalezince, péče o sirotky, box 5477.

maternity hospital asked for admission to the cheapest third class.[8] The reason for this was that if a woman wanted to be admitted for free, not only was she obliged to provide her body to medical students, but she was also supposed to function as a wet nurse in the foundling hospital for at least four subsequent months.[9]

The fee was paid upon arrival at the hospital. By paying this fee, single mothers freed themselves from their maternal duties. Their new-born children were then taken away from them and transferred to a special room where they were looked after by wet nurses. Interestingly, the first names of these children could be chosen by their mothers if they wanted to. In cases that the mother had not done so, a midwife chose a name for the child. The children of non-paying mothers were kept for some time together with their biological mothers due to the need to determine whether the woman was capable and suitable for temporary service as a wet nurse in the foundling hospital. Single mothers had the opportunity to buy themselves out of the obligation to breastfeed and their children were then admitted free of charge, because they had already provided their bodies for learning purposes. The overall effort of the institute aimed at allowing women to return to work as soon as possible.

Apart from the children born in the maternity hospital, babies born in other institutes (such as prisons, hospitals, poorhouses, etc.) could also be admitted to the foundling hospital. Their admission had to be approved by the Czech Gubernium (a supreme administrative authority in the Czech Lands between 1763–1849. Later the decision was made by the provincial governorate) and both legitimate and illegitimate children had the chance to be accepted. Children born in other institutions were taken into the foundling hospital at the request of the directorate of the facility where they had been born. That particular institution was also obliged to examine the situation of the child's parents. First and foremost, the origin of the parents and their length of stay in Prague had to be determined. A key prerequisite for admitting a child into the foundling hospital for free was either permanent residence, or at least a 10-year long stay in Prague. In cases of poor parents who came from the countryside and had no relatives in Prague, their home village or the manorial lords were obliged to care for such dependent children. The care and raising of the child then fully depended on his parents' home village and its landowners.[10] The child could be handed over to the foundling hospital for a pre-assessed fee,

---

[8] NA, The Provincial Maternity Hospital (further referred to as ZPN), Protocols of the female patients, books 140–177.
[9] Bayer, Beschreibung, p. 124.
[10] NA, ČG-Publ., box 5477.

which was set at 50 Fl. When the manorial lords and later the home village did not intend to pay this fee, the concerned child could be sent back to his home village (where he legally belonged). Thus the home village and its lords were then obliged to ensure both food provision and accommodation for the child.

Furthermore, children could be put into the foundling hospital also because of the imprisonment of their parents. In this case, the upper threshold for admitting such child was the age of 15 years, later decreased to 12 years (from 1805). Representatives of a given home village were required to pick up the child from prison, where he was temporarily placed together with his parents. If the home village did not react to the notification within 8 days, that child was then placed in orphan care either at the expense of the home village or expenses of the child's relatives. Childcare for offspring of either imprisoned or diseased persons did not last long, usually matching the imprisonment period of the parents or hospitalisation in the case of single mothers. In general, hospitals or prisons were not considered suitable places for children. That was the regulation of the governorate. In practice, however, the situation was significantly different. If a nursing mother was imprisoned for a short time, she ended up in prison together with her child. The child was kept with his mother, who had to provide his sustenance.

Another group of children who were in the care of the foundling hospital were children born outside any institutional facility. These children were referred to as "children from outside" (Kinder vom Aussen). Typically, their age ranged from infancy to 12 years – i.e. children deemed too young to provide for themselves. The age limit was lowered for the last time in 1873 and then only children under the age of 6 could stay in the foundling hospital.[11] This group consisted of both legitimate and illegitimate children of either widowed or single females. These women usually made their request directly to the Czech Gubernium, which, being the administrator of the foundling hospital, had the right to decide on the acceptance of a given child. Afterwards, the Czech Gubernium forwarded the request for further processing to the directorate of the foundling hospital, but we can also track a reverse practice in contemporary documents.

The applicants for admission of a child into institutional care were then interrogated and the findings were documented in so-called "interrogation protocols." These official records contained basic information such as the name of the applicant, marital status, occupation and reasons for the request. The applicant was obliged to fulfil three main duties: to present a "certificate of poverty", to demonstrate that she was either born or had

---

[11] Decision of the Czech provincial parliament of December 3, 1872.

lived for at least 10 years in Prague and finally, she had to submit a certificate of good morals. The directorate subsequently decided whether or not the applicant had met the conditions for a child's admission into the foundling hospital. The foundling hospital with the maternity hospital were conceived as a joint-institute designed primarily for Prague and its residents, therefore both the affiliation to Prague and lack of assets formed the basis for an applicant's right to place her offspring into state care for free. The entire admission process lasted two to three weeks. If necessary, the directorate of the foundling hospital was entitled to admit any child temporarily and carry out the entrance procedure later.[12] This provisional acceptance mainly concerned illegitimate children not born at the maternity hospital whose lives were in immediate danger. Judging from the preserved requests for admission to the foundling hospital, the requests for accepting orphans originating from full families outweighed applications made by single mothers.[13] The larger number of applications for admission of children originally from complete families was probably caused by a general awareness among single mothers that the authorities preferred childbirths in the maternity hospital. Applications for admission of children of married couples were mostly filed by widows.

If a single mother gave birth outside the maternity hospital and decided to put her child in the foundling hospital, she had to file a request, in which she had to prove her moral integrity, lack of financial resources and also her long-term stay in Prague. Even if the single mother was born in Prague or lived in the city for a long period, and therefore her offspring had a right to a free admission to orphan care, it was examined whether her relatives could pay the admission fee for her child. Furthermore, the directorate of the foundling hospital also examined if the father of the child (if his name was given) could pay the admission fee. Single mothers who decided to submit a request for admitting their children to the care of the foundling hospital had been forced to do so by adverse circumstances. They usually justified their request by their inability to take care of their offspring. In addition, they emphasised efforts to gain employment. They perceived the foundling hospital to be a guarantor for better care than they could provide themselves. Female applicants who did not come from Prague sometimes offered to pay a certain sum for the acceptance of their offspring by this facility. They wanted to entrust their children to the care of the state and thus indicated how they had received the money and declared that they were not able to pay a higher amount than that offer. In

---

[12] NA, ZPN, a collection of the documents issued by the Provincial Maternity Hospital in Prague, book 10.

[13] NA, ČG-Publ., 1806–1815, boxes 5477 and 5478.

addition, they supported their claim by presenting their "certificate of poverty." The fee for admitting a child whose mother did not have permanent residence in Prague, was set at 50 Fl. It was possible to reduce the amount in exceptional cases.[14] The fact that the applicants were aware of this possibility is well testified by the tone of preserved applications.

The foundling hospital rarely admitted children who had both parents, but it was theoretically possible. Despite a ban issued by the governorate on July 14, 1805 under no. 23875, the foundling hospital cared for several children whose parents were both still alive. Such applications were granted with regard to the current situation of parents who, because of illness or absence of a breadwinner, happened to be in a difficult life situation. These children were mostly taken temporarily until the family situation improved, meaning that their parents either recovered or the family breadwinner returned home. Their financial and personal situation was monitored every six months and when some improvement had occurred, the child was returned to his family. In the case of a death of a parent/parents, this child could stay in the care of the foundling hospital.[15]

Apart from parents and relatives, there were other subjects which could apply for admitting a child into the foundling hospital – e.g. a legal guardian who had got into a difficult financial situation, a parish priest or a city administration. This situation occurred when the child was either completely orphaned or abandoned. We find cases where a parish priest made the request on behalf of a single mother and the application stated the reasons for admitting that child. Applications by parish priests were considered credible, and therefore the child's mother was not subjected to further questioning.

Applications for admission of both legitimate and illegitimate children were granted only if the applicant consented to surrender the child into state care. If the applicant was against submitting the child into state care and asked merely for some sort of financial support, she was mostly rejected. In general, such support stood against the directive rules and the applicant was given advice to ask at her home village council (where she legally belonged in terms of permanent residence).

Obviously, the foundling hospital was accepting children who were found in and around Prague, i.e. true foundlings. The court decree from 1788 created 63 places destined for children born or abandoned in Prague. The city administration paid an annual fee of 375 Fl. as cover for the care for such foundlings.[16] Every child who was born outside the maternity

---

[14] NA, ČG-Publ., 1806-1815, boxes 5477 and 5478.
[15] Ibid.
[16] NA, ČG-Publ., 1806–1815, box 5477.

hospital and was brought into the foundling hospital had to possess a certificate of baptism. If any doubts about his christening appeared, then the child had to be baptised immediately. And when the first name and a surname of the child remained unknown, the child was given a new full name.[17]

After being admitted to the foundling hospital, the children received a guardian. The directorate of the foundling hospital fulfilled this role – actually it was indirectly the state, which became "a father" to the child. Furthermore, the government officials made decisions on the future of these children and they also oversaw their education. Putting a child in the custody of the foundling hospital meant a certain guarantee that the child would be properly cared for, at least in the first phase of life. And this could not be guaranteed by his relatives nor by the municipality nor by the manorial lords. Yet these subjects did form the first instance which could be contacted in case of need, but none of them could provide continual care for such children. All the children who came to be included in the system of national orphan care received decent care in a uniform manner during the entire existence of the foundling hospital.

Anyone who handed over a child to the care of the foundling hospital, was entitled to receive information regarding his future fate. After presenting a so-called "cut-out ticket" (*Ausschnittszettel*), which stated the protocol number of the child, the one who had brought it in obtained information on the current situation of the child. Mothers could be told the address of the foster parents to whom the child had been entrusted. A single mother who was interested in the fate of her child could visit him and his foster parents. The foundling hospital directorate instructed the mothers to act respectfully and obediently during visits to the foster parents. If the biological mother found inconsistencies in the care of her child, she was supposed to report them to the directorate. Thus the single mothers actually acted as supervisors of foster parents in a way.[18] Unfortunately, our archival sources do not tell us whether such incidents actually occurred.

The children who were born in the maternity hospital were transferred to the foundling hospital between the fourth and eighth day after birth. They arrived together with their indigent mothers, who started to work as wet nurses. Each infant was examined and registered into the "foundling protocol." The new-born was then assigned a protocol number called a "foundling mark." This was basically a piece of paper in the shape of

---

[17] NA, ČG-Publ. 1796–1805, no. 90/4 and 90/5, Issues concerning the maternity hospital and the foundling hospital, box 3510.
[18] NA, ZPN, Instruktionen für die Gebär u. Findelanstalt zu Prag 1835, book 14.

either a circle of a square with the personal number of the child. This hung
around the child's neck to avoid any case of mistaken identity.[19]

The children did not stay in the foundling hospital for long. The
directorate always tried to transfer them into the care of foster parents as
soon as possible. Originally, the children were supposed to be entrusted
only to foster parents residing in the country, to become more resistant to
all sorts of diseases and to live a moral life. Yet the rule that the children
should be cared for only by foster parents residing outside of Prague could
be violated if there was either a shortage of foster parents or a longer
period of adverse weather.[20] Nevertheless, a constant lack of foster parents
from rural areas eventually led to the issuing of permission to entrust the
children to foster parents in Prague.[21] Ill and weak children remained in
the care of the foundling hospital until their condition improved. It was
generally thought that an ill child would be better cared for in an
institution than at somebody's house. Thus the foundling hospital probably
became the very first state institution in the Czech Lands which
systematically dealt with childhood diseases.

When the foundling hospital had children capable of transportation to
foster care in its care, it was announced via a public announcement. Priests
were supposed to assist in acquiring new foster parents – their duty was to
inform the faithful that there was a need for accepting children into foster
care. Individuals who were interested in receiving a foster child registered
either with their manorial lords or through the regional office. The
application for the child had to enclose a certificate of morality, which was
issued jointly by a parish priest and by the manorial lords.

An integral part of the application was confirmation that the applicant
had recently given birth, and therefore was able to breastfeed. This
certificate was issued free of charge. The priest who signed the certificate
also became responsible for a child who was about to be entrusted to that
foster mother. Another condition for obtaining a child from the foundling
hospital was the Catholic faith of both foster parents.[22] If such a potential
foster mother was found to be fit for custody, she was then told by the
regional office; at the same time, she was informed when to pick up the
child from the foundling hospital in Prague. The actual handover of
children to new parents from rural areas could be carried out on Mondays,

---

[19] Ibid.
[20] Ibid. Article no. 62.
[21] A regulation from October 30, 1840. NA, ZPN, a book of regulations (1832–
1841), book 4, p. 197.
[22] NA, ZPN, a book of regulations (1808–1841), book 1.

Wednesdays and Fridays. The applicants from Prague were supposed to pick up their foster child on Tuesdays, Thursdays and Saturdays.[23]

Any female applying for a foster child had to arrive at the directorate of the foundling hospital in person. There was an official who was familiar with children suitable for transfer into foster care. The main duty of this officer was to verify all the required documents, enter her personal data into the protocol and issue a permit, which allowed for the release of a child from the foundling hospital. Before the child was actually entrusted to her, a prospective foster mother had to undergo an examination, as to whether she was really able to breastfeed. This examination was conducted by a midwife. Afterwards, each foster mother had to loudly recite an oath that she would care for the child, breastfeed him and treat him as her own. At the same time, she had to sign a so-called "contract on the child", which contained the principles of proper foster care.[24] Then she received a "label of the child," which stated the child's full name, date of birth and his number in the foundling protocol. She was supposed to have these two documents in her possession as long as the baby stayed in her care. If she no longer cared for the child for any reason, she was obliged to return these two documents to the foundling hospital.

The directorate of the foundling hospital tried to vaccinate all children against smallpox before their transfer to foster families. The policy then did not allow for immunisation against this illness before new-borns reached the age of 30 days.[25] But in fact, foster parents frequently received much younger infants. Once their overall health condition and the weather made it possible, the child was offered to foster care. Thus the foster parents were often given one-week or two-week-old babies. As a result of this practice, most of the children who came into foster care were not vaccinated. Foster parents living near Prague had to have the child vaccinated later in the foundling hospital. Those who came from distant places were obliged to have their foster child vaccinated by an authorised doctor near their residence and send the confirmation to the directorate. Thus the directorate kept track of the immunisation status of all the children ever sent to foster care.

Foster mothers who picked up an infant from the foundling hospital until 1880 received generous baby supplies. The foster mother could keep these if the child in her care survived the first year of life. In the event the child died before reaching one year, the foster mother had to return all

---

[23] NA, ZPN, a book of regulations (1808–1841), book 1, p. 20.
[24] NA, ZPN, a book of regulations (1832–1841), book 4.
[25] NA, ZPN, Instruktionen für die Gebär und Findelanstalt zu Prag, 1835, book 14, Instructions for the head doctor of the foundling hospital, Article no. 43.

baby supplies to the foundling hospital. A foster mother who managed to
nurse the child in her care until the age of 1 year, received an extra
financial bonus.[26] The prospect of receiving this bonus and the baby
supplies was supposed to act as a guarantee that a foundling would be well
cared for.

Furthermore, foster parents were financially motivated by the receiving
of a regular allowance. Its amount was graded according to the age of the
child, for infants under 1 year it was 24 Fl. per year, for a child 1–10 years
old it was 15 Fl. and for children to the age of 15 the amount was set at 12
Fl. annually. The allowance was reduced symmetrically with the
increasing age of the child, because older children were assumed to be
able to assist foster parents at work. The amount was paid to foster parents
in monthly intervals by the parish priests. Each payment of the allowance
was recorded in the contract.

The foundling hospital sometimes placed older children in foster care
as well. These were children who either had returned from previous foster
parents, or children brought up outside the foundling hospital. As these
children were no longer babies, they could be entrusted to either foster
mothers who were not breastfeeding at that moment or to foster families
which were already caring for one child. The directorate did not provide
any additional supplies for older children and thus in some cases, the child
owned only those clothes he was currently wearing. Yet if the new foster
parents cared well for these older children, they could obtain an allowance
for clothing, paid by the foundling hospital.[27] At the same time, the
directorate of the foundling hospital tried to encourage foster parents to
keep the children even after the age of 15. Moreover, foster families could
even receive a more generous allowance when they accepted a disabled
child.[28]

Most foster mothers came from poor rural areas.[29] They usually
belonged to the lower strata of society, typically had 5–6 children and
tended to care for one or two foundlings of different ages. The allowance
paid for the foster care was a welcome source of extra income for these
families. Some foster mothers had to walk several days to get to Prague for

[26] NA, ČG-Publ. 1796–1805, box 3510.
[27] NA, ZPN, a collection of documents issued by the Provincial Maternity Hospital
in Prague, book 10.
[28] Ibid.
[29] Marie Červinková-Riegrová, O nalezencích v Čechách, přednáška v Měšťanské
besedě v Praze dne 16. ledna 1888 [About foundlings in the Czech Lands. A
lecture in Měšťanská beseda in Prague], (Praha: M. Červinková-Riegrová, 1888),
p. 2.

the baby. Obviously, such a long journey from Prague to the new home meant great risk for the infant, since he was in danger of either hypothermia or dehydration. Sadly enough, some children died before they reached their destination.

A constant lack of foster parents accompanied the foundling hospital throughout its entire existence. Such a deficit of suitable candidates was widely perceived as a sensitive issue, especially given the high mortality rate in the facility. Early transfer to foster care was seen as prevention against mortality. For this reason, the directorate asked the city authorities as well as manorial lords to actively cooperate on the issue of foundling care. Yet the directorate continually faced numerous challenges in its quest to succeed in saving children's lives. The archival sources from the 1820s and 1830s contain many written complaints addressed to the directorate claiming that rural landlords did not support foster care at their estate and that they even completely opposed the idea of placing children into foster care in their territory.[30] To make the situation worse, the allowance for raising children in foster care did not keep pace with rising prices.[31]

The biggest problem was finding those foster mothers who would be able to breastfeed the baby. A high death rate in the foundling hospital prompted the provincial authorities to act. In 1805, the allowance for breastfed infants was increased by 7 Kreutzer a day. Such an increase in financial support was intended to encourage prospective foster mothers to accept children under 1 year of age. The contemporary experience proved that even an illegitimate child had a greater chance of survival after reaching that threshold.

Any child could be repeatedly returned to the foundling hospital and again entrusted to other foster parents. The possibility of returning – so-called "Restitution" – was enshrined in a contract that the foundling hospital always signed with foster parents. Foster parents who wanted to return the child to the foundling hospital in Prague were obliged to notify the directorate a month in advance as well as state the reason why they had decided to give up raising that particular child.[32]

After a child reached the age of 6 in foster care, his foster parents were required to send him to school. A foundling had the right to free textbooks and his foster parents were exempt from paying tuition fees.[33] The child

---

[30] NA, ZPN, a collection of the documents issued by the Provincial Maternity Hospital in Prague 1808–1841, book 1.

[31] ČG-Publ., 1806–1815, box 5477.

[32] NA, ZPN, a book of regulations of the Provincial Maternity Hospital, book 10.

[33] NA, Zemský výbor [The Land Committee], (further referred to as ZV), No. 34/33 – The Prague maternity hospital and a foundling hospital, varia, 1794–1850,

was then supposed to be educated according to his abilities, skills and physical strength. Yet the reality was often far different from the wishes of the creator of the reforms. Complaints frequently arose about the neglect of schooling for foundlings until the 1870s, despite the fact that foster children should have been regularly supervised by a parish priest.[34] Some parish priests did not fulfil this obligation at all and therefore the foster children usually did not attend school because they could work in the field or around the house. It can be said that the issue of educating foundlings was not satisfactorily resolved until 1872 (in this year, the length of foster care for foundlings was shortened to 6 years).

Obviously, providing medical assistance in the case of illness of a child was among the basic responsibilities of foster parents. If the foundling died, the foster parents had to report to the manorial lords and the parish priests who consequently notified the administration of the foundling hospital through the regional office. Even in these cases, we find attempts to conceal the death of a foster child by the foster parents, or to present their own child to act as the foundling, for which they would then wrongfully keep receiving the allowance. Such embezzlement was regarded as theft, for which not only foster parents were held accountable, but also the home village, which had to pay damages – its responsibility was to supervise the foundlings and their foster parents and they had failed to do so.[35]

In the case of either the death of the child or his return to the institute, the parish priest had two duties to carry out: first, he was obliged to review the financial issues (allowance payments) and to make a list of all items that the child owned. If that child was younger than 1 year, the parish priest was supposed to collect the baby supplies from the foster parents and return them to the directorate of the foundling hospital in Prague. In general, parish priests were fully responsible for the overall management of the care for foundlings residing within their parish. In addition to paying allowances to the foster parents, they were furthermore supposed to supervise the care of foundlings and supervise foster parents regularly, discuss all related issues and keep convincing them to keep the child in their care. In cases where they discovered discrepancies in raising the child during a visit to a foster family, the priests were supposed to reprimand the foster parents. If they found major offences such as neglect, they were obliged to notify the authorities. Every six months the parish priests sent statements summarising the payments of allowances to the directorate in

box 623.
[34] E.g. NA, ZPN, The book of standards 1841–1865, book 5, p. 230.
[35] NA, ČG-Publ. 1796–1805, box 3510.

Prague. In addition, they were required to report on the state of foundlings. Yet some parish priests completely failed to meet these obligations. Foundlings from some foster families returned to the foundling hospital badly dressed and without any education at all. Thus the directorate of the foundling hospital tried to change this situation by introducing the institution of "Foundling/Orphan's Fathers" whose task was to oversee the moral and intellectual development of foster children. These "fathers" were supposed to work together with parish priests. Yet in some parishes, this function was held only by a priest himself. Generally, the issue regarding the supervision of raising foundlings had not been satisfactorily resolved by the end of the 19th century.[36]

In connection with both the transition of the foundling hospital under the provincial administration and with shortening the duration of foster care to the age of 6 in 1872, it was decided to implement so-called "two-third care." This system was a complete novelty in the care for foundlings – a child might be entrusted to his biological mother or maternal relatives, who would then receive two-thirds the amount of the standard allowance. The family would receive this financial support until the child reached the age of 4 in the care of his mother or relatives. A necessary condition for entrusting the child to his own mother was her "proper, moral" life and good mental shape.[37] A child from the foundling hospital could be entrusted into the two-third care only upon personal request by his mother or his blood relatives. These individuals were then obliged to prove that they were able to care for a child, i.e. that they were endowed with adequate accommodation, suitable for a small child.

As we can see, the Prague foundling hospital fulfilled an important role in the city's system of care for the poor by playing the role of guardian for uncared-for children, entrusted them to foster families and paid for their care. Furthermore, this facility covered medical care for these abandoned children, and initiated and supervised their vaccinations as well as their education. In addition, the foundling hospital admitted children born outside the maternity hospital throughout its entire existence. It also functioned, albeit in a limited way, as an orphanage. Thanks to the introduction of the two-third care, the foundling hospital enabled biological mothers or other blood relatives to become much more engaged in raising and educating their offspring. By doing so, the institution actually fulfilled an important role in the protective custody of endangered children.

---

[36] NA, ZPN, The development, organisation and agenda of the institute 1893–1949, box 2.

[37] NA, ZPN, the book of documents I., book 10, p. 381.

In addition to care for children, the foundling hospital also became involved in care for single mothers. In 1833, a mediation office of wet nurses (so-called *Ammen-Comptoir*) was established, whose task was to prevent a "disaster"[38] in the event that the mother could not breastfeed or if an incorrect choice of a wet nurse occurred. This mediation office constantly oversaw the medical condition of the wet nurses, and its officers also controlled the way they handled infants.[39.] And who could become a wet nurse? They were either single mothers who gave birth in the maternity hospital or other females whose children lived in the foundling hospital. Widows and other married women living in Prague could also do the job, but single mothers were preferred. The aim was to provide them with a paid job, and thereby give them the means to earn a living. By establishing the mediation office, the foundling hospital expanded its care for single mothers who had expressed their interest in becoming wet nurses. Thus the foundling hospital represented a much-needed part of the system of care for the poor by caring for endangered children as well as for some of their mothers. Over time, the institution also gained an important place in providing health care in Prague.

---

[38] NA, ZPN, a book of standards (1808–1841), book 1, a report from 1833, pp. 82–90.
[39] Gottfried Rittershain, Zweiter Jahresbericht der königl. böhmischen Landesfindelanstalt in Prag (Prag 1866), p. 99.

CHAPTER THIRTEEN

THE REGISTER OF WORKERS IN A CITY AS A TOOL OF THE CARE FOR THE POOR: THE CITY OF BRNO AS A CASE STUDY[1]

ZDEŇKA STOKLÁSKOVÁ

Abstract: The methodological starting point of the study is an analysis of the police records of inhabitants, which function as a restrictive measure, i.e. as a tool used by municipalities in order to have as small a number of latently needy persons as possible. The targeted effort of municipalities (larger agglomerations) to keep the number of persons granted permanent residency in such cities at the absolute minimum is shown in the example of representative cases of wage workers in Brno and Olomouc. This tendency, a sort of "social indifference" towards the fate of "retired, old, and useless" workers – who were often after a lifetime of work in the city forced to leave for their home rural communities, which had no means to look after them – was not unusual.

The title of the contribution evokes the presumption that the subject of the interpretation will be collaboration by the police in caring for the poor. However, the methodological starting point here is the opposite: to expose the police register as a set of restrictive measures, as an instrument used by the Brno Municipal Authority to ensure that the town had as few latently needful persons as possible.

The right to poverty support as a civil right

Care for the poor in towns is inherently related to the state social system, which began to emerge in the Czech Lands no later than in the middle of the 18th century. The Theresian and Josephine reforms gradually took away care for the poor from private organisations and

---

[1] The publication was carried out as a part of the project of excellence Centre for Cross-Disciplinary Research into Cultural Phenomena in the Central European History: Image, Communication, Behaviour (Czech Science Foundation, Reg. no. 14-36521G).

subjects, i.e. primarily the church and generous donors from the ranks of the affluent population. Occasional and random charity care was replaced by organised and systematic social work, dividing subjects who were to be supported by the appropriate institutions as much as possible, according to level of need. Why did the state take away care for the poor from private hands and make its own monopoly from it? Did these actions not abolish a certain long-term, albeit irregular and scattered, flow of funds in favour of the poor?

Enlightenment legislators certainly saw this danger, but a much more important aspect of the modern period was the vision of a new man, equal before the law, which was supported by the abolition of serfdom in the year 1781, the Civil Code of 1786, and the General Civil Code of the year 1811, according to which "every human being has an innate, intellectually-given right, and therefore must be regarded as a person."[2] However, the term "human being" had a special meaning at the start of the 19th century, as it did not belong among common legal concepts; instead, terms tended to be used such as *"Individuum"*, *"Inwohner"* [domestic inhabitant, within the meaning of a domestic state citizen, not domestic in the sense of a municipality], *"Bürger"* [burgher], eventually *"Staatsbürger"* [state citizen] and of course *"Untertan"* [subject]. The term human being undoubtedly also included women, which previous concepts had not. "Under legally prescribed conditions, every person is able to acquire rights."[3]

These rights also meant the right to basic human treatment: i.e. the right to birth, marriage and burial in a cemetery, and basic assistance in the event of poverty, old age and illness. On the one hand, the right to birth was supported by punishment for abortion, on the other hand primarily by prevention, i.e. an effort to improve the social status of unmarried mothers and illegitimate children, or more precisely to transfer part of the responsibility to the father of the illegitimate child, and last but not least options for the mothers of unwanted children, to give birth to their child for free and leave it in the care of the state.

---

[2] "Jeder Mensch hat angeborne, schon durch die Vernunft einleuchtende Rechte, und ist daher als eine Person zu betrachten." Allgemeines Bürgerliches Gesetzbuch für die gesammten Deutschen Erbländer der Oesterreichischen Monarchie III., Wien 1811, (further referred to as ABGB 1811), Article 16, Seiner Majestät des Kaisers Franz Gesetze und Verfassungen im Justiz-Fache. Für die deutschen Staaten der Oesterreichischen Monarchie, (hereinafter: Justizgesetzsammlung), dritte Fortsetzung (1804–1811), no. 946, p. 278.

[3] "Jedermann ist unter den von Gesetzen vorgeschriebenen Bedingungen fähig, Rechte zu erwerben." ABGB 1811, Article 18, Justizgesetzsammlung, dritte Fortsetzung (1804–1811), no. 946, p. 278.

The right to marriage was supported by the abolition of serfdom, so the nobility could no longer deny unpropertied engaged couples marriage, as had previously occurred to a large extent. In this way, dominions tried to prevent the expansion of the unpropertied population class, which from the mid-18th century was also supported by legal regulations. "In order to limit the unrestricted conclusion of marriages by persons without resources and without livelihoods, permission to marry cannot be granted to anyone unless they bring confirmation of the means in which they intend to support themselves."[4] One might also speculate that the very prevention of the possibility of concluding marriage contributed to the birth of some children outside wedlock. After the abolition of serfdom, the nobility lost this control mechanism. The issue of the influence of political offices on the conclusion of marriages after the abolition of serfdom in the year 1781 so far remains unexamined; nevertheless, certain efforts by the state to prevent the conclusion of marriages by persons who could not declare the manner of their livelihood is also evident in the 19th century.

The right and obligation (as it was not only humane, but also hygienic aspects that played a role here) to be buried in a cemetery was guaranteed by Josephine legislation. So-called "donkey burials", i.e. burials outside cemeteries, which had formerly been realised by non-Catholics due to the Catholic population's opposition, were no longer allowed. These facts are also documented by entries in Registers of Births and Deaths – "buried at the cross above the village", "buried beside the Way of the Cross" or even "buried like a lout."[5] For example, in the years 1673–1680, 11% of all deceased in Nové Město in Moravia were buried outside cemeteries. A dignified burial was also enabled by the state's pressure for the reduction of fees for religious ceremonies, which had formed a significant part of funeral expenses. Disproportionately high fees, which were demanded even from the poorest classes, were scathingly criticised by Enlightenment authors, according to whom man came into the world for free, so he should also leave the world for free. "How did it happen that this process, which in itself seems to be a mere police act, fell under spiritual authority, and how were fees for the entry into this valley of tears introduced,

---

[4] "Die freie Zusammenverheurathung der gewerb- und mittellosen Leute einzuschränken, ist keinem, ohne beigebrachte Urkunden, wie sie sich erhlich zu nähren gedenken, hierzu die Erlaubnis zu ertheilen." Decree dated the 1st of July 1746, *Kaiserlich-Königliches Theresianisches Gesetzbuch enthaltend die Gesetze von den Jahren 1740 bis 1780*, 3rd edition, Wien: Mößle 1789; hereinafter the laws of Maria Theresa, vol. 1 (1789), no. 35, p. 33.

[5] Eva Melmuková, *Patent zvaný toleranční* [Letters Patent of Religious Tolerance], (Praha: Mladá fronta, 1999), p. 178.

particularly the burdensome duty that we have to pay at the time of our
departure; we must look for the traces of this process in the late centuries
of Christianity. [...] So it often happens that a man who kept his family
debt-free throughout his whole life plunges it into debt by his death.
Funeral fees were really so excessive that they were burdensome even for
the lowest class. When you see a family whose father is lying dead on a
plank and the orphaned under-age children are crying for bread, while the
helpless mother brings the last of their possessions to a pawn shop, to
satisfy the parish priest who does not want to bury her husband for free
with a few guldens, then it's surely pardonable if a person who sees this
scene calls such priests hard and heartless people."[6]

Funeral expenses represented a disproportionate financial burden for
the family of the deceased, as shown by an unpropertied boy's memory of
a funeral. "Within a short time my brother Frankie became sick, and he
was sick for four weeks. Father asked for a doctor to be brought from
Vožice; some Mr. Schuch. He came around three times. The last time he
said that Frankie was beyond help, that he'd be dead within two days at
most. It happened. Two days later, Frankie died. [...] My poor parents
lamented the boy. And they cried even more, as they didn't know how
they'd bury the poor fellow. My poor parents didn't have a single
groschen. [...] Father said: "I'll go to my brother, hopefully he won't
throw me out; when there's work again I'll pay him everything back." [...]
There was no other way, father had to go to this wicked brother and he
pleaded earnestly with him, that he knew that his boy had died, and could
he give him a few gold coins so he can bury him. His brother started

---

[6] "Wie es aber zugieng, daß eine Handlung, die an sich eine blosse Polizeysache zu
seyn scheint, in die geistliche Gerichtsbarkeit gezogen wurde, wie und wann die
Mäuthen, die wir beym Eingang in dieses Jammerthal, und besonders der
drückende Esitozoll, den wir beym Ausgang entrichten mußten, eingeführet
worden, davon wären wohl die Spuren in den späteren Jahrhunderten der
Christenheit aufzusuchen. (...) Da ereignete sich dann oft, daß ein Mann, der seine
Familie durch sein ganzes Leben schuldenfrey erhielt, sie durch seinen Tod in die
Schulden stürzte. Die Begräbnistaxen waren wirklich so überspannt, daß sie auch
für die niedrigste Klasse drückend seyn mußten, und wenn man dann so eine
unglückliche Familie sah, wo hier der Vater auf dem Brett lag, dort die verwaisten
unmündigen Kinder um Brod schrien, indessen die hilflose Mutter ihre letzte
Habschaft dem Versatzamt zuträgt, um mit den wenigen Gulden den Pfarrer, der
weil er diese wenigen Gulden weiß, den Mann nicht gratis begraben will, zu
befriedigen, und wenn man dann bey dem Anblick so einer Scene in edeln
Unwillen auffährt, und diese Priester harte, gefühllose Menschen nennet, so ist es
gewiß sehr verzeihlich." [Joseph Richter] Obermayr, *Bildergalerie katholischer
Mißbräuche*, Frankfurt – Leipzig 1784, p. 80–81 and 85.

shouting at him, saying "I don't have any money. Take him away in a sack and bury him yourself."[7] The boy's funeral could only be conducted with the help of a financial loan from a local teacher who even brought pupils with him, probably so that they would sing at the ceremony for free.

The right to basic poverty support tended to be theoretical under the conditions of the emerging modern state, but it was a reason for the transfer of poverty care into the hands of the state, as the basic postulate here was equality: i.e. the right to some kind of – in the Enlightenment period rather theoretical – poverty support for every person. This right could not be realised without a basic register of the population and its domestic jurisdiction, as the domestic municipality became the only subject from which the needful poor person could expect help.

The legal and ideological prerequisites for the realisation of basic poverty care, and their criticism

Poverty care cannot be realised without a basic register of the population. With the abolition of serfdom in the year 1781,[8] the state lost the possibility of an elementary control mechanism, which could only be replaced with difficulty. Even before the announcement of the abolition of serfdom, laws were being prepared to control the movement of inhabitants. The most important appears to be the Conscription and Recruiting District System [*Konskriptions- und Werbbezirksystem*], published on September 27, 1781. In the short interim period, i.e. slightly over one month before the announcement of the abolition of serfdom, the nobility also assumed responsibility for migrating subjects, as the dominions were obliged to prevent the disappearance of men capable of serving in the army. The dominion guaranteed the eventually incorrectly issued permits to move to unconscripted lands, or abroad, with a pecuniary fine amounting to 150 to 300 guldens.

---

[7] *Paměti babičky Kavalírové* [The Memories of Grandmother Kavalírová], ed. Otakar Vlasák (Praha: Český spisovavatel, 1993, 10th edition), pp. 53–54. František Adler, the author's brother, died at the age of thirteen in the year 1819. The same source states the price of the funeral of an older woman (the author's mother-in-law), probably in the 1840s, as 80 guldens; (a good housemaid's monthly earnings amounted to 5–6 guldens).

[8] The Letters Patent of Abolishing of Serfdom dated November 1st, 1781, *Handbuch aller unter der Regierung des Kaisers Joseph des II. für die k.k. Erbländer ergangenen Verordnungen und Gesetze in einer systematischen Verbindung*, Wien 1780-1789, hereinafter the laws of Joseph II (thematic collection), vol. 1 (1785), p. 74ff.

After the abolition of serfdom, fear of subjects disappearing continued to exist. Instead of the all-ensuring control mechanism of serfdom, other means of record-keeping and control were chosen. Such an instrument, actually a relic of aristocratic power structures, became dismissal certificates, which were issued free of charge by the nobility to subjects who wanted to move. Whether the nobility could exert pressure (if the move was undesirable) remains merely a proposition, given the current state of research. The so-called Regulations for the Subjects of Krain and Special Status (for door-to-door trade) for the Dominions of Gottschee and Reifnitz[9] show actual problems and intervention by the state (in the sense of regulation) in aristocratic power. [10]

However, the dominions guaranteed that qualified persons would not leave the land. In theory, no nobility was allowed to receive a foreign subject without a dismissal certificate, as it was within the dominions' competency to request a dismissal certificate from the "old" nobility for the "new" nobility. The interpretation of the ascertained facts is problematic; one can assume that the preserved archival sources document only legal migration. The most important legal reason for the issue of dismissal certificates was marriage to the subject of another nobility, and the subsequent move to the territory of one of the fiancés' nobilities. This process is documented by Pavel Cibulka for the South Moravian dominion of Lundenburg (Břeclav): 90% of the total identified 268 persons who wanted to settle in the Liechtenstein dominion of Břeclav in the years 1783–1826 did so for reasons of marriage. [11]

The newly created structure of care for the poor was thoughtfully connected to other areas of state administration, which mainly manifested itself in the military and in religious organisations. The lost war against Prussia, and the considerable loss of the state's "industrial heart" – Silesia – connected with it, showed Maria Theresa the unsustainable situation in the army, and most importantly in the economy. Both factors are related to the number and status of the population. Many thinkers "around the throne" found themselves under the influence of population theories which were fashionable at the time, according to which one of the most important factors of economic development was represented by the largest population

---

[9] Now Kočevje and Ribnik in Slovenia.
[10] "Untertansregulativ für Krain" of September 13, 1782, the law of Joseph II (thematic collection), vol. 1 (1785), pp. 77–79.
[11] Pavel Cibulka, "Eine Herrschaft in Mähren," in *Grenze und Staat. Paßwesen, Staatsbürgerschaft, Heimatrecht und Fremdengesetzgebung in der österreichischen Monarchie (1750-1867)*, eds. Waltraud Heindl and Edith Saurer (Wien: Böhlau, 2000), pp. 721–787, here 778–779.

possible. The promoted growth in the number of inhabitants as quickly as possible, regardless of the poor classes' diet, was scathingly criticised by contemporaries: "Under the assumption that the number of inhabitants in the land can be doubled or tripled, individuals will gain very little; whereby the main gain is for the sovereign, who has more subjects, and who can enhance the lustre of his throne and rap his neighbours over the knuckles more easily." The criticism was aimed not only at the population theories themselves, but also against the propagators of these ideas, who were described as incompetent and extravagant men who lacked the courage to live according to their own ideas. "First of all I came to one populationist. His attractive theories left me with the expectation that I would find him at the side of an honourable woman, in a circle of well-fed children. What a sight! The ardent populationist lay on the bed with three surgeons standing beside him, who were just getting ready to render him permanently unusable for populating. He had fared miserably in the infertile common places of life [brothels] and he wrote his essay only to be able to pay for the pills and drinks that were to help him stand on his feet again, so he could wander the land like a shadow for another few months."[12]

As a result of reforms in health care, hygiene and care for the poor, the number of inhabitants rose sharply. In the year 1770, even before the economically-motivated abolition of serfdom, a conscription of the male population in certain Austrian lands was carried out. [13] The purpose of this conscription, which was performed due to pressure by co-regent Joseph, was clearly connected with the army. However, the functioning of the army was contingent on the condition of the state economy, which among other things meant the size of the population, its health, education and average age.

The purpose of the conscription of 1777 was to determine the status of the entire population, including groups of inhabitants which had previously not been of interest to the state, such as women and Jews. For the first time in the history of the Austrian Empire, not only was the number of inhabitants of most non-Hungarian lands ascertained, but also their age, occupation, family status, creed, and most importantly so-called political domicile, i.e. social affiliation. In the year 1777, legal principles

---

[12] Both quotations: Johann Pezzl, *Marokkanische Briefe* (Frankfurt – Leipzig, 1785), pp. 19 and 23–24.

[13] These lands continued to be called the "old conscripted lands." For our purpose, let's quickly summarize that the "old conscripted lands" are identical to the later Cisleithania, albeit with the exception of Tyrol, Vorarlberg and Austrian Littoral, until the year 1818 also Trieste and of course Salzburg.

were created for a later domestic law, even though under the continuing patrimonial system this supported the dichotomy of subjects responsible for the socially needful. Especially problematic was the fact that the area of social care involved competing subjects, which in practice led to a decade-long "economic battle" in certain areas (such as, for example, deportation to the community/municipality of permanent residence) between nobilities and municipalities, ending only with the abolition of the patrimonial system.

Of special interest in this context is the Family Code [*Gesindeordnung*] of 1782,[14] which systemised the legal status of the lower classes of the population under the new conditions for the abolition of serfdom. The now free former serfs could decide on their own affairs without the nobility's consent (moving, marriage, education), but the state wanted to retain complete control of the population, so that it could count, tax and most importantly find the people again, which was important for the army, as the largest part of the troops came from the unpropertied classes.

Unrestricted labour mobility, which was highest in the poorest section of the population, corresponded to the plans of the ruling circles, which were interested in dynamic economic development. This attitude is evident as early as September 1781 (i.e. before the abolition of serfdom): "There is therefore no intention, in any case, to place obstacles in the path of someone, whether it's in trade, commerce or their journey; on the contrary, everyone should be provided with the best possible progress and support. Thus, nobody may be prevented from travelling where they like, whether it's to trade or attend to their affairs, in the land where they were born or live, or according to circumstances to another conscripted or unconscripted land or even abroad, if it happens with observation and preservation of good order and the necessary caution, and if they arrange a permit in the appropriate location in advance."[15]

---

[14] Family Code for rural families in Bohemia, Moravia and Silesia dated February 8, 1782, the laws of Joseph II, vol. 1 (1785), p. 84.

[15] "Es ist aber deswegen keineswegs die Absicht, jemanden, es sei in Geschäften, im Handel oder Wander, oder auf auch sonst eine Art, einige Hindernis in Weg zu legen, sondern im Gegentheile vielmehr einem ieden allen nur möglichen Vorschub und Beförderung hierinnfalls zu verschaffen. Daher ist es auch niemanden verwehrt, sich Geschäfte und Verrichtungen halber in dem Lande, wo er geboren oder ansässig ist, hinzubegeben, wo er will, oder nach Umständen auch in ein anderes konskribiertes oder unkonskribiertes, ia selbst in ein auswärtiges Land zu verfügen, wenn es unter Beobachtung der zur Erhaltung der guten Ordnung nöthigen Vorsicht geschieht, und wenn sich deswegen vorher gehörigen Orts um die Erlaubnis gemeldet wird. " Conscription and Recruiting District System, the laws of Joseph II (thematic collection), vol. 3 (1785), pp. 40–141, here pp. 60–61.

The comprehensive control mechanism of serfdom had to be replaced with other tools, starting with an inspection of the register of classes which were not bound by property. Servants' books were introduced in September 1782, in which the basic unit was defined as the municipality – not the nobility – as was the case with passports, exile passports, dismissal certificates and other personal documents. Thus, one of the factors of the new order in the field of social affairs is evident here. The municipality becomes the centre of order, record-keeping, security and care.

Co-ordinators of poverty care above municipal level but independent of the dominion had to be defined, because the municipalities and nobilities represented competing subjects in care for the poor; in addition to this, difficultly resolvable situations could arise if the municipality was located in the territory of two or three dominions. This problem was solved in connection with another reform – the new organisation of parishes. Parish districts were mostly identical to poverty districts, because putting the co-ordination of poverty care in parish priests' hands seemed to be logical and natural. Parish priests became so-called "fathers of the poor", even though this function was not linked to an ecclesiastic person. Thus, the Catholic Church, which had lost some of its influence in the social sphere as a result of the Josephine reforms, was once again involved in poverty care.

The creation of state-organised poverty care was connected with the structure of the army. In 1781, independent recruiting districts were established within the nobility,[16] whose primary function was naturally the constant "supply" of the army with young men. The current status of the population was to be ascertained by regular revisions which took place between the end of February and the end of May. In order to place the whole process in the context of the current status of the army, heads of households were ordered to verbally report every change in their family to the appropriate office within fourteen days.[17] The report was to be made on a Sunday or a public holiday, probably so as not to disrupt the working day with the journey to the office and back, which demonstrates the curious, but typical, thrift of Josephinism. The reporting obligations did not include only the birth, marriage or death of a family member, but also moving or change of service. Copies of population books were held by the nobility and district commissioners. For neglecting to comply with the verbal reporting obligation within fourteen days, a fine of 30 Kreutzer was stipulated for the nobility, clergy, burghers and "VIPs", while the fathers

---

[16] Ibid. p. 40–141.
[17] Ibid. p. 50. The voluntary reporting of changes in the composition of household members was already published in the Court Decree of June 26, 1779.

of serf families were punished with 24 hours' imprisonment. It seems that a written report was not required.

Special attention was given to soldiers sent home for an unlimited period of time, whose health was to be inspected. The potential costs of treatment were to be covered by the administration only under the assumption that the cured soldier could return to the regiment. In other cases, the army did not pay the medical expenses, which in fact meant that the costs had to be covered by the municipality (or that the treatment was not agreed to at all). This postulate confirms the transfer of the costs of poverty and health care to (mostly rural) municipalities, which provided the most recruits. The poor stratum of the population, which nobody wanted to have or secure, was represented by military veterans, as the common perception was that they were paying for men without morals or a work ethic. "The core of the nation lives in its heyday years unmarried, idle, grown wild and taught only one art, which is to beat a person to death; upon return to its rural cottage, it spreads violence and shameful diseases among its neighbours."[18] Contemporary laws, in which vagrants and beggars are grouped together with military ex-servicemen, correspond to this satirical and critical view.

The regular recruitment had an unwanted side effect, but one which was welcomed by the state – it served as an effective brake on pauperisation, because unpropertied men who were recruited were not available on the marriage market. The weakness of the entire system, in which the poor, and more importantly, the healthy section of the population was excluded from the process of starting families because of the realisation of the state's costly military ambitions, was exposed even by contemporaries. "Because only weaklings and adolescents from peasant families are allowed into trade and marriage undisturbed, the nation is facing the danger of becoming a republic of limping, cross-eyed, humpbacked dwarves with crooked legs and crippled arms in just a few generations."[19]

---

[18] "Der Kern der Nation lebt in seinen blühendsten Jahren unverheiratet, müßig, verwildert, in der einzigen Kunst todzuschlagen geübt; verbreitet bei seiner Zurückkehr in die ländliche Hütte Wildheit und schändliche Krankheiten unter seine Nachbarschaft." Pezzl, *Marokkanische Briefe*, pp. 26–27.

[19] "Da bloß die Schwächlinge und Auswüchse der ländlichen Familien ungestört zu Gewerbe und Ehe gelassen werden, läuft eine solche Nation Gefahr, in einigen Generationen in eine Republik von hinkenden, schielenden, höckerichten, krummbeinichten, lahmhändigen Zwergen verwandelt zu werden." Ibid, pp. 243–244.

The state was not only interested in a constant influx of young healthy men, but also in how and where it could (again) find such men who were conscripted, or suitable for conscription, as they devoted themselves to their professions and education, which was vitally necessary for economic development. Thus, military authorities became an inseparable part of the comprehensive migration control mechanism, particularly of the population's poor classes.

How such a mechanism of finding (again) a man who might be suitable for military service took place was described in his memoirs by journeyman wheelwright František Kebrdle, who at the time found himself on a wandering pilgrimage in Styria. "At the beginning of March [1845] I received a message from home that I must report for conscription in the month of May. I was saddened by the report, but that's the way it had to be. So I decided I would be home for the Easter holidays. I got ready, and after Passion Sunday [5th Sunday of Lent], i.e. fourteen days before the holidays, on Monday, I set off on my way back. [...] The suffering I endured, snow was falling the whole way, and especially from Budweis to Písek there were snowdrifts, those nights, my boots soaked. In Padrť I stopped at my uncle Svoboda's [...] and I stayed in his place overnight; the next day, on Wednesday, I crawled home through Strašice knee-deep in snow. I came home, and there was nobody home in the room. [...] Just then my mother came into the room and she couldn't recognise me, my whole body looked like it was bronzed from the cold and my face was swollen [...]."[20]

Population groups not important for the army were also controlled, but only formally. In women's passports, the number of the recruiting district was entered (zero was entered instead of the protocol number), such as for example in the passport of Ursula Bernreuter, a maid. The passport was issued in the year 1846 by the dominion in Drnholec, and served the sixteen-year-old woman as a travel document so that she could carry out her profession (she travelled with her employers). The fact that the passport was issued for all the conscripted lands shows that the holder was viewed as a person necessary for the state. (Fig. 13-1)

In the 19th century, a tendency towards the domestic principle of poverty care (which emerged in the Josephine period) also existed. The conscription patent in the year 1804 merely intensified the "search for order" in the area of jurisdiction and the poverty care associated with it. Foreigners were divided into the following categories: from the same or other district of the same land, from another conscripted land, from an

---

[20] František Kebrdle, *Memoirs*, National Technical Museum Archive, Collection of Memoirs and Manuscripts, no. 1609, pp. 14–16.

unconscripted land, or from abroad. In the classification of unmarried persons without parents, nobles, the "unfit" and women were singled out; military service was expected from the rest of the male population. The more detailed division of foreigners shows the state's efforts to territorially classify both domestic and foreign persons. In the case of its own state citizens this engagement served for more sophisticated involvement for the state mechanism's needs, while for foreigners it created a legal basis so that, if necessary, they would not have to be socially provided for.

Restrictions motivated by the effort to have as few needful persons as possible in the town

Domestic right was motivated by the idea that there should be at least one place in the state from which a person cannot be expelled, and that there is at least one institution to which a needful poor person can turn if necessary. However, this unquestionably good postulate was difficult to realise in a society whose life was dictated by economic pace. Poverty was inseparably connected with industrialisation, so in its early phases a fear of beggars and vagrants outweighed the advantages of a wider selection of work opportunities for the population. In the 1720s, the Lower Austrian town of Tulln spoke out against the establishment of workshops, because with them "various immoral women and other vermin would come into the town, and it would be impossible to get domestic staff."[21] Fears of poverty and its possible radicalisation were not only present in the propertied class; they were also expressed by the Minister of the Police, Johann von Pergen: "These types of people, without livelihood and to a large extent also without good morals, who have nothing to lose and can only gain from revolution, can be controlled only by banning the establishment of factories and marriages".[22] Pergen's stance evoked embarrassment and one could even say horror in advocates of liberalism, represented by the Court Chamber; they protested (but only after their imaginary victory over Pergen in the year 1809; at this time, the influence of the already "worn out" Minister Pergen was weakening, which made the advocates of liberalisation more powerful) against the debasement of factory workers as

---

[21] Wolfgang Häusler, "Von der Manufaktur zum Maschinensturm. Industrielle Dynamik und sozialer Wandel im Raum von Wien," in *Wien im Vormärz* (= Forschungen und Beiträge zur Wiener Stadtgeschichte, Band 8), ed. Felix Czeike (Wien – München: Komissionsverlag Jugend und Volk, 1980), p. 49.
[22] Quoted according to: Roman Sandgruber, *Ökonomie und Politik. Österreichische Wirtschaftsgeschichte vom Mittelalter bis zur Gegenwart* (Wien: Ueberreuter, 1995), pp. 175–176.

a class with poor morals: "No master, no factory owner accepts people into idleness. They employ them in great numbers, and permanently. However, a diligent and hard-working man, as scandalous as his behaviour may seem, is not dangerous to the state alliance or to morals."[23]

The Court Chamber did not have any fear of factory workers. However, the towns which profited from the work did, as they feared the possible entitlement to social support.[24] This is clearly shown by the statutes of large towns, which were bestowed in the Czech Lands in the year 1850 on Prague, Liberec, Brno, Olomouc and Opava. In these statutes, the acquisition of domestic right was stipulated only on the basis of an "explicit voluntary admission", which was characterised as a legal act between the municipality and the individual person, whereby from the municipality's side it required the municipal authority's consent and depended only on the municipality's free will; therefore, there was no right of appeal against the withholding of domestic right. [25] After all, a year earlier, the Provisional Municipal Act was passed, by which the acquisition of a new domestic jurisdiction was advantageous for the poor classes as never before.

One must look at the historical context of the Provisional Municipal Act of 1849. Its very name reveals that its approval by Parliament was expected, enshrined in the Constitution, which, as we know, never occurred.[26] It was these very revolutionary factors of the Provisional Municipal Act that influenced the very advantageous statutory deadline for the acceptance of the new domestic jurisdiction; in other words, the formulation of the Act was advantageous for the unpropertied classes. The entitlement to admission into another domestic union arose after just four years of an Austrian state citizen's tacit usucaption without a domestic certificate, or with a domestic certificate whose validity had already expired.

This first advantageous opportunity was used by a certain Johann Suchy, a cloth-cutting journeyman from Pilsen, who worked in the

---

[23] Johann Slokar, *Geschichte der österreichischen Industrie und ihrer Förderung unter Kaiser Franz I.* (Wien: Verlag von F. Tempsky, 1914), p. 50.

[24] Enshrined as rights in Article 22 of the Provisional Municipal Act of 1849.

[25] Josef Ulbrich, *Lehrbuch des Oesterreichischen Staatsrechts* (Wien: C. Konegen, 1883), p. 260.

[26] The Imperial, so-called March Constitution was adopted on March 4, 1849, and the Provisional Municipal Act was issued on March 17, 1849. In the foreword to the Provisional Municipal Act, the Emperor refers to Article 33 of the recently published Constitution, which relates to municipalities. *Allgemeines Reich-Gesetz- und Regierungsblatt*, 1849, no. 170, pp. 203–222.

Offermann family's factory in Brno at least from March 13, 1848 to
January 5, 1867. On August 22, 1852 (i.e. four years after the adoption of
the Provisional Municipal Act, which was the shortest possible period)
Johann Suchy was admitted into the domestic union of the town of Brno,
whereby he became entitled to possible social assistance, which was
timely for him because he was already 68 years of age. Nevertheless, he
continued to work for the Offermanns until he was 83, which in his
physically intensive trade was very admirable. His labour "value" is also
shown by the fact that he had a time-unrestricted "certificate," as the Brno
police called it; probably a permit to reside in the town of Brno. As an
employee in Offermann's textile factory, the largest enterprise in Brno,
Johann Suchy could also look forward to possible support from the social
support fund and sickness fund, which Karl Offermann established for his
employees.[27] Johann Suchy's newly-acquired domestic jurisdiction is
documented by his conscription certificate. (Cf. fig. 13-3, Conscription
certificate for Johann Suchy, dated August 22, 1825.[28])

Provisions for poverty

Such favourable conditions for admission into the domestic union did
not exist in the Austrian state system before or since; their validity was
ended by the Municipal Act of 1859, which left the four-year usucaption
deadline (the so-called *Quadrinierung*), but restricted it with an instrument
very important for the poorest classes: i.e. the entitlement did not arise if
the person in question received poverty support during the "waiting
period." The authors of this restriction based it on the postulate that those
who are a burden on public benefaction do not have the right to request
domestic jurisdiction and the social support connected with it, as these
should be granted only to persons who deserve them by their work or

---

[27] Karl (von) Offermann (1792–1869), son of textile entrepreneur Johann Heinrich
Offermann (1748–1793), took over the company, which his father had established,
in the year 1819 when it was already in its heyday, and this boom continued under
his administration. The modernisation of the factory enabled not only further
development, but also extensive social activity for the enterprise's employees. In
1863 Karl Offermann was made a peer. Cf. Bohumír Smutný, *Brněnští podnikatelé
a jejich podniky 1764–1948* [Brno Entrepreneurs and their Businesses 1764–1948]
(Brno: Statutární město Brno and Archiv města Brna, 2012), pp. 296–301, here p.
297.
[28] "Johann Suchy erscheint N. 10 der Bäckergasse einheimisch konskribirt und
nach Brünn zuständig. Konskriptions Amt Brünn 22. August 852 (Bretler)", MPA,
Police Directorate, B 26, Factory and Wage Labour Records (1848), no. 569.

otherwise, e.g. by the purchase of real estate or carrying on a trade or commerce. That this fact was actually monitored is proven by the confirmation issued for a certain Josefa Sucha by the Imperial-Royal Support Institute in Brno in the year 1854: "We hereby confirm that Josefa Sucha of Bystrc in Moravia was supported in the Brno Imperial-Royal Support Institute from December 13 to December 21, 1854."[29] Of interest in this case is the fact that the confirmation was issued four and a half years before the publication of the Municipal Act, which introduced such restrictions. (Fig. 13-4, Confirmation for Josefa Sucha, MPA, B 26, no. 569.)

Continuous employment

The applicant for the domestic right should enjoy an unblemished reputation, which for the poor was not as much of a problem as the following condition: they must not be in arrears with the payment of landowner taxes and municipal levies. For unpropertied persons, a significant restrictive fact was the condition that the applicant for admission into the municipal union had to prove the continuous operation (in the case of craftsmen, traders, etc.) of their business, or a continuous source of income – i.e. employment, which ensured the livelihood of their person or the entire family for the entire period. In the case of unpropertied applicants for domestic right, proof of continuous employment was apparently required.

This significant factor was very carefully monitored by the municipal authority, as shown by the example of Teresie Kunz of Libavá in Moravia. The twenty-seven-year-old grey-eyed blonde maid entered the service of a certain professor Eigel in Olomouc on February 7, 1850. On April 10, 1854 she left the service. Both the start and the termination of the service was reported by the woman to the police immediately on the following days, where she requested an extension of residence during the period of her unemployment (to April 25, 1854). The renewed residence permit (of April 30,1854), which was granted retrospectively when she reported her new service (for a certain Ms. Hurník, also in the town of Oloumouc) on May 1, 1854, shows that the town did not defend itself against "unsuspicious" poor people, even when they were unemployed, because Teresie Kunz owned a valid domestic certificate, which "protected" the town against her possible entitlement to poverty support.[30]

---

[29] Moravian Provincial Archives in Brno (MPA), Police Directorate, B 26, Factory and Wage Labour Records (1849), no. 570.
[30] State District Archive of Olomouc (SOkA), Archive of the Town of Olomouc, Book of Domestic Staff Records (1853), Sign. 3231, no. 4292.

The same procedural steps are documented by the case of Maria Amalia Kovarzik, a fourteen-year-old worker in a factory for the production of plush in Brno, who was unemployed from her dismissal by her first employer – the Schöller brothers – on March 7, until September 16, 1848.[31] There is no proof that she received poverty support; her residence permit was merely extended for her period of unemployment. Although Maria Amalia was born in Brno, her jurisdiction was in Domašov, as it was in this village in the judicial district of Ivančice that her parents had domestic rights. By interrupting her employment, she excluded herself from eventual entitlement to the granting of domestic jurisdiction, which however, given her age, she could not yet claim independently. She managed to acquire Brno domestic jurisdiction later, in the year 1855. Because she was still a minor on this date, it could only come about by her marriage or the subsequent marriage of her mother.[32] Maria Amalia Kowarzik continued to work in the town of Brno without changing employers: after her past unemployment she worked from September 16, 1848 in the Auspitz family's textile factory, and from September 30, 1877 for the company Spitz.[33] Nothing is known about her fate after that; in our context, the important factor is that she was no longer registered by the police as a domestic person.

Police protocols document very thorough record-keeping (and also compliance by workers) of residency and work permits. Josef Neufuss, a thirty-seven-year old head waiter from Sobotka in Bohemia, worked from March 8, 1850 for a certain Thomas Wlk in the town of Olomouc. He came to his employer with a "fresh" domestic certificate which had been issued only the day before. He ended his employment on February 25, 1853, but he reported this fact to the police ten days earlier; according to the police protocol he left for his domestic municipality on the day his employment ended, which for the police was an important and monitored

---

[31] The workshop and later factory of the Schöller brothers, established in the year 1819, was one of the largest textile enterprises in Brno. In the year 1826, the owners set up health insurance for their employees. Smutný, *Brněnští podnikatelé*, p. 381.

[32] "Maria Kowarzik ist in Nr. 5 am Mühlgraben einheimisch und zuständig konskribiert. Konsk. Amt Brünn am 12. 9. 1855." MPA, Police Directorate B 26, Book of Protocols (1848), no. 569. On her own marriage or the remarriage of her mother, I conclude from the police official's notes that she lived with her mother, whereas previous notes had mentioned both her parents. Her father was probably no longer alive. The change of residence indicates either a different social situation, or one of them entering into marriage.

[33] For more on the famous textile industry entrepreneurs Auspitz and Spitz, see: Smutný, *Brněnští podnikatelé*, pp. 24–26 and 416–417.

circumstance. After all, as an unemployed person, and later also with an "expired" domestic certificate, he could have been a burden on the municipal social system. Josef Neufuss appeared in Olomouc again the following year (March 11, 1854) and once again found employment in his profession. The police had no objections against him staying and working in the town, because he once again came with a new domestic certificate.[34]

Mandatory change of domestic jurisdiction

According to the law, women had to assume their husband's domestic jurisdiction, without being able to choose or keep their original one. The law was motivated by the effort that the whole family, i.e. including children if applicable, would have the same domestic right. However, this clear postulate brought some families fundamental existential problems. A woman born in a town where she also worked had to mandatorily assume her husband's domestic jurisdiction after marriage, who was a "foreigner" in the town, whereby she excluded herself from the possibility of receiving social support from the town in case of need.

The fact that the woman received a different domestic jurisdiction by marriage was recorded by the police, especially if she became a citizen of a town in this way, as was the case with Katharina Matouschek, who was born in Brno but had domestic jurisdiction in Těšovice in Bohemia.[35] This fact may be explained by Katharina Matouschek's parents living in Brno without acquiring Brno political domicile. On July 15, 1848, Katharina Matouschek, who was fourteen at the time, was granted permission to work as a "*nopperin*"[36] in the Schöller brothers' textile factory. Katharina lived with her mother in Horní Cejl (now Francouzská Street), inhabited at the time mainly by poor workmen. Her work permit was repeatedly extended until her marriage; on the same day on which she acquired Brno domestic jurisdiction, this information was entered in the Brno Police Directorate's protocols of factory workers. Her husband, linen weaver Melichar, held Brno domestic jurisdiction, which in this way was also transferred to her, and this was confirmed by the Brno conscription authority. "Das Katharina Melichar im Hause N. 17 am Teichdamm einheimisch konskribirt, und anher zuständig ist, wird bestätigt. Konsk-

---

[34] SOkA Olomouc, Archive of the Town of Olomouc, Book of Domestic Staff Records (1853), Sign. 3231, no. 4292.

[35] After the abolition of the patrimonial system, Těšovice (Teschwitz) became part of the Vítkov municipality in the year 1850 (until 1878); during the years 1960–1991 it was a part of Sokolov.

[36] A worker who removes knots from the cloth.

Amt Brünn am 19. Oktober 1853. (Bretler)."[37] Katharina Melichar continued to work in several textile factories (Strakosch, Hirsch, Bauer), until she returned to the Scholler brothers' company in the year 1869. From the perspective of police records, it's a remarkable fact that no entries exist of additional residency permit and work permit extensions, which confirms the assumption that these documents were requested only from workers who were not members of the Brno municipality.

Restrictions on the acquisition of domestic right by usucaption

"Admission to the domestic union takes place tacitly, by the foreign Austrian state citizen's usucaption, without a domestic certificate or with a certificate which has already expired, and who resided continuously in the municipality for four years."[38] The municipal authorities defended themselves fiercely against a growth in the number of unpropertied persons, who would automatically tacitly acquire an entitlement to domestic right by usucaption. An especially effective weapon used by them was the regular inspection of the personal documents with which the workers came to the town. They monitored the validity periods of the presented documents, especially domestic certificates, as the expiration of the domestic certificates' validity was automatically followed by an usucaption period, after whose expiry admission to the domestic union could be claimed. The town of Brno defended itself thoroughly on this very point. On the basis of analysis of the preserved personal details of wage workers in Brno (this involves mainly factory workers and domestic staff), one can make the hypothetical conclusion that entitlement by tacit usucaption was very difficult to acquire, as the police probably verified every year whether the worker had a valid document. If they did not, they were probably asked to have it re-issued by their domestic municipality, to which they were entitled free of charge every four years. As soon as the domestic, usually rural, municipality issued the new document, the town was once again "protected" against a latent claim to domestic jurisdiction by usucaption. In this context, they also inspected whether the workers

---

[37] MPA, B 26, Factory and Wage Labour Records (1848), no. 569 and 621.
[38] "Die Aufnahme in den Gemeindeverband erfolgt stillschweigend durch Duldung eines ohne Heimatschein, oder mit einem bereits erloschenen Heimatscheine sich durch vier Jahr ununterbrochen in der Gemeinde aufhaltenden, die österreichische Staatsbürgerschaft besitzenden Fremden." Letters Patent of March 17, 1849, Article 12, *Allgemeines Reichsgesetz- und Regierungsblatt für das Kaiserthum Oestereich*, no. 170, pp. 203–222, here p. 205.

were carrying on the type of profession which was recorded upon their arrival in Brno.

That was not always the case. Some women, after losing their jobs as cooks, nannies, maids or maidservants were forced to work in factories, or in worse cases as labourers, such as for example 34-year old Anna Kolaczek of Rychnov who, as a maid, acquired a domestic certificate from her municipality on December 18, 1851; on January 2, 1852 her legal residence was confirmed by the Brno Police Directorate. On September 14, 1853, apparently after losing her job as a maid, she was forced to start work as a labourer in a factory; she confirmed her change of job title to the police in Brno on September 26, 1853 and to the District Representative in Rychnov on December 10, 1853.[39]

Other women, after losing their livelihoods and housing, which maids always lost simultaneously, were cast into such social conditions that they were not able to return to their previous lives from them, as was the case with twenty-six-year-old Maria Vaniczek, who stooped from a maid to a labourer and finally a prostitute. For our context, let's briefly summarise her life story. The unmarried daughter of a shepherd in Dobřínsko in the Znojmo region, she lived and worked with her parents until she was twenty, helped out in the household and earned some extra money by manual work.[40] After her father's death, she worked as a maid in the nearby village of Krumlov. However, two years later she lost her job and went to Vienna to work as a maid, which she managed to do. After some time she was dismissed. Because she did not find work and had nowhere to live, she could not request an extension of her residency permit. She got into a vicious circle from which it was difficult to find a way out: she was without work, without a roof over her head and without documents (and money), whereby all these factors were mutually connected. When requesting an extension of a residency permit, one had to have both employment and housing. And it was at this very moment that Maria Vaniczek crossed the invisible line of an "honest way" of earning a livelihood from which, as it showed, there was no way back. She began to procure means of subsistence by petty theft and occasional prostitution, initially combined with casual work as a maidservant and labourer. On August 9, 1839 she was arrested in the Josephstadt district of Vienna, and a protocol was written up about her. She admitted that she had already been arrested three times. She stated that she was on her way back home from Hungary, where she had served her cousin until his death. The

---

[39] MPA, B 26, Factory and Wage Labour Records (1848), no. 569.
[40] MPA, F 177, Dominion of Moravský Krumlov, box 376, inv. no. 6 (exile files 1839–1841).

evening or night time of her arrest, which was certainly not accidental, was repeated during all contact with the control organs. Maria was deported home and punished with five blows of the cat-o'-nine-tails. The Viennese municipal authority asked her village to take the necessary measures to prevent her return to Vienna.

This obviously did not happen, because on October 4, 1839 she was arrested in Josephstadt again. She worked in the garden centre of a certain Theresia Schumann, where she also spent the night. From archive sources it is not completely clear whether this time she prostituted herself in Vienna again or, as she herself stated in the protocol, merely sold her body to two foremen to pay for her journey to Vienna. During this "payment" she probably caught a sexually transmitted disease. She was once again deported to Dobřínsko, where she was questioned. She regretted the fact that she fell into immoral society, but she saw herself as a victim of her social situation: she herself would not have chosen such a path, but circumstances forced her to act this way. She spent two days in prison and then she was released home.

In the following year (1840) she was arrested in the suburbs of Vienna three times, whereby she was also treated in the General Hospital (probably in the sexually transmitted disease department). Each time she was deported home. It was only when she was questioned for the last time that it transpired that her domestic municipality did not want to grant her long-term residence, under the threat that if she did not obey they would banish her mother, who as a beggar probably lived at the municipality's expense, from Dobřínsko. One can assume that, under the law, both women held political domicile in Dobřínsko, whereby they would also be entitled to social assistance there. This case shows the ways in which the municipalities tried to rid themselves of burdensome persons, although they were entitled to stay in them.

What Maria Waniczek probably did not realise was the fact that her "exile tourism" was resulting in considerable expenditure for her small municipality (in the year 1869, Dobřínsko had 386 inhabitants); thus, the municipal representatives' disapproving attitude towards her is easily understandable. In a broader framework, this case can serve to demonstrate the financial situation of small Moravian municipalities, which barely had the resources to provide for needful persons at home, because many citizens did not live at home in their productive age, but in large agglomerations. The municipal authorities missed out on the levies from their productive period; in addition, they had to provide for their "retired" citizens when they were sent by the industrial towns back to their domestic municipalities after they "ceased to be of use." In Moravia in the year

1869, 80 percent of the population lived in a different municipality than that in which they were born[41] (the place of birth was usually also the place of political domicile, because it was very difficult for unpropertied persons to acquire a different domestic jurisdiction). For Dobřínsko, the proportion of persons absent in their productive age may even have been higher than 80 percent, as it was a small municipality close to Vienna.[42]

The sample "respectable person" working in the town

What did the "prototype of the respectable person", who searched for work in the town, look like? The representative typical "sample", at least according to the Brno Police Directorate archives, was a woman 20-30 years of age, of Catholic faith, unmarried, who came from a municipality near the town of Brno. Her typical appearance was described as a woman of medium build with proportionate facial features, brown hair and grey or blue-grey eyes, a healthy colour in her face without any special identification characteristics, sometimes with a command of German in addition to "Moravian" language. One of these women, for example, was twenty-three-year-old Karoline König of Náměšť, who came to Brno in the year 1849 with a domestic certificate from her municipality and looked for work as a maid, which for several years she actually carried out.[43]

Given the fact that pictorial documentation of the workers could not be procured, the description of the persons was a necessary supplement to identification, but it was prepared by a purely subjective evaluator, so the same person could appear different according to two various identifiers. Veronika Kratochvil, a thirty-seven-year-old widow from Ponětovice (at the time still Puntovice) in the Brno region, who worked in several textile factories in Brno as a worker who wound the material onto spools [Feinspulerin], had blue eyes and blonde hair according to the police official's description but, according to the description of the municipal representative who issued the domestic certificate, she had chestnut hair and grey eyes.[44] Sometimes the municipal representatives inappropriately showed an ignorance of the Czech language; the note "married", referring to a man, is relatively common for women, but less common were

---

[41] Heinrich Rauchberg, "Sociale Wanderungen in Oesterreich," *Mährisches Gewerbeblatt* 15 (1893), p. 9ff.

[42] The quoted statistical data comes from a later period, because no statistics exist for the 1840s. On the basis of my own research, I can hypothetically presume that the data for the forties probably does not differ greatly from later statistics.

[43] MPA, B 26, Factory and Wage Labour Records (1849), no. 570.

[44] MPA, B 26, Factory and Wage Labour Records (1848), no. 569.

incorrect terms in the description of persons, such as for example in the
case of a certain Anna Kolaczek of Rychnov, who according to the
description had "red" eyes and hair. (Cf. fig. 13-5).[45]

What was the literacy of wage workers in Brno? Unfortunately,
preserved archive sources do not allow a deeper analysis of this interesting
factor, because the police files themselves did not record this fact. A
certain level of literacy can be concluded from the fact that the
identification document is furnished with a handwritten signature, but such
evidence – in the vast majority of cases the domestic certificate – was
preserved only rarely. Surprisingly, however, substitute symbols (three
crosses) appear instead of the signature even in the mid-19th century, from
which partial secondary analphabetism can be concluded, i.e. that the
workers could read, but over time they lost the knowledge of writing they
acquired in school. However, partial secondary analphabetism, which
could be expected of older persons, particularly women, also appears in
the case of younger men. Examples are Franz Dobšák, a twenty-one-year-
old cloth cutter from Otnice near Brno, and thirty-four-year-old
maidservant Barbara Navratil of Sviny by Křižanov, neither of whom
could sign their domestic certificate.[46]

Statistical evaluation of the wage labour register

For the statistical evaluation, 1,313 wage workers from the Brno Police
Directorate factory and wage labour protocols were analysed. The
analysed factor is the persons' origin, i.e. the workers' domicile. The
"turning point" years of 1847–1849 were deliberately chosen, in order to
observe the possible influence of the abolition of vassalage and the
breakdown of the patrimonial system on the inhabitants' mobility.[47] No
influence whatsoever was discovered in this regard. Inhabitants' mobility
during the existence of the patrimonial system was actually higher than in
the years 1848 and 1849. In the year 1847 the Brno police registered 744
workers, compared to just 249 in the year 1848 and 320 in the year 1849.
(Cf. fig. 13-6, Factory and wage workers in Brno 1847–1849).

---

[45] Ibid.
[46] MPA, B 26, Factory and Wage Labour Records (both from the year 1848), no.
569 and 477.
[47] Allerhöchstes Patent vom 7. September 1848. Aufhebung der Untertänigkeitsbandes
und Entlastung des bäuerlichen Besitzes in *Seiner k. k. Majestät Ferdinand des
Ersten politische Gesetze und Verordnungen für sämmtliche Provinzen des
Oesterreichischen Kaiserstaates, mit Ausnahme von Ungarn und Siebenbürgen.*,
vol. 67, Wien 1851, no. 112, p. 285ff.

This conclusion corresponds to (the author's) other research on the mobility of the unpropertied classes of the population. In accordance with the ruling circles, the nobility never prevented their subjects' labour mobility, especially in the case of work migration which allowed for daily or weekly travel home. This fact is proven by police officials' entries in protocols: "travels home daily" or "travels home on Saturdays." The latter workers usually did not have housing in the town, but spent the night directly in the factory buildings. Under normal conditions, domestic staff lived in their employers' apartments.

In the observed context – the wage labour register in the town as a factor in care for the poor – it's particularly important that for the municipal authority it did not play a role where the workers' domiciles were. Police data on workers was to serve not only as an overview of foreign (i.e. not from Brno) workers, but also represented a legal and informative base for eventual banishment or deportation. For the police, it played no role whether the workers came from the suburbs of Brno, Moravian villages, other Crown lands, Hungarian lands or foreign countries. The only thing that was important was that they did not have political jurisdiction in Brno, which meant that they were not entitled to eventual material assistance in the event of illness, poverty or death of their breadwinner.

This completely clear tendency, which can be demonstrated not only for Brno but also for Olomouc,[48] shows the considerable effort the towns made to have as few needful persons as possible in their registers. The main instrument for the achievement of this goal was the detailed record-keeping of factory and wage workers who did not have domestic jurisdiction in the town.

Conclusion

Most of the analysed factors, which are so far almost untouched by archive research, show that the laws very often merely codified actual official procedures, which had probably already been practised for a long time, i.e. that the practice preceded the legal provisions. In a broader context, this development can be viewed as one of the characteristics of the ongoing liberalisation of economy and society, whose roots probably reach much deeper than is known from current historical research.

---

[48] SOkA Olomouc, Archive of the City of Olomouc, Domestic Staff Protocols (1853–1857), no. 3231–3239, no. 4292–4300.

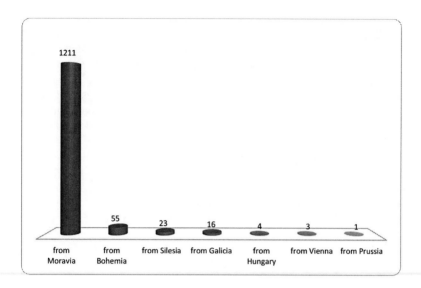

Fig 13-1 Factory and wage workers in Brno 1847–1849 (Moravian Provincial Archives in Brno, B 26, Factory and Wage Labour Records (1848–1849), no. 568, 569 and 570.)

Fig. 13-2 (next page) Passport of Ursula Bernreuter of October 26, 1846 (Moravian Provincial Archives in Brno, B 95, Moravian-Silesian Governor's Office, no. 1/9, box 358).

K. K. Gubernial - Gebiet Mähren und Schlesien.

Kreis _____   Werbbezirks Nro. _3_

Pass Nro. _309_   Protokolls Nro. _____

Reise-Paß

für _Ursula Bernreuter_

Charakter, Gewerbe oder Beschäftigung _Dienstmagd_

gebürtig aus _Trobovwez_   Zweck der Reise:

Geburtsjahr _1830_   _In Dienst_

Religion _katholisch_

Stand _ledig_

Statur _klein_

Gesicht _rund_

Haare _blond_

Augen _blau_   Mit diese _reiset auf gegenwärtigen
Reisepaß:_

Mund _gewöhnlich_

Nase _länglich_

besondere Kennzeichen _keine_

Dermalen Wohnort _Trobowej_ Haus-Nro. _178_

Dessen eigenhändige Namensunterschrift _____

Derselbe reiset von hier über _____ nach _____

Dieser Reisepaß ist giltig auf _Ein Jahr_

Alle löblichen Civil- und Militär-Behörden werden dienstfreundschaftlichst ersucht den Innhaber dieses Passes nach Bestimmungsort frey und ungehindert pass- und repassiren und nöthigen Falls allen Vorschub geneigtest angedeihen zu lassen, wobei man sich zu aller Gegenwillfährigkeit erbietet.

Ausgefertigt von _____

Dürrnholz vom _26. Oktober
1846_

Jede Verfälschung dieses Reise-Passes sie mag an welcher Stelle oder aus welcher Absicht immer vorgenommen werden, ist zu Folge allerhöchster Entschließung vom 19. August 1818, Gubernial-Cirkular vom 11. Juni 1819 Zahl 14446 ein Verbrechen, das nach den §§. 178 und 181 des Strafgesetzbuches ersten Theils bestraft wird.

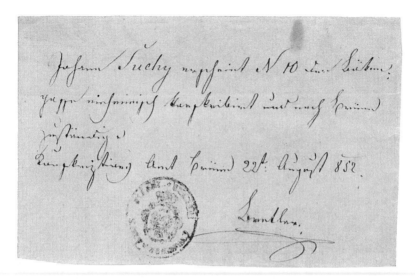

Fig. 13-3 Conscription certificate for Johann Suchy of August 22, 1852 (Factory and wage workers in Brno 1847–1849, Moravian Provincial Archives in Brno, B 26, Factory and Wage Labour Records, 1848, no. 569.)

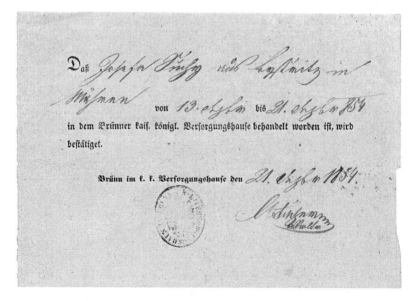

Fig. 13-4 Confirmation for Josefa Sucha (Moravian Provincial Archives in Brno, B 26, Factory and Wage Labour Records (1848), no. 569.)

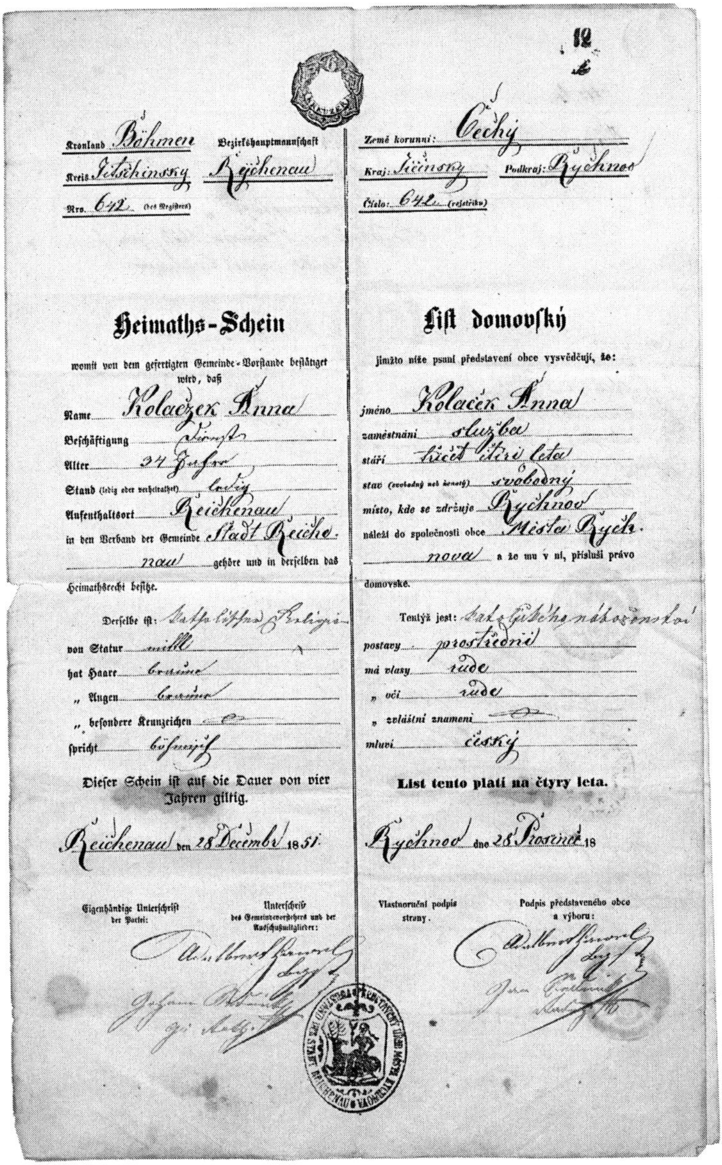

Kronland Böhmen — Bezirkshauptmannschaft Rychenau
Kreis Jitschinsky — Nro. 642 (des Registers)

Země korunní: Čechy
Kraj: Jičinsky — Podkraj: Rychnow
Číslo: 642 (rejstříku)

Heimaths-Schein

womit von dem gefertigten Gemeinde-Vorstande bestätiget wird, daß

Name: Kolaczek Anna
Beschäftigung: Dienst
Alter: 34 Jahre
Stand (ledig oder verheiratet): ledig
Aufenthaltsort: Reichenau
in den Verband der Gemeinde Stadt Reichenau gehöre und in derselben das Heimathsrecht besitze.

Derselbe ist: katholischer Religion
von Statur: mittel
hat Haare: braune
„ Augen: braune
„ besondere Kennzeichen: —
spricht: böhmisch

Dieser Schein ist auf die Dauer von vier Jahren giltig.

Reichenau den 28 December 1851.

Eigenhändige Unterschrift der Partei:
Unterschrift des Gemeindevorstehers und der Ausschußmitglieder:

List domovský

jímžto níže psané představení obce vysvědčuje, že:

jméno: Kolaček Anna
zaměstnání: služba
stáří: třicet čtyři leta
stav (svobodný neb ženatý): svobodný
místo, kde se zdržuje: Rychnow
náleží do společnosti obce Města Rychnowa a že mu v ní přísluší právo domovské.

Tentýž jest: katolického náboženství
postavy: prostřední
má vlasy: rude
„ oči: rude
„ zvláštní znamení: —
mluví: česky

List tento platí na čtyry leta.

Rychnow dne 28 Prosince 18

Vlastnoruční podpis strany.
Podpis představeného obce a výboru:

Fig. 13-5 Domestic certificate for Anna Kolaczek of December 28, 1851 (Moravian Provincial Archives in Brno, B 26, Factory and Wage Labour Records (1848), no. 569.)

CHAPTER FOURTEEN

KATHOLISCHES KRANKENHAUSWESEN IN DEN STÄDTEN DES RUHRREVIERS BIS ZUM ERSTEN WELTKRIEG[1]

ARNE THOMSEN

The Catholic hospital system in the cities of the Ruhr region before the First World War

Abstract: The Ruhr region was undergoing an economic transformation from agricultural to industrial during the mid-19th century. Increased immigration, brought about by this change, made apparent the lack of health care facilities in the region. Since the municipalities were not able to establish hospitals to a sufficient extent, the Catholic as well as Protestant communities began founding their own facilities. In doing so, a competition occurred between single entities that offered health services (and among which also belonged mining fraternities). Charitable reasons, which mainly included having health care as widely available as possible, stood above religious motives. After all, the entire Ruhr region developed differently in many aspects than other regions in Germany due to its population of various denominations and of multinational origin.

Das Erscheinungsbild des Ruhrgebiets um die Mitte des 19. Jahrhunderts kann sich nicht deutlicher von heutigen Bildern des industriellen Ballungsraumes unterscheiden. Dörfliche und kleinstädtische Strukturen waren vorherrschend, Infrastruktur und Verkehrssystem unterentwickelt. Industrialisierung und Urbanisierung hatten die agrarisch geprägte Region des späteren „Reviers" noch nicht erreicht. Die ortsansässige Bevölkerung musste Notsituationen zum größten Teil durch familiäre Sozialbindungen

---

[1] Bei dem folgenden Beitrag handelt es sich um eine leicht gekürzte und redigierte Version des Aufsatzes "Der Beginn des katholischen Krankenhausfrühlings im Ruhrrevier," in *Wirtschaft und Gemeinschaft. Konfessionelle und neureligiöse Gemeinsinnsmodelle im 19. und 20. Jahrhundert*, Hrsg. Swen Steinberg und Winfried Müller (Bielefeld: transcript, 2014), S. 63–77.

oder nachbarschaftliche Solidarität auffangen. Entsprechend der Bevölkerungszahl existierten in der Region nur wenige traditionelle Hospitäler. Im Gegensatz zu anderen Gegenden Deutschlands war das spätere Revier ursprünglich ein dünn besiedeltes Gebiet. Bis zur Jahrhundertwende erreichte keine Stadt trotz eines enormen Bevölkerungswachstums die 100.000-Einwohner-Grenze. 1910 gab es dagegen mit Essen, Duisburg, Dortmund, Gelsenkirchen, Bochum, Mülheim und Hamborn bereits sieben Großstädte mit sechsstelliger Einwohnerzahl.[2] Im Jahre 1843 zählte das Ruhrgebiet dagegen lediglich 236.000 Einwohner und damit bloß ca. 15.000 Bürger mehr als nach dem Wiener Kongress von 1815.

Die um 1840 aufkommende Industrialisierung führte zu spürbaren Umstrukturierungen des agrarisch geprägten Raumes an Rhein, Ruhr und Emscher. Das Ruhrgebiet musste einen explosionsartigen Bevölkerungszuwachs verkraften. Die Einwohnerzahl Gelsenkirchens beispielsweise stieg von 1855 bis 1875 von 1.030 auf über 11.000 oder um 995 % an.[3] Auch andere Städte vervielfachten ihre Bevölkerung:

Tabelle 14-1: Bevölkerungsentwicklung einzelner Städte laut amtlicher Statistik (nach Gebietsständen gerundet auf Tausend)[4]

	Bochum	Dortmund	Essen
um 1850	17.000	31.000	9.000
um 1870	56.000	109.000	137.000
um 1910	234.000	584.000	295.000

Zigtausende Menschen, hauptsächlich aus den Ostprovinzen und aus ländlichen Regionen Deutschlands stammend, strömten in die Region, um überwiegend in den neu entstehenden Bergwerken und Stahlwerken tätig zu werden. Sie verließen die ärmlichen ländlichen Verhältnisse und erhofften für sich und ihre Kinder einen sozialen Aufstieg in der Stadt. Die Landwirtschaft konnte ihnen aufgrund von technischen Modernisierungen kein Auskommen mehr bieten und barg die Gefahr des Pauperismus. Andererseits gab es in der Stadt mehr gesundheitliche Risiken für die Zuwanderer.

---

[2] Vgl. Jörg Vögele et al., "Hygiene – Ein Zugang zur Industrialisierungs- und Urbanisierungsgeschichte des Ruhrgebiets," *Forum Industriedenkmalpflege und Geschichtskultur* 2 (2004): S. 15–21.
[3] Vgl. Barbara Lueg-Hoffmann, *Das Krankenhaus- und Medizinalwesen der Stadt Gelsenkirchen im 19. Jahrhundert* (Herzogenrath: Murken-Altrogge, 1992), S. 4.
[4] Zahlen aus: Vögele et al., "Hygiene," S. 16.

Schnell entwickelte sich durch den Urbanisierungsprozess ein akuter
Bedarf an Gesundheitsleistungen, da teilweise häusliche Pflegetraditionen
und -kenntnisse in der industriellen, städtischen Kleinfamilie nicht mehr
bekannt waren.[5] Die Zuständigkeiten für stadthygienische Maßnahmen
waren im frühen 19. Jahrhundert zwischen Staat und Gemeinde noch
wenig austariert. Dazu kamen finanzielle Probleme und mangelnde
technische Erfahrung.[6] Die Gemeinde Gelsenkirchen beispielsweise
bekam über Jahrzehnte ihre Abwasserentsorgung nicht in den Griff, was
zu vielen Erkrankungen ihrer Bürger führte.[7] Der Stadtteil Horst galt um
die Jahrhundertwende aufgrund des dortigen Emscherbruchs als
„Fiebernest"[8] und war nach einer Reichsstatistik die deutsche Gemeinde
mit der schlechtesten gesundheitlichen Infrastruktur. Die Patientenzahlen
und die Pflegetage im ansässigen St. Josephs-Hospital verzehnfachten sich
seit der Gründung 1889 (94 Kranke / 2017 Pflegetage) bis 1900 (952
Kranke / 26244 Pflegetage).[9] Da andere Städte des Deutschen Reiches
aber vergleichbare Statistiken zur Krankheits- und Sterbehäufigkeit
aufwiesen, war der Handlungsdruck auf die Gelsenkirchener Behörden in
der Gesundheitsvorsorge bis zum Ausbruch der Typhusepidemie von 1901
nicht besonders ausgeprägt.[10]

Der preußische Staat sah sich nur eingeschränkt dafür verantwortlich,
seinen Untertanen Unterstützung im Krankheitsfall zukommen zu lassen.
Die öffentliche Hand scheute sich vor finanziellen Verpflichtungen im
Bereich der medizinischen Infrastruktur und der Fürsorgetätigkeit und
wurde zumeist nur bei Epidemien und ansteckenden Krankheiten aktiv.
Das Krankenhauswesen war neben Wasserversorgung, Kanalisation,
Abfallbeseitigung etc. nur ein Teil des öffentlichen Gesundheitswesens.

---

[5] Vgl. Joachim Wiemeyer, *Krankenhausfinanzierung und Krankenhausplanung in
der Bundesrepublik Deutschland* (Berlin: Duncker und Humblot, 1984), S. 15.
[6] Vgl. Anne Irmgard Hardy, *Ärzte, Ingenieure und städtische Gesundheit.
Medizinische Theorien in der Hygienebewegung des 19. Jahrhunderts* (Frankfurt
am Main et al.: Campus-Verlag, 2005), S. 91.
[7] Zur öffentlichen Gesundheitsvorsorge in Gelsenkirchen siehe die ausführliche
Studie von Martin Weyer-von Schoultz, *Stadt und Gesundheit im Ruhrgebiet
1850–1929. Verstädterung und kommunale Gesundheitspolitik dargestellt am
Beispiel der jungen Industriestadt Gelsenkirchen* (Essen: Klartext, 1994).
[8] Elmar Hilchenbach, "Ärzte im Vest Recklinghausen," (Diss. med., Ruhr-
Universität Bochum, 1988), S. 227.
[9] Vgl. Arne Thomsen, *Katholisches Krankenhauswesen im Ruhrrevier.
Entwicklungen und Akteure von den Anfängen der Industrialisierung bis zum
Ersten Weltkrieg* (Münster: Aschendorff, 2012), S. 51.
[10] Vgl. Weyer-von Schoultz, *Stadt und Gesundheit im Ruhrgebiet*, S. 138 f.

Die Gesetze, die das Krankenhauswesen berührten, waren keinesfalls auf die Bismarck'sche Sozialgesetzgebung der 1880er Jahre beschränkt. Im Gegenteil, die Zuständigkeiten in der Gesundheitspolitik mussten über mehrere Jahrzehnte zwischen Staat und Kommunen ausdifferenziert werden. Die preußische Regierung nahm die Gemeinden mit Gesetzen und Rechtsverordnungen zur Sozialpolitik zunehmend in die Pflicht, sich um die Armen zu kümmern. Ein Ausgangspunkt ist das Allgemeine Preußische Landrecht von 1794, das nach dem Wiener Kongress von 1815 auch auf dem Gebiet des heutigen Ruhrgebietes eingeführt wurde. Im Preußischen Landrecht wurde festgehalten, dass Hospitäler „unter dem besonderen Schutz des Staates"[11] stehen. Für diese Rechtsleistung konnten die Einrichtungen jederzeit von Staatsvertretern kontrolliert werden. Weiter wurde eine allgemeine öffentliche Fürsorgepflicht gegenüber den Armen Teil des Gesetzeswerkes. Zudem sah die preußische Städteordnung von 1808 vor, dass die Kommune u. a. Sorge für die Krankenpflege der Armen tragen musste.[12] Allerdings wurde diese Anordnung praktisch kaum kontrolliert. Mit der Verabschiedung der preußischen Verfassung von 1850 erhielten Religionsgemeinschaften das Recht, eigene Wohltätigkeitsanstalten zu unterhalten. Zudem fielen bedeutende rechtliche Niederlassungsbestimmungen weg und die Einrichtungen standen nicht mehr unter direkter staatlicher Aufsicht.

Bis Mitte des 19. Jahrhunderts verbesserte sich die Versorgung der Einwohner Preußens mit Krankenhäusern. Kam 1834 auf 56.000 Einwohner ein Krankenhaus, war im Jahr 1853 eine Anstalt durchschnittlich für 24.000 preußische Untertanen zuständig.[13] Diese Zahlen sind aber nicht besonders aussagekräftig, da sie keine Informationen über die Bettenkapazität der einzelnen Krankenhäuser beinhalten. Eine Umwandlung vom Hospital zum Krankenhaus vollzog sich nur in einigen Großstädten.[14] Im

---

[11] *Allgemeines Landrecht für die Preußischen Staaten von 1794,* Hrsg. Hans Hattenhauer (Frankfurt am Main: Metzner, 1970), S. 664 (2. Teil, 19. Titel Von Armenanstalten, und andern milden Stiftungen, § 32).
[12] Vgl. Ralf Stremmel, *"Gesundheit – unser einziger Reichtum"? Kommunale Gesundheits- und Umweltpolitik 1800–1945 am Beispiel Solingen* (Solingen: Selbstverlag Stadtarchiv, 1993), S. 20.
[13] Vgl. Heinz Goerke, "Personelle und arbeitstechnische Gegebenheiten im Krankenhaus des 19. Jahrhunderts," in *Studien zur Krankenhausgeschichte im 19. Jahrhundert im Hinblick auf die Entwicklung in Deutschland,* Hrsg. Hans Schadewaldt (Göttingen: Vandenhoeck und Ruprecht, 1976), S. 65.
[14] Vgl. Christoph Johannes Schweikardt, *Die Entwicklung der Krankenpflege zur staatlich anerkannten Tätigkeit im 19. und frühen 20. Jahrhundert. Das Zusammenwirken von Modernisierungsbestrebungen, ärztlicher Dominanz, konfessioneller Selbstbehauptung und Vorgaben preußischer Regierungspolitik*

Ruhrgebiet sind dagegen ausnahmslos Neugründungen zu verzeichnen.
Ausgelöst durch Industrialisierung und Urbanisierung sind hier – im
Gegensatz zu anderen Regionen Deutschlands[15] – nahezu alle
Krankenhäuser in der zweiten Hälfte des 19. Jahrhunderts, dem „Zeitalter
ununterbrochener Krankenhausgründungen"[16], entstanden. Auch im
Bereich des Krankenhauswesens kann das rheinisch-westfälische
Industriegebiet somit als eine „verspätete Region"[17] bezeichnet werden.
Die Verzögerung erklärt sich aus der zuvor vorherrschenden ländlichen,
bevölkerungsarmen Struktur der Region.

Im Ruhrgebiet existierten im 19. und zu Beginn des 20. Jahrhunderts
deutlich mehr konfessionelle als kommunale Krankenhäuser. Dieses
Phänomen ist, wenn auch in abgeschwächter Form, im gesamten
Rheinland und Westfalen zu konstatieren. Im übrigen Preußen war das
Verhältnis dagegen umgekehrt.[18] Krankenhausgründungen nahmen zu,
wenn der Bergbau in die jeweilige Region kam. Dabei muss die zum Teil
lange Planungszeit der Anstalten berücksichtigt werden. Der für Preußen
konstatierte „Trend in Richtung kommunaler Trägerschaft"[19] ist im
Untersuchungsgebiet nicht feststellbar. Anders als etwa in Düsseldorf gab

---

(München: Martin Meidenbauer, 2008), S. 41.

[15] Reinhard Spree vertritt die These, dass in allen deutschen Staaten mehr
Krankenhäuser in der ersten als in der zweiten Hälfte des 19. Jahrhunderts
gegründet wurden. Vgl. Reinhard Spree, "Krankenhausentwicklung und
Sozialpolitik in Deutschland während des 19. Jahrhunderts," *Historische
Zeitschrift* 260 (1995): S. 76. Die Behauptung van der Lochts, dass das moderne
Essener Krankenhauswesen Mitte der 1820er Jahre begann, ist unrichtig. Zu
diesem Zeitpunkt setzte nur die Diskussion über die Zukunft der Beginenkonvente
ein. Vgl. Volker van der Locht, *Von der karitativen Fürsorge zum ärztlichen
Selektionsblick. Zur Sozialgeschichte der Motivstruktur der Behindertenfürsorge
am Beispiel des Essener Franz-Sales-Hauses* (Opladen: Leske und Budrich, 1997),
S. 89.

[16] Werner Frese und M. Albinata Peters, *Die Ausbreitung der Kongregation der
Krankenschwestern nach der Dritten Regel des hl. Franziskus* (Münster:
Mutterhaus der Krankenschwestern vom Hl. Franziskus, 1988), S. 141.

[17] So der Titel des Aufsatzes von Karl Rohe, "Die ‚verspätete' Region. Thesen und
Hypothesen zur Wahlentwicklung im Ruhrgebiet vor 1914," in *Probleme
politischer Partizipation im Modernisierungsprozeß*, Hrsg. Peter Steinbach
(Stuttgart: Klett-Cotta, 1982), S. 231–252.

[18] Vgl. Irmgard Müller, "Die Entwicklung des Gesundheitswesens im Ruhrgebiet,"
Rubin. Wissenschaftsmagazin der Ruhr-Universität Bochum 1 (1991): S. 38–45.

[19] Beate Witzler, *Großstadt und Hygiene. Kommunale Gesundheitspolitik in der
Epoche der Urbanisierung* (Stuttgart: Steiner, 1995), S. 32.

es im Revier vor einer „Konfessionalisierung des Krankenhauswesens [keinen Versuch der] Kommunalisierung".[20]

Dennoch entstanden im Ruhrgebiet weitaus mehr katholische Krankenanstalten als in katholisch geprägten Gegenden im Süden Deutschlands oder in Österreich.[21] Die Dichte an katholischen Krankenhäusern in einer Region hängt demzufolge weniger vom Anteil der Katholiken in der Bevölkerung, sondern vom Industrialisierungs- und Urbanisierungsgrad des Gebietes ab.[22] 85 katholische Krankenhäuser wurden bis zum Ausbruch des Ersten Weltkrieges im Gebiet des heutigen Regionalverbands Ruhr gegründet. Damit existierten 1914 im rheinisch-westfälischen Industriegebiet doppelt so viele moderne katholische Hospitäler wie 1850 im gesamten Gebiet des Deutschen Reiches.[23] Auch heutzutage besitzt kaum eine andere europäische Region eine vergleichbar hohe Krankenhausdichte.

Im rheinisch-westfälischen Industriegebiet dominierten im Vergleich zum übrigen Preußen wie auch zu anderen Landesteilen Deutschlands konfessionelle Hospitäler. Von diesen Einrichtungen standen die meisten in katholischer Trägerschaft. Weitet man den Blick auf die benachbarten Gebiete des Ruhrgebiets aus, waren im Jahre 1913, am Vorabend des Ersten Weltkrieges, 43 % aller katholischen Krankenhäuser des Deutschen Reichs in der preußischen Rheinprovinz oder in Westfalen beheimatet.[24] In zahlreichen Städten des Ruhrreviers gab es nur ein evangelisches, aber mehrere katholische Krankenhäuser.

Eine sinnvolle Gesamtplanung und ein raumplanerisches Krankenhausbaukonzept sind im rheinisch-westfälischen Industriegebiet

---

[20] Fritz Dross, *Krankenhaus und lokale Politik 1770–1850. Das Beispiel Düsseldorf* (Essen: Klartext, 2004), S. 240.

[21] Vgl. Hans-Jürgen Brandt, "Katholische Kirche und Urbanisation im deutschen Kaiserreich," *Blätter für deutsche Landesgeschichte. Neue Folge des Korrespondenzblattes* 128 (1992): S. 221–239.

[22] Antonius Liedhegener konstatiert zu Recht, dass es nur wenige Arbeiten zum Verhältnis von religiösen Vorstellungen und Verhaltensweisen auf der einen Seite und den Urbanisierungsprozessen auf der anderen Seite gibt. Vgl. Antonius Liedhegener, *Christentum und Urbanisierung. Katholiken und Protestanten in Münster und Bochum 1830–1933* (Paderborn et al.: F. Schöningh, 1997), S. 25.

[23] Vgl. Karl Gabriel, "Sozial-katholische Bewegung," in *Zeitzeichen. 150 Jahre Deutsche Katholikentage 1848–1998. Mit einem Bildteil „150 Jahre Katholikentage im Bild"*, Hrsg. Ulrich von Hehl und Friedrich Kronenberg (Paderborn et al.: Schöningh, 1999), S. 106.

[24] Vgl. Catherine Maurer, *Der Caritasverband zwischen Kaiserreich und Weimarer Republik. Zur Sozial- und Mentalitätsgeschichte des caritativen Katholizismus in Deutschland* (Freiburg im Breisgau: Lambertus, 2008), S. 93.

weder von staatlicher noch von kommunaler oder kirchlicher Seite erkennbar. Ebenso wenig kann eine übergeordnete Strategie, katholische Krankenhäuser als Gegenpol zu den negativen Auswüchsen von Verstädterung und Industrialisierung zu gründen, ausgemacht werden.[25] Die Diözesen hatten keine genauen Vorstellungen über den Bestand an Sozialeinrichtungen in ihrem Bistum.[26] Im Fokus der Kirchenobrigkeit standen vielmehr religiöse und andere sozialpolitische Themen. So konnte im gesamten Ruhrgebiet auch kein organisiertes Netzwerk katholischer Hospitäler entstehen.[27] Von kirchlicher Seite versuchte in der Region allein Bischof Johann Georg Müller (1798–1870), den Prozess im Bistum Münster bis zu seinem Tod zu lenken.[28] Nach der Jahrhundertwende kamen nur noch vereinzelt Anstalten zur katholischen Krankenhauslandschaft des Ruhrgebiets hinzu. Es war eine gewisse Sättigung erreicht worden, und die Kirchengemeinden, die sich die Errichtung eines Krankenhauses zum Ziel gesetzt hatten, hatten ihre Pläne zumeist schon verwirklicht. Die Kongregationen, die weiter expandieren wollten und dies aufgrund eines Mitgliederwachstums auch konnten, wichen daher auf andere Felder aus. Die Klemensschwestern beispielsweise engagierten sich wieder stärker auf dem Gebiet der ambulanten Krankenpflege.[29]

[25] Siehe dazu Wilhelm Damberg, "Kirchliche Zeitgeschichte Westfalens, der Schweiz, Belgiens und der Niederlande. Das katholische Beispiel," *Westfälische Forschungen* 42 (1992): S. 445–465.
[26] Vgl. Ewald Frie, "Katholische Wohlfahrtskultur im Wilhelminischen Reich: Der ‚Charitasverband für das katholische Deutschland', die Vinzenzvereine und der ‚kommunale Sozialliberalismus'," in *Soziale Reform im Kaiserreich. Protestantismus, Katholizismus und Sozialpolitik*, Hrsg. Jochen-Christoph Kaiser und Wilfried Loth (Stuttgart et al.: Kohlhammer, 1997), S. 184–201.
[27] Wagener-Esser behauptet das Gegenteil für das Bistum Münster, zu dem vor der Gründung des Ruhrbistums 1957 Teile des Ruhrgebiets gehörten und auch heute noch gehören. Vgl. Meike Wagener-Esser, *Organisierte Barmherzigkeit und Seelenheil. Das caritative Sozialnetzwerk im Bistum Münster von 1803 bis zur Gründung des Diözesancaritasverbands 1916* (Altenberge: Oros-Verlag, 1999), S. 97.
[28] Vgl. Erwin Gatz, *Kirche und Krankenpflege im 19. Jahrhundert. Katholische Bewegung und karitativer Aufbruch in den preussischen Provinzen Rheinland und Westfalen* (München et al.: Schöningh, 1971), S. 574 f.; Meike Wagener-Esser, "Barmherzigkeit als Beruf(ung): Entstehung und Entwicklung des karitativen Sozialnetzwerks im Bistum Münster," in *Konfessionelle Armutsdiskurse und Armenfürsorgepraktiken im langen 19. Jahrhundert*, Hrsg. Bernhard Schneider (Frankfurt am Main: Lang, 2009), S. 227–246.
[29] Vgl. Wolfgang Schaffer, "Ordensentwicklung seit dem 19. Jahrhundert," in *Geschichtlicher Atlas der Rheinlande, 11. Lieferung, Beiheft IX/5*, Hrsg. Franz

Die christlich-caritative Motivation der katholischen Bevölkerung und das Bedürfnis, im Krankheitsfall für eine Versorgung des Nächsten zu sorgen, konnten sich im sozialen Engagement für eine Hospitalgründung ausdrücken. Die Spende für ein Krankenhausprojekt gehörte dazu, egal wie schlecht die persönliche finanzielle Situation war. Selbstheiligung und die Erlangung des ewigen Seelenheils waren für im katholischen Milieu verwurzelte Bürger erstrebenswerte Ziele, die sie durch Almosen in Form von Stiftungen und Spenden zu erreichen versuchten. Vorbild war der Aufruf des späteren Mainzer Bischofs Ketteler, der die soziale Frage zur Aufgabe der Kirche erklärte.[30] Ein Krankenhaus war für viele Kirchengemeinden neben einer Kirche und einer Schule die wichtigste Errungenschaft und trug zur Stabilisierung des katholischen Milieus bei.[31]

Die Initiative für den Krankenhausbau ging zumeist vom Gemeindepfarrer aus, während sich die Diözesen weitestgehend zurückhielten. Diese caritativen Basisinitiativen reagierten, ähnlich der frühen Kirche, auf Notlagen der Gesellschaft. In einigen Gemeinden wurde so ein Krankenhausbauverein gegründet, dem der örtliche Pfarrer vorstand: In nahezu der Hälfte der 85 „modernen" Hospitäler des Untersuchungsgebietes war Letzterer der Verantwortliche für das lokale Krankenhausprojekt.[32] Er verstand den Krankenhausbau als Dienstleistung für seine stark anwachsende Gemeinde. Die hohe Identifikation des Pfarrers mit dieser war für das Entstehen der meisten modernen Hospitäler somit von entscheidender Bedeutung. So notierte der Gladbecker Pfarrer Franz Nonn (1832–1898), als das Krankenhausprojekt in seiner Gemeinde auf Gegnerschaft stieß: „Ich muss es machen, wie die Mutter, welche die Kinder wäscht, auch wenn sie schreien".[33]

Irsigler (Bonn: Habelt-Verlag, 2008), S. 7.

[30] Vgl. Wilhelm Damberg, "Das 19. Jahrhundert," in *Das Bistum Essen. 1958–2008. Eine illustrierte Kirchengeschichte der Region von den Anfängen des Christentums bis zur Gegenwart*, Hrsg. Wilhelm Damberg et al. (Münster: Aschendorff, 2008), S. 117–150. Siehe auch Bernhard Schneider, "Katholische Armutsdiskurse und Praktiken der Armenfürsorge im gesellschaftlichen Wandel des 19. Jahrhunderts und das Paradigma der Zivilgesellschaft," in *Zwischen Fürsorge und Seelsorge. Christliche Kirchen in den europäischen Zivilgesellschaften seit dem 18. Jahrhundert*, Hrsg. Arnd Bauerkämper und Jürgen Nautz (Frankfurt am Main: Campus-Verlag, 2009), S. 79–111.

[31] Vgl. Brandt, "Katholische Kirche und Urbanisation," S. 228 f. Liedhegener, *Christentum und Urbanisierung*, S. 505, bezeichnet den Krankenhausbau als spezifische Seelsorgeform.

[32] Siehe dazu Thomsen, *Katholisches Krankenhauswesen*, S. 68–74.

[33] Zitiert nach Wagener-Esser, *Organisierte Barmherzigkeit und Seelenheil*, S. 217.

Eine der ersten Handlungen eines Krankenhausvorstands war das Verfassen eines Statuts. Dieses war notwendig für das Erlangen der bischöflichen und staatlichen Genehmigung und wurde normalerweise schon vor Baubeginn angefertigt. Genauso wichtig war ein Vertrag mit einer Kongregation zur Übernahme der Krankenpflege. Denn die Schwestern kamen nur auf Anfrage in die neuen Einrichtungen. Ohne die Bereitschaft Barmherziger Schwestern, die Krankenpflege und in einzelnen Fällen auch die Trägerschaft zu übernehmen, wären zahlreiche Krankenhäuser der Region erst später oder gar nicht eröffnet worden. Katholische Ordensschwestern waren vor der Eröffnung moderner Krankenanstalten ambulant in den Wohnhäusern der Kranken oder in speziellen Behandlungsräumen tätig. Diese Arbeit war meist wenig effizient und aufgrund der schlechten Transportwege und großen Entfernungen überaus zeitaufwendig. Der Beitrag der Ordensschwestern zur Niedrighaltung der Pflegekosten war für das wirtschaftliche Überleben einzelner Häuser überaus wichtig. Die Krankenpflegerinnen kannten keinen Heimatbesuch und wurden keinesfalls adäquat entlohnt. Ein Gehalt hätte auch den Konstitutionen ihrer Kongregation widersprochen. Dies bedeutete einen enormen Wettbewerbsvorteil gegenüber nichtkonfessionellen Krankenanstalten. Die Ansteckungsgefahr und ausufernde Arbeitszeiten waren weitere unattraktive Begleiterscheinungen der Schwesterntätigkeit. Ihr religiöses Leben mit dem Ziel der Selbstheiligung gab den Schwestern aber den Willen und die Kraft, die miserablen Arbeitsbedingungen zu ertragen. Nichtreligiöse Aspekte für die Entscheidung zum Ordenseintritt waren die Selbstverwirklichung etwa durch eine Ausbildung zur Krankenschwester und ein allgemeiner sozialer Aufstieg.[34] Die Unterbringung der Schwestern im Hospital war oft schwierig. Ihr Wunsch nach einem abgetrennten Wohntrakt verwirklichte sich zum Teil erst mehrere Jahrzehnte nach Eröffnung der Einrichtung.

Von Seiten der Kommunen konnten die Bauherren nur wenig unterstützende Mittel erwarten. Die Städte des Ruhrgebiets waren durch die rasche Entwicklung zur urbanen und schwerindustriellen Region und die damit verbundene Bevölkerungsexplosion überfordert und in der Regel dankbar, wenn andere für den Krankenhausbau aufkamen. Wegen der erwiesenen Nützlichkeit der jeweiligen Krankenhäuser erklärten sich die Kommunen aber rasch bereit, durch jährliche Zuschüsse oder anderen Beihilfen die neuen konfessionellen Einrichtungen zu unterstützen. In

---

[34] Vgl. Relinde Meiwes, "Religiosität und Arbeit als Lebensform für katholische Frauen. Kongregationen im 19. Jahrhundert," in: *Frauen unter dem Patriarchat der Kirchen. Katholikinnen und Protestantinnen im 19. und 20. Jahrhundert*, Hrsg. Irmtraud Götz von Olenhusen (Stuttgart et al.: Kohlhammer, 1995), S. 69–88.

Duisburg konnte das Städtische Krankenhaus, das aufgrund der Räumlichkeiten keine Geschlechtertrennung der Patienten ermöglichte, dank der Existenz zweier konfessioneller Krankenhäuser geschlossen werden.[35] Ähnlich waren die Verhältnisse in Gelsenkirchen und Essen.

Die Finanzierung des jeweiligen Bauwerks erfolgte zumeist aus – zum Teil konfessionsübergreifend eingeworbenen – Spenden und Erbschaften. Für notwendige Kredite konnten die Vermögenswerte der Kirchengemeinde belastet werden. Einige örtliche Bergwerke lieferten das nötige Heizmaterial zum Unkostenpreis oder gratis, beteiligten sich aber erst dann an den Kosten für Bauprojekte, nachdem das Krankenhaus seinen Nutzen erwiesen hatte. Die Deckung der laufenden Kosten versuchten die Krankenhausverwaltungen neben anderen Einnahmen – etwa über Lotterien und Basare – durch den Verkauf von „Abonnements" für den Krankheitsfall zu regeln. Solche Abonnements, eine Art „Frühform der Krankenversicherung auf freiwilliger Basis"[36], sicherten die Unterbringung bei ernsthafter Erkrankung und konnten von Privatpersonen oder von Unternehmen für ihre Arbeiter erworben werden. Für die Krankenhäuser bedeuteten aber Einnahmen aus der Armenfürsorge eine wichtigere Einnahmequelle als Zahlungen von Privatpatienten. Gelegentlich verzichteten die Hospitäler auch auf Kostenerstattung oder nahmen Naturalien als Aufnahmegebühr an.[37]

Ungeachtet aller finanziellen und materiellen Zuwendungen blieb die finanzielle Situation nahezu aller Häuser durch vielfältige Kostensteigerungen permanent angespannt. Auf Mahnungen und Verbesserungsvorschläge von behördlicher Seite, ausgesprochen insbesondere während der jährlichen Revisionen des amtsärztlichen Kreisarztes, konnte wegen fehlender Mittel oftmals erst mit mehrjähriger Verspätung reagiert werden. Die armseligen Verhältnisse erforderten von allen Bediensteten Pioniergeist und die „Fähigkeit zur Improvisation".[38] Benötigte etwa das Krankenhaus in Essen-Bergeborbeck eine Badewanne, so musste diese extra aus einem benachbarten Kloster angeliefert werden.[39] In der Anfangszeit des

---

[35] Vgl. Ulrich Stüttgen, *Die Entwicklung des Krankenhauswesens der Stadt Duisburg vom 14. bis zu 19. Jahrhundert (Vom Gasthaus-Hospital zum ersten Städtischen Krankenhaus)* (Münster: Murken, 1976), S. 90.

[36] Gatz, *Kirche und Krankenpflege*, S. 554.

[37] Vgl. Wagener-Esser, *Organisierte Barmherzigkeit und Seelenheil*, S. 296 f.

[38] Hans-Jürgen Brandt, "Barmherzigkeit in Person. Wie reich Gelsenkirchen mit den armen Schwestern aus Dernbach war," in *„Maria, Hilfe der Christen". Hospital und Kapelle in Gelsenkirchen. Ein geschichtliches und spirituelles Lesebuch*, Hrsg. Manfred Paas et al. (Lindenberg im Allgäu: Kunstverlag Fink, 2006), S. 15.

[39] Vgl. Albrecht Schennen, "Zur Frühgeschichte der Essener Krankenhäuser im 19.

Hamborner St. Johannes-Hospital mussten Kranke gar ihr eigenes Bett
mitbringen. Zum Teil behandelten die Ärzte die gewöhnlichen
Krankenhauspatienten seinerzeit noch ehrenamtlich. Ihre Einkünfte
erzielten sie mit Privatpatienten außerhalb und innerhalb der Klinik. Feste
Dienstzeiten waren unbekannt und ein Austausch mit Fachkollegen nur
selten möglich. Den Krankenhausträgern fehlten noch die finanziellen
Mittel, die Ärzte ganztägig an ihre Kliniken zu binden. Die Bismarck'sche
Sozialgesetzgebung der 1880er Jahre trug später aber wesentlich zur
finanziellen Entlastung der Hospitäler bei und beendete die Zufälligkeit
der Einnahmehöhen.

Für die Patienten, die bei persönlicher Mittellosigkeit bis zur Einführung
der Sozialversicherung auch kostenlos behandelt wurden, waren die neuen
Einrichtungen sprichwörtlich ein Segen, denn in der Stadt gab es mehr
gesundheitliche Risiken für die Zuwanderer. Der typische Patient des
Ruhrgebietskrankenhauses im langen 19. Jahrhundert rekrutierte sich aus
der Gruppe der sog. „labouring poor", war männlich, unverheiratet,
ortsfremd und im arbeitsfähigen Alter zwischen 15 und 30 Jahren. Er
konnte im Krankheitsfall, häufig ausgelöst durch einen beruflichen Unfall
in einer in der näheren Umgebung gelegenen Zeche, nicht auf familiäre
Unterstützung hoffen. Ziel des Krankenhausaufenthalts war die
schnellstmögliche Genesung und damit auch die Wiederherstellung der
Arbeitskraft.[40] Dies war im Interesse von Patient und Arbeitgeber
zugleich, gab es doch nur, wenn überhaupt, ein äußerst geringes
Krankengeld – auch dieser Zustand sollte sich nach Einführung der
Gesetzlichen Krankenversicherung 1883 bessern. Etwaige Angehörige des
Industriearbeiters waren allerdings noch nicht mitversichert. Für sie und
für Nichtversicherte sprang bei Bedarf an stationärer Krankenpflege die
städtische Armenkasse ein. In letzterem Fall konnte der Patient aber sein
allgemeines Wahlrecht verlieren.[41] Der Anteil von Frauen an den
Krankenhauspatienten blieb bis zum Ausbruch des Ersten Weltkrieges
deutlich niedriger als der Anteil männlicher Patienten, auch da die Statuten
der Häuser neben Geisteskranken die Aufnahme von Wöchnerinnen und

---

Jahrhundert," *Beiträge zur Geschichte von Stadt und Stift Essen* 85 (1970): S. 99–
166.
[40] Vgl. Jörg Vögele, *Sozialgeschichte städtischer Gesundheitsverhältnisse während
der Urbanisierung* (Berlin: Duncker und Humblot, 2001), S. 355.
[41] Vgl. Bernd Josef Wagner, "‚Um die Leiden der Menschen zu lindern, bedarf es
nicht eitler Pracht': Zur Finanzierung der Krankenhauspflege in Preußen," in:
*Krankenhaus-Report   19.   Jahrhundert.   Krankenhausträger,
Krankenhausfinanzierung, Krankenhauspatienten*, Hrsg. Alfons Labisch und
Reinhard Spree (Frankfurt am Main et al.: Campus-Verlag, 2001), S. 41–68.

Säuglingen ausschlossen. Darin unterschied sich das damalige vom heutigen Krankenhaus. Wenn es die Räumlichkeiten zuließen, wurden bereits in den Anfangsjahren der jeweiligen Einrichtungen Einzelzimmer eingerichtet. Dadurch sollte die wohlhabende Bevölkerung angelockt werden, die ansonsten im Krankheitsfall bis zur Entwicklung moderner medizinischer Apparaturen eine Behandlung im eigenen Haus vorzog. Des Weiteren führten die Krankenhäuser ein Dreiklassensystem in der Pflege ein, dessen Auswirkungen sich am deutlichsten in der ungleichen Ausstattung der Patientenzimmer zeigten.[42] Patienten der 1. Klasse waren Selbstzahler und belegten ein Ein-Bett-Zimmer. In der 2. Klasse mussten sich die zumeist als Kassenmitglieder versicherten Kranken das Zimmer zu zweit oder dritt teilen. Für die Patienten der 3. Klasse zahlte zumeist die Armenkasse. Die dortige Begrenzung der Bettenzahl wurde durch die Größe des Krankensaales vorgegeben.

Die Bevölkerung strömte, nach kurzer Zeit des Abwartens, aufgrund von Mundpropaganda in die Krankenhäuser. Das bereits erwähnte erste Essener Krankenhaus besaß zu Beginn des Betriebes 1844 fünf Betten, die in den ersten 12 Monaten von nur 34 Kranken in Anspruch genommen wurden. 1855, eine Dekade nach der Gründung, hatte die Einrichtung aber schon eine Auslastung von über 1.000 Kranken im Jahr aufzuweisen. Die Krankenhäuser benötigten so, aufgrund steigender Patientenzahlen und neuer technisch-sanitärer Möglichkeiten, oftmals schon kurze Zeit nach Fertigstellung einen Aus- oder Neubau. Bauliche Mängel und Unzulänglichkeiten der Erstbauten waren zum Teil festzustellen und Resultat fehlender Expertise, besonders in medizinisch-hygienischer Hinsicht gewesen.

Mit dem Ansteigen der Patientenzahl nahm auch die Anzahl der Krankenpflegerinnen zu. So ist ein paralleles Wachstum von Krankenhäusern und Kongregationen zu beobachten. Die Krankenhausvorstände baten die jeweiligen Mutterhäuser der Pflegekongregationen wiederholt um die Sendung weiterer Schwestern. Dem konnte aufgrund der hohen Nachfrage nicht immer stattgegeben werden. Bei den Münsteraner Clemensschwestern existierte gar eine Warteliste mit Anfragen von Gemeinden.[43] Weltliche Krankenschwestern gab es zur damaligen Zeit selten, der Beruf galt

---

[42] Am Allgemeinen Krankenhaus Hamburg existierten sogar vier Pflegeklassen. Vgl. Reinhard Spree, "Die Finanzierung von Krankenhäusern in Deutschland während des 19. Jahrhunderts," in *Struktur und Dimension. Festschrift für Karl Heinrich Kaufhold zum 65. Geburtstag II.*, Hrsg. Hans-Jürgen Gerhard (Stuttgart: Steiner, 1997), S. 413–446, hier S. 417.

[43] Vgl. Wagener-Esser, *Organisierte Barmherzigkeit und Seelenheil*, S. 279.

aufgrund der Belastungen als unattraktiv. Außerdem existierten bis zum Beginn des 20. Jahrhunderts kaum Ausbildungsmöglichkeiten außerhalb religiöser Genossenschaften.

In einzelnen Städten des Ruhrgebiets ist ein paralleler Krankenhausbau von katholischer und evangelischer Seite dokumentiert. Dass hierbei die konfessionelle Rivalität wie in anderen Regionen Preußens die entscheidende Rolle gespielt hat, ist aber zu bezweifeln – wenngleich sie sicherlich, wie auch die innerkatholische Konkurrenz zwischen den Kirchengemeinden, nicht ohne Bedeutung war. So sind beispielsweise Beschwerden der evangelischen Gemeinde Duisburg über Konversionsversuche im katholischen St. Vincenz-Hospital der Stadt erhalten.[44] Hauptursache des Phänomens des gleichzeitigen Krankenhausbaus war aber wohl ein eminenter sozialer Bedarf, dem die Kommunalverwaltungen aufgrund eingeschränkter finanzieller Handlungsmöglichkeiten nicht nachkommen konnten. Die kirchlichen Bauherren wollten einen gesundheitlichen Notstand vermeiden oder zumindest lindern. Bis zur Eröffnung des ersten Gelsenkirchener Krankenhauses mussten Kranke aber einen mehrere Stunden dauernden Transport in die Hospitäler der Umgebung in Kauf nehmen.[45] Da weder Katholiken noch Protestanten in Gelsenkirchen alleine in der Lage waren, ein Krankenhaus zu finanzieren und ein Gemeinschaftshospital keine Mehrheit fand, einigte man sich auf eine katholische Einrichtung, zu dessen Finanzierung auch von evangelischer und jüdischer Seite beigetragen wurde. Der erfolgreiche Gründungsprozess des katholischen Krankenhauses ermutigte dann die evangelische Seite ihrerseits ein eigenes Krankenhausbauprojekt zu verwirklichen.[46]

Die zuvor rudimentäre ärztliche Versorgung des Ruhrgebietes konnte durch die neuen katholischen Krankenanstalten deutlich verbessert werden. Am Vorabend des Ersten Weltkrieges waren die katholischen Hospitäler in der Krankenhauslandschaft der Region fest etabliert. Das Ruhrrevier war zu diesem Zeitpunkt mit Krankenanstalten weitgehend versorgt und für die Verpflegung von verwundeten Soldaten gerüstet.

---

[44] Vgl. Thomsen, *Katholisches Krankenhauswesen,* S. 77.

[45] Am 1. Juli 1857 wurde der Bergtagelöhner Ferdinand K. nach einer Transportzeit von drei Stunden mit einer Fraktur in das Bochumer St. Elisabeth-Hospital eingeliefert, 1856 der Bergarbeiter Heinrich F. nach einer ebenso langen Beförderungszeit. Vgl. Herm[ann] Schulte, "Der Wattverband. Nach eigenen Erfahrungen," *Deutsche Klinik* 13 (1860): S. 65–67, 76–77, 85–87.

[46] Vgl. Lueg-Hoffmann, *Das Krankenhaus- und Medizinalwesen der Stadt Gelsenkirchen,* S. 55.

CHAPTER FIFTEEN

OBDACHLOSIGKEIT, WOHNUNGSELEND UND WOHNUNGSNOT: DER WOHNREFORMDISKURS IN DER HABSBURGERMONARCHIE AM BEISPIEL WIENS UND BUDAPESTS 1848–1914

ULRIKE HARMAT

Homelessness, poverty and a housing shortage: Discourse on housing reform in the Habsburg monarchy in Vienna and Budapest, 1848–1914

Abstract: The paper deals with "housing issues" concerning the lower social strata of Vienna and Budapest in the period from 1848 to 1918. Housing, in general, was at that time significantly affected by various developments such as demographic changes, migration to cities, urbanisation, the spread of new ideas about the concept of family, state influence on housing, etc. In connection with the increased urbanisation in Vienna and Budapest, as well as in many other cities, the demand for apartments grew faster than their supply. The housing conditions of the lower, working classes in Budapest as well as in Vienna were affected by general overcrowding as well as by a lack of healthy and inexpensive small apartments. As shown in the example of treating homelessness, the measures against poverty were initially limited to mere repressive police actions. In addition, the housing shortage was at first handled within the framework of health and safety policy measures, based on thinking of bourgeois reformers on housing and the social sphere. Their primary goal was to ensure the stability of social conditions in general.

Im Jahre 1894 nahm der Nationalökonom und Finanzwissenschaftler Eugen von Philippovich die letzte Volkszählung zum Anlass, den

Wohnverhältnissen in Wien eine eigene Broschüre zu widmen.[1] Die
Ergebnisse der Volkszählung 1890 sowie der Bericht des Leiters des
städtischen statistischen Amtes, Stephan Sedlaczek,[2] hatten Philippovich
alarmiert. Die Volkszählung 1890 habe gezeigt, „dass wir in Oesterreich,
und speziell in Wien, Wohnungsverhältnisse von so krasser Natur haben,
dass niemand, der für die Entwickelung der Zukunft ein Interesse hat und
der ein wenig mitfühlt mit den Leiden der Bevölkerung, daran achtlos
vorübergehen kann".[3] Im Hinblick auf die Wohnungsfrage weisen die
Stellungnahmen Philippovichs eine für den bürgerlichen Wohnreformdiskurs
typische Konstante auf: die Warnung vor dem politischen Radikalismus,
der aus solchen Wohnverhältnissen erwachsen könnte.

In seiner Schrift *Wirtschaftlicher Fortschritt und Kulturentwicklung*
aus dem Jahre 1892 hatte Philippovich darauf hingewiesen, dass die
Hauptfrage der Kulturentwicklung sei, inwieweit sie sich auf die
Lebensführung der Einzelnen und ihrer Familien auswirke. So hätten sich
zwar in den letzten Jahrzehnten in mancher Hinsicht Fortschritte
eingestellt, nicht jedoch in dem Ausmaße, dass dadurch die Nachteile, die
die Neuordnung der Wirtschaftsverhältnisse mit sich gebracht habe,
ausgeglichen worden wären. Gerade aus den Kreisen der Arbeiter und
Angestellten, deren Lage sich nach vielen Seiten verbessert habe
(gestiegene Löhne, bessere Arbeitsbedingungen etc.) würden nicht
grundlos Rufe nach sozialen Reformen ertönen, da die Verbesserungen
etwa bei Ernährung, Kleidung etc. durch die „elenden Wohnungsverhältnisse
der großen Städte mit ihren das ganze Familienleben und die Reinheit der
Gesinnung vernichtenden Wirkungen" aufgehoben worden wären.[4]

Dabei hatte Philippovich vor allem den proletarischen Charakter des
Bettgeherwesens im Auge: „Ein nicht kleiner Teil der Bevölkerung der
großen Städte hat überhaupt keine Wohnung, sondern nur Schlafstätten
und wechselt häufig seinen Schlafplatz von Nacht zu Nacht. [...]
Ungenügende Zahl von Wohnungen, hohe Preise, schlechte
Beschaffenheit, Ueberfüllung mit Menschen erzeugen in den Städten
Mißstände, welche in gesundheitlicher, gemütlicher und sittlicher Hinsicht
jeden Fortschritt verwehren."[5] Mit Blick auf den Sozialismus warnte

---

[1] Eugen von Philippovich, *Wiener Wohnungsverhältnisse* (Berlin: Heymann,
1894).
[2] Stephan Sedlaczek, *Die Wohn-Verhältnisse in Wien. Ergebnisse der
Volkszählung vom 31. December 1890* (Wien: Magistrat, 1893).
[3] Philippovich, *Wiener Wohnungsverhältnisse*, S. 7.
[4] Eugen von Philippovich, *Wirtschaftlicher Fortschritt und Kulturentwicklung*
(Freiburg i. Br.: Mohr, 1892), S. 27 f.
[5] Ebenda, S. 39.

Philippovich vor dem „agitatorischen Brand", den ein politischer Radikalismus aufgrund einer „einseitigen Weltanschauung" hier entfalten könnte und der geeignet sei, nicht nur die auf das Privateigentum gegründete Gesellschaftsordnung, „sondern auch die geistigen und sittlichen Kräfte zu zerstören, die die Träger eines erreichbaren Fortschrittes werden könnten."[6]

Ähnlich hatte auch der Statistiker Heinrich Rauchberg argumentiert, als er darauf hinwies, dass das „socialistische Gesellschaftsideal" den Arbeitern in umso hellerem Licht erstrahlen würde, je trostloser die Wohnverhältnisse sich gestalteten. Wer jedoch – wie es der Standpunkt der bürgerlichen Parteien sei – auf dem Boden der gegenwärtigen Gesellschaftsordnung stehe und nur eine schrittweise Entwicklung derselben für möglich halte, der müsse die Lösung des Problems innerhalb dieser versuchen. Man dürfe sich jedoch nicht darauf beschränken, nur die auffälligsten Symptome des Übels zu bekämpfen.[7] Auch Rauchberg warnte vor der Zersetzung des Familienlebens durch die Anwesenheit „wildfremder Leute" und sah die „Geschlossenheit und Reinheit des Familienlebens" in Gefahr. Er warnte davor, dass diese Zustände zu einem sozialistischen Familienideal hinleiten könnten.[8]

Die zeitgenössischen Schriften des 19. Jahrhunderts fassten die Wohnungsverhältnisse der arbeitenden Bevölkerung in der Regel unter dem Begriff der „Wohnungsfrage" zusammen. Die „Wohnungsnot" im Allgemeinen, schrieb Friedrich Engels 1872, sei nichts dem modernen Proletariat gegenüber allen früheren unterdrückten Klassen „Eigenthümliches", sondern habe alle unterdrückten Klassen aller Zeiten gleich betroffen. Neu hingegen sei die „eigenthümliche Verschärfung, die die schlechten Wohnungsverhältnisse der Arbeiter durch den plötzlichen Andrang der Bevölkerung nach den großen Städten erlitten" hätten.[9]

Das Problem der unzureichenden Wohnungsversorgung erreichte im Verlaufe der Industrialisierung mit ihrer Zusammenballung riesiger Menschenmassen in gewerblich-industriellen Zentren neue Dimensionen. Wohnungsnot wurde so zum „Charakteristikum aller rasch wachsenden größeren Städte".[10] Obgleich sämtliche ärmeren Schichten (Arbeiter,

---

[6] Ebenda, S. 55 f.
[7] Heinrich Rauchberg, *Die Kaiser Franz Josef I.-Jubiläums-Stiftung für Volkswohnungen und Wohlfahrts-Einrichtungen* (Wien: Hölder, 1897), S. 9.
[8] Ebenda, S. 5.
[9] Friedrich Engels, *Zur Wohnungsfrage. Separatdruck aus dem „Volksstaat" von 1872* (Hottingen und Zürich: Verl. d. Volksbuchhandlung, 1887[2]), S. 11.
[10] Vgl. Peter Feldbauer et al., "Arbeiterwohnungsfrage, Wohnungspolitik und Mietrechtsreform in Österreich am Beispiel Wiens (1890–1916)," in *Wege zur*

Handwerker, Kleingewerbetreibende, niedrige Beamte) unter dem Mangel an Wohnungen litten, verschärften vor allem die Arbeiter die Nachfrage nach billigem Wohnraum, da sie einerseits den Kern der in die städtischen Zentren wandernden Massen bildeten, andererseits die wachsende Dominanz freier, industriekapitalistischer Arbeitsverhältnisse den Bedarf an Wohnraum steigerte. „An die Stelle des ledigen, bei seinem Meister, in Herbergen oder als Bettgeher lebenden Gesellen trat der verheiratete Arbeiter, der nicht nur sich, sondern auch Frau und Kinder unterzubringen hatte",[11] was die Anforderungen an Qualität und Größe der Arbeiterwohnungen veränderte.

Industrialisierung und Urbanisierung führten in den Städten auch zu einer verstärkten sozialräumlichen Gliederung, die einerseits „die sozialen Ungleichheiten der Gesellschaft ausdrückte und visualisierte", andererseits „diese selbst reproduzierte".[12] Die Citybildung verdrängte die zuvor in den Innenstädten ansässige Bevölkerung und an Stelle älterer Wohnhaustypen entstand in der City der Typus des mit hochwertigen Wohnungen ausgestatteten Wohn- und Geschäftshauses. Die europäischen Städte waren gekennzeichnet durch Arbeiterviertel mit „eng zusammenstehenden, zum Teil verfallenden Gebäuden, übersetzten Wohnungen, dunklen Gassen und Hinterhöfen sowie schlecht belüftbaren Arbeitermietshäusern".[13]

Einen zentralen Ausgangspunkt für die Auseinandersetzung mit der Wohnungsfrage bildeten die regelmäßig durchgeführten Volkszählungen sowie Seuchen und Epidemien, die in den großen Städten auftraten, und die „zyklisch offen in Erscheinung tretende Obdachlosigkeit": „Während der Staat zunächst noch weitgehend passiv blieb, war auf kommunaler Ebene in den beiden Hauptstädten und in anderen größeren Städten schon vor der Jahrhundertwende ein gewisser Ausbau von Einrichtungen der armenfürsorgerisch geprägten Obdachlosenpolitik zu verzeichnen."[14] Ab der Jahrhundertwende verschoben sich die Perspektiven der Reformdiskussion

Arbeitsrechtsgeschichte, Hrsg. Harald Steindl (Frankfurt am Main: Klostermann, 1984), S. 369–414, hier S. 370.
[11] Ebenda, S. 370.
[12] Vgl. Adelheid von Saldern, "Wohnen in der europäischen Großstadt 1900–1939. Eine Einführung," in *Wohnen in der Großstadt 1900–1939. Wohnsituation und Modernisierung im europäischen Vergleich*, Hrsg. Alena Janatková und Hanna Kozińska-Witt (Stuttgart: Steiner, 2006), S. 11–38, hier S. 16.
[13] Ebenda, S. 16.
[14] Gerhard Melinz und Susan Zimmermann, "Mit den Waffen der Sozialpolitik? Wohnungspolitischer Interventionismus in Österreich und Ungarn von 1889 bis in die 1930er Jahre," in *Europäische Wohnungspolitik in vergleichender Perspektive 1900–1939*, Hrsg. Clemens Zimmermann (Stuttgart: Fraunhofer-IRB-Verl., 1997), S. 85–129, hier S. 88.

und man setzte sich „verstärkt mit den wirtschaftlichen und gesellschaftlichen Ursachen der unzureichenden Wohnungsversorgung der Unterschichten und mit Fragen einer möglichen öffentlichen Intervention zugunsten der Verbesserung der Kleinwohnungsversorgung auseinander".[15]

Der bürgerliche Wohnreformdiskurs: zwischen Kleinhaus und Mietskaserne

Der vor allem seit den 1860er Jahren einsetzende Diskurs der bürgerlichen Wohnreformer verstand – wie im Folgenden gezeigt werden soll – Wohnungspolitik in erster Linie als „Defensivpolitik" und hoffte, damit „die Stabilität des aufbrechenden Gesellschaftssystems" erhalten zu können.[16] Einen zentralen Aspekt der Wohnreformdiskussion bzw. der Wohnbaudiskussion bildete vor allem der Gegensatz von Kleinhaus (Einfamilienhaus) und Mietshaus (Mietskaserne/Zinskaserne).

Noch weit über die Mitte des 19. Jahrhunderts hinaus wohnte die Mehrheit der Menschen in den Städten und auf dem Land in Kleinhäusern. Wenige Jahrzehnte später wurden eben diese Wohnverhältnisse der vorindustriellen Zeit von der bürgerlichen Wohnreformbewegung in einem verklärten Licht gesehen: „Unter dem Schock eines seit der Jahrhundertwende rapid voranschreitenden Verstädterungsprozesses, in dessen Folge sich die Mietskaserne als typische Form städtischen Arbeiterwohnens durchsetzte, forderten sowohl konservative als auch liberale Sozial- und Wohnreformer eine Besinnung auf die Wohnform des Kleinhauses."[17]

Die instabilen Arbeitsverhältnisse des 19. Jahrhunderts, die die Mobilität der Arbeiter erforderten, ließen letztlich aber die Mietwohnung, die dem Arbeiter im Unterschied zum Eigenheim mehr Bewegungsfreiheit gab, als geeignetste Form des Wohnens erscheinen. Das Mieterdasein wurde im Verlauf der Industrialisierung, wie Thomas Nipperday schreibt,

---

[15] Ebenda, S. 88.

[16] Wolfgang Hösl, "Die Anfänge der gemeinnützigen und genossenschaftlichen Bautätigkeit in Wien. Eine Studie über die Motive, die soziale Relevanz und die Entwicklung der gemeinnützigen und genossenschaftlichen Baubewegung in Wien bis 1918 I.," (Diss. phil., Universität Wien, 1979), S. 20.

[17] Robert Hoffmann, "Kleinhaus und Eigenheim in historischer Perspektive. Ein Überblick zur österreichischen Entwicklung," in *Festschrift Guido Müller. Geograph und Landesforscher*, Hrsg. Wolfgang Sitte und Hermann Suida (Salzburg: Inst. für Geographie, 1997), S. 71–95, hier S. 75.

„ein Konstitutivum, ja schließlich der vorherrschende Zug des modernen
städtischen Lebens".[18]
Im Zuge der Verstädterung stieg die Wohnungsnachfrage in vielen
Städten rascher als das Wohnungsangebot, was zu einem Anwachsen des
Untermiet- und Bettgeherwesens führte und den bürgerlichen
Wohnungsreformern den Angelpunkt ihrer Kritik bot, die nicht selten von
einem „tüchtigen Schuss Agrarromantik"[19] begleitet war. Sie versprachen
sich nämlich von der Reetablierung des Eigenhauses das, was ihrer
Ansicht nach durch die Wohnverhältnisse des Industriezeitalters zerstört
worden war, „ein nach bürgerlichem Vorbild in Besitz, Gesundheit, Moral,
Staatstreue und Heimatbewusstsein stabilisiertes Familienleben des
Arbeiterstandes"[20].
In den wohnungspolitischen Debatten des 19. Jahrhunderts wurde die
Propagierung des Kleinhauses mit wohnungspolitischen Absichten
verbunden und zum Teil auch als Instrument zur Bewältigung der sozialen
Frage als solcher verstanden. Dem Massenmietshaus wurde seine
Existenzberechtigung in erster Linie nur auf Grund ökonomischer Zwänge
zuerkannt. Der Gegensatz von Kleinhaus und Mietskaserne bezeichnete
also „nicht nur zwei besondere Bauformen, sondern auch gegensätzliche
wohnungs- und sozialpolitische Positionen".[21] Die Wohnungsfrage wurde
von den meisten zeitgenössischen bürgerlichen Sozial- und Wohnreformern
zunächst vor allem als „ein Problem der Deklassierung bürgerlicher
Schichten und der Gewährleistung eines standesgemäßen Wohn- und
Lebensniveaus für in finanzielle Nöte geratene Kleinbürgerfamilien oder
Witwen von Beamten und Handwerksmeistern" betrachtet.[22]
Zu Beginn der franzisko-josephinischen Ära war man sich allgemein
darüber im Klaren, dass gegen die Wohnungsnot der unteren
Bevölkerungsschichten etwas unternommen werden müsse. Bereits im

[18] Zitiert nach ebenda, S. 78.
[19] Hans J. Teuteberg, "Eigenheim oder Mietskaserne: Ein Zielkonflikt deutscher
Wohnungsreformer 1850–1914," in *Innerstädtische Differenzierung und Prozesse
im 19. und 20. Jahrhundert. Geographische und historische Aspekte*, Hrsg. Heinz
Heineberg (Köln und Wien: Böhlau, 1987), S. 21–56, hier S. 23.
[20] Hoffmann, "Kleinhaus und Eigenheim," S. 80.
[21] Renate Kastorff-Viehmann, "Kleinhaus und Mietskaserne," in *Wohnen im
Wandel. Beiträge zur Geschichte des Alltags in der bürgerlichen Gesellschaft*,
Hrsg. Lutz Niethammer (Wuppertal: Hammer, 1979), S. 271–291, hier S. 272.
[22] Andreas R. Hofmann, "Von der Spekulation zur Intervention. Formen des
Arbeiterwohnungsbaus in Lodz und Brünn vor und nach dem Ersten Weltkrieg," in
*Wohnen in der Großstadt 1900–1939. Wohnsituation und Modernisierung im
europäischen Vergleich*, Hrsg. Alena Janatková und Hanna Kozińska-Witt
(Stuttgart: Steiner, 2006), S. 225–248, hier S. 225.

Jahre 1857 warnte Bernhard Friedmann eindringlich vor den Folgen der Wiener Wohnungnot.[23] Friedmann setzte sich in seiner Schrift mit dem kleinbürgerlichen Abstieg auseinander. Es ging ihm in erster Linie um die Sicherung des Wohlstandes eines „arbeitsamen Mittelstandes" und um gesamtstaatliche wirtschaftliche Stabilität, den Schutz vor willkürlichen Mietzinserhöhungen und um die Bedürfnisse der Beamten. Er thematisierte dabei vor allem die zunehmende Mobilisierung der Bevölkerung infolge der Mietzinserhöhungen.

„Kein Bewohner der Vorstädte fühlt sich jetzt von einem [Miet]Quartale zum andern sicher auf seinem ‚Grund', in seiner Straße, zwischen seinen vier Mauern. [...] Von einer Wohnung kann daher kaum mehr die Rede sein, höchstens von einem temporären Obdache, von steinernen Zelten, welche unablässig ihre Besitzer wechseln. Niemand kann sich eines ‚zu Hause' rühmen oder erfreuen [...]. So geht ein Zug der Unruhe und der Beängstigung durch die ganze Bewohnerschaft Wiens, ein flüchtiges Nomadenleben tritt an die Stelle einer ruhigen, angesessenen, bürgerlichen Existenz [...]."[24]

Seine Sorge betraf in erster Linie die „standesmäßige Lebensweise" der gesamten Staatsdienerschaft und „die Gefahr der Demoralisierung". Die bürgerlichen Haushaltungen würden mehr und mehr aus den wohnlicheren, reinlich gehaltenen Behausungen hinaus- und in die „physisch und sittlich ungesunde Nachbarschaft des Pöbels hineingedrängt."[25]

Wolfgang Hösl und Gottfried Pirhofer haben in ihrer auf Wien bezogenen Studie gezeigt, dass in der Früh- und Hochgründerzeit tatsächlich nur für das (Klein-)Bürgertum eine Wohnungsfrage existierte.[26] Infolge der Wohnungsknappheit und Verteuerung sei ein „etabliertes Lebensgelände" des Kleinbürgertums (nämlich Familie und Innerlichkeit) ins Wanken geraten. Demgegenüber sei das Wohnungselend der Arbeiterschichten in der Früh- und Hochgründerzeit in gewisser Weise „zeitlos und nur ein Moment einer durchgängig katastrophalen Situation" gewesen.[27] Das Wohnungselend war demnach „keineswegs ein spezifisches Problem der nach 1870 überproportional anwachsenden Arbeiterschaft", sondern betraf alle Bewohner der kleinen und kleinsten

[23] Bernhard Friedmann, *Die Wohnungsnot in Wien* (Wien: Wallishausser, 1857).
[24] Ebenda, S. 5.
[25] Ebenda, S. 10.
[26] Vgl. Wolfgang Hösl und Gottfried Pirhofer, *Wohnen in Wien 1848–1938. Studien zur Konstitution des Massenwohnens* (Wien: Deuticke, 1988), S 14.
[27] Ebenda, S. 14.

Unterkünfte, deren Anteil am Wiener Wohnungsbestand vor Kriegsausbruch „immer noch 75 Prozent betrug".[28]

Im Jahre 1884 veranstaltete Maximilian Steiner, der Gründer des „Vereins für Arbeiterhäuser" eine Enquete, „um durch Einzelnachweise die Wohnungsverhältnisse der minderbemittelten Classen zu kennzeichnen".[29] In die Enquete sollten jene Wohnungen einbezogen werden, welche für Personen bestimmt waren, „die unter dem kleinen Bürgerstande, aber über dem eigentlichen Taglöhner rangiren": gewerbliche Hilfsarbeiter, Diurnisten, Geschäftsdiener, Briefträger und andere Arbeiter oder Kleingewerbetreibende, welche durchschnittlich 40 bis 75 fl. pro Monat erhielten. Die Wohnungsverhältnisse dieser Bevölkerungsschichten waren, wie Steiner berichtete, „die allerschlimmsten": „Die Wohnungen derselben kamen per Quadratmeter Wohnfläche theurer zu stehen als diejenigen der noch Aermeren; auch consumirt der Wohnungszins eine grössere Quote des Gesammt-Einkommens als dies bei der nächst höheren, sowie bei der nächst niedrigeren Bevölkerungsschichte der Fall ist." Abgesehen davon wurden auch erschreckende Wohn- und Lebensverhältnisse festgestellt: „Ehemalige Stallungen, hölzerne Gartenhäuschen, nasse Kellergewölbe, Dachräume, welche nicht einmal durch Holzwände vor der zwischen den Dachziegeln eindringenden Winterkälte geschützt waren, fanden sich vermiethet und zwar zu vollen Preisen."[30] Die meisten dieser Räume waren eng und niedrig; die zu ebener Erde gelegenen Wohnungen feucht, die Hauskanäle vernachlässigt und übelriechend. Zu den schlimmsten Missständen gehörte die Überfüllung. Außerdem waren die Bewohner dieser Wohnungen ständig im Wohnungswechsel begriffen. Es wurden „Schlaf-Locale" festgestellt, in denen in einem einzigen Zimmer 23 Personen „zu Bett" gingen. Dennoch schreckten die Behörden in manchen Fällen vor einer sanitätspolizeilichen Räumung zurück, weil man nicht ohne Grund befürchtete, dass durch die Delogierung das Elend noch vergrößert würde.

Der Mangel an kleinen und bezahlbaren Wohnungen war jedoch nicht nur von der Produktion der Bauindustrie abhängig. Wie Feldbauer nachwies, konnte der Wohnungsmangel in der ersten Hälfte der 1870er Jahre trotz der „Rekordproduktion der Bauindustrie" nicht gemildert werden, sondern verschärfte sich noch laufend weiter. Der Mangel an kleinen Wohnungen und die extrem hohen Mietzinse führten zu einem lebhaften Wohnungswechsel zu jedem Zinstermin, was sich auch an der

---

[28] Feldbauer et al., "Arbeiterwohnungsfrage," S. 372.

[29] Maximilian Steiner, Der „Verein für Arbeiterhäuser" in Wien. Ein Beitrag zur Wohnungsfrage (Wien: Ver. f. Arbeiterh., 1896), S. 4.

[30] Ebenda, S. 6 f.

Zahl der gerichtlichen Delogierungen nachweisen lässt.[31] Die Bautätigkeit hatte sich besonders auf den Stadterweiterungsrayon konzentriert, wo man „infolge administrativer Begünstigungen und der zu erwartenden zahlungskräftigen Mieter hohe und sichere Profite erhoffte".[32]

1860 nahmen der Kunsthistoriker Rudolf von Eitelberger und der Architekt Heinrich von Ferstel die geplante Stadterweiterung zum Anlass und publizierten die Schrift: „Das bürgerliche Wohnhaus und das Zinshaus". Die Autoren sahen die Familie, die für sie „die erste und heiligste Schöpfung des bürgerlichen Lebens" darstellte, bedroht. Sie hoben den Besitz eines eigenen Hauses für die Bedeutung der Familie hervor und zogen gegen die „monströse Zinshaus-Architektur"[33] zu Felde. Der von ihnen entworfene Plan für ein Wohnhaus bezog sich vor allem auf die Bedürfnisse des Mittelstandes (Handwerker und Geschäftsleute); die Wohnverhältnisse der Arbeiter fanden keinerlei Beachtung. Eine Grundvoraussetzung bildete für sie die Abgeschlossenheit der Privatwohnung bzw. des Hauses; diese sei, so argumentierten sie, nicht nur eine ästhetische Anforderung, sondern auch eine der Sittlichkeit.

Die Schrift Eitelbergers und Ferstels reflektiert, wie Hannes Stekl schreibt, „den zeitgenössischen gesellschafts- und wirtschaftspolitischen Diskurs".[34] Ähnlich wie bei Friedmann ging es auch hier um die Sicherung des Wohlstandes eines „arbeitenden Mittelstandes", um wirtschaftliche Stabilität, Entproletarisierung und Unterdrückung revolutionärer Neigungen durch Haus- oder Wohnungseigentum. Dabei ignorierte man, dass der „gebildete Mittelstand" und die „wohlhabende Bürgerklasse" nur zum Teil die Leidtragenden des Wohnungsdefizits waren, das vor allem auf dem Mangel an Kleinwohnungen (mit einem Jahreszins von bis zu 400 Gulden) beruhte und hauptsächlich einkommensschwache Lohnarbeiter und Kleingewerbetreibende traf. Demgegenüber propagierte man ein bürgerliches Familienleitbild. Wohnungseigentum wurde als „Postulat der öffentlichen Moral" und somit als Garant politischer Sicherheit betrachtet. Die Elemente der „Bewegung und Unruhe", die die Autoren vor allem in

---

[31] Peter Feldbauer, *Stadtwachstum und Wohnungsnot. Determinanten unzureichender Wohnungsversorgung in Wien 1848 bis 1914* (Wien: Verlag für Geschichte und Politik, 1977), S. 145.

[32] Ebenda, S. 147.

[33] Rudolf von Eitelberger und Heinrich Ferstel, *Das bürgerliche Wohnhaus und das Zinshaus. Ein Vorschlag aus Anlaß der Erweiterung der innern Stadt Wien's* (Wien: Gerold, 1860), S. 11.

[34] Hannes Stekl, ",Bürgerliches Wohnhaus' und Cottagesiedlungen. Alternativen zur Architektur der Wiener Ringstraße," *Österreich in Geschichte und Literatur* 53/1 (2009): S. 2–20, hier S. 9.

den besitzlosen Klassen identifizierten, sollten dadurch neutralisiert werden.

Auf dieser Linie lag auch die ein Jahrzehnt später veröffentlichte Schrift des bekannten Wohnungsreformers Emil Sax, der sich 1869 mit den Wohnungszuständen der arbeitenden Klassen befasste[35] und als Vater der Reformbewegung bezeichnet wurde. Zirka zehn Jahre nach der Schrift Friedmanns leitete Sax seine Broschüre zum Neubau Wiens mit den Worten ein: „Die Wohnungsnoth ist in Wien zu einer bleibenden Calamität geworden. [...] Sie ist in Aller Munde, weil eben Jeder darunter leidet."[36] Sax ordnete die neuen Dimensionen des Wohnungselends nicht mehr allein den spezifischen Verhältnissen in Wien, sondern den im Gefolge der Industrialisierung international phasenverschoben auftretenden Problemen des beschleunigten Stadtwachstums zu und richtete sein Augenmerk zunächst auf jene Faktoren, welche das Funktionieren des Wohnungsmarktes prinzipiell und im konkreten Fall vereiteln konnten.[37]

Auch Sax ging es in erster Linie um eine Stabilisierung der herrschenden gesellschaftlichen Verhältnisse und die Verhinderung revolutionärer Strömungen. Größtes Gewicht legte Sax dabei auf die Eigentumserwerbung. Er forderte die Abkehr vom „Casernement" und propagierte das englische Cottage-System. Eine vollständige Lösung der Wohnungsfrage sei nur dann möglich, wenn es gelänge, die Arbeiter im weitesten Umfange zu Eigentümern ihrer Wohnungen zu machen. Der Arbeiter würde, so schrieb Sax, „Capitalist" und könne so aus der besitzlosen in die Klasse der Besitzenden aufsteigen.[38] Passagen wie diese riefen den energischen Widerspruch seitens Friedrich Engels hervor, der Sax' Vorschläge mit zum Teil beißendem Spott kommentierte. Für die Arbeiter in den Großstädten, so führte Engels aus, sei Mobilität die „erste Lebensbedingung" und Grundbesitz nur eine Fessel: „Verschafft ihnen eigene Häuser, kettet sie wieder an die Scholle, und ihr brecht ihre Widerstandskraft gegen die Lohnherabdrückung der Fabrikanten."[39]

Sax dürfte sich auch selbst der Grenzen seines Systems bewusst gewesen sein, denn er gestand ein, dass Cottage und Casernement zwei Extreme darstellten, die Raum für Übergänge ließen. Es war ihm klar, dass

---

[35] Emil Sax, *Die Wohnungszustände der arbeitenden Classen und ihre Reform* (Wien: Pichler, 1869).

[36] Emil Sax, *Der Neubau Wien's im Zusammenhange mit der Donau-Regulirung. Ein Vorschlag zur gründlichen Behebung der Wohnungsnoth* (Wien: A. Pichler's Witwe & Sohn, 1869), S. 5.

[37] Vgl. Feldbauer, *Stadtwachstum und Wohnungsnot*, S. 214.

[38] Sax, *Wohnungszustände*, S. 63.

[39] Engels, *Zur Wohnungsfrage*, 33.

die reine Cottage-Bauweise für die Arbeiter aus Kostengründen nicht möglich war, und er schlug für die Unterschichten eine Zwischenform von Zinskaserne und Cottage vor. Das Programm von Sax – und die dahinter stehende Ideologie – blieben bis ins 20. Jahrhundert bestimmend für die Reformdebatte.[40] Trotz aller Einsicht in die gegebenen ökonomischen Bedingungen blieb das Kleinhaus der „wohnungspolitische Favorit"[41] der konservativ geprägten Wohnreformer.

Auch Maximilian Steiner führte bei einem 1884 gehaltenen Vortrag vor dem Ingenieur- und Architektenverein den „sittlich-ökonomischen Niedergang" der Bevölkerung auf die ungünstigen Wohnungsverhältnisse zurück: „Dadurch geht der moralische Halt verloren, den die Liebe zum häuslichen Heerd gewähren [!] und die schlechten Keime wandern wie das Contagium einer Seuche aus einem Haus in das andere."[42] Wie Sax propagierte er „in offener Kampfansage an die sozialistische Arbeiterbewegung"[43] den Bau von Einfamilienhäusern mit Garten, an denen die Mieter allmählich das Eigentumsrecht erwerben sollten.[44] Damit wollte er den Facharbeiter „in das kleinbürgerliche Lebensmodell integrieren und gegen ‚anarchistische Umtriebe' immunisieren.[45] Dafür gründete Steiner 1886 den „Verein für Arbeiterhäuser", der nach diesem Muster Einfamilienhäuser erbauen sollte.

Obdachlosigkeit und Obdachlosenpolitik

All diesen theoretischen Überlegungen einer idealen Wohnform standen die Realitäten des Wohnungselendes der Unterschichten in den

---

[40] Auch Heinrich Reschauer und Mathias Ratkowsky ging es bei ihren Vorschlägen in erster Linie um die Stabilität der gesellschaftlichen Verhältnisse, die sie durch die schlechten Wohnverhältnisse in den Großstädten gefährdet sahen. Vgl. Heinrich Reschauer, *Vorschlag zur raschen und vollständigen Beseitigung der Wohnungsnoth in Wien* (Wien: Selbstverl., 1871); Mathias G. Ratkowsky, *Die zur Reform der Wohnungs-Zustände in grossen Städten nothwendigen Massregeln der Gesetzgebung und Verwaltung. Mit besonderer Rücksicht auf die Verhältnisse Wiens* (Wien: Beck, 1871).

[41] Renate Kastorff-Viehmann, "Kleinhaus und Mietskaserne," S. 277.

[42] Maximilian Steiner, *Ueber die Errichtung von Arbeiterwohnungen in Wien. Ein Vortrag, gehalten im „Oesterr. Ingenieur- und Architekten-Verein" zu Wien am 15. März 1884* (Wien: s. t., 1884), S. 8.

[43] Gottfried Pirhofer, "Linien einer kulturpolitischen Auseinandersetzung in der Geschichte des Wiener Arbeiterwohnungsbaues," *Wiener Geschichtsblätter* 33/1 (1978): S. 1–23, hier S. 18.

[44] Steiner, *Der „Verein für Arbeiterhäuser"*, S. 10.

[45] Pirhofer, "Linien," S. 18.

wachsenden Städten gegenüber. Arbeitslosigkeit, Zuwanderung, Delogierungen und Wohnungsmangel stellten im spätgründerzeitlichen Wien zehntausende Personen aus den Unterschichten vor das Problem, nicht genau zu wissen, wo sie in den nächsten Tagen schlafen sollten. Der Großteil der Obdachlosen Wiens war „fremdzuständig", was bedeutete, dass der Betroffene nicht das Wiener Heimatrecht innehatte.[46] In Wien gab es ein paar Dutzend Massenquartiere, die zumeist stark überfüllt, schmutzig, jedoch billig waren und den Vorteil besaßen, dass strenge Hausregeln unbekannt waren. Wesentlich besser ausgestattet waren die Obdachlosenasyle mit ihren riesigen Schlafsälen, von denen es um die Jahrhundertwende zwei gab: das städtische in Favoriten und das Asyl des Asylvereins für Obdachlose im dritten Bezirk.

Nachdem im Winter 1867/1868 die Zustände unhaltbar geworden waren, versuchte der bereits erwähnte Maximilian Steiner, der als Schriftführer des „Asylvereins für Obdachlose" fungierte, durch private Wohltätigkeit Abhilfe zu schaffen. In der Geschichte des Vereins heißt es dazu: „Der mächtige Zustrom der Bevölkerung nach Wien, welcher um die Mitte der Sechzigerjahre erfolgte, zog eine drückende Wohnungsnoth nach sich. Es kam so weit, dass ganze Familien im Flussbette der Wien, unter Brücken und in den Ausfallsthoren der Canäle campierten; Andere begaben sich freiwillig in polizeilichen Gewahrsam oder verlangten ‚per Schub' fortgeschickt zu werden. Der Stadtphysikat und die Sicherheitspolizei standen rathlos der wachsenden Bedrängnis gegenüber."[47]

Besonders elend war die Unterbringung der Taglöhner-Massen im Zuge der mehrjährigen, 1869/1870 begonnenen Arbeiten zur Donauregulierung. Vermutlich erst unter dem Druck der Presse und der Gemeinde errichtete die so genannte Donauregulierungsunternehmung für einen Teil der Arbeiter Baracken aus Holz. Neben diesen Baracken gab es laut Bericht des Wiener Stadtphysikates „Erdhütten [...] an der Böschung des neu aufgeschütteten Dammes"; diese bestanden „aus Brettern und Pfosten, nach oben in einem spitzen Winkel zusammenlaufend und von

---

[46] Das Heimatrecht war Voraussetzung für die Unterstützung eines Armen aus öffentlichen Mitteln. Vgl. zum Folgenden Michael John, "Obdachlosigkeit – Massenerscheinung und Unruheherd im Wien der Spätgründerzeit," in *Glücklich ist, wer vergißt ...? Das andere Wien um 1900*, Hrsg. Hubert Ch. Ehalt, Gernot Heiß und Hannes Stehl (Wien et al.: Hermann Böhlaus Nachf., 1986), S. 173–194, hier S. 173.

[47] *Der „Asylverein für Obdachlose" 1870–1903* (Wien: Selbstverlag, 1903), S. 9. Der Verein stand „unter dem Allerhöchsten Protectorate Sr. k. u. k. Apostolischen Majestät des Kaisers".

außen ganz mit Erde bedeckt."[48] Nach Beendigung der Arbeiten wurden diese Baracken teilweise stehen gelassen und Asylplätze für Obdachlose.

Bei der Gründung des „Asylvereins für Obdachlose" gab es zunächst Probleme. Während die Vereinsstatuten sofort genehmigt wurden, machte die zuständige Behörde bei der Genehmigung der Hausordnung Probleme, da – anders als beim städtischen Asyl, bei dem sich jeder Obdachlose ausweisen und seine Heimatzuständigkeit angeben musste – hier jeder Obdachlose Aufnahme finden sollte, ohne nach Herkunft, Stand und Namen befragt zu werden. Erst nachdem die Proponenten ankündigten, dass man in diesem Fall von der Vereinsgründung absehen würde, wurde die proponierte Hausordnung schließlich bewilligt. Das bedeutete, dass das Asyl für Obdachlose „von den polizeilichen Meldevorschriften und Streifungen grundsätzlich eximirt" wurde.[49]

Das erste Asylhaus wurde am 13. Dezember 1870 eröffnet und war zunächst für obdachlose Frauen und Kinder bestimmt, ein Jahr später folgte ein zweites für obdachlose Männer.[50] Die Obdachlosen, die bei Eintritt und Austritt aus dem Asyl Suppe und Brot erhielten, durften insgesamt fünf aufeinanderfolgende Nächte im Asyl verweilen und sollten während dieser Zeit Arbeit und Unterkunft suchen bzw. sich die Mittel zur Abreise verschaffen; eine längere Verweildauer, so wurde argumentierte, würde zu „Apathie und trägem Zuwarten" führen. Wie aus dem Vereinsbericht hervorgeht, zogen die meisten Obdachlosen das Asyl des Asylvereins dem städtischen Asyl vor, wo die Verwaltung über jeden „Insassen" einen Kataster führte und ihn über die Gründe seiner Obdachlosigkeit „einvernehmen" konnte. Im städtischen Asyl befand sich eine Polizeiwachstube und 34 uniformierte „Aufseher" überwachten die Obdachlosen. Nach Ablauf der maximalen Aufenthaltsdauer von sieben Tagen konnte der Obdachlose, sofern er noch immer keine Unterkunft gefunden hatte, in das im gleichen Komplex liegende berüchtigte „Werkhaus" abgeschoben werden. Diese „an offene Repression grenzende"[51] Maßnahme hielt selbst die „berücksichtigenswerten Armen"[52] vom städtischen Asyl ab.

Der Ausdruck „berücksichtigungswert" deutet bereits an, dass man glaubte, die Spreu vom Weizen trennen zu müssen, sowohl bei der gesamten Armutsproblematik als auch bei der Obdachlosigkeit. Man anerkannte einerseits den Fürsorgegedanken der Gemeinde, wandte sich

---

[48] Zitiert nach Hösl und Pirhofer, *Wohnen in Wien*, S. 13.
[49] *Der „Asylverein für Obdachlose" 1870–1903*, S. 12.
[50] Ebenda, S. 13.
[51] John, "Obdachlosigkeit," S. 182.
[52] *Der „Asylverein für Obdachlose" 1870–1903*, S. 12.

aber gegen jene Familien, „die sich das ganze Jahr hindurch in
Wärmestuben, Asylen und Kanälen aufhalten" und deren Mitglieder
„Geldaushilfen zum Zwecke der Aufnahme einer Wohnung [...] zur
Gänze vertränken".[53]

Der Versuch, die Schuld an der Misere bei den Betroffenen selbst zu
suchen, war keineswegs neu. Schon Emil Sax hatte den Hauptgrund für
die untragbaren Wohnzustände auch in dem individuellen Fehlverhalten
und der mangelnden Einsicht der Betroffenen geortet, die versuchten,
„möglichst wenig für die Wohnung auszugeben, während sie daneben auf
Trunk und allerlei eitle Vergnügungen ihr Einkommen in wahrhaft
sündlicher Weise verschleudern".[54] Sax nahm zwar die untersten
Schichten – die, „um nicht ganz obdachlos zu bleiben, wo und wie immer
ein Nachtlager zu suchen bemüssigt und in dieser Beziehung völlig wehr-
und hilflos sind" – von seiner Kritik aus. Die differenzierende
Grundhaltung gegenüber den Armen jedoch scheint ein fester Bestandteil
der Diskussion gewesen zu sein und schlug sich, vielleicht unbewusst, in
den Formulierungen selbst wohlmeinender Zeitgenossen nieder – etwa in
einer Wortmeldung des Sozialdemokraten Jakob Reumann, der von der
„Unterstützung unschuldig [!] obdachlos gewordener Familien" sprach.[55]

Auch die organisierte Privatwohltätigkeit versuchte, „Schmarotzer"
auszusondern, und sah sich aus sozialpädagogischen Motiven der
„individualisierenden" Methode verpflichtet. Der Philanthropische Verein
verlangte sogar eine schriftliche Begründung der Bewerbung. Dieser
Verein sowie der Katholische Wohltätigkeitsverband errichteten aufgrund
der steigenden Obdachlosigkeit seit der Jahrhundertwende zusätzlich
Familienasyle. Der Philanthropische Verein beschäftigte in diesem
Zusammenhang so genannte Recherchenten, die über die Aufnahme
entschieden, nachdem sie Erkundigungen über den Bewerber eingeholt
hatten.[56]

Die Neu- und Zubauten nach 1900 signalisieren den wachsenden
Bedarf. Immer wieder mussten Obdachlose wegen Überfüllung der Asyle

---

[53] So der Wiener Bürgermeister anlässlich einer Anfrage wegen der repressiven
Vorgangsweise der Behörden gegenüber 70 obdachlosen Familien während der
großen Wohnungsnot 1910/11, zitiert bei John, "Obdachlosigkeit," S. 181.
[54] Sax, *Wohnungszustände,* S. 28.
[55] Das Zitat bei John, "Obdachlosigkeit," S. 181.
[56] Auch der Asylverein für Obdachlose errichtete ein eigenes Familienasyl für 32
Familien. Eine Auflistung der diversen Einrichtungen für Obdachlose findet sich
bei Raimund Fürlinger, *Obdachlosigkeit und Obdachlosenfürsorge. Eine
Denkschrift und ein Mahnruf zur Fürsorge für die Zeit nach dem Kriege* (Wien: s.
t., 1916.

abgewiesen werden. Nach einer Erhebung des Katholischen Wohltätigkeitsverbandes waren im Jahre 1911 im Durchschnitt in Wien täglich 2.403 Personen in Obdachlosenfürsorge. Zehn Jahre zuvor, als es in Wien nur das städtische Asyl und das private Asyl für Obdachlose gab, waren es pro Tag 284.[57] Im Jahre 1911 waren insgesamt 117.602 Kinder von der Obdachlosigkeit betroffen.

Diejenigen, die keinen Platz in den Asylen fanden, nächtigten an den verschiedensten Plätzen. „Der Schreiber dieser Zeilen", so heißt es in einem Bericht aus dem Jahre 1905, „hat jahrelanges Studium gerade diesen Großstadtbürgern zugewendet, er hat sie in ihren Höhlen und Schlupfwinkeln, in ihren Erdlöchern und in den Misthaufen der Gärtner in der Brigittenau und Erdberg aufgesucht, im Ziegelofen und in dem Kahnschuppen am Donaukanal, in den Auen und wo sie sonst noch unterkriechen, diese Verlorenen […]."[58] Immer wieder wurden Obdachlose tot aufgefunden, die erfroren waren.

Wie Michael John zeigt, nahmen sich Zeitungs- und Sensationsjournalisten mit Vorliebe dieser Thematik an. Der Schriftsteller und Journalist Emil Kläger veröffentlichte z. B. 1908 ein Buch mit dem „reißerischen und denunziatorischen" Titel *Durch die Quartiere des Elends und Verbrechens: ein Wanderbuch aus dem Jenseits.*[59] Der bedeutendste Sozialreporter dieser Zeit, Max Winter, berichtete über die *Höhlenbewohner in Wien* unter anderem anhand des Beispiels der Brigittenauer Obdachlosenkolonie. Die Obdachlosen nächtigten in einem drei Quadratmeter großen Erdloch: „Dennoch schlafen in diesem Raume vier so arme Teufel und früher schliefen hier gar acht Trogledyten, acht Höhlenbewohner der Großstadt, eng aneinandergepreßt die Leiber, um dadurch gegen die Kälte Schutz zu finden. Acht Menschen! Seid ihr wirklich noch Menschen, ihr armen Tiere in Menschengestalt, für die es keinen ‚Tierschutzverein' gibt, die die Polizei ruhig verderben läßt, weil sie ihnen kein anderes Obdach als den stinkigen überfüllten Polizeiarrest bieten kann."[60] John weist darauf hin, dass die politische Relevanz dieser Sozialreportagen, abgesehen von der Stärkung der Privatwohltätigkeit, verschwindend gering war. Die Verfasser waren von unterschiedlichen Motiven geleitet, vom „Aufrütteln", von der Stärkung der Privatwohltätigkeit

---

[57] Ebenda, S. 4, 7. Vgl. *Die Armenpflege. Mitteilungen aus dem Gebiete der freiwilligen Armenpflege* 1/6 (1903): S. 11 f.

[58] *Die Armenpflege* 3/1 (1905), S. 2.

[59] Emil Kläger, *Durch die Quartiere des Elends und Verbrechens: ein Wanderbuch aus dem Jenseits* (Wien: Mitschke), 1908.

[60] Max Winter, *Höhlenbewohner in Wien. Brigittenauer Wohn- und Sittenbilder aus der Luegerzeit* (Wien: Vorwärts, 1927), S. 40.

durch Spenden des liberalen und philantrophischen Bürgertums, der persönlichen Profilierung als Schriftsteller bzw. Journalist bis hin zur Selbstdarstellung.[61] Die Adressaten waren Intellektuelle, das Kleinbürgertum und das liberale Bürgertum. Die Schriften dienten in gewisser Weise „der Entdeckung des Elends."[62]

Die Maßnahmen, die man gegen Not und Elend traf, waren in erster Linie polizeilicher Einsatz bzw. offene Repression in Form von Abschiebung, Werkhaus oder Arrest. Im Hintergrund stand die Befürchtung, dass die unteren Schichten für die bürgerliche Welt zu einer Bedrohung werden könnten: sanitär, mental, in krimineller und letztlich revolutionärer Form.

Dieser Zugang, die Folgen der großstädtischen Wohnungsmisere mittels repressiv-polizeilicher Maßnahmen bzw. bescheidener Fürsorgemaßnahmen zu verdrängen, zeigte sich auch in Budapest. Wie Susan Zimmermann nachgewiesen hat, stand auch dort bis nach der Jahrhundertwende Wohnungspolitik vor allem im Zeichen von Seuchenabwehr, gesundheitspolizeilich motivierter Durchsetzung minimaler Forderungen der Wohnungshygiene und Garantie der öffentlichen Sicherheit und Ordnung. Obdachlosigkeit blieb daher für die hauptstädtischen Behörden zunächst „nur in ihrer Erscheinungsform als Vagaboundage unausgesprochener Gegenstand kommunaler Politik und armenpolizeilicher Verdrängungsstrategien".[63] Seit den 1880er Jahren ging die Budapester Stadtverwaltung allmählich zu einer Politik der Unterstützung privater Aktivitäten in der Obdachlosenfürsorge über. Das einzige Obdachlosenasyl, das seit 1876 existierte, war auf Initiative einer Freimaurer-Gesellschaft entstanden. Dieser „Verein Asyl für Obdachlose" wurde ab 1880 regelmäßig vom Rat der Hauptstadt unterstützt. Ab Mitte der 1880er Jahre zeichnete sich dann ein „Übergang zur Erweiterung der behördlichen Unterstützung privater Obdachlosenfürsorge und zum Notwohnungsbau ab".[64]

Obwohl die Kommune ihrem Vorsatz treu blieb, dass ein direktes behördliches Eingreifen nach Möglichkeit vermieden werden sollte, bemühte sie sich dennoch um eine stärkere Unterstützung privater Initiativen. Sie stellte dem „Verein Asyl für Obdachlose" ein Grundstück

---

[61] John, "Obdachlosigkeit," S. 178.

[62] Ebenda.

[63] Vgl. zum Folgenden Susan Zimmermann, *Prächtige Armut. Fürsorge, Kinderschutz und Sozialreform in Budapest. Das „sozialpolitische Laboratorium" der Doppelmonarchie im Vergleich zu Wien 1873–1914* (Sigmaringen: Thorbecke), 1997, S. 134.

[64] Ebenda, S. 135.

zur Verfügung und bewilligte einen jährlichen Zuschuss von 5.000 Gulden für die Tilgung des Kredits zur Bestreitung der Baukosten. 1888 wurde das zweite Asyl des Vereins eröffnet, dem 1892 und 1894 zwei weitere folgten. Beim Umgang mit der Problematik zeigt sich, dass die Ansätze einer Obdachlosenfürsorge der Kommune stärker auf die Versorgung männlicher als weiblicher Obdachloser abzielten, obwohl das Problem der stellungslosen, hauptsächlich weiblichen Dienstboten, die sich bei den so genannten „Dienstbotenvermittlern" und „Herbergen" aufhielten, bekannt war. Zimmermann führt dies auf die „geschlechtsspezifisch unterschiedlich bewertete ‚Bedrohlichkeit' von durch Obdachlosigkeit auf die Straße getriebenen Männern und ‚Frauen'" zurück sowie auf die herrschenden Vorstellungen bezüglich „spezifisch weiblicher Methoden" der Beschaffung von Beherbergung durch „unmoralisches" Treiben.[65]

Es waren vor allem die beiden Choleraepidemien von 1886 und insbesondere von 1892, die die Gemeinde dazu brachten, von ihrer Haltung abzugehen. Man bekannte sich von nun an zumindest zum Notwohnungsbau in Eigenregie und sogar zu dem Vorhaben, notfalls selbst ‚Musterhäuser' für den Arbeiterwohnbau zu errichten.[66] Die ersten Notstandswohnungen, die in den Jahren 1886 und 1892 erbaut wurden, waren einfache ebenerdige Holzbaracken, die teils aus Familienzimmern (Wohnküchen), teils aus großen gemeinsamen Schlafsälen bestanden. 1893 konnten in den vorhandenen Notstandsbaracken rund 1.500 Personen untergebracht werden.[67] Ein Bruch mit den herkömmlichen Formen kommunaler Wohnungspolitik zeichnete sich, wie noch gezeigt werden soll, erst ab dem Jahre 1906 ab.

Wohnungsverhältnisse der Unterschichten

Ein Blick auf die Wohnverhältnisse der unteren bzw. der Arbeiterschichten in Budapest zeigt, dass hier – ähnlich wie im österreichischen Teil der Monarchie und hier vor allem in Wien – Wohnungsmangel bzw. Wohnungsüberbelegung sowie der Mangel an gesundheitlich einwandfreien und billigen Kleinwohnungen das Hauptproblem darstellten. Noch im Jahr 1911 betrug der Anteil der bloß aus einem Zimmer bestehenden Wohnungen in Budapest mehr als die Hälfte (54,4 %), der Anteil der Zweizimmerwohnungen belief sich auf rund ein Viertel (24,4 %). Das heißt, dass diese beiden Gruppen

---

[65] Ebenda, S. 138.
[66] Ebenda, S. 139.
[67] Albert Werkner, "Der Kleinwohnungsbau in Budapest," (Diss. phil., Universität Leipzig, Weida i. Thür 1913), S. 71, 94.

zusammen nahezu vier Fünftel sämtlicher Wohnungen ausmachten. In diesen kleinsten Wohnungen lebten 76 % der Budapester Bevölkerung (50,2 % in Einzimmerwohnungen, 25,8 % in Zweizimmer-wohnungen).[68] Mehr als ein Drittel der Budapester Bevölkerung lebte 1911 in überfüllten Wohnungen, ein weiteres Drittel in sehr gedrängten Wohnverhältnissen und nur weniger als ein Drittel lebte unter günstigen Verhältnissen (d. h. zwei Bewohner pro Zimmer).[69]

Wie in Wien zeigte sich auch in Budapest die bekannte Tatsache, dass die Mietpreise eines Wohnraumes in den allerkleinsten Wohnungen höher waren als in den mittelgroßen und daher die kapitalschwächeren Mieter relativ höhere Mieten zu entrichten hatten. Die Tatsache, dass je geringer das Einkommen, desto größer der Teil war, der davon für die Wohnbedürfnisse verwendet werden musste, bestätigte auch eine von der Budapester Allgemeinen Bezirks-Arbeiter-Krankenkasse in den Jahren 1905/1906 durchgeführte Wohnungsenquete. Anlässlich dieser Enquete wurden die Wohnungen von 1.604 kranken Arbeitern untersucht und dabei ernüchternde Tatsachen vorgefunden. In nahezu der Hälfte der Zimmer entfielen auf einen Bewohner weniger als 10 m^3 Luftraum, auf 6.970 Personen entfielen bloß 3.734 Betten. Hinsichtlich der Mietpreise stellten sich die Kellerwohnungen als die teuersten dar.[70]

Arbeiterinnen (Fabrikarbeiterinnen, Näherinnen), deren durchschnittliches jährliches Einkommen 450 bis 650 Kronen betrug, mussten als Hauptmieterinnen für ihre Wohnung 27,5 bis 38,4 % davon entrichten. Die am niedrigsten entlohnten männlichen Arbeiter (Taglöhner, Mühlenarbeiter, Schuster) verwendeten hierfür als Hauptmieter 26 % ihres Einkommens. Als Zimmermieter hatten die Arbeiter 20,4 %, als Bettgeher 13,9 % ihres Einkommens für das Wohnen aufzuwenden.

Auch hier bestätigte sich der bekannte Teufelskreis: Ohne Untermieter und Bettgeher waren die Arbeiter nicht in der Lage, ihre wöchentlichen Mieten zu bezahlen. Gleichzeitig führte die Aufnahme von Untermietern und Bettgehern in die kleinen Wohnungen zu einer zusätzlichen Überbelegung. Im Jahre 1906 hatten in Budapest 36,8 % der Arbeiterwohnungen Untermieter und Bettgeher. Die Hälfte der Haushalte

---

[68] Ebenda, S. 15 ff.
[69] Ebenda, S. 22 f. Die Kriterien für die Feststellung der Überfüllung variierten jedoch bei den einzelnen Zählungen. So wurden etwa im Jahre 1870 nur jene Wohnungen als überfüllt angesehen, bei welchen auf ein Zimmer durchschnittlich mehr als fünf Personen entfielen, ab 1881 galten jene als überfüllt, in welchen vier und mehr Bewohner auf einen Wohnraum (Zimmer, Küche, Kammer, Vorzimmer) entfielen.
[70] Ebenda, S. 28.

(51,9 %) mit Untermietern und Bettgehern waren Einzimmerwohnungen.[71] Gábor Gyáni gelangte aufgrund seiner Untersuchung der Wohnungsverhältnisse der Budapester Arbeiter zu folgender Einschätzung: „In one way or another, every member of the working class was permanently or temporarily part of the system of lodging and bed-tenancy. The newly arrived workers lodged or rented a bed until they established a family and their livelihood. After a certain amount of time, they became tenants and from that point they shared their own homes with strangers. "[72]

Es war vor allem das Bettgeherwesen, das – wie bereits erwähnt – seitens der bürgerlichen Wohnreformer als vermeintliche Ursache des sittlichen Verfalls betrachtet wurde, da es, wie man behauptete, das Familienleben zersetze. Johann Böhm, der spätere Vorsitzende des Österreichischen Gewerkschaftsbundes, erinnert sich daran, dass um 1900 in Wien die meisten Arbeiter und kleinen Angestellten, die mit ihren Familien eine aus Zimmer und Küche bestehende Wohnung innehatten, Untermieter aufnehmen mussten, da der Arbeitsverdienst nicht ausreichte, um den Zins zu bezahlen:

„Eine aus Zimmer und Gangküche bestehende Wohnung kostete in der Regel 12 bis 15 Gulden pro Monat, eine solche aus Zimmer, Kabinett und Küche 14 bis 18 Gulden, vereinzelt wohl auch 20 Gulden pro Monat. Bei einem Durchschnittseinkommen von 10 bis 12 Gulden pro Woche betrug der Monatszins also mehr als einen Wochenlohn. Um ihn aufbringen zu können, mußten Untermieter und Bettgeher mithelfen. Es war keine Seltenheit, daß Familien von fünf oder mehr Personen in einem einzigen Zimmer schliefen und in der Gangküche auf einem Notbett, das tagsüber weggeräumt werden mußte, noch ein oder zwei Bettgeher. An den Haustoren aller Häuser waren Zettel angeschlagen, auf denen angekündigt war, daß Schlafstellen zu vermieten seien. […] Nicht nur das Heer der Wanderarbeiter, sondern auch viele ständig in Wien ansässige Menschen haben sich zeit ihres Lebens als Bettgeher durch das Leben gerettet."[73]

Ein Bettgeher brachte ungefähr ein Viertel der Miete für eine Zimmer-Küche-Wohnung ein. Es waren daher auch vorwiegend die ärmeren Schichten der Bevölkerung, welche Mitbewohner aufnahmen. Von den 119 Wiener Arbeiterfamilien, die sich in den Jahren 1912 bis 1914 zur Führung von Haushaltsbüchern bereit erklärt hatten, beherbergte rund ein Drittel Untermieter oder Bettgeher, und zwar meist mehr als einen. Dabei

---

[71] Gábor Gyáni, *Parlor and Kitchen. Housing and Domestic Culture in Budapest 1870–1940* (Budapest: Central European Univ. Press), 2002, S. 151.
[72] Ebenda, S. 152.
[73] Johann Böhm, *Erinnerungen aus meinem Leben* (Wien: Verl. d. Österreich. Gewerkschaftsbundes, 1953), S. 66.

geht aus den Unterlagen deutlich hervor, dass es in erster Linie finanzielle Gründe waren, die zur Aufnahme von Mitbewohnern motivierten.[74]

Dass es offensichtlich nicht schwer war, als Bettgeher eine Schlafstelle zu finden, zeigt der Hinweis Böhms, dass an den Toren aller Wohnhäuser Zettel angeschlagen waren, auf denen angekündigt war, dass Schlafstellen zu vermieten seien.[75] Der Umfang des zur Verfügung stehenden Raumes spielte dabei keine Rolle. „Gerade in den kleinen, für Wien typischen Zimmer-Küche-Wohnungen waren häufig Bettgeher anzutreffen."[76] Dass die Mieter dieser Schlafstellen keinerlei Komfort erwarten durften, geht aus einer Beschreibung Adelheid Popps, einer der Gründerinnen der sozialdemokratischen Frauenbewegung in Wien, hervor. Popp berichtet aus eigener Erfahrung über die Aufnahme eines Bettgehers in das Kabinett, das sie mit ihrer Mutter gemietet hatte: „Auch mein jüngerer Bruder kam wieder zu uns und brachte einen Kollegen mit, mit dem er sein Bett teilte. So waren wir vier Personen in einem kleinen Raum, der nicht einmal ein Fenster hatte, sondern das Licht nur durch die Fensterscheiben erhielt, die sich in der Tür befanden." In einem Bett schliefen Adelheid Popp und ihre Mutter, und in dem zweiten, „dessen Fußende an unser Kopfteil stieß", Bruder und Bettgeher.[77]

Während die so genannten Aftermieter einen in sich abgeschlossenen Teil der Wohnung oder zumindest einen bestimmten Wohnungsbestandteil in Aftermiete nahmen, waren die Bettgeher solche Personen, die keine eigene Räumlichkeit, sondern nur eine Schlafstelle mieteten. Das bedeutet, dass diejenigen, die Aftermieter aufnahmen, nicht zwangsläufig zu den schlecht Situierten gehören mussten, sich sogar aus wirtschaftlich Vermögenden rekrutieren konnten, während die so genannten Bettgeher eindeutig zu den Ärmsten der Bevölkerung zählten.

In Wien wies ein Viertel aller Haushaltungen so genannte Aftermieter oder Bettgeher auf, und nicht weniger als 12,5 % der Wiener Bevölkerung lebten 1900 in fremden Haushalten. Dazu kam ein ständiger Wohnungswechsel. Fast ein Viertel aller Wohnungen Wiens wurde jährlich gerichtlich gekündigt, davon die überwiegende Zahl auf 14 Tage oder noch kürzere Frist.[78] Mehr als ein Drittel der Wiener Wohnungen bestanden, abgesehen von der Küche, nur aus einem Raum. In solchen

---

[74] Josef Ehmer und Peter Feldbauer, "Arbeiterwohnen im 19. Jahrhundert," *Beiträge zur historischen Sozialkunde* 9/3 (Juli–September 1979): S. 57–62, hier S. 59.

[75] Böhm, *Erinnerungen*, S. 61.

[76] Ehmer und Feldbauer, "Arbeiterwohnen," S. 59.

[77] Adelheid Popp, *Jugend einer Arbeiterin* (Berlin et al.: Dietz, 1977), S. 36.

[78] Vgl. dazu Rauchberg, *Die Kaiser Franz Josef I. – Jubiläums-Stiftung*, S. 5 f.

Kleinstwohnungen lebten 43 % der Bevölkerung. Von diesen Wohnungen waren 17 % überbelegt, da sie von sechs und mehr Personen bewohnt wurden.

Im Vergleich Wien – Budapest lässt sich feststellen, dass sich die Wiener Situation hinsichtlich des Wohnungsbelags günstiger darstellte. So entfielen im Jahre 1880 in Wien auf 3,5 % aller Wohnungen vier oder mehr Personen pro Bestandteil (Zimmer), in Budapest traf dieses Kriterium im Jahre 1881 auf 6,6 % zu. Dieser Unterschied wurde bis zu Beginn des zwanzigsten Jahrhunderts nicht aufgehoben. 1910 wohnten in 29 % der Wiener Zimmer-Küche-Wohnungen mehr als vier Personen; in Budapest traf dies 1911 auf 41,3 % der Zimmer-Küche-Haushaltungen zu.[79] Für die Unterschichten Wiens war vor allem die Senkung des Wohnungsbelags in den Wohnungen mit nur einem Bestandteil von Bedeutung. Dennoch waren für die Masse der Kleinwohnungsbenützer weder ein eigener Abort, Gas und elektrisches Licht noch eine Badegelegenheit Realität. 1910 lebten noch rund 28.000 Menschen in Wien in circa 7.000 Kellerwohnungen – mehr als zur Mitte des 19. Jahrhunderts.[80]

Im Jahre 1894 hatte Eugen von Philippovich in Wien eine private Wohnungserhebung durchgeführt, die sich auf 48 einräumige, 49 zweiräumige (Zimmer oder Kammer und Küche) sowie vier dreiräumige (Zimmer, Kammer, Küche) Wohnungen erstreckte.[81] Von all diesen Wohnungen hatten nur drei (darunter zwei dreiräumige) den Minimalluftraum und eine genügende Bodenfläche. Das Luft- und Raumdefizit betrug im Durchschnitt aller Wohnungen 28,8 % des Minimalraumes und 36 % der Minimalbodenfläche, war aber in vielen Fällen noch größer. In 19 der untersuchten 48 einräumigen Wohnungen stand den Bewohnern nicht einmal die Hälfte des als Existenzminimum notwendigen Luftraumes zur Verfügung, in einigen nicht einmal ein Drittel.[82]

Das österreichische Arbeiterwohnungsgesetz (1892) stellte bestimmte Minimalanforderungen an die Arbeiterwohnungen, für deren Bau die

---

[79] Michael John, *Wohnverhältnisse sozialer Unterschichten im Wien Kaiser Franz Josephs* (Wien: Europaverlag, 1984), S. 143 f.

[80] Ebenda, S. 152.

[81] Zum Folgenden Philippovich, *Wiener Wohnungsverhältnisse,* S. 16 ff.

[82] Der Oberste Sanitätsrat und die Gesellschaft der Ärzte hatten unter anderem folgende Mindestanforderungen erarbeitet: Jede Wohnung musste mit einer Küche versehen sein. Bei Bemessung der Größe der Wohnräume sollte für jede über ein Jahr alte Person ein Luftraum von mindestens zehn Kubikmetern und eine Grundfläche von mindestens vier Quadratmetern veranschlagt werden.

vorgesehene Steuerbefreiung in Anspruch genommen werden konnte. Paragraph 4 des Gesetzes bestimmte: „Der bewohnbare Raum einer einzelnen Wohnung darf, wenn dieselbe nur ein einziges Gelass enthält, nicht weniger als 15 und nicht mehr als 30 m², bei Wohnungen, welche aus mehreren Räumen bestehen, nicht weniger als 40 und nicht mehr als 75 m² betragen." Der Mietzins für einen Quadratmeter Wohnraum durfte in Wien höchstens 1 fl. 75 kr. ö.W., in Orten mit mehr als 10.000 Einwohnern 1 fl. 15 kr., in allen anderen Orten 80 kr. betragen. Hinsichtlich der vom Gesetz geforderten Bodenfläche blieben 33 der 48 von Philippovich erhobenen einräumigen Wohnungen unter den Anforderungen, wobei der Gesetzgeber mit Sicherheit nicht davon ausgegangen war, dass diese von drei bis sechs Personen bewohnt sein sollten. Bei den zweiräumigen Wohnungen wurden die Minimalforderungen in 47 von 49 Fällen nicht erfüllt.

Philippovichs Wohnungsbeschreibungen zeigen die „Kümmerlichkeit menschlichen Lebens", so etwa in einem zweistöckigen Haus auf der Meidlinger Hauptstraße, in welchem er die Kellerwohnungen besichtigte:

„Eine Durchfahrt führt [...] in einen zweiten Hof. Von ihr aus führt rechts eine Stiege in den Keller, nach zwei Wendungen sind wir unten. Rechts und links gehen schmale, etwa 75 Centimeter breite Gänge, die den Zutritt zu den Kellerwohnungen vermitteln. Das Licht fällt in diesen Gang durch hoch angebrachte, in den zweiten Hof führende Fenster. [...] Wir treten durch eine Thür in einen stark verdunkelten Raum von 4:3,5 Meter Grundfläche. Rechts in der Ecke, in der Höhe von über 2 Metern vom Boden befindet sich ein Fenster, das eindringender Kälte wegen zur Hälfte verdeckt ist, so dass etwa ein halber Quadratmeter Fensterfläche Licht spendet. [...] Die schief einfallenden Lichtstrahlen fallen auf ein altes Sopha, auf dem sich einige nackte Kinder herumtrieben. Im Halbdunkel ist eine Frau beschäftigt an einem Tische Wäsche zu bügeln, der Raum selbst hängt voll davon und nimmt von dem bischen Licht noch weg. Der zweite, durch diese in ein Wohnzimmer verwandelte Küche zugängliche Raum geht nach der anderen Hofseite. Er ist durch zwei Fenster gleicher Konstruktion, wie die geschilderte, stärker belichtet, größer und geräumiger, aber kahl und öde. Über das notwendigste Bettzeug, einen Tisch, einen Kasten geht die Einrichtung nicht. Hier wohnt die Hauptpartei, die Küchenbewohner sind Aftermieter. Dort sind es 6, hier 5 Personen, zwei Elternpaare und 7 Kinder, deren Heim unter der Erde liegt. So reiht sich in diesem Keller noch Raum an Raum, etwa 10 Wohnungen mit 29 Erwachsenen und 34 Kindern umfassend."[83]

---

[83] Philippovich, *Wiener Wohnungsverhältnisse*, S. 19 f.

Hinzu kamen noch „entsetzliche Abtrittsverhältnisse". Für die Kellerwohnungen mit ihrer Bewohnerschaft war kein eigener „Abort" vorhanden. Die Leute mussten über die Stiege in den zweiten Hof gehen und die Toiletten benützen, die dort für die Bewohner des Erdgeschosses des Hinterhauses errichtet worden waren. Es waren insgesamt drei, die auf 100 bis 120 Personen entfielen. Sie waren „dunkel und in so entsetzlichem Zustande, dass der Unrat unter den Thüren herausläuft".[84]

Ähnliche Verhältnisse fanden sich auch in vielen anderen der von Philippovich aufgesuchten Häuser. Philippovich weist darauf hin, dass es sich hierbei nicht um eigentliche Armen-, sondern um Arbeiterwohnungen handelte. Sie alle waren gekennzeichnet durch die nur notdürftigste Einrichtung:

„Von der Fülle der Produktion auf allen Gebieten des Hausrats dringt nichts in diese Schichten der Bevölkerung. Sie haben nur im Gebrauch, was zum Leben unentbehrlich ist, und das nicht immer in ausreichendem Maße. Keine Spur eines Schmuckes, einer Zierde, eines Gegenstandes, der nur der Freude und dem Behagen dienen soll. Die Wohnung ist nur die Schutzdecke vor den Unbilden der Witterung, ein Nachtlager, das bei der Enge, in der sich die Menschen drängen, bei dem Mangel an Ruhe, an Luft, an Reinlichkeit nur dem erschöpftesten Körper zur Ruhestätte werden kann. [...] Es fehlt alles, was wir als Grundlage gesunden bürgerlichen Lebens anzusehen gewohnt sind: die selbständige Existenz der Familie, die besondere Fürsorge für die Grundbedürfnisse des täglichen Lebens, für die Erkrankten und Pflegebedürftigen, die Wahrung der Schamhaftigkeit durch Trennung der Geschlechter, Verhüllung des Geschlechtslebens der Eltern vor den Kindern, die erzieherische Fürsorge der Eltern für die Kinder in Stunden der Ruhe und Erholung. Diese Wohnungen bieten keine Behaglichkeit und keine Erquickung. Wer in sie hinabgesunken oder hineingeboren wurde, muss körperlich und geistig verkümmern und verwelken oder verwildern."[85]

Ähnliche Zustände, die Gustav Schmoller für die deutschen Städte beschrieben hatte, führten schließlich zu dessen „Mahnruf". Darin wies Schmoller auf die Folgen dieser Wohnzustände hin, die die unteren Schichten des großstädtischen Fabrikproletariats notgedrungen auf ein Niveau der „Barbarei und Bestialität, der Rohheit und des Rowdytums" zurücksinken lassen würden. Von solchen Zuständen drohe die größte Gefahr für die Kultur. Die Lehren der Sozialdemokratie und des

---

[84] Ebenda, S. 20.
[85] Ebenda, S. 26.

Anarchismus würden erst gefährlich, wenn sie auf einen Boden fielen, der
so „entmenschlicht und entsetzlich" sei.[86]

Auch wenn der Einwand, dass es sich, unter sozialen Aspekten
betrachtet, bei der Erhebung von Philippovich um eine „Ansammlung von
Deklassierten"[87] (verelendetes Handwerk, von trunksüchtigen Männern
verlassene Frauen und Kinder, Bettgeher, Witwen, Taglöhner, Heimarbeiter,
Arbeitsunfähige, Kranke und Alte) handelte und sich darin keine einzige
industrielle Facharbeiter-Familie fand, nicht ganz von der Hand zu weisen
ist, so zeigen doch auch viele andere Berichte, dass „die Existenz und auch
quantitative Bedeutung des Elends" nicht bestreitbar ist. Hösl und Pirhofer
haben in ihrer Analyse die Vermutung ausgesprochen, dass die
Darstellung dieser „schaurigen Bilder", eingebettet in Statistik, Emotionen
mobilisieren sollte und die Strategie verfolgte, die industriellen
Facharbeiter-Wohnverhältnisse systematisch zu verbessern. Gleichzeitig
hätte sie jedoch „fatale" Konsequenzen für das Bild gehabt, das von den
Arbeiterpopulationen der Spätgründerzeit geprägt worden sei. So fänden
sich hier Formulierungen wie: „verkümmerte und verwilderte oder
verwelkte"; „nicht wie Menschen wohnten, sondern wie Ungeziefer
nisteten sie"; „die Kellermenschen ans Licht zu bringen" und
dergleichen.[88] Für Deutschland weisen Hartmut Häußermann und Walter
Siebel demgegenüber darauf hin, dass die neuesten sozialhistorischen
Arbeiten „insgesamt auf eine Revision der Verelendungsthesen hinauslaufen
und aufzeigen, dass die Verbesserungen der Wohnungsversorgung schon
in der Zeit vor dem Ersten Weltkrieg bis zu den extrem unterversorgten
städtischen Schichten durchgesickert" seien.[89]

Ein ähnlicher Aspekt, den Gyáni in Bezug auf Budapest hervorhebt,
bezieht sich auf die kulturelle Assimilation der unteren Schichten der
Arbeiterklasse an jene der Industriearbeiter, die schon früher einen
höheren Status erreichten. Er konstatiert zwischen den einzelnen Schichten
der Arbeiterklasse eine Kluft, die sich auch in den Wohnverhältnissen
zeigte und je nach Besitz, Einkommen und Arbeitsplatz variierte. Diese
Differenzierung fehlte häufig in der öffentlichen Wahrnehmung:

---

[86] Gustav Schmoller, "Ein Mahnruf in der Wohnungsfrage (1887)," in Gustav
Schmoller, *Zur Social- und Gewerbepolitik der Gegenwart. Reden und Aufsätze*
(Leipzig: Duncker & Humblot, 1890), S. 342–371, hier S. 348.
[87] Vgl. dazu Hösl und Pirhofer, *Wohnen in Wien*, S. 60 f.
[88] Ebenda, S. 61.
[89] Vgl. Hartmut Häußermann und Walter Siebel, *Soziologie des Wohnens. Eine
Einführung in Wandel und Ausdifferenzierung des Wohnens* (München et al.:
Juventa-Verl., 2000²).

"Middle-class professionals and the general public held a number of popular beliefs about the workers, beliefs formed from a certain social distance. They believed that the working class, with their difficult financial situation, overcrowded flats, and over-sociable private lives, were a hotbed of deviance and emotional and intellectual emptiness. They felt that the conditions of working-class life resulted in barbarism and uncivilised behaviour. This is a simplistic picture of the lower social classes, but one which remains popular. "[90]

Daher war man auch überrascht, wenn man bei der Besichtigung der Wohnungen Spuren von Komfort und Charme vorfand, wie z. B. in den Wohnungen der Arbeiter der Schiffswerft in Óbuda. In den meisten Wohnungen herrschten mustergültige Ordnung und Sauberkeit. Die Möbel der Arbeiterwohnungen waren ärmlich, aber ordentlich. Es waren einige Blumentöpfe in den Fenstern und an manchen Orten machten „blendend weiße Spitzenvorhänge" die Arbeiterwohnung gemütlich.[91] Die Fokussierung auf die (sub)proletarischen „Elendsränder", die häufig plakative Bilder vermittelten, umfassten eben nicht die ganze Bandbreite der Lebens- und Wohnbedingungen, worauf auch schon Pirhofer und Hösl[92] hingewiesen haben. Dadurch wird vielfach der Blick darauf verstellt, dass es sich auch bei der Arbeiterschaft nicht um eine sozial homogene Klasse handelte, sondern es je nach der Zugehörigkeit zu verschiedenen Branchen und auch innerhalb dieser je nach Verwendung eine Reihe von Abstufungen gab. So stellte etwa Hedwig Lemberger anlässlich ihrer Erhebung der Lebenshaltung der Verlags- und Fabrikarbeiterschaft fest:

„Zwischen der Schicht jener Arbeiterfamilien, die in geordneten Verhältnissen leben, d. h. ohne Schulden durchkommen, den Mietzins pünktlich bezahlen und auch eine nette Stube haben, der Bettdecken und eine Tischdecke ein ganz wohnliches Aussehen verleihen, bis hinab zu jenen Kreisen, deren Habseligkeiten ins Versatzamt wandern müssen und die wegen rückständiger Zinszahlung einem ständigen Logiswechsel unterworfen sind, wobei ihnen ein Handwägelchen zum Aufladen ihres dürftigen Hausrates genügt, findet sich ebenso gut eine ganze Reihe von Abstufungen, wie sie sich zwischen jenen bürgerlichen Kreisen ergeben, die wir zu den ‚oberen Zehntausend' zu rechnen pflegen, und dem kleinen Beamtentum, dessen Haushaltsführung weit kärglicher ist, als die des wohlhabenden Kleinbürgertums. Allerdings lösen die in ihrer großen Mehrheit bedrückend traurigen Lebensverhältnisse trotz ihrer mehrfachen

[90] Gyáni, *Parlor and Kitchen*, S. 175.
[91] Ebenda, S. 176.
[92] Hösl und Pirhofer, *Wohnen in Wien*, S. 60 f.

Abstufungen von Dürftigkeit und Elend zunächst den Eindruck
scheinbarer Gleichförmigkeit in uns aus."[93]

Das immer wiederkehrende Thema im Reformdiskurs, der Hinweis auf
die „unsittlichen Zustände" in den Arbeiterwohnungen, die „Nähe der
Geschlechter", das „unverhüllte Geschlechtsleben", die „Vermischung
familienfremder Leiber" etc., die den Verhältnissen in den Zinskasernen
zugeordnet wurden – all dies war nach Ansicht von Hösl und Piringer in
der Spätgründerzeit bereits eine extreme Ausnahme: So zeigten Interviews
im Rahmen von „oral history" und dokumentierte Fotos von Innenräumen
und Bewohnern für die durchschnittlichen Verhältnisse eher das Bild einer
ziemlich strikten hygienisch-sexuellen Ordnung.[94]

Die Beschwörung der „Geschlossenheit und Reinheit des Familienlebens",
die es zu bewahren bzw. wiederherzustellen gelte, sowie die – unter
anderem – von Philippovich und Rauchberg formulierte Sorge, dass diese
Zustände zu einem sozialistischen Familienideal hinleiten könnten, waren,
wie sich zeigen sollte, unbegründet. Wie Pirhofer nachweist, gelang es der
sozialistischen Arbeiterbewegung nicht, die agrarischen Traditionen
sinnlich-solidarischer Lebensweisen im neuen städtischen Kontext zu
einem eigenen autonomen „Familienideal" zu entwickeln, für das man
Wohnsysteme hätte fordern können – auch wenn von Seiten der
konservativen Sozialreformer auf die Gegnerschaft der „radicalen
Arbeiterbewegung" hingewiesen wurde.[95] Zwar habe man das „Recht auf
Wohnung" im Wahlprogramm gefordert. Wie die Wohn- und Lebensform
hingegen aussehen sollte, war „durch die kulturpolitische Entscheidung
(bzw. das Fehlen einer dezidierten Gegenentscheidung)" „weitgehend
präjudiziert" und bildete keinen Punkt der Auseinandersetzung.[96]
Vielmehr habe das kleinbürgerliche Wohn- und Lebensmodell das
fehlende „sozialistische Familienideal" ersetzt. An anderer Stelle schreibt
Pirhofer im Zusammenhang mit der Wohnbaupolitik der
sozialdemokratischen Arbeiterbewegung in der Ersten Republik: „So ist,
was häufig als Symbol eines kulturell, womöglich politisch autonomen

---

[93] Hedwig Lemberger, *Die Wiener Wäsche-Industrie* (Wien: Deuticke, 1907), S.
219 f.
[94] Hösl und Pirhofer, *Wohnen in Wien*, S. 70.
[95] So z. B. von Max Steiner, dem Gründer des 1886 errichteten „Vereins für
Arbeiterhäuser," der sich zum Ziel setzte, das Einfamilienhaus als Wohnform für
die Arbeiterklasse einzuführen. Vgl. Steiner, *Der „Verein für Arbeiterhäuser"*;
vgl. auch Renate Schweitzer, "Der staatlich geförderte, der kommunale und der
gemeinnützige Wohnungs- und Siedlungsbau in Österreich bis 1945 I.," (Diss.,
Technische UniversitätWien, 1972), S. 396–402.
[96] Pirhofer, "Linien," S. 20.

‚Lagers' gilt, bereits durchdrungen von den ordnungspolitischen Konzepten der konservativen bürgerlichen Sozialreformer des 19. Jahrhunderts, deren Beharren auf die je abgeschlossene Einzelwohnung sich in der Auseinandersetzung um die Entwicklung des Arbeiterwohnungsbaues gegen die philantropisch-antikapitalistischen Sozialutopisten und deren Modelle von Gemeinschaftshäusern ideologisch durchgesetzt hatte."[97]

Die Sozialdemokratin Therese Schlesinger formulierte bereits 1912 die neuen Aufgaben der Arbeitergenossenschaften und forderte die Arbeiterschaft auf, endlich „an die Erfüllung einer Kulturmission" zu schreiten. In einem Artikel in der sozialdemokratischen Zeitschrift *Der Kampf* trat sie vor allem gegen die „herrschende, unrationelle und kulturwidrige Form der proletarischen Hauswirtschaft" auf.[98] Schlesinger trat demnach für eine zeitgemäße Umgestaltung derselben ein. Die Überfüllung der Proletarierwohnungen, deren häufigster Typus die Zimmer-Küche-Wohnung sei, wäre selbst dann noch gesundheitsgefährdend, wenn diese nur zum Wohnen und Schlafen benützt würden; dass sie aber zugleich als Werkstätten für alle hauswirtschaftlichen Arbeiten dienen müssten, mache sie in noch höherem Maße sanitätswidrig. Die organisierte Arbeiterschaft habe es verabsäumt, dem häuslichen Jammer des Proletariats auf den Leib zu rücken. Wenn sie nun daran gehe, Wohnhäuser zu erbauen, so dränge sich die Frage auf:

„Sollen wirklich in diesen Häusern dem alten häuslichen Jammer der besitzlosen Klassen neue Heimstätten errichtet werden? Soll dort die gleiche Vergeudung von Kraft und Material vor sich gehen wie in den traurigen Wohnhöhlen, die das private Kapital den Arbeiterfamilien bietet? Sollen auch dort in zwanzig engen Küchen auf zwanzig kleinen Herden zwanzig dünne Suppen brodeln, darüber auf zwanzig Wäscheleinen flüchtig gereinigte Windeln, Kinderhemden und Abwischtücher trocknen und die Zeit und Kraft von zwanzig abgeplagten Weibern schmählich missbraucht werden?"[99]

Schlesinger forderte daher das Gemeinschaftshaus und die „Zentralhauswirtschaft", somit eine rationalere Organisation des Wohnens, die „mit der die Frauen zermalmenden Barbarei des Zwerghaushaltes" aufräumen sollte.[100]

---

[97] Ebenda, S. 3.
[98] Therese Schlesinger, "Eine Aufgabe der Arbeiter-Baugenossenschaften," *Der Kampf. Sozialdemokratische Monatsschrift* 6 (Oktober 1912 bis September 1913): S. 131–135, hier S. 133.
[99] Ebenda, S. 133.
[100] Therese Schlesinger, "Krieg und Einzelhaushalt," *Der Kampf.*

Die Sozialdemokraten hatten erst im Kommunalprogramm aus dem Jahre 1896, als sie bei den Gemeinderatswahlen kandidierten, programmatische Forderungen zur Wohnungsfrage formuliert. „Bis dahin wurde Kommunalpolitik als ‚Krähwinkelpolitik' abgelehnt."[101] Das in der *Arbeiter-Zeitung* veröffentlichte kommunale Programm forderte unter Punkt 7 (Wohnungspolizei) eine fünfjährlich zu erhebende Wohnungsstatistik über den Zustand der Wohnungen, die Art des Zusammenwohnens und die Mietpreise, weiters die Förderung des Baus von gesunden Wohnhäusern sowie die Verhinderung der Vermietung sanitätswidriger Wohnungen und eine regelmäßige Wohnungsinspektion. Außerdem sollte die Kommune ihr Grundeigentum „durch Erwerbung unverbauter Grundstücke in großem Maßstabe" vermehren und darauf systematisch Häuser mit billigen Wohnungen errichten.[102]

Dieses Minimalprogramm blieb im Wesentlichen bis zum Parteitag 1907 unverändert. Auf diesem legte der Wiener Gemeinderat Leopold Winarsky erstmals eine „marxistische Analyse" und einen etwas ausgebauten Forderungskatalog vor. 1911 präzisierte Winarsky dann seine Vorschläge in der Broschüre *Wohnungsteuerung und Wohnungselend*.[103] Für die Sozialdemokratie stellte sich demnach die Wohnungsfrage „nur als ein Teil der sozialen Frage" dar: „Sie weiß, daß ihre endgültige Lösung nur möglich sein wird nach Ueberwindung der kapitalistischen Klassenherrschaft und Ueberführung des Grundes und des Bodens, ebenso wie der Wohnhäuser in den gemeinschaftlichen Besitz des arbeitenden Volkes." Ungeachtet dieser langfristigen Ziele sollte es aber auch möglich sein, schon „in der kapitalistischen Gesellschaft" Reformen durchzuführen, die der arbeitenden Bevölkerung eine menschenwürdige Wohnung verschaffen könnten.[104] Eine der Hauptforderungen Winarskys betraf die

---

Sozialdemokratische Monatsschrift 8 (Jänner 1915 bis Dezember 1915): S. 403–411, hier S. 408. Zum Konflikt um das Familien-Einküchenhaus, das die radikale Frauenbewegung um Auguste Fickert bereits 1905 auf das Programm setzte, vgl. Pirhofer, "Linien," S. 4 ff.

[101] Feldbauer et al., "Arbeiterwohnungsfrage," S. 391.

[102] *Arbeiter-Zeitung. Zentralorgan der österreichischen Sozialdemokratie* 8/32 (1896): S. 1.

[103] Leopold Winarsky, *Wohnungsteuerung und Wohnungselend* (Wien: Verl. der Wiener Volksbuchh., 1911).

[104] Ebenda, S. 23. Gefordert wurde z. B. die Erbauung von Häusern mit billigen Kleinwohnungen in eigener Regie durch die Gemeinden, die Beseitigung der Hauszinssteuer und ihren Erlass durch eine Wertzuwachssteuer und Bauplatzabgabe sowie die Erlassung eines Reichswohnungsgesetzes für die Schaffung von Bauordnungen, für die Wohnungsinspektion und die Ausdehnung des Enteignungsrechtes der Gemeinden.

„Brechung der Hausherrenherrschaft" in den Gemeindevertretungen durch Einführung des allgemeinen und gleichen Wahlrechtes für alle Gemeindewahlen.

Die sozialdemokratische „Realpolitik" blieb trotz aller Bemühungen weitgehend folgenlos, „abgesehen vom latenten Druck, den ihre Forderungen möglicherweise auf die christlich-soziale Mehrheit im Gemeinderat ausübte".[105]

Maßnahmen gegen die Wohnungsnot in Wien

Im Jahr 1896 wurde die „Kaiser Franz Josef I.-Jubiläumsstiftung für Volkswohnungen und Wohlfahrtseinrichtungen" gegründet.[106] Das Aktionsprogramm der Stiftung sah den Bau von Musterhäusern vor, an denen die Typen, Verwaltungsgrundsätze und Rentabilität erprobt werden sollten. Dabei entschied man bereits in der Vorbereitungsphase die alte Streitfrage, ob Cottage- oder große Miethäuser erbaut werden sollten, zugunsten von freistehenden oder reihenweise angeordneten Miethäusern, was Rauchberg wie folgt begründete: „Das Cottage-Familienhaus bleibt zwar das Ideal; aber nach einem bekannten Worte des Grafen Taaffe ist das Ideal das, was man eben nicht haben kann. Familienhäuser sind bei uns nicht einmal dem Mittelstande zugänglich. Wollte man Arbeiterhäuser nach diesem Principe erbauen, so wäre der finanzielle Misserfolg unvermeidlich."[107]

Die Höhe der Mietzinse sollte so berechnet sein, dass das Reinerträgnis einer billigen Verzinsung des in sämtlichen Anlagen der Stiftung investierten Kapitals entsprach, und man strebte eine vierprozentige Verzinsung der Gesamtinvestitionen an. Dies wurde als Merkmal der „Gemeinnützigkeit" ausgegeben. Die Stiftung wollte durch dieses Prinzip der Gemeinnützigkeit vorführen, „dass schon die gegenwärtige Wirthschaftsverfassung eine Lösung der Wohnungsfrage zulässt" und dass Wohltätigkeit hier nicht am Platze sei.[108] Dies entsprach ganz der „five per cent philanthropy", die Octavia Hill, die berühmte Vorkämpferin der Londoner Wohnungsbewegung, vertrat. Hill lehnte auf dem Gebiet der

---

[105] Feldbauer et al., "Arbeiterwohnungsfrage," S. 402.
[106] Vgl. zur Vorgeschichte der Gründung Rauchberg, *Die Kaiser Franz Josef I. – Jubiläums-Stiftung*, dort im Anhang der Stiftbrief, S. 35–44; weiters Hösl, "Die Anfänge," S. 65–94; *Erster Jahres-Bericht der Kaiser Franz Joseph I. Jubiläums-Stiftung für Volkswohnungen und Wohlfahrts-Einrichtungen für das Jahr 1896* (Wien: s. t., 1897).
[107] Rauchberg, *Die Kaiser Franz Josef I. – Jubiläums-Stiftung*, S. 19 f.
[108] Ebenda, S. 23.

Wohnungsbewegung jegliche Form der Wohltätigkeit ab „and from beginning to end she argued that for reform to be effective it had to be conducted along profitable lines. Otherwise the independence of the working classes would be sapped […]. Her ideal, which so captured the imagination of her generation, was a combination of 'philanthropic instinct' and 'business aptitude.'"[109]

Die Jubiläums-Stiftung stellte „das erste, auch von höchsten Gesellschaftskreisen zur Kenntnis genommene und finanziell geförderte Projekt" zu Linderung der Wohnungsnot in Wien dar.[110] Unter den Gründern waren prominente Ökonomen, Architekten und Mittelstandspolitiker. Die sozialpolitischen Absichten liefen auf eine „Hilfe zur Selbsthilfe" hinaus, wobei die Stoßrichtung vor allem gegen „anarchistische Selbsthilfebewegungen" und gegen den sozialdemokratischen Kampf um die Macht im Staate als „radikale Variante der Selbsthilfe"[111] gerichtet war.

Der Kreis der Personen, für welche die Stiftungshäuser bestimmt sein sollten, umfasste laut Stiftbrief Lohnarbeiter, gewerbliche oder Handlungsgehilfen und sonstige Personen mit kärglichem Einkommen.[112] Für diese waren auch Wohlfahrtseinrichtungen geplant, die zu einer Hebung der gesamten Lebenshaltung beitragen sollten, wie etwa: Badeanstalten, Kinderbewahranstalten und Kindergärten, Plätze für Jugendspiele und körperliche Übungen, Krankenzimmer, Konsumgenossenschaften, Lehr- und Vortragszimmer, die Aufstellung von Volksbibliotheken etc. Finanziert wurde das Projekt zum Teil aus dem Stadterweiterungsfonds, ein – wie Renate Banik-Schweitzer schreibt – „stark verspäteter Beitrag der Ringstraßenzeit zur Bekämpfung der wirklichen Wohnungsnot".[113]

Im Mai 1901 wurde die erste Wohnhausanlage, der „Stiftungshof", fertig gestellt. Gleichzeitig begann man mit dem Bau eines zweiten Hofes (Lobmeyrhof). Insgesamt wies die „Breitenseer-Kolonie", wie sie überall

---

[109] Zur Tätigkeit von Octavia Hill, die eine rigide Kontrolle über ihre Mieter ausübte, siehe Anthony S. Wohl, "Octavia Hill and the Homes of the London Poor," *Journal of British Studies* 10/2 (1971): S. 105–131, hier S. 127 f.

[110] Siehe dazu Feldbauer et al., "Arbeiterwohnungsfrage," S. 395.

[111] Ebenda, S. 395.

[112] § 2 des Stiftbriefes bei Rauchberg, *Die Kaiser Franz Josef I. – Jubiläums-Stiftung*, S. 38.

[113] Renate Banik-Schweitzer, "Die Kleinwohnungsfrage in Wien um die Jahrhundertwende," in *Die Kleinwohnungsfrage. Zu den Ursprüngen des sozialen Wohnungsbaus in Europa*, Hrsg. Juan Rodríguez-Lores und Gerhard Fehl (Hamburg: Christians, 1987), S. 431–450, hier S. 434.

genannt wurde, 482 Wohnungen auf.[114] Daneben gab es noch zwei Ledigenheime und zwei Männerheime. Die Ledigenheime waren „eine zivilisatorische Verbesserung" gegenüber dem üblichen Untermieter- und Bettgeherleben und bedeuteten eine „Anhebung um eine oder mehrere Stufen in der sozialräumlichen Hierarchie".[115] Gleichzeitig gewährleisteten sie das oft geforderte „reine Familienleben", da in den Familienwohnungen ein Verbot der Untervermietung herrschte. Die Einzelzimmer waren sieben bis vierzehn Quadratmeter groß und zweckmäßig, aber ohne Luxus eingerichtet (Eisenbett, Kasten, Tisch mit zwei Sesseln, Spiegel, Waschtisch, Ausgusseimer, Wasserflasche etc.). Es gab ein eigenes Dienstpersonal, das die Zimmer sauber hielt; gegen einen kleinen Zuschlag wurde auch die private Wäsche gewaschen. Außerdem gab es Frühstücksküchen mit Kochherden sowie Gesellschaftsräume mit Speise-, Arbeits-, Spiel- und Schreibtischen.

Ganz allgemein unterschieden sich die Jubiläumshäuser in ihrer Grundrissgestaltung erheblich vom spekulativen Massenwohnbau: Die Gangküchenwohnung „existierte nicht mehr".[116] Die Wohnungen waren zwar nicht größer als früher, jedoch lagen nur mehr vier von ihnen an einem Stiegenhaus, die Küchen waren also direkt zu belüften und zu belichten. Jede Wohnung verfügte über ein eigenes WC, allerdings lag es bei der Hälfte der Wohnungen immer noch im Stiegenhaus. Was die soziale Schichtung der Mieter anlangt, so wurde festgestellt, dass die „eigentliche Arbeiterschaft", also die Industriearbeiter und „Lohnarbeiter", die die Stiftung ansprechen wollte, sich die Wohnungen in den Stiftungshäusern nicht leisten konnte.[117]

Das staatliche Engagement beschränkte sich bis zur Jahrhundertwende auf Steuererleichterungen für den Wohnungsbau. Zwei Reichsgesetze sahen Steuererleichterungen für den Bau von Arbeiterwohnungen vor, doch beschränkten sie gleichzeitig die Renditen so stark, dass sich niemand zu einer nennenswerten Bautätigkeit bereitfand.[118] Mit dem Gesetz vom 9. Februar 1892[119] wurde in Österreich zwar ein erster Schritt sozialer Fürsorge auf dem Gebiet des Wohnungswesens unternommen,

---

[114] Hösl, "Die Anfänge," S. 82.
[115] Hösl und Pirhofer, *Wohnen in Wien*, S. 85 f.
[116] Banik-Schweitzer, "Die Kleinwohnungsfrage," S. 436.
[117] Dazu sowie zur Höhe der Mieten Hösl, "Die Anfänge," S. 84–88.
[118] Banik-Schweitzer, "Die Kleinwohnungsfrage," S. 440.
[119] Gesetz vom 9. Februar 1892, Reichsgesetzblatt (weiter RGBl.) 37/ 7. 2. 1892, betreffend Begünstigungen für Neubauten mit Arbeiterwohnungen. Die §§ 4 und 5 enthielten Bestimmungen über Wohnungsgröße sowie den jährlichen Mietzins pro m².

doch handelte es sich dabei lediglich um ein Steuerbegünstigungsgesetz, da es den Arbeiterwohnhäusern unter gewissen Voraussetzungen die vierundzwanzigjährige Befreiung von der Gebäudesteuer und von nahezu allen Umlagen einräumte. Seine Mängel waren jedoch derart, dass während der zehnjährigen Geltungsdauer des Gesetzes in kaum 400 Fällen davon Gebrauch gemacht wurde. Ein wesentlicher Mangel bestand darin, dass es nicht die in den Häusern wohnenden Arbeiter, sondern den Eigentümer, also den Vermieter, als den eigentlichen Träger der gewährten Begünstigung auffasste; außerdem wurden die Maximalzinse derart niedrig angesetzt, dass mit den diesen Mietzinsen entsprechenden Kapitalien Gebäude mit der geforderten sanitären Ausstattung nicht erbaut werden konnten. Hinzu kam, dass Gebäude, in denen die Wohnungen unentgeltlich überlassen wurden, vom Gesetz nicht erfasst wurden.[120] Mit diesem Gesetz verfolgte man die Absicht, der Spekulation durch Festlegung einer Mietzinsobergrenze bei geförderten Wohnungen einen Riegel vorzuschieben.[121] Der Misserfolg des Gesetzes führte schließlich zu einer Novelle und zum Gesetz vom 8. Juli 1902, in dem die Bestimmung über die Mietzinsobergrenze nicht mehr enthalten war.[122] Der Kern des Gesetzes von 1892 blieb jedoch erhalten. Steuererleichterung und Steuerbefreiung wurden noch immer als zentrales Mittel der Wohnbauförderung betrachtet und die 24-jährige Befreiung von der Hauszins- und Gebäudesteuer blieb bestehen.

Eine eigentliche Wohnungsfürsorge setzte in Österreich erst im Jahre 1907 mit der Gründung der „Zentralstelle für Wohnungsreform in Österreich" (ZWÖ) ein. Einer der Initiatoren der Zentralstelle war Heinrich Rauchberg, der anlässlich der konstituierenden Versammlung einen Vortrag hielt, in welchem er erklärte, dass die Wohnungsfrage nicht nur eine Frage der Arbeiterklasse und der Unbemittelten sei, sondern „eine ganz allgemeine Kulturangelegenheit".[123] Theodor Bach, einer der

---

[120] Franz von Meinzingen und Franz Pauer, *Die Wohnungsfürsorgegesetze nebst einschlägigen Verordnungen, Erlässen und Publikationen* (Wien: Manz, 1912), S. 1.

[121] Hermann Kepplinger, "Zur Finanzierungsgeschichte des Arbeiterwohnbaus in Österreich bis 1945 unter besonderer Berücksichtigung des Wohnbaus in Linz," in *Wohnen in Linz. Zur Geschichte des Linzer Arbeiterwohnbaues von den Anfängen bis 1945*, Hrsg. Brigitte Kepplinger (Wien et al.: Böhlau, 1989), S. 103–143, hier S. 106.

[122] Gesetz vom 8. Juli 1902, RGBl. 144/ 8. 7. 1902, betreffend Begünstigungen für Gebäude mit gesunden und billigen Arbeiterwohnungen.

[123] Heinrich Rauchberg, *Ziele und Wege der Wohnungsreform in Österreich. Erweiterte Fassung des Vortrages gehalten von Professor Dr. Heinrich Rauchberg anlässlich der konstituierenden Versammlung der Zentralstelle für*

Architekten der Jubiläumshäuser und Professor an der Technischen Hochschule Prag, fasste die stadtplanerischen Reformvorstellungen der ZWÖ zusammen. Gefördert werden sollten vor allem das Einfamilienhaus und das Kleinwohnungshaus:

„Wir brauchen vor allem mehr Licht und mehr Luft! Wir wollen nicht mehr in zusammengepressten, licht- und luftermangelnden, dabei mietüberlasteten Wohnungen oder Zinskasernen inmitten eines endlosen Gewirres von Straßen wohnen, sondern auch in freundlichen, gesunden Häusern, in vom Grün der Natur belebten Gebieten, die uns – wenn möglich – eine Erleichterung der Mietlasten und die Aussicht auf größere Beständigkeit bieten [...]. Wir wollen, um das gesundheitliche Niveau unseres Wohnens zu heben, die durchschnittliche Höhenlage unserer Wohnungen vom Zentrum zur Peripherie allmählig senken und danach verhindern, daß das vielstöckige Zinshaus aus der engverbauten Stadt noch mehr eindringe in die Randverbauung, als dies bedauerlicherweise bereits geschehen ist."[124]

Die Tätigkeit der Zentralstelle war nicht auf Wien begrenzt, sondern umfasste auch die Kronländer, in denen die örtlichen Interessen in Zweigvereinen organisiert wurden, die sich wieder zu Landesverbänden zusammenschließen sollten. Es kann angenommen werden, dass die Existenz der Zentralstelle mit ein Anlass dafür war, die Wohnungsfürsorgeagenda in das im selben Jahr gegründete Ministerium für öffentliche Arbeiten aufzunehmen und ein eigenes Departement für Wohnungsfürsorge zu schaffen. „Bahnbrechend" wirkte die Zentralstelle bei der Vorbereitung des staatlichen Kleinwohnungsfürsorgefonds, der zur Basis des staatlichen Wohnbauförderungssystems der Ersten und auch noch der Zweiten Republik werden sollte.[125]

Mit der Einrichtung des Departments für Wohnungsfürsorge war das Wohnungsproblem zwar amtlicherseits zur Kenntnis genommen worden, konkrete und wirksame Maßnahmen ließen jedoch noch immer auf sich warten. Ein Aufschwung der genossenschaftlichen Bautätigkeit trat erst ein, „als verschiedene gesellschaftliche Institutionen einzelnen Baugenossenschaften entsprechende Kredite einräumten".[126]

Wohnungsreform in Österreich (Wien: Selbstverl. Zentralstelle für Wohnungsreform in Österreich, 1907), S. 9; vgl. auch Hösl, "Die Anfänge," S. 123–161.

[124] Theodor Bach, zitiert nach Banik-Schweitzer, "Die Kleinwohnungsfrage," S. 438. Eine ähnliche Kritik der Zinskaserne findet sich auch bei Rauchberg, *Ziele und Wege der Wohnungsreform*, S. 12.

[125] Banik-Schweitzer, "Die Kleinwohnungsfrage," S. 438.

[126] Kepplinger, "Finanzierungsgeschichte," S. 109. Dies waren zunächst die

Am 22. Dezember 1910 erhielt schließlich das *Gesetz betreffend die Errichtung eines Wohnungsfürsorgefonds* die kaiserliche Sanktion.[127] Die Sozialdemokratie agierte dabei als „Interessenwahrerin des Industriebürgertums im vollen Bewusstsein der Tatsache, daß der Wohnungsfürsorgefonds nur einer kleinen Minderheit ihrer Anhänger zugute kommen würde".[128] Insbesondere für die schlechter entlohnten Schichten konnte man davon wenig erwarten. Viele einfache Mitglieder der Partei glaubten, der Wohnungsfürsorgefonds würde die Bildung von Arbeitergenossenschaften fördern. Diese hätten jedoch, um in den Genuss der Unterstützung zu kommen, 10 % der Baukosten aus eigenen Mitteln aufbringen müssen, was „utopisch anmutete"; der nicht von Arbeitern getragene gemeinnützige Wohnungsbau kam somit nur für die „Arbeiteraristokratie" in Frage.[129]

Der Wohnungsfürsorgefonds wurde vom Ministerium für öffentliche Arbeiten verwaltet. Die durch ihn angebotene staatliche Finanzierungshilfe förderte die Entstehung zahlreicher gemeinnütziger Baugenossenschaften. Allein 1912 wurden mehr als 130 Baugenossenschaften gegründet.[130] Als wesentliches Mittel zur Verbesserung des Wohnungsproblems betrachtete man die Beschaffung billigen Baulandes und propagierte nach ausländischen Vorbildern die Einführung des Baurechtes in Österreich. Nachdem der damalige Justizminister Franz Klein im Jahre 1908 eine Enquete veranstaltet hatte, jedoch mit seinen Bemühungen zur Einführung des Erbbaurechtes gescheitert war, brachte seine neuerliche Initiative im Jahre 1911 endlich den gewünschten Erfolg.[131] Das Baurecht wurde von der Novelle zum Allgemeinen Bürgerlichen Gesetzbuch losgelöst und zu

---

Arbeiter-Unfallversicherungsanstalten sowie das Pensions- und Provisionsinstitut der k. k. Staatsbahnen. Die erste Aktivität größeren Umfangs wurde mit der Gründung des „Kaiser Franz Joseph I.-Regierungsjubiläumsfonds" im Jahr 1908 initiiert, der mit vier Millionen Kronen aus dem Budgetüberschuss des Jahres 1906 dotiert war und gemeinnützigen Baugenossenschaften Hypothekardarlehen zur Verfügung stellte. Allerdings wurden nur Wohnungen für Staatsbeamte gefördert. Zwischen 1908 und 1910 wurden in Österreich 45 Beamtengenossenschaften gegründet.

[127] Gesetz vom 22. Dezember 1910, RGBl. 242/ 22. 12. 1910, betreffend die Einrichtung eines Wohnungsfürsorgefonds.

[128] Banik-Schweitzer, "Die Kleinwohnungsfrage," S. 440.

[129] Ebenda, S. 440 f.

[130] Kepplinger, "Finanzierungsgeschichte," S. 111.

[131] Franz Baltzarek, "Franz Klein als Wirtschafts- und Sozialpolitiker," in *Forschungsband Franz Klein (1854–1926). Leben und Wirken. Beiträge des Symposiums „Franz Klein zum 60. Todestag"*, Hrsg. Herbert Hofmeister (Wien: Manz, 1988), S. 173–182, hier S. 178.

einer eigenen Gesetzesvorlage gemacht. Unter der Bezeichnung „Baurecht" erlangte das Erbbaurecht 1912 Gesetzeskraft.[132] Beim „Erbbaurecht" ging es darum, unter bestimmten Voraussetzungen ein Baurecht auf fremdem Grund durchzusetzen. Das Baurecht selbst war ein dingliches, vererbliches und veräußerliches Recht, auf einem Grundstück ein Bauwerk zu haben; es konnte für die Zeitdauer von mindestens 30 und maximal 80 Jahren eingeräumt werden.

Die Förderungsmaßnahmen, die darauf abzielten, die Kapitalbeschaffung für den gemeinnützigen Wohnbau zu erleichtern, brachten nicht den erwarteten Erfolg.[133] Ein Grund dafür lag darin, dass infolge des angespannten Kapitalmarktes ab 1912 die Sparkassen keine Hypothekardarlehen mehr gewährten. Ein weiterer Punkt, der für die geringe praktische Bedeutung der Reformmaßnahmen verantwortlich war, hing damit zusammen, dass von den im Gesetz angesprochenen Bauträgern nur die Baugenossenschaften praktisch tätig wurden, während sich die Gemeinden bis auf wenige Ausnahmen nicht direkt im Wohnbau engagierten. Dies hatte zur Folge, dass sich der Kreis derjenigen, die in den Genuss einer geförderten Wohnung kommen konnten, auf einige wenige Berufsgruppen beschränkte, und zwar auf diejenigen, die das Privileg eines regelmäßigen und gesicherten Einkommens hatten. Dies waren vor allem Staatsbedienstete und Angestellte. „Für die meisten Arbeiterfamilien war aufgrund der instabilen Einkommenssituation der Beitritt zu einer Wohnbaugenossenschaft mit den daraus erwachsenden langfristigen Verpflichtungen unmöglich; eine entsprechende Wohnung oder gar ein Eigenhaus befand sich außerhalb der Möglichkeiten."[134] Die meisten Baugenossenschaften, die vor dem Ersten Weltkrieg gegründet wurden, waren daher auch Beamten- bzw. Angestelltengenossenschaften. Die Konsequenz daraus war, dass eben jene Bevölkerungsgruppen, die am stärksten von unzulänglichen Wohnungsverhältnissen betroffen waren, durch die Wohnbauförderungsgesetze kaum eine Verbesserung ihrer Situation erfuhren.

Mieterstreiks und Hausboykott in Budapest

Die europäischen Großstädte des ausgehenden 19. und frühen 20. Jahrhunderts hatten alle mit dem Problem der enormen Zuwanderung zu kämpfen. Im letzten Viertel des 19. Jahrhunderts zählte Budapest zu jenen europäischen Großstädten, deren Bevölkerung am stärksten gewachsen

---

[132] Gesetz vom 26. April 1912, RGBl. 86/ 26. 4. 1912, betreffend das Baurecht.
[133] Vgl. dazu Kepplinger, "Finanzierungsgeschichte," S. 111 f.
[134] Ebenda, S. 112.

war. Am größten war der Bevölkerungszuwachs zwischen den Jahren 1890 und 1900, in denen die Bevölkerungszahl Budapests von 492.237 auf 717.681 Personen stieg.[135] Die Baukonjunktur wirkte sich zeitversetzt auf den Wohnungsmarkt aus. Die Krise am Wohnungsmarkt zeigte sich vor allem an der Zahl der leerstehenden Wohnungen, die 1909 mit der Zahl von 284 den Tiefstand erreichte. Eine zusätzliche Verschlechterung des Wohnungsmarktes für die Unterschichten ergab sich aus dem abnehmenden Anteil leerstehender Ein- und Zweizimmerwohnungen. Der Anteil der Einzimmerwohnungen an den leerstehenden Wohnungen betrug in den Jahren 1901 bis 1907 zwischen 55 und 70 %, 1911 waren es nur mehr 25,6 %.[136] Aufgrund der langanhaltenden Baukrise war ab dem Jahr 1904 absehbar, dass sich die Lage auf dem Wohnungsmarkt zuspitzen würde. Anders als in Wien, wo sich der Wohndichte-Wert zwischen 1880 und 1910 leicht verbesserte, verschlechterte sich die Situation in Budapest, wo z. B. im Arbeiterbezirk Ferencváros (Franzstadt) 1891 40,15 % der Bevölkerung in Wohnungen mit vier und mehr Personen pro Wohnungsbestandteil wohnten.[137]

In den Jahren 1906 bis 1911 versuchten die Budapester Mieter durch vielfältige Aktionen der Monopolstellung der Hausherren entgegenzuwirken. Besonders drückend wirkte sich der ständige Anstieg der Mietpreise aus, der bei jedem Quartalwechsel regelmäßig eintrat. Gleichzeitig wurde statt der bisher vierteljährlichen oder monatlichen Vermietung nunmehr die wöchentliche Vermietung eingeführt, was wiederum mit einer Zinssteigerung einherging.[138] Als die Hausbesitzer eine weitere Erhöhung selbst nicht mehr für möglich hielten, schoben sich zwischen Hausbesitzer und Mieter Mittelspersonen, so genannte „Generalmieter", „zweifelhafte Existenzen", die das ganze Haus gegen Zusicherung einer höheren Summe

---

[135] Vgl. Gábor Gyáni, "Budapest," in *Housing the Workers 1850–1914. A Comparative Perspective*, Hrsg. Martin J. Daunton (London und New York: Leicester Univ. Pr., 1990), S. 149–181, hier S. 157.

[136] Vgl. zum Folgenden Albert Lichtblau, "Boykott – Krawall – Gewalt – Demonstration: Die Budapester Mieterbewegung 1906 bis 1912 und exkursive Vergleiche zu ähnlichen Vorgängen in Wien," *Archiv. Jahrbuch des Vereins für Geschichte der Arbeiterbewegung* 8 (1992): S 65–81, hier S. 67.

[137] Siehe dazu John, *Wohnverhältnisse*, S. 143 f.; Sedlaczek, *Wohn-Verhältnisse in Wien*, S. 86–89; Carl Hugo Lindemann, "Die Wohnungsstatistik von Wien und Budapest," in *Verhandlungen des Vereins für Socialpolitik über die Wohnungsfrage und die Handelspolitik*, (Leipzig: Duncker & Humblot, 1902), Anhang S. 371–392, hier S. 383 ff.

[138] Gábor Gyáni, "Budapest," S. 173.

mieteten und dann ihrerseits die Mietzinse der einzelnen Wohnungen erhöhten.[139]

Nach der Jahrhundertwende hatte der rapide Rückgang von leerstehenden Wohnungen in Budapest das Verhältnis zwischen Hausbesitzern und Mietern[140] noch verschärft. 1904 konnte die Sozialdemokratische Partei für eine Veranstaltung gegen den Wohnungswucher bereits 15.000 Personen mobilisieren. Erstmals drohte man mit dem Streik der Wohnungsmieter, und die *Volksstimme*, das Blatt der Sozialdemokraten, konnte über den Fall eines Hausboykotts berichten, der erfolgreich mit der Herabsetzung der Miete endete.[141] Im August 1906 leiteten die Budapester Sozialdemokraten eine Bewegung gegen die Wohnungsteuerungen ein. Laut Polizeibericht versammelten sich am 19. August 1906 40.000 Personen und forderten in einer Resolution vom Magistrat, dass dieser „einem Entwurf Geltung verschaffe, in welchem die Preise der Wohnungen je nach ihrer Größe und Lage festzusetzen sind. Ansonsten werde man ab 1. Februar 1907 gezwungen sein, die Bezahlung der heutigen unerhört hohen Wohnungsmieten zu verweigern."[142] Dieses Ultimatum blieb nicht ohne Folgen. Ende August 1906 fand im Stadthaus eine Konferenz über die Budapester Wohnungsnot statt. Der seit April 1906 amtierende Bürgermeister István Bárczy kündigte im September 1906 eine Wohnbauaktion der Gemeinde an, die bereits 1907 einsetzen sollte. Es wurde der Bau von 200 kommunalen Kleinwohnungen beschlossen, die jedoch erst 1909 fertiggestellt waren. Die Methode des Hausboykotts wurde auch in den folgenden Jahren angewandt. Im Februar 1909 lösten Mietsteigerungen zu Quartalsbeginn wutentbrannte Reaktionen der Mieter aus. Dabei wurden innerhalb einer Woche drei Mietshäuser von den Mietern und Leuten aus der Nachbarschaft demoliert. Neben dem Boykott wandten die Mieter auch die Methode des Mietstreiks an: „Sie zahlten keine oder nur einen Teil der Miete, bis sich der Hausbesitzer oder Pächter zu einer Rücknahme der Mietsteigerung entschloss. Gleichzeitig stellten sie das Haus unter Boykott."[143] Das Ziel war ein Jahresvertrag für das betreffende Haus, durch welchen die Mieter vor Kündigung und Mietsteigerungen bewahrt werden sollten.[144]

---

[139] Werkner, "Der Kleinwohnungsbau," S. 3.
[140] Zum Folgenden siehe Lichtblau, "Boykott," S. 70 ff.
[141] Zimmermann, *Prächtige Armut*, S. 246.
[142] Zitiert nach Lichtblau, "Boykott," S. 71.
[143] Ebenda, S. 73. Die Mieterstreiks hatten durchaus Erfolg. 81 % der Streiks zwischen März 1910 und März 1911 endeten erfolgreich für die Mieter und nur 5 % mit Delogierungen.
[144] Zu den Budapester Mieterstreiks siehe auch: Michael John, *Hausherrenmacht*

Besonderes Aufsehen erregte der Mieterstreik im sogenannten „Hétház"
(Siebenhaus), einem besonders charakteristischen Gebäudekomplex im
Arbeiterbezirk „Angyalföld", der 500 Mietparteien und etwa 2000
Menschen beherbergte und der Budapester Hauptstädtischen Sparkasse
gehörte. Am Beispiel des „Hétház" zeigt sich auch die für diese Form des
Widerstandes charakteristische Solidarität der Betroffenen, welche – die
gesellschaftlichen Unterschiede außer Acht lassend – in den Monaten des
Streiks gemeinsam als Hausgemeinschaft auftraten.[145] Im April 1910 brach
der erste Streik aus. Die wegen der Mietrückstände auferlegten Sanktionen
schmiedeten die Mieter des Hauses zusammen. „Infolge der immer
wiederkehrenden Delogierungen im ‚Siebenhaus' lebten jetzt in der einen
oder anderen Wohnung 20–25 Menschen, die sich in ihren Wohnungen
zusammenpferchten", heißt es in einem zeitgenössischen Bericht.[146] Der
Schriftsteller Lajos Kassak, der mit seiner Mutter und Schwester im
„Hétház" wohnte, erinnert sich an diese Zeit: „Es begann mit ‚Wander'-
Versammlungen, mit Reden und mit Gesang und am Ersten verweigerten
die Bewohner einhellig die Bezahlung der Miete [...]." Die Bewegung
verwandelte sich binnen kurzem in einen wahrhaften Karneval:

„Bald begann die Katzenmusik in den Häusern [...]. Wir gingen von
Haus zu Haus. Silberstein (‚die Seele der Bewegung') hielt Ansprachen,
die Männer standen in der Mitte des Hofes und sangen Arbeiterlieder, die
Frauen machten auf den Gängen einen ohrenbetäubenden Lärm mit
Kochlöffeln, kaputten Töpfen und mit schäbigen Blechstücken. Auf diese
Weise ging es bis zehn, elf Uhr, dann zogen wir uns in unsere Nester
zurück, um auf den nächsten Tag zu warten."[147]

---

und Mieterelend. Wohnverhältnisse und Wohnerfahrung der Unterschichten in
Wien 1890–1923 (Wien: Verl. für Gesellschaftskritik, 1982), S. 45–53.

[145] Gyáni weist darauf hin, dass nicht nur die Mieter der proletarischen
Mietskasernen unter den steigenden Mieten litten, sondern auch Angehörige der
unteren Mittelklasse: "When the petty bourgeoisie resided with workers in the
same building, the barriers separating them from each other during times of peace
immediately lost their significance in the common struggle against the landlord or
house-renter. An entire ritual protest came into existence which made the everyday
life in each of the houses very like a permanent carnival." Gyáni, "Budapest," S.
177.

[146] Zitiert ebenda, S. 177.

[147] Zitiert nach Gábor Gyáni, "Großstadterfahrung am Beispiel Budapests," in Die
Habsburgermonarchie 1848–1918 9/1. Teilband 1. Soziale Strukturen. Von der
feudal-agrarischen zur bürgerlich-industriellen Gesellschaft. Lebens- und
Arbeitswelten in der industriellen Revolution, Hrsg. Helmut Rumpler und Peter
Urbanitsch (Wien: Verl. der Österr. Akad. der Wiss., 2010), S. 539–560, hier S. 551.

Als im Oktober 1910 die Sparkasse versuchte, einigen Mietern zu kündigen, verweigerten die Mieter erneut die Zahlung. Neue Mieter, die den Hausboykott durchbrachen, wurden verprügelt. Ende November 1910 wurden 29 Parteien delogiert. Sie errichteten daraufhin im Freien ein Lager, wo sie auch übernachteten. „Der Solidarisierungseffekt war enorm: Es wurden Lebensmittel, Brennholz und Geld gespendet."[148] Nach vier Tagen brachen die Delogierten das Lager ab und fanden Unterkunft in kommunalen Notbaracken. Nach etlichen Mieterstreiks im Jahre 1911, die mittels Delogierung abgewürgt wurden, erlahmte die Bewegung schließlich.

Die Budapester Mieterstreiks dienten den Wiener Streiks als Vorbild, sie unterschieden sich jedoch nach der Einschätzung von John „in der Ausführung und im Effekt" sehr nachhaltig: „[W]ährend es in Wien als Folge der Mieterstreiks keinerlei gesetzgeberische Aktivitäten oder Sofortmaßnahmen gab, die Mieterstreiks nicht sehr heftig waren, und auch gegenüber den Hausherren nicht zu besonderen Erfolgen führten, war das in Budapest [...] anders."[149] In Wien gab es nur wenige besonders gewalttätige Auseinandersetzungen. Die Sozialdemokraten versuchten „aus Angst vor einer Zersplitterung der Kräfte"[150] die Bewegung unter Kontrolle zu bringen und sie durch Gründung des Mietervereins in institutionelle Kanäle zu lenken: „Die unmittelbaren Erfolge, wie in Budapest, blieben eigentlich aus."[151]

Auch die Budapester Sozialdemokraten hatten bis 1910 die Methode des Mieterstreiks gemieden, da die Hausbesitzer das Recht hatten, auch Gebrauchsgegenstände zu pfänden. Daher beschränkte man sich zunächst auf den Hausboykott. Erst die Reform des Pfandrechtes zu Gunsten der Mieter veranlasste die Sozialdemokraten, auf die Taktik des Mieterstreiks umzuschwenken.[152] Der Aufbau einer Mieterorganisation war in Budapest, anders als in Wien, nicht möglich, da es den Sozialdemokraten untersagt war, einen eigenen Parteiapparat aufzubauen. Organisatorisch basierte die Partei auf den Gewerkschaften und war daher in einer ungünstigeren Position als ihre Genossen in der cisleithanischen Reichshälfte, die seit 1897 im Reichsrat und seit 1900 im Wiener Gemeinderat vertreten waren. Daher waren die Sozialdemokraten in Ungarn stärker „auf außerparlamentarische Aktionen" angewiesen, um ihre Stärke zu

---

[148] Lichtblau, "Boykott," S. 74.
[149] John, *Hausherrenmacht*, S.41.
[150] Lichtblau, "Boykott," S. 75.
[151] John, *Hausherrenmacht*, S. 41.
[152] Lichtblau, "Boykott," S. 77. Zum Pfand- und Rückhalterecht der Vermieter siehe: Zimmermann, *Prächtige Armut*, S. 267 f.

demonstrieren, während sich die österreichischen Sozialdemokraten
bereits „auf dem Weg zur parlamentarischen Machteroberung" sahen und
daher versuchten, die Mieterbewegung in geregelte und legale Bahnen der
Mieterorganisation zu leiten.[153]

Maßnahmen gegen die Wohnungsnot in Budapest

Die Wohnungsnot in der ungarischen Hauptstadt war „deutlich
zugespitzter als in Wien und anderen westlich gelegenen Großstädten" und
die Wohnungsfrage stellte sich daher in der Zeit vor dem Ersten
Weltkrieg, wie gezeigt, „als besonders konflikthaft" dar.[154]

Die offizielle „Wohnbauförderung" beschränkte sich auch hier zunächst
hauptsächlich auf Steuererleichterungen und -befreiungen für Hausbesitzer. In
seinem Bericht auf dem internationalen Wohnungskongress in Wien 1910
kritisierte Emerich Ferenczi, der Wohnungsexperte des Budapester
Bürgermeisters István Bárczy, dass die Bestimmungen betreffend das
Wohnungswesen alle unter einem gemeinsamen Fehler leiden würden,
nämlich dass sie „nur nebensächlich in den Rahmen verschiedener Gesetze
eingefügt wurden und daher einer zielbewussten Einheitlichkeit
entbehren."[155] Tatsächlich erschöpfte sich die staatliche ungarische
Wohnungsgesetzgebung in der Schaffung von Teilmaßnahmen und
behandelte diese Materie hauptsächlich im Zusammenhang mit der
Regelung anderer Verwaltungsangelegenheiten.

Für die Entwicklung des Kleinwohnungsbaus in Budapest war dagegen
das Gesetz betreffend die Förderung der Entwicklung der Hauptstadt
Budapest von Bedeutung (Gesetzesartikel XLVIII/1908). Dieses Gesetz
bezweckte, den Haushalt der Hauptstadt durch Zusicherung
verschiedenartiger Begünstigungen zu ordnen. Es gewährte weiters den in
einigen zentralen Stadtteilen errichteten Neubauten weitgehende
Steuerbefreiungen. Der in diesem Zusammenhang wichtige § 12 war im
ursprünglichen Gesetzestext nicht vorgesehen und wurde erst nachträglich
in das Gesetz aufgenommen. Er lautete: „Alle jene Wohngebäude, die die
Hauptstadt zu dem Zwecke erbaut, um sie zu einem ihren Selbstkosten
entsprechenden Mietzins zu vermieten, sind so lange von der staatlichen

---

[153] Lichtblau, "Boykott," S. 79 f.

[154] Melinz und Zimmermann, "Mit den Waffen der Sozialpolitik?," S. 86.

[155] Emerich Ferenczi, "Die Fortschritte des Wohnungswesens in Ungarn in den
letzten fünf Jahren," in *Bericht über den IX. internationalen Wohnungskongress.
Wien, 30. Mai bis 3. Juni 1910 I.*, Hrsg. Bureau des Kongresses (Wien: Verl. der
Zentralstelle für Wohnungsreform in Österreich, 1911), S. 1043–1061, hier S.
1044.

Gebäudesteuer befreit, als die Mietsummen das Maß der Selbstkosten tatsächlich übersteigen."[156] Mit diesem Paragraphen war ein alter Wunsch der Stadtverwaltung verwirklicht, die bereits im Jahre 1897 für vier von ihr erbaute Arbeiterwohnhäuser die Steuerfreiheit erbeten hatte, was jedoch vom Finanzminister mit Hinweis auf die Absicht, ein alle Seiten der Wohnungsfrage umfassendes Gesetz zu schaffen, abgelehnt wurde.[157] Der zitierte Paragraph war die Grundlage für die im Jahr 1909 einsetzende große Wohnungsaktion der Budapester Stadtverwaltung.

Für den Beginn und die Ausführung des Bauprogramms war aufgrund der begrenzten Autonomie der Hauptstadt Budapest die Kooperation mit der Regierung eine „unentbehrliche Voraussetzung". Es war daher ein Glücksfall, dass „genau in der kritischen Phase von Beschluss und Anlaufen des Programms in der Person von Sándor Wekerle ein Politiker an der Spitze der Regierung stand, der selbst ein Anhänger und Vorkämpfer des massierten Wohnungsbaus war".[158] Das Ergebnis dieser Zusammenarbeit war das erwähnte Gesetz XLVIII/1908, mit dem der Hauptstadt unter anderem die Steuerbefreiung für kommunalen Wohnbau bei Vermietung zum Selbstkostenpreis zugesichert wurde. Zur Erzielung von Miethöhen, die die Aufwandsneutralität für die Gemeinde sicherstellten und zumindest für einen Teil der Arbeiterbevölkerung erschwinglich sein sollten, waren diese Begünstigungen unerlässlich.[159]

Damit war der Umschwung in der staatlichen Wohnungspolitik eingeläutet, in Budapest selbst war jedoch mit dem Gesetz von 1908 noch nicht die letzte Hürde genommen. Dies erfolgte erst am 7. April 1909, als sich die außerordentliche Vollversammlung des Hauptstädtischen Munizipalausschusses für das vom Rat in einigen Punkten abgeänderte Bárczy'sche Bauprogramm aussprach. Die Entscheidung vom April 1909 läutete das kommunale Wohnbauprogramm der Jahre 1909 bis 1913 ein, bedeutete einen „Bruch mit dem Althergebrachten" und stellte gleichzeitig eine Art „Feuerwehraktion" dar.[160] Der Umschwung in der

---

[156] Werkner, "Der Kleinwohnungsbau," S. 44.

[157] Ebenda, S. 78 ff.

[158] András Sipos, "Bürgermeister István Bárczy und die öffentlichen sozialen Bauprojekte in Budapest am Anfang des 20. Jahrhunderts," in *Budapest und Wien. Technischer Fortschritt und urbaner Aufschwung im 19. Jahrhundert*, Hrsg. Peter Csendes und András Sipos (Wien et al.: Deuticke, 2003), S. 197–205, hier S. 201.

[159] 1909 wurden ähnliche Bestimmungen für alle Städte und Gemeinden erlassen. Vgl. Zimmermann, *Prächtige Armut*, S. 254.

[160] Ebenda, S. 259. Zu den Vorschlägen Bárczys vgl. Werkner, "Der Kleinwohnungsbau," S. 79 f. Demnach sollte die Bautätigkeit der Hauptstadt insgesamt acht Gruppen von Bauten umfassen: 3 Notstandsbaracken, 3

hauptstädtischen Wohnungspolitik war vor allem auch eine Folge der Mieterbewegung, die – wie bereits ausgeführt – im Februar 1909 eskalierte und sich in Hausboykotts bis hin zu Zertrümmerungsaktionen äußerte.[161] Die Sozialdemokratie, die die Mieterbewegung unterstützte, forderte in Memoranden den Übergang zum kommunalen Wohnbau, die Einführung der Mietzinsbeschränkungen, eine neue kommunale Bodenpolitik und die Schaffung eines Wohnungsamtes. Nur unter Ausnützung dieses äußeren Drucks durch die „Revolution der Mieter" konnten István Bárczy und seine Mitarbeiter ihre radikale Lösung in den kommunalen Entscheidungsgremien durchsetzen. „Während die konservativen Gegner von einem gefährlichen Schritt in Richtung Sozialismus sprachen, wiesen Bárczy und sein Kreis darauf hin, dass die Belastungsfähigkeit der Gesellschaft – die in den westlichen Städten vorhanden war – in Budapest fehle."[162]

Nach Angaben von Ferenczi vermehrte die Bauaktion der Hauptstadt zwischen 1907 und 1913 die Zahl der Wohnungen um 4.816.[163] Hinzu kamen noch ein Volkshotel, ein Volkshaus, Notwohnungen und die durch die Schulbauten in der gleichen Periode frei gewordenen Privatwohnungen, womit durch die Bautätigkeit der Gemeinde insgesamt 6.500 Wohnungen hinzukamen, was nahezu einem Viertel der gesamten Wohnungsproduktion in den Jahren 1909 bis 1913 entsprach.

Für die völlig unbemittelten Schichten der Bevölkerung (ungelernte Arbeiter etc.) wurden aus Kostengründen ebenerdige bzw. einstöckige Kleinwohnungskolonien erbaut. Ein Teil dieser Kolonien wurde auf leeren Baugründen im Innern der Stadt, der größere Teil jedoch auf den billigen,

---

Barackensäle, 5 Volkshotels (Ledigenheime), 2 Volksheime, 30 Kleinwohnungshäuser, Wohnungen für die Angestellten der Hauptstadt, darunter 30 größere Häuser und 370 Familienhäuser, 13 gewöhnliche Mietshäuser und 90 Schulbauten. Letztere Maßnahme war darauf zurückzuführen, dass die Wohnungsnot in Budapest u. a. auch dadurch verstärkt wurde, dass viele öffentliche Behörden und Anstalten – auch Schulen – in Mietshäusern untergebracht wurden. Im Jahre 1909 nahmen die kommunalen Schulen etwa 500 Mietwohnungen in Anspruch.

[161] Vgl. dazu Gyáni, *Parlor and Kitchen*, S. 162; Zimmermann, *Prächtige Armut*, S. 250 ff., 255. Vgl. auch Lichtblau, "Boykott," S. 65–81.

[162] Sipos, "Bürgermeister István Bárczy," S. 200.

[163] Darunter 20 Kleinwohnungshäuser (mit insgesamt 1.636 Wohnungen), 4 Beamtenwohnhäuser (mit 313 Wohnungen), ein Werkstättenmietshaus (mit 61 Wohnungen), eine Künstlerkolonie (mit 27 Wohnungen) und 16 Kleinwohnungskolonien (mit insgesamt 2.779 Wohnungen). Die Angaben bei Emerich Ferenczi, "Boden- und Wohnungsreform in Budapest," *Jahrbuch der Bodenreform. Vierteljahreshefte* 12 (1916): S. 106.

an die bebauten Stadtteile angrenzenden Grundstücken erstellt. Einige dieser Kolonien bildeten kleine Gemeinden, die mit verschiedenen für die Allgemeinheit notwendigen Einrichtungen versehen waren. Der Großteil der ebenerdigen Häuser der Kleinwohnungskolonien bestand aus Einzimmerwohnungen, es gab jedoch auch einige wenige mit zwei Zimmern. Zu dem größten Teil der Wohnungen gehörte eine besondere Speisekammer, ein Klosett oder Bodenabteil. Zu den Einzimmerwohnungen gehörte ein gemeinsames Badezimmer, während die Zweizimmerwohnungen einen eigenen Baderaum besaßen.

Bei der Festsetzung der Wohnungsmieten ging man, wie Ferenczi berichtet, „nicht von den Herstellungskosten der einzelnen Wohnungen aus, sondern von der Leistungsfähigkeit der Mieter".[164] Trotz des weit größeren Komforts waren die Mieten der kommunalen Kleinwohnungen daher viel geringer als jene in den minderwertigen Mietshäusern der Umgebung. Dem Bettgeher- bzw. Schlafgängerwesen versuchte man durch die Errichtung eines Volkshotels im VI. Bezirk abzuhelfen, das am 17. Februar 1912 eröffnet wurde. Der Grundgedanke dieser Institution war, den Bewohnern für die Nacht ein besonderes Schlafabteil zu bieten, für all ihre sonstigen Bedürfnisse jedoch durch Bereitstellung gemeinsamer Räumlichkeiten zu sorgen.

Erwähnenswert ist in diesem Zusammenhang, dass es ein wesentliches Element des „Volksaufklärungskonzeptes" von Bárczy war, den Armen und Obdachlosen eine ästhetisch ansprechende Umgebung zu verschaffen, indem in den für sie gebauten Anlagen auch künstlerischen Aspekten Raum gegeben werden sollte. So wurde etwa das Volkshotel mit Wandgemälden von Mariska Undi ausgestattet. Der Kritik an dieser „Luxusausführung" begegnete Bárczy in seiner Eröffnungsrede wie folgt: „Die Beachtung des ästhetischen Aspekts, die Gemälde und andere Einrichtungsgegenstände von künstlerischem Niveau dienten nicht für die Pracht, sondern dafür, die Herberge warm und gemütlich zu machen, denn so entsprach sie ihrer Funktion besser und konnte für die ärmsten Leute eher ein richtiges Heim werden, als mit einer kalten, kasernenmäßigen Einrichtung."[165]

Auch in Ungarn suchte man nach Alternativen zu den Mietskasernen, wobei man sich auch hier die englischen Gartenstädte als Vorbild nahm. Als ein „Paradebeispiel" einer solchen Gartenstadt in der österreichisch-ungarischen Monarchie wird die „Staatliche Arbeitersiedlung Kispest"[166]

---

[164] Ebenda, S. 108. Zu den Kleinwohnungskolonien vgl. auch Werkner, "Der Kleinwohnungsbau," S. 85 f.

[165] Zitiert nach Sipos, "Bürgermeister István Bárczy," S. 204.

[166] Ilona Sármány-Parsons, "Gartenstadtidee und Villenkolonien in Budapest im

bei Budapest angeführt. Dabei konnte man jedoch nicht einfach das Beispiel der englischen „garden cities", die für die kapitalstarke Mittelschicht gebaut wurden, nachahmen, sondern musste auf die spezifischen gesellschaftlichen Voraussetzungen vor Ort reagieren. Die Arbeitersiedlung Kispest ist untrennbar mit dem Namen von Sándor Wekerle verbunden („Wekerle-Siedlung"). Wekerle war als amtierender Ministerpräsident und Finanzminister seit Anfang 1908 auch Vorsitzender des „Rates der Hauptstadt für öffentliche Arbeiten" geworden und kontrollierte damit sämtliche Bereiche des Entstehens der Arbeitersiedlung.[167]

Angesichts des Wohnungsmangels verfolgte man damit das Ziel, den unteren Schichten auf Staatskosten einen erschwinglichen Wohnraum zur Verfügung zu stellen, der auch den Anspruch auf eine gesunde Wohnweise („Licht und Luft") erfüllen sollte. Der Gesetzesartikel XXIX/1908 stellte dem Finanzminister für den Bau von Arbeiterhäusern einen durch eine Anleihe zu deckenden Kredit von zwölf Millionen Kronen zur Verfügung, um auf den in Kispest und dem Bezirk Óhegy angekauften Grundstücken „Arbeiterhäuser in einfacher Ausführung" errichten zu lassen und dieselben an Arbeiter bzw. Angestellte staatlicher und anderer Fabrikbetriebe zu vermieten.[168] Die Häuser sollten in staatlichem Eigentum verbleiben und künftig von jeder Steuer befreit sein. Nach den Angaben von Ferenczi sollten auf der Kolonie 1.084 Häuser errichtet werden, darunter 755 ebenerdige, 328 ein- und mehrstöckige. Diese Häuser sollten insgesamt 4.665 Wohnungen enthalten. Ende Dezember 1915 waren 953 Häuser fertig gestellt.[169] Um die Anlage möglichst abwechslungsreich zu gestalten, entwarf man insgesamt 48 unterschiedliche Häusertypen: „Verschiedene Häusergrößen, volkstümlich gestaltete Fassaden, eine uneinheitliche Anordnung auf den Grundstücken und verschiedenartige Anlagen der Gärten vermieden jede Eintönigkeit und gaben der Siedlung ein ansprechendes Äußeres."[170] Trotz mancher Abstriche, so resümiert Ilona Sármany-Parsons, sei die Wekerle-Siedlung eine der ersten Gartenstadtsiedlungen gewesen, „die in einem Guss geplant war und ein alternatives, naturnahes und Gemeinschaft schaffendes

---

Zeitalter des Dualismus," *Österreich in Geschichte und Literatur* 53 (2009): S. 39–54, hier S. 49.
[167] Géza von Geyr, "Die Wekerlesiedlung in Budapest. Staatliche Arbeitersiedlung und Gartenstadt," *Ungarn-Jahrbuch* 17 (1989): S. 71–94, hier S .79.
[168] Ferenczi, "Boden- und Wohnungsreform," S. 81–120, hier S. 101.
[169] Ebenda, S. 102. Die Zahlenangaben für die geplanten Häuser differieren; vgl. von Geyr, "Die Wekerlesiedlung," S. 81 und Sármány-Parsons, "Gartenstadtidee," S. 51.
[170] Vgl. die Abbildungen 1–9, in von Geyr, "Die Wekerlesiedlung," S. 89–94.

städtebauliches Ideal verwirklichte".[171] Die Wohnungen wurden hauptsächlich an Arbeiter der Staatsbetriebe, vor allem der staatlichen Maschinenfabrik und der Hauptwerkstätte der Ungarischen Staatsbahn vermietet. Die Mieten wurden vom Finanzministerium so minimal berechnet, dass sie weit unter den üblichen Preisen in Budapest und seiner Umgebung lagen und für Arbeiter mit kleinem Einkommen bezahlbar waren.[172]

* * *

Zieht man abschließend einen Vergleich zwischen Wien und Budapest, so lässt sich feststellen, dass die gesellschaftlichen und politischen Auseinandersetzungen mit der unzureichenden Wohnungsversorgung im Unterschied zu Ungarn in Österreich „keine quantitativ ins Gewicht fallenden und im internationalen Vergleich bedeutsamen öffentlichen Eigenbauprogramme" hervorbrachten. Was hingegen die staatliche und kommunale Unterstützung von nicht (ausschließlich) privatkapitalistisch-gewinnorientiertem Kleinwohnungsbau betraf, so weisen Zimmermann/Melinz darauf hin, dass in Österreich zugunsten der Bevölkerung der städtisch-industriellen Zonen „unverkennbar mehr als in Ungarn" geschah.[173] Durch die Einrichtung des staatlichen Wohnungsfürsorgefonds wurde die Kreditbeschaffung für die gemeinnützige Bautätigkeit erleichtert. Letztere erfuhr 1913 in Wien erstmals einen lebhaften Aufschwung, sodass nach vorsichtigen Schätzungen etwa ein Fünftel der gesamten Wohnungsproduktion auf ihr Konto ging. Die Verabschiedung des (Erb)Baurechts im Jahre 1912 sollte kapitalschwachen Bauherren den Aufwand für den Grundkauf ersparen und so die Herstellung von billigen und gesunden Wohnungen anregen.

In den Gemeindegremien bestimmten jedoch noch immer die besitzbürgerlichen Schichten die Kommunalpolitik. So auch in Wien, wo die Christlich-Sozialen und Liberalen darauf beharrten, dass die Produktion und Verteilung von Wohnungen eine privatwirtschaftliche bzw. genossenschaftliche Aufgabe sei.[174] Die Mieterbewegung der Jahre

---

[171] Sármány-Parsons, "Gartenstadtidee," S. 54.

[172] Der Mietpreis für eine Einzimmerwohnung mit Nebenräumen, Gartenteil, Hof- und Wasserverbrauch belief sich in der Siedlung auf 140 Kronen pro Jahr, während bei fast der Hälfte der etwa 71.000 Budapester Einzimmerwohnungen die Mietpreise bei 400 Kronen jährlich lagen (bei Zweizimmerwohnungen belief sich das Verhältnis auf 220 bzw. 700 Kronen). Vgl. von Geyr, "Die Wekerlesiedlung," S. 84 f.

[173] Melinz und Zimmermann, "Mit den Waffen der Sozialpolitik?," S. 98.

[174] Vgl. dazu Feldbauer et al., "Arbeiterwohnungsfrage," S. 400.

1910 und 1911 brachte jedoch auch die regierenden Christlich-Sozialen
unter Legitimationsdruck und zum Überdenken ihrer Haltung. Außerdem
führte die Einleitung von Notstandsmaßnahmen im Jahre 1911 zu
Konflikten zwischen der Partei und den Hausherren, deren Fraktion
innerhalb der Partei an Macht verlor.

CHAPTER SIXTEEN

ARMUT, ARMENFÜRSORGE UND KATHOLISCHE IDENTITÄT IM DEUTSCHSPRACHIGEN KATHOLIZISMUS DER ERSTEN HÄLFTE DES 19. JAHRHUNDERTS

BERNHARD SCHNEIDER

Poverty, care for the poor and Catholic identity in German speaking Catholicism in the 19th century

Abstract: The article first discusses poverty and care for the poor in German Catholic areas between the years 1800–1850. Secondly, it explains the daily practice in the care for the poor in two regions of Southern Germany in the period between 1800–1870. The perception of poverty and care for the poor is further explained. The article also summarises discussions about different forms of care for the poor and its specifically confessional profile, the possibilities of cooperation with the state as well as with other confessions.

Die Geschichte der Armut und der Armenfürsorge ist lang, und die Geschichte einer vom Christentum geprägten Wahrnehmung von Armen und Armut ist es in Europa ebenfalls. Bis in die Mitte des 20. Jahrhunderts hinein wurde Armut auch von Armen anders erlebt, je nachdem, ob diese einen kirchlichen Hintergrund hatten oder nicht. Die bekannte deutsche Schriftstellerin Ulla Hahn hat das aus eigenem Erleben für die 1960er Jahre in ihrem erfolgreichen autobiographischen Roman „Aufbruch" vor wenigen Jahren sehr eindrucksvoll beschrieben.[1] Auch für die Kirchen selbst war und ist das Feld der sozialen Hilfen ein zentraler Bestandteil des Handelns. In Deutschland stellen die beiden großen Dachverbände

---

[1] Ulla Hahn, *Aufbruch* (München: Deutsche Verlags-Anstalt, 2009) bzw. (München: Dt. Taschenbuch-Verlag 2011) Taschenbuchausgabe, hier S. 106 f.

kirchlicher sozialer Dienste („Deutscher Caritasverband" und „Diakonie / Diakonisches Werk") die größten nicht-staatlichen Arbeitgeber. Mit einem Papst, der sich selbst nach dem armen Franz von Assisi nennt und der als Erzbischof von Buenos Aires als „Vater der Armen" bezeichnet wurde, ist Armut im Moment im katholischen Diskurs wieder besonders populär und beflügelt die Kirche. Das hat aber sogleich in der säkularen Presse auch Stimmen auf den Plan gerufen, die der katholischen Kirche ein besonderes Verdienst in der Armenfürsorge absprachen. In Gestalt des medial sehr präsenten und in der deutschen Wissenschaftslandschaft hoch dekorierten protestantischen Theologen Friedrich Wilhelm Graf warf man dem Katholizismus in Lateinamerika in der Armutsfrage trotz der von den lateinamerikanischen Bischofssynoden programmatisch formulierten „Option für die Armen" förmlich Versagen vor. Graf titelte: „Für die Armen gibt's nur Barmherzigkeit".[2] Graf nannte auch gleich die besseren Helfer: die Pfingstkirchen, die durch Leistung und Askese den Armen den Weg wiesen, der Armut zu entrinnen und in den Mittelstand aufsteigen. Dazu gäbe es manches zu sagen, aber das soll hier nicht das Thema sein.

Diese Kontroverse zeigt paradigmatisch: Armut und Armenfürsorge stehen mit dem Selbstverständnis, mit der Identität des Christentums in Verbindung. Sie zeigt auch: Der Umgang mit Armut und Armen avanciert (manchmal) zum Richtmaß, um Leistung oder Versagen einer Kirche zu messen. Man könnte den Eindruck gewinnen, ein Wort des später führenden katholischen Sozialreformers sei auf die Gegenwart gemünzt: Wilhelm Emmanuel von Ketteler sprach 1848 vom „edlen Wettkampf der Liebe und Barmherzigkeit".[3] Er verlangte damit Chancengleichheit für die katholische Kirche und ihr karitatives Wirken in Deutschland im Angesicht staatlicher Beschränkungen. Dabei hatte er aber auch den Wettstreit der Konfessionskirchen im Blick. Und natürlich war er überzeugt, der Katholizismus werde sich in einem solchen Wettkampf

[2] *Frankfurter Allgemeine Sonntagszeitung* 24. März 2013, S. 30 (Wirtschaft). Wiederabdruck: Friedrich Wilhelm Graf, "Theologie des Reichtums statt Option für die Armen. Die Ökonomie der Pfingstkirchen," in *Arme Kirche – Kirche für die Armen: ein Widerspruch?*, Hrsg. Jörg Alt und Klaus Väthröder (Würzburg: Echter 2014), S. 198–202.
[3] Wilhelm Emmanuel von Ketteler, "Entwurf einer Rede über die Unabhängigkeit der Kirche vom Staat zur 1. Lesung der Grundrechte (Artikel III)," in Wilhelm Emmanuel von Ketteler, *Nachgelassene und anonyme Schriften*, Hrsg. Erwin Iserloh (Mainz: Hase & Koehler, 1985), S. 104–109, hier 108 f. Zum Kontext des Textes vgl. Karsten Petersen, *„Ich höre den Ruf nach Freiheit." Wilhelm Emmanuel von Ketteler und die Freiheitsforderungen seiner Zeit. Eine Studie zum Verhältnis von konservativem Katholizismus und Moderne* (Paderborn et al.: Schöningh, 2005), hier besonders S. 174 f.

siegreich durchsetzen. Kettelers Aussage war eine jener Reaktionen auf die Armutsfrage im 19. Jahrhundert, um die es in meinem Beitrag geht. Dieser Beitrag stellt die Ergebnisse des von mir geleiteten Projekts „Armenfürsorge und katholische Identität. Armut und Arme im katholischen Deutschland des frühen 19. Jahrhunderts" vor. Es war seit 2005 Teil des von der Deutschen Forschungsgemeinschaft (DFG) an der Universität Trier geförderten Sonderforschungsbereichs (SFB) „Fremdheit und Armut. Wandel von Inklusions- und Exklusionsformen von der Antike bis zur Gegenwart".[4] Am 31. Dezember 2012 endeten das Projekt und der Sonderforschungsbereich planmäßig.

Der Ertrag meines Projekts findet sich zum einen in einer Datenbank wieder, in der rund 6.000 Dokumente inventarisiert sind. Für rund 1.800 Dokumente sind Quellenauszüge oder Volltexte in dieser Datenbank hinterlegt. Darüber hinaus entstanden eine ganze Serie von wissenschaftlichen Qualifikationsschriften (Diplomarbeiten, wissenschaftliche Prüfungsarbeiten sowie drei Dissertationen), zwei Tagungsbände sowie einige weitere Beiträge in Zeitschriften, einem Ausstellungshandbuch und in Sammelwerken, die teils von Mitgliedern des Trierer Sonderforschungsbereichs, teils von anderen Wissenschaftlern im In- und Ausland herausgegeben wurden.[5] Wie bei solchen Forschungsverbünden üblich, sind damit kontinuierlich auch schon Zwischenergebnisse publiziert worden, die sich bis zum Ende des Projekts weithin bestätigten. Was im Folgenden auf ausdrücklichen Wunsch der Herausgeber des

---

[4] Einen Gesamtüberblick bietet "Forschungsprogramm," Sonderforschungsbereich 600 „Fremdheit und Armut, in: Forschungszentrum Europa. Strukturen langer Dauer und Gegenwartsprobleme, Universität Trier," abgerufen am 9. März 2016, <http://www.fze.uni-trier.de/de/presse-und-service/archiv/sfb-600/forschungsprogramm>. Viele Ergebnisse der verschiedenen Projekte des SFBs bieten die Bände der Reihe *Inklusion / Exklusion. Studien zu Fremdheit und Armut von der Antike bis zur Gegenwart* im Verlag Peter Lang.

[5] Die bis 2013 erschienenen Publikationen des Projektleiters (Bernhard Schneider) und des Projektteams (Antje Bräcker, Ingmar Franz, Michaela Maurer bzw. jetzt Michaela Collinet, Christian Schröder) sind in der Gesamtbibliographie des Forschungszentrums Europa der Universität Trier verzeichnet. Vgl. "Gesamtbibliographie in: Forschungszentrum Europa. Strukturen langer Dauer und Gegenwartsprobleme [online], Universität Trier," abgerufen am 9. März 2016, <http://www.fze.uni-trier.de/de/presse-und-service/gesamtbibliographie>. Zu ergänzen ist der Aufsatz Bernhard Schneider, "Armutsdiskurse, Armenfürsorge und Industrialisierung im ‚deutschen' Katholizismus während des langen 19. Jahrhunderts," in *Wirtschaft und Gemeinschaft. Konfessionelle und neureligiöse Gemeinsinnsmodelle im 19. und 20. Jahrhundert*, Hrsg. Swen Steinberg und Winfried Müller (Bielefeld: transcript, 2014), S. 35–62.

vorliegenden Bandes präsentiert wird, ist dementsprechend nicht gänzlich neu, sondern stützt sich intensiv auf die früheren Projektpublikationen und schreibt diese weiter fort. Im Rahmen des vorliegenden Beitrags ist es selbstverständlich auch nur möglich, einige zentrale Ergebnisse summarisch zu präsentieren, während der genaue Nachweis aus den Quellen wie auch die argumentative Entfaltung und tiefergehende Interpretation der einzelnen Aspekte den einzelnen Forschungsarbeiten vorbehalten bleiben muss.

Fragestellung und Methode

Ausgehen mussten die Forschungen unseres Projekts von einem doppelten Hintergrund.[6] Zum einen hatte sich durch die Französische Revolution und die ihr folgende Säkularisation die gesellschaftliche Stellung der katholischen Kirche in großen Teilen des deutschsprachigen Raumes erheblich verändert. Verbunden damit gab es sowohl Säkularisierungstendenzen in einzelnen Bevölkerungsgruppen als auch neue religiöse Aufbrüche und eine fortbestehende kirchliche Bindung in großen Teilen der katholischen Bevölkerung.[7] Zum anderen war die erste Hälfte des 19. Jahrhunderts durch großes Bevölkerungswachstum und wirtschaftliche Umbrüche gekennzeichnet, die mit massiven Subsistenzkrisen und einer unübersehbaren Massenarmut verbunden waren, für die dann bereits von den Zeitgenossen das neue Wort „Pauperismus" gebraucht wurde. Damit brachte man sprachlich zum Ausdruck, dass diese Form und dieses Ausmaß an Verarmung als neuartig

---

[6] Der Forschungsansatz unseres Projekts ist näher beschrieben in Bernhard Schneider, "Armut und Konfession. Ergebnisse und Perspektiven (kirchen-) historischer Forschungen zum Armutsproblem unter besonderer Berücksichtigung des 19. Jahrhunderts und des deutschen Katholizismus," in *Konfessionelle Armutsdiskurse und Armenfürsorgepraktiken im langen 19. Jahrhundert*, Hrsg. Bernhard Schneider (Frankfurt am Main: Peter Lang 2009), S. 9–57, hier S. 23–31. Ich folge im Text diesem Beitrag weitgehend, auch ohne dies im Detail weiter kenntlich zu machen.

[7] Zu den Veränderungen vgl. einführend Karl Hausberger, *Reichskirche – Staatskirche – „Papstkirche". Der Weg der deutschen Kirche im 19. Jahrhundert* (Regensburg: Pustet, 2008); Bernhard Schneider, "Reform of Piety in German Catholicism, 1780–1920," in *Piety and Modernity*, Hrsg. Anders Jarlert (Leuven: Leuven University Press, 2012), S. 193–224, hier S. 193–205. Mit weitem europäischen Horizont jetzt Rudolf Schlögl, *Alter Glaube und moderne Welt. Europäisches Christentum im Umbruch 1750–1850* (Frankfurt am Main: Sischer, 2013).

erschienen.[8] Mit der einsetzenden Industrialisierung kamen zu diesen klassischen Hungerkrisen noch die neuen Konjunkturkrisen hinzu. Deutlich spürbar wurden sie für die breite Masse der Bevölkerung im Untersuchungsraum wegen der vergleichsweise spät einsetzenden Industrialisierung ab der Jahrhundertmitte.[9] Die Untersuchungszeit war auf diese Weise eine Umbruchs- und eine Übergangszeit, in der um adäquate Antworten auf die sich zuspitzenden sozialen Probleme vielfältig gerungen wurde, ohne dass die Konturen eines neuen sozialen Sicherungssystems bereits klar erkennbar waren.[10]

Diese Situation wirft die Frage auf, wie sich die Katholiken und ihre Kirche denn dieser Situation stellten und mit ihr auseinandersetzten. Konkreter noch: Wie setzten sie sich mit der Problematik massenhafter Armut auseinander angesichts der Tatsache, dass die alte gesellschaftliche Ordnung, in der im katholischen Bereich kirchliche Institutionen die wesentlichen Träger der Armenfürsorge gewesen waren, nicht mehr existierte? Die Deutung von Armut wie Überlegungen zum Umgang mit ihr und den Armen müssten doch in einer Kirche, die sich in der eigenen Geschichte immer wieder als „Mutter der Armen" verstanden hatte, in einer solchen zugespitzten Situation auf der Agenda gestanden haben. Das war die Ausgangsannahme, die uns fragen ließ, ob es so etwas wie einen Armutsdiskurs im deutschen Katholizismus dieser Zeit gab und welches Bild von Armut und Armen mit welcher Semantik in ihm gezeichnet würde. Verbanden sich mit der Armenfrage bestimmte gesellschafts- und kirchenpolitische Vorstellungen? Auch danach war zu fragen, zumal der Katholizismus in der ersten Hälfte des 19. Jahrhunderts im deutschsprachigen Raum noch ein erhebliches Maß an Pluralität theologischer und kirchenpolitischer Strömungen kannte. Außerdem war in der ersten Hälfte des 19. Jahrhunderts bekanntlich noch keine offizielle

---

[8] Vgl. Günther Schulz, „Armut und Armenpolitik in Deutschland im frühen 19. Jahrhundert", *Historisches Jahrbuch* 115 (1995), S. 388–410; Karl H. Metz, *Die Geschichte der sozialen Sicherheit* (Stuttgart: Kohlhammer, 2008). Zur Begriffsgeschichte ausführlich Werner Conze, "Art. Proletariat, Pöbel, Pauperismus," in *Geschichtliche Grundbegriffe. Historisches Lexikon zur politisch-sozialen Sprache in Deutschland* Bd. 5, Hrsg. Otto Brunner et al. (Stuttgart: Klett-Cotta, 1984), S. 27–68.
[9] Vgl. Wilhelm Abel, *Massenarmut und Hungerkrisen im vorindustriellen Deutschland* (Göttingen: Vandenhoeck und Ruprecht, 1986). Zur Datierung der „Industriellen Revolution" in Deutschland um 1840/50 vgl. Hans-Ulrich Wehler, *Deutsche Gesellschaftsgeschichte* Bd. 2 *1815–1845/49* (München: Beck, 1996), S. 613–640, hier S. 613 f.
[10] Siehe Schulz, "Armut und Armenpolitik," S. 388–410; Metz, *Die Geschichte der sozialen Sicherheit.*

kirchliche Soziallehre vorhanden, vielmehr bildete sich eine solche erst im letzten Drittel des 19. Jahrhunderts aus.[11] Gleichzeitig erschien es spannend zu sein, diesen Armutsdiskurs auch daraufhin zu durchleuchten, ob und inwiefern in ihm Aussagen vorkamen, mit denen so etwas wie eine katholische Selbstbeschreibung vorgenommen wurde, um Identität zu konstruieren.[12] Eine wichtige Grundannahme bestand bei allen unseren Forschungen – wie auch denen des gesamten Sonderforschungsbereichs – darin, Armut nicht als einfachen Tatbestand vorhandener Not anzusehen. Wahrnehmungen und Deutungsmuster, Semantiken und Repräsentationen machen erst faktisch vorhandenen Mangel zu dem, was jeweils als Armut gilt.[13] Dementsprechend bezeichnet der Begriff „Armut" weder in der Vergangenheit noch in der Gegenwart einen einheitlichen Sachverhalt.

Methodisch war das Projekt in diesem Bereich als historische Diskursanalyse angelegt.[14] Eine gewisse Erweiterung besteht darin, dass die historische Semantik einerseits und die Stereotypenforschung andererseits als Verfahren einbezogen werden. Wir gingen daher z. T. in Verbindung mit anderen Teilprojekten des SFB gezielt auch Wandlungen auf begrifflicher Ebene nach, speziell dem Wortfeld „Caritas" (Nächstenliebe; Barmherzigkeit, Wohltätigkeit).[15] Zum anderen sollte in den Blick kommen, ob sich Zuschreibungen so verdichten, dass sie stereotypischen Charakter annehmen (z. B. „würdige Arme"; „ehrbare Arme"; der müßiggehende Bettler; der Arme als gefährliches Subjekt).

---

[11] Vgl. Franz Josef Stegmann und Peter Langhorst, "Geschichte der sozialen Ideen im deutschen Katholizismus," in *Geschichte der sozialen Ideen in Deutschland*, Hrsg. Helga Grebing (Essen: Klartext-Verlag, 2000), S. 599–862.
[12] Zu unserem Verständnis von Identität als kommunikativer Konstruktion vgl. Schneider, "Armut und Konfession," S. 25.
[13] Vgl. Lutz Raphael, "Armut zwischen Ausschluss und Solidarität. Europäische Traditionen und Tendenzen seit der Spätantike," in *Armut – Perspektiven in Kunst und Gesellschaft. Begleitband zur Ausstellung*, Hrsg. Herbert Uerlings et al. (Darmstadt: Primus-Verlag, 2011), S. 23–31 hier S. 31. Siehe zum Armutsbegriff in lexikalischer Kürze auch Sebastian Schmidt, „Armut", in *ebenda*, S. 40 f.
[14] Unter Diskurs verstehen die Forschungen meines Projektes im Anschluss an die jüngere diskursanalytische Theoriebildung (Landwehr; Eder) einen Komplex von (sprachlichen) Hervorbringungen zu einem bestimmten Thema während einer bestimmten Zeit und in einem bestimmten Raum. Dieser Komplex weist spezifische Regelmäßigkeiten auf, die das Thema systematisch organisieren. Vgl. Achim Landwehr, *Geschichte des Sagbaren. Einführung in die Historische Diskursanalyse* (Frankfurt am Main: Campus-Verlag, 2008), S. 92 f.
[15] Vgl. *Caritas – Barmherzigkeit – Diakonie. Studien zu Begriffen und Konzepten des Helfens in der Geschichte des Christentums vom Neuen Testament bis ins späte 20. Jahrhundert*, Hrsg. Michaela Collinet (Münster: Lit, 2014).

In einer zweiten Projektphase haben wir diese Fragestellung dann ausgeweitet auf die Praxis des Helfens, denn Diskurse verweisen auf Praktiken und sind mit ihnen vielfältig verwoben. So begegnen im untersuchten publizistischen Quellenkorpus unzählige Nachrichten über einzelne lokale karitative Maßnahmen, aber auch reflektierende Artikel, die etwa die Praxis der Armenfürsorge an einem bestimmten Ort beleuchten. Akteure vor Ort beteiligten sich mitunter direkt mit Berichten über ihre Arbeit und warben um Unterstützung und Nachahmung. Andererseits propagierten Autoren in der katholischen Presse auch bestimmte Formen des Helfens, die zumindest ihrer Meinung nach noch nicht genügend in der Praxis verankert waren. Konkret untersucht wurden in Form eines historischen Regionalvergleichs zwei deutsche Regionen unterschiedlichen Profils: das Saarland und Südbaden. Von Interesse war in diesem Zusammenhang zunächst, welche kirchlichen Akteure und Institutionen in diesen Räumen im Bereich der Armenfürsorge auf welche Weise wirkten und ob sich dabei bestimmte Konzepte von Armut und Armenfürsorge erkennen ließen. Darüber hinaus war zu beachten, wie sich diese Akteure und Institutionen gegenüber kommunalen-staatlichen oder auch zu anderskonfessionellen Akteuren und Institutionen verhielten. Es galt schließlich zu überprüfen, ob in der Untersuchungszeit die Bedeutung kirchlicher Akteure und Institutionen in der Armenfürsorge vor Ort tatsächlich marginal war, wie man in der Literatur lesen konnte.[16]

Zur Sprache des Helfens: Caritas, Wohltätigkeit, Nächstenliebe

Wenn es heute darum geht, die kirchliche Hilfstätigkeit in sozialen Notlagen im katholischen Bereich oder auch die religiös motivierten Hilfen katholischer Christen und Christinnen begrifflich zu fassen, fällt den meisten Beobachtern sicher das Wort „Caritas" ein. Die begriffsgeschichtlichen Studien im Trierer Sonderforschungsbereich belegen dagegen, dass dieser Begriff, obwohl in der Geschichte des Christentums seit frühchristlicher Zeit präsent,[17] in der ersten Hälfte des 19. Jahrhunderts in den zahlreich untersuchten katholischen Quellen zur Armuts- und Armenfürsorgeproblematik praktisch keine Rolle spielte.[18]

---

[16] Vgl. Schulz, "Armut und Armenpolitik," S. 402.

[17] Siehe Andreas Müller, „‚Caritas' im Neuen Testament und in der Alten Kirche," in *Caritas – Barmherzigkeit – Diakonie. Studien zu Begriffen und Konzepten des Helfens in der Geschichte des Christentums vom Neuen Testament bis ins späte 20. Jahrhundert*, Hrsg. Michaela Collinet (Münster: Lit, 2014), S. 17–47.

[18] Vgl. Antje Bräcker et al., "Vom Almosen zur Solidarität. Begriffe und Konzepte

Der Begriff „Caritas" war in der christlichen Tradition inhaltlich so weit,
dass er damit wenig geeignet erschien, das spezifisch helfende Tun in den
vielfältigen sozialen Nöten adäquat zum Ausdruck zu bringen. Stärker
theologisch geprägte Quellen wie Gebetbücher, Predigten oder Katechismen
bedienten sich in der von uns untersuchten Zeit traditionsreicher Vokabeln
wie „Almosen", „Almosengeben", „Barmherzigkeit" / „Werke der
Barmherzigkeit" oder „Nächstenliebe", wenn sie das Thema erörterten.[19]
In publizistischen Quellen, aber auch in pastoraltheologischen
Handbüchern dieser Zeit dominiert eine neutralere Begrifflichkeit. Hier
spricht man dann gerne von „Mildtätigkeit" oder „Wohltätigkeit". Die
stärker religiös geprägten Vokabeln fehlen aber keineswegs. Um den
spezifisch religiösen Charakter des Helfens zum Ausdruck zu bringen, fügt
man den neutralen Begriffen nicht selten das Adjektiv „christlich" hinzu.
Die Quellen akzentuieren im Kontext der genannten Begriffe regelmäßig
das Handeln, damit vor allem Nächstenliebe oder Barmherzigkeit nicht
einfach als Gefühl erscheinen.[20] In Einzelfällen versuchten
strengkirchlich-ultramontan ausgerichtete Autoren auch das christlich
helfende Handeln von zeitgenössischen Formen philanthropischer Hilfe
terminologisch abzugrenzen. In solchen Texten stehen „christliche Liebe"
bzw. „Barmherzigkeit" dann den negativ bewerteten säkularen Termini
„Menschenliebe" und „Humanität" gegenüber.[21]

Diskurse um Armut und Armenfürsorge

Unsere Forschungen haben ergeben, dass sich um die verschiedenen
Quellensorten zwei Teildiskurse gruppieren, die einen deutlich
unterschiedlichen Charakter aufweisen und abweichenden Diskursregeln
unterliegen.[22] Man kann sie als liturgisch-paränetischen Teildiskurs
einerseits und als politisch-kirchenpolitischen Teildiskurs andererseits

---

des Helfens im Katholizismus von der Aufklärung bis ins späte 20. Jahrhundert,"
in *Caritas – Barmherzigkeit – Diakonie. Studien zu Begriffen und Konzepten des
Helfens in der Geschichte des Christentums vom Neuen Testament bis ins späte 20.
Jahrhundert*, Hrsg. Michaela Collinet (Münster: Lit, 2014), S. 161–185, hier S.
164 f. Zur Begrifflichkeit in den Verkündigungstexten ausführlich Michaela
Collinet, *Frohe Botschaft für die Armen? Armut und Armenfürsorge in der
katholischen Verkündigung des späten 18. und frühen 19. Jahrhunderts* (Stuttgart:
Kohlhammer, 2015), S. 187–199.
[19] Vgl. dazu und zum Folgenden Bräcker et al., "Vom Almosen zur Solidarität," S.
165.
[20] Vgl. ebenda, S. 166 f.
[21] Vgl. ebenda, S. 169.
[22] Erste knappe Charakterisierung bei Schneider, "Armut und Konfession," S. 40.

bezeichnen. Im Folgenden beschreibe und erläutere ich diese beiden Teildiskurse gestützt auf die verschiedenen im Projekt entstandenen Qualifikationsschriften.

a) Armut und Armenfürsorge in katholischen Hirtenbriefen und Predigten

In ihrer Dissertation hat Michaela Maurer (jetzt Michaela Collinet) den Nachweis erbracht, dass Armut und Arme in katholischen Predigten aus der ersten Hälfte des 19. Jahrhunderts in beachtlichem Umfang zum Thema wurden. In den von ihr ausgewerteten Predigten (2.836) gingen 24 % in irgendeiner Form darauf ein.[23] Die Prediger, die auf diese Thematik eingingen, beschäftigten sich allerdings in höchst unterschiedlichem Umfang mit ihr. Bei rund der Hälfte dieser Predigten blieben Arme und Armut ein Randthema, bei einem guten Drittel waren sie ein wichtiges, aber nicht das Hauptthema. Die Aussagen zu Armut und Armenfürsorge waren hier überwiegend eingebunden in die Erörterung von Fragen des Glaubens und der Moral. Zum ausschließlichen Gegenstand avancierte die Armutsfrage in 11 % der Predigten mit Bezug zu dieser Frage. Auch in diesen Predigten geht es meist um theologische Aspekte des Themas – die Pflicht zur Nächstenliebe und das daraus folgende Handeln; die kirchliche Lehre vom Almosen und den guten, barmherzigen Werken –, während Fragen der Praxis kirchlicher oder auch kommunaler-staatlicher Armenfürsorge wenig Aufmerksamkeit fanden.[24] Bezogen auf das Gesamtkorpus von fast 3.000 Predigten sind die 71 Predigten mit Schwerpunkt Armut / Armenfürsorge eine bescheidene Ausbeute. Sicherlich kann man daher mit gutem Grund davon sprechen, Armut sei eine nur untergeordnete Perspektive für die katholischen Prediger in der untersuchten Zeit gewesen. Dies gilt im Übrigen für die beiden kirchenpolitischen und theologischen Hauptströmungen im zeitgenössischen Katholizismus gleichermaßen, also für Prediger spätaufklärerischer wie für Prediger strengkirchlich-ultramontaner Ausrichtung.[25]

Auch in dem im 18. Jahrhundert aufkommenden neuen Kommunikationsinstrument der Hirtenbriefe, mit dem sich die Bischöfe

---

[23] Vgl. dazu und zum Folgenden Collinet, *Frohe Botschaft*, S. 89–95. Vgl. auch Michaela Maurer, "Armenfürsorge in der katholischen Verkündigung vom späten 18. bis zur Mitte des 19. Jahrhunderts," in *Konfessionen in den west- und mitteleuropäischen Sozialsystemen im langen 19. Jahrhundert*, Hrsg. Michaela Maurer und Bernhard Schneider (Münster: Lit, 2013), S. 41–57.

[24] Vgl. Collinet, *Frohe Botschaft*, S. 93 f.

[25] Ebenda, S. 93.

vermehrt an ihren Klerus oder / und an die Gläubigen wandten,[26] waren
Ausführungen zu unserem Thema anzutreffen, sogar in deutlich größerer
Intensität als bei den Predigten.[27] 62 % der 151 untersuchten Hirtenbriefe
hatten es im Blick. Thematischer Schwerpunkt waren Armut und
Armenfürsorge allerdings wieder nur im kleinsten Teil dieses Korpus. 7 %
der Hirtenbriefe, die auf diese Thematik eingingen, machten sie zum
Hauptthema. Bemerkenswert ist bei dieser Quellengruppe, dass sich mit
einer Ausnahme nur Hirtenbriefe intensiv mit der Armutsproblematik
auseinandersetzten, die in der Mitte des 1840er Jahre entstanden. Sie
reagierten ganz offenkundig auf die große Hungersnot der Jahre 1846/47
und auf die wachsende soziale Unruhe in Deutschland in diesem
Jahrzehnt.[28] In den Hirtenbriefen dieser Zeit begegnen deshalb auch
konzeptionelle Überlegungen zur Bekämpfung der Armut, die zuvor kaum
eine Rolle spielten.[29]

In diesen Verkündigungstexten herrschte eine Darstellungsweise vor,
die Armut als individuelles Problem einer Person oder einer Familie
erscheinen lässt, während die Dimension eines gesamtgesellschaftlichen
Problems erst ganz spät am Ende der Untersuchungszeit in den Texten
sichtbar wird. In umfassenden akuten Krisen wie Hungersnöten oder
Epidemien gerieten auch diese Momente in das Blickfeld der
Verkündigung.[30] „Bei der Deutung dieser Massenarmut aber auch der
individuellen Armutssituationen überwiegen sittlich-moralische
Interpretationsmuster. Da die Geistlichen Armut als eine im göttlichen
Heilsplan vorgesehene und bleibende gesellschaftliche Realität ansehen,
streben sie keine strukturelle Lösung des Armutsproblems, sondern eine
Linderung der Not an. Es gehen die Meinungen jedoch darüber
auseinander, ob die Linderung durch individuelle Akte der Nächstenliebe,

---

[26] Charakterisierung dieses Quellentyps bei ebenda, S. 86–88.
[27] Vgl. ebenda, S. 95–98. Eine erste kompakte Auswertung der Hirtenbriefe bietet
Michaela Maurer, "‚Vater der Armen'?! Arme und Armut in der Verkündigung
katholischer Bischöfe," in Konfessionelle Armutsdiskurse und
Armenfürsorgepraktiken im langen 19. Jahrhundert, Hrsg. Bernhard Schneider
(Frankfurt am Main: Peter Lang 2009), S. 98–118.
[28] Vgl. Collinet, Frohe Botschaft, S. 97 f.; Maurer, "‚Vater der Armen'?!," S. 93.
[29] Vgl. Collinet, Frohe Botschaft, S. 97; Maurer, "‚Vater der Armen'?!," S. 108–
111.
[30] Vgl. Collinet, Frohe Botschaft, S. 100 f. Zeitgenössische Stimmen zum
Pauperismusproblem finden sich dokumentiert bei Liselotte Dilcher, Der deutsche
Pauperismus und seine Literatur (Frankfurt am Main: Privatdruck, 1957); Die
Eigentumslosen. Der deutsche Pauperismus und die Emanzipationskrise in
Darstellungen und Deutungen der zeitgenössischen Literatur, Hrsg. Carl Jantke
und Dietrich Hilger (Freiburg und München: Alber, 1965).

durch die Arbeit staatlicher Institutionen oder das Wirken kirchlicher Armenfürsorgeeinrichtungen gewährleistet werden sollte."[31]

Diese Meinungsunterschiede spiegeln nicht nur individuell abweichende Positionen der einzelnen Verkündiger – Priester und Bischöfe – wider, sondern in ihnen kommt auch die kirchenpolitisch-theologische Verankerung der Akteure zum Ausdruck. Am meisten beachtet werden über alle Divergenzen hinweg die „verschiedenen Formen persönlicher Nächstenliebe",[32] zu denen durchgängig aufgerufen wird und zu denen genauso regelmäßig auch Formen der immateriellen Hilfe gezählt werden.[33] Für die Verkündigungstexte typisch ist dabei, dass sie nicht nur die Situation der Armen in den Blick nehmen, sondern vielmehr auch stark die Seite der Gebenden. In den unzähligen Appellen zur tätigen Nächstenliebe geht es ganz zentral um das Seelenheil der Menschen, zu dem die aus Gottes- und Nächstenliebe erbrachten klassischen „Werke der Barmherzigkeit" (nach dem Matthäusevangelium Mt 25, 31–46) nach Meinung nahezu aller Autoren ganz entscheidend beitragen. Armut erscheint in dieser Perspektive als regelrecht notwendig, damit die Reichen durch ihre den Armen im Geist christlicher Nächstenliebe erwiesene Hilfe eine Heilschance haben.[34] Damit knüpft die kirchliche Verkündigung des frühen 19. Jahrhunderts direkt an biblische Vorstellungen und an Argumentationsmuster aus der Spätantike an, die sich in Predigten und Schriften griechischer wie lateinischer Kirchenväter finden.[35]

Die öffentlich-institutionalisierte Armenfürsorge erfährt eine positive Würdigung fast ausschließlich in Verkündigungstexten katholisch-aufklärerischer Provenienz. Sie schließen eng an die einschlägigen Tendenzen frühneuzeitlicher Armenfürsorge auch in katholischen Territorien an, das Armenwesen straffer zu gestalten, genauer zu regeln und es dabei zu zentralisieren. Auch das im 18. Jahrhundert in diesem Zusammenhang wachsende Interesse an Armutsprävention durch Bildungsmaßnahmen findet einen Nachhall in den untersuchten Quellen.[36] Bei den strengkirchlich-ultramontanen Autoren findet sich dagegen das größte Interesse an einer spezifisch kirchlichen Praxis der Armenfürsorge.

---

[31] Maurer, "Armenfürsorge," S. 42.

[32] Ebenda, S. 44.

[33] Vgl. dazu und zum Folgenden ebenda, S. 42–47.

[34] Vgl. Collinet, *Frohe Botschaft*, S. 110–113.

[35] Vgl. Maurer, "Armenfürsorge," S. 42–44. Zur Tradition dieser Argumentationsmuster vgl. Oliver Müller, *Vom Almosen zum Spendenmarkt. Sozialethische Aspekte christlicher Spendenkultur* (Freiburg im Breisgau: Lambertus, 2005).

[36] Siehe Maurer, "Armenfürsorge," S. 47–51.

Sie rekurrieren dafür insbesondere auf die Tradition karitativ tätiger Orden
und Kongregationen, die in Predigten und Hirtenbriefen dieser Provenienz
in höchsten Tönen gelobt und als Ideal der Armenfürsorge präsentiert
werden.[37] Der von den Orden in christlichem Geist geleisteten Hilfe
gebührt nach Meinung dieser Autoren entschieden der Vorrang vor einer
säkularen, wofür sie sowohl die geschichtlichen Erfahrungen als auch die
Erfahrungen der eigenen Gegenwart als Belege anführen. Selbstlose und
opferbereite Armenfürsorge aus religiösem Geist könne den Armen am
besten dienen und entfalte bei ihnen auch die besten Wirkungen, da sie
sich nicht in einer bloß materiellen Gabe erschöpfe, sondern diese mit
liebender Zuwendung, geistlichem Trost und religiös-moralischer
Unterweisung verknüpfe.

In der von den Autoren im liturgisch-paränetischen Armutsdiskurs
gepflegten Semantik artikuliert sich eine große Wertschätzung der
Bedürftigen, denen durch eine theologisch differenzierte Inklusionssemantik
(soteriologische, christologische, schöpfungstheologische und
ekklesiologische Inklusion) Würde zugesprochen wird.[38] Der Begriff der
Würde oder gar der Menschenwürde begegnet in den untersuchten Texten
jedoch nur selten. Eine derartige Wertschätzung wurde von den
Geistlichen allerdings an gewisse Bedingungen geknüpft und traf nicht
automatisch jeden, der bedürftig war. Dafür steht auch in der
Untersuchungszeit die seit der Spätantike bekannte Unterscheidung von
„wahren" Armen und „falschen" Armen bzw. „starken" Bettlern, die seit
dem Spätmittelalter besonders häufig verwandt wurde.[39] Eine spezifisch
religiöse Exklusionssemantik ist wenig verbreitet, und sie trifft auch mehr
die Reichen als die Armen.[40] Der zentrale Modus religiöser Exklusion ist
derjenige, der über den Begriff der Sünde vorgenommen wird. Die
kritisierten Sünden der Reichen sind dabei Hartherzigkeit,
verschwenderisches Luxusleben und fehlende Nächstenliebe. Fehlender
Arbeitswille oder die Vortäuschung von Bedürftigkeit, aber auch fehlende
Frömmigkeit und eine damit verbundene Haltung fehlender demütiger

---

[37] Vgl. dazu und zum Folgenden ebenda, S. 51–56.

[38] Dazu und zum Folgenden Collinet, *Frohe Botschaft*, S. 132–141.

[39] Siehe dazu ebenda, S. 116–121. Zur spätmittelalterlichen und frühneuzeitlichen
Verwendung vgl. z. B. Sebastian Schmidt, "Die Abschaffung der Armut – das
frühneuzeitliche Inklusionsprogramm und seine Exklusionen am Beispiel der
Geistlichen Kurfürstentümer Trier, Köln und Mainz," in *Zwischen Ausschluss und
Solidarität. Modi der Inklusion/Exklusion von Fremden und Armen in Europa seit
der Spätantike*, Hrsg. Lutz Raphael und Herbert Uerlings (Frankfurt am Main et
al.: Lang, 2008), S. 241–274, hier bes. S. 247–249, 254 f.

[40] Vgl. Collinet, *Frohe Botschaft*, S. 140 f.

Annahme der Not charakterisieren den Unterschied von würdigen bzw. unwürdigen Armen. „Anders als in der Praxis der kommunalen und staatlichen Armenfürsorge führt die genannte Unterscheidung aber nicht in allen Verkündigungstexten zur grundsätzlichen Ablehnung der unwürdigen Armen als Unterstützungsempfänger."[41] Meist steht für die abgelehnten unwürdigen Armen der Begriff des Bettlers, teils um kriminalisierende Zuschreibungen erweitert, doch gibt es auch eine Verwendung dieses Begriffs ohne negative Konnotation, bei der Bettler als Synonym für Arme stehen.

Zum Thema in Predigten und Hirtenbriefen werden vor allem die würdigen Armen, die stark topoihaft als arme Witwen und Waisen präsentiert werden.[42] Sie repräsentieren jene Gruppe der „verschämten Hausarmen", d. h. der sesshaften tugendhaften Armen, die nach Ansicht der Autoren am stärksten unter Armut litten. Ihnen wurde in der neuzeitlichen Armenfürsorge am ehesten gesellschaftliche Akzeptanz entgegengebracht. Daneben kommen ebenfalls arme Alte und arme Kranke in den Blick, deren Probleme teils eingehend erörtert werden. Beiden Gruppen gemeinsam ist, dass ihnen die Fähigkeit abgeht, durch Arbeit für den eigenen Lebensunterhalt zu sorgen. Das macht sie grundsätzlich unterstützungswürdig. Als vergleichsweise neue Armutsgruppe begegnen die arbeitenden Armen, worunter die Autoren allerdings noch vorwiegend Tagelöhner und Dienstboten verstehen. Auch ihre Not wird individuell gedeutet (entweder wegen eines Fehlverhaltens der Dienstherren oder wegen der eigenen Vergehen) und nicht strukturell. „Die Wahrnehmung einer trotz Arbeit bestehenden extremen Notlage einer großen Gruppe von Menschen, wie sie die Pauperismusdefinition [...] beschreibt, zeigt sich in den Predigten und Hirtenbriefen der späten 1840er und 1850er Jahre."[43]

Als wesentliche Diskursregeln im liturgisch-paränetischen Armutsdiskurs ergeben sich zusammenfassend die folgenden:

- die Wahrnehmung materieller Armut als individuelles Schicksal und nicht als eine breite Bevölkerungsschichten betreffende Massenarmut;
- die moraltheologische Deutung von Armut im Blick auf den Einzelnen (als Strafe, Prüfung etc.) sowie im Blick auf die Gesellschaft die geschichtstheologische Deutung als Folge des Abfalls von Kirche und Glaube;

---

[41] Ebenda, S. 116.
[42] Vgl. ebenda, S. 122–132.
[43] Ebenda, S. 131.

• die verstärkte Ausrichtung der Verkündigungstexte auf die zur
Wohltätigkeit verpflichteten Reichen als Adressatengruppe.

b) Armut und Armenfürsorge in der katholischen Presse

Der zweite Teildiskurs begegnet in der katholischen Presse.[44] Eine
solche katholische Presse etablierte sich allmählich im Verlauf der ersten
Hälfte des 19. Jahrhunderts aus eher dürftigen Anfängen.[45] Sie wies dabei
ein beachtliches Spektrum unterschiedlicher Typen auf: streng
wissenschaftlich-theologische Fachorgane standen neben eher für die
seelsorgliche Praxis gedachten Zeitschriften, diese wiederum neben stark
kirchenpolitisch ausgerichteten, und auch eher der religiösen Erbauung
dienende Titel fehlten nicht.[46] Bestanden viele dieser Zeitschriften nur
wenige Jahre, so gelang es einigen wenigen Titeln, sich über Jahrzehnte
am Markt zu behaupten. Knapp 40 derartige Zeitschriften wurden in
unserem Forschungsprojekt integral ausgewertet, wobei wir Wert darauf
legten, die verschiedenen Typen zu berücksichtigen und eine angemessene
regionale Streuung zu gewährleisten. Besonders war darauf zu achten,
auch die unterschiedlichen theologischen und kirchenpolitischen Lager mit
den ihnen nahestehenden Organen abzudecken.[47] Als Schwierigkeit erwies
sich dabei der Umstand, dass der Boom katholischer Zeitschriften in den
1830er und 1840er Jahren fast nur einem einzigen innerkatholischen Lager
zugute kam, nämlich den strengkirchlich-ultramontan ausgerichteten
Kreisen. Sie errangen in dieser Zeit die publizistische Meinungsführerschaft,
während die noch in den ersten beiden Jahrzehnten prominente katholische

---

[44] Die Auswertung dieses Teildiskurses erfolgt schwerpunktmäßig durch eine
Dissertation von Ingmar Franz. Diese war bei Abschluss des vorliegenden
Manuskripts noch nicht vollständig beendet, so dass manche wichtigen Aspekte
des Themas noch nicht zu erörtern sind. Eine erste Darstellung zentraler
Ergebnisse bietet Ingmar Franz, "Katholische Publizistik und die Diskurse um
Armut und Soziale Frage bis zum Kulturkampf," in *Konfessionen in den west- und
mitteleuropäischen Sozialsystemen im langen 19. Jahrhundert*, Hrsg. Michaela
Maurer und Bernhard Schneider (Münster: Lit, 2013), S. 59–92. Auf diesem
Beitrag basiert das gesamte Kapitel. Wo ich nicht im Einzelnen auf diesen Beitrag
oder auf andere Arbeiten des Projekts verweise, stütze ich mich auf die vorläufige
Fassung einzelner Teilkapitel der Dissertation von Herrn Franz.
[45] Eine kurze Pressegeschichte bietet Bernhard Schneider, *Katholiken auf die
Barrikaden? Europäische Revolutionen und deutsche katholische Presse 1815–
1848* (Paderborn et al.: Schöningh, 1998), S. 44–94.
[46] Zur Typologie und Programmatik vgl. ebenda, S. 58–73.
[47] Dazu und zum Folgenden erste Hinweise bei Franz, "Katholische Publizistik," S.
60 f.

Spätaufklärung gleichzeitig in der Presse stark an Boden verlor. Um diesem Ungleichgewicht etwas entgegenzuwirken, haben wir in unserem Korpus alle vorhandenen 11 katholisch-aufklärerischen Zeitschriften berücksichtigt und (nur) eine Auswahl von 25 strengkirchlich-ultramontanen. Gleichwohl ist auch bei den von uns entdeckten Texten zur Armenfrage die ultramontane Sicht allein schon quantitativ dominant. Ebenso ergibt sich aus der geschilderten Entwicklung der katholischen Presse, dass die Jahre ab 1830 in unserem Quellenkorpus deutlich stärker dokumentiert sind als die beiden ersten Jahrzehnte des Jahrhunderts.

Mit den Zeitschriften haben wir eine auf breite Rezeption angelegte Quellengruppe vor uns, die auch einen nachweislich beachtlich großen Verbreitungsgrad erreichte, denn man darf ab den 1830er Jahren von einem Lesepublikum von ca. 200.000 Menschen ausgehen.[48] Mit den Zeitschriften begegnet uns eine Quellengruppe mit einer vergleichsweise hohen Aktualität und zeitlichen Nähe auch zu plötzlichen Ereignissen wie Epidemien oder akuten Hungerkrisen, und sie reagieren auch rascher und intensiver auf neue Entwicklungen wie die beginnende Industrialisierung.[49]

Auch der Armutsdiskurs in den untersuchten Zeitschriften ist ein religiös geprägter Diskurs, aber er ist kein theologischer Fachdiskurs, denn eine fachtheologische Auseinandersetzung erfolgt kaum und die Adressaten vieler Zeitschriften waren auch nicht speziell Fachtheologen. Gerade die stärker wissenschaftlich ausgerichteten Organe beschäftigen sich am wenigstens mit dem Thema Armut. Die Zeitschriftenbeiträge weisen ein breites Spektrum an literarischen Formen auf, in denen sie sich mit dem Thema Armut auseinandersetzen: Kurze Nachrichten, Miszellen, ausführliche Artikel oder Artikelserien, Rezensionen und Korrespondentenberichte, ja sogar einzelne Gedichte lassen sich in unserem reichhaltigen Material finden.[50]

Weit stärker als in den Quellen des liturgisch-paränetischen Teildiskurses fokussierte die katholische Presse auf die praktischen und (kirchen-)politischen Aspekte der Problematik. Exemplarisch deutlich wird dies in den vergleichsweise zahlreichen Artikeln der zwischen 1804 und 1827 erscheinenden spätaufklärerischen, praktisch-theologisch ausgerichteten Zeitschrift *Archiv für die Pastoralkonferenzen*.[51] In dieser

---

[48] Zur Berechnung dieses Verbreitungsgrades vgl. Schneider, *Katholiken*, S. 73–85.

[49] Mit diesem Aspekt beschäftigt sich näher Schneider, "Armutsdiskurse, Armenfürsorge und Industrialisierung," hier bes. S. 49–57.

[50] Vgl. Schneider, "Armut und Konfession," S. 38.

[51] Siehe als erste Auswertung Patrick Bircher und Bernhard Schneider, "Katholische Armutsdiskurse im frühen 19. Jahrhundert," in *Zwischen Ausschluss*

behandelt das Gros der Beiträge Stiftungen, Wohltätigkeitsvereine und
Anstalten der Armenfürsorge sowie armenpolitische Fragen. Hier stellten
die Autoren – alle Priester – ihre bereits realisierten Projekte oder
Konzepte für die künftige Gestaltung der Armenfürsorgepraxis vor und
präsentierten sich so als Sozialexperten. Dahinter treten Ausführungen zur
Almosentheologie und zum Prinzip christlicher Nächstenliebe deutlich
zurück.

Auch im politisch-kirchenpolitischen Teildiskurs begegnen Arme in
verschiedenen Kategorisierungen, mit denen spezifische Zuschreibungen
verbunden sind.[52] So spricht man von selbstverschuldet Armen, weil sie
sich durch eigenes Fehlverhalten in die Armutssituation gebracht hätten,
und unverschuldet Armen, die ohne eigenes Zutun in Not geraten seien.
Von verschämten Armen (Hausarmen), die sich schämen, öffentlich als
Arme erkannt zu werden, ist ebenso die Rede wie von unverschämten
Armen, die lieber dem Bettel nachgehen, als zu arbeiten. Auch die binäre
Formel von den würdigen und den unwürdigen Armen findet sich. Mit
diesen verschiedenen Kategorien ist der Zugang zu Hilfen bzw. deren
Verweigerung eng verknüpft, sie erweisen sich also als Modi von
Inklusion und Exklusion. Konkret lehnen viele Texte es ab, arbeitsfähigen
Armen Hilfe zu gewähren, da sie nicht wirklich bedürftig seien und sich
selbst helfen könnten. Bestenfalls sollte man ihnen in eng begrenztem
Umfang helfen. Deutlicher noch als in den meisten Verkündigungstexten
kommt dies einem Verdikt über das Betteln gleich. Spannungsfrei bleiben
die Texte bei diesen Bemühungen um eine Grenzziehung nicht immer. So
kann selbst innerhalb eines einzigen Textes einerseits das Ideal einer
prinzipiell uneingeschränkten, universal geltenden Nächstenliebe
beschworen werden, während andererseits die Unterscheidung von
wahren, würdigen Armen und unwürdigen Armen benutzt wird, um den
Kreis der Hilfeberechtigten zu begrenzen.[53] Kompliziert wurde es
spätestens im konkreten Einzelfall in der Praxis. Konnte man als in der
Armenfürsorge wirkender Priester wirklich Bettlern, selbst wenn man

---

und Solidarität. Modi der Inklusion/Exklusion von Fremden und Armen in Europa seit der Spätantike, Hrsg. Lutz Raphael und Herbert Uerlings (Frankfurt am Main et al.: Lang, 2008), S. 311–339, hier bes. S. 315–329 (die einzelnen Zahlen bei der Quantifizierung sind nun durch die Forschungen von Ingmar Franz teilweise überholt, die inhaltlichen Aussagen bleiben davon unberührt gültig). Als englische Fassung: Patrick Bircher und Bernhard Schneider, "Catholic poverty discourses in the early nineteenth century," in *Strangers and Poor People*, Hrsg. Andreas Gestrich et al. (Frankfurt am Main: Lang, 2009), S. 343–369.
[52] Vgl. dazu und zum Folgenden Franz, "Katholische Publizistik," S. 62–66.
[53] Vgl. Bircher und Schneider, "Katholische Armutsdiskurse," S. 328; Bircher und Schneider, "Catholic poverty discourses," S. 358.

berechtigte Zweifel an ihrer Unterstützungswürdigkeit hatte, die Hilfe einfach verweigern? Musste man nicht auch hier versuchen, in einer Kombination von materieller Hilfe und moralisch-religiöser Belehrung und Ermahnung diese zu bessern und auf einen guten Weg zu bringen? In einem Artikel wurde genau dies empfohlen.[54]

Vor diesem komplizierten Hintergrund sind auch die im politisch-kirchenpolitischen Teildiskurs so bedeutsamen Ausführungen über konkrete Formen und Institutionen der Armenhilfe zu sehen. Bei diesen Fragen werden dann auch markante Unterschiede zwischen der spätaufklärerischen und der strengkirchlich-ultramontanen Presse erkennbar. Armenfürsorge war für beide Lager ein wichtiges Feld kirchlichen Engagements und Selbstverständnisses, aber eben mit spezifischen Akzentuierungen.

Der katholischen Spätaufklärung nahestehende Autoren sprechen sich nachdrücklich für eine organisierte Armenfürsorge auf lokaler Ebene aus, bei der Kommune und Kirche Hand in Hand arbeiten.[55] Sie greifen in ihren Vorschlägen über eine bloße Linderung der vorhandenen Not hinaus und entfalten zum Teil ein regelrechtes Programm zur Armutsprävention, mit dem auch das notorische Problem des Bettelns beseitigt werden sollte. Erzieherische und sozialdisziplinierende Komponenten fügen sich in den meisten Beiträgen zusammen bis hin zur Idee von Sittengerichten einerseits und der Einrichtung von sogenannten „Industrieschulen" andererseits, in denen man bestimmte Fertigkeiten in Handwerk und Gewerbe erlernen sollte. Gerade Kinder aus armen Familien und das oft ja ebenfalls noch sehr junge Dienstbotenpersonal avancierten zu einer bevorzugten Klientel für derartige Bemühungen. Da Arbeitsmangel und zum Lebensunterhalt nicht ausreichende Löhne (das Phänomen der „labouring poor") in diesem Teildiskurs deutlicher als in den Verkündigungstexten als Probleme wahrgenommen werden, finden sich auch dazu verschiedentlich Überlegungen. Das schloss gleichzeitig den Gedanken ein, Arme notfalls auch zur Arbeit in Arbeitsanstalten zu

---

[54] Vgl. einen Text aus dem Jahr 1810, in dem dieses Dilemma erörtert wird, bei Franz, "Katholische Publizistik," S. 66.

[55] Siehe dazu und zum Folgenden Bircher und Schneider, "Katholische Armutsdiskurse," S. 320–329; Bircher und Schneider, "Catholic poverty discourses," S. 350–359; Franz, "Katholische Publizistik," S. 66–69; Bernhard Schneider, "Katholische Armutsdiskurse und Praktiken der Armenfürsorge im gesellschaftlichen Wandel des 19. Jahrhunderts und das Paradigma der Zivilgesellschaft," in *Zwischen Fürsorge und Seelsorge. Christliche Kirchen in den europäischen Zivilgesellschaften seit dem 18. Jahrhundert*, Hrsg. Arnd Bauerkämper und Jürgen Nautz (Frankfurt am Main: Campus-Verlag, 2009), S. 79–111, hier S. 82–84.

zwingen.[56] In dieser Hinsicht führten die katholischen Spätaufklärer die
Diskurse und Praktiken im katholischen Deutschland des 18. Jahrhunderts
fort.[57] In der spätaufklärerischen Presse wurde in den ersten Jahrzehnten
des 19. Jahrhunderts vereinzelt selbst darüber diskutiert, ob es im Kampf
gegen die Armut helfe, mehr Fabriken zu errichten und die Fabrikarbeit zu
fördern. Die Meinungen gingen in dieser Hinsicht weit auseinander, bis
hin zum Ruf nach staatlichen Maßnahmen gegen die zunehmend
eingesetzten Maschinen, da diese Arbeitsplätze vernichteten.[58]

Im Rahmen dieser katholisch-aufklärerischen Konzepte zur
Armenfürsorge galt es weithin als selbstverständlich, dass Kirche und
Staat, Pfarrer und Bürgermeister, zusammenwirken.[59] Dementsprechend
hieß man in diesen Kreisen staatliches Engagement gut und verlangte nach
ihm. Armenfürsorge erscheint als ein wesentliches Element guter
Herrschaft, die sich um das Wohlergehen der Menschen als Staatsziel zu
sorgen hatte. Ein rein staatliches Armenfürsorgewesen lag dagegen
jenseits des Horizonts, und selbst gegenüber verpflichtenden Abgaben für
das Armenwesen trug man teilweise erhebliche Bedenken. Ebenso wenig
pochte man in den katholisch-aufklärerischen Texten auf ein spezifisch
katholisches Armenwesen oder auf eine Sonderrolle des Klerus in der
Armenfürsorge. Das sollte offenkundig im gemischtkonfessionellen
Südwesten Deutschlands, wo das Gros der spätaufklärerischen
Zeitschriften erschien, die Anschlussfähigkeit der Kirche an den Staat und
sein Wirken im sozialen Bereich erleichtern. Gleichzeitig ist aber auch die
Tendenz zu erkennen, „eine rein säkulare Philanthropie wie auch eine
gänzlich von der Kirche losgelöste öffentliche Armenfürsorge" auf diese
Weise zu verhindern.[60]

In der strengkirchlich-ultramontanen Presse war das Wirken der Kirche
und vieler einzelner Katholiken und Katholikinnen in der Armenfürsorge

---

[56] Einige Textbelege dazu bei Schneider, "Armutsdiskurse, Armenfürsorge und
Industrialisierung," S. 44.
[57] Vgl. Schmidt, "Abschaffung der Armut," S. 257 f; Bernhard Schneider,
"Christliche Verbrüderung und tätige Nächstenliebe – Armenfürsorge und
Bruderschaften im Horizont der katholischen Aufklärung," in *Armut und
Armenfürsorge in der Frühen Neuzeit*, Hrsg. Konrad Krimm et al. (Ostfildern:
Thorbecke, 2011), S. 237–257.
[58] Näher dazu Schneider, "Armutsdiskurse, Armenfürsorge und Industrialisierung,"
S. 51.
[59] Zum Folgenden Franz, "Katholische Publizistik," S. 82; Bircher und Schneider,
"Katholische Armutsdiskurse," S. 320–329; Bircher und Schneider, "Catholic
poverty discourses," S. 350–359; Schneider, "Katholische Armutsdiskurse und
Praktiken der Armenfürsorge," S. 83.
[60] Ebenda.

ein Beweismittel.[61] In teils langen historischen Rückblicken und mit manchen Zitaten aus dem Fundus der kirchlichen Überlieferung strich man mit sichtbarem Stolz die erbrachten Leistungen der katholischen Kirche in der Geschichte der Armenfürsorge heraus. Damit versuchten die Autoren direkt oder indirekt zu zeigen, dass die Kirche für dieses Feld zuständig sei und auch über die erforderliche Handlungskompetenz verfüge. Trotz allem durch Revolution und Säkularisation erlittenen Schaden gelte das – so lautet die mal ausgesprochene, mal nur angedeutete Folgerung – auch für die eigene Gegenwart. Dementsprechend treten zur historischen Beweisführung Erörterungen über die Gegenwart und den Zustand der Gesellschaft allgemein und des Armenwesens im Besonderen hinzu. Die ultramontanen Autoren sind bei manchen Differenzen im Detail von einer Grundannahme überzeugt: Die soziale Problematik, Hungerkrisen und Massenarmut haben im Kern eine religiös-sittliche Dimension. Mit Goethes Faust gesprochen liegt dort des Pudels Kern. Die innerhalb dieses Denkmodells folgerichtige Konsequenz lautet dann: Eine erfolgversprechende Auseinandersetzung mit den sozialen Nöten ist nur vom Boden des katholischen Glaubens aus und nur mit den traditionsreichen Mitteln kirchlicher Armenfürsorge zu leisten.[62]

Als solche Mittel der Armenfürsorge propagieren die strengkirchlich-ultramontanen Zeitschriften exzessiv vor allem das Wirken karitativ tätiger Orden und Kongregationen, was sich vor allem auf Frauenorden und Frauenkongregationen bezog, die man gerne pauschal unter dem Namen „Barmherzige Schwestern" zusammenfasste.[63] Eine erste quantifizierende Auswertung von acht ultramontanen Zeitschriften zwischen 1828 und 1850 wies 187 Beiträge allein zu den Barmherzigen Schwestern nach,[64] doch liegt die Gesamtzahl der Beiträge im gesamten Korpus weit höher, wie die Dissertation von Ingmar Franz zeigen wird.[65] Die ultramontane

---

[61] Die Ausführungen dieses Abschnitts greifen allgemein zurück auf Bircher und Schneider, "Katholische Armutsdiskurse," S. 334–340; Bircher und Schneider, "Catholic poverty discourses," S. 360–369; Schneider, "Katholische Armutsdiskurse und Praktiken der Armenfürsorge," S. 85–89.
[62] Siehe näher außer der in Anm. 61 genannten Literatur auch Franz, "Katholische Publizistik," S. 69–91; Schneider, "Armutsdiskurse, Armenfürsorge und Industrialisierung," S. 57–60.
[63] Dazu und zum Folgenden Franz, "Katholische Publizistik," S. 69–76; Bernhard Schneider, "The Catholic poor relief discourse and the feminization of Caritas in early nineteenth-century Germany," in Gender and Christianity in Modern Europe, Hrsg. Patrick Pasture et al. (Leuven: Leuven University Press, 2012), S. 35–55, bes. S. 39–50.
[64] Zahlen bei Franz, "Katholische Publizistik," S. 71.
[65] Ein von Herrn Franz im Rahmen seines Dissertationsvorhabens bereits erstelltes

Presse beschäftigte sich mit den karitativen Orden kontinuierlich, wobei
sich der Beginn der 1830er Jahre und die Mitte der 1840er Jahre als
Höhepunkte der Berichterstattung zeigen. Die besondere Eignung der
Schwestern, ihre Effizienz in der Führung von Hospitälern und anderen
Armen- und Krankenfürsorgeeinrichtungen, ihr unermüdlicher und zudem
kostengünstiger Einsatz werden stark betont. Sie erscheinen im scharfen
Kontrast zu den sehr negativ charakterisierten weltlichen Pflegekräften,
die gegen Lohn arbeiten, aber auch im Vergleich zu den protestantischen
Diakonissen als die besten Helferinnen im Dienst der Armen und Kranken.
Verantwortlich macht die katholische Presse dafür ihre religiöse Berufung
zu einem lebenslangen jungfräulichen Leben, das sie allein Christus und
den ihnen anvertrauten Armen und Kranken widmeten. Durch diese
Lebensweise könnten die Schwestern auch die doppelte Dimension der
Nöte der ihnen Anvertrauten bearbeiten: Sie leisteten leiblich-materielle
und – ganz entscheidend – auch geistlich-religiöse Hilfe. Angesichts dieser
ihrer Meinung nach unübersehbaren Vorteile warb die strengkirchlich-
ultramontane Presse mit großem Elan dafür, in möglichst vielen Ländern
und Kommunen weibliche karitative Orden und Kongregationen wieder
einzuführen und ihnen die Armen- und Krankenfürsorge anzuvertrauen.
Gleichzeitig setzte sie sich intensiv mit Widerständen auseinander, die
diesem Ansinnen in der Praxis entgegenstanden. Mit dem Argument der
sozialen Nützlichkeit sollte – so kann man resümieren – den durch die
Säkularisation im deutschsprachigen Raum stark in Mitleidenschaft
gezogenen Orden wieder die freie Niederlassung und damit ein
anerkannter Ort in der nachrevolutionären Gesellschaft verschafft
werden.[66]
    Neben den Barmherzigen Schwestern fanden seit dem Ende der 1830er
Jahre karitative Vereine verstärkt Aufmerksamkeit in der strengkirchlich-
ultramontanen Presse. Unter diesen stieß der Vinzenzverein auf das größte
Interesse.[67] Auch in diesem Fall war das Interesse mit der deutlich

---

Diagramm kommt allein für die 1840er Jahre auf über 200 Beiträge.
[66] Vgl. allgemein zur Entwicklung des Ordenswesens im 19. Jahrhundert *Klöster
und Ordensgemeinschaften*, Hrsg. Erwin Gatz (Freiburg im Breisgau: Herder,
2006). Speziell zu den karitativen Frauengemeinschaften Relinde Meiwes,
Arbeiterinnen des Herrn. Katholische Frauenkongregationen im 19. Jahrhundert
(Frankfurt am Main: Campus-Verlag, 2000). Zur diskursiven Auseinandersetzung
um die Orden im frühen 19. Jahrhundert vgl. Uwe Scharfenecker, "Mönchtum und
Ordenswesen im Spiegel der katholischen Publizistik Südwestdeutschlands vom
Ende des 18. bis zur Mitte des 19. Jahrhunderts," *Rottenburger Jahrbuch für
Kirchengeschichte* 9 (1990): S. 235–246.
[67] Dazu Franz, "Katholische Publizistik," S. 76–81 und ausführlich Ingmar Franz,
"Der Vinzenzverein im kirchenpolitischen Diskurs deutscher katholischer

erkennbaren Absicht verbunden, für diese Vereinigung zu werben und Gründungen im deutschsprachigen Raum zu stimulieren. Man reagierte also in den Zeitschriften nur leicht zeitversetzt auf ein neues Modell der Hilfe, denn der erste Vinzenzverein war erst 1833 in Paris entstanden.[68] Bei aller Betonung der Tradition kirchlicher Armenpflege konnte man also im strengkirchlich-ultramontanen Armutsdiskurs auch neue Wege akzeptieren, sofern sie zu dieser Tradition passten und sich in das hierarchisch-kirchliche Gefüge einordneten. Für die ultramontanen Autoren war das beim Vinzenzverein gegeben, der auch in seinem Handeln dem von diesen Autoren favorisierten Konzept der Armenfürsorge entsprach. Es war ein Handeln aus religiöser Motivation heraus, es war ein freies Wirken und nicht Teil der staatlichen Armenfürsorge, und es war eine Kombination wiederum von materieller Hilfe und moralisch-religiöser Unterweisung und Tröstung. Dadurch sollte die von den strengkirchlich-ultramontanen Autoren erhoffte und erwünschte gesellschaftliche Erneuerung Fortschritte erzielen. Zugleich zeigt dieses Beispiel eine Eigenheit des ultramontanen Armutsdiskurses: seine internationale Weite. Entwicklungen im französischen Katholizismus oder im Kirchenstaat oder auch in England und Irland fanden hohe Beachtung und wurden vielfältig kommentiert.[69]

Wie schon die bisherigen Ausführungen deutlich gemacht haben sollten, argumentierte man im Armutsdiskurs der strengkirchlich-ultramontanen Presse pointiert konfessionell und engagierte sich für eine eigenständige kirchliche Armenfürsorge. Damit korrespondieren die erheblichen Vorbehalte gegenüber einem staatlichen Wirken im Bereich des Armenwesens.[70] Dieses wird als kalt, lieblos und auf Zwang basierend dargestellt, das Arme und Reiche entzweie, anstatt sie wie im Gedanken der christlichen Nächstenliebe miteinander zu verbinden. Zudem ginge diese staatliche, auf Armensteuern gestützte Hilfstätigkeit als bloße materielle Hilfe am Kern des Armutsproblems vorbei. Damit reihen sich

Zeitungen und Zeitschriften zwischen 1842 und 1851," in *Konfessionelle Armutsdiskurse und Armenfürsorgepraktiken im langen 19. Jahrhundert*, Hrsg. Bernhard Schneider (Frankfurt am Main: Peter Lang 2009), S. 119–153.

[68] Vgl. zu seiner Geschichte Matthieu Brejon de Lavergnée, *La Société Saint-Vincent-de-Paul au XIXᵉ siècle. 1833–1871* (Paris: Le Cerf, 2008).

[69] Beispiele für die Rezeption von Entwicklungen im Kirchenstaat bei Franz, "Katholische Publizistik," S. 85 f. Zu England und Irland erste Hinweise ebenda, S. 90 f.

[70] Vgl. ebenda, S. 82–84, 88–91; Bircher und Schneider, "Katholische Armutsdiskurse," S. 337 f.; Bircher und Schneider, "Catholic poverty discourses," S. 366 f; Schneider, "Katholische Armutsdiskurse und Praktiken der Armenfürsorge," S. 85–89.

die Überlegungen der strengkirchlich-ultramontanen Autoren zur Armenfürsorge ein in ihren Kampf gegen einen omnipotenten Staat und für die Freiheit der Kirche von staatlicher Bevormundung.[71] Das schloss wenigstens in einigen Beiträgen aus den 1840er Jahren vor dem Hintergrund der Dimensionen des Pauperismus allerdings nicht aus, dass dem Staat auch eine Funktion im Bereich des Armenwesens zugestanden wurde; dieser durfte hier jedoch nicht dominieren. In einem Text aus dem Jahr 1847 wird in diesem Zusammenhang dem Grundsatz nach das Prinzip der Subsidiarität entwickelt.[72]

Armut und katholische Armenfürsorge in der Praxis: Regionale Fallstudien

Ging es in den voraufgegangenen Kapiteln um Armutsdiskurse im Katholizismus des deutschsprachigen Raums, so sollen hier einige wichtige Ergebnisse jener Teiluntersuchung meines Projekts vorgestellt werden, die sich mit der praktischen Beteiligung katholischer Initiativen an der Armenfürsorge zwischen 1803 und 1870 beschäftigte.[73] Auch dabei sollte im Blick bleiben, ob es zwischen den beiden zeitgenössischen Hauptströmungen Unterschiede in der Armenfürsorge gab. Deshalb wurden zwei Regionen in Südwestdeutschland bearbeitet und anschließend miteinander verglichen, von denen die eine stärker von katholisch-aufklärerischen Strömungen beeinflusst war (der südliche Teil des Großherzogtums Baden), während die andere (Saarregion in der damaligen preußischen Rheinprovinz) davon nur schwach berührt war und einem eher traditionellen Katholizismus verhaftet blieb, der sich dann früher als in Südbaden ultramontanen Ideen und Praktiken öffnete.[74] Um den Regionalvergleich zu realisieren und dabei auch – wie gewünscht –

---

[71] Zur generellen Ausrichtung der ultramontanen Kreise vgl. *Ultramontanismus. Tendenzen der Forschung*, Hrsg. Gisela Fleckenstein und Joachim Schmiedl (Paderborn: Bonifatius, 2005).

[72] Die einschlägigen Texte bei Schneider, "Katholische Armutsdiskurse und Praktiken der Armenfürsorge," S. 86 f.

[73] Vgl Christian Schröder, *Armenfürsorge und katholische Identität. Südbaden und die Saarregion im historischen Vergleich (1803–1870)* (Berlin: Lit, 2014). Einige Ergebnisse der Untersuchung bietet Christian Schröder, "Kooperation – Konfrontation – Koexistenz. Katholische Armenfürsorge in Deutschland zwischen Spätaufklärung und Ultramontanismus," in *Konfessionen in den west- und mitteleuropäischen Sozialsystemen im langen 19. Jahrhundert*, Hrsg. Michaela Maurer und Bernhard Schneider (Münster: Lit, 2013), S. 143–162.

[74] Vgl. Schröder, "Kooperation – Konfrontation – Koexistenz," S. 144 f.

die lokale Ebene in den Blick zu bekommen, wurden je sieben Fallstudien für beide untersuchten Regionen bearbeitet. Sie repräsentieren innerhalb der jeweiligen Region Orte mit möglichst unterschiedlichem Profil (Stadt – Dorf; städtische Zentren – Kleinstädte usw.).

In Südbaden mit seiner meist spätaufklärerischen Pfarrerschaft lässt sich eine starke Rolle der Kirche in der Armenfürsorge aufzeigen. Sie war seit 1820 sogar gesetzlich in der Form festgeschrieben, dass in den lokalen Stiftungsräten, die alle Stiftungen – kirchliche wie weltliche – verwalteten, der örtliche Pfarrer nicht nur Mitglied war, sondern diesem vorstand.[75] Oft verwahrte er auch die Akten im Pfarrhaus. Damit war der Einfluss auf die vor Ort in aller Regel bedeutsamsten Ressourcen zur Armenfürsorge groß, was sich erst im Horizont des badischen Kulturkampfs ab den 1850er Jahren allmählich änderte. Bereits die Konstruktion der Stiftungsräte, in denen neben dem Pfarrer auch der Bürgermeister wirkte, zeigt, wie die Grenzen zwischen öffentlicher (kommunaler) und kirchlicher Armenfürsorge verschwammen und die Pfarrer auch Funktionen von Staatsbeamten wahrnahmen. Dafür gab es im südbadischen Raum verschiedene wichtige historische Vorbilder, besonders das Pfarrarmeninstitut im josephinischen Vorderösterreich und das 1800 maßgeblich von einem katholischen Priester geschaffene Freiburger Modell der Armenfürsorge.[76]

Die Fallstudien zeigen über dieses amtliche Wirken hinaus ein bemerkenswertes persönliches Engagement der südbadischen Pfarrerschaft im Bereich der Armenfürsorge, das natürlich auch von der Persönlichkeit und den finanziellen Möglichkeiten der einzelnen Pfarrer abhing. Katholische Priester waren in den untersuchten Orten nicht selten überaus großzügige Stifter, die Ausbildungsstätten für Jungen und Mädchen (z. B. Heinrich Sautier in Freiburg; Ignaz Heinrich von Wessenberg in Konstanz) oder auch neue Krankenhäuser (Pantaleon Rosmann in Breisach) finanzierten.[77]

Charakteristisch für das Wirken der katholischen Spätaufklärer in Südbaden waren die Identifikation der bürgerlichen und der christlichen

---

[75] Ebenda, S. 146; Schröder, *Armenfürsorge,* S. 37 f.

[76] Vgl. dazu ausführlich Schneider, "Christliche Verbrüderung und tätige Nächstenliebe," S. 237–257; Schröder, "Kooperation – Konfrontation – Koexistenz," S. 147 f. Ausführlich zu Ferdinand Weiß als Reformer des Freiburger Armenwesens Schröder, *Armenfürsorge,* S. 54–60.

[77] Zu Rosmann vgl. Schröder, "Kooperation – Konfrontation – Koexistenz," S. 148 f.; zu Wessenbergs Engagement für den Verein zur Rettung verwahrloster Kinder vgl. ebenda, S. 151 f.; zu Sautier vgl. ebenda, S. 152 f. Ausführlicher jeweils Schröder, *Armenfürsorge,* S. 66–72 (Sautier), S. 39 f., 92–95 (Wessenberg), S. 106–114 (Rosmann).

Tugenden sowie die Ausrichtung ihres Handelns zugleich auf die Gesellschaft und den Staat. Darin realisierten sich zwar staatskirchliche Tendenzen, aber „die religiöse Dimension der karitativen Hilfe für die Armen ging dabei nicht im Nutzen für Staat und Gesellschaft auf, sondern blieb eine für das persönliche Heil relevante Handlung."[78] Diese sozial so stark engagierten Priester sahen ihr Handeln dezidiert als kirchliches Handeln an den Armen und eigneten sich in eigenen Reflexionen mitunter traditionsreiche theologische Vorstellungen an (der Priester als Vater der Armen; das im Priesteramt erworbene Vermögen als Gut der Armen).[79] Das bedeutete allerdings gerade nicht eine konfessionelle Zuspitzung. Zu den weiteren Charakteristika in Südbaden zählt vielmehr eine Offenheit für überkonfessionelle Zusammenarbeit in der Armenfürsorge, die dann ab der Jahrhundertmitte allerdings in einem Klima wachsender Rekonfessionalisierung kaum mehr möglich war. Nun wuchs das Bestreben in beiden christlichen Konfessionen, eigene Einrichtungen mit klarem konfessionellem Profil zu etablieren.[80]

Trotz dieser intensiven Verflechtung von Kirche, Kommune und Staat in der Armenfürsorge blieben allerdings Konflikte keineswegs völlig aus. Es gab wegen der faktischen Bedeutung und der hohen symbolischen Qualität durchaus Auseinandersetzungen, meist um Fragen der Zuständigkeit. So wurde in Konstanz die Verwaltung des dortigen Spitals, der wichtigsten Institution der Armen- und Krankenfürsorge, zu einem heftigen Streitpunkt zwischen Repräsentanten des liberalen Bürgertums und dem katholischen Klerus.[81] In Breisach widersetzte sich der Gemeinderat lange den Krankenhausplänen von Pfarrer Rosmann, weil er finanzielle Folgekosten fürchtete.[82] Im beginnenden badischen Kulturkampf verschärften sich diese Konflikte nach der Jahrhundertmitte deutlich, wobei neben dem Ringen um Zuständigkeit nun auch inhaltliche Differenzen deutlicher erkennbar wurden. Selbst in dieser kämpferischen Konstellation wollten allerdings auch diejenigen, die den kirchlichen Einfluss im Armenwesen beschränken und die Stiftungen stärker unter staatliche Kontrolle zu bringen beabsichtigten, nicht auf das Wirken von Barmherzigen Schwestern in konkreten lokalen Armen- und Krankenfürsorgeeinrichtungen verzichten. Diese waren schlicht das Personal mit der besten fachlichen Eignung.[83]

---

[78] Schröder, "Kooperation – Konfrontation – Koexistenz," S. 147.
[79] Siehe ebenda, S. 149 f.
[80] Vgl. ebenda, S. 151–153.
[81] Siehe Schröder, *Armenfürsorge,* S. 77–81.
[82] Vgl. Schröder, "Kooperation – Konfrontation – Koexistenz," S. 148 f.
[83] Das zeigt die Fallstudie zu Meßkirch anschaulich. Vgl. Schröder,

Die Armenfürsorge vollzog sich in der Saarregion in rechtlich wie politisch und auch wirtschaftlich gänzlich anderen Rahmenbedingungen als denjenigen, die in Südbaden gegeben waren. Lange Zeit wirkte wegen der zeitweiligen Zugehörigkeit dieser Region zu Frankreich (zwischen 1794 und 1814) noch die französische Revolutionsgesetzgebung nach. Diese hatte die Armen- und Krankenfürsorge als eine zentralisierte staatliche Aufgabe definiert. Pfarrer konnten an ihr gewissermaßen als externe Experten beteiligt werden, jedoch erlangten sie nie jene Position als Leiter dieser Fürsorge, die ihnen in Südbaden das Stiftungsgesetz von 1820 zuwies.[84] Dennoch spielten die Pfarrer auch an der Saar in der öffentlichen Armenfürsorge faktisch eine beachtliche Rolle, und zwar auch deshalb, weil sie den übergeordneten staatlichen Verwaltungsbehörden zunehmend als Experten galten, auf deren Wissen über den Zustand der Bevölkerung nicht verzichtet werden durfte.[85] Darüber hinaus war eine beachtliche Zahl katholischer Laien in teils sehr großem Umfang in der Armenfürsorge engagiert, wobei sie dies erkennbar aus religiösen Motiven heraus taten. Dieses Engagement machte es häufig erst möglich, ein kirchliches Armenwesen zu profilieren. Da sowohl Männer als auch Frauen in dieser Richtung tätig waren, kann insoweit nicht von einer Feminisierung der Caritas gesprochen werden. Durch das Wirken der Barmherzigen Schwestern erhielt die Armenfürsorge an der Saar ab der Jahrhundertmitte dann in wachsendem Maße ein weibliches Gesicht.

Stärker als in Südbaden war die Bevölkerung konfessionell gemischt, und wirtschaftlich entstand hier relativ früh ein starker industrieller Kern (Montanindustrie). Daraus resultierten ausgeprägte konfessionelle Konflikte im Armenwesen, wobei meist strittig war, ob eine bestimmte Einrichtung (die alten Hospitäler) konfessionellen Charakter hatte oder nicht und ob dementsprechend die jeweils andere Konfession an deren Verwaltung beteiligt sein durfte. Strittig war mitunter auch, ob katholische „Barmherzige Schwestern" die Leitung eines Hospitals übernehmen durften. Unstrittig war dagegen gewöhnlich, Arme durch solche Einrichtungen auch über die Konfessionsgrenzen hinweg zu versorgen.[86] Da die staatliche Verwaltung in der zu Preußen gehörenden Region protestantisch dominiert war, erhielten solche Konflikte auch eine zusätzliche Dimension, so dass sich in stark katholisch geprägten Gemeinden im Ringen um den Status von Armen- und Krankenfürsorge-einrichtungen auch ein Kirche-Staat-Konflikt und der Konflikt zwischen

---

Armenfürsorge, S. 175–178.

[84] Siehe Schröder, "Kooperation – Konfrontation – Koexistenz," S. 153 f.

[85] Dazu und zum Folgenden Schröder, *Armenfürsorge,* S. 310 f.

[86] Beispiele Schröder, "Kooperation – Konfrontation – Koexistenz," S. 154–158.

der lokalen katholischen Verwaltung und den übergeordneten staatlichen Instanzen Bahn brach. Früher und insgesamt stärker als in Südbaden zeigt sich vor diesem Hintergrund in der Saarregion die Tendenz, eigenständige, katholische Einrichtungen zu gründen.[87]

„Neben diesen Tendenzen zur Abgrenzung von protestantischen und staatlichen Armenfürsorgebemühungen dürfen jedoch beachtliche Kooperationsmodelle innerhalb des Saarkatholizismus nicht übersehen werden. Diese begegnen allerdings – im Unterschied zu Baden – weniger in Form überkonfessioneller Vereinigungen. Stattdessen konnte es in rein katholischen Orten zu einem bemerkenswerten Zusammenspiel von kommunalem, bürgerlichem und katholischem Engagement für die lokalen Armen kommen.“[88] Besonders prägnant war diese Kooperation im saarländischen Ort Wallerfangen, wo es eine frühe Form betrieblicher sozialer Sicherung durch die Unternehmerfamilien Villeroy und Galhau gab, die darüber hinaus auch einen pfarrlichen Armenverein förderten. Diesen unterstützten auch Bürgermeister und Gemeinderat. Seit 1848 leiteten „Barmherzige Schwestern" die vom Armenverein getragenen Einrichtungen für Arme, Kranke und Kinder.[89]

Zentren der Armenfürsorge waren im Übrigen in Südbaden wie an der Saar die aus der vorrevolutionären Zeit stammenden Hospitäler (Spitäler), die teils bis in das Mittelalter zurückreichten. Sie durchliefen in der Untersuchungszeit eine allmähliche Transformation und Modernisierung, deren Ausmaß und Tempo jedoch von Ort zu Ort unterschiedlich war. Bis in die Mitte des Jahrhunderts hinein waren insbesondere auf dem Land und in kleineren Städten viele dieser Einrichtungen noch multifunktional und wenig organisiert. Sie sorgten für verschiedene Gruppen (von Waisenkindern bis zu alten und gebrechlichen Menschen), waren nicht selten aber auch an der offenen Armenfürsorge beteiligt, d. h. halfen den außerhalb des Hospitals lebenden Armen und Kranken aus dem Stiftungsvermögen mit Nahrungsmitteln, Kleidern oder Medikamenten. Kirchliche Akteure – Priester wie Schwestern – waren wichtige Akteure bei solchen Transformationsprozessen und trugen so zur Professionalisierung und Modernisierung der Armen- und Krankenfürsorge wesentlich bei.[90]

---

[87] Ebenda, S. 158.
[88] Ebenda, S. 159.
[89] Ebenda, S. 159 f.; Schröder, *Armenfürsorge*, S. 222–238 sowie Christian Schröder, "Armenfürsorge und katholische Identität. Wallerfangen im 19. Jahrhundert," *Archiv für mittelrheinische Kirchengeschichte* 63 (2011): S. 213–249.
[90] Schröder, *Armenfürsorge*, S. 181 f. (Südbaden), S. 311–313 (Saar).

Bilanzierende Perspektiven

Aus den vielen Einzelergebnissen in unserem Forschungsprojekt lassen sich an dieser Stelle einige bilanzierende Perspektiven in fast thesenartiger Verdichtung formulieren.[91]

1. Armut und Arme waren im deutschen Katholizismus des 19. Jahrhunderts nicht einfach vergessen, weder in den Diskursen noch in der Praxis. Das karitative Engagement in verschiedenen Formen – teils eingebunden in öffentliche Strukturen und Einrichtungen, teils unabhängig davon – und der damit verbundene Aufbau bzw. Ausbau von Fürsorgeinstitutionen waren ein bemerkenswerter und anerkennenswerter Dienst an den Armen. Eine wirkliche „Option für die Armen", also eine Perspektivierung des gesamten kirchlichen Denkens und Handelns unter dem Vorrang von Armenhilfe und Gerechtigkeit bestand jedoch nicht.

2. Armutsdeutung und Armenfürsorge erfolgten in der Untersuchungszeit lange vornehmlich in einer religiös-moralischen Ausrichtung und fokussiert auf das einzelne Individuum. Systemtheoretisch gesprochen bot das Funktionssystem Religion damit die von ihm erwarteten Leistungen: Armen wurden Sinnperspektiven für ihr Schicksal offeriert, ihnen wurde Würde zugeschrieben, sie erhielten eine religiöse Inklusionszusage. Ferner wurde nicht wenigen Armen in ihrer Not konkret geholfen. Der Armutsdiskurs – insbesondere der liturgisch-paränetische – wie auch die Praxis der Nächstenliebe waren dabei über lange Strecken gesellschaftlich konservativ. Die theologische Sinn-Ordnung und deren Stabilisierung standen im Vordergrund, nicht der politisch-gesellschaftliche Wandel oder Strukturreformen.[92]

3. Unpolitisch waren der Armutsdiskurs und die Armenfürsorgepraxis damit aber nicht. Sie waren vielfältig mit anderen Problemkomplexen verknüpft. Das in der jüngsten Zeit laut gewordene Plädoyer für einen verschränkungsgeschichtlichen Zugang in der Beschäftigung mit Religion und Kirche erhält hierdurch aus der laufenden Forschung Unterstützung.[93]

---

[91] Ich knüpfe hier an meine Zwischenbilanz von 2009 an, die durch den Fortgang der Forschungen bestätigt wurde, und verarbeite die Einsichten aus meinen eigenen jüngeren Aufsätzen sowie die klugen Zusammenfassungen der Dissertationen meiner Promovenden. Vgl. Schneider, "Armut und Konfession," S. 38–42; Collinet, *Frohe Botschaft*, S. 268–275; Schröder, *Armenfürsorge*, S. 317–325.

[92] So auch Collinet, *Frohe Botschaft*, S. 274 f.

[93] Vgl. Franziska Metzger, "Plädoyer für einen verschränkungsgeschichtlichen Blick auf den Schweizer Katholizismus zur Zeit des Nationalsozialismus," in *Widerstand? Forschungsperspektiven auf das Verhältnis von Katholizismus und Nationalsozialismus*, Hrsg. Andreas Henkelmann und Nicole Priesching

Kritik an der Gesellschaft, am Staat oder an der Wirtschaft konnte besonders im politisch-kirchenpolitischen Armutsdiskurs deutlich formuliert werden. Die verbreitete Armut wie die unzureichende Armenfürsorge waren dann insbesondere in strengkirchlich-ultramontanen Kreisen Zeichen für die Entchristlichung der Gesellschaft, die einer Rechristianisierung bedürfe. Auch die Wirtschaft, inkl. der Industrie, benötige, so zeigten sich viele katholische Stimmen überzeugt, eine Verchristlichung. Politisch war dieser Armutsdiskurs nicht zuletzt auch in der Forderung der strengkirchlich-ultramontanen Kreise nach Freiheit der Kirche in der Armenfürsorge und in ihrer teils schroffen Ablehnung von Armensteuern, Armengesetzen und einer ausgebauten staatlichen Armenverwaltung. Politisch waren ebenso der spätaufklärerische Armutsdiskurs und die Armenfürsorgepraxis, denn sie waren ein klares politisches Signal zur Integration der Kirche in die bestehende nachrevolutionäre Gesellschaft und die nach 1800 neu entstehenden Staaten. Diese Integration schloss eine enge Zusammenarbeit ein, allerdings unter verantwortlicher Beteiligung der Kirche und ihres Klerus.

4. Die Präsenz kirchlicher Akteure in der Armenfürsorge war im Vergleich zu der Zeit vor der Säkularisation stark verändert. Präsent war die Kirche nun nicht mehr in Gestalt der geistlichen Landesherren, die in ihrer doppelten Funktion als Bischöfe und Fürsten oder Äbte und Fürsten bis zum Untergang des Alten Reiches eine mehr oder weniger katholisch geprägte Armenfürsorge realisiert hatten. Nach der Säkularisation repräsentierten auch nicht mehr die zahllosen Abteien und Klöster, die vorher als Anlaufstellen für Arme nicht selten wichtiger gewesen waren als die landesherrlichen oder kommunalen Einrichtungen der Armenfürsorge, kirchliche Armenfürsorge. Diese Präsenz sicherte nun zunächst einmal der Klerus, besonders der Pfarrer. Seine Stellung als Experte im Armenwesen war allgemein anerkannt und ließ ihn vor Ort zu einer Schnittstelle zwischen Armen, Kirche, Gemeinde und Staat werden, wobei die rechtliche Form, in der diese Position gegossen wurde, divergierte. Das priesterliche Selbstbild wies in dieser Hinsicht keine Einheitlichkeit auf, so wenig wie das Maß, in dem sich die katholischen Priester karitativ engagierten und sich als Väter und Sachwalter der Armen verstanden. Hinzu kamen als Repräsentantinnen kirchlicher Armenfürsorge im öffentlichen Raum vor allem seit den 1840er Jahren die sogenannten „Barmherzigen Schwestern", für die zunächst vor allem die strengkirchlich-ultramontanen Kreise massiv geworben hatten. An den Schwestern kam man aber auch sehr bald sonst nicht mehr vorbei, weil sie zu dieser Zeit in der Armen- und Krankenfürsorge für viele

(Saarbrücken: Universaar, 2010), S. 195–238.

Verantwortliche als konkurrenzlos gut und günstig erschienen. Sie profilierten diesen Sektor als christlichen Liebesdienst und als weibliche Domäne, was bis heute – auch mit negativen Folgen – nachwirkt.[94] Im ultramontanen Katholizismus profilierte sich schließlich auch karitatives Laienengagement im Sinne einer dezidiert kirchlichen Armenfürsorge.

5. Armutsdiskurse und Armenfürsorgepraxis leisteten damit einen Beitrag, um die Kirche in der postrevolutionären Gesellschaft neu zu positionieren. Der Nachweis gesellschaftlicher Nützlichkeit von Kirche und Glaube wurde diskursiv postuliert und mit einer Fülle von karitativen Initiativen und Institutionen auch einzulösen versucht. Indem man auf einer religiösen Deutung der Armutsfrage beharrte und darauf bestand, dass sie nur aus christlicher Liebe zu lösen sei, formulierte man zugleich einen Anspruch: nämlich in zentralen gesellschaftlichen und politischen Fragen Kompetenz zu besitzen, an deren Lösung mindestens beteiligt zu werden und Kirche und Religion so nicht auf einen kleinen Sektor privater Religiosität oder des öffentlichen Kultes einschränken zu lassen. Das galt nicht nur für die strengkirchlich-ultramontanen Kreise. Bei allem Bemühen um Anschlussfähigkeit an den zeitgenössischen Armutsdiskurs und bei aller Kooperation mit Kommunen und Staat und bei aller gesellschaftlicher Einbindung und Orientierung des seelsorglichen Handelns war die Armenfürsorge auch für die der katholischen Aufklärung zuzurechnenden Kreise ein kirchliches Handeln. Dazu fundierten sie ihre Praxis theologisch und schlossen an Begründungsmuster aus der Bibel und der kirchlichen Überlieferung an. All dies trug dazu bei, die Position der Kirche als öffentlicher und nützlicher Anstalt zu sichern, wie dies unisono, wenn auch mit teils anderer Begründung und Zielsetzung, katholisch-spätaufklärerische und strengkirchlich-ultramontane Autoren in ihren Beiträgen postulierten.

6. Eine Säkularisierung der Armenfürsorge, eine „Entkirchlichung der Barmherzigkeit" war keine Option, egal in welchem kirchlichen Lager. Beide Lager gingen von einer kirchlichen „Kernkompetenz" im Bereich der Armenfürsorge aus.[95] Das starke kirchliche Engagement im Bereich des sozialen Helfens, der Aufbau breit gefächerter kirchlicher Fürsorgeinstitutionen und der entschiedene Kampf strengkirchlich-

---

[94] Zu einigen kritischen Aspekten – die Wahrnehmung von Pflege als aufopferungsvoller Liebesdienst statt als hoch qualifizierter Beruf mit Anspruch auf entsprechende Entlohnung – vgl. Schneider, "The Catholic poor relief," S. 39 f.

[95] Beide Begriffe nach Hermann-Josef Große Kracht, "Sozialer Katholizismus und demokratischer Wohlfahrtsstaat. Klärungsversuche zur Geschichte und Gegenwart einer ungewollten Wahlverwandtschaft," *Jahrbuch für christliche Sozialwissenschaften* 46 (2005): S. 45–97, hier S. 57, 63.

ultramontaner katholischer Kreise gegen eine alleinige staatliche Alleinzuständigkeit trugen mittelbar zum charakteristischen dualen deutschen Sozialstaatssystem bei, das freie, nicht-staatliche Formen der Wohltätigkeit und Fürsorge ausdrücklich vorsieht und ihnen seit der Weimarer Zeit sogar einen Vorrang zubilligt.[96]

Allzu schroff kann man bis zur Jahrhundertmitte die Grenzen zwischen öffentlicher und kirchlicher Armenfürsorge jedoch nicht ziehen, und zwar nach dem, was Christian Schröder für die Praxis aufgezeigt hat, aber auch nach dem, was sich für den spätaufklärerischen Teil des Armutsdiskurses ergeben hat. Das gilt in doppelter Perspektive: Zum einen wollte man zum Teil ja gar keine separierte kirchliche Armenfürsorge aufbauen, weil man keine Trennung zwischen Kirche, Gesellschaft und Staat sah (katholische Spätaufklärung). Zum anderen betrachteten auch öffentliche Akteure vor Ort (Bürgermeister, Gemeinderäte und Mitglieder von Stiftungsräten oder Armenkommissionen) wenigstens in überwiegend katholischen Gemeinden die lokalen Einrichtungen der Armenfürsorge als ihre katholischen Hospitäler und reklamierten dies gegebenenfalls gegenüber höheren Instanzen außerhalb der Gemeinde. Um die Jahrhundertmitte geriet allerdings auch der Bereich der sozialen Hilfen zunehmend unter einen gewissen Abgrenzungsdruck. Im strengkirchlich-ultramontanen Armutsdiskurs kann man diesen Trend schon deutlich früher erkennen, so dass hier der Diskurs der Praxis anscheinend vorauslief und diese erkennbar beeinflusste.[97]

7. In der Armenfürsorgepraxis wie in den katholischen Armutsdiskursen kann man den Versuch sehen, eine die funktionale Differenzierung überbrückende gesamtgesellschaftliche Integrationsleistung zu erbringen und so den verloren gegangenen Anspruch auf Gesamtdeutung zu restaurieren. Insofern lässt sich auch die Bourdieu'sche Vorstellung von „Diskursen" als Ringen um die Wirklichkeitsdeutung auf die katholischen Armutsdiskurse anwenden.

---

[96] Dazu ausführlich Schneider, "Katholische Armutsdiskurse und Praktiken der Armenfürsorge," bes. S. 98–103.

[97] Dass diese Dynamik der Abgrenzung auch außerhalb des deutschen Sprachraums zunahm, verdeutlichen die Beiträge in *Konfessionen in den west- und mitteleuropäischen Sozialsystemen im langen 19. Jahrhundert*, Hrsg. Michaela Maurer und Bernhard Schneider (Münster: Lit, 2013). Vgl. dazu auch meine bilanzierenden Bemerkungen Bernhard Schneider, "Konfessionen in den west- und mitteleuropäischen Sozialsystemen im langen 19. Jahrhundert. Ein edler Wettkampf der Barmherzigkeit? Einleitung und Zwischenbilanz," in *ebenda*, S. 13–37, hier S. 32–34.

8. Für die katholische Kirche hatte diese Entwicklung selbst erhebliche Konsequenzen. Der Ausbau der karitativen Organisationen führte zu einer funktionalen Binnendifferenzierung im Funktionssystem Religion/Kirche. Sie machte es möglich, insgesamt sehr geschickt auf die funktionale Ausdifferenzierung der Gesellschaft zu reagieren und dieser nachgefragte Leistungen anzubieten. Der Preis dafür waren einige seit dem späten 19. Jahrhundert im deutschen Katholizismus bis heute nicht verstummende Klagen: die Klage über die Verselbstständigung dieses Sektors einerseits; die Klage über den Verlust an karitativem Bewusstsein in den Gemeinden und bei den einzelnen Christen andererseits. Die jüngsten Leitbilddiskussionen in Caritas (und Diakonie) belegen die Aktualität dieser Problematik.

9. Im Blick auf die gesamte Entwicklung zeigt sich, dass der karitative Aufbruch im deutschen Katholizismus von der Basis ausging. Bischöfe wie Päpste stützten ihn erst sehr viel später ab und gaben ihm dann amtliche Autorität. Anders gewendet: Die amtlichen kirchlichen Autoritäten zeigten sich lange allzu wenig engagiert.

10. Summa summarum waren Armutsdiskurse und praktizierte Armenfürsorge im deutschen Katholizismus des 19. Jahrhunderts Teil eines Ringens um Identität. Bei diesem Ringen war auch die konfessionelle Konkurrenz im Blick. Identität wurde in den katholisch-aufklärerischen Diskursen und Armenfürsorgepraktiken allerdings weniger über negative Abgrenzung aufgebaut, so dass Kooperationen mit andersconfessionellen Personen und Institutionen ausdrücklich möglich waren. Für den strengkirchlich-ultramontanen Versuch der Identitätsstiftung war neben dem Rekurs auf die Kirchengeschichte auch die betonte Abgrenzung nach außen ein wichtiges Element. Im „Wettkampf der Barmherzigkeit" – mal edel, mal weniger edel geführt – sollte nach innen wie nach außen die Richtigkeit und Überlegenheit des eigenen Weges bewiesen werden.

CHAPTER SEVENTEEN

„SO ABER UNTER DIR SEIN WIRD EIN DÜRFTIGER [...] SO VERHÄRTE NICHT DEIN HERZ, UND VERSCHLIEßE NICHT DEINE HAND VOR DEINEM DÜRFTIGEN BRUDER" – DAS ARMENWESEN DER PRAGER JÜDISCHEN GEMEINDE IN DER ZWEITEN HÄLFTE DES 19. JAHRHUNDERTS[1]

MARTINA NIEDHAMMER

"If any of your brethren approaches you for help, your heart will not be closed and you will not shut your hand": poverty in the Prague Jewish community in the second half of the 19th century

Abstract: The paper examines the care for the poor within the Jewish religious community in the 19th century, with an emphasis on the coexistence of communal and religious institutions. The focus is therefore on later periods, not on the often postulated specificity of Jewish care for the poor which is captured, for example, in the Maimonides regulations or in the legal code of Schulchan Aruch. The paper is devoted to the rather neglected problems of care for the poor organised within the Jewish community, which was characterised by a multitude of diverse institutions (inheritances, private donations and various forms of the care provided by the community) which all were subjected to the so-called "Poor Committee."

---

[1] Dtn 15, 7. Zitiert in der Übersetzung nach Ludwig Philippson: *Die Israelitische Bibel. Enthaltend den heiligen Urtext, die deutsche Übertragung, die allgemeine, ausführliche Erläuterung mit mehr als 500 englischen Holzschnitten. Erster Theil: Die fünf Bücher Moscheh*, Hrsg. Ludwig Philippson, Leipzig 1844.

Due to the parallelism of municipal and Jewish facilities for combating poverty, the paper focuses on two aspects: firstly, on communication between the Committee and the municipal authorities in endowment issues and secondly, the paper deals with the reaction of the Committee on modernisation pressures from the side of the city government (increasing in the late 19th century and stemming from the overall congestion of the system of the care for the poor).

There were apparently clashes between the Jewish community and municipal authorities and their mutual communication was noticeably sporadic. Yet in areas of common interest, their relationship became pragmatic and both were ready to cooperate. However, in the case of the reorganisation of the care for the poor, it was the opposite. The Committee apparently did not follow local municipal patterns, e.g. the Elberfeld system. Instead, relying on examples from the Jewish environment, local Jewish leaders advocated for other ways of modernisation including those implemented across Jewish communities in Germany.

Als der Prager Hausbesitzer und Gold- und Silberwarenfabrikant Michael Goldschmidt am 8. September 1856 starb, hinterließ er Frau und Tochter, jedoch offenbar keinen Sohn, der für ihn das Kaddisch – das zentrale Gebet des jüdischen Totengedenkens – hätte sprechen können. Deshalb hatte er bereits zu Lebzeiten vorgesorgt und „zum Frommen [s]einer Seele" testamentarisch verfügt, dass zehn arme unbescholtene Männer jährlich an seinem Todestag für ihn beten und im Gegenzug jeweils fünf Gulden erhalten sollten.[2] Mit der Auswahl dieses Minjans[3] hatte Goldschmidt nicht etwa den Testamentsvollstrecker, sondern die Repräsentanz der Prager israelitischen Kultusgemeinde beauftragt. Sie sollte geeignete Kandidaten aus zwei Prager Synagogengemeinden, denen der Verstorbene nahegestanden hatte, per Los bestimmen und die jährlichen Geldauszahlungen an die Betenden bis zu deren Tod veranlassen.[4]

---

[2] Archiv židovského muzea v Praze (Archiv des Jüdischen Museums in Prag, weiter AŽMP), Židovská náboženská obec v Praze (Jüdische Kultusgemeinde in Prag, weiter ŽnoP), Poslední vůle, legáty (Letztwillige Verfügungen, Legate), (1855–1917), Sign. 128456, Schreiben des k. k. Landesgerichtspräsidenten an die Repräsentanz der Prager israelitischen Kultusgemeinde, Prag, 6.12.1856; Beilage: Auszug aus dem Testamente des am 8. September 1856 in Prag verstorbenen Michael Goldschmidt, Prag, 14.10.1856.
[3] Minjan = das für einen jüdischen Gottesdienst erforderliche Quorum von mindestens zehn religiös mündigen Männern.
[4] AŽMP, ŽnoP, Poslední vůle, legáty (1855–1917), Sign. 128456, Schreiben des k. k. Landesgerichtspräsidenten an die Repräsentanz der Prager israelitischen Kultusgemeinde, Prag, 6.12.1856; Beilage: Auszug aus dem Testamente des am 8.

Michael Goldschmidts Legat, über das die Repräsentanz wenige Monate nach seinem Ableben durch das Landesgericht Prag informiert wurde, war jedoch keineswegs ein Einzelfall. Vielmehr war es Teil eines umfangreichen privaten jüdischen Stiftungswesens für bedürftige Gemeindemitglieder, das die Prager Kultusgemeinde treuhänderisch verwaltete.

Dazu gehörten im Wesentlichen zwei Gruppen: Zum einen Vermächtnisse in Form von Geld- oder (seltener) Sachspenden, die anlässlich bestimmter Fest- oder Gedenktage alljährlich wiederkehrend verteilt bzw. als Stipendien verliehen wurden. Beispielhaft ließen sich hierfür die eben erwähnte Gebetsstiftung des Michael Goldschmidt, aber auch Brautausstattungs- und Bekleidungsstiftungen für mittellose junge Mädchen und Kinder anführen. Zum zweiten Typus gehörten institutionalisierte Stiftungshäuser, die Bedürftigen eine kostenlose Unterkunft und teilweise auch Verpflegung boten.

Aufgabe der Kultusgemeinderepräsentanz war es, die Prager Gemeinde oder – für den Fall, dass die Stiftung nicht auf die böhmische Hauptstadt allein beschränkt war – auch auswärtige Gemeinden in der Monarchie rechtzeitig über eine Ausschreibung mittels Aushang in den Synagogen und Annoncen in den einschlägigen Tageszeitungen zu informieren. Die einlaufenden Bewerbungen um Unterstützung aus dem Fonds mussten sodann auf die Rechtmäßigkeit ihres Anspruchs, d. h. die tatsächliche Bedürftigkeit und Ehrbarkeit des Interessenten, sowie ggf. auf weitere satzungsgemäße Voraussetzungen überprüft und schließlich potentielle Empfänger ausgewählt werden. Im Falle der Wohnungsstifte hatte die Repräsentanz zudem darauf zu achten, dass das Zusammenleben der Hausbewohner möglichst reibungslos verlief. Eventuell auftretende Streitigkeiten musste sie schlichten. Nicht zuletzt war die Repräsentanz dazu verpflichtet, das Stiftungskapital ordnungsgemäß zu verwalten, um regelmäßige Ausschüttungen zu garantieren.

Will man den Jahresabschlüssen für das Armenwesen Glauben schenken, so leistete die Prager israelitische Kultusgemeinde jedoch auch aus eigenen Mitteln Beträchtliches: So unterstützte sie zahlreiche bedürftige Gemeindemitglieder mit regelmäßigen Geldgaben und Mietzuschüssen, punktuell half sie zudem notleidenden durchreisenden Juden, d. h. ortsfremden Glaubensgenossen.[5] Die dafür benötigten Gelder

---

September 1856 in Prag verstorbenen Michael Goldschmidt, Prag, 14.10.1856.

[5] Vgl. die Ausgabenverzeichnisse in den von der Repräsentanz veröffentlichten Jahresausweisen zum Armenwesen. Diese Ausweise erschienen nachweislich mindestens seit dem Jahr 1858. Einzelne Jahresausweise sind im AŽMP, ŽnoP in diversen Akten erhalten. Siehe auch Fußnote 25.

stammten zum Teil direkt aus der Kultuskasse, zum Teil wurden dafür einmalige Spenden anlässlich von Beschneidungs-, Hochzeits- und Beerdigungsfeierlichkeiten verwendet.[6] Ausschließlich aus dem Gemeindeetat bestritten wurde hingegen die traditionelle Verköstigung Armer bzw. sozialer Randgruppen – jüdischer Soldaten sowie Insassen von Gefängnissen, Kranken- und Irrenanstalten – zu Pessach und am Vorabend des Jom Kippur.[7] Auf Zuschüsse aus dem Kultusetat angewiesen waren darüber hinaus eine Reihe kleinerer Wohltätigkeitseinrichtungen, wie der Krankenpflegeverein Bikur Cholim, der unentgeltlich Medikamente ausgab. Da sein eigener Fonds die dafür anfallenden Kosten nicht immer decken konnte, glich die Kultuskasse die entstandenen Defizite regelmäßig aus.[8]

Die Fürsorgearbeit aus Mitteln des Gemeindeetats sowie die Verwaltung derjenigen privaten Stiftungen, die der Aufsicht der Kultusgemeinde anvertraut worden waren, bildeten das institutionelle und finanzielle Rückgrat des jüdischen Armenwesens. Beide Bereiche, insbesondere das Stiftungswesen, sind bereits relativ gut erforscht.[9] Weitaus weniger weiß man hingegen über die innergemeindliche Organisation sowie die praktische Durchführung der Armenfürsorge – über die der Armenpflege zugrunde liegenden Strukturen, die Vergabepraktiken oder die Kommunikation mit Behörden und öffentlichen Fürsorgeeinrichtungen.

Im Folgenden soll daher die Arbeit der sog. Armenkommission zwischen 1850 und 1900 in den Blick genommen werden, die in Prag – ähnlich wie in anderen jüdischen Gemeinden – für die Umsetzung des Armenwesens zuständig war. Sie bestand aus Mitgliedern der Kultusgemeinderepräsentanz und zählte um die Mitte des 19. Jahrhunderts fünf Personen.[10] Im Laufe der Jahrzehnte wurde sie jedoch auf mehr als

---

[6] Ebenda.

[7] Ebenda.

[8] Ebenda.

[9] Jüngst z. B. *Jüdische Wohlfahrtsstiftungen. Initiativen jüdischer Stifterinnen und Stifter zwischen Wohltätigkeit und sozialer Reform*, Hrsg. Andreas Ludwig und Kurt Schilde (Frankfurt am Main: Fachholschulverlag, 2010). Speziell zu Prag im 19. Jahrhundert vgl. Elisabeth Malleier, "Beiträge zur Organisation von Krankenpflege in der jüdischen Gemeinde in Prag im 19. und zu Beginn des 20 Jahrhunderts," *Judaica Bohemiae* 44 (2009): S. 83–103 sowie Martina Niedhammer, "'Dass dieses Haus halb von Juden, halb von Christen bewohnt werde.' Interreligiöse Stiftungen im jüdischen Bürgertum am Beispiel Prags in der zweiten Hälfte des 19. Jahrhunderts," *Český časopis historický* 111 (2013): S. 563–578.

[10] *Geschäftsordnung für die Repräsentanz der Prager israelitischen Cultus-*

das Doppelte erweitert: So gehörten ihr einem Rechenschaftsausweis aus dem Jahre 1887 zufolge elf Mitglieder an, allesamt Männer.[11]

Die Arbeit der Kommission, die mit den alltäglichen Schwierigkeiten des Prager jüdischen Armenwesens unmittelbar konfrontiert war, scheint in zweifacher Hinsicht interessant. Angesichts der relativen Geschlossenheit des jüdischen, innergemeindlich organisierten Wohlfahrtssystems, das von öffentlichen Sozialeinrichtungen weitgehend unabhängig war, stellt sich die Frage nach dem praktischen Umgang mit dieser Parallelstruktur: Arbeiteten konfessionelle und kommunale Organe in bestimmten Bereichen der Wohlfahrtspflege zusammen? Inwiefern gab es Überschneidungen zwischen privater und öffentlicher Wohltätigkeit, d. h. nahmen Mitglieder der Prager jüdischen Gemeinde auch die städtische Armenfürsorge in Anspruch? Und wie reagierte die Armenkommission auf den im letzten Drittel des 19. Jahrhunderts vermehrt spürbar werdenden Modernisierungsdruck, der letztlich aus einer Überlastung des hergebrachten Wohlfahrtssystems resultierte und keineswegs nur kommunale Einrichtungen betraf? Beiden Aspekten, der Frage nach dem Wechselspiel zwischen der Kultusgemeinde und städtischen Institutionen im Bereich der Armenpflege sowie der Frage nach einer Reorganisation des Prager jüdischen Armenwesens, soll mit Fokus auf die Koexistenz kommunaler und konfessioneller Fürsorgesysteme nachgegangen werden.

Tatsächlich waren die Berührungspunkte zwischen öffentlicher und religiös motivierter Armenfürsorge, wie sie die Prager Kultusgemeinde betrieb, in der zweiten Hälfte des 19. Jahrhunderts vordergründig gering. Das 1868 vom böhmischen Landtag verabschiedete Armengesetz definierte die öffentliche Armenpflege nicht nur als minimalistisch, sondern auch als subsidiär, was bedeutete, dass sie einerseits nur das zum Überleben unbedingt Erforderliche zur Verfügung stellte und andererseits erst dann eintrat, wenn kein Anspruch auf Unterstützung von dritter Seite – an Verwandte, Vereine oder Stiftungen – bestand.[12] Deswegen war es nicht zuletzt Aufgabe der Kultusgemeinde, ihren in Armut geratenen Gemeindemitgliedern zu helfen, wenngleich Böhmen im Unterschied zu einigen anderen Kronländern nicht vorsah, dass Armenstifte und

---

Gemeinde. *Angenommen mit Sitzungsbeschluß vom 10. September 1865*, Prag 1865, S. 15, § 62.

[11] AŽMP, ŽnoP, Reorganizace chudinství, vandrovní žebrota – účty, komise (Reorganisation des Armenwesens, Wanderbettel – Belege, Kommissionen), Sign. 128385, *Das Armenwesen der Prager israelitischen Cultusgemeinde im Jahre 1886* (Prag: s. t., 1887), S. [II].

[12] Landes-Gesetzblatt für das Königreich Böhmen 1868, XXIV. Stück, Nr. 59, § 1 und 2.

Privatvereine offenlegten, welche Personen von ihnen unterstützt wurden.[13]

Dem Prager Magistrat war daher nicht näher bekannt, wer die Armenfürsorge der Kultusgemeinde in Anspruch nahm. Das legen zumindest Schreiben des Bürgermeisters an die Repräsentanz nahe, in denen die Kultusgemeinde beauftragt wurde, an jüdische Arme Gelder zu verteilen, die im Zuge von Spendensammlungen eingenommen und vom Stadtrat zur Verteilung „an verschämte Arme jeder Confession" bestimmt worden waren.[14] Ähnlich ging man auch im Falle nichtpersonalisierter Vermächtnisse vor, die Angehörige verschiedener Religionsgemeinschaften bedachten. Das zeigt das Beispiel der Franziska Geitler Edle von Armingen, die bei ihrem Tod 1870 testamentarisch 100 Gulden „zur Vertheilung an arme Leute in der Josefstadt" bestimmt hatte.[15] Da die Verstorbene, die selbst vom Judentum zum Christentum konvertiert war,[16] die Empfänger innerhalb des gleichermaßen von Juden wie von Christen bewohnten Stadtviertels nicht näher bestimmt hatte, verfügte der Prager Bürgermeister, dass der Betrag unter beiden Konfessionen aufgeteilt werden solle. Die für die jüdischen Bedürftigen bestimmten Gelder konnte die Kultusgemeinderepräsentanz nach eigenem Ermessen verteilen.[17]

---

[13] Vgl. Ernst Mischler, "Armenpflege. Die öffentliche Armenversorgung," in *Österreichisches Staatswörterbuch. Handbuch des gesamten österreichischen öffentlichen Rechtes* Bd. 1., Hrsg. Ernst Mischler und Josef Ulbrich, (Wien: A. Holder, 1905²), S. 324–337, hier S. 334.

[14] Vgl. AŽMP, ŽnoP, Chudinství, soukromé dary (Armenwesen, Spenden von Privatleuten), Sign. 128404a, Note des Prager Bürgermeisters Wenzel Wanka an die Repräsentanz der Prager israelitischen Kultusgemeinde, Prag, 21.1.1859. In derselben Akte finden sich zahlreiche weitere Belege für ein analoges Vorgehen des Magistrats in ähnlichen Fällen. Ein Aufruf des Bürgermeisters an die Kultusgemeinde aus dem Jahr 1868, sich an einer allgemeinen Armenkonskription zu beteiligen, indem sie alle von ihr unterstützen Personen mittels eines vorgefertigten Formulars an die Stadt Prag melde, scheint folgenlos geblieben zu sein, vgl. AŽMP, ŽnoP, Reorganizace chudinství, vandrovní žebrota – účty, komise, Sign. 128385, Schreiben des Bürgermeisters Karl Leopold Klaudy an die Repräsentanz der Prager israelitischen Kultusgemeinde, Prag, 18.2.1868.

[15] AŽMP, ŽnoP, Poslední vůle, legáty (1855–1917), Sign. 128456, Schreiben des Prager Bürgermeisters Franz Dittrich an die Repräsentanz der Prager israelitischen Kultusgemeinde, Prag, 1.8.1870.

[16] Vgl. Jan Županič, *Židovská šlechta podunajské monarchie mezi davidovou hvězdou a křížem* [Jüdischer Adel der Donaumonarchie zwischen Davidstern und Kreuz] (Praha: Nakladatelství Lidové noviny, 2012), S. 246. Franziska (geb. 1797) war mit Sigmund Christian Geitler von Armingen (urspr. Samuel Jeitteles, 1790–1861) verheiratet, der sich 1828 hatte taufen lassen.

[17] AŽMP, ŽnoP, Poslední vůle, legáty (1855–1917), Sign. 128456, Schreiben des

Abgesehen von diesen Beispielen arbeitete man aus Sicht der Kultusgemeinde mit den kommunalen Behörden im Bereich des Armenwesens vor allem dann zusammen, wenn es um die Ausschreibung interkonfessioneller Stiftungsplätze ging, für die nicht nur jüdische, sondern auch christliche Bewerber gesucht werden mussten. Mit der Auswahl der Letzteren wurde häufig der Prager Stadtrat betraut.[18]

Ein weiterer potentieller Berührungspunkt zwischen dem jüdischen Armenwesen und öffentlichen Stellen ergab sich aus der Tatsache, dass Bewerber um Stipendien und Stiftungsplätze bei der Prager Kultusgemeinde an höherer Stelle Rekurs einlegen konnten, wenn sie an der Vergabepraktik der Gemeinde begründete Zweifel hegten.[19] So wandte sich etwa Sofie Flekeles aus Wien am 26. Mai 1884 an die Prager Statthalterei in deren Eigenschaft als Stiftungsaufsichtsbehörde und beschwerte sich, dass ihr die bereits zugesagte Unterstützung aus der von der Kultusgemeinde verwalteten Markus Fischer'schen Brautausstattungsstiftung nicht ausgezahlt worden sei.[20] Ihren Einspruch begründete Sofie Flekeles damit, dass sie zum Zeitpunkt der Bewerbung alle dafür notwendigen Voraussetzungen erfüllt habe, da sie eine ledige Braut gewesen und nachweislich mit dem Stifter verwandt sei.[21] Auf Aufforderung des Magistrats musste sich die Repräsentanz daraufhin zu dem Fall äußern. In ihrer Antwort bezog sich diese nicht nur auf die Statuten der Stiftung, sondern auch auf den Stiftungsvorsteher Wolf Wiener, der sich bei der

---

Prager Bürgermeisters Franz Dittrich an die Repräsentanz der Prager israelitischen Kultusgemeinde, Prag, 1.8.1870.

[18] Vgl. etwa das Beispiel der 1865 von Leopold von Portheim, einem Prager jüdischen Fabrikanten, gegründeten Armenstiftung, die arme, arbeitsunfähige Prager Familienväter und -mütter christlicher und jüdischer Religionszugehörigkeit paritätisch bedachte. Die Auswahl der christlichen Stiftlinge oblag nach dem Willen des Stifters dem Magistrat, während sich die jüdischen Bewerber der Kultusgemeinderepräsentanz vorstellen mussten. AŽMP, ŽnoP, Esther Presseles z Portheimů (Bestand Esther Presseles von Portheim), Sign. 128453, Leopold von Portheim'sche Armenstiftung, Ausschreibung, Prag, 2.6.1866.

[19] Reichs-Gesetz-Blatt für das Kaiserthum Österreich 10/1853, Beilage C, § 35 sowie Rudolf Herrmann Herrnritt, "Stiftungen," in Österreichisches Staatswörterbuch. Handbuch des gesamten österreichischen öffentlichen Rechtes Bd. 4, Hrsg. Ernst Mischler und Josef Ulbrich (Wien: A. Holder, 1909[2]), S. 484–491, hier S. 486. Stiftungsaufsichtsbehörde und damit erste Instanz war die Statthalterei, deren Entscheidungen vom Bezirksamt, d. h. im Prager Falle vom Magistrat, umgesetzt werden mussten.

[20] AŽMP, ŽnoP, Fišlova výbava pro nevěsty (Fischer'sche Brautausstattungsstiftung), Sign. 128395. Der Vorgang erschließt sich retrospektiv aus der Korrespondenz zwischen der Prager Kultusgemeinde und dem Magistrat, siehe unten.

[21] Ebenda.

Familie der Bewerberin persönlich nach deren Verhältnissen erkundigt hatte.[22] Dabei habe er jedoch, so die Repräsentanz, feststellen müssen, dass Sofie Flekeles bereits wenige Tage nach ihrer Bewerbung um die Brautausstattungsstiftung geheiratet hatte, sodass sie bei der geplanten Verleihung am Todestag des Stifters nicht mehr ledig gewesen sei.[23] Diese Argumentation überzeugte offenbar, denn der Magistrat teilte der Repräsentanz schließlich mit, dass Sofie Flekeles' Einspruch abgelehnt worden sei.[24]

Der umfangreiche Schriftwechsel zwischen der erfolglosen Bewerberin, der Kultusgemeinderepräsentanz und den Prager Behörden belegt nicht nur die Zähigkeit, mit der Bedürftige ihre Anliegen teilweise verfolgten. Er beleuchtet auch die relativ reibungslose Zusammenarbeit zwischen der Kultusgemeinde und den städtischen Behörden, die sich an der vergleichsweise zügigen Erledigung des Falls in nicht ganz viereinhalb Monaten ablesen lässt.

Mittelbar verweist der Blick auf die Behörden jedoch auch auf grundsätzliche Unterschiede im Umgang mit Bedürftigen, die im Bereich der privaten bzw. konfessionellen und der öffentlichen Armenfürsorge bestanden. So grenzte sich die öffentliche Armenpflege mit ihrem bereits erwähnten Prinzip des Minimalismus bewusst von der privaten Wohltätigkeit ab.

Die private Armenfürsorge basierte hingegen auf dem Grundsatz der Mildtätigkeit und war daher in der Lage, zuweilen auch auf individuelle Bedürfnisse Bedürftiger einzugehen, die jenseits des vom Gesetzgeber gewährten Minimums lagen.[25] Das zeigt das Schreiben des Wolf Plohn,

---

[22] Ebenda, Schreiben der Repräsentanz der Prager israelitischen Kultusgemeinde an den Prager Magistrat, 2.7.1884 sowie Schreiben des Stiftungsvorstehers Wolf Wiener an die Repräsentanz der Prager israelitischen Kultusgemeinde, Wien, 18.5.1884.

[23] Ebenda.

[24] Ebenda, Schreiben des Prager Magistrats an die Repräsentanz der Prager israelitischen Kultusgemeinde, Prag, 7.10.1884.

[25] Dies betont z. B. der von der Repräsentanz veröffentlichte Jahresausweis über Ein- und Ausgaben im Bereich des Armenwesens für das Jahr 1885: AŽMP, ŽnoP, Reorganizace chudinství, vandrovní žebrota – účty, komise, Sign. 128385, Das Armenwesen der Prager israelitischen Cultusgemeinde im Jahre 1885, S. [1]. Das 1890 in Jena erschienene *Handwörterbuch der Staatswissenschaften* definiert die Mildtätigkeit als entscheidendes Abgrenzungskriterium zwischen öffentlicher und privater Armenfürsorge: „Durch Gewährung der öffentlichen Unterstützung soll eine als notwendig anerkannte staatliche Pflicht erfüllt, nicht aber Mildthätigkeit geübt werden. Eine durch das Gesetz angeordnete Mildthätigkeit würde des für mildthätige Gaben charakteristischen Momentes der Freiwilligkeit entbehren. Die

der die Armenkommission der Kultusgemeinde im April 1880 um eine zusätzliche Mahlzeit ersuchte, da er bereits 52 Jahre alt, erwerbsunfähig und „nicht im Stande [sei], vom Hausiren mit Zündhölzchen sich den nötigsten Lebensunterhalt zu verschaffen". Plohn räumte zwar ein, dass er bereits zweimal pro Tag eine Suppe aus der „Volksküche"[26] erhalte, doch könne er davon „nicht leben".[27] Zunächst waren die Mitglieder der Armenkommission, die das Bittgesuch Plohns noch am selben Tag von der Repräsentanz zugestellt bekamen, uneins darüber, wie es zu beantworten sei. So erblickte ein Kommissionsmitglied in der Gewährung von Extramahlzeiten eine unangemessene Besserstellung einzelner Armer gegenüber der Mehrheit der Bedürftigen innerhalb der Kultusgemeinde.[28] Demgegenüber verwies ein anderes Kommissionsmitglied auf die intensiven Bemühungen des Bittstellers, sich mithilfe einer kleinen Verkaufstätigkeit eigenes Geld hinzuzuverdienen. Darüber hinaus sei Plohn sehr fromm und der Enkel eines Rabbiners.[29] Insbesondere dieser Hinweis, aber auch die Tatsache, dass Wolf Plohn gewissermaßen eine Hilfe zur Selbsthilfe anstrebte, waren offenbar ausschlaggebend dafür, dass Plohn die zusätzliche Mahlzeit letztlich doch bewilligt wurde.[30]

Etwas anders gelagert war der Fall des Juda Schüttenhofer, eines Mitglieds der Prager jüdischen Gemeinde, der, schwer erkrankt und beinahe blind, völlig auf fremde Unterstützung angewiesen war. Der Prager Magistrat hatte ihn deshalb im städtischen Siechenhaus am Karlstor untergebracht, was bedeutete, dass er auch alle finanziellen Lasten der

---

öffentlichen Gelder sollen im Interesse der Gesamtheit, [sic] nicht zu mildthätigen Zwecken verwendet werden. Es ist daher durchaus rationell, wenn durch staatliche Festsetzung der Maximalgrenze, bis zu welcher die öffentliche Unterstützung gehen darf, den Armenbehörden eine unverrückbare Schranke gezogen wird, damit sie nicht aus der Tasche der Steuerzahler Gelder für Zwecke verwenden, welche außerhalb der öffentlichen Fürsorgepflicht liegen und für welche dem Staat kein Recht zur Erhebung von Zwangsbeiträgen zusteht." Paul Felix Aschrott, "Armenwesen. Einleitung," in *Handwörterbuch der Staatswissenschaften* Bd. 1, *Abbau – Autorrecht*, Hrsg. Johannes Conrad et al. (Jena: Fischer, 1890), S. 819–823, hier S. 823.

[26] Es ist unklar, welche Institution damit gemeint ist. Möglicherweise wurde Plohn vom Suppenverein „Mechalke Tarnegolim" unterstützt.

[27] AŽMP, ŽnoP, Žádosti chudých o přijetí do ústavu (Anträge Bedürftiger auf Aufnahme in die Armenfürsorge), Sign. 128431, Schreiben des Wolf Plohn an die Repräsentanz der Prager israelitischen Kultusgemeinde, Prag, 5.4.1880.

[28] Ebenda, Notiz des Philipp Schwab, Prag, 6.4.1880 [später durchgestrichen].

[29] Ebenda, Notiz des David Zappert, Prag, 6.4.1880.

[30] Ebenda, Entwurf des Bewilligungsschreibens der Kultusgemeinderepräsentanz an Wolf Plohn, Prag, 2.5.1880.

Versorgung Schüttenhofers übernommen hatte. Wie Schüttenhofer jedoch am 2. August 1881 an die Repräsentanz der Kultusgemeinde schrieb, hatte er das städtische Siechenhaus eigenmächtig verlassen, da ihm dort eine Lebensführung nach den rituellen Vorschriften des orthodoxen Judentums nicht möglich war.[31] Daher bat er nun um eine „vollständige" Versorgung durch die Prager israelitische Kultusgemeinde. Diese wurde ihm denn auch umgehend gewährt,[32] obwohl der jüdische Armenfonds dadurch letztlich finanzielle Verpflichtungen der Prager Stadtgemeinde übernahm.

Die Beispiele Wolf Plohns und Juda Schüttenhofers machen deutlich, dass die Armenkommission der Prager jüdischen Gemeinde über gewisse Handlungsspielräume verfügte. Diese erlaubten ihr, den Einzelnen und seine persönliche Situation weitaus mehr zu berücksichtigen, als dies die öffentliche Armenfürsorge tun konnte, deren Anliegen weniger der Arme selbst als vielmehr die Sicherstellung der öffentlichen Ordnung war. Darüber hinaus verdeutlichen die Fälle Plohns und Schüttenhofers, dass Arme durchaus eigenes „Kapital" in die Verhandlung mit Fürsorgeeinrichtungen einbringen konnten, das ihre Aussichten auf Unterstützung deutlich verbesserte – im Falle der jüdischen Gemeinde war dies etwa ein besonders religiöser Lebenswandel.

Ungeachtet ihrer größeren Flexibilität in Einzelfällen stand die Armenkommission der Prager israelitischen Kultusgemeinde jedoch letztlich vor ähnlichen Problemen wie die öffentliche Armenfürsorge: Angesichts der Vielzahl der Bedürftigen waren die finanziellen Mittel knapp. Zudem hatte die Armenkommission keineswegs die Kontrolle über das gesamte Armenwesen der Gemeinde. Kleine innergemeindliche Wohltätigkeitsvereine sowie Almosen einzelner Gemeindemitglieder unterliefen regelmäßig ihre Arbeit. Wiederholt wurden daher Stimmen laut, die die Ungerechtigkeit des bestehenden Versorgungssystems für Bedürftige kritisierten, indem sie darauf hinwiesen, dass beileibe nicht jeder, der Almosen erhalte, dieselben auch tatsächlich benötige oder aber in moralischer Hinsicht verdiene. Plastisch veranschaulicht dies ein anonymes Beschwerdeschreiben an die Kultusgemeinderepräsentanz aus dem Jahre 1889, in dem ein gewisser Karl Brod und seine Ehefrau Anna beschuldigt wurden, Unterstützungsgelder der Gemeinde zu erhalten,

---

[31] Ebenda, Schreiben des Juda Schüttenhofer an die Repräsentanz der Prager israelitischen Kultusgemeinde, Prag, 2.8.1881.
[32] Ebenda, Notizen dreier Mitglieder der Armenkommission, Prag, 8.–12.9.1881 sowie Entwurf des Bewilligungsschreibens der Kultusgemeinderepräsentanz vom 14.9.1881 auf der Rückseite von Schüttenhofers Schreiben.

obwohl sie „Sparkassa Büchel" [sic] sowie ein Haus in Goltsch-Jenikau (*Golčův Jeníkov*) besäßen.[33]

In einem zweiten Schritt sollen daher knapp die Reformbestrebungen der Repräsentanz im ausgehenden 19. Jahrhundert skizziert werden. Sie stehen in engem ideellem Zusammenhang mit den Reformen, die in Österreich auf dem Gebiet der öffentlichen Wohlfahrtspflege ergriffen wurden, ohne dass sich jedoch in dieser Frage eine Zusammenarbeit zwischen kommunalen Behörden und der Kultusgemeinde nachweisen ließe.

Seit dem letzten Drittel des 19. Jahrhunderts versuchte die Armenkommission, die Vergabe von Spendengeldern innerhalb der Gemeinde zu zentralisieren. Ziel war einerseits, das Spendenaufkommen zu steigern, da Spendenwillige nun feste Geldbeträge für Bedürftige bei der Kommission hinterlegen konnten. Andererseits sollte auf diesem Weg eine höhere Verteilungsgerechtigkeit erreicht werden, indem die Kommission alle von ihr für würdig erachteten Armen gleichermaßen bedachte. 1870 wurde daher ein vorgedrucktes Rundschreiben an alle Gemeindemitglieder versandt. Darin forderte die Armenkommission dazu auf, ihr monatlich oder vierteljährlich feste Geldbeträge zur Verteilung an Bedürftige zukommen zu lassen. Die Vorzüge, die dieses System gegenüber dem herkömmlichen individuellen Almosengeben habe, pries die Kommission in leuchtenden Farben:

---

[33] AŽMP, ŽonP, Reorganizace chudinství, vandrovní žebrota – účty, komise, Sign. 128385, anonymes Schreiben an die „Israelitische Kultus-Gemeinde [sic] der Josefstadt in Prag", o. O., undatiert [eingegangen bei der Repräsentanz am 1.7.1889 und vom Präsidenten Arnold Rosenbacher noch am selben Tag an die Armenkommission überstellt]. Auf das Problem, dass die Armenkommission immer wieder Gefahr lief, den Überblick über die von ihr Unterstützten zu verlieren, weshalb mitunter die „Falschen" bedacht wurden, verweisen auch zwei aus den Jahren 1904 und 1905 erhaltene, streng vertraulich geführte Verzeichnisse. Sie listen Personen auf, die aus sittlichen oder rituellen Gründen keine Almosen erhalten sollten, da sie als kriminell eingestuft wurden, des Landes verwiesen worden waren oder nicht jüdisch bzw. getauft waren. AŽMP, ŽonP, Žádosti chudých o přijetí do ústavu, Sign. 128431, Streng vertraulich, Liste Nr. 7 vom 21.4.1904 und Liste Nr. 10 vom 7.2.1905. Ähnliche Verzeichnisse („Warnlisten") wurden von der Prager Kultusgemeinde auch in späteren Jahren erstellt, etwa Mitte der 1930er Jahren, als verstärkt jüdische Flüchtlinge aus dem nationalsozialistischen Deutschland in der Tschechoslowakei Zuflucht suchten, vgl. Kateřina Čapková und Michal Frankl, *Unsichere Zuflucht. Die Tschechoslowakei und ihre Flüchtlinge aus NS-Deutschland und Österreich 1933–1938* (Wien u. a.: Böhlau Verlag, 2012), S. 197–199.

„Wenn man sieht, wie sich vor den israelitischen Festtagen, am Neumonde, bei freudigen oder betrübenden Familienangelegenheiten die mitunter höchst unverschämten Armen sich zu Ihnen schaarenweise hinandrängen – wodurch mitunter schon öffentliche Scandale erregt wurden – wenn man ferner berücksichtigt, wie diese Schaaren oder einzelne Bettler Sie oft mitten in Ihren Geschäften unterbrechen, Ihnen Ihre theure Zeit rauben – so dürfte es Ihnen gewiß willkommen sein, wenn Sie von diesen zudringlichen Individuen befreit werden und doch dabei die Überzeugung haben, daß das, was Ihr gutes Herz den Unglücklichen spenden wollte, denselben auch gewissenhaft zukommt."[34]

Der Versuch der Armenkommission, Spender und Empfänger mittels einer Stigmatisierung des Letzteren zu trennen und auf diese Weise das vordem persönliche Verhältnis zwischen Almosengeber und Bedürftigem zu versachlichen, war jedoch nicht von Erfolg gekrönt. Nur ein Jahr später teilte die Armenkommission in einer öffentlichen Kundmachung mit, dass sie den „bereits einmal gemachten, aber wegen der leider nur schwachen Beteiligung aufgegebenen Versuch zur Beseitigung des immer mehr um sich greifenden Bettelunfugs" wiederhole und anlässlich des Purimfestes[35] erneut um Spenden zur Almosenverteilung bitte.[36] Ganz offenbar lag für viele Gemeindemitglieder ein wesentlicher Anreiz des Spendens gerade im unmittelbaren Kontakt mit dem Armen, dessen Dankbarkeit und Loyalität sich der Schenkende bei dieser Gelegenheit versichern konnte. Genau dieser Aspekt aber entfiel bei einer zentralisierten Almosenvergabe, wie sie den Kommissionsmitgliedern vorschwebte. Auch in späteren Jahren sah sich die Repräsentanz daher genötigt, die Gemeinde daran zu erinnern, dass es alleinige Aufgabe der Armenkommission sei, Spendengelder zu verteilen – „so ungern wir dem Einzelnen das edle Vergnügen schmälern möchten, eigenhändig Almosen zu geben."[37]

Eine tiefergreifende Reform des Armenwesens wurde von der Kultusgemeinde erst um die Jahrhundertwende in Angriff genommen. Vorausgegangen war eine längere interne Diskussion zwischen der

---

[34] AŽMP, ŽonP, Reorganizace chudinství, vandrovní žebrota – účty, komise, Sign. 128385, Euer Wohlgeboren! Rundschreiben der Armenkommission der Prager israelitischen Kultusgemeinde, Prag, 28.1.1870 [Vordruck].

[35] Purim = freudiger Feiertag zum Gedenken an die Errettung der persischen Juden. Es ist eine religiöse Pflicht, an diesem Tag Almosen zu geben.

[36] AŽMP, ŽonP, Reorganizace chudinství, vandrovní žebrota – účty, komise, Sign. 128385, Kundmachung der Commission zur Verwaltung des Armenwesens, Prag, 9.2.1871.

[37] AŽMP, ŽnoP, Reorganizace chudinství, vandrovní žebrota – účty, komise, Sign. 128385, Das Armenwesen der Prager israelitischen Cultusgemeinde im Jahre 1885, S. [2].

Repräsentanz und verschiedenen jüdischen Wohltätigkeitsvereinen.[38]
Letztlich durchsetzen konnte sich ein detaillierter Reformvorschlag der
Loge „Bohemia" des B'nai B'rith-Ordens[39] vom 13. Dezember 1899. Der
31-seitige Entwurf sah eine Bündelung aller Prager jüdischen
Wohltätigkeitsvereine vor, „damit die Zersplitterung der Hilfsmittel
aufhöre, die Mittel vereinigt, die Controle [sic] erleichtert, und – was heute
oft der Fall ist – nicht einzelne Leute bevorzugt werden, die bei der
Inanspruchnahme der Wohlthätigkeit gewerbsmäßig vorgehen [...]".[40] Vor
allem aber regte der Orden an, das Armenwesen der Prager jüdischen
Gemeinde nach dem Elberfelder System umzugestalten.[41]

Dieses dezentrale Modell der Armenfürsorge basierte auf dem
Engagement ehrenamtlicher Armenpfleger und propagierte eine Anleitung
zur Selbsthilfe.[42] Seit Ende der 1880er Jahre war es erfolgreich in einigen
böhmischen Städten, wie etwa Reichenberg, Aussig oder Karlsbad,
etabliert worden.[43] Dennoch bezog sich die „Bohemia" in ihrem Vorschlag

---

[38] Vgl. dazu die Schreiben einzelner Wohltätigkeitsvereine an die
Kultusgemeinderepräsentanz sowie das Protokoll der am 21.5.1903 im Prager
jüdischen Rathaus veranstalteten Sitzung des Comités zur Reorganisation des
Armenwesens, dem Vertreter aller Prager Synagogen und der einzelnen
Wohlfahrtsinstitute angehörten, AŽMP, ŽnoP, Reorganizace chudinství, vandrovní
žebrota – účty, komise, Sign. 128385.
[39] Die Loge „Bohemia" wurde 1893 als erste Prager Niederlassung des B'nai
B'rith-Ordens gegründet. Erklärtes Ziel des Ordens ist neben der Bekämpfung des
Antisemitismus die Förderung von Toleranz und Humanität, u. a. mit den Mitteln
der Wohltätigkeit. Zum Selbstverständnis der B'nai B'rith (hebr. Söhne des
Bundes) in den böhmischen Ländern vgl. Kateřina Čapková, "Jewish Elites in the
19th and 20th Centuries. The B'nai B'rith Order in Central Europe," *Judaica
Bohemiae* 36 (2000): S. 119–142.
[40] AŽMP, ŽnoP, Reorganizace chudinství, vandrovní žebrota – účty, komise, Sign.
128385, Schreiben der B'nai B'rith-Loge „Bohemia" an die Repräsentanz der
Prager israelitischen Kultusgemeinde, Prag, 13.12.1899.
[41] Ebenda.
[42] Sabine Hering und Richard Münchmeier, *Geschichte der Sozialen Arbeit. Eine
Einführung* (Weinheim und München: Juventa Verlag, 2005³), S. 30f.
[43] Vgl. Ernst Mischler, "Einleitung. Übersicht über die Armenpflege und die
private Wohlthätigkeit in Österreich," in *Österreichs Wohlfahrts-Einrichtungen
1848–1898. Festschrift zu Ehren des 50jährigen Regierungs-Jubiläums Seiner k. u.
k. Apostolischen Majestät des Kaisers Franz Joseph I.*, Hrsg. v. d. unter dem
höchsten Protectorate Sr. k. u. k. Hoheit des durchlauchtigsten Herrn Erzherzog
Otto stehenden Commission der Österreichischen Wohlfahrts-Ausstellung Wien
1898 (Wien: A. Hölder, 1899), S. VII–XLII, hier S. XXVIII. Die Stadt Prag führte
das Elberfelder System nicht ein, was möglicherweise daran lag, dass sich dieses
aufgrund der hohen Mobilität der Stadtbevölkerung und der notorischen

nicht auf kommunale Vorbilder aus der Region, sondern auf die innerjüdischen Beispiele der Kultusgemeinden von Köln, Frankfurt und Berlin. Nach dem Muster des Berliner „jüdische[n] Stellungsvermittlungscomité[s]" wollte man zudem ein jüdisches „Arbeitsvermittlungsbureau" für Arbeitssuchende einrichten, das ein „Verzeichnis verläßlicher jüdischer Arbeiter und Handwerker mit genauer Specialisirung ihrer Arbeitsfähigkeit" anlegen sollte, die bei Bedarf weiterempfohlen werden konnten.[44]

Es bleibt unklar, weshalb die Prager Kultusgemeinde nicht zumindest in diesem Punkt eine Zusammenarbeit mit der Stadt Prag erwog, die nur ein Jahr vorher, 1898, eine nicht-gewerbliche Arbeitsvermittlung eingerichtet hatte.[45] Als die Reorganisation des Prager jüdischen Armenwesens im Jahre 1903 abgeschlossen war, war von einer irgendwie gearteten kommunalen Einflussnahme oder Interferenz trotz offensichtlicher struktureller Anleihen bei der städtischen Sozialpolitik in den erhaltenen Quellen keine Rede.

Vielmehr hatten bereits die Mitglieder des B'nai B'rith-Ordens in ihrem Reformvorschlag aus dem Jahre 1899 die Errichtung eines jüdischen „Rechtscomités" angemahnt, das prüfen sollte, inwieweit der Staat, das Land Böhmen und die Stadt Prag ihren Verpflichtungen gegenüber den Armen nachkämen.[46] „[N]achdem ein großer Theil des von Juden gezahlten Steuerguldens für die jetzt nur Andersgläubigen zukommenden Wohlthaten verwendet wird", sollten gegebenenfalls entsprechende Rechtsmittel zur Wahrung jüdischer Ansprüche ergriffen werden.[47]

Ganz offensichtlich wurden die kommunalen Behörden im Zuge der Reorganisation des Prager jüdischen Armenwesens eher als Gegenspieler

---

Überforderung der ehrenamtlichen Helfer für Großstädte zunehmend als impraktikabel erwies. Hering und Münchmeier, *Geschichte der sozialen Arbeit*, S. 32.

[44] AŽMP, ŽnoP, Reorganizace chudinství, vandrovní žebrota – účty, komise, Sign. 128385, Schreiben der B'nai B'rith-Loge „Bohemia" an die Repräsentanz der Prager israelitischen Kultusgemeinde, Prag, 13.12.1899.

[45] *Die Arbeitsvermittlung in Österreich*, Hrsg. Statistisches Department im k. k. Handelsministerium (Wien: A. Hölder, 1898), S. 275f.

[46] AŽMP, ŽnoP, Reorganizace chudinství, vandrovní žebrota – účty, komise, Sign. 128385, Schreiben der B'nai B'rith-Loge „Bohemia" an die Repräsentanz der Prager israelitischen Kultusgemeinde, Prag, 13.12.1899.

[47] Ebenda. Dieses Argument steht freilich im Widerspruch zum Wesen der Steuer, die „ohne spezielle Gegenleistung" erbracht werden muss. Vgl. Robert Meyer, "Abgaben," in *Österreichisches Staatswörterbuch* Bd. 1., Hrsg. Mischler und Ulbrich, S. 7–18, hier S. 8.

denn als Ideengeber gesehen. Dies mag angesichts der zwar beschränkten, aber nicht uneffektiven Kommunikation zwischen der jüdischen Gemeinde und der Stadt Prag in Stiftungsangelegenheiten überraschen. Um jedoch ermessen zu können, inwiefern die Haltung der Prager israelitischen Kultusgemeinde gegenüber der Stadtgemeinde repräsentativ für das jüdische Armenwesen Zisleithaniens im späten 19. Jahrhundert war, bedürfte es weiterer vergleichender lokaler Studien.[48]

An dieser Stelle lässt sich anhand der überlieferten Akten der Prager Kultusgemeinde lediglich festhalten, dass ihr Versuch, das Armenwesen zu reformieren – mochte er auch scheinbar losgelöst von kommunalen Initiativen erfolgt sein – innerjüdisch durchaus eine gewisse Strahlkraft entwickelte: So langte 1903 aus den Vereinigten Staaten ein Schreiben der „United Hebrew Charities of the City of New York" in der Kultusgemeinderepräsentanz ein.[49] Wie darin zu lesen war, hatte man von den Bestrebungen zu einer „improved method of distributing charity and of granting relief among your worthy poor" erfahren und bat nun um entsprechende schriftliche Unterlagen.[50]

---

[48] Generell scheint eine Verbindung öffentlicher und konfessioneller Armenpflege um 1900 in der österreichischen Reichshälfte noch kaum vorhanden. Eine Ausnahme stellt laut Mischler lediglich der „Landesverband für Wohlthätigkeit in [sic] Steiermark" dar, der als Dachorganisation öffentlicher und kirchlicher Institutionen über Unterstützungsmöglichkeiten informierte und eine Arbeitsvermittlung betrieb. Mischler, "Einleitung. Übersicht über die Armenpflege," S. XXXVIII.
[49] AŽMP, ŽnoP, Reorganizace chudinství, vandrovní žebrota – účty, komise, Sign. 128385, Schreiben der United Hebrew Charities of the City of New York an die Yiddishe Cultus Gemeinde, Prague, Hungary [sic], New York, 22.6.1903.
[50] Ebenda.

CHAPTER EIGHTEEN

ARMUTSPOLITIK, ANTIZIGANISMUS UND WOHLFAHRT IN CISLEITHANIEN ZWISCHEN 1900 UND 1914

MARIUS WEIGL

Poverty policy, Anti-Gypsyism and the general welfare in Cisleithania between 1900 and 1914

Abstract: A criticism of poverty policy as well as of the entire system of social care coming from lower authorities culminated in Cisleithania around the year of 1900. It was related to the persisting economic crisis in Bohemia and Moravia, and to the migration of its labour to Vienna. However, a turnaround in social issues happened in Cisleithania at that time. This turnaround was manifested in two areas: first, in an attempt to reorganise the original municipal social system into a new one, run by the state. And second, the professionalisation of the police occurred. This paper demonstrates how a politically calculated usage of the stereotype of a "Gypsy" served to shape powers/competences in the sphere of social care as well as in that of the police. The article further documents the potential arbitrariness on the side of authorities, which could easily affect people under the definition of being a "Gypsy" on the eve of the First World War.

Seit den Arbeiten von Michael Zimmermann, Wolfgang Ayaß und Leo Lucassen haben die historiographischen Forschungen zu Antiziganismus die Ambivalenz der Armutspolitik zwischen Wohlfahrt und Kriminalitätsprävention betont.[1] Zu Beginn des 20. Jahrhunderts wurden

---

[1] Michael Zimmermann, Rassenutopie und Genozid. Die nationalsozialistische „Lösung der Zigeunerfrage" (Hamburg: Christians,1996); Zwischen Erziehung und Vernichtung. Zigeunerpolitik und Zigeunerforschung im Europa des 20. Jahrhunderts, Hrsg. Michael Zimmermann (Stuttgart: Steiner, 2007); Wolfgang Ayaß, „‚Ein Gebot der nationalen Arbeitsdisziplin', Die Aktion ‚Arbeitsscheu Reich' 1938," in Feindererklärung und Prävention. Kriminalbiologie, Zigeunerforschung und Asozialenpolitik, Hrsg. Wolfgang Ayaß et. al. (Berlin:

in Mähren und im Besonderen in Böhmen und Niederösterreich eine radikale Anti-Zigeuner-Politik verfolgt und Impulse für andere Kronländer gesetzt. Um die Positionen der Statthaltereien in Prag, Brünn und in Wien sowie deren Unterbehörden zu erörtern, muss zwischen den Institutionen, sozialen Lebenswelten und Akteuren differenziert werden.

Die Kronländer hatten zwar dieselbe Gesetzeslage – hier von Belang sind das Heimatrecht von 1863[2] und dessen Novellierung von 1896,[3] das Schubgesetz von 1871,[4] das Landstreichergesetz von 1873[5] und das modifizierte Landstreichergesetz von 1885[6] sowie im Speziellen der „Erlass zur Bekämpfung des Zigeunerunwesens" von 1888. Jedoch wurden die Gesetze aufgrund regionaler und sozioökonomischer Faktoren, wie des Bedarfs an ambulantem Gewerbe und Saisonarbeiter/-innen, der Arbeitslosigkeit in den Industriegebieten in Böhmen und Mähren, der Nähe zu Ungarn, welches als „Heimatland der Zigeuner" imaginiert wurde, der zunehmenden Bedeutung der Polizeidirektionen in Wien und Prag bezüglich der Einführung von Zigeunerevidenzen sowie ferner der sozialen Frage und der Krise der Armenfürsorge, die auf dem Heimatrecht aufbaute, unterschiedlich angewendet.

Rotbuch-Verlag, 1988); Leo Lucassen, Zigeuner. Die Geschichte eines polizeilichen Ordnungsbegriffes in Deutschland 1700–1945 (Köln et al.: Böhlau, 1996); Leo Lucassen et al., Gypsies and other itinerant groups. A socio-historical approach (Basingstocke: Macmillan 2001); Martin Luchterhandt, Der Weg nach Birkenau. Entstehung und Verlauf der nationalsozialistischen Verfolgung der „Zigeuner" (Lübeck: Schmidt-Römhild, 2000); Florian Freund et al., Oberösterreich und die Zigeuner. Politik gegen eine Minderheit im 19. und 20. Jahrhundert (Linz: OÖLA, 2010); Florian Freund et al., Vermögensentzug, Restitution und Entschädigung der Roma und Sinti (Wien: Oldenbourg, 2004); Marius Weigl, „‚Für die öffentliche Sicherheit.' Zur Genese der antiziganistischen Norm in Österreich zwischen 1918 und 1938" (Diplomarbeit, Universität Wien, 2012).

[2] Reichsgesetzblatt (weiter RGBl.) 105/1863, Gesetz vom 3. December 1863 betreffend die Regelung der Heimatverhältnisse.

[3] RGBl. 222/1896, Gesetz vom 5. December 1896, wodurch einige Bestimmungen des Gesetzes vom 3. December 1863 (R.G.Bl.Nr.105), betreffend die Regelung der Heimatverhältnisse, abgeändert werden.

[4] RGBl. 88/1871, Gesetz vom 27. Juli 1871 in Betreff der Regelung der polizeilichen Abschaffung und des Schubwesens.

[5] RGBl. 10/1873, Gesetz vom 10. Mai 1873, womit polizeistrafrechtliche Bestimmungen wider Arbeitsscheue und Landstreicher erlassen werden.

[6] RGBl. 89/1885, Gesetz vom 24. Mai 1885, womit strafrechtliche Bestimmungen in Betreff der Zulässigkeit der Anhaltung in Zwangsarbeits- und Besserungsanstalten getroffen werden.

Die Bekämpfung der erfundenen „Zigeunerplage"

Der Zigeunererlass von 1888 war einerseits eine Anleitung für Behörden, welche Gesetze bei „Zigeunern" angewendet werden sollten (so u. a. das Schubgesetz 1871, die Landstreichergesetze von 1873 und 1885 und das Tierseuchengesetz von 1880), aber andererseits in zwei Punkten eine Ausnahmeregelung. Erstens konnten Waren und Geld von „Zigeunern" beschlagnahmt und für die Schubkosten verwendet werden. Zweitens sollten jene, die eine österreichische Staatsbürgerschaft hatten, denen man aber keine Heimatzuständigkeit nachweisen konnte oder wollte, entgegen dem Heimatrechtsgesetz 1863 keiner Heimatgemeinde zugewiesen werden. Jedes Jahr sollten die Länderbehörden dem Ministerium des Innern in Wien einen Bericht über das „Zigeunerunwesen" senden.[7]

Fast alle dieser Berichte an das Ministerium des Innern in Wien waren zwischen 1900 und 1914 entweder rein deskriptiv und enthielten keinerlei Vorschläge oder Problematisierungen oder sie sprachen von einem Abnehmen des „Zigeunerunwesens". Nur drei Kronländer bildeten die Ausnahme. Die Landesregierung in Krain fokussierte in der Darstellung des lokalen „Zigeunerunwesens" auf die in Krain heimatberechtigten und nicht in den Grenzregionen aufgegriffenen „Zigeuner". Die Krainer „Zigeuner" sollten in den ökonomisch schwächeren Gemeinden angesiedelt und ihre Arbeitskraft für öffentliche Bauten, den Ausbau der Infrastruktur sowie Erntearbeiten verwendet werden.[8] Anfangs versprach

---

[7] "K. k. Ministerium des Innern, Erlass zur Bekämpfung des Zigeunerunwesens, 14.9.1888, Z. 14015 ex 1887," in Die polizeilichen Vorschriften Niederösterreichs. Nach dem Stande vom 1. September 1927 II., Hrsg. Friedrich Meister (Wien: Im Selbstverlag des Amtes der n. ö. Landesregierung, 1927), S. 1069.
[8] Österreichisches Staatsarchiv (weiter ÖStA), Allgemeines Verwaltungsarchiv (weiter AVA), Ministerium des Innern, Allgemein, Kt. 2118 20/2 Nr. 10.423-901 Zl. 6.811, k. k. Landesregierung für Krain, Laibach, 16.2.1902, k. k. Ministerium des Innern, Landesstellen berichten zum ho. Beteilungserlasse Z. 4604-02 in Gemäßheit dem ho. Circular-Erlasse v. 14/9.888 Z 14015-87 und v. 20/6.1900 Z 18036 über die im Jahre 1901 in Bezug auf das Zigeuner-Unwesen gemachten Wahrnehmungen und getroffenen Verfügungen; ebenda, Nr. 5.039-03, k. k. Landespräsident für Krain, Laibach, 31.1.1903; ebenda, Nr. 8.188, k. k. Landesregierung für Krain, Laibach, 22.2.1904; ebenda, Kt. Nr. 6.892-05, k. k. Landesregierung für Krain, Laibach, 13.2.1905; ebenda, Nr. 14.825 Zl. 10.525, k. k. Landesregierung für Krain, Laibach, 3.3.1906, K. k. MdI, Berichte der Landeschefs in 1) Lemberg, 2) Laibach, 3) Troppau, 4) Wien, 5) Zara und 6) Graz ad h.o. Z. 14.015ex1887 über die im Jahre 1905 in der Bekämpfung des Zigeunerunwesens erzielten Erfolge; ebenda, Nr. 8.096, k. k. Landesregierung für Krain, Laibach, 2.3.1909; ebenda, Kt. 2119 20/2 Nr. 4.973-910, k. k.

sich die Krainer Landesregierung eine „Lösung des Zigeunerunwesens"
durch Arbeit und Erziehung zur Arbeit bei den Jugendlichen, aber dieses
selbstgemachte Versprechen konnte wegen der eigenen repressiven
Sozialpolitik (schlechtere Bezahlung, Zuteilung der Lehrherren) nicht
eingehalten werden. Zu Beginn des zweiten Jahrzehnts des 20.
Jahrhunderts wurde der Ton in den Berichten rauer, zugleich wurden
„Unverbesserlichkeit" wie „Kriminalität" der „Zigeuner" betont und
entsprechende Maßnahmen gefordert – auch gegen jene fremden
„Zigeuner", die an der Grenze aufgegriffen wurden. Nachdem überdies
Brandlegungen klischeehaft „Zigeunern" angelastet worden waren und die
Gendarmerie unter Beteiligung der Zivilbevölkerung Streifungen
durchgeführt hatte, kam es 1911 sogar zu einem pogromartigen Mord an
einem böhmischen Handelsagenten.[9] In ihren Jahresberichten über die
öffentliche Sicherheit verlor die Landesregierung allerdings kein Wort
über ein etwaiges „Zigeunerunwesen".[10]

Eine weitere Statthalterei, die ab 1900 sowohl eine zunehmende
„Zigeuner-" als auch „Landstreicherplage" zum Thema machte, war jene
für Tirol und Vorarlberg. Ihr zufolge endete dieses Problem im Jahr 1912
abrupt, wobei aber ohnehin wohl nur Deutschtirol betroffen gewesen sei.
Aus dem Vergleich zwischen den Sicherheitsberichten und den Berichten
über die „Bekämpfung des Zigeunerunwesens" geht hervor, dass es sich

---

Landesregierung für Krain, Laibach, 6.2.1910, Betreff: Bekämpfung des
Zigeunerunwesens im Jahre 1909 erzielte Erfolge; ebenda, Nr. 6.133-11, k. k.
Landesregierung für Krain, Laibach, 17.2.1911, Betreff: Die bei der Bekämpfung
des Zigeunerunwesens im Jahre 1910 erzielten Erfolge; ebenda, Nr. 9.876-912, k.
k. Landesregierung für Krain, Laibach, 16.3.1912; ebenda, Nr. 7.293-13, k. k.
Landesregierung für Krain, Laibach, 25.2.1913.
[9] ÖStA, AVA, Ministerium des Innern, Allgemein, 20/2 Kt. 2119 Nr. 9.876-912,
Tages-Rapport, 25.9.1911, k. k. Landesregierung für Krain, Laibach, 16.3.1912.
[10] ÖStA, AVA, Ministerium des Innern, Präsidium, Kt. 1979 20/4 Nr
615/M.I./1900, k. k. Landesregierung in Krain, Laibach, 1.2.1900; ebenda, Nr.
3.120/M.I./1901, k. k. Landespräsidium in Krain, Laibach, 19.4.1901; ebenda, Nr.
1.857/M.I./1902, k. k. Landespräsidium in Krain, Laibach, 11.3.1902; ebenda, Nr.
1.352/M.I./1903, k. k. Landespräsidium für Krain, Laibach, 24.2.1903; ebenda, Nr.
1.075/M.I./1904, k. k. Landespräsidium in Krain, Laibach 15.2.1904; ebenda, Nr.
743/M.I./1905, k. k. Landespräsidium in Krain, Laibach, 3.2.1905; ebenda, Nr.
1.1282/M.I./1906, k. k. Landespräsidium in Krain, Laibach, 8.2.1906; ebenda, Kt.
1980 20/4 Nr. 1.048/M.I./1907, k. k. Landespräsidium für Krain, Laibach
4.2.1907; ebenda, Nr. 1.561/M.I./1908, k. k. Landespräsidium in Krain, Laibach,
19.2.1908; ebenda, Nr. 4.641/M.I./1909, k. k. Landespräsidium in Laibach,
10.4.1909; ebenda, Nr. 1.901/M.I./1910, k. k. Landespräsidium in Laibach,
21.2.1910; ebenda, Nr. 3.592/M.I./1911, k. k. Landespräsidium in Laibach,
12.4.1911; ebenda, Nr. 1.457/M.I., k. k. Landespräsidium in Laibach, 6.2.1911.

offenbar vielmehr um ein „Landstreicherunwesen" gehandelt hatte, das
vor allem durch reichsdeutsche Handwerksburschen bedingt gewesen sein
soll.[11]
Die Statthalterei in Böhmen wiederum forderte sowohl in ihren
Berichten über die öffentliche Sicherheit als auch in den jährlichen
Berichten über die „Bekämpfung des Zigeunerunwesens" das
Innenministerium dazu auf, strengere Maßnahmen zu ergreifen und ein
Ausnahmegesetz gegen „Zigeuner" zu erlassen. Primär richtete sich das
Vorgehen der böhmischen Sicherheitsbehörden gegen dort
heimatberechtigte „Zigeuner". Diese wurden zu öffentlichen Arbeiten
herangezogen und in Zwangsarbeitsanstalten eingewiesen. Darüber hinaus
wurden kontinuierlich Landesstreifungen von der Gendarmerie
durchgeführt. Dabei wurden böhmische „Zigeuner" nach Niederösterreich
abgedrängt; das führte wiederum zu Konflikten mit der dortigen
Gendarmerie. Aber auch sogenannte böhmische „Halbzigeuner" –

---

[11] ÖStA, AVA, Ministerium des Innern, Allgemein, Kt. 2118 20/2 Nr. 4.604;
ebenda, Nr. 4.604 Zl. 3.036-907, k. k. Statthalterei für Tirol und Vorarlberg,
Innsbruck, 27.1.1902, k. k. Ministerium des Innern, Statthalter in Innsbruck und
Landesregierung in Klagenfurt berichtet in Gemäßheit den ho. Erlasse v. 14/9.888
Z. 14015 und v. 20/6.1900 Z. 18036 über die im Jahre 1901 in Bezug auf das
Zigeuner-Unwesen gemachten Wahrnehmungen; ebenda, Nr. 5.542-03, k. k.
Statthalterei für Tirol und Vorarlberg, Innsbruck, 2.2.1903; ebenda, Nr. 4.873-04,
k. k. Statthalterei für Tirol und Vorarlberg, Innsbruck, 30.1.1904; ebenda, Nr.
6.395-05, k. k. Statthalterei für Tirol und Vorarlberg, Innsbruck, 6.2.1905; ebenda,
Nr. 7.480 ex 1906 Zl. 5.934, k. k. Statthalterei für Tirol und Vorarlberg, Innsbruck,
1.2.1906; ebenda, Nr. 21.505-08, k. k. Statthalterei für Tirol und Vorarlberg,
Innsbruck, 31.5.1908; ebenda, Nr. 29.778-09, k. k. Statthalterei für Tirol und
Vorarlberg, Innsbruck, 10.8.1909; ebenda, Kt. 2119 20/2 Nr. 5.691-13, k. k.
Statthalterei für Tirol und Vorarlberg, Innsbruck, 7.2.1913; ebenda, Präsidium, Kt.
1979 20/4 Nr. 820/M.I./1900, k. k. Statthalterei für Tirol und Vorarlberg,
Innsbruck, 10.2.1900; ebenda, 20/4 Nr. 1.254/M.I./1901, k. k. Statthalterei für
Tirol und Vorarlberg, Innsbruck 31.2.[sic]1.1901; ebenda, Nr. 707/M.I./1902, k. k.
Statthalterei für Tirol und Vorarlberg, Innsbruck, 24.1.1902; ebenda, Nr.
651/M.I./1903, k. k. Statthalterei für Tirol und Vorarlberg, Innsbruck, 25.1.1903;
ebenda, Nr. 702/M.I./1904, k. k. Statthalterei für Tirol und Vorarlberg, Innsbruck,
29.1.1904; ebenda, Nr. 1.418/M.I./1906, k. k. Statthalterei für Tirol und
Vorarlberg, Innsbruck 12.2.1906; ebenda, Kt. 1980 20/4 Nr. 1.875/M.I./1907, k. k.
Statthalterei für Tirol und Vorarlberg, Innsbruck, 25.2.1907; ebenda, Nr.
2.853/M.I./1908, k. k. Statthalterei für Tirol und Vorarlberg, Innsbruck 28.3.1908;
ebenda, Nr. 7.424/M.I./1909, k. k. Statthalterei für Tirol und Vorarlberg,
Innsbruck, 23.6.1909; ebenda, Kt. 1904 20 Nr. 3.149/M.I., k. k. Statthalterei für
Tirol und Vorarlberg, Innsbruck, 8.3.1913, Betreff: Sicherheitsbericht pro 1912.

Schleifer, Geschirrhändler und Riemenhändler12 – tauchten in den niederösterreichischen Gemeinden an der Grenze zu Böhmen auf. Die Statthalterei in Prag wies im Übrigen für die „Bekämpfung des Zigeunerunwesens" wie auch für die des „Landstreicherunwesens" die höchsten Zahlen aus.

Tabelle 18-1: Anzahl der Abstrafungen auf Basis des Landstreichergesetzes von 1885 und des Zigeunererlasses von 1888 in Böhmen

Jahr	Landstrei-cherei	Bettel	Arbeits-scheu	„Zigeuner" (Landstreicherei, Bettel; 1901, 1904 und 1905 auch Diebstahl, weil nicht differenziert)
1901	19.389[13]	11.831[14]	1.086[15]	3.196[16]
1904	19.163[17]	14.904[18]	649[19]	3.826[20]
1905	16.467[21]	15.342[22]	542[23]	2.857[24]

[12] ÖStA, AVA, Ministerium des Innern-Allgemein, 20/2 Kt. 2118, K. k. n.ö. Statthalterei, Wien, 11.3.1906, Zigeunerunwesen, Bekämpfung, Nr.14.825-ex 1906 Zl. 11.1695.
[13] ÖStA, AVA, Ministerium des Innern, Präsidium, Kt. 1979 20/4 Nr. 5.121/M.I./1902, Ausweis über die Anzahl jener Individuen, gegen welche in dem Solarjahre 1901 auf Grund des Gesetzes vom 10. Mai 1873, R.G.Bl. No. 108, R.G.Bl. No. 89 und vom 24. Mai 1885 R.G.Bl. No. 90 vorgegangen wurde, K. k. Statthalterei in Böhmen, Prag, 4.7.1902.
[14] Ebenda.
[15] Ebenda.
[16] ÖStA, AVA, Ministerium des Innern, Allgemein, Kt. 2118 20/2 Nr. 10.423-901, k. k. Ministerium des Innern, Landesstellen berichten zum ho. Beteilungserlasse Z 4604-02 in Gemäßheit der ho. Circular-Erlässe v. 14/9. 888 Z 14015-87 und v. 20/6 1900 Z 18036 über die im Jahre 1901 in Bezug auf das Zigeuner-Unwesen gemachten Wahrnehmungen und getroffenen Verfügungen, k. k. Statthalterei in Böhmen, Prag, 12.3.1902.
[17] ÖStA, AVA, Ministerium des Innern, Präsidium, Kt. 1979 20/4 Nr. 2.991/M.I./1905 Ausweis über die Anzahl derjeniger Individuen, gegen die im Solarjahre 1904 im Grunde der Gesetze vom 10. Mai 1873, R.G.Bl. No. 108, vom 24. Mai 1885, R.G.Bl. No. 89 und vom 24. Mai 1885, R.G.Bl. No. 90 vorgegangen wurde, k. k. Statthalterei in Böhmen, Prag, 5.5.1905.
[18] Ebenda.
[19] Ebenda.
[20] ÖStA, AVA, Ministerium des Innern, Allgemein, Kt. 2118 20/2 Nr. 14020/05 Zl. 17.956/05, k. k. Ministerium des Innern, k. k. Statthalterei in Böhmen, Prag, 12.4.1905.
[21] ÖStA, AVA, Ministerium des Innern, Präsidium, Kt. 1979 20/4 Nr. 5.249/M.I./1906, Ausweis über die Anzahl derjenigen Individuen der im Solarjahre

1909	13.640[25]	13.402[26]	140[27]	2.961[28]

Das von Dillmann 1905 herausgegebene „Zigeuner-Buch" inspirierte im selben Jahr die Forderung nach einer Revision der 1890 angelegten Zigeunerevidenzen. Vereinzelt wurden diesbezüglich bereits Versuche unternommen, wie etwa von dem Gendarmerieposten in den Königlichen Weinbergen, der 1910 eine mit 500 Karten versehene Zigeunerevidenz einführte.[29] Schon 1904 wurden die ersten Schritte von der Staatsanwaltschaft in Prag für ein derartiges Registrierungssystem in die Wege geleitet.[30] Und auch die Bezirkshauptmannschaft Tachau übte sich 1905 in den ersten Schritten der Daktyloskopie von „Zigeunern".[31]

1905 im Grunde der Gesetze vom 10. Mai 1873, R.G.Bl. No. 108, vom 24. Mai 1885, R.G.Bl. No. 89 und vom 24. Mai 1885, R.G.Bl. No. 90, k. k. Statthalterei in Böhmen, Ausweis für das Soljahr [sic] 1905 vorgegangen wurde, k. k. Statthalterei in Böhmen, Prag, 3.6.1906.

[22] Ebenda.

[23] Ebenda.

[24] ÖStA, AVA, Ministerium des Innern, Allgemein, Kt. 2118 20/2 Nr. 14.825-ex1906 Zl. 5.281, k. k. Ministerium des Innern, Berichte der Landeschefs in 1., Lemberg, 2., Laibach, 3., Troppau, 4., Wien, 5., Zara und 6. Graz ad h.o. Z. 14.015ex1887 über die im Jahre 1905 in der Bekämpfung des Zigeunerunwesens erzielten Erfolge, k. k. Statthalterei, in Böhmen, Prag, 1.2.1906.

[25] ÖStA, AVA, Ministerium des Innern, Präsidium, Kt. 1980 20/4 Nr. 5.555/M.I./1910, Ausweis über die Anzahl derjenigen Individuen, gegen die im Solarjahre 1909 im Grunde der Gesetze vom 10.V.1873, R.G.Bl. No. 108, 24./5 1885, R.G.Bl. No. 89 und vom 24. Mai 1885, R.G.Bl. No. 90 vorgegangen wurde, k. k. Statthalterei in Böhmen, Prag, 30. 5. 1910, Zustand der öffentlichen Sicherheit im Jahre 1909.

[26] Ebenda.

[27] Ebenda.

[28] ÖStA, AVA, Ministerium des Innern, Allgemein, Kt. 2119 20/2 Nr. 21.371-11, k. k. Statthalterei in Böhmen, Prag, 31.5.1910, Zigeunerunwesen, Jahresbericht pro 1909.

[29] ÖStA, AVA, Ministerium des Innern, Allgemein, Kt. 2119 20/2 Nr. 25.401/1911 Zl. 25.401, k. k. Statthalterei in Böhmen, Prag, 22.7.1911, Zigeunerunwesen, Jahresbericht pro 1910.

[30] ÖStA, AVA, Ministerium des Innern, Allgemein, Kt. 2118 20/2 Nr. 33529/1904 Z. 12.554 Post exped., Einsichtsakt des JM betreffend Einführung einer Zentralevidenz für abgestrafte Zigeuner in Böhmen, Wien, 28.7.1904.

[31] ÖStA, AVA, Ministerium des Innern, Allgemein, Kt. 2118 20/2 Nr. 14.825-ex1906 Zl. 5.281, k. k. Ministerium des Innern, Berichte der Landeschefs in 1., Lemberg, 2., Laibach, 3., Troppau, 4., Wien, 5., Zara und 6. Graz ad h.o. Z. 14.015ex1887 über die im Jahre 1905 in der Bekämpfung des Zigeunerunwesens

In Niederösterreich zielte die Abschiebepraxis der Gendarmerie nicht nur auf aus Böhmen abgedrängte „Zigeuner" und „Halbzigeuner", sondern auch auf solche Personen, die von den Sicherheitsbehörden zwar als „Zigeuner" erachtet wurden, jedoch als Ernte- und Saisonarbeiter/-innen hier eine Arbeit fanden. Gleiches traf auf ungarische, aber vor allem mährische „Zigeuner" zu. In diesem Rahmen kam es zu Konflikten zwischen Großgrundbesitzern und Behörden, weil Erstere an billigen Arbeitskräften interessiert waren, die Gendarmerie sowie die Bezirksbehörden jedoch in den „Zigeunern" eine Gefahr für die öffentliche Sicherheit sahen. Die Gendarmerie hatte durch die Abdrängungen und Abschiebungen allerdings das letzte Wort. Das Hin und Her wie auch die von der Statthalterei in Wien bemängelte fehlende Auslastung der Zwangsarbeitsanstalt in Korneuburg führten im Jahr 1908 schließlich zu der Praxis der Überstellung von in Böhmen verurteilten „Zigeunern" in diese Anstalt.[32] Dabei sollten die Kosten zwischen den Kronländern und der Staatskasse aufgeteilt werden, da jegliche „Zigeuner" unabhängig von der Heimatzuständigkeit in Korneuburg eingeliefert werden sollten. Dieser Vorschlag wurde schon 1904 seitens der niederösterreichischen Statthalterei ihrem böhmischen Pendant unterbreitet, das ihn als eine für „die Wohlfahrt der Länder und seiner Bewohner fördernde Aktion"[33] bezeichnete.

Da auch zwischen „Halbzigeunern" und „Zigeunern" unterschieden wurde, muss auf die Verwendung des Terminus „Zigeuner" als polizeilicher Ordnungsbegriff bei Fahndungen genauer eingegangen werden. Die Ambiguität der biologistischen Kategorisierung anhand von Zigeunernamen, wie sie etwa der Kriminalwissenschaftler Hans Gross vornahm[34], zeigte sich schon in den Ausschreibungen des Zentralen Polizeiblattes. Anhand der häufigsten Namen Daniel, Malik und Ružička in Verbindung mit einem mobilen Gewerbe oder der Fahndung wegen Landstreicherei, Bettel, Diebstahl etc. lässt sich dies exemplifizieren. In den Fahndungen der

---

erzielten Erfolge, k. k. Statthalterei, in Böhmen, Prag, 1. 2. 1906.

[32] ÖStA, AVA, Ministerium des Innern, Allgemein, Kt. 2118 20/2 17.378-09, k. k. Statthalterei in Böhmen, Prag, 10.5.1909 Ausserlandschaffung einer Zigeunertruppe; ebenda, Nr. 40.043/08, k. k. Ministerium des Innern, Wien, 24.12.1908, Statthalterei in Prag betreffend die Bestreitung der Hälfte der mit der Anhaltung von 60 Zigeunern in der Zwangsarbeitsanstalt Korneuburg verbundenen Kosten.

[33] ÖStA, AVA, Ministerium des Innern, Allgemein, Kt. 2118 20/2 Nr. 17.956/05 Zl. 14.020/05, k. k. Statthalterei in Böhmen, Prag, 27.3.1905.

[34] Hans Gross, Handbuch für Untersuchungsrichter als System der Kriminalistik I., Hrsg. Erwein Höpler (München et al.: Schweitzer, 1922), S. 454–480 ("IX. Abschnitt. Die Zigeuner; ihr Wesen ihre Eigenschaften").

böhmischen, niederösterreichischen und mährischen Sicherheitsbehörden wurde in unserem Untersuchungszeitraum der Name Daniel 128-mal als „Zigeuner" etikettiert und 16-mal nicht, der Name Malik 35-mal und 14-mal nicht und der Name Ružička 83-mal und 40-mal nicht.

Die Verbindung dieser Familiennamen, wie auch anderer Namen, mit dem polizeilichen Ordnungsbegriff „Zigeuner" kam ausschließlich im Kontext mit mobilen Berufen, Arbeitsmigration oder Arbeitslosigkeit vor. Da durchgängig mobile Gewerbe und das strikte Verbot der Ausübung mit dem „Zigeunerunwesen" in Zusammenhang gebracht wurden, können bei den Ausschreibungen von „Zigeunern" und/oder mobilen Gewerbetreibenden regionale Unterschiede verdeutlicht werden.

Auch im Vergleich der Fahndungen in den Kronländern können die regionalen Unterschiede veranschaulicht werden. Von den 303 Ausschreibungen böhmischer Behörden in den Jahren 1900–1913 wurden 179 als „Zigeuner", 116 nicht als solche und 8 als „Landstreicher" bzw. „Vagant" etikettiert. 192 der ausgeschriebenen Personen waren laut Fahndung in Böhmen heimatberechtigt. Ein ähnliches Bild zeichnet sich für Mähren ab: Im Rahmen von 476 Ausschreibungen wurde nach 297 Personen als „Zigeuner" (gegenüber 166 „Nicht-Zigeunern") und nach 13 als „Landstreicher"/„Vagant" gefahndet. Über die Hälfte jener „Zigeuner" mit nachgewiesenen Heimatgemeinden stammte aus Mähren (170). Bei den relativ wenigen 182 Ausschreibungen von niederösterreichischen Behörden wurden 70 als „Zigeuner", aber 108 nicht als „Zigeuner", 1 als „Landstreicherin" und 3 als „Bettler/-innen" beschrieben. Von diesen stammten nur 9 aus diesem Kronland.

Tabelle 18-2: Fahndungen von „Zigeunern". Vergleich von Böhmen, Mähren und Niederösterreich (1900–1913)

Kron-land	Fahn-dungen insgesamt	Mobiles Gewerbe/ Saisonar-beit	„Zigeu-ner" mit Beruf	„Zigeu-ner" ohne Beruf	„Zigeu-nerin-nen" mit Beruf	„Zigeu-nerinnen" ohne Beruf	„Land-streicher"/ „Vagant"/ „Bettler"	ohne individuelle Angaben (z. B. „Zigeunerb anden", „-familien" o der Kinder)
Böhmen	303	116	18	98	2	51	8	10
Mähren	476	166	33	174	3	80	13	7
Nieder-öster-reich	182	108	20	22	6	8	4	14

Quelle: Eigene Zählung auf Basis des Zentral-Polizeilichen Fahndungsblattes

Wien (1900–1913).[35]

---

[35] K. k. Polizeidirektion Wien, Zentral-Polizeiliches Fahndungsblatt, Wien [Nr./Datum]: 3/26.1.1900; 9/15.2.1900; 10/17.2.1900; 14/2.3.1900; 18/10.3.1900; 32/26.4.1900; 33/28.4.1900; 37/10.5.1900; 45/7.6.1900; 50/23.6.1900; 59/11.7.1900; 73/16.8.1900; 80/29.8.1900; 83/7.9.1900; 93/5.10.1900; 94/8.10.1900; 96/12.10.1900; 124/14.12.1900; 138/28.12.1900; 2/15.1.1901; 7/4.2.1901; 8/6.2.1901; 17/4.3.1901; 21/16.3.1901; 46/7.6.1901; 48/10.6.1901; 49/12.6.1901; 55/21.6.1901; 59/28.6.1901; 61/5.7.1901; 61/5.7.1901; 65/11.7.1901; 82/22.8.1901; 85/2.9.1901; 117/20.9.1901; 94/27.9.1901; 99/11.10.1901; 100/15.10.1901; 108/30.10.1901; 115/16.11.1901; 117/20.11.1901; 119/25.11.1901; 141/29.12.1901; 143/31.12.1901; 17/4.3.1902; 21/18.3.1902; 24/27.3.1902; 31/14.4.1902; 36/23.4.1902; 37/25.4.1902; 40/3.5.1902; 43/12.5.1902; 49/30.5.1902; 53/11.6.1902; 67/15.7.1902; 71/24.7.1902; 100/6.8.1902; 89/11.9.1902; 192/17.9.1902; 95/25.9.1902; 96/27.9.1902; 113/4.11.1902; 121/28.11.1902; 131/5.12.1902; 134/22.12.1902; 39/29.12.1902; 2/12.1.1903; 4/20.1.1903; 7/27.1.1903; 10/3.2.1903; 15/17.2.1903; 16/19.2.1903; 27/30.3.1903; 79/3.4.1903; 31/10.4.1903; 34/18.4.1903; 38/28.4.1903; 48/30.5.1903; 49/4.6.1903; 50/6.6.1903; 57/24.6.1903; 68/21.7.1903; 77/8.8.1903; 80/13.8.1903; 83/22.8.1903; 94/21.9.1903; 129/30.9.1903; 100/6.10.1903; 113/30.10.1903; 118/10.11.1903; 121/16.11.1903; 126/26.11.1903; 140/16.12.1903; 145/29.12.1903; 1/10.1.1904; 2/12.1.1904; 3/14.1.1904; 6/21.1.1904; 7/25.1.1904; 12/8.2.1904; 18/26.2.1904; 30/30.3.1904; 34/12.4.1904; 37/19.4.1904; 43/5.5.1904; 43/5.5.1904; 45/11.5.1904; 55/8.6.1904; 56/10.6.1904; 62/23.6.1904; 65/27.6.1904; 69/7.7.1904; 71/9.7.1904; 78/25.7.1904; 82/3.8.1904; 91/25.8.1904; 96/2.9.1904; 98/6.9.1904; 102/14.9.1904; 104/19.9.1904; 115/8.10.1904; 116/10.10.1904; 123/20.10.1904; 128/28.10.1904; 147/3.12.1904; 154/14.12.1904; 161/23.12.1904; 161/23.12.1904; 3/18.1.1905; 4/21.1.1905; 9/1.2.1905; 16/17.2.1905; 17/22.2.1905; 28/29.3.1905; 31/4.4.1905; 39/18.4.1905; 45/4.5.1905; 51/19.5.1905; 54/26.5.1905; 55/30.5.1905; 60/14.6.1905; 61/17.7.1905; 77/18.7.1905; 78/19.7.1905; 80/22.7.1905; 81/25.7.1905; 66/28.7.1905; 86/3.8.1905; 93/16.8.1905; 94/19.8.1905; 97/25.8.1905; 105/7.9.1905; 116/28.9.1905; 121/9.10.1905; 129/21.10.1905; 154/30.11.1905; 157/3.12.1905; 158/4.12.1905; 168/20.12.1905; 172/28.12.1905; 3/18.1.1906; 5/22.1.1906; 9/31.1.1906; 10/3.2.1906; 23/8.3.1906; 49/5.5.1906; 53/12.5.1906; 57/21.5.1906; 62/31.5.1906; 78/5.6.1906; 69/18.6.1906; 79/6.7.1906; 37/21.7.1906; 89/26.7.1906; 90/28.7.1906; 97/10.8.1906; 98/13.8.1906; 99/17.8.1906; 102/26.8.1906; 103/28.8.1906; 111/12.9.1906; 122/4.10.1906; 127/11.10.1906; 131/17.10.1906; 138/26.10.1906; 144/6.11.1906; 148/10.11.1906; 153/20.11.1906; 159/28.11.1906; 161/1.12.1906; 162/3.12.1906; 165/7.12.1906; 168/12.12.1906; 172/19.12.1906; 173/20.12.1906; 176/27.12.1906; 177/28.12.1906; 178/29.12.1906; 7/18.1.1907; 15/8.2.1907; 19/21.2.1907; 20/25.2.1907; 20/25.2.1907; 21/26.2.1907; 21/26.2.1907; 28/9.3.1907; 31/18.3.1907; 45/23.4.1907; 58/23.5.1907; 65/5.6.1907; 68/11.6.1907; 74/24.6.1907; 75/26.6.1907; 78/3.7.1907; 78/3.7.1907; 81/8.7.1907; 89/22.7.1907;

90/24.7.1907; 99/9.8.1907; 101/12.8.1907; 102/14.8.1907; 103/17.8.1907;
103/17.8.1907; 105/24.8.1907; 107/27.8.1907; 120/18.9.1907; 121/19.9.1907;
122/21.9.1907; 125/28.9.1907; 133/12.10.1907; 142/28.10.1907; 147/2.11.1907;
151/12.11.1907; 153/16.11.1907; 162/30.11.1907; 171/11.12.1907;
157/23.12.1907; 181/30.12.1907; 182/31.12.1907; 1/7.1.1908; 3/13.1.1908;
19/8.2.1908; 21/13.2.1908; 28/29.2.1908; 31/10.3.1908; 31/10.3.1908;
33/13.3.1908; 36/19.3.1908; 40/26.3.1908; 42/30.3.1908; 47/10.4.1908;
38/23.4.1908; 57/29.4.1908; 60/6.5.1908; 61/7.5.1908; 63/9.5.1908; 67/16.5.1908;
70/23.5.1908; 72/27.5.1908; 73/30.5.1908; 85/26.6.1908; 86/30.6.1908;
91/7.7.1908; 94/11.7.1908; 96/18.7.1908; 103/29.7.1908; 104/31.7.1908;
130/18.9.1908; 131/21.9.1908; 142/7.10.1908; 149/17.10.1908; 150/20.10.1908;
152/23.10.1908; 153/24.10.1908; 155/28.10.1908; 157/30.10.1908;
175/25.11.1908; 191/18.12.1908; 196/24.12.1908; 7/14.1.1909; 9/16.1.1909;
35/27.2.1909; 42/13.3.1909; 50/31.3.1909; 52/6.4.1909; 62/24.4.1909;
65/30.4.1909; 70/10.5.1909; 72/12.5.1909; 79/27.5.1909; 80/28.5.1909;
92/17.6.1909; 93/18.6.1909; 94/19.6.1909;104/8.7.1909; 116/26.7.1909;
117/27.7.1909; 119/29.7.1909; 123/13.8.1909; 132/20.8.1909; 136/28.8.1909;
146/14.9.1909; 148/17.9.1909; 154/27.9.1909; 164/14.10.1909; 167/20.10.1909;
175/3.11.1909; 178/8.11.1909; 178/8.11.1909; 182/13.11.1909; 195/2.12.1909;
201/10.12.1909; 209/21.12.1909; 219/30.12.1909; 3/13.1.1910; 3/13.1.1910;
15/31.1.1910; 18/7.2.1910; 22/16.2.1910; 23/17.2.1910; 25/21.2.1910;
36/10.3.1910; 39/14.3.1910; 43/22.3.1910; 46/29.3.1910; 47/30.3.1910;
53/13.4.1910; 54/15.4.1910; 59/23.4.1910; 61/28.4.1910; 62/30.4.1910;
64/4.5.1910; 70/14.5.1910; 71/18.5.1910; 79/6.6.1910; 86/16.6.1910;
93/27.6.1910; 98/5.7.1910; 100/8.7.1910; 106/15.7.1910; 113/26.7.1910;
114/30.7.1910; 117/5.8.1910; 118/6.8.1910; 126/25.8.1910; 129/30.8.1910;
138/13.9.1910; 139/14.9.1910; 143/20.9.1910; 147/26.9.1910; 154/4.10.1910;
158/10.10.1910; 159/12.10.1910; 163/18.10.1910; 165/21.10.1910;
169/29.10.1910; 176/10.11.1910; 178/12.11.1910; 184/23.11.1910;
185/24.11.1910; 188/29.11.1910; 190/2.12.1910; 196/13.12.1910; 205/26.12.1910;
205/26.12.1910; 4/16.1.1911; 15/7.2.1911; 18/13.2.1911; 21/18.2.1911;
25/28.2.1911; 26/7.3.1911; 29/13.3.1911; 33/21.3.1911; 39/4.4.1911; 39/6.4.1911;
39/8.4.1911; 41/11.4.1911; 46/25.4.1911; 59/27.5.1911; 60/29.5.1911;
65/10.6.1911; 68/19.6.1911; 70/26.6.1911; 71/27.6.1911; 80/18.7.1911;
87/31.7.1911; 91/5.8.1911; 96/11.8.1911; 96/11.8.1911; 108/7.9.1911;
116/21.9.1911; 120/3.10.1911; 121/4.10.1911; 126/11.10.1911; 130/17.10.1911;
131/19.10.1911; 134/25.10.1911; 135/27.10.1911; 137/3.11.1911; 142/10.11.1911;
143/11.11.1911; 144/14.11.1911; 151/27.11.1911; 155/4.12.1911; 162/15.12.1911;
163/16.12.1911; 164/17.12.1911; 166/19.12.1911; 167/20.12.1911;
168/22.12.1911; 173/28.12.1911; 14/29.1.1912; 24/23.2.1912; 25/24.2.1912;
28/1.3.1912; 29/2.3.1912; 30/5.3.1912; 31/8.3.1912; 34/15.3.1912; 48/2.4.1912;
44/6.4.1912; 50/26.4.1912; 52/30.4.1912; 57/11.5.1912;
71/13.6.1912;73/17.6.1912; 75/21.6.1912; 76/26.6.1912;
84/10.7.1912;87/15.7.1912; 92/23.7.1912; 96/30.7.1912; 129/7.8.1912;
103/14.8.1912; 106/20.8.1912; 113/3.9.1912; 115/7.9.1912;117/11.9.1912;

Bei den aus Mähren ausgeschriebenen „Zigeunern" waren die meisten Taglöhner/-innen (12); jene, die nicht auf diese Art beschrieben wurden, waren überwiegend Komödianten/-innen (22). Unter den 6 ausgeschriebenen „Zigeunern" in Böhmen waren 4 Riemenhandwerker, 1 Sängerin und 1 Krämerin. Wie in Mähren wiesen Komödianten/-innen die höchste Zahl (16) bei den nicht als „Zigeuner" Etikettierten auf. Die in Niederösterreich ausgeschriebenen „Zigeuner" waren überwiegend Musiker/-innen (15). Bei den nicht als „Zigeuner" bezeichneten Personen waren die meisten Taglöhner/-innen (19). Diese Zahlen sollen nicht als absolut verstanden werden, sondern lediglich die Ambivalenz des polizeilichen Ordnungsbegriffes „Zigeuner" und seinen Verwendungskontext aufzeigen.

Dass die Fahndungspraxis durchaus mit den Berichten über die „Bekämpfung des Zigeunerunwesens" teilweise im Widerspruch stand, darf nicht verwundern, sondern weist einmal mehr darauf hin, dass das Konstrukt des „Zigeuners" eine Ambivalenz der Moderne ist.[36] Dennoch lassen sich die harschen Vorgehensweisen der böhmischen und mährischen Sicherheitsbehörden herausfiltern – mit dem Unterschied, dass das Potenzial der polizeilichen Alltagspraxis in Mähren stärker als in Böhmen ausgeschöpft wurde, die Statthalterei in Prag jedoch zusätzlich neue Wege gehen wollte.

Die ständige Thematisierung und partielle Umsetzung der Einweisung von „Zigeunern" in Zwangsarbeitsanstalten fand auch international Resonanz. 1909 richtete der Schweizer Bundesrat auf Anraten der Schweizer Polizei an Österreich-Ungarn, Frankreich, Italien sowie an das Deutsche Reich den Vorschlag einer Konferenz zur „internationalen Lösung der Zigeunerfrage", weil das europäische „Zigeunerproblem" nach eigener Einschätzung ein zentraleuropäisches sei. Um dem Wunsch des ungarischen Innenministeriums zu entsprechen, stimmte das österreichische Ministerium des Innern dem zu, erwähnte jedoch die „erfolgreichen Maßnahmen" in Cisleithanien und die Tatsache, dass es eigentlich kein „Zigeunerunwesen" mehr gebe. Im Unterschied zu den

119/13.9.1912; 138/22.10.1912; 143/30.10.1912; 160/20.11.1912; 157/26.11.1912; 166/12.12.1912; 169/15.12.1912; 3/13.1.1913; 7/18.1.1913; 8/20.1.1913; 15/31.1.1913; 19/7.2.1913; 24/17.2.1913; 26/20.2.1913; 30/27.2.1913; 34/7.3.1913; 47/5.4.1913; 62/9.5.1913; 63/10.5.1913; 65/15.5.1913; 67/17.5.1913; 73/29.5.1913; 78/6.6.1913; 86/19.6.1913; 93/30.6.1913; 96/8.7.1913; 97/9.7.1913; 108/29.7.1913;116/12.8.1913; 124/27.8.1913; 126/29.8.1913; 153/16.10.1913; 127/17.11.1913; 177/22.11.1913; 183/1.12.1913;184/2.12.1913; 190/10.12.1913; 202/29.12.1913.
[36] Zygmunt Bauman, Moderne und Ambivalenz. Das Ende der Eindeutigkeit (Hamburg: Hamburger Ed., 2005), S. 16, 22.

Aussagen der böhmischen Statthalterei hätten die massiven Einweisungen von „Zigeunern" in Zwangsarbeitsanstalten keine Erfolgsaussichten. Da die polizeilichen Alltagspraktiken sowohl in den österreichischen Kronländern wie auch im Deutschen Reich auf das Abdrängen und Abschieben in andere Gebiete ausgerichtet waren, wurde jedoch letztlich keine Konferenz abgehalten.

Unabhängig von der nicht umgesetzten internationalen Konferenz hatten jene ans Deutsche Reich angrenzenden Bezirkshauptmannschaften in Böhmen schon im Jahr 1907 mit den bayrischen, sächsischen und preußischen Nachbargemeinden eine grenzübergreifende „Bekämpfung des Zigeunerunwesens" angedacht. Die jeweils abzuschiebenden „Zigeuner" sollten nahtlos an die nächste Sicherheitsbehörde auf der anderen Seite der Grenze übergeben werden. Aufgrund der spezifischen regionalen Differenzen und des Ersten Weltkriegs kam es allerdings nicht zu einer Umsetzung der geplanten Zusammenarbeit.

Obwohl die Behörden in Mähren mit den polizeilichen Alltagspraktiken der böhmischen und niederösterreichischen Amtskollegen konfrontiert worden waren, wurden weder ein „Zigeuner-" noch ein „Landstreicherunwesen" angesprochen. Abschiebungen, aber vor allem die Einweisung in Zwangsarbeitsanstalten, wie aus dem Zahlenvergleich von Abschiebungen, Einweisungen und Fahndungen hervorgeht, waren ohnehin an der Tagesordnung.

Tabelle 18-3: Anzahl der Abstrafungen auf Basis des Landstreichergesetzes von 1885 und des Zigeunererlasses von 1888 in Mähren

Jahr	Landstreicherei	Bettel	Arbeitsscheu	„Zigeuner"
1900	6.915[37]	4.278[38]	183[39]	1.175[40]
1902	6.349[41]	4.658[42]	89[43]	1.291[44]

[37] ÖStA, AVA, Ministerium des Innern, Präsidium, Kt. 1979 20/4 Nr. 1.935/M.I./1901, Ausweis über die Anzahl derjenigen Individuen, gegen welche im Solarjahre 1901 im Grunde der Gesetze vom 10. Mai 1873, R.G.Bl. No. 108, vom 24. Mai 1885, R.G.Bl. No. 89 und vom 24. Mai 1885, R.G.Bl. No. 90 vorgegangen wurde, k. k. Statthalter Präsidium für Mähren, Brünn, 6.3.1901.
[38] Ebenda.
[39] Ebenda.
[40] ÖStA, AVA, Ministerium des Innern, Allgemein, Kt. 2118 20/2 Nr. 10.423-901 Zl. 7.479 k. k. mährische Statthalterei, Brünn, 19.2.1902.
[41] ÖStA, AVA, Ministerium des Innern, Präsidium, Kt. 1979 20/4 Nr. 1.133/M.I./1904, Ausweis über die Anzahl derjenigen Individuen, gegen welche im Solarjahre 1903 im Grunde des Gesetzes vom 10. Mai 1873, R.G.Bl. No. 108, vom 24. Mai 1885, R.G.Bl. No. 89 und vom 24. Mai 1885, R.G.Bl. No 90

1903	7.873[45]	5.952[46]	k. A.[47]	1.039[48]
1904	4.958[49]	5.741[50]	345[51]	865[52]
1905	4.378[53]	5.164[54]	129[55]	683[56]

Das zeigt sich auch im Beschluss des mährischen Landtags vom 29. Oktober 1908, über die landesstatistische Erhebung Mährens eine genaue bevölkerungsstatistische Erfassung von „Zigeunern" durchzuführen. Nach einem Verzeichnis der mährischen Statthalterei gab es in 139 Gemeinden heimatberechtigte „Zigeuner" oder auch Wohnsitze von „Zigeunern". Am 10. Dezember 1909 wurden an diese Gemeinden Erhebungsformulare ausgegeben, welche bis zum 1. März 1910 ausgefüllt werden sollten.[57]

---

vorgegangen wurde, k. k. Statthalterei Präsidium für Mähren, Brünn, 17.2.1904.

[42] Ebenda.

[43] Ebenda.

[44] ÖStA, AVA, Ministerium des Innern, Allgemein, Kt. 2118 20/2 Nr. 9.251-03, k. k. mährische Statthalterei, Brünn, 26.2.1903.

[45] ÖStA, AVA, Ministerium des Innern, Präsidium, Kt. 1979 20/4 Nr. 1.133/M.I./1904, Ausweis über die Anzahl derjenigen Individuen, gegen welche im Solarjahre 1903 im Grunde des Gesetzes vom 10. Mai 1873, R.G.Bl. No. 108, vom 24. Mai 1885, R.G.Bl. No. 89 und vom 24. Mai 1885, R.G.Bl. No 90 vorgegangen wurde, k. k. Statthalterei Präsidium für Mähren, Brünn, 17.2.1904.

[46] Ebenda.

[47] Ebenda.

[48] ÖStA, AVA, Ministerium des Innern, Allgemein, Kt. 2118 20/2 Nr. 8.725/05 Zl. 8.512, k. k. mährische Statthalterei, Brünn, 23.2.1905.

[49] ÖStA, AVA, Ministerium des Innern, Präsidium, Kt. 1979 20/4 Nr. 1.254/M.I./1905, Ausweis über die Anzahl derjenigen Individuen, gegen welche im Solarjahre 1904 im Grunde des Gesetzes vom 10. Mai 1873, R.G.Bl. No. 108, vom 24. Mai 1885, R.G.Bl. No. 89, und vom 24. Mai 1885, R.G.Bl. No. 90 vorgegangen wurde, k. k. Statthalterei Präsidium für Mähren, Brünn, 25.2.1905.

[50] Ebenda.

[51] Ebenda.

[52] ÖStA, AVA, Ministerium des Innern, Allgemein, Kt. 2118 20/2 Nr. 8.725/05 Zl. 8.512, k. k. mährische Statthalterei, Brünn, 23.2.1905.

[53] ÖStA, AVA, Ministerium des Innern, Präsidium, Kt. 1979 20/4 Nr. 1.619/M.I./1906, Ausweis über die Anzahl derjenigen Individuen, gegen welche im Solarjahre 1905 im Grunde des Gesetzes vom 10. Mai 1873, R.G.Bl. No. 108, vom 24. Mai 1885, R.G.Bl. No. 89 und vom 24. Mai 1885, R.G.Bl. No. 90 vorgegangen wurde, k. k. Statthalterei Präsidium für Mähren, Brünn, 17.2.1906.

[54] Ebenda.

[55] Ebenda.

[56] ÖStA, AVA, Ministerium des Innern, Allgemein, Kt. 2118 20/2 Nr. 7.480 ex 1906 Zl. 7.480, k. k. mährische Statthalterei, 14.2.1906.

[57] Statistische Monatschrift Neue Folge XV. Zählung der in Mähren

Anhand des Formulars sollten die „verschiedenen Personaldaten, wie z. B. Umgangssprache, Religion, Erwerb, Schulbesuch der Kinder usw., zur Erhebung gelangen".[58] Das Ergebnis dieser Zählung sollte in der *Statistischen Monatszeitschrift* bekanntgegeben werden, jedoch blieb eine Publikation aus. Ebenso kam es zu keiner Veröffentlichung in den *Statistischen Jahrbüchern der autonomen Landesverwaltung* in den im Reichsrate vertretenen Königreichen und Ländern. Ob tatsächlich eine genaue Zählung stattfand, kann bezweifelt werden. Es ist zwar nicht von der Hand zu weisen, dass diese Erfassung mit der Vorbereitung der 1910 durchgeführten Volkszählung in Österreich-Ungarn in Verbindung stand, von den mährischen Behörden wurden jedoch 1910 keinerlei Schritte in diese Richtung unternommen. Hingegen wurden die jüdischen Gemeinden Mährens bei der Auswertung des Zensus während des Ersten Weltkriegs eigens ausgewiesen.[59]

Das Statistische Landesamt des Königreichs Böhmen publizierte 1908 eine umfassende statistische Auswertung bezüglich Armenfürsorge, Wohlfahrtseinrichtungen, Jugendfürsorge, Zwangsarbeits- und Besserungsanstalten, schubpolizeilicher Agenden usw. Unter anderem wurden Bettler/-innen und „Landstreicher" eigens erfasst, aber von „Zigeunern" war keine Rede.[60] Und auch aus Böhmen kamen 1910 im Zuge der durchzuführenden Bevölkerungserfassung andere Anregungen. Die „Deutsche Landeskommission für Kinderschutz und Jugendfürsorge in Böhmen" unter der Federführung von Obersanitätsrat Dr. Alois Epstein regte im Sinne der Jugendwohlfahrt eine Erhebung aller in Pflege befindlichen Kinder und Jugendlichen an.[61] Damit bekräftigte er mehr oder minder nur den Erlass des Innenministeriums vom 11. August 1909,

---

heimatberechtigten Zigeuner (Brünn: K. k. Statistische Zentral-Kommission, 1910), S. 66.
[58] Ebenda, S. 66.
[59] ÖStA, AVA, Ministerium des Innern, Allgemein, Kt. 2372 33/1 Nr. 35.707/15, k. k. Justizministerium, Wien, 5.7.1915, k. k. Ministerium des Innern, Vorrede zum Allg. Verzeichnisse der Ortsgemeinden und Orthschaften nach den Ergebnissen der Volkszählung vom 31. September 1910, Wien, 15.7.1915.
[60] Das Armenwesen im Königreiche Böhmen am Anfang des XX. Jahrhundertes (Prag: Calve in Komm., 1908).
[61] ÖStA, AVA, Ministerium des Innern, Allgemein, Kt. 2364 33/1 Nr. 635/1910, k. k. Ministerium des Innern, Volkszählung 1910. Statistische Zentralkommission, betreffend die Zählung von Pflegekindern, Wien, 26.7.1910, 33/1 Nr. 25.479/1910 Kt. 2364; k. k. Ministerium des Innern, Obersanitätsrat Dr. Alois Epstein legt vor einen Separatabdruck aus der Zeitschrift für Kinderschutz und Jugendfürsorge über die statistische Ermittlung der in fremder Pflege befindlichen Kinder bei der Volkszählung 1910, Wien, 20.1.1910.

der eine Erhebung der Kinderschutz- und Jugendfürsorgeanstalten angeordnet hatte.[62] Aber auch die Statthalterei in Prag unterstrich die kriminalpräventive Bedeutung der Erfassung der sozialen Verhältnisse der Arbeiter/-innenschicht nicht nur in Prag, sondern ausgedehnt auf alle Vororte, da Letztere nicht nur zum Prager Polizeirayon gehörten, sondern gerade in diesen Vororten die Arbeiter/-innenschicht lebte.[63]

Wohlfahrt und Kriminalitätsprävention

Wenngleich die Statthalterei Böhmens durchwegs ein härteres Vorgehen in der „Bekämpfung des Zigeunerunwesens" gesetzlich anvisierte und ein überaus restriktives Vorgehen in der polizeilichen Alltagspraxis umgesetzt wurde, übte sie an der bestehenden Armenfürsorge Kritik. Die harschen Maßnahmen in Böhmen wie auch in Mähren müssen im Kontext der Wirtschaftskrise und der zunehmenden Verarmung und Arbeitslosigkeit in den Hauptindustriegebieten Cisleithaniens betrachtet werden. Letztere wurden auch von beiden Statthaltereien im Zuge der zunehmenden bzw. anhaltenden Verurteilungen wegen Landstreicherei und Bettel als Ursache benannt. Daneben wurde die Institution der Naturalverpflegsstationen von beiden Statthaltereien, vor allem aber von derjenigen in Prag, positiv als Steuerungsmittel gegen die Landstreicherei hervorgehoben. Als Kern der „unverbesserlichen Landstreicher" wurden stets die „Zigeuner" genannt, wobei die von der Statthalterei Böhmen ausgewiesenen Zahlen dazu im Widerspruch standen. Auch die Forderungen nach einer strengen Handhabe von Lizenzen für ein mobiles Gewerbe im Zuge der „Bekämpfung der Landstreicherplage" lesen sich ident zu jenen der „Zigeunerplage".

Neben der Forderung nach einem Ausnahmegesetz für „Zigeuner" brachte die Statthalterei Böhmens beim Innenministerium auch den Vorschlag zur Änderung des Wohlfahrtssystems ein und kritisierte dabei vor allem das Schubsystem, das nicht disziplinierend auf das „gefährliche" Individuum einwirke. Stattdessen sollte, so die Statthalterei, ein

---

[62] ÖStA, AVA, Ministerium des Innern, Allgemein, Kt. 2364 33/1 Nr. 5747/1910, k. k. Statthalterei Wien, Kinderschutz- und Jugendfürsorge-Anstalten – Statistik, Wien, 11.2.1910, k. k. Ministerium des Innern, Statthalterei in Wien betreffend der Drucksorten für die Erhebung der Kinderschutz- und Jugendfürsorgeanstalten.
[63] ÖStA, AVA, Ministerium des Innern, Allgemein, Kt. 2365 33/1 Nr. 44.538/1910, k. k. Ministerium des Innern, Volkszählung 1910, Statthalterei in Prag betreffend der Wohnungs- und Häuserverhältnisse im Prager Polizeirayon, Wien, 28.11.1910.

Aufenthaltsrecht, eine Arbeitslosen- wie auch eine Invaliditätsversorgung eingeführt werden, die auch die Armenverbände deutlich entlasten würden. Überdies wurde ein Vorschlag für die Einweisung in Zwangsarbeits- und Besserungsanstalten auf zivilrechtlichem Weg und über die Entziehung der Fürsorge eingebracht.

Bezogen auf „Arbeitsscheue" musste nach Einschätzung der böhmischen Statthalterei zur „Bekämpfung der Landstreicherplage" das Netz zwischen Zwangsarbeits- und Besserungsanstalten auf der einen und den Naturalverpflegsstationen und der Arbeitsvermittlung auf der anderen Seite ausgebaut werden. Dabei sollte aber strikt zwischen „Arbeitswilligen" und „Arbeitsscheuen" unterschieden werden. Ein Wegsperren der Letzteren böte nichtsdestotrotz keinen Ausweg, weil die Kosten zu hoch seien. Auch das Ansammeln von „Arbeitsscheuen" wurde von der Statthalterei befürchtet. So schlugen einige Länderbehörden eine Dezentralisierung der Zwangsarbeitsanstalten vor. Die Kosten für die kleinen und verteilten Zwangsarbeitsanstalten als „staatliche Institutionen" sollte demnach in erster Linie der Staat tragen. Zusätzlich wurde eine eventuelle Deckung des Arbeitskräftemangels in der Landwirtschaft als positiver Effekt erwartet.[64] Die Statthalterei in Prag war die einzige politische Landesinstanz, die die „Bekämpfung des Zigeunerunwesens" mit der sozialen Frage in Verbindung setzte und wiederholt ein Ausnahmegesetz forderte.[65] Entsprechend bezeichnete sie die „Zigeuner" zwar einerseits als „Landstreicher im wahren Sinne des Wortes"; andererseits jedoch wurden „Zigeuner" angesiedelt und arbeiteten als Tagelöhner/-innen und Saisonarbeiter/-innen.

Im Zuge der Erhebungen des Ministeriums des Innern von 1907 und 1908 äußerten sich alle Landesregierungen und Statthaltereien (von Mähren und der Bukowina liegen keine Stellungnahmen vor) gegen diese Änderung. Im Widerspruch zu der niederösterreichischen Statthalterei und dem Landesausschuss nahm die Wiener Polizeidirektion einen anderen Standpunkt ein. Das Schubwesen wurde zwar als notwendig erachtet, auf lange Sicht aber wurde das Aufenthaltsrecht oder ein Unterstützungswohnsitz als zweckdienlicheres System angesehen. In Wien wurde weder ein „Landstreicher-" noch ein „Zigeunerunwesen" problematisiert, dafür aber ein „Bettlerunwesen" festgestellt. Während in den Jahren 1900 bis 1902 noch Abschiebungen bzw. Abschaffungen von der Wiener Polizei als Mittel der Kriminalitätsprävention präferiert

[64] ÖStA, AVA, Ministerium des Innern, Allgemein, Kt. 2115 20/2 Nr. 19.381-09, k. k. Statthalterei in Böhmen, Prag, 20.5.1909, Reform des Schubgesetzes und der Gesetze über die Zwangsarbeitsanstalten.
[65] Ebenda.

wurden,[66] wandte sie sich ab der zweiten Hälfte der 1900er Jahre von der ausschließlichen Kriminalisierung der Bettler/-innen ab und deren Überwachung zu. Die Verbindung von Arbeitslosigkeit und Delikten wurde so in einem größeren Bild erfasst.[67]

Die Polizeidirektion äußerte sich recht früh zu den Vorschlägen der böhmischen Statthalterei und schlug vor, Abschiebungen auf „Härtefälle" („Arbeitsscheue", „Dirnen", „Bettler") zu begrenzen und dadurch Kosten zu reduzieren. Zusätzlich wurde 1907 eine Zusammenarbeit mit dem städtischen Arbeits- und Dienstvermittlungsamt für eine gemeinsame Bekämpfung der Arbeitslosigkeit von Zugereisten anvisiert.[68] Jedoch wurde auch unterstellt, dass viele „Arbeitsscheue" sich nicht arbeitssuchend meldeten, um sich der Schubbehandlung nach § 1 des Landstreichergesetzes von 1885 entziehen zu können. Auch die böhmische Statthalterei bediente sich dieser Unterstellung, als sie die zivilgerichtliche Entmündigung und die Einweisung von „Arbeitsscheuen" in Zwangsarbeits- und Besserungsanstalten vorschlug.[69]

Etliche Vereine zur sozialen Pflege und Institutionen wurden in die Kriminalitätsprävention eingebunden, wie etwa Asylhäuser oder Werk- und Armenhäuser. Darüber hinaus war die Überwachung von Arbeitsvermittlungsstellen ein Mittel, um den Frauen- und Mädchenhandel bei der Anwerbung von Dienstbotinnen zu verhindern.[70] Der schon 1906

[66] ÖStA, AVA, Ministerium des Innern, Präsidium, 20/4 Kt. 1979 Nr. 2.823/M.I./1900, k. k. Polizeidirektion Wien, 18. 3. 1900, k. k. niederösterreichische Statthalterei, Wien, 8.5.1900; ebenda, Nr. 3.235/M.I./1901, k. k. Polizeidirektion Wien, 24.2.1901, k. k. niederösterreichische Statthalterei, Wien, 24.4.1901; ebenda Nr. 2.481/M.I./1902, k. k. Polizeidirektion Wien, 14.3.1902, k. k. niederösterreichische Statthalterei, Wien, 31.3.1901 [sic, recte 1902].
[67] ÖStA, AVA, Ministerium des Innern, Präsidium, Kt. 1980 20/4 Nr. 2.330/M.I./1907, k. k. Polizeidirektion Wien, 17.1.1907, Sicherheitsbericht für das Jahr 1906, k. k. niederösterreichische Statthalterei, Wien, 14.3.1907, Stand der öffentlichen Sicherheit und Handhabung der Vagabundengesetze im Jahre 1906.
[68] ÖStA, AVA, Ministerium des Innern, Präsidium, Kt. 1980 20/4 Nr. 2.347/M.I/1908, k. k. Polizeidirektion Wien, 25.1.1908, Sicherheitsbericht für das Jahr 1907, k. k. niederösterreichische Statthalterei, Wien, 16.3.1908, Stand der öffentlichen Sicherheit und Handhabung des Vagabundengesetzes im Jahre 1907.
[69] ÖStA, AVA, Ministerium des Innern, Allgemein, Kt. 2115 20/2 Nr. 41.211-908, k. k. Polizei Direktion in Wien, 10.12.1907, Zwangsarbeits- und Schubwesen, Gesetzesänderung, K. k. n. ö. Statthalterei, Wien, 14.11.1908, Zwangsarbeits- und Schubwesen, Gesetzesänderung.
[70] Über die Lebensverhältnisse von Dienstbotinnen in Österreich zwischen 1918 und 1938 unter der Berücksichtigung der politischen Zäsuren 1918 und 1934 arbeitet zurzeit Jessica Richter im Rahmen ihrer Dissertation.

und 1907 in den polizeilichen Fokus gekommene Straßenbettel von Kindern führte 1909 zur Installierung der polizeilichen Jugendfürsorge[71] in Wien. Dieser Prozess ging mit der Professionalisierung der Polizei, besonders jener in Wien, Hand in Hand. So wurde 1899 das Erkennungsamt bei der Polizeidirektion Wien eingerichtet, um eine systematische Erfassung von Verbrecher/-innen (Anthropometrie, Daktyloskopie, Verbrecheralbum) zu ermöglichen.[72]

Dass sich die Wiener Polizei der sozialen Frage widmete, soll aber keine Abnahme der Kriminalisierung implizieren. Vielmehr kann dies als Ausweitung der polizeilichen Alltagspraxis verstanden werden – Alf Lüdtke zufolge erfüllte die Polizei neben ihrer Funktion als Exekutive in Bezug auf die Wohlfahrtseinrichtungen nach wie vor die indirekte Funktion als „Gesamtorganisation des Staates" im Sinne der „guten Policey".[73]

Da es zu keiner Gesetzesreform kam, wurde 1912 der Versuch unternommen, die Kosten für die Zwangsarbeitsanstalten anders aufzuteilen. Diese Idee folgte der Praxis zwischen Niederösterreich und Böhmen. Auch hier blieb es jedoch bei dem Versuch. Erst durch den Ersten Weltkrieg konnten die angedachten Schritte schließlich umgesetzt werden: die Errichtung der „Zigeunerkonzentrationsstationen" zuerst in Hainburg,[74] später dann in Weyerburg[75] – beide also in Niederösterreich.

Fazit

Die „Bekämpfung des Zigeunerunwesens" in Cisleithanien von 1900 bis 1914 muss im Kontext der Metamorphose der sozialen Frage betrachtet werden. Infolge der anhaltenden Wirtschaftskrise in den zentralen Industriegebieten Cisleithaniens und der zunehmenden Deklassierung in

---

[71] Über die Konzeptualisierung der polizeilichen Jugendfürsorge in Wien und vor allem ihre institutionelle Entfaltung während des Nationalsozialismus verfasst zurzeit Ina Friedmann ihre Dissertation.

[72] ÖStA, AVA, Ministerium des Innern, Präsidium, Kt. 1979 20/4 Nr. 2.823/M.I./1900, k. k. Polizeidirektion Wien, 18.3.1900, k. k. niederösterreichische Statthalterei, Wien, 8.5.1900.

[73] Alf Lüdtke, "Zurück zur ‚Policey'? Sicherheit und Ordnung in Polizeibegriff und Polizeipraxis – vom 18. bis ins 21. Jahrhundert," in Polizei, Recht und Geschichte. Europäische Aspekte einer wechselvollen Entwicklung (Beiträge des 14. Kolloquiums zur Polizeigeschichte), Hrsg. Helmut Gebhardt (Graz: Leykam, 2006), S. 14–16.

[74] Siehe Walter Mentzel, "Kriegsflüchtlinge in Cisleithanien im Ersten Weltkrieg" (Dissertation, Universität Wien, 1997), S. 259.

[75] Vgl. Weigl, "‚Für die öffentliche Sicherheit', S. 96.

Verbindung mit Arbeitsmigration wurde das Bedrohungsszenario des „Zigeunerunwesens" vor allem in Böhmen als Argument für die Reformierung des Sozial- wie auch des Polizeiwesens vorgeschoben. Zum Schluss sei noch am Rande erwähnt, dass die Statthalterei in Prag im Sicherheitsbericht für 1900 nicht etwa „Zigeuner" als Grund für das „Landstreicherunwesen" anführte, sondern „daß speziell in der jüngeren Generation Arbeitsunlust und Hang zum liederlichen Lebenswandel wahrnehmbar"[76] seien.

---

[76] ÖStA, AVA, Ministerium des Innern, Präsidium, Kt. 1979 20/4 Nr. 6.683/M.I./1900, k. k. Statthalterei in Böhmen, 30.10.1900.

CHAPTER NINETEEN

DIE KRAKAUER KOMMUNALPOLITIK
GEGENÜBER DER JÜDISCHEN GEMEINDE
IN DER ZWEITEN POLNISCHEN REPUBLIK,
1918–1939

HANNA KOZIŃSKA-WITT

Krakow municipal policy towards the Jewish community during the Second Polish Republic, 1918–1939

Abstract: The article deals with the history of Krakow's government at the time of the Second Polish Republic, with particular attention paid to the representatives of the Jewish community in the city parliament. The author furthermore examines municipal social policy as well as subsidies paid by the city treasury in favour of Jewish charitable facilities. Decisive factors that influenced changes of Krakow's city policy towards its Jewish community are cited as: first, the global economic crisis, second, the newly established authoritarian regime of Marshal Piłsudski and finally, a growing chauvinism.

In meinem Beitrag gehe ich in drei Schritten vor: Zunächst werde ich die Geschichte der Krakauer Selbstverwaltung skizzieren, wobei die Stellung der Juden in dieser näher beleuchtet wird. Anschließend stelle ich die kommunale Subventionierung der Institutionen der jüdischen Gemeinde dar und versuche, die Windungen der Subventionierungspolitik in den allgemeinen politischen Kontext einzubetten. In einem letzten Schritt kommentiere ich schließlich den Krakauer Fall.

Juden in der Krakauer Selbstverwaltung

Krakau zählte im Jahr 1921 ca. 184.000 und im Jahre 1939 ca. 259.000 Einwohner, von denen ungefähr 25 % Mitglieder der jüdischen Gemeinde waren. Einige der lokalen jüdischen Milieus, nämlich die Orthodoxen, die

Wirtschaftseliten und die Intelligenz (*Inteligencja*), waren seit der galizischen Zeit in der Selbstverwaltung repräsentiert.[1] Während in anderen Regionen des neuen polnischen Staates, insbesondere in den ehemaligen russischen und preußischen Teilungsgebieten, die Selbstverwaltungsstrukturen nach dem Ersten Weltkrieg ganz neu aufgebaut werden mussten, konnte in Krakau (wie auch in anderen Teilen des ehemaligen Galizien) an die bestehenden Strukturen angeknüpft werden.[2]

Für Krakau bedeutete dies, dass die Stadt weiterhin von einem liberalen, zensusabhängigen Gremium verwaltet wurde, jedenfalls in den ersten 13 Jahren, d. h. bis 1931. Den Kern dieser Struktur bildete ein „Klub der Bürgerlichen" (*klub mieszczan*). Diese informelle Kaderpartei gruppierte Repräsentanten der gebildeten und vermögenden Stadteinwohner ohne Konfessionsunterschied. Einen Teil dieses Klubs bildeten jüdische Repräsentanten, von denen viele der sog. „Partei der Assimilatoren" angehörten.[3] So wurde eine politische Gruppierung genannt, deren Anhänger sich jüdisch fühlten und die Interessen der Juden vertraten, dies jedoch im Rahmen der existierenden Rechtsstrukturen und in der Kooperation mit den nicht-jüdischen Stadträten taten (heute würde man sie

[1] Im Jahre 1914 saßen im Krakauer Stadtparlament 67 Christen und 20 Juden: Irena Homola-Skąpska, "Kuria inteligencji w krakowskiej Radzie Miejskiej (1866–1914)" [Die Inteligencja-Kurie im Krakauer Stadtparlament (1866–1914)], in dies., Z dziejów Krakowa, Galicji i Śląska Cieszyńskiego. Wybór pism historycznych [Aus der Geschichte Krakaus, Galiziens und des Teschener Schlesien. Eine Auswahl historischer Schriften] (Kraków – Warszawa: Księgarnia Akademicka 2007), S. 41–87, hier S. 77.
[2] Elżbieta Adamczyk, "Samorząd Krakowa i jego władze" [Die Krakauer Selbstverwaltung und ihre Behörden], in Dzieje Krakowa [Geschichte Krakaus] Bd. 4: Kraków w latach 1918–1939 [Krakau in den Jahren 1918–1939], Hrsg. Janina Bieniarzówna und Jan M. Małecki (Kraków: Wydawnictwo Literackie, 1997), S. 51–58; Elżbieta Adamczyk, Gospodarka komunalna miasta Krakowa w okresie II Rzeczypospolitej [Die Kommunalwirtschaft der Stadt Krakau in der Periode der Zweiten Republik] (Kraków: Wydawnictwo Uniwersytetu Jagiellońskiego, 1997), S. 63; Hanna Kozińska-Witt, "Udział Żydów w wyborach do Rady m. Krakowa i w jej składzie w okresie Drugiej Rzeczypospolitej – prasowa wersja wydarzeń" [Die Teilnahme der Juden an den Wahlen zum Rat der Stadt Krakau und an deren Zusammensetzung in der Periode der Zweiten Republik – die Sicht der Presse], Kwartalnik Historii Żydów 4 (2013): S. 647–678.
[3] Łukasz Tomasz Sroka, Żydzi w Krakowie. Studium o elicie miasta 1850–1918 [Juden in Krakau, eine Studie über die Stadtelite] (Kraków: Wydawnictwo Naukowe Akademii Pedagogicznej, 2008), S. 113–133; Simon Segal, The New Poland and the Jews (New York: Furman, 1938), S. 184.

„Integrationisten" nennen).[4] Jüdische Stadträte vertraten zwar auch jüdische Belange, gleichzeitig aber wurden sie als Repräsentanten der ganzen Stadtgemeinde angesehen. Das war insoweit verständlich, als diese Juden in der Regel nicht im jüdischen Stadtviertel wohnten. Seit dem Anfang des 20. Jahrhunderts stellte dieses Milieu überdies dauerhaft den Posten des Stadtvizepräsidenten.[5] Die Vertreter der modernen Parteien, d. h. der Sozialisten und der Christdemokraten, befanden sich im Stadtparlament in der Minderheit und bildeten dort eine schwache Opposition.

An diesen Machtverhältnissen änderte die Entstehung des neuen Staates zuerst nur wenig.[6] Weit mehr Bedeutung hatte die Tatsache, dass bereits während des Ersten Weltkrieges der Prozess der großflächigen Eingemeindungen abgeschlossen war, denn dadurch wurden das zensusabhängige Stadtparlament um Vertreter der neuen Stadtteile erweitert. Im Jahr 1919 wurde dem Stadtparlament noch eine zusätzliche vierte Kurie des allgemeinen Wahlrechts hinzugefügt, die sich aus Mitgliedern der im nationalen Parlament vertretenen modernen Parteien rekrutierte. Auf diese Weise wurde die Dominanz der Bürgerlichen in Krakau zwar geschwächt, nichtsdestotrotz bestand sie weiterhin. Die Vertreter der modernen Parteien drängten jedoch auf eine Reform, von der sie sich einen Machtzuwachs versprachen.

Die Existenz eines administrativen „liberalen Reservats", wie das Krakauer Stadtparlament von seinen Gegnern genannt wurde, war nicht nur Gegenstand der mündlichen Kritik. Zwischen 1924 und 1926 unternahmen die stets majorisierten Anhänger der modernen Parteien den Versuch einer gewaltsamen Modernisierung, indem das Stadtparlament aufgelöst und durch einen nominierten Kommissarischen Rat (*Rada Przyboczna przy komisarzu rządowym*) ersetzt wurde.[7] Dieses Gremium bestand aus Vertretern der modernen Massenparteien. Auf diese Art und

---

[4] Ezra Mendelsohn, On Modern Jewish Politics (New York: Oxford University Press, 1993), S. 16. Kritisch über den Begriff "Assimilation" Antony Polonsky, The Jews in Poland and Russia Bd. 1: 1350–1881 (Oxford: The Littman Library of Jewish Civilization, 2010), S. 184.

[5] Sroka, Żydzi w Krakowie, S. 130 f. Man hatte auf diesen Posten im Jahr 1905 den Ingenieur Józef Sare (1850–1929) gewählt, der bis zu seinem Tod Vizepräsident blieb, siehe Czesław Brzoza und Kamil Stephan, "Józef Sare," in Krakowianie. Wybitni Żydzi krakowscy XIV–XX w. [Krakauer. Die herausragenden Krakauer Juden des 14.–20. Jhs.], Hrsg. Agnieszka Kutylak (Kraków: Muzeum Historyczne Miasta Krakowa, 2006), S. 92–95.

[6] Czesław Brzoza, "Jewish Participation in elections to Kraków City Council," Polin 23 (2010): S. 213–239.

[7] Adamczyk, Gospodarka komunalna, S. 66–72.

Weise fand sich auch der erste Zionist in der Stadtvertretung ein.[8] Die
Einsetzung des Kommissarischen Rates wurde jedoch für rechtswidrig
befunden, sodass das alte Stadtparlament im April 1926, kurz vor dem
Mai-Umsturz durch Józef Piłsudski, kraft des Urteils des Höchsten
Verwaltungsgerichts (*Najwyższy Trybunał Administracyjny*) wieder ins
Amt eingesetzt wurde.

Der Mai-Umsturz veränderte die Situation in Krakau allerdings nicht.
Der Autoritarismus des „Kleinen Diktators", wie Piłsudski von Anthony
Polonsky genannt wurde,[9] hatte zunächst wenig Auswirkung auf die
Provinz. Die einzige sichtbare Folge war, dass der ganze „Klub der
Bürgerlichen" opportunistisch der informellen „Piłsudski-Partei", d. h.
dem „Parteilosen Block der Zusammenarbeit mit der Regierung"
(*Bezpartyjny Blok Współpracy z Rządem* – BBWR), beitrat.[10] Somit wurde
eine der wichtigsten Großstädte der Zweiten Republik weiterhin von den
nun „maskierten Liberalen" verwaltet. Die Macht der Selbstverwaltung
wurde jedoch im Staatsinneren immer mehr ausgehöhlt, während diejenige
der übergeordneten administrativen Provinzinstanzen, d. h. der
Woiwodschaften, an Bedeutung gewann. Dies war mit der allgemeinen
Stärkung des Autoritarismus, mit dem Etatismus und dem
Interventionismus nach 1926 verbunden, die die Demokratie im jungen
Staat ernsthaft bedrohten. Der vor kurzem verstorbene Zeithistoriker
Andrzej Garlicki fasste diese Tendenz zusammen, indem er urteilte, dass
die Zweite Republik immer mehr die Demokratie eingeschränkt,
gleichzeitig aber den Anschein davon weiterhin bewahrt habe.[11] Die
Schwächung der Selbstverwaltung wurde in Krakau von dem biologischen
Prozess der Alterung und des Ablebens der z. T. greisen Stadträte
begleitet.

Im Jahre 1931 wurde das alte Stadtparlament schließlich endgültig
aufgelöst und durch ein kommissarisches Organ (*Rada Przyboczna*)
ersetzt, dessen nominierte Mitglieder einzig aus dem Piłsudski-Lager (der

---

[8] Brzoza, "Jewish Participation," S. 218.

[9] Wie im Titel des Buches: Antony Polonsky, The Little Dictators: The History of
Eastern Europe since 1918 (London: Routledge & Kegan Paul, 1975).

[10] Czesław Brzoza, "Kraków polityczny" [Das politische Krakau], in Dzieje
Krakowa [Geschichte Krakaus] Bd. 4: Kraków w latach 1918–1939 [Krakau in den
Jahren 1918–1939], Hrsg. Janina Bieniarzówna und Jan M. Małecki (Kraków:
Wydawnictwo Literackie, 1997), S. 109. BBWR war eine „Sammelpartei", die alle
gruppiert hat, die Piłsudski unterstützten, unabhängig von deren politischen Partei-
Zugehörigkeit.

[11] Andrzej Garlicki, Piękne lata trzydzieste [Die schönen Dreißigerjahre]
(Warszawa: Prószyński, 2008), S. 9.

sog. *Sanacja*) kamen.[12] Die ersten demokratischen Wahlen fanden im Jahr 1933 statt, das daraus resultierende Stadtparlament (*Tymczasowa Rada Miejska*) wurde wieder von der *Sanacja* dominiert. Die Selbstverwaltungskompetenzen wurden in dieser Periode immer stärker beschnitten und die administrativen Strukturen im Jahr 1933 kraft des sog. „Vereinigenden Gesetzes" (*ustawa scaleniowa*) im ganzen Staat vereinheitlicht.[13] Wie in der gesamtstaatlichen Öffentlichkeit wurde auch in den Sitzungen des Krakauer Stadtparlamentes der Antisemitismus als „cultural code" immer breiter akzeptiert und angewandt.[14]

Die *Sanacja*-Bewegung war von ihrem Selbstverständnis her nicht antisemitisch, vielmehr wurde Piłsudski von mehreren jüdischen Milieus unterstützt.[15] Der Marschall schien politisch die einzige Alternative zu den Nationaldemokraten mit ihren Schwesterparteien dazustellen. Unter den kommunalen Piłsudski-Anhängern in Krakau befanden sich somit auch jüdische Stadtverordnete, die zwei verschiedenen politischen Lagern angehörten.[16] Einige dieser sog. „Regierungsjuden" (*Żydzi rządowi*) waren Mitglieder der *Sanacja*-Bewegung selbst; bei ihnen handelte es sich zum Beispiel um Kombattanten, die zusammen mit Piłsudski gekämpft hatten. Die anderen hingen dem sog. Allgemeinen Zionismus an, einer Richtung, die im Unterschied zu anderen regionalen zionistischen Fraktionen auf die Kooperation mit Nicht-Juden ausgerichtet war.[17] Außer diesen Vertretern der modernen politischen Milieus gab es im Stadtparlament auch noch Repräsentanten der jüdischen Orthodoxie, mit der die *Sanacja* in den Dreißigerjahren ein Abkommen schloss.

Diese Konstellation hatte zur Folge, dass auch in der demokratischen Periode die herrschende Mehrheit im Krakauer Stadtparlament von einem Bündnis aus miteinander kooperierenden Juden und Nicht-Juden gestellt wurde. Dies war für diese Zeit untypisch, führte die Demokratisierung doch generell zu einer Ethnisierung der Politik und damit normalerweise

---

[12] Adamczyk, Gospodarka komunalna, S. 75–77; Brzoza, "Jewish Participation," S. 220 f.

[13] Eigentlich „Ustawa o częściowej zmianie ustroju samorządu terytorialnego z 23 marca 1933 r."

[14] Zum Begriff „cultural code" siehe Shulamit Volkov, Jüdisches Leben und Antisemitismus im 19. und 20. Jahrhundert (München: Beck, 1990), S. 13–36.

[15] Szymon Rudnicki, "Żydzi a Józef Piłsudski" [Juden und Józef Piłsudski], in ders., Równi, ale niezupełnie [Gleich, aber nicht vollständig] (Warszawa: Stowarzyszenie Midrasz, 2008), S. 116–134.

[16] Brzoza, "Jewish Participation," S. 222.

[17] Szymon Rudnicki, Żydzi w parlamencie II Rzeczypospolitej [Juden im Parlament der Zweiten Republik] (Warszawa: Wydawnictwo Sejmowe, 2004), S. 324 f., 331.

zu einer Verschlechterung der politischen Situation der Minderheiten, d. h. in diesem Fall der Juden.

Die Sozialisten (10) und der Bund (1)[18], die den Autoritarismus bekämpften, waren im Stadtparlament mit insgesamt elf Stadtdeputierten vertreten. Die nationalistische Opposition im Krakauer Stadtparlament war sehr schwach und bestand eigentlich nur aus zwei Stadträten, einem Christdemokraten und einem Nationaldemokraten, die jedoch sehr aktiv waren und gegen Juden hetzten. Dadurch konnte sich der verbale Antisemitismus in den Verhandlungen stärker als zuvor etablieren, u. a. auch deswegen, weil der Antisemitismus zum Ausdruck der oppositionellen Haltung gegenüber der *Sanacja* geworden war.[19] Indem man „die Juden" angriff, die als Verbündete der *Sanacja* wahrgenommen wurden, konnte man diese kritisieren, ohne sich in Gefahr der direkten Konfrontation zu bringen.

Wie im gesamten öffentlichen Raum nahm der Antisemitismus nach dem Tode Piłsudskis im Jahr 1935 auch in den Sitzungen des Krakauer Stadtparlamentes weiterhin sichtbar zu. Zugleich intensivierte der Tod des Marschalls den Machtkampf im Lager seiner Nachfolger. Eine der drei miteinander um Piłsudskis Nachfolge konkurrierenden *Sanacja*-Fraktionen erblickte in der Übernahme des Antisemitismus des nationalen Lagers ihre Chance, eine breite gesellschaftliche Unterstützung im ganzen Staat zu gewinnen und dadurch an die Macht zu gelangen.[20] Da auch die Krakauer *Sanacja* diese Wandlung durchlief, konnten jüdische Stadtdeputierte schließlich nicht mehr mit dem Regierungslager der Nach-Piłsudski-Zeit kooperieren und mussten sich auf andere Weise verbünden.

Diese Entwicklung erreichte ihren Höhepunkt im letzten Wahlkampf zum Stadtparlament im Dezember 1938. Wie in keiner Kampagne zuvor bildete der Antisemitismus den zentralen Punkt des Wahlkampfes. Die Wahlkandidaten wurden als Antisemiten oder Nicht-Antisemiten vorgestellt. Aus dieser Wahl ging ein Stadtparlament hervor, das aus zwei

---

[18] Der Bund (Allgemeiner Jüdischer Arbeiterbund in Polen, Litauen und Russland, jidd. Algemeyner Yidisher Arbeter Bund in Lite, Poyln un Rusland), gegr. im Jahr 1897 in Vilnius, war eine jüdische sozialistische Arbeiterpartei, die in den Industriezentren sehr bedeutend war. Siehe dazu Daniel Blatman, "Bund", The YIVO Encyclopedia of Jews in Eastern Europe, abgerufen am 2. August 2016, <http://www.yivoencyclopedia.org/article.aspx/Bund>.

[19] Jerzy Tomaszewski, "Niepodległa Rzeczypospolita" [Unabhängige Republik], in Najnowsze dzieje Żydów w Polsce w zarysie (do 1950r.) [Ein Abriss der neuesten Geschichte der Juden in Polen (bis 1950)], Hrsg. Jerzy Tomaszewski (Warszawa: PWN, 1993), S. 208.

[20] Andrzej Friszke, O kształt niepodległej [Über die Gestalt der Unabhängigen], (Warszawa: Biblioteka "Więzi," 1989), S. 180–182 und 258 f.

gleichstarken Fraktionen bestand: einer rechten, die aus der neuen, post-Piłsudski'schen „Regierungspartei" (*Obóz Zjednoczenia Narodowego –* OZN) und den Nationaldemokraten bestand, und einer linken, die von den Sozialisten und „den Juden" gebildet wurde. Unter die „Juden" subsumierte man die Zionisten, Orthodoxen, aber auch Gruppierungen wie die Kombattanten oder die sog. Neo-Assimilatoren, die zuvor mit der Regierungspartei kooperiert hatten.[21] Das Stadtparlament war bis zum Ausbruch des Zweiten Weltkrieges aufgrund seiner Zusammensetzung beschlussunfähig und bildete ein Forum sinnloser Debatten, während derer die eine Seite den Antisemitismus propagierte, die andere ihn wiederum verwarf. Der zionistische Stadtdeputierte Juda Zimmerman fasste diese Entwicklung zusammen, indem er feststellte, dass jede im Stadtparlament gehaltene Rede entweder mit der Judenfrage begonnen oder aber mit ihr beendet wurde.[22]

Kommunale Subventionen

Haben diese Entwicklungen die städtische Subventionierungspolitik gegenüber der jüdischen Gemeinde beeinflusst? Kann man an der Höhe der Subventionen die jeweils aktuelle politische Positionierung der Parteien und Milieus in der Stadtvertretung oder im polnischen Staat ablesen?

Die Frage ist bedeutsam, da die Zweite Polnische Republik von Anfang an die Sozialpolitik an die Kommunen abschob und diese dafür verantwortlich machte, ihren Bedürftigen Hilfe zu leisten. Das schrieb das Gesetz über die Sozialpolitik aus dem Jahre 1923 fest.[23] Die galizische Gesetzgebung machte aus den kleinpolnischen Kommunen eine Avantgarde dieser Entwicklung, denn diese waren schon lange vor der

[21] Brzoza, "Jewish Participation," S. 228 f.
[22] "Mamy prawa ludzkie aby żyć na tej ziemi" [Wir haben Menschenrechte, um auf diesem Boden zu leben], Nowy Dziennik, July 6,1939, S. 13.
[23] "Ustawa o opiece społecznej z dn. 16 sierpnia 1923" [Das Gesetz über die Sozialhilfe vom 16. August 1923], in Zbiór ustaw i rozporządzeń dotyczących opieki społecznych, (Warszawa: Sejm, 1927); Melanja Bornstein-Łychowska, 10 lat polityki społecznej państwa polskiego, 1918–1928 [10 Jahre Sozialpolitik des polnischen Staates, 1918–1928] (Warszawa: Min. Pracy i Opieki Społecznej, 1928), S. 54; Ewa Leś, Zarys historii dobroczynności i filantropii w Polsce [Ein Abriss der Geschichte von Wohltätigkeit und Philanthropie in Polen] (Warszawa: Prószyński, 2001), S. 82; Janusz Radwan-Pragłowski und Krzysztof Frysztacki, Miłosierdzie i praktyka. Społeczne dzieje pomocy człowiekowi [Barmherzigkeit und Praxis. Eine Gesellschaftsgeschichte der Hilfeleistungen für den Menschen] (Kraków: "Śląsk" Wydawnictwo Naukowe, 2009), S. 399–402.

Entstehung des polnischen Staates für ihre Bedürftigen selbst zuständig gewesen.[24] Obwohl das Gesetz von 1923 erst im Jahr 1927 seine ausführenden Bestimmungen erhielt,[25] gab es in Krakau daher ältere Traditionen der Sozialpolitik, auf welche die Selbstverwaltung nun zurückgreifen konnte.

Im liberalen Krakauer Stadtstatut, das 1866 eingeführt worden war und mit manchen Veränderungen bis 1931 in Kraft blieb, gab es einen gesonderten Abschnitt (VI.), der sich mit der Kommunalpolitik gegenüber der jüdischen Gemeinde befasste.[26] Demnach war die jüdische Gemeinde selbst dafür verantwortlich, Institutionen zu unterhalten, die die Bedürfnisse ihrer Mitglieder deckten. Darunter fielen auch die Hilfeleistungen an bedürftige Juden.

Wenn man bedenkt, dass die Monarchie im liberalen Geiste eine Entkonfessionalisierung der öffentlichen Sphäre anstrebte und die Macht der Kirchen beschneiden wollte, erscheint dies auf den ersten Blick paradox. Der Abschnitt VI. drückte allerdings eine allgemeine europäische Tendenz aus: Friedrich Lenger weist darauf hin, dass auch in Deutschland vor dem Ersten Weltkrieg bedürftige Juden ausschließlich von den jüdischen Wohltätigkeitsvereinen versorgt wurden, obwohl dies theoretisch auch nicht-jüdische Vereine leisten mussten.[27]

Das Gesetz, das die soziale Verantwortung an die Konfessionsgemeinden abschob, entstand wahrscheinlich u. a. aus dem Bewusstsein, dass die Gründung und die aktive Unterstützung von Hilfsorganisationen die

---

[24] Hanna Kozińska-Witt, "Samorządowa polityka przyznawania subwencji wobec potrzeb żydowskich mieszkańców Krakowa (1918–1939): Proza budżetów samorządowych, a dyskurs publicystyczny" [Die Subventionierungspolitik der Selbstverwaltung angesichts der Bedürfnisse der jüdischen Einwohner Krakaus (1918–1939): die Prosa der Selbstverwaltungsbudgets und der Pressediskurs], Kwartalnik Historii Żydów 255 (2015): S. 413–445. Das ehemalige Kronland Galizien wurde in der Zweiten Polnischen Republik in drei Woiwodschaften unterteilt, eine davon war die kleinpolnische Woiwodschaft (województwo małopolskie) mit dem Woiwodschaftssitz in Krakau.
[25] Maks Schaff, "Jubileusz" [Das Jubileum], Przegląd społeczny 3 (1933): S. 41–50, hier S. 45 f.
[26] "Dział VI" [Teil VI], in Tymczasowy Statut miasta stołecznego Krakowa [Vorläufiges Statut der Hauptstadt Krakau] (Kraków: s. t., 1866), S. 31 f., ebenfalls abgedruckt in Statut gminny miasta Krakowa. Wydanie nieoficjalne dla użytku wewnętrznego gminy miasta Krakowa [Das Gemeindestatut der Stadt Krakau. Inoffizielle Ausgabe zum inneren Gebrauch der Gemeinde der Stadt Krakau] (Kraków: s. t., 1931), S. 45 f.
[27] Friedrich Lenger, European Cities in the modern Era, 1850–1914 (Leiden und London: Brill, 2012), S. 172.

religiöse Pflicht eines jeden bekennenden Juden ist. Deswegen gab es „schon immer" in jeder jüdischen Gemeinde eine Fülle von wohltätigen Vereinen, die man nun für die moderne Sozialpolitik in Anspruch nehmen konnte. Die religiöse Pflicht wurde so in eine administrative Verpflichtung umgewandelt: Die jüdische Konfessionsgemeinde wurde nun gesetzlich dazu angehalten, Institutionen dieser Art zu gründen und zu unterhalten.[28] Die Munizipalität behielt zwar die Kontrolle, es stand ihr aber frei, inwieweit sie sich im sozialen Bereich engagierte. Wie Jerzy Tomaszewski schreibt, fühlten sich die staatlichen Behörden aufgrund der Tatsache, dass innerhalb der konfessionellen Gemeinden Hilfsorganisationen existierten, aus der eigenen Pflicht entlassen.[29]

Sofern die jüdische Gemeinde durch die Aktivitäten philanthropischer Vereine den Pflichten der Munizipalität nachkam, konnte dies als Übertragung der Aufgaben von der Kommune auf die Konfessionsgemeinde verstanden werden.[30] In einem solchen Fall war die Erstere dazu verpflichtet, der jeweiligen Religionsgemeinde ausreichende Finanzmittel bereitzustellen, damit diese ihren Aufgaben nachgehen konnte. Wahrscheinlich ist daraus die Tradition der dauerhaften Subventionierung mancher konfessionellen Institutionen entstanden: des Krankenhauses, des Waisenheims, des Altersheims, des Ritualbades und des Friedhofs. Diese wurde auch im polnischen Staat fortgesetzt (siehe die Tabelle im Anhang).[31] Manche der damit verbundenen Ausgaben zählten zu den sog. „Panzerausgaben"

---

[28] Krystyna Samsonowska, Wyznaniowe gminy żydowskie i ich społeczności w województwie krakowskim (1918–1939) [Jüdische Konfessionsgemeinden und ihre Milieus in der Krakauer Woiwodschaft (1918–1939)], (Kraków: Societas Vistulana, 2005), S. 22.
[29] Jerzy Tomaszewski, "Żydzi w strukturach społeczeństwa obywatelskiego: Polska w XX w." [Juden in den Strukturen der Staatsbürgergesellschaft: Polen im 20. Jh.], in Židé v české a polské občanské společnosti = Żydzi w polskim i czeskim społeczeństwie obywatelskim [Juden in der tschechischen und polnischen Zivilgesellschaft], Hrsg. Jerzy Tomaszewski und Jaroslav Valenta (Praha: Univerzita Karlova, Filozofická fakulta, 1999), S. 79–101, hier S. 94.
[30] Adamczyk, Gospodarka komunalna, S. 130.
[31] Budżet wydatków i dochodów gm. M. Krakowa za lata [Das Budget der Ausgaben und der Einnahmen der Stadtgemeinde Krakau für die Jahre] 1918–19; 1921, 1925, 1926, 1927/8, 1928/9, 1929/30, 1930/1, 1931/2, 1933/4, 1934/5, 1937/8, 1938/9 (Kraków: Gmina Miejska Kraków, 1919–1939); Zamknięcia rachunkowe funduszów gm. M. Krakowa oraz funduszów pod zarządem tejże zostających za lata [Die Rechnungsabschlüsse der Fonds der Stadtgemeinde Krakau und derjenigen Fonds, die sich unter ihrer Verwaltung befinden für die Jahre] 1920, 1921, 1922, 1923, 1924, 1925, 1926, 1927/8, 1929/30, 1930/1, 1931/2, 1932/3, 1933/4, 1934/5 (Kraków: Gmina Miejska Kraków, 1921–1936).

(*wydatki opancerzone*), die in jedes Budget aufgenommen wurden. Waren in der Vergangenheit außerdem mehrere Kleininitiativen unterstützt worden, so wurden diese Kleinförderungen nach dem Jahr 1919 gezielt gebündelt.[32]

Zuerst muss unterstrichen werden, dass die Subventionierung zwar regelmäßig erfolgte, aber recht gering ausfiel. Sie machte einen unbedeutenden Prozentsatz des kommunalen Budgets aus. So betrug z. B. im Jahr 1937 das Gesamtbudget 15 Mio. zł, wovon 10.000 zł für die jüdischen Initiativen bestimmt waren.[33] Nach den Berechnungen von Joseph Marcus wurden z. B. die jüdischen Krankenhäuser hauptsächlich durch Patientengebühren (58 %), Subventionen der jüdischen Konfessionsgemeinden (19 %), Spenden aus dem Ausland (11 %) und kommunale Subventionen (5 %) finanziert.[34] Für jüdische Institutionen waren jedoch diese knappen Gelder aufgrund ihrer Regelmäßigkeitsgarantie eine sehr wichtige Finanzquelle. Sie waren umso wichtiger, als der Staat jüdische Institutionen in der Regel nicht unterstützte. Das finanzielle Engagement des „internationalen Judentums" bei den Hilfeleistungen bis zum Jahr 1923, als das Gesetz über die Sozialpolitik deren Finanzierung den Kommunen übertrug, schien dabei eine bequeme Erklärung dafür zu liefern, warum der polnische Staat den jüdischen Hilfsorganisationen jegliche Hilfe verweigerte: Da die Juden von den Auslandsjuden versorgt würden, könne sich der Staat auf die Hilfe für diejenigen konzentrieren, die keine Chance auf den Erhalt von Leistungen Fremder haben. Es ist ein Desiderat der künftigen Forschung, zu untersuchen, inwieweit diese Einstellung die konfessionelle Aufteilung der Hilfsleistungen bestätigt und zur Ethnisierung der Sozialpolitik beigetragen hat.

Es muss nochmals unterstrichen werden, dass Juden weiterhin ihre Institutionen mehrheitlich privat gründeten und unterhielten. Sie bekamen weit größere Finanzspritzen aus dem Ausland als von ihrem eigenen Staat, wie z. B. in Krakau in dem Falle des Baus eines neuen jüdischen Hospitals oder aber der Errichtung des dringend benötigten neuen Friedhofs. In diesen Fällen zahlte die Munizipalität nur vereinzelt größere Summen an die Gemeinde aus.

---

[32] Budżet wydatków i dochodów gm. M. Krakowa na okres od 1.07.1918 do 30.06.1919 r. i od 1.07. do 31.12.1919 [Ausgaben- und Einnahmenbudget der Stadtgemeinde Krakau für die Periode vom 1.7.1918 bis zum 30.6.1919 und vom 1.7. bis zum 31.12.1919] (Kraków: Gmina Miejska Kraków, 1919), S. 102–162.

[33] "Debata polityczna na Ratuszu krakowskim" [Eine politische Debatte im Krakauer Rathaus], Nasz Przegląd September 25, 1937, S. 9.

[34] Joseph Marcus, Social and Political History of Jews in Poland, 1919–1939 (Berlin: Mouton Publ., 1983), S. 143.

Im Jahre 1927 wurde eine Anordnung herausgegeben, die den jüdischen Gemeinden ihren ausschließlich konfessionellen Charakter bestätigte.[35] Zwar konnten die Gemeinden weiterhin Hilfeleistungen initiieren und durchführen. Die Behörden konnten nun aber solche Aktionen verbieten, die keinen ausgesprochen konfessionellen Charakter besaßen (z. B. von den Zionisten initiierte moderne Initiativen wie den jüdischen Turnverein). In einem solchen Falle musste die Munizipalität die Aktionen nicht unterstützen, was wiederum einen bequemen Grund für weitere Unterlassungen schuf. In diesem Jahr wurden auch die Ausführungsbestimmungen zum Gesetz des Jahres 1923 verabschiedet, die die Stadtkommunen dazu verpflichteten, den Konfessionsgemeinden bei der Bewältigung der sozialen Aufgaben unter die Arme zu greifen (s. o.).

Im Jahre 1930 begann die Stadt Krakau, manche nicht-konfessionellen Kulturinitiativen innerhalb der jüdischen Gemeinde zu unterstützen, wie das Theater und das Museum. Einerseits hat das mit der Herrschaft der *Sanacja* zu tun, deren Mitglieder sich für moderne, des Öfteren auch zionistische Initiativen manifest aussprachen. Andererseits handelte es sich in beiden Fällen um Initiativen, die sehr pro-polnisch waren. Das Theater spielte polnische Klassiker in Jiddisch, und das Museum sollte die polnisch-jüdische Symbiose veranschaulichen. Es wurden zusätzlich weitere zionistische Kulturinitiativen unterstützt, wie z. B. die Ausstellungstätigkeit der „Vereinigung der Jüdischen Künstler, Maler und Bildhauer in Krakau" (*Zrzeszenie Żydowskich Artystów Malarzy i Rzeźbiarzy w Krakowie*).[36]

Sehr interessant ist die Förderung der religiösen Schulen, die in den Dreißigerjahren sichtbar wurde, als die *Sanacja* mit den Orthodoxen einen Pakt schloss und damit den konfessionellen Charakter der jüdischen Gemeinde stärkte. Von der Kommune wurde nun gleichzeitig sowohl die religiöse (Talmud-Tora-Schulen) als auch die säkulare jüdische Kultur (zionistische oder aber bundistische Initiativen, s.o.) gefördert. Durch diese Unterstützungspraxis konnte der Staat seine übergeordnete, neutrale Position gegenüber den unterschiedlichen Judenheiten manifestieren.

Den Wendepunkt in der Subventionierungspolitik bildete das Jahr 1929, als die Weltwirtschaftskrise ausbrach. Die Spätfolge war, dass manche Subventionen gekürzt werden mussten, was seit dem Budgetjahr 1932/33 deutlich sichtbar ist. Gleichzeitig wurde im Jahr 1931 vom

---

[35] Tomaszewski, "Niepodległa Rzeczypospolita," S. 188 f; Marcus, Social and Political History, S. 331; Rudnicki, Żydzi w parlamencie, S. 300.

[36] Natasza Styrna, Zrzeszenie Żydowskich Artystów Malarzy i Rzeźbiarzy w Krakowie (1931–1939) [Vereinigung der Jüdischen Künstler, Maler und Bildhauer in Krakau (1931–1939)] (Warszawa: Wydawnictwo Neriton 2009), S. 106.

Ministerium für Konfessionen und Öffentliche Aufklärung eine
Anordnung herausgegeben (*okólnik* Nr. V.4773/31), dass die
Konfessionsgemeinden alle Sozialinstitute und Einrichtungen in die eigene
Verantwortung übernehmen sollten, die sich in ihren Bezirken befanden.[37]
Allerdings wurde in einem weiteren Punkt den Gemeinden verboten,
Gelder auszugeben, bevor sie ihre Schulden beglichen haben. Somit
besaßen die Gemeinden zwar theoretisch ihre Institute, konnten diese
praktisch aber weder finanzieren noch verwalten.

Das erwähnte „Vereinigende Gesetz" von 1933 nahm den städtischen
Kommunen schließlich den Rest ihrer Autonomie und machte sie zu
ausführenden Organen der Staatspolitik. Die neue Richtlinie der
Subventionsvergabe wurde mit der Verfassung vom April 1935 und mit
dem ausführenden Gesetz von 1936 neu geregelt.[38] Damit wurde die
kommunale Finanzpolitik weit mehr als bisher vom Staat vorgegeben und
kontrolliert, was vor allem eine Empfehlung zur Sparsamkeit bedeutete.
Als Erste waren die öffentliche Gesundheit und die Sozialpolitik davon
betroffen.[39]

Während sich die Situation im Jahr 1936 erholte und die allgemeinen
Sozialausgaben immer höher wurden, blieben die Subventionen für
jüdische Initiativen klein oder wurden immer weiter gekürzt.[40] Dabei
verarmte die jüdische Gemeinde in Krakau zusehends, die Unterhaltung
der entsprechenden Institutionen wurde zu einem ernsten Problem. Dies
hatte drei Gründe: Erstens wurde die Gemeinde mit einer weiteren
Provinzgemeinde (Podgórze) zusammengeschlossen, die unvermögend
war und deren Mitglieder weniger Gemeindesteuer zahlten.[41] Zweitens
wollte man den Gemeinden das rituelle Schächten verbieten, das die

---

[37] "Czego żądamy?" [Was fordern wir?], Przegląd społeczny 3 (1933): S. 121–136,
hier S. 134.
[38] Marcus, Social and Political History, S. 240; Adamczyk, Gospodarka
komunalna, S. 78.
[39] Archiwum Państwowe w Krakowie (Staatsarchiv Krakau, weiter APKr), Urząd
Wojewódzki w Krakowie [Woiwodschaftsamt Krakau] (weiter UWKr), Sign.
29/206/527, Zbiór okólników [Zirkularbestand], Okólnik nr SF 1-2/35, Kraków
21.01.1935: O gospodarce finansowo-budżetowej oraz ustalaniu i zatwierdzaniu
preliminowanych budżetów związków samorządowych [Zirkular Nr. SF 1-2/35,
Krakau, den 21. Januar 1935: Von der Finanz-Budgetwirtschaft und von der
Beschließung und der Bestätigung der präliminierten Budgets der
Selbstverwaltungsverbände], S. 333.
[40] Tomaszewski, "Żydzi w strukturach społeczeństwa," S. 94; Marcus, Social and
Political History, S. 143.
[41] "Posiedzenie budżetowe" [Die Budgetsitzung], Gazeta Gminna 1 (1938): S. 1–6,
hier S. 1 f.

Hauptquelle ihrer Einkommen darstellte.[42] Und drittens schritt die Pauperisierung der Gemeindemitglieder voran, die keine Berechtigung auf staatliche Unterstützung hatten und deswegen von den konfessionellen Gemeinden unterstützt wurden. Die Munizipalität schien diese Prozesse zu ignorieren und zahlte im besten Falle die Subventionen in der bisher gewohnten Höhe aus.

Die Ausgaben wurden nun pauschalisiert: Die Kommunen durften die privaten oder konfessionellen Institutionen mit Sozialaufgaben beauftragen, wobei sie sich an die allgemein geltenden Gesetze zu halten hatten.[43] Man ordnete aus diesem Grund eine Reduktion der bisherigen Subventionen an.[44] Diese Anordnung führte dazu, dass sich in den letzten Jahren der Zweiten Republik (seit 1936/37) das Subventionierungssystem radikal änderte. Subventioniert wurden jetzt nicht einzelne Initiativen, wie Krankenhäuser usw., sondern man stellte eine pauschale Summe zur Verfügung, um die Kranken und die armen Erwachsenen oder Kinder einer Konfession zu versorgen. Außerdem unterstützte man mit einer pauschalen Subvention die jüdische Kultur und Ausbildung. So delegierte man die Aufgabe, wie diese Summen verteilt werden sollten, an die jüdische Gemeinde und verdrängte den Entscheidungsprozess aus der kommunalen Selbstverwaltung. Man kann dies als einen weiteren Versuch der Separierung der beiden Gesellschaften interpretieren. Um gegen die Verringerung der kommunalen Subventionen für jüdische Institutionen zu protestieren, weigerten sich die jüdischen Stadtverordneten (vier Zionisten und ein Bundist) im Jahre 1936 zum ersten Mal, das geplante Stadtbudget zu bestätigen.[45]

---

[42] Szymon Rudnicki, "Ubój rytualny jako problem polityczny" [Das Schächten als ein politisches Problem], in ders., Równi, ale niezupełnie [Gleich, aber nicht ganz] (Warszawa: Stowarzyszenie Midrasz, 2008), S. 157–172.

[43] Maks Schaff, "Równowaga budżetów i gospodarki komunalnej – a opieka społeczna" [Das Gleichgewicht der Budgets und der kommunalen Wirtschaft in Bezug auf die Sozialpolitik], Przegląd społeczny 10–11 (1935): S. 221.

[44] APKr, UWKr, sign. 29/206/527, Zbiór okólników [Zirkularbestand], Okólnik nr SF 11-11-6, Warszawa, 8 luty 1935: O gospodarce finansowo-budżetowej związków samorządowych [Zirkular Nr. SF 11-11-6, Warschau, den 8. Febr. 1935: Von der Finanz-Budgetwirtschaft der Selbstverwaltungsverbände], S. 380.

[45] "Radni żydowscy powstrzymują się od głosowania nad budżetem m. Krakowa" [Jüdische Stadtdeputierte enthalten sich der Abstimmung über das Budget der Stadt Krakau], Nowy Dziennik, 23. April, 1936, S. 14.

Fazit

Welche Schlüsse können wir aus der hier geschilderten städtischen Subventionspraxis ziehen? Erstens veranschaulicht sie eine konfessionelle Trennung der Stadt. Ich denke, dass diese Trennung an sich traditionell und nicht-diskriminatorisch war. Sie wurde jedoch immer mehr als eine Separierung verstanden und gewann damit ein diskriminatorisches Potential.

Die konfessionellen Initiativen wurden wenig unterstützt, die moderne Sozialpolitik sollte säkularisiert und konfessionell neutral betrieben werden. Dies blieb jedoch Theorie, denn die Sozialpolitik war weiterhin konfessionell verankert. So wie der Staat die existierenden Selbstverwaltungsstrukturen nützte, um sich der sozialen Verantwortung zu entziehen, nützten die Kommunen die konfessionellen Hilfsnetzwerke, um sich der unangenehmen Pflichten zu entledigen. Der Fisch schien jedoch vom Kopf her zu stinken, denn die Staatspolitik ermunterte diese Entwicklung. So kann an den kommunalpolitischen Leitlinien die allgemeine innenpolitische Tendenz abgelesen werden: Die Kommunen wandelten sich von relativ autonomen Strukturen kraft des wachsenden Interventionismus zu ausführenden Organen der Staatsverwaltung. So wie die Staatspolitik mit ihrem Etatismus und der Neigung zur „nationalen Wirtschaft" wurde auch die kommunale Sozialpolitik zusehends diskriminatorisch. In der polnischen Realität bedeutete dies eine Ethnisierung der Sozialpolitik: Die jüdischen Initiativen wurden weit weniger unterstützt als diejenigen der „eigenen" Katholiken. Eine Forderung an die künftige Forschung wäre eine Analyse, ob diese konfessionell definierte Diskriminierung in einem ähnlichen Maße auch andere Glaubensgruppen betraf.

Das Fatale dabei war, dass im jüdischen Falle die konfessionellen Institutionen in besonders breitem Umfang soziale Aufgaben übernahmen, die eigentlich andere Instanzen hätten erledigen sollen. Dadurch entstand für die Stadt die Möglichkeit, sich zu entlasten, indem man gar nicht erst versuchte, diese Aufgaben wahrzunehmen oder zu finanzieren. Zwar waren die Interessenvertreter der jüdischen Milieus in der Krakauer Selbstverwaltung verbal gleichberechtigt. Realpolitisch und finanziell jedoch wurden ihre Anliegen verkannt und denen der nicht-jüdischen Mehrheit untergeordnet.

Tabelle 19-1: Städtische Subventionen sowohl für Institutionen, die innerhalb der jüdischen Konfessionsgemeinde tätig waren, als auch für diejenigen, die sich außerhalb der Gemeinde befanden[46]

Städtische Subventionen	1918/19	1920/21 P	1920/21 B	1921/22 P	1921/22 B	1925/26 P	1925/26 B	1926/27 P	1926/27 B	1927/28 P	1927/28 B	1928/29 P	1928/29 B	1929/30 P	1929/30 B	1930/31 P	1930/31 B
Jüdisches Krankenhaus	1.500			1.500		200	200	1.000		1.000		2.000	2.000	5.000	5.000	5.000	5.000
Waisenheim	3.240			21.600		1.000	1.000	1.000		1.000		1.200	1.000	1.200	1.200	1.200	2.000
Altersheim	1.000	700				100	100	300		1.000		1.000	0	1.000	1.000	1.000	2.000
Ritualbad																	
Friedhof								5.000						10.000	10.000	10.000	20.000
Waisenheimbund	3.000	2.100		5.000			867	1.233		1.626					5.000		
Talmud Tora (E)	200	140		200										1.000	1.000	1.500	1.500
Talmud Tora (R)														1.000	1.000	1.000	1.000
Berufsschule										300		300	300	1.000	1.000	2.000	2.000
Arbeitsbeschaffungsmaßnahmen					20.000					20.000		2.300	2.300	2.000	2.000	2.000	2.000
Ferienlager	500	350		1.000													
Studentenheim														1.000	1.000		
Theater														5.000	5.000	5.000	0
Museum														5.000	5.000	5.000	0

[46] Die Förderung für die Haushaltsjahre 1918–1920 ist in Kronen [*korona*], für die Jahre 1920–1922 in polnischen Mark [*marka polska*] angegeben. Das Haushaltsjahr 1925/26 fiel in die Periode der Währungsreform und ist in Dollar gerechnet. Ab dem Haushaltsjahr 1926/27 Angaben in polnischen Złoty.

Städtische Subventionen	1931/32		1932/33		1933/34		1934/35		1935/36		1936/37		1937/38	
	P	B	P	B	P	B	P	B	P	B	P	B	P	B
Krankenhaus	5.000	5.000	4.000	3.000	3.000		3.000	2.400	3.000				3.000	
Waisenheim	2.000	2.000	1.000	991	750		500	0	400	400	200		200	
Altersheim	2.000	2.000	2.000	1.600	2.000		2.000	1.700	2.000	15.000	1.800		1.800	
Ritualbad	10.000	0	2.000	0	1.500		1.000	800	850					
Friedhof	20.000	10.000			10.000		1.000	0						
Waisenheimbund					5.000								955	
Talmud Tora (E)[47]			3.500	2.847			3.000	2.552		800	400		400	
Talmud Tora (R)[48]			1.500	1.025			1.000	750		200	200		200	
Berufsschule	2.000	2.000	1.000	750			500	250	250	250	250		250	
Arbeitsbeschaffungsmaßnahmen	2.000	0												
Ferienlager														
Studentenheim	1.000	500												
Theater	5.000	3.500	4.000	3.000	3.500		2.500	1.500	2.500	1.575	1.250		1.250	
Museum	15.000	6.000			3.500									

Quelle: Budżet wydatków i dochodów gm. M. Krakowa za lata [Das Budget der Ausgaben und der Einnahmen der Stadtgemeinde Krakau für die Jahre] 1918–19; 1921, 1925, 1926, 1927/8, 1928/9, 1929/30, 1930/1, 1931/2, 1933/4, 1934/5, 1937/8, 1938/9; Zamknięcia rachunkowe funduszów gm. M. Krakowa oraz funduszów pod zarządem tejże zostających za lata [Die Rechnungsabschlüsse der Fonds der Stadtgemeinde Krakau und derjenigen Fonds, die sich unter ihrer Verwaltung befinden für die Jahre] 1920, 1921, 1922, 1923, 1924, 1925, 1926, 1927/8, 1929/30, 1930/1, 1931/2, 1932/3, 1933/4, 1934/5.

Die Spalte „P" (präliminiert) nennt die Summen, die im Voraus geplant, die Spalte „B" (budgetiert) diejenigen, die tatsächlich ausgezahlt wurden. Es ist bekannt, dass manche Subventionen als „außergewöhnliche Ausgaben" geführt wurden. In solchen Fällen war es nicht möglich, diese Gelder eindeutig den jüdischen Initiativen zuzuordnen. Es gab vereinzelt Fälle, in denen die ausgezahlten Summen höher als die präliminierten waren: wie z. B. für das Waisenheim im Jahr 1930/31. Die Erhöhung dieser Subvention wurde während einer gewöhnlichen Stadtparlamentssitzung beschlossen. Seit 1932/33 wurden die Subventionen immer geringer, diese Tendenz hielt bis zum Ende der Zweiten Republik an.

---

[47] Talmud-Tora-Schule in Kazimierz (E).
[48] Talmud-Tora-Schule in Podgórze (R).

CHAPTER TWENTY

NO MORE POORHOUSES AND SPITALS, BUT SOCIAL CARE: THE MASARYK HOMES IN PRAGUE-KRČ

HANA MÁŠOVÁ

Abstract: How to solve an old problem anew: Prague city hall decided to radically reform care for the poor – instead of a few poorhouses and hospitals for incurables, the city built joint facilities of health and social care in the 1920s, outfitting them in an unprecedented way. Their primary purpose was to care for the low-income elderly, the chronically ill and those children most in need. Support of these social groups was widely perceived as an obligation of society, not as charity. Public polls, gathering experience from abroad and the recommendations of local experts preceded the construction itself and both positive and negative views on this central caregiving institution continued to be considered throughout its entire existence.

I intend to outline a general conception of the construction of the Masaryk Homes, also known as the Central Caregiving Institute of Prague. Not only was it a remarkable project, which had no parallel in Central Europe at its time, but it also meant the realisation of a new concept of social care. The impetus was the formation of Greater Prague.

The Masaryk Homes were built in Prague in the 1920s for its socially needy persons. Since the 1860s, care for the helpless was under the competence of the municipality/village where that particular person had their primary residency. The needy were not only orphans and the elderly poor, but public hospitals were not allowed to receive the terminally ill, so chronically ill, patients with tuberculosis and those with cancer, rheumatics, cardiac patients, diabetics, etc. all badly needed assistance. If they themselves or other "obliged persons" were not able to provide them with the means of life, they were supposed to be cared for by their primary residency municipalities/villages. This was, however, often carried out in a very dismal way. Suitable facilities did not meet the demand and there were frequently only a few beds. Hospitals/spitals or poorhouses – these names were used synonymously – frequently did not cover even basic material needs and sadly enough, their inmates sometimes had no choice but to go begging.

The city of Prague did not find itself in an easy situation at the time of the birth of Czechoslovakia. In 1920 (1922) the city grew to 37 new districts, up from the 8 existing residential districts. The new capital extended not only in area, but its population tripled and increased to 750,000 inhabitants. Prague was in fact the 11th largest city in Europe at that time. Obviously, the influx of population to Prague from all over the Czech Lands further increased the number of those seeking help.

The obligation attributable to Prague – being a primary residence municipality – to take care of the needy thus acquired a new, theretofore unseen dimension. The number of applicants who were legally entitled to receive assistance was constantly increasing and free places for persons in need were disappearing. Moreover, not all the newly connected parts of Prague ran poorhouses and hospitals for incurables. Some of the existing facilities had to be closed down due to being in a state of serious disrepair. At least 600 new places in social care facilities were urgently needed just to reach pre-war levels. This shortage was primarily caused by the devastation of war, yet in some municipalities even basic (mandatory) care for the poor was being dealt with in a totally undignified manner even before the war. All the contrasts between the old parts of Greater Prague and its new districts became palpable: the difference in the level of provided municipal social care was reflected in the financial capacities of individual parts of the city, "the level of understanding the issues of modern times"[1] was inconsistent, the degree of social engagement with the municipal government varied as well and objectively, the composition of the population of a given part of Prague also played a role. At the time of the preparation of the act of establishing the capital city of Prague, poorhouses or hospitals operated in only 13 parts of the city. Some had a capacity of only 3 to 4 persons (Braník, Vinohrady, Vysočany), some could accommodate 6 (Michle, Vršovice) or 7 persons (Záběhlice). They were fully occupied, "even though they were such miserable institutions and their existence was a direct mockery of social slogans of modern times, and some of them were easily overtaken by any wretched shelter for the poor in the poorest rural areas."[2] Due to their sheer incompetence and

---

[1] Petr Zenkl, "Městská sociální péče" [Municipal social care], in *Praha v obnoveném státě československém* [Prague in the restored Czechoslovak state], (Praha: The city council of Prague, 1936), p. 422.
[2] Ibid., p. 444.

unsuitability, 7 poorhouses (and the hospital for incurables in Nusle) were immediately closed down. Thus Prague was left with only poorhouses in Bubeneč, Karlín, in Prague's New Town, Smíchov, Vinohrady and in Žižkov with a total of 814 places. One hospital for incurables operated in Karlov, added to by former district hospitals for incurables in Smíchov and in Počernice with a total of 435 places. Altogether, the Prague social net could count 1240 places in its facilities. The chances of being placed in these few remaining facilities dramatically declined at the beginning of the 1920s. By contrast, requests for placing the needy in these caregiving institutions mounted and applicants were forced to wait for a vacant place until somebody died.

What was groundbreaking was a new approach to the problems of the poor. Also, the terminology was different: instead of using a general term "pauperism", we began to talk about a "social question." Whether it was related to the principles on which the new republic was being built, or to the number of socially minded politicians in the city administration or to "the level of understanding the issues of modern times", simply the fact that society consisted of different social classes was reflected as a call upon those more fortunate to those less so. Those individuals in need should not continue to be dependent on random mercy. The elderly should be entitled to an award for a lifetime of work, even though they did not manage to accumulate any property from which they could live now. Children and adolescents – the second most vulnerable group – disadvantaged by either poverty or by illness, needed the help and assistance of society in cases where such support could not be provided by their relatives. To put it bluntly, it was the duty of the municipality, and no longer mere charity.

New general attitudes were manifest even in the names of the institutions that were being established by municipalities for their needy inhabitants. Traditional terms such as a "poorhouse" or "spital" were gradually squeezed out by new ones such as "nursing home, hospital, caregiving institution, social institution"; all these names intermingled and were used synonymously. As a result, the word "poorhouse" vanished from the contemporary language for good. Nice sounding words such as "home, homes, the Masaryk Homes", became widely applied not only in Prague, but in many other cities across Czechoslovakia that also wanted to have their caregiving facility named after Tomáš Garrigue Masaryk.

The authorities where the idea of founding a central caregiving institution for the city of Prague came into being were jointly the Central Social Board and the Central Social Office – two new bodies of social administration which replaced the original Directorate. They were created

under the new social code of Prague on January 1, 1924.³ Petr Zenkl, a
national socialist, experienced and energetic politician and a social worker,
was elected the first chairman of the Central Social Board.

PhDr. Petr Zenkl (*1884 Tábor–†1975 Washington, USA), worked as
a teacher until 1918, and was active also as a cultural worker – chairman
of the lecture department of the *Osvětový svaz* [Union for Education of the
Public], chairman of the Committee for the celebrations of Jan Hus in
1914–1915, editor of educational literature, etc. He became member of the
Karlín district council in 1913 (a mayor of this part of Prague since 1919).
Later he was elected a member of the city council and in 1937 he was
elected mayor of Greater Prague. He was convinced that social care was
not charity, but an obligation of society. "By the establishment of this new
institution, the municipality of Prague has met one of its most pressing
obligations towards its weak and vulnerable citizens. This institute shows
that Prague wants to be aware of its obligations to act as a model, because
it is a state capital and it shall serve as an example to other cities. [...] This
particular institute furthermore intends to prove that the Czechoslovak
nation, which regained its independence and eagerly awaited freedom,
wants to get out of misery and liberate those who cannot provide for
themselves. The institute in Krč shall be also a sort of proof that the
municipality of Prague is aware of the challenges faced by modern
municipalities in the field of social care. In addition, it shall be a memorial
to the gratitude of its citizens that Prague had become the capital of an
independent Czechoslovak State, an expression of gratitude by those who
can now enjoy the freedom of Czechoslovakia to those who sacrificed
their lives and their work for the Czechoslovak State."⁴

The central council of the capital city of Prague approved Zenkl's
proposal to found the Central Institute of Social Welfare in Krč on April
12, 1926. This proposed institute had been featured in the investment
programme for the next 50 years from the year 1924, but still the idea of a
central institute had been far from commonplace. There were actually two
ways to make up for the missing places in shelters for the elderly and in
hospitals for incurables: either to rebuild or newly build small institutions

---

³ The Central Social Office [Ústřední sociální úřad, further referred to as CSO], set
up on January 1, 1924 functioned until 1949, when it was closed. In its archival
collections stored in Prague City Archives (AHMP) are specifically earmarked
documents concerning the construction and management of the Central Caregiving
Institute [Ústřední zaopatřovací ústav] in Krč. In addition, there is a collection of
documents issued by the CSO, sign. III-3, boxes 215–260; and CSO sign. II-7/b,
boxes 162–173.
⁴ Zenkl, "Městská sociální péče," pp. 449–450.

in places where they were lacking, or to aggregate these services into one large building, i.e. to found one central caregiving institution for the whole city. The first option was propped up by long tradition and experience. Yet organisational, economic and medical reasons spoke in favour of the latter: central laundry, central kitchen, etc., buying in bulk, easier oversight and control, separation of the ill from the healthy, investment savings and the possibility to use potentially vacant buildings. The temptation to build on greenfield sites, i.e. erecting completely new facilities, along with the possibility to plan everything to the very last detail, played a significant role. There was an enormous chance to realise all these bold plans without much compromise. Such unwanted compromises would inevitably occur during reconstruction and the modifications of existing buildings. As it turns out, some idealistic notions accompanying the design of the Masaryk Homes had to give way to reality, but not many.

In its time, such a conception was a world rarity

Advice and suggestions had been sought at home and abroad before the final decision was made. In the summer of 1924, the Foreign Ministry approached the consulates and embassies in all developed European countries in order to obtain information on how the issues of social care were being addressed in European capitals as well as in some other major cities (especially Vienna, Paris, London, Bucharest, Moscow, St. Petersburg, Belgrade, Munich, Berlin, Leipzig, Hamburg, Brussels, Frankfurt, Geneva, Zurich, Dresden, Copenhagen, Stockholm, Amsterdam, Rome, etc.).[5] The ministry was asked to send "to the community of Prague the most detailed material on either municipal or other institutions of social care for adults as well as for the youth – orphanages, convalescent homes, and hospitals for poor and ill children, homes for neglected and debauched youth, etc. And poorhouses and hospitals for incurables, etc. Especially desirable is information regarding the existence of a facility called a "Central Caregiving (Social) Institute" and which institutions were concentrated in its framework, in what way and with what results."[6]

Those cities were also asked to report on the following points: (1) how is poverty being eradicated and if begging is anyhow limited/controlled; (2) if any financial support exists for the elderly poor; (3) if there is some sort of labour introduced in poorhouses, how it is organised and how it is

---

[5] AHMP, CSO III-3, box 243, a letter of Central Social Board of July 20, 1924 to the department of correspondence with foreign countries of the Presidium of the Council and Municipal Office of the Capital City of Prague.
[6] Ibid.

controlled; (4) if the abovementioned municipalities care for school children to stay in the fresh air also in other times apart from school holidays; (5) if there is any support for adolescents employed in small businesses, factories, shops, etc. (6) if any dormitories for homeless people are established and maintained.[7]

In a letter from Berlin (12 pages and 35 attachments) it was explicitly written that "a similar institute in Berlin does not operate and will not be established. Establishing a similar central social institution is recommended to smaller cities, but the capital city that counts with the growth of the population, could make use of such central pavilion-like institution only for a limited time as it could not keep up with innovations and it would further limit the independence of individual social sectors."[8] Nor could the report from London offer a relevant example – local institutes were established and maintained mainly by private charities as it was determined by specific historical developments in England. Other records indicate the amount of materials sent, mostly from German and Swiss cities. Yet none of them mentioned any facility like the one proposed in Prague. Furthermore, an extensive amount of material on social institutions arrived from Saxony; 39 folders of information on institutions, regula, annual reports, schedules, etc. were delivered from Switzerland. A stenographic report on the meeting in the Bavarian Chamber arrived from Munich, and one copy of the *Administratiff Annuaire de Belgique* was delivered from Brussels.

Responses varied widely, but all of them shared one thing in common: no such central facility existed, and no plans were in development to establish one. Yet in Prague the decision was made to found such an institution. Its updated plan copied at least some of the technical achievements attained abroad, in compliance with the original intent to raise the future central social care facility at the most advanced level. At the beginning of the following year (on January 31, 1925), the Prague city council officially approached and asked for advice from domestic experts on social issues. 30 experts in the field of social and health issues were interviewed – from the ministerial level to managers of particular institutions across the country. They were supposed to share their experience so that architects could familiarise themselves with all the suggestions on how to organise the constitution of the buildings. Special requirements and recommendations on the various questions of institutional care were taken into account as well. The experts were further asked for tips concerning the project of a facility "which shall on a large

---

[7] Ibid.
[8] Ibid.

scale resolve the socially important question of caregiving in old age and in disease."[9]

Ing. Bohumír Kozák, a functionalist architect, was chosen in an anonymous tender to design the Masaryk Homes. Kozák then submitted an offer for project work and on February 27, 1926 he presented the entire project to the city representatives. Thus the construction of the Central Caregiving Institute in Krč could be launched and the construction itself started on July 16, 1926. The opening ceremony of the newly built facility took place on October 28, 1928 as a part of the celebrations for the 10th anniversary of the Republic. That same year, the facility was given a new name by a Decree of the City Council of September 21, 1928 – and was officially declared "the Masaryk Homes – Social Institutes of the Capital City of Prague."[10]

The first residents settled into the brand new compound on May 13, 1929, i.e. less than a year after the grand opening of the Masaryk Homes. Within barely one month – from May 13 to June 6, 1929 – 1125 people were successively relocated by bus and 196 people by an ambulance of the Red Cross, following rigorous timetables. All of them came from the abolished Prague poorhouses and hospitals for incurables.

The construction itself as well as the management of the Masaryk Homes are well documented. There are 50 boxes of documents in the Archives of the City of Prague containing materials related to its construction and management. The other material consists of films (documentary and fiction), radio recordings, annual publications, promotional leaflets as well as fictional publications. These documents were already largely in demand at the time of their origination, because the interest in the operating of such a new type of institute was great.[11] Just as the builders were inspired at home and abroad (Zlín, Ostrava, etc.), other cities wanted to see and learn as well, if not about the entire complex of facilities, then at least some details. After all, the Masaryk Homes were

---

[9] Ibid.

[10] Presidential Office was asked to approve the renaming of the Institute theretofore called the "Central Caregiving Institution of the Capital City of Prague" to the new name "Masaryk Homes – Social Institutions of the Capital City of Prague." Zenkl's proposal was raised at a meeting of the City Council on September 21, 1928. AHMP, CSO III-3, box 227.

[11] A visit by Egyptian King Fu'ad in 1929, visits by travellers and others – experts from England, America, France and Sweden, etc. – their visits had to be curtailed to prevent disturbance to residents and were, of course, possible only after receiving permits. See the permits issued to participants of the First International Congress for Medical Technology and City Hygiene. Protocols of February 7, 1930. AHMP CSO III-3, boxes 226, 247, 249, 250, 252.

built with the intention that Prague would serve as a model of how to handle social issues across the entire country. Moreover, Prague wanted not only to solve problems attributable to it as a community, but also those that would be at some point dealt with by larger administrative units.

Regarding the technical construction of the facility, we can say that originally it was planned as a pavilion facility for 2,400 people, a number which was considered the ideal maximum, whereas going beyond that could have adverse effects. The collection of 21 buildings consisted of a total of 10 pavilions for the poor (6 for the elderly, one of the buildings cared for married couples, and 4 pavilions for ill persons, originally for about 1,700 people), furthermore there was a children's convalescent home with a forest kindergarten for 200 children, children's hospital for 150 children, a children's sanatorium for 100 children under 6 years of age, other buildings – administrative, social, ceremonial – all equipped with the latest technologies and located around a park plaza accessible through the colonnade. Around the compound were orchards, forest, and a stream – a pure functionalist harmony of yellow and white in a green area. "It was a purpose, light, air, cleanliness. Smooth white facades, variegated with yellow fireclay plates – which protect the windows and openings in general – act cheerfully and bring a colourful impression against the background of green hillsides of the Kunratice forest. A road, running around the institute, is doped and made dust-free."[12]

Funding of this project was entirely the burden of the City of Prague. On December 21, 1926 the Ministry of Social Welfare announced that it could not grant the request for a financial subsidy raised by the Central Social Office. Thus the Central Social Board suggested that the construction would utilise all legally relevant funds and their yields – for example, funds for orphan care, funds for poorhouses and gifts, bequests and loans. For the sake of the Masaryk Homes in Krč, funds of former poorhouses in Nové Město, Karlín, Žižkov, Vinohrady, Smíchov, Nusle, Vršovice as well as a part of the orphan's fund were merged, amounting to 2,644,900 Czechoslovak crowns [CZK]. Financial gifts and bequests in favour of various social care facilities were actually quite frequent. A new fund, called "The Fund of the Masaryk Homes in Krč" was set up and all financial resources of the abovementioned resources were channelled into it. Interest coming from these resources continued to be used as ordinary income of the Masaryk Homes.[13] The system of tenders was practised

---

[12] P. Zenkl, "Městská sociální péče," p. 449. Ottův slovník nové doby 5/1 [Otto's New Encyclopedia], 1st edition, s.v. "Praha" [Prague], pp. 16–17: "it is an imposing and impressive facility with cutting-edge achievements."

[13] E.g. utilization of the financial gift by Board of Aldermen [i.e. community

from the beginning of the project in order to "to build the Homes as cheaply as possible, but not to let cheapness be to the detriment of the quality of work"[14] and contracts were signed with municipal companies. The money, raised by selling the buildings of emptied poorhouses and hospitals for incurables – they became vacated thanks to the existence of the Masaryk Homes – was also included in the budget. Originally, in April 1926, the city council authorised the construction of the Masaryk Homes with an estimated cost of 80 million CZK (construction costs 75 million and the interior equipment of 5 million CZK). Yet the entire construction turned out to be much more expensive. During the construction itself, the initial general programme was enhanced by a few new objects (quarantine, apartments, greenhouse, swimming pool, summer dining room, hydrotherapy, coroner's office, etc.). Moreover, unforeseen circumstances which had not been known at the beginning of construction, occurred as well (dewatering, an improved boiler room, a two-month construction strike in 1927 – resulting in delays as well as in the increase in the cost of construction and materials). Yet the most important factor was that it was decided to build and equip this facility in one stroke – instead of the originally planned construction in stages. In October 1928, the city council calculated the cost at 105 million CZK. Four years later, in October 1932, when the final settlement of the construction of the Masaryk Homes was reviewed by a special commission, the current cost reached 108 million CZK. Another unexpected expense was the building bunkers in case of frost and expanding the number of beds by another 300. Negotiations with construction companies were very difficult, yet successful (e.g. one company had submitted an invoice charging the city 27 million CZK, and after negotiations, it was reduced to about 5.5 million CZK[15]). By the end of 1933, an increase to a total of CZK 113,762,245 had been expected. But when we take into account the modernity and generosity of the amenities, we can only agree that the construction of the Masaryk Homes was accomplished quite economically. An average cost of 50,000 CZK per one bed in a hospital stood as the standard across the whole country. In well-

---

representatives] of September 13, 1915, to commemorate the 85th birthday of Emperor Franz Josef I. This gift enabled the setting up of an orphan's fund (after the war it was funded by donations made during civil marriages). Furthermore, municipal loans from the Central Institute of Insurance [Ústřední pojišťovna] and the Pension Institute of Employees in Health Insurance Companies [Pensijní ústav zaměstnanců nemocenských pojišťoven]. AHMP CSO III-3, boxes 240, 243, 248, 257 and others.

[14] AHMP CSO III-3, box 229.

[15] AHMP CSO III-3, box 257.

equipped district hospitals, the cost of one bed ranged from 44,000 to
54,000 CZK and in the Masaryk Homes, the price was about 38,000 CZK,
including equipment.[16] It is obvious that the municipality had every right
to feel truly outraged by an article entitled "The Prague municipality
blows millions" in the Pražský Večerník [Prague Evening Journal] from
October 6, 1928.

A change in the original plan – we can also call it a compromise –
occurred in terms of the number of inmates in the Homes. First, the
number of 2,000 places for adults and 450 for children was considered to
be ideal. Yet from the beginning it was envisaged that, if necessary, the
Homes would be gradually expanded. In 1931, the commission decided to
increase the number of beds in such a way that "rooms of 8 beds will
become rooms for 9 or 10 persons, etc., thus the nursing home will gain
295 new beds, and the hospital for incurables will gain 71 new beds."[17]
Furthermore, a quarantine-isolation ward for children as well as a
dormitory for nurses were built later and because of constantly increasing
demand by applicants, who were willing and able to pay for their stay in
the Homes, the construction of a pavilion for paying inmates was agreed to
– the "Baxa's pavilion" in the late 1930s.

Yet this number was soon exceeded as well and amounted to 3,500
persons. The introduction of social insurance did not lead to a decrease in
the need for beds in the Homes. The only change was that more inmates
could financially contribute to their institutional care.

Transformation of the Homes into a hospital

As we already know, the Masaryk Homes did not merely have a
function as social care provider, but also as a medical provider. Since the
mid-1920s, an agreement existed between the municipality and the
Ministry of Education under which the city of Prague entrusted the
medical treatment of the inmates in its two largest social care institutions
(the St. Bartholomew poorhouse and the hospital for incurables in Karlov)
to the Medical Faculty at Charles University. The faculty thus acquired
much needed space as well as a great research opportunity for two of its
clinics – the Haškovec Clinic for Nervous Disorders and the Eiselt
Institute for Diseases of Old Age. The agreement was transferred to the
Masaryk Homes upon their completion – in terms of technical equipment,
the Homes were excellently prepared for medical needs – laboratories, X-

---
[16] Ibid.
[17] A report from the commission meeting of June 5, 1931, AHMP CSO III-3, box
255.

ray and operating theatres represented the top work in the field. A certain disadvantage was in the method of selecting inmates – patients were eligible for placement in the Masaryk Homes only if they had permanent residency in Prague and the social situation of their family was unsatisfactory, but on the other hand, these criteria resulted in the unity of homogeneous patients for scientific comparison and statistical calculations.

The Dean's Office of the Medical Faculty proposed the establishment of two research departments for its two clinics within the compound of the Masaryk Homes. Additionally, another research department was later set up for Professor Pešina's clinic for children's diseases. Thanks to this agreement, one world-unique research facility could prosper: The Institute for Diseases of Old Age (renamed as a Clinic in 1929), which entirely moved into the compound of the Homes. The clinics also divided competencies among themselves: they took turns in administering a central emergency service, Eiselt's clinic was responsible for laboratory inventory, whereas a dissecting-room and histological laboratory clinic were administered by Haškovec's clinic. Physicians were also obliged to participate in assessment procedures when selecting candidates for placement. The medical staff (doctors) gained accommodation and board at the Masaryk Homes upon obligation to supervise the food provision from a medical standpoint. Altogether, three clinics of the Medical Faculty had their research departments in the Masaryk Homes: neurological, geriatric and children's. Professor Eiselt's geriatric clinic actually existed thanks only to the possibility of functioning in the Homes.

Interestingly, in the 1930s new problems – in today's language the issue of social beds and geriatric care – became prevalent and more urgent than solving the problems of the poor. From the opening of the Homes, there had been an acute, rising need for new permanent beds, especially for the chronically ill. In 1931, Petr Zenkl noted that "the facility is not [large] enough today – the elderly are pushed away by diseased persons."[18] He further stated elsewhere, that "The short existence of the institute has already shown us what had been envisaged by its founder, namely that in the future there would be more and more incurably ill inmates, and that all buildings used so far only to accommodate the aged must be equipped at such a high level that they could be transformed into hospitals whenever the need arises. Therefore, even pavilions for the elderly [...] are equipped with all sanitary facilities, similarly to the hospital pavilions."[19]

---

[18] A report from the commission meeting of June 5, 1931. AHMP, CSO III, box 255.

[19] Petr Zenkl, "Masarykovy domovy. Sociální ústavy hlavního města Prahy Praha-

When planning the entire project of the Homes, their founders had already thought ahead to possible changes not only in social legislation, but also in the progress of providing public health services, and in particular in the development of society in general. Therefore, the Central Caregiving Institutes, originally built for the urgent resolution of poverty problems, had from the beginning sufficient technical prerequisites to be turned into a hospital in a better (as it was at that time expected) future.

The first pavilions to be gradually transformed into a hospital were the ones dedicated to children's care – actually, they mostly already functioned as a hospital in the late 1930s. Then a sudden and violent transformation of the Homes occurred during the occupation, as its Czech director and certain other employees were dismissed at the beginning of the occupation of the Czech Lands. On September 1, 1939 – in the context of mass dismissal of employees of municipal employees of Prague – František Veidiš, the Homes' director, was dismissed. A German national, G. Ludwig, was appointed as temporary head of the Homes. She later became the facility director. The Germans consequently occupied a part of the Homes and seized them for their fellows. In 1941, the first pavilions of the facility began to serve as a German Luftwaffe military hospital. Soon enough, hundreds of beds were seized for injured Wehrmacht soldiers. The original patients were evicted, leaving together with their caregivers and physicians.

After the war, some of the original patients returned back to the facility. Yet due to its equipment, the Krč compound was again used as a hospital – now for the Red Army soldiers, returnees from concentration camps and the like. A complete conversion to a hospital was only a question of a few years. Such a transformation was almost inevitable, as the ideological plan by Petr Zenkl reckoned that when social issues were overcome, the Masaryk homes would be turned into a hospital and therefore both medical technology and medical care played an important role in the Homes from the beginning of their operation. In essence, a process which had been originally endowed at the inception of the Homes: the intention to serve the ill when one does not need to solve the problem of the poor, was finished off during the 1940s and 1950s.

Krč" [Masaryk Homes. Social insitutions of the Capital City of Prague], Československá nemocnice 1/5–6 (1931), p. 7, offprint. See also Růžena Pelantová, "Velkolepé sociální dílo" [A magnificent social work], in Pražský primátor: památce dr. P. Zenkla, bývalého několikanásobného primátora hl. města Prahy [Prague's Mayor]. In memory of Dr P. Zenkl, former multiple mayor of the Capital City of Prague], ed. Jožka Pejskar (Praha: Vl. nákl., 1993).

In 1947, the city administration provided two pavilions to Bulovka hospital: one of the hospital pavilions started to function as a lung surgery ward and the Baxa pavilion was transformed into the obstetric and neonatal ward. In the subsequent years of 1947–1953, a complete re-profiling of the hospital and experimental research facility was accomplished. Furthermore, departmental scientific research institutes of the Ministry of Health were established, added to by a facility of the Institute for Further Education of Physicians and Pharmacists (the name of the complex was then abbreviated to SOLOÚ – *Státní odborné léčebné a ošetřovací ústavy v Krči* – State Specialised Medical Care Institutions in Krč). The last renaming – this time instead of the name "District Hospital in Prague 14" – was officially installed in May 1954: the hospital was named after Dr. Josef Thomayer. In 1971, the IKEM (The Institute of Clinical and Experimental Medicine), an outstanding research and clinical facility, came into being as a result of the prior integration of six independent research institutes. Between 1984 and 2012, the whole compound was called Thomayer Hospital with a Health Centre and since 2012 it has been officially called "Thomayer Hospital." Additionally, a three-storey nuclear shelter, which was built between 1952 and 1962, was completely turned into an underground hospital (including operating rooms and 70 beds, an irradiation device for cancer patients and a factory of solutions for pharmaceutical purposes).

In the immediate vicinity of the Thomayer Hospital with its clinical research wards, there is an exceptional complex of transplant medical facilities. However, it seems as if things are completely reversed: hospice beds are now urgently needed for the terminally ill, some – we do not always precisely know what exactly – facilities for the "socially excluded." ... Yet the complex of the former Masaryk Homes cannot solve these issues.

In conclusion: The idea of the Masaryk Homes clearly demonstrates that in the 1920s the representatives of Greater Prague understood their social responsibility towards weaker members of the then society – and that they were even able to foresee the further development of society. And what about now, a hundred years later?[20]

---

[20] The contribution is based on archival research along with the author's articles on the Masaryk Homes: Hana Mášová, "O stavbě Masarykových domovů, sociálních ústavů hlavního města Prahy" [On the construction of the Masaryk Homes, Social Institutions of the Capital City of Prague], Dějiny vědy a techniky 29, no. 4 (1996): pp. 101–116; Hana Mášová, "Masarykovy domovy a pražská lékařská fakulta" [Masaryk Homes and Prague's Medical Faculty], Časopis lékařů českých 138, no. 4 (1999): pp. 122–123; Hana Mášová, "Masarykovy domovy – velkorysý projekt řešení sociální péče v hlavním městě předválečné ČSR" [the Masaryk Homes – A magnificent project to solve the social care within the capital city of inter-war Czechoslovakia], Zdravotnické noviny 49, no. 18 (2000): pp. 8–9.

SELECTED BIBLIOGRAPHY:

VÁCLAVA HORČÁKOVÁ

Abel, Wilhelm. *Massenarmut und Hungerkrisen im vorindustriellen Deutschland.* Göttingen: Vandenhoeck und Ruprecht, 1986.

Acemoglu, Daron, and Robinson, James A. *Why nations fail. The origins of power, prosperity, and poverty.* London: Profile, 2013.

Althammer, Beate, Raphael, Lutz, and Stazic-Wendt, Tamara, eds. *Rescuing the vulnerable. Poverty, welfare and social ties in modern Europe.* New York; Oxford: Berghahn, 2016.

Ammerer, Gerhard, Schlenkrich, Elke, Veits-Falk, Sabine, and Weiß, Alfred Stefan, Hrsg. *Armut auf dem Lande. Mitteleuropa vom Spätmittelalter bis zur Mitte des 19. Jahrhunderts.* Wien: Böhlau Verlag, [2010].

Arbeitskreis "Repräsentationen", Hrsg. *Die "andere" Familie. Repräsentationskritische Analysen von der Frühen Neuzeit bis zur Gegenwart.* Frankfurt am Main: Lang, 2013.

Armut in der reichen Stadt. Herausgegeben vom Dresdner Geschichtsverein e. V., Dresden: Dresdner Geschichtsverein, 2007. (Dresdner Hefte. Beiträge zur Kulturgeschichte; 26 Jahrg., Heft 89, 1/2007)

Augustyniak, Urszula, and Karpiński, Andrzej. *Charitas. Miłosierdzie i opieka społeczna w ideologii, normach postępowania i praktyce społeczności wyznaniowych w Rzeczypospolitej XVI–XVIII wieku.* Warszawa: Wydawnictwo Naukowe Semper, 1999.

Balvín, Jaroslav. *Sociální pedagogika a její dvě české osobnosti: Miroslav Dědič a Přemysl Pitter.* Praha: Radix, spol. s r.o., 2015.

Barciak, Antoni, ed., *Curatores pauperum. Źrodła i tradycje kultury charytatywnej Europy Środkowej.* Katowice: Instytut Górnoslaski, 2004.

Bauerkämper, Arnd, and Nautz, Jürgen, Hg. *Zwischen Fürsorge und Seelsorge. Christliche Kirchen in den europäischen Zivilgesellschaften seit dem 18. Jahrhundert.* Frankfurt am Main, New York, NY: Campus-Verl., 2009.

Brakelmann, Günter. *Die soziale Frage des 19. Jahrhunderts.* 5., unveränd. Aufl., Bielefeld: Luther-Verlag, 1975.

Bruckmüller, Ernst, Hrsg. *Armut und Reichtum in der Geschichte Österreichs.* Wien: Böhlau; München: Oldenburg, 2010. (Österreich-Archiv. Schriftenreihe des Instituts für Österreichkunde.)

Bruckmüller, Ernst. *Sozialgeschichte Österreichs.* 2. Aufl., Wien – München: Oldenbourg, 2000.

Buquoy, Margarete. *Hrabě Buquoy, sociální reformátor doby osvícenství.* 2. vyd. Feldkirchen-Westerham: Buquoy, 2007.

Castel, Robert. *Die Metamorphosen der sozialen Frage. Eine Chronik der Lohnarbeit.* Konstanz: UVK 2000.

Castel, Robert, and Dörre, Klaus, Hg. *Prekarität, Abstieg, Ausgrenzung. Die soziale Frage am Beginn des 21. Jahrhunderts.* Frankfurt am Main/New York: Campus, 2009.

Čapka, František. *Odbory v českých zemích v letech 1918–1948.* Brno: Masarykova univerzita, 2008.

Cohen, Daniel. *The wealth of the world and the poverty of nations.* Cambridge: Massachusetts Institute of Technology, 1998.

Collinet, Michaela. *Frohe Botschaft für die Armen? Armut und Armenfürsorge in der katholischen Verkündigung des späten 18. und frühen 19. Jahrhunderts.* Stuttgart: Kohlhammer, 2015.

Collinet, Michaela, Hrsg. *Caritas – Barmherzigkeit – Diakonie. Studien zu Begriffen und Konzepten des Helfens in der Geschichte des Christentums vom Neuen Testament bis ins späte 20. Jahrhundert,* Münster: Lit, 2014.

Cuřínová, Ludmila. *Medicína a sociální činnost.* Praha: Scientia, 2002.

Czeike, Felix. *Wirtschafts- und Sozialpolitik der Gemeinde Wien in der ersten Republik (1919–1934). T. 1, 2.* Wien: Verl. f. Jugend u. Volk, 1958–1959.

Daunton, Martin J., ed., *Housing the Workers 1850–1914. A Comparative Perspective.* London and New York: Leicester Univ. Pr., 1990.

Denk, Ulrike. *Alltag zwischen Studieren und Betteln. Die Kodrei Golberg, ein studentisches Armenhaus an der Universität Wien, in der Frühen Neuzeit.* Mit 9 Abbildungen. Göttingen: V&R unipress; [Wien]: Vienna University Press, 2013.

Deyl, Zdeněk. *Soupis literatury k sociálním dějinám ČSR 1918–1938. Díl 1., Sociální politika. Díl 2. Sociální poměry. Díl 3., Sociální hnutí.* Praha: Ústav československých a světových dějin ČSAV v Praze, 1973, 1975, 1979.

Dilcher, Liselotte. *Der deutsche Pauperismus und seine Literatur.* Frankfurt am Main: Privatdruck, 1957.

Dross, Fritz. *Krankenhaus und lokale Politik 1770–1850. Das Beispiel Düsseldorf.* Essen: Klartext, 2004.

Emminghaus, Arwed. *Das Armenwesen und die Armengesetzgebung in europäischen Staaten.* Berlin: F. A. Herbig, 1870.

Eser, Susanne F. *Verwaltet und verwahrt – Armenpolitik und Arme in Augsburg. Vom Ende der reichsstädtischen Zeit bis zum ersten Weltkrieg.* Sigmaringen: Thorbecke, 1996.

Farmer, Sharon A., Hrsg. *Approaches to poverty in medieval Europe. Complexities, contradictions, transformations, c. 1100–1500.* Turnhout: Brepols, [2016].

Fejtová, Olga, and Hlavačka, Milan, Hrsg. *Stadt und Armut im langen 19. Jahrhundert.* Berlin: Deutsches Institut für Urbanistik, 2014. (Informationen zur modernen Stadtgeschichte 2)

Feldbauer, Peter. *Kinderelend in Wien. Von der Armenkinderplege zur Jugendfürsorge 17. – 19. Jahrhundert.* Wien: Verlag für Gesellschaftskritik, 1980. (Österreichische Texte zur Gesellschaftskritik, 1)

441

Feuerstein, Christiane. *Vom Armenhaus zur sozialen Infrastruktur. Altersversorgung in Wien.* Weitra, Verl. Bibliothek der Provinz, Ed. Seidengasse, 2009.

Fialová, Ivana, and Tvrdoňová, Daniela, eds. *Od špitála k nemocnici. Zdravotníctvo, sociálna starostlivosť a osveta v dejinách Slovenska.* Bratislava: Slovenský národný archív, 2013.

Fischer-Martin, Nora, and Fischer, Gerhard, Hrsg. *Die Blumen des Bösen. Band II, Eine Geschichte der Armut in Wien, Prag, Budapest und Triest in den Jahren 1693–1873.* Wien: Daedalus, 1994.

Fischer, Wolfram. *Armut in der Geschichte. Erscheinungsformen und Lösungsversuche der "Sozialen Frage" in Europa seit dem Mittelalter.* Göttingen: Vandenhoeck & Ruprecht, 1982. (Kleine Vandenhoeck-Reihe; 1476)

Fontaine, Laurence. *L'économie morale. Pauvreté, crédit et confiance dans l'Europe préindustrielle.* Paris: Gallimard, 2008.

Fontaine, Laurence. *The moral economy. Poverty, credit, and trust in early modern Europe.* New York, NY: Cambridge University Press, 2014.

Freund, Florian et al. *Oberösterreich und die Zigeuner. Politik gegen eine Minderheit im 19. und 20. Jahrhundert.* Linz: OÖLA, 2010.

Freund, Florian et al. *Vermögensentzug, Restitution und Entschädigung der Roma und Sinti.* Wien: Oldenbourg, 2004.

Fuchs, Rachel G. *Gender and poverty in nineteenth-century Europe.* Cambridge: Cambridge University Press, 2005. (New approaches to European history; 35)

Gajek, Eva Maria, and Lorke, Christoph, Hrsg. *Soziale Ungleichheit im Visier. Wahrnehmung und Deutung von Armut und Reichtum seit 1945.* Frankfurt am Main; New York: Campus Verlag, 2016.

Gatz, Erwin. *Kirche und Krankenpflege im 19. Jahrhundert. Katholische Bewegung und karitativer Aufbruch in den preussischen Provinzen Rheinland und Westfalen.* München et al.: Schöningh, 1971.

Geremek, Bronisław. *Geschichte der Armut. Elend und Barmherzigkeit in Europa.* München: Artemis Verlag, 1988.

Geremek, Bronisław. *Litość i szubienica. Dzieje Nędzy i Miłosierdzia.* Warszawa: Czytelnik, 1989. (Wielkie problemy dziejów człowieka)

Geremek, Bronisław. *Slitování a šibenice. Dějiny chudoby a milosrdenství.* Praha: Argo, 1999.

Geremek, Bronisław. *Świat "opery żebraczej". Obraz włóczęgów i nędzarzy w literaturach europejskich XV–XVII wieku.* Warszawa: Państwowy Instytut Wydawniczy, 1989.

Gestrich, Andreas, King, Steven, and Raphael, Lutz, eds. *Being poor in modern Europe, Historical perspectives 1800–1940.* Oxford: P. Lang, 2006.

Gestrich, Andreas, Hurren, Elizabeth and King, Steven, eds. *Poverty and sickness in modern Europe. Narratives of the sick poor, 1780–1938*, London, New York: Continuum, 2012.

Gestrich, Andreas, Hrsg. *Strangers and poor people. Changing patterns of inclusion and exclusion in Europe and the Mediterranean World from classical antiquity to the present day.* Frankfurt am Main: Lang, 2009.

Grebing, Helga, Hrsg. *Geschichte der sozialen Ideen in Deutschland*, Essen: Klartext-Verlag, 2005.

Gruner, Wolf. *Öffentliche Wohlfahrt und Judenverfolgung. Wechselwirkung lokaler und zentraler Politik im NS – Staat (1933–42)*. München: Oldenbourg, 2002.

Hahn, Sylvia, Lobner, Nadja, and Sedmak, Clemens, Hg. *Armut in Europa, 1500–2000.* Innsbruck; Wien; Bozen: StudienVerlag, 2010. (Querschnitte: Einführungstexte zur Sozial-, Wirtschafts- und Kulturgeschichte; Bd. 25)

Hahn, Sylvia. *Migration – Arbeit – Geschlecht. Arbeitsmigration in Mitteleuropa vom 17. bis zum Beginn des 20. Jahrhunderts.* Göttingen: V&R Unipress, 2008.

Halířová, Martina. *Sociální patologie a ochrana dětství v Čechách od dob osvícenství do roku 1914. Disciplinace jako součást ochrany dětství.* Pardubice: Univerzita Pardubice, Fakulta filozofická, 2012. (Monographica. 10)

Hardy, Anne Irmgard. *Ärzte, Ingenieure und städtische Gesundheit. Medizinische Theorien in der Hygienebewegung des 19. Jahrhunderts.* Frankfurt am Main et al.: Campus-Verlag, 2005.

Heindl, Waltraud et alii, Hg. *Eliten und Außenseiter in Österreich und Ungarn.* Köln; Weimar: Böhlau, 2001.

Henke, Robert. *Poverty and charity in early modern theater and performance.* Iowa City; University of Iowa Press, [2015].

Hering, Sabine, and Münchmeier, Richard. *Geschichte der Sozialen Arbeit. Eine Einführung.* 5. Aufl. Weinheim und München: Juventa Verlag, 2014.

Hering, Sabine, ed., *Social Care under State Socialism (1945–1989). Ambitions, Ambiguities and Mismanagement.* Opladen: Barbara Budrich Verlag, 2009.

Hesse, Horst. *Die sogenannte Sozialgesetzgebung Bayerns Ende der sechziger Jahre des 19. Jahrhunderts. Ein Beitr. z. Strukturanalyse d. bürgerl. Gesellschaft.* München: Stadtarchiv, 1971.

von Hippel, Wolfgang. *Armut, Unterschichten, Randgruppen in der Frühen Neuzeit.* München: Oldenbourg, 1995.

Hlavačka, Milan, Cibulka, Pavel et alii., *Chudinství a chudoba jako sociálně historický fenomén. Ambivalence dobových perspektiv, individuální a kolektivní strategie chudých a instrumentária řešení.* Praha: Historický ústav, 2013. (Práce Historického ústavu AV ČR. Opera Instituti Historici Pragae. Řada A, Monographia; 46)

Hlavačka, Milan, Cibulka, Pavel et alii, *Sociální myšlení a sociální praxe v českých zemích 1781–1939. Ideje, legislativa, instituce.* Praha: Historický ústav, 2015. (Práce Historického ústavu AV ČR. Opera Instituti Historici Pragae. Řada A, Monographia; Svazek 54)

Hojda, Zdeněk, Ottlová, Marta, and Prahl, Roman, eds. *Útisk, charita, vyloučení. Sociální 19. století. Sborník příspěvků z 34. ročníku mezioborového sympozia k problematice 19. století. Plzeň, 27. 2. – 1. 3. 2014.* Praha: Academia, 2015.

Horst, Ulrich. *Evangelische Armut und Kirche. Thomas von Aquin und die Armutskontroversen des 13. und beginnenden 14. Jahrhunderts.* Berlin:

Akademie-Verlag, 1992. (Quellen und Forschungen zur Geschichte des Dominikanerordens. Neue Folge; Bd. 1)

Hübner, Peter, and Hübner, Christa. *Sozialismus als soziale Frage: Sozialpolitik in der DDR und Polen, 1968–1976.* Mit einem Beitrag von Christoph Boyer zur Tschechoslowakei. Köln: Böhlau, 2008. (Zeithistorische Studien, Bd. 45.)

Iseli, Andrea. *Gute Policey. Öffentliche Ordnung in der Frühen Neuzeit.* Stuttgart: Ulmer, 2009.

Jantke, Carl, and Hilger, Dietrich, Hrsg. *Die Eigentumslosen. Der deutsche Pauperismus und die Emanzipationskrise in Darstellungen und Deutungen der zeitgenössischen Literatur.* Freiburg und München: Alber, 1965.

Jemelka, Martin et allli. *Ostravské dělnické kolonie. Sv. 1–3.* Ostrava: Filozofická fakulta Ostravské univerzity v Ostravě, 2011–2015.

Jíšová, Kateřina, ed. *Milosrdenství ve středověkých městech. Barmherzigkeit in der mittelalterlichen Städten. Charity in late medieval cities.* Praha: Scriptorium: Archiv hlavního města Prahy, 2013. (Documenta Pragensia. Supplementum, 4, 2013)

John, Michael. *Hausherrenmacht und Mieterelend. Wohnverhältnisse und Wohnerfahrung der Unterschichten in Wien 1890–1923.* Wien: Verl. für Gesellschaftskritik, 1982.

Jörg, Christian. *Teure, Hunger, grosses Sterben. Hungersnöte und Versorgungskrisen in den Städten des Reiches während des 15. Jahrhunderts,* Stuttgart: Hiersemann, 2008. (Monographien zur Geschichte des Mittelalters. 55)

Jütte, Robert. *Arme, Bettler, Beutelschneider. Eine Sozialgeschichte der Armut in der Frühen Neuzeit.* Weimar: Hermann Böhlaus Nachfolger, 2000.

Jütte, Robert. *Obrigkeitliche Armenfürsorge in deutschen Reichsstädten der frühen Neuzeit. Städt. Armenwesen in Frankfurt am Main u. Köln.* Köln; Wien: Böhlau, 1984.

Klopp, Wiard. *Leben und Wirken des Sozialpolitikers Karl Freiherr von Vogelsang,* Wien 1930.

Kocka, Jürgen, Puhle, Hans-Jürgen, and Klaus Tenfelde, Hrsg., *Von der Arbeiterbewegung zum modernen Sozialstaat. Festschrift für Gerhard A. Ritter zum 65. Geburtstag.* München u. a.: Saur, 1994.

Kodymová, Pavla. *Historie české sociální práce v letech 1918–1948.* Praha: Karolinum, 2013.

Krauß, Martin. *Armenwesen und Gesundheitsfürsorge in Mannheim vor der Industrialisierung 1750–1850/60.* Sigmaringen: Thorbecke, 1993.

Krimm, Konrad et al., Hrsg. *Armut und Fürsorge in der Frühen Neuzeit.* Ostfildern: Thorbecke, 2011.

Kučera, Martin. *Chudých budete mít vždy mezi sebou. Olomoucké domy milosrdenství v první polovině 20. století.* Olomouc: Memoria Olomouc, 2014.

Kühberger, Christoph, and Sedmak, Clemens, Hg., *Aktuelle Tendenzen der historischen Armutsforschung.* Wien: Lit, 2005. (Geschichte. Forschung und Wissenschaft; Bd. 10)

Ledvinka, Václav and Pešek, Jiří, eds. *Ponížení a odstrčení. Města versus katastrofy. Sborník příspěvků z 8. vědeckého zasedání Archivu hlavního města*

444   Selected Bibliography

Prahy, konaného ve dnech 2. a 3. října 1990 a 13. vědeckého zasedání Archivu hlavního města Prahy ve dnech 3. a 4. října 1995. Praha: Scriptorium, 1998.

Lis, Catharina and Soly, Hugo. *Poverty and capitalism in pre-industrial Europe* . Hassocks: Harvester Press, 1979. (Pre-industrial Europe, 1350–1850)

van der Locht, Volker. *Von der karitativen Fürsorge zum ärztlichen Selektionsblick. Zur Sozialgeschichte der Motivstruktur der Behindertenfürsorge am Beispiel des Essener Franz-Sales-Hauses.* Opladen: Leske und Budrich, 1997.

Lucassen, Leo et al. *Gypsies and other itinerant groups. A socio-historical approach.* Basingstoke: Macmillan, 2001.

Lucassen, Leo. *Zigeuner. Die Geschichte eines polizeilichen Ordnungsbegriffes in Deutschland 1700–1945.* Köln et al.: Böhlau, 1996.

Ludwig, Andreas, and Schilde, Kurt, Hrsg. *Jüdische Wohlfahrtsstiftungen. Initiativen jüdischer Stifterinnen und Stifter zwischen Wohltätigkeit und sozialer Reform.* Frankfurt am Main: Fachholschulverlag, 2010.

Martínek, Miloslav. "Přehled vývoje rakouského zákonodárství v oblasti chudinství, zdravotnictví a sociální správy." *Sborník k dějinám 19. a 20. století* 4 (1977): 63–85.

Maurer, Michaela, and Schneider, Bernhard, Hg. *Konfessionen in den west- und mitteleuropäischen Sozialsystemen im langen 19. Jahrhundert,* Münster: Lit, 2013.

Mazur, Elżbieta. *Dobroczynność w Warszawie 19 wieku.* Warszawa Instytut archeologii i etnologii Polskiej akademii nauk, 1999.

Metz, Karl H. *Die Geschichte der sozialen Sicherheit.* Stuttgart: Kohlhammer, 2008.

Militzer-Schwenger, Lisgret. *Armenerziehung durch Arbeit. Eine Untersuchung am Beispiel des württembergischen Schwarzwaldkreises 1806–1914.* Tübingen: Tübinger Vereinigung für Volkskunde, 1979. (Untersuchungen des Ludwig-Uhland-Instituts der Universität Tübingen; 48)

Müller, Oliver. *Vom Almosen zum Spendenmarkt. Sozialethische Aspekte christlicher Spendenkultur.* Freiburg im Breisgau: Lambertus, 2005.

Neuhold, Leopold, and Neureiter, Livia, Hg. *Muss arm sein? Armut als Ärgernis und Herausforderung.* Innsbruck; Wien: Tyrolia-Verlag, [2008]. (Theologie im kulturellen Dialog, 15)

Newman, Lucile F., ed. *Hunger in history. Food shortage, poverty, and deprivation.* Cambridge (USA): Blackwell, 1990.

Pankoke, Eckart. *Die Arbeitsfrage. Arbeitsmoral, Beschäftigungskrisen und Wohlfahrtspolitik im Industriezeitalter.* Frankfurt am Main: Suhrkamp 1990.

Pauly, Michel. *Peregrinorum, pauperum ac aliorum transeuntium receptaculum. Hospitäler zwischen Maas und Rhein im Mittelalter.* Stuttgart: Franz Steiner Verlag, 2007. (Beihefte der Vierteljahrschrift für Sozial- und Wirtschaftsgeschichte 190.)

Pawlowsky, Verena. *Mutter ledig – Vater Staat; das Gebär- und Findelhaus in Wien 1784 – 1910.* Innsbruck; Wien; München: Studien-Verl., 2001.

Plum, Werner. *Diskussionen über Massenarmut in der Frühindustrialisierung.* Bonn – Bad Godesberg: Forschungsinstitut der Friedrich-Ebert-Stiftung, 1977. (Hefte aus dem Forschungsinstitut der Friedrich-Ebert-Stiftung)

Pokorný, Antonín. *1000 let chudinství v Praze. Letmý pohled zpět na jeden úsek kultury českého srdce.* Praha: nákladem vlastním, [1940].

Radtke, Wolfgang. *Armut in Berlin. Die sozialpolitischen Ansätze Christian von Rothers und der Königlichen Seehandlung im vormärzlichen Preussen.* Berlin: Akad. – Verlag, 1993.

Rákosník, Jakub. *Odvrácená tvář meziválečné prosperity. Nezaměstnanost v Československu v letech 1918–1938.* Praha: Univerzita Karlova, 2008.

Rákosník, Jakub, and Tomeš, Igor et alii. *Sociální stát v Československu: právně-institucionální vývoj v letech 1918–1992.* Praha: Auditorium, 2012.

Rákosník, Jakub. *Sovětizace sociálního státu. Lidově demokratický režim a sociální práva občanů v Československu 1945–1960.* Praha: Filosofická fakulta Univerzity Karlovy, 2010.

Raphael, Lutz and Uerlings, Herbert, Hrsg. *Zwischen Ausschluss und Solidarität. Modi der Inklusion/Exklusion von Fremden und Armen in Europa seit der Spätantike.* Frankfurt am Main et al.: Lang, 2008.

Ritter, Gerhard. *Der Sozialstaat. Entstehung und Entwicklung im internationalen Vergleich. 3., erweiterte Auflage.* München: Oldenbourg, 2010.

Ritter, Gerhard A. *Soziale Frage und Sozialpolitik in Deutschland seit Beginn des 19. Jahrhunderts,* Opladen: Leske u. Budrich, 1998.

Rodríguez-Lores, Juan, and Fehl, Gerhard, Hrsg. *Die Kleinwohnungsfrage. Zu den Ursprüngen des sozialen Wohnungsbaus in Europa.* Hamburg: Christians, 1987.

Ruda, Frank. *Hegel's Rabble. An investigation into Hegel's philosophy of right.* London: New Delhi; New York: Sydney: Bloomsbury, 2013.

Rumpler, Helmut, and Urbanitsch, Peter, Hrsg. *Die Habsburgermonarchie 1848–1918 9/1. Teilband 1. Soziale Strukturen. Von der feudal-agrarischen zur bürgerlich-industriellen Gesellschaft. Lebens- und Arbeitswelten in der industriellen Revolution.* Wien: Verl. der Österr. Akad. der Wiss., 2010.

Sachße, Christoph, and Tennstedt, Florian, *Bettler, Gauner und Proleten. Armut und Armenfürsorge in deutsche Geschichte.* Reinbek b. Hamburg: Rowohlt, 1983.

Sachße, Christoph, and Tennstedt, Florian. *Gechichte der Armenfürsorge in Deutschland. Band 1–4,* Stuttgart; Berlin; Köln; Mainz: Kohlhammer, 1980–2012.

Sachße, Christoph, and Tennstedt, Florian, Hrsg. *Soziale Sicherheit und soziale Disziplinierung. Beiträge zu einer historischen Theorie der Sozialpolitik.* Frankfurt am Main: Suhrkamp, 1986. (Edition Suhrkamp. Neue Folge; 323)

Scheutz, Martin, Sommerlechner, Andrea, Weigl, Herwig, and Weiss, Alfred Stefan, Hrsg., *Europäisches Spitalwesen. Institutionelle Fürsorge in Mittelalter und Früher Neuzeit. Hospitals and Institutional Care in Medieval and Early Modern Europe.* Wien; München: R. Oldenbourg Verlag, 2008. (Mitteilungen des Instituts für Österreichische Geschichtsforschung, Ergänzungsband; 51)

Scheutz, Martin, and Weiss, Alfred Stefan. *Spital als Lebensform: Österreichische Spitalordnungen und Spitalinstruktionen der Neuzeit. T. 1–2.* Wien: Böhlau, 2015. (Universität Wien. Institut für Österreichische Geschichtsforschung: Quelleneditionen des Instituts für Österreichische Geschichtsforschung; Bd. 15)

Schmidt, Sebastian, Hrsg. *Arme und ihre Lebensperspektiven in der Frühen Neuzeit.* Frankfurt, M.; Berlin; Bern; Bruxelles; New York, NY; Oxford; Wien: Lang, 2008.

Schmidt, Sebastian [et al.], Hg. *Norm und Praxis der Armenfürsorge in Spätmittelalter und früher Neuzeit.* Stuttgart: Franz Steiner Verlag, 2006. (Vierteljahrschrift für Sozial- und Wirtschaftsgeschichte. Beihefte; Nr. 189)

Schneider, Bernhard, Hrsg. *Konfessionelle Armutsdiskurse und Armenfürsorgepraktiken im langen 19. Jahrhundert.* Frankfurt am Main: Peter Lang, 2009.

Schofield, Phillipp, and Lambrecht, Thijs, eds. *Credit and the rural economy in north-western Europe, c. 1200 – c. 1850.* Turnhout: Brepols, 2009.

Schulz, Günther, Hrsg. *Arm und Reich. Zur gesellschaftlichen und wirtschaftlichen Ungleichheit in der Geschichte.* Stuttgart: Steiner, 2015.

Schweikardt, Christoph Johannes. *Die Entwicklung der Krankenpflege zur staatlich anerkannten Tätigkeit im 19. und frühen 20. Jahrhundert. Das Zusammenwirken von Modernisierungsbestrebungen, ärztlicher Dominanz, konfessioneller Selbstbehauptung und Vorgaben preußischer Regierungspolitik.* München: Martin Meidenbauer, 2008.

Šmerda, Hynek. *Křesťanská charita v běhu věků. (Od počátku do doby vrcholného středověku s přihlédnutím k situaci na jižní Moravě).* České Budějovice: Nakladatelství Jih, 2010.

Sroka, Łukasz Tomasz. *Żydzi w Krakowie. Studium o elicie miasta 1850–1918.* Kraków: Wydawnictwo Naukowe Akademii Pedagogicznej, 2008.

Štefko, Martin, ed. *Česká škola sociální politiky v souvislostech.* Praha: Univerzita Karlova v Praze, Právnická fakulta, 2015.

Steinhauser, Werner. *Geschichte der Sozialarbeiterausbildung.* Wien: ÖKSA, 1993.

Stekl, Hannes. *Österreichs Zucht- und Arbeitshäuser 1671–1920. Institutionen zwischen Fürsorge und Strafvollzug.* Wien: Verlag für Geschichte und Politik, 1978.

Štěpek, Jiří. *Sto let přídělových systémů na území bývalého Československa 1915–2015. Část 1, (1915–1945).* Praha: Národohospodářský ústav Josefa Hlávky, 2014. faksim. (Studie Národohospodářského ústavu Josefa Hlávky; 7/2014)

Stokláskova, Zdeňka. *Cizincem na Moravě. Zákonodárství a praxe pro cizince na Moravě 1750–1867.* Brno: Matice moravská, 2007. (Knižnice Matice moravské. 22.)

Svoboda, František. *Tři archetypy evropské sociální politiky.* Brno: Masarykova univerzita, 2012.

Svobodný, Petr, and Hlaváčková, Ludmila. *Pražské špitály a nemocnice.* Praha: Nakl. Lidové noviny, 1999. (Knižnice Dějin a současnosti. 8.)

Tálos, Emmerich. *Staatliche Sozialpolitik in Österreich. Rekonstruktion und Analyse.* Wien: Verlag für Gesellschaftskritik, 1981.

Thernstrom, Stephan. *Poverty and progress. Social mobility in 19. Century City.* Cambridge: Harvard University Press, 1964.

Tönnis, Ferdinand. *Die Entwicklung der sozialen Frage bis zum Weltkriege,* Unveränd. Nachdr. d. 4., verb. Aufl., Berlin u. Leipzig, de Gruyter, 1926, Berlin: de Gruyter, 1989.

Torres, Luc, and Rabaey, Hélène, eds., *Pauvres et pauvreté en Europe à l'époque moderne. (XVI–XVIIIe siècle).* Paris: Classiques Garnier, 2016.

Uerlings, Herbert et alii, Hrsg., *Armut. Perspektiven in Kunst und Gesellschaft. 10. April 2011 – 31. Juli 2011. Eine Ausstellung des Sonderforschungsbereichs 600 "Fremdheit und Armut", Universität Trier in Kooperation mit dem Stadtmuseum Simeonstift Trier und dem Rheinischen Landesmuseum Trier. Begleitband zur Ausstellung.* Darmstadt: Primus Verlag, 2011.

Wagener-Esser, Meike. *Organisierte Barmherzigkeit und Seelenheil. Das caritative Sozialnetzwerk im Bistum Münster von 1803 bis zur Gründung des Diözesancaritasverbands 1916.* Altenberge: Oros-Verlag, 1999.

Witzler, Beate. *Großstadt und Hygiene. Kommunale Gesundheitspolitik in der Epoche der Urbanisierung.* Stuttgart: Steiner, 1995.

Wolfgruber, Gudrun. *Von der Fürsorge zur Sozialarbeit. Wiener Jugendwohlfahrt im 20. Jahrhundert.* Wien: Löcker, 2013.

Young, Michael. *The rise of the meritocracy 1870–2033. An essay on education and equality.* Harmondsworth, Penguin Books 1961.

Zelinka, Inge. *Der autoritäre Sozialstaat. Machtgewinn durch Mitgefühl in der Genese staatlicher Fürsorge.* Münster: LIT Verlag, 2005.

Zimmermann, Michael, Hrsg. *Zwischen Erziehung und Vernichtung. Zigeunerpolitik und Zigeunerforschung im Europa des 20. Jahrhunderts.* Stuttgart: Steiner, 2007.

Zimmermann, Susan. *Prächtige Armut. Fürsorge, Kinderschutz und Sozialreform in Budapest. Das "sozialpolitische Laboratorium" der Doppelmonarchie im Vergleich zu Wien 1873–1914.* Sigmaringen: Thorbecke, 1997.

Zudová-Lešková, Zlatica, and Voráček, Emil et al., *Theory and practice of the welfare state in Europe in 20th century.* Prague: Historický ústav, 2014. (Práce Historického ústavu AV ČR. Opera Instituti Historici Pragae. Řada A, Monographia; vol. 49)

CONTRIBUTORS

Antonie DOLEŽALOVÁ, associate professor, The Institute of Economic Studies, Charles University, Prague, e-mail: antonie.dolezalova@gmail.com

Werner DROBESCH, professor, Institute of History, Alpen-Adria-University, Klagenfurt, e-mail: Werner.Drobesch@aau.at

Gabriela DUDEKOVÁ, senior researcher, Institute of History, Slovak Academy of Sciences, Bratislava, e-mail: gabriela.dudekova@savba.sk

Olga FEJTOVÁ, deputy director, Prague City Archives, Prague, e-mail: Olga.Fejtova@praha.eu

Florian GRAFL, PhD student, University Giessen, Giessen, e-mail: Florian.Grafl@geschichte.uni-giessen.de

Martina HALÍŘOVÁ, lecturer, Institute of History, University Pardubice, Pardubice, e-mail: martina.halirova@upce.cz

Ulrike HARMAT, senior researcher, Institut für Neuzeit- und Zeitgeschichtsforschung, Austrian Academy of Sciences, Vienna, e-mail: Ulrike.Harmat@oeaw.ac.at

Peter HEUMOS, Moosburg, e-mail: peter.heumos@live.de

Milan HLAVAČKA, professor, Institute of History, Czech Academy of Sciences, Prague, e-mail: hlavacka@hiu.cas.cz

Hanna KOZIŃSKA-WITT, unit leader, Aleksander Brückner Zentrum für Polenstudien, Halle (Salle), e-mail: kozinska@web.de

Hana MÁŠOVÁ, lecturer, Institute for History of Medicine and Foreign Languages, Charles University, Prague, e-mail: hana.masova@lf1.cuni.cz

Zdeněk R. NEŠPOR, researcher, Institute of Sociology, Czech Academy of Sciences, Prague, e-mail: Zdenek.Nespor@soc.cas.cz

Martina NIEDHAMMER, research associate, Collegium Carolinum, Munich, e-mail: martina.niedhammer@collegium-carolinum.de

Jakub RÁKOSNÍK, assistant professor, Institute of Economic and Social History, Charles University, Prague, e-mail: jakub.rakosnik@ff.cuni.cz

Karel ŘEHÁČEK, unit leader, State Provincial Archives in Pilsen, Pilsen, e-mail: rehacek@soaplzen.cz

Bernhard SCHNEIDER, professor, University Trier, Trier, e-mail: schneid0@uni-trier.de

Zdeňka STOKLÁSKOVÁ, lecturer, Department of History, Masaryk University, Brno, e-mail: stoklas@phil.muni.cz

Arne THOMSEN, student, Ostwestfalen-Lippe University of Applied Sciences, Lemgo, e-mail: arne.thomsen@gmx.de

Andreas WEIGL, head of department, Provincial and Municipal Archive of the City of Vienna, e-mail: andreas.weigl@wien.gv.at

Marius WEIGL, PhD student, IFF University Klagenfurt, Klagenfurt/Wien, e-mail: marius.weigl@univie.ac.at